RECREATION and LEISURE:

Issues in An Era of Change
Third Edition

RECREATION and LEISURE:

Issues in An Era of Change
Third Edition

edited by:

Thomas L. Goodale
George Mason University

and

Peter A. Witt
University of North Texas

VENTURE PUBLISHING, INC.
State College, PA 16801

Cover Design: Sikorski Design
Production: Bonnie Godbey
Printing and Binding: BookCrafters, Chelsea, MI

Library of Congress Catalogue Card Number 90-71927
ISBN 0-910251-42-8

Distributed outside North America
by E. & F. N. Spon Ltd.
11 New Fetter Lane
London, England EC4P 4EE

TABLE OF CONTENTS

End of Table of Contents

PREFACE

The genesis of this, the third edition of *Recreation and Leisure: Issues in an Era of Change*, was a conversation between the co-editors about twelve years ago. Since then, change has given us a whole new vocabulary for daily discourse: glasnost, perestroika, apartheid, Solidarity, Tiananmen Square, Pacific Rim, Golan Heights, European Economic Community, Free Trade Agreement, Third World debt, Iran-Contra, Graham-Rudman, bailouts, AIDS, crack cocaine, AK47's, ozone depletion, greenhouse effect (and Green Party), nuclear winter, junk bonds, catastrophic health insurance, steroids, cholesterol. That vocabulary reflects an era of change and suggests continuing change. More than that, it reflects a nation and a world reconfigured politically, economically and socially. The Berlin Wall has become a fence with gates. Ceausescu is gone; Noriega is incarcerated; New York has a black Mayor; once confederate Virginia, a black Governor.

Less dramatic, of course, but nonetheless evident to observers of the field of parks, recreation and leisure services, are changes in the field. The outlines of a new configuration are, as yet, unclear, although much has changed. Privatization of public services; the spectre of liability and deep pocket awards; cost recovery and revenue generation; marketing and entrepreneurship; tourism and the travel/hospitality industry; pre-school, day care, and after school programs, fewer and smaller college and university curricula; a more insistent critique (including the feminist critique of androcentrism) of concepts, practices, and research in the field; more open discussion of purpose and the role of values and ethics in our field—these are among the preoccupations of the past decade or so. Conversely, less is heard about leisure education and counselling, for example, or about enabling, facilitating or, more recently, empowerment. The program of accrediting college and university curricula has been, by most accounts and criteria, a success even if still ignored by many in the field and opposed by some. Those in the therapeutic sector of the field have made much progress, again by most accounts and criteria, in developing professional registration and certification of therapeutic recreation personnel. Broader environmental concerns have re-surfaced.

In short, the field of parks, recreation and leisure services has changed markedly in the past decade or so. That was and is inevitable—the world has changed. That being the case, it is easy to become "caught up" in the present and near future, scanning for trends, positioning for the waves and whirls of change to come, and trying to be relevant. The consequence is temporarity and, before long, obsolescence.

Yet change is not the only constant, and attention to other constants helps maintain steerage amidst waves and whirls. Among those other constants are the themes and issues which characterize the human experience, not over brief periods but long ones, not in one applied field but in society. How do we arrive at the meaning of things, and who are the arbiters? What are the prerogatives of individuals, professions, institutions, corporations and the state, and what are their responsibilities to one another? What is wealth and how should it be distributed? What is our place in and obligation to the earth, the cosmos, the future? What marks successful professions, fields and agencies? What marks successful lives? And what of all this filters through the porous bounds of parks, recreation and leisure studies and services?

We were convinced, twelve years ago, that a book devoted to issues in our field could be valuable in many ways: compensating for the relative dearth of such material in the literature; adding the thoughtful essay to a literature comprised mainly of introductory texts, empirical research or how to go about day to day tasks; combatting the temporary and obsolescence from being caught up in the whirl of events; encouraging eclectic but somehow integrated and comprehensive approaches to fundamental questions; encouraging deliberation of why, rather than what and how park, recreation and leisure services are rendered. We are still convinced that such a book could be valuable in those ways. But we recognized those were lofty ambitions and were prepared to settle for stimulating some thought and discussion in a few classrooms, offices, coffee shops, and bars.

Judged by these modest criteria, the initial and revised editions of "Issues" were successful enough to encourage us and Venture Publishing to try again. This is our third try. An anthology comprised of original work from the pens and keyboards of 32 contributors may never quite congeal in the well shaped mould one envisions for it. But we think we are getting close. Recalling that a camel is a horse put together by a committee, we thought of the initial (1980) volume as a camel with many humps. The revised (1985) edition had fewer humps: this edition has fewer still, and if not yet a horse, it is a better likeness.

Of the 33 chapters here, 24 appeared in the 1985 edition. A few of those have been substantially revised, but most remain intact or with minor editorial changes. Despite appropriate criticisms, such as the use of gender specific pronouns, we and the authors think they have withstood most of the ravages of recent years. Five chapters from the revised edition were deleted, mainly because of our inability to situate and integrate material nonetheless valuable in other respects. Seven new chapters have been added, each a significant addition, each timely but in some ways also timeless. We have also brought back a section, attempted in the first edition but deleted from the second, focused upon research. It includes two chapters resurrected from the initial volume, three new chapters, and four chapters carried over from the revised edition. The new material and the change from three sub-themes to four has meant some resequencing of material as well, and there are four more chapters here than in earlier editions.

The four sub-themes, in brief, focus upon basic concepts and their meanings, the provision of parks and recreation services, the profession and the preparation of professionals, and research into parks, recreation and leisure. The last section points out, among other things, the importance of conceptual clarity, leading us not in a circle so much as a continuing dialogue about these four principal themes, each informing and informed by the other. Section IV directs a feedback loop to Section I.

The sequence of sections and chapters was derived from a logic comprised of such considerations as progressions, reinforcement, contrast, and complementarity. Yet there is no enjoinder to read every chapter, much less read them in the sequence presented here. Earlier editions have been used as a text or as supplementary readings for a variety of courses. Depending on needs and interests, some sections and chapters will be more pertinent than others. Sections I and IV are, for example, a bit more conceptual, theoretical, and philosophical than the other sections. Those 16 chapters may form a core for a graduate level issues course while the 17 chapters in Sections II and III might form the core of an undergraduate issues course. In short, a variety of adaptions are possible.

The only enjoinder is to read and reflect, discuss and debate matters of fundamental and enduring significance. If some of the authors and essays presented here stimulate that, good. And if in all this someone finds a good thought and with it makes a good difference, we could ask no more. On the other hand, we should ask no less of those holding out the promise of fulfilling life for us all.

T. L. G. & P. A. W.

End of Preface

(turn to p. 1 ———→)

SECTION I

Clarifying Concepts: The Ongoing Struggle for Understanding

INTRODUCTION

Most books on almost any subject begin by defining the basic terms to be utilized and making distinctions between key concepts that need to be introduced. This practice is presumed necessary as it permits a sense of common understanding among the readers. Books on recreation and leisure are no exception to this general pattern. Unfortunately, after reading most definitions of terms like play, recreation or leisure, the reader is often left with the vague sense that though much has been said, little has been communicated, and definitional and conceptual understanding continues to be elusive. Part of the morass is due to differing opinions about what the fundamental terms in our field mean and part is due to the complexity of the concepts with which we are dealing.

But if the field of recreation and leisure is to advance and mature, we must continue the struggle for conceptual clarity, if not agreement. Clarity ultimately forms the basis for practice and evaluation of whether services and systems have met stated goals and objectives.

One of the purposes, then, of this opening section is to focus attention on some of the basic concepts that are used in our field. For example: Arnold (1) delves into the background and interrelationship of recreation, leisure and play; Farina (2) and Goodale (3) examine time and free time; Bregha (4) analyzes obligation and freedom; Smith (6) looks at pleasure; and Michaelis (5) assesses play and creativity.

The combined efforts of these authors add considerable support to material presented in later sections of the book which notes the crippling consequences of failing to define our terms or clarify our concepts. Thus, the wrestling with meaning sets the stage and tone for efforts in the other sections of the book to describe needed services, professional practices, and research.

Several other themes emerge through the articles in this section. One of these is the necessity to balance objective and subjective conceptualizations and evidence for our key concepts and terms. Farina (2) and Goodale (3), for example, point out the extraordinary complexity of the concept of time. In a society such as ours—technologic, interrelated, and interdependent—time as a quantity is inescapable. As a commodity measurable with uncommon precisions, we know the mechanistic, objective side of time well. Godbey's (11) discussion of "time deepening" is an example of further efforts to combat time scarcity and understand patterns of time usage that occur over a person's life.

On the other hand there is a subjective, aesthetic and experiential side to time. While more difficult to grasp, it may be far more important because the "problem of leisure" is perhaps not so much a problem of quantity of time but of quality. This is clear, as Farina (2) points out, in the two most common qualifiers attached to the word time, as in "free" time and "leisure" time. Beyond any objective meaning these adjectives are laden with qualitative, evaluative and emotive content. Ultimately, Farina suggests that leisure is probably better understood in relation to freedom rather than time.

Freedom, and what to do with it, thus becomes another dominant theme of this section. Bregha (4) raises the issue of whether we are dealing with freedom from, i.e., freedom from work and other obligations, or freedom to, i.e., freedom to choose what to do. Bregha ultimately asks: How much freedom do we really have? What are the conditions of freedom? What are the internal as well as external barriers to choosing freely?

The fragile nature of freedom to becomes a dominant issue for several other authors in this and succeeding sections as well. For example, Michaelis (5) describes the conditions that can destroy playfulness as one moves through childhood and into adulthood, while Bishop and Jeanrenaud (15) discuss the many potential roadblocks to creativity and the difficulty in its preservation. In Section III, Reynolds (22) points to the social potential of our service system as a significant negative influence on the freedom to, while Lord, Hutchison and VanDerbeck (21) chastise professionals per se for presenting significant restraints on leisure and the ability to choose.

The goal of leisure is another dominant theme. Bregha (4) notes that goalless leisure is a contradiction and that time uses are not equal in quality, morality or social relevance. Smith (5) makes a similar observation in stating that sensate pleasure is inferior to intellectual pleasure. But not all intellectual pleasure is good because the product of it may be twisted or destructive. This is also noted by Goodale (7) in his discussion of the strong link in Aristotle's philosophy between leisure, ethics and the exercise of virtue. Thus, we are once again involved in the age-old task of distinguishing means from ends. But Aristotle clearly separated leisure from amusement and recreative pastime.

Goodale (3) extends this discussion by asking "Is there enough time?" which naturally leads to an inquiry of what use we wish to make of our time. Goodale asks us to consider if there is more time than life—if we use time in the wisest and most meaningful ways—all of which of course leads us back to the question of who sets the standards. Most of us have the freedom to do with our time as we please, but are there uses of time, and thus our freedom, that are more human and meaningful?

Dustin, McEvoy and Schultz (8) conclude the section by asking if there is a standard by which we can assess if one form of recreation is more appropriate for involvement than another. While they acknowledge the importance of free time as providing the opportunity to do what one wishes, they also note that "freedom also demands a sense of obligation to do the right thing." But what is the right thing and who is to be the judge? They conclude that judging the right thing by a standard of what brings pleasure, the hedonistic error, leads to inappropriate involvements. Rather they propose that the right thing is what is really good for us. Thus, the judgement of the goodness or badness of specific involvement rests with its impact on the larger community, i.e., those involvements which contribute to the "physical and mental health, the sense of being loved and loving, the feelings of belonging and self-esteem, and the growth and development of life in its entirety." This perspective places leisure in another realm from amusements, to which Smith (6) answers, "here, here."

In the words of poet Alexander Pope: "Amusement is the happiness of those who cannot think." That is one way to summarize Aristotle's philosophy on that subject. It is also an appropriate summary of Smith's (6) analysis of the "Biological Basis of Pleasure" and its implications. Smith raises several issues related to the goal of leisure and its end, pleasure, by discussing the neurophysiologic evidence which points to human beings as distinguishable from other animals by their ability to derive pleasure from thought. He describes the fact that too many of us involve ourselves in sensate, hedonistic and even narcissistic pleasures, increasingly ignoring the potential of deriving pleasure through thought. These pursuits he sees as sub-human and not in the best interests of human development and purpose. Those who seek sensory pleasures, which probably include us all to greater or lesser degrees, could reply to the effect that we are, after all only (or merely) human. But then there are those who have suggested that in light of the many problems and challenges confronting man, being only (or merely) human may not be enough.

Smith's discussion of the biological basis of pleasure also points to the potential for recent research into brain functioning to supply important new information about the purposes and value of play and leisure. Michaelis (5) also sees the potential descriptive value of this emerging information, noting the primacy of the right brain and of the affective, non-rational mode of thinking to play and creativity. The ultimate need to integrate right and left, cognitive and affective, and rational and non-rational elements also brings us back to the objective-subjective distinction regarding leisure.

In total, the time has come to think seriously about what and how we think, what we mean, what we intend, what we do and what happens as a result. Leisure, recreation and play can and often do mean and imply different things; means and ends of leisure and of service delivery need to be distinguished; and the disparity between objective and subjective experience resolved.

(no keep)

p. 4 is blank.

Chapter 1

The Dilemma of Meaning

Serena Arnold

Almost everyone believes that he or she has an adequate understanding of the words leisure, recreation and play. Even though we may have carefully and logically thought through their meanings, we can find ourselves unable to interpret what others may be implying by their usage. Many persons will have ready definitions and argue that leisure is time off the job, time free from requirements of life and time in which they may choose to do what they like. Recreation will be reported as closely allied with sports and games, and if you ask for an identification of recreations, more often than not you will be provided with the names of diversions perceived as means for escape from routine. It will be asserted that play is an activity of children, the opposite of work or the antithesis of attention to duty. Some have suggested that play is the work of children. We frequently hear that Americans work hard at their play and their work is the recreation. At the same time, some persons will assert that they have no time for leisure.

If the reader feels comfortable with our more common definitions of leisure, recreation, play, and also the word work, and believes that he or she can precisely understand what the authors of chapters within this book have meant in their usage, there is no reason to pursue further the following material. If, on the other hand, there are inconsistencies in meanings, a simple exercise of categorization of what each writer tends to be implying by use of these terms will illustrate clearly a need for greater precision in definition.

The purpose of this article, therefore, is to search for clarity, in our understanding of the words leisure, recreation and play, as well as work. If those words are ambiguous and we are unsure of our symbols, it will follow that our thinking will be illogical and our intent confusing. Particularly is this true when we attempt to carry out research pertaining to leisure, recreation or play. If we are to communicate with any degree of scientific intent, we must come to grips with semantic representations. For there is ample evidence that we use words when we think. Imagine if you will, how much confusion could be engendered if a chemist left us to surmise what he meant when he said, "You will be using $C_3H_3(NO_2)_2$ in this experiment?"

Our ability to communicate through symbols is a definite attribute that separates human beings from other creatures. Words are symbols, just as the number two is a symbol. If we fail to understand the meaning of the symbols we use, there is little hope for an orderly comprehension of conceptual realities or actions. In other words, it is essential that we think through what we mean when we speak or write about leisure, recreation and play, just as you would need to know that our chemist was speaking of nitroglycerine. While the consequences might be different, the needs are similar.

To assert that recreation is re-creation, leisure is free time and play a non-productive activity, and all three have their opposites in work, is to compound errors made in the 18th and 19th centuries in which these terms were used in relation to industrialized production. Knowledge of how words have developed into present day terminology will come from tracing their historical significances and symbolic usages. It clarifies where we are and what needs to be done to properly understand what is being said or written. The science of semantics provides us the tools.

Only recently have there been serious attempts to analyze the discrete meanings of leisure, recreation and play. For the most part, these terms have been used with emotive intent rather than by reason of their symbolic content—that is, the signs they contain (significance). Many of us have not been aware that there is a difference between what is loosely meant by a term and its symbolic meaning of significance. The two approaches are often confused, just as the definition of a word is often confused with a description of what it represents. Some persons find it difficult to accept the fact that a standard dictionary does not contain definitions, but rather synonyms.

Culminating from centuries of usage and changing moral codes and mores, the terms we are discussing have undergone a variety of adaptations resulting in a mixture of imprecision. To bring concrete thinking out of generalizations and to separate meanings presents a formidable task. While the English language is considered to be rich and expressive from a literary view, ambiguous terms with imprecise connotations are precarious for scientific applications. So much of what has been written concerning leisure, recreation and play fits better into journalistic convenience than into a scientific mode that provides us explanations. For these reasons, attempts have been made to coin new terms or find a single representative term, but none has gained wide acceptance. For a time, I advocated coining the term Ludinetics for academic study of recreation; the logic being that the Latin *ludus*, for play and *etics*, the study of, made operational sense. However, I soon reasoned that with such esoterics, I could not avoid confronting the hackneyed terms I wished to clarify; therefore, the dilemma was merely exacerbated.

The field of recreation is not alone with semantic difficulties. Traditional disciplines are still fraught with agonies of definition. In medicine, for example, the term sick has no precise meaning, nor have the terms illness, handicapped or health. Recently, 25 physicians were interviewed and asked to define sick. The resulting conclusion was that the term meant "something was not working." For the medical profession, the word had meaning only to the extent that it was broken down into referents and these referents isolated and made definitive through laboratory investigation. Viability and respectability of any field is not found in its designation per se, but rather by the specificity of its concepts and concreteness of its research. It is by such contributions to knowledge that more preciseness and better research is developed. Testing, substantiated by competent observers, is a continuing process in every viable field.

One of the immense challenges for recreation professionals is to understand the field so well that they are capable of delimiting terms into elements that are applicable to research methods. One law of research is that when a problem is stated as a generalization, the resulting conclusion can only be a greater generalization. The umbrella under which we presently reside as a profession is far too expansive for concrete research purposes. As long as recreation is anything done for pleasure within free time, as long as leisure is wedded to time, and as long as play is activities of fun and games, there are no boundaries. We may find solace in designing facilities and developing and managing parks and playgrounds, but how do we evaluate them in terms of purpose? What specifically, were our aims, objectives or goals?

It seems to me that all facets of the field of recreation, leisure and play are infested by our looseness of meaning in the terms presently being applied. As the title of this publication suggests, we are in an era of change and if we fail to update our concepts of what we mean by recreation, leisure and play, there are reasons to believe that our efforts to become a mature profession will become less effective rather than more. We have been saying this for years, but the difficulties we face are much older and more far-reaching. It means setting aside traditions within our profession, becoming radical, perhaps, in changing our ways of thinking and daring to challenge the *status quo*. As I travel about the country, I cannot avoid contemplating how it happens that our concepts of children's playgrounds show very few differences from those established in 17th century Boston. Resisting change is a human foible and fear its strongest ally.

The intent of this article, therefore, is a limited investigation into the history of the terms we habitually apply to our field and a search for the sources from which they have emanated. Such a review may seem dull and academic, for there are many who shy away from semantics, believing that expedience is a more practical and rewarding enterprise. In passing, however, the very connotation of freedom with which we have traditionally interpreted leisure and recreation may well have a bearing on the maddening increase in misuse of park and recreation amenities. At one time, historically speaking, leisure was license; campus, playground; ludicrous an aspect of play; games the fetes of gladiators within Roman colosseums. Residuals from the past in respect to language are especially slow to disappear.

Academic study of recreation, leisure and play is little more than a few decades old. During this time research consisted predominantly of descriptive studies depicting the status quo. Considerable emphasis was placed on leadership, administration and management practices, but these studies were predicated on the premise that recreation was understood through spiritual and moral values or a contributing factor to self-improvement or prevention of social ills.

Of late, there is greater frequency of studies directed toward basic research. Hopefully, we have passed the stage where we carried out surveys in which we asked a constituency, "What does recreation (or leisure or play) mean to you?" Within such quests, we learned that our constituency knew no more than we about definitions. Again, through a process of maturing, we went on many searches to discover what persons did for their recreations, and furthermore, what constituted their leisure pursuits. We did discover one essential fact from these efforts, however, and that was that our population reported activities as broad as life itself. I well remember a nation-wide study to discover the most popular recreation of the American people. The finding showed that swimming headed the list. When I investigated further, it was revealed that the study was conducted during July and August. On the other hand, I also found that the researcher failed to instruct his population as to the meaning of recreation. Again, an erroneous premise that everyone knows its meaning.

Another example of lack of interpretation may be found in the statement "leisure is one of our leading industries." An exciting statement, is it not, but if analyzed, one must ask the question, is leisure a commodity to be bought and sold in the marketplace? Is leisure a thing, and if so what are its referents? Inasmuch as the fast food industry is included in the research that reported on the economic value of leisure, one could well ask the question, does eating out mean an increase or decrease in the amount of leisure one has? Clearly, it depends upon the definition given to leisure. If we consider leisure as the opposite of employment for financial gain, then leisure must be exchanged for the time taken to earn enough money to pay for eating out. This dichotomy would not occur if we ceased using time as a measure for leisure or as a thing to be calculated as a leisure referent.

There are numerous examples of failing to clarify meaning. A recent review of 123 studies of play revealed that only 19 authors attempted to define the term within their methodology. To say that we expect everyone to know what is meant by play, is to avoid the issue. Additionally, to state that play-recreation-leisure is simply an attitude, a way of life, or a state of mind, is to provide richness through poetics, but little in substance. A fair and unbiased illustration is to review all of the so-called theories of play and compare the differences.

Our dilemma, therefore, lies in subjectivity without definition. We have been unable to name recreation, play or leisure as a thing that can be counted or measured. In an effort to quantify recreation experiences, I was a participant in an effort to experiment with use of sphygmomanometers to measure changes in blood pressure during periods of play activity, but conclusions were invalid due to contaminating influences by members of the research team. Apparently, play, according to our definition, could not be superimposed by persons outside and apart from the players themselves and neither could there be interference with the progress of play. All participants expressed the loss of freedom and an absence of a "spirit of play," hence the technique was abandoned.

There is instructive value in recognizing our limitations in terms of being able to gain accurate information on human behavior under controlled conditions. Objectivity is illusive at best, and if we do not recognize subjectivity for its tell-tale signs, we will be blithely on our way believing that defining terms is an inconsequential exercise. We must know, however, that we are not alone with our problems of definition and meaning. Ogden and Richards stated the problem concisely when they wrote:

". . . the approach to meaning, far more than the approach to such problems as those of physics, requires a thorough-going investigation of language. Every advance in physics has been at the expense of some generally accepted piece of meta-physical explanation which had enshrined itself in a convenient, universally practiced symbolic shorthand. But the confusion and obstruction due to such shorthand expressions and to the naive theories they protect and keep alive is greater in psychology, and especially in the theory of knowledge, than elsewhere; because no problem is so infected with so-called metaphysical difficulties—due here, as always, to an approach to a question through symbols without initial investigation of their function."[1]

The authors could have written equally well for recreation. Only in the last few years are we becoming aware of our own symbolic shorthand. In a field as subjective as recreation, evolving as it did through a type of missionary zeal and moralistic appeal by enthusiastic supporters, generalizations were acceptable. To sever our ties with emotionally laden nomenclature requires awareness of words and their meanings. By this I do not mean to debase emotionality in any sense of the word; I only plead to knowing the difference between an emotionally laden term and an objective one and their different uses. Linguistic modes are powerfully contagious and there needs to be a few iconoclasts who question and resist the prevailing influence. To listen as well as to read words with acute awareness of their referents and symbols is similar to the mathematician who responds to equations and understands their symbols as meaningful or not. Let us begin now by exploring the meanings of our terms as they originated.

RECREATION AS AN ABSTRACTION

The term recreation is an abstract symbol and thus resists modeling into a series of sub-referents without resorting to further abstractions. In this sense, it could be argued that recreation has no meaning in reality because it does not represent a description of a thing or object. It eludes measurement or quantification. Furthermore, its boundaries are unlimited in terms of the number of referents that could be brought to mind. The word could be said to be a conditional symbol of varying magnitude, as on a continuum. It raises problems not unlike those associated with beauty or pleasure; it becomes a plaything of the mind.

If we assert that recreation represents revitalization of the individual because he has participated in certain activities, we place upon the symbol a qualitative measure, a degree of worth or value—hence a morality. The assumption implies that creativity is good and non-creativity is bad, at least it suggests that non-creativity is not recreative. The question arises, how did recreation become associated with good or bad?

As an English word, it arose from Middle English of the 14th century and was adopted from Old French. Remembering our history, this was a period of moral upheaval that gave rise to the Reformation. Originally, however, the term recreation stemmed from Latin, *recreatio*. From the history of the English language, we find that literary words stemming from French and incorporated into English were expressions of the upper class. Thus recreation had use, not to peasants and laborers, but to those who enjoyed the privileges of higher social position. If there were a word in the idiom of commoners that connoted recreation in the sense of refreshment, revitalization, or entertainment, it has eluded me. All of these words, including amusement, were of French-Latin extraction. On the other hand, the Germanic "rest" is likely from Germanic "*rast*" which referred to ceasing work or the absence of motion—to be at ease.

In Latin, *recreatio* carried a connotation of restoration or recovery from something. Its root is in the word *re-creo* (to create again) to refresh, invigorate, or revive. Further references include such inferences as to amuse oneself after obligation: *laxandi levandique animi gratia*, having to do with pleasant respite. Without neuroscientific evidence, the word with which we are dealing has a metaphysical content. If we are to accept the various synonyms given, we would need to substantiate activity as a means for attaining relaxation or rest. The assumption would produce a dichotomy: rest from activity or a cessation of movement on the one hand and diverting activity on the other.

In the study of word meanings, and accepting the canon that thought is dependent upon symbols, we should try to find a word to mean the opposite of recreation. If we selected the referent, revitalization or refreshment, the antonyms fatigue and exhaustion would come to mind. If, however, we accept the Latin root *creare*, the antonym would be to exterminate or annihilate. Further, the

Latin word *creo* has the meaning of bringing forth and quite clearly symbolizes work (fabricate). With the root word for recreation relating to work, it would require considerable imagination to establish re-creation as the antithesis of work. Furthermore, in usage, the word create was associated with the Divine Creator and re-create with being re-born of the spirit, of being made anew or cleansed of sin. In this sense, the word recreation was ontological rather than a name for some activity as such. In essence, then, it was a word associated with the nature of being, or reality.

During the 16th and 17th centuries, recreation began to be used to represent activities that provided both spiritual and physical refreshment for industrial workers after hours of debilitating toil. It was during the industrial revolution when the word became a referent for both a state of being and activities of a diversionary nature which were espoused by advocates as essential to maintaining health of workers confined in factories for the majority of their waking hours. In Germany, and to a lesser degree in England, physical exercise was promoted and took root among groups outside of factory workers, *per se*. The saying, "healthy body, healthy mind" became an acceptable precept. In England, field sports were widespread means for diversionary activity and were for a time discouraged or prohibited by entrepreneurs because workers would leave their machines to participate in group contests. In 19th century United States, social problems attributed to child labor and tenement living led to the advent of the "play movement" which was to prosper and include more than sports and more than activities only for children. By this advent, however, recreation did not lose its moral connotation, but rather the notion of recreation being a curative process for unfavorable conditions was strengthened. With secular support, recreation became popularized on the basis of being a preventive and as such was useful to satisfy the emotive needs entrepreneurs, the moralistic interests of reformers, and the philosophic proclivities of intellectuals. From these early stages, Patrick proposed the "recreation or relaxation theory of play" and recreation as opposed to work became an ingrained notion in this country.[2] While I find no support for such liberties with word meanings and no precedents set in our language stemming from other languages, particularly from Latin or Greek, we seem to persist in choosing work as the antonym for recreation as well as for leisure or play. If we were to continue to depend on the general population for assistance in defining recreation, we would have paid little attention to those who have insisted that their work was their recreation.

LEISURE IDEALS

Turning to Greece and particularly the writings of Aristotle for discourses on leisure and its ideal, we find that leisure was a basis for culture. Historically and profoundly, leisure was a way of personal growth and social attainment of the "good life," particularly in Athens during the 5th century B.C. This was the period often referred to as the "Golden Age" or the "Age of Pericles," the time during which the Parthenon was constructed and various intellectual and aesthetic advances were made. The importance of Greek culture to any study of Western civilization and Occidental thought cannot be minimized. Our system of reasoning is of Green origin, to say nothing of political influences on our own form of government or on arts and sciences. Approximately 10 percent of the English language is Greek, including much of our nomenclature associated with leisure. The Greek term *schole* (leisure) has since evolved into words such as school, scholar, scholastic, and a host of terms we use in daily conversation. Curiously, however, we possess no counterpart to the Greek *ascholia* (un-leisure) which of course was the antonym for leisure and necessary to the Greeks to insure clarity.

Anthenian society was centered around leisure, or in our terms, centered in freedom from labors associated with everyday maintenance necessities. At this point, we must keep in mind that during this period of Greek history, there was no industrial manufacturing as such. The social system was supported by a slave population which was rationalized as essential to citizen freedom to reach a state of *arete* (the nearest English translation being virtue). *Arete* represented "excellence in all things" and, in the Homeric period, symbolized the ideal for which all citizens must strive: attainment of the highest good of which humans were capable. Leisure, therefore, was "opportunity" for realization of that ideal. The complexity of meaning of the term *schole* was in the wholeness of its concept, in its life-giving inferences and universality. More recently, Jaegar, in his scholarly work, explores these concepts fully, relating them to the central meaning of the term culture.[3] Pieper also asserted that leisure was the basis of culture and implied that the term recreation as commonly used in our society has been erroneously attached to leisure due to the fact that it reflected certain states of prescribed activity.[4] de Grazia also supported the same contention.[5]

In classical Greece, leisure was not time available to be employed, nor was it a means to an end outside and apart from itself. It would have been incomprehensible to Aristotle for a person to state, "Now I have leisure for some activity." Neither was work considered the opposite of leisure, for the word work was *erg*, the root meaning for output of energy, in other words, a system of measuring expenditure of energy. A state of toil, (our term for labor) can be found in the Greek counterpart: slave. Thus we draw from early Greek culture our emotive referents associated with distaste for work and labor, representing something somewhat less than the good life and in itself demeaning to the human spirit.

Although we cling with passion to the idea of freedom, we also center our lives around work, and in our attempts to integrate the two—freedom and work/labor, we have created a dichotomy of semantic complexity which contributes to misunderstandings and inconsistencies. The framers of our Constitution, many of whom were scholars of Greek, held that the pursuit of happiness was the American ideal, but did not anticipate that Americans would become slaves to technology rather than technology replacing the slavery of Athens. We have great difficulty conceiving of a highly advanced civilization where labor was not the center of life. In this sense we have adopted Greek terms, but turned full circle from their meanings.

Finding referents by which to clarify the Greek meaning for leisure requires study of the first chapter of Aristotle's *Metaphysics*.[6] There is evidence that the important referent for *schole* is found in the word contemplation. This term does not , however, symbolize inactivity by posturing oneself as the Thinker, but rather it meant to observe, view, behold. Contemplation has a close association, etymologically, with Greek *theoria* referred to being a spectator at festivals and it is interesting that during the Periclean period, poor people were given money or "passes" by government to attend the theater. The *theorikos* were those who traveled to see men and things and reflect upon them as one would speculate or postulate an explanation for a phenomenon. In our modern sense , it would apply if we attended the World Series baseball games to reflect on the scene in order to gain insights into the character of American culture. Contemplation meant more than merely reflecting on phenomena and perceiving man's place in the scheme of things; it carried the connotation of participation-reflection. Attendance at a festival such as the Olympian Festival was a highly religious experience and a culmination of all that was Greek. The *theorikos* were persons of action, and through their beholding of phenomena, innovations within the culture arose. Thus, philosophy was an action oriented process which to the Greeks was fundamental to knowledge. To dissuade ourselves of the notion that contemplation did not result in action and that leisure was inaction, we need only to turn to archaeological discoveries that clearly reveal the Greeks' contribution to technology. Brumbaugh published an impressive account of machines, gadgets and a variety of inventions that were precursors of our clocks as well as mechanical toys.[7] Leisure, then, fits well into the Greek scheme of aesthetics as experiential integration of thought and action. An idea alone was insignificant without action.

In Latin derivations of leisure we find that important diversions occurred which affected our current concepts of leisure. The dominance of Rome over Greece was military and economic rather than intellectual. Greek philosophers and teachers perpetuated their system of education and left lasting marks on Roman literature, religion and language. While the Greeks were profoundly aesthetic and idealists for the most part, the Romans, above all else, were pragmatic—or as we say, practical. Therefore, any infusion of ideals held in regard to leisure by the Greeks was selectively accepted in terms of how these ideals could become subservient to practicality and applicable to a pragmatic philosophy. As was said by a Roman general, "Greeks die in bed, while Romans die on the battlefield."

Leisure, in the modern sense, came from Latin *licere* and by way of French *leisir*, Middle English *licere*, to its present spelling. The root word, *licere*, meaning to be permitted, evolved into the word license. Leisure literally meant "permission" as applied to "opportunity" afforded that was free from a legal occupation. Roman intellectuals such as Cicero and Ovid, however, invoked *otium* as signifying the idea of leisure. *Otium* was associated with contemplation and opportunity for freedom from time as well as freedom from occupation. As we have the word "leisurely" to describe a manner, there was the Latin *otiose*. There was also the word *vaco* which symbolized emptiness, to be free from, and as Cicero used the word, to have occasion for something, or to have leisure. Our word vacation comes from the same root. The English phrase, "free living" could be represented by *licentia* which for Ovid implied dissoluteness or licentiousness.

The counterpart for Greek *schole* was the Latin *schola* and, according to classical references, *ludus literarum* and *ludus discendi*, literally mean to be free of books. Later, *schola* was to become associated with a sect of scholars or disciples, and thus the word discipline referred to activities at *schola*. In this sense, learning and scholarship were representative of leisure as well as the absence of a legal occupation. Much later, *schola* came to indicate a place where learned lectures and discussions took place and hence disciplines as studies.

For some time after Greece was conquered by Rome, young Roman patricians were sent to Athens for schooling and *ludus* (play) became a referent for schooling and learning. From this emerged our word campus as the center of learning—playground. It is highly instructive to us in the field of recreation that both leisure and play in the Greek and Roman sense were linked closely to education or learning. Contemplation or reflection would take place only when a condition of leisure was experienced. Leisure could not be forced, it could not occur under servitude, it was non-material and therefore a non-business-like condition. It was opportunity for knowledge and culturation. *Artes liberales* has the meaning of leisure in its finest sense.

We must remember that Roman writers such as Ovid, Seneca, Virgil and Cicero were profoundly affected by Greek culture, and therefore reflected a selective point of view. Their philosophies do not necessarily reflect the thinking of either the populace or the ruling classes. It was after disintegration of the Roman Empire that *otium* was considered circumspect in terms of Christian moral codes. Christian adherents who wrote had witnessed license within leisure as it had been practiced, and condemned festivals and spectacles during the wanning years of Roman civilization. On the other hand, *otium* was to fuse with the contemplative life within monasteries and continued to have an association with learning and discipline. Leisure was strictly controlled within monastic life and the doctrine of work was to become a means for purification of the spirit. The word work took on attributes of being a prevention as well as a cure for transgressions in both individuals and social groups.

Centuries later, the economist Veblen attached to leisure the notion of free time and created the term "leisure class."[8] From his treatise by the same name, and through the respect given to his theories by sociologists, Veblen left his mark on American thinking in regard to leisure. At this time, and henceforward, leisure became synonymous with free time, unproductiveness and absence from the necessity to work; in fact as unwillingness to work, or laziness. Many became disdainful of the wealthy who had freedom from toil, while others envied their comfortable position in society. This was a popularized ideality not unlike that held by Puritans of new England. It may have been, as Hall suggested, that opposition to pursuits of the wealthy was not so much that the pursuits themselves were evil, but that envy resulted in recriminative acts against the group that had opportunity to pursue interests that the less advantaged would have liked to pursue.[9]

On the other hand, Veblen's influence on writers in the field of recreation and leisure brought about the common definition of leisure still being published in Fairchild's *Dictionary of Sociology* in which it is defined as time remaining after the necessities of life are attended to,[10] hence the notion that leisure as time is quantitatively determined. Any semantic faithfulness to its roots and origin has been abrogated. Without removing leisure from time as a referent, without discontinuing to use the phrases, "leisure time," "free time," "using leisure" and a host of other phrases propositional to quantities of time, leisure will continue to be considered a commodity to be used, bought or sold. In this sense, time becomes the central issue and not leisure. From a point of language, time and leisure are anomalies, just as "good leisure" or "bad leisure" are anachronisms for those of us who prefer to maintain that leisure is an experience. It becomes our problem, if we believe this, to sort out referents that hold true to the classical notion of *arete*.

PLAY AS A SYMBOL

There is no single idea to be expressed by the word play, any more than for the words discussed previously, but the concept of play is far more universal than either leisure or recreation. While the other two terms applied only to humans, play extends to include animals. It is therefore instructive to keep in mind the juncture with the gamboling and frolicking of animals as well as humankind.

The English word play etymologically came from Anglo-Saxon *plage* and *plegan*, literally symbolizing play and to play. The word came from those commoners of Britain and not from the litany of aristocracy, therefore it has no equivalent in French, Latin or Greek word roots. While I know of no author who has undertaken an analysis of recreation and leisure to any exhaustive degree, Huizinga has provided us with a classic treatise on play.[11] I often lament that among the readers of his work, by far the greater number are outside the field of leisure and recreation. My own research tends to support Huizinga's contention that the word, stemming from German idioms and fusing with English, provides us with many more referents than simply to move swiftly, frolic, or play a game for amusement. Etymologically, the word encompasses the whole spectrum of ways of playing, modes of playing and conditions of playing. Bringing together referents from a variety of languages, the case may be established that play has a focal meaning of a harmonious mix of shear fantasy and powerful realism. A review of some 52 referents supports this contention.

There appears to be a generic term for play that represents all play and all forms of play. The basic Greek word was *paidia* (play), which referred to the play of children, with its roots in child *(pid)*. In literary usage, however, *paidia* had an extended meaning to represent the belief that one must be as a child to play. This influence is illustrated by Plato when he wrote, ". . . man is God's plaything, and that is the best part of him." He noted that life must be lived as play, playing certain games, making sacrifices, singing and dancing, then man will be able to propitiate the gods . . ." In this discourse, Plate was referring to a much higher order of play than mere "child's play."

We find the same extended usage for play in association with education and culture, for we find the same root in *paideia*. There is no doubt that the Greeks considered education as a life-long concern integrated into community and *arete*. According to some authorities, the word *paideia* literally meant culture.[12] It is apparent from Plato's writings that learning and play were inseparably bound together, that the former was a natural outgrowth of a play motive in life, and that play extended from the child's level to the highest realms of aesthetic and religious experience. Symbols referring to play were for the most part derivations of *paidia*. Suffixes were to indicate playing, playful, plaything, attendance at school, rearing of children, teaching and instruction, as well as to take part in festivals (which included athletics and drama-poetry along with music and dance). The Greeks attached no morality to play and there was no antonym to connote "unplay." Curiously, they had no linguistic equivalent to our word game or sport. For the Greeks, there was only the Olympian Festival and no such expression "Olympic Games." While they may have not understood play an better than we, they recognized it in all aspects of life and nurtured it.

Not unlike classical Greek, but even more inclusive, we find that in Latin there was one universal word to express the whole realm of play, that being *ludus*. The word stem comes from *ludere*, of which *ludus* is a referent. Play was not drawn from the root for child, but rather from a breadth of concepts and at all ages and all levels of society. *Ludus* covered aspects of drama, gambling, games, festivals, athletics, school and learning, satire and comedy, as well as activities associated with parades and public celebrations for amusement. Other derivations cover the realm of unreality or conditions illusionary or fanciful. Cicero used the word *ludimagister* or schoolmaster, hence a direct link with education as was the case with leisure and the Greek derivations.

The word *alea* represented a game of dice and later was to become a referent for chance or hazard. To play, *ludo*, indicated that one could play in a variety of ways, including dice, for purposes of amusement, to banter in conversation, or deceive or delude another with tricks. In classical Latin, there was no word for game in the literal sense, only *ludus*. Game is of English origin as is the term sport. Although we loosely term festival and circuses of Roman times as "public games," they are literally known as *ludus* (play).

Curiously, we find only faint tracings of the original classical Latin *ludus* in the Romance languages. Our words ludicrous, ludibrious and other derivations carry overtones of play, but in a limited sense. Interestingly, we have a game called *Ludo*, which is related to parcheesi and carries the notion of play. Backgammon is often given as the source for game, or originally, *gammon*, but this may only be claimed due to the sound-alike effect. It seems that in our search for meaning of recreation, leisure and play, we find a central theme among all characteristics indicated in the historical tracings of those languages most nearly associated with our own. This theme converges in play, the phenomenon most interesting and intriguing to me. It would appear, then, that play is the experience attributed to recreation and sought through leisure. By systematized observation and autobiographic investigations, we are able to distinguish play from among other behaviors, be it animal or humankind. When you and I play, we are conscious of the experience and are not self-deceiving. By focusing on play to understand concepts generally associated with leisure and recreation, there is no linguistic violence committed against the other terms. The major handicap that I have found is in derisive connotations of an emotive nature among those who fail to understand the universality and significance of play. I am convinced that these handicaps will pass if we become more committed to a research approach.

Of the three terms, play is the most immediately recognized as action oriented. It is the most universal among all cultures, for all languages have a symbol for play, both written and spoken, and no society in the history of written language has ignored play. In a literal sense, we can accept the common phrase, "Americans work hard at their play," as being linguistically correct—we put a great many ergs into it. If, on the other hand, such play is more of a fetish, then there may be a different assessment made. The fact that the word play comes to us through the language of "common folk" and subjugated peoples, helps explain emotive responses to it by intellectuals and upper classes in England and thence America. It might be said that in more recent times, only the disenfranchised person played (including children and animals) while the more advantaged recreated and had leisure.

CONCLUSIONS

This has been a very cursory treatment of the evolution of terms in the field of recreation, but nevertheless, it should provide evidence that we are truly faced with a dilemma as to the meanings of the words central to any discussion of recreation, leisure or play. My theme has been a plea for semantic understanding to clarify intended uses of these terms, especially as we attempt to carry out, through research, assessments of what the field is contributing to society. It has been my contention that we unknowingly add to misunderstanding by failing to clarify our definitions, both among ourselves and with the public. We are often like the person, who when asked what he meant by a certain statement has responded by saying, "You know what I mean" or "I know what I mean, I just can't explain it." If we fail to know the meaning of words necessary to explain a point, then we can presume that the person's thinking is fuzzy. Fuzzy thinking generally produces fuzzy notions, for when we think we use symbols (words).

It is not surprising that we resist being asked to explain that we mean. Not only are we verbally bombarded with words through television and radio, but we are also surrounded by the printed word for most of our waking hours.

To listen carefully and analyze what we hear may soon become a lost art, and then when someone errs and says, "There has been a breakdown in communication," it will be a fact and not just an excuse for failure. Sometimes when we ask for clarification we become more confused and then simply shut down our ears in defense. As an illustration of defending oneself from onslaughts of words which have no meaning for us, a lady clerk in a large office where there were a number of other workers, was asked, "How can you concentrate on what you are doing when there is so much conversation going on around you?" Her answer was, "I don't hear them. I turn it off."

How many of us truly listen and analyze what a politician is saying during campaigns? How many analyze the words he uses? Rather, too many persons take in superficial impressions of how he looks at people, his dress, and how convincingly he delivers his words. Long ago, despots learned the art of orating without using words that had clear-cut and precise meanings and were able to evade or shelter the facts. For example, for a time Americans were not at war in Vietnam, we were maintaining a police action and many less discerning persons believed it.

Too often the journalistic mood of the writer arises and colorful words are sprinkled across the pages. They read so well, it is hoped that no one will questions their accuracy. How delightful it sounds when we sell recreation and leisure as a vehicle for contentment and happiness. Who can be against happiness, against joyful living, against satisfaction with oneself? The gritty part comes when someone asks us to explain what we mean. It has often been said that the person who asks another for clarity is the worst sort of bore, if not simply rude. Only a few of us have lost enough timidity to insist.

As children we learned our language first by imitation and we often misled our parents by using words that they should have realized we did not understand. We also learned to use words in a correct sense without knowing their meanings, to say nothing of skipping the hard ones in our school texts. It is well understood that language is highly contagious, and we must guard against adopting jargon and nonsense statements without examination.

Influences have been many and varied as to reasons for our dilemma in meaning. Not the least of them stems from emotionally laden explanations of the importance of recreation, leisure and play by the early founders of the recreation movement. During the beginning stages of any social movement, stimulating emotional responses among people is far more productive in drawing attention and adherents than any intellectual approach could possibly be. Today, however, recreation has gained acceptance as an institution in America and it is now time for dispassionate analysis. Changes in methods of communication are coming so rapidly that we will be forced to play catch-up to be understood. If we believe, as our early leaders did, that recreation, leisure and play contributed to fulfillment of living, then we need to ask "how" and "why." This can happen only by developing new theories and testing them through research. In light of present individual and social needs, we must not only recognize the holes in other's symbolic reasoning, but also in our own.

REFERENCES

1. Ogend, C. K. and Richards, P. A. *The Meaning of Meanings, A Study of the Significance of Language Upon thought and the Science of Symbolism.* New York: Harcourt Brace, 1923, p. 12.
2. Patrick, G. T. W. *The Psychology of Relaxation.* Boston: Houghton Mifflin, 1916, p. 15.
3. Jaeger, W. *Paideia: The Ideals of Greek Culture.* (Gilbert Highet, Trans.), New York: Oxford University Press, 1939.
4. Pieper, J. *Leisure: The Basis of Culture.* New York: The New American Library, 1963.
5. de Grazia, S. *Of Time, Work and Leisure.* New York: The Twentieth Century Fund, 1962, p. 264.
6. Aristotle. *Metaphysics*, Chapter 1.
7. Brumbaugh, R. S. *Ancient Greek Gadgets and Machines.* New York: Thomas Cromwell Co., 1966, pp. ix-x.
8. Veblen, T. *The Theory of the Leisure Class.* New York: The Macmillan Co., 1899.
9. Hall, T. C. *The Religious Background of American Culture.* Boston: Houghton Mifflin, 1930, Chapter 1.

10. Fairchild, H. P. (Ed.). *Dictionary of Sociology*. New York: Philosophical Library, 1944, p. 175.
11. Huizinga, J. *Homo Ludens: A Study of the Play Element in Culture*. Boston: Beacon Press, 1955, Chapter 11.
12. Jaeger, W. *Op. Cit.*

End of Chapter 1

Chapter 2

Perceptions of Time

John Farina

Time, as a concept, has caused insomnia to philosophers, artists, and social and physical scientists from the beginnings of recorded thought. Yet for the ordinary man the concept itself presents no problem. He knows what time it is—he received a watch for Christmas. He knows when he starts and quits work—he punches in. He knows when the buses, trains and aircraft come and go. He has a fair sense of what sixty miles per hour means both objectively and subjectively. The calendar gives him some idea where he is on the continuum of history. On occasion he has too much time and, perhaps more frequently, he has not enough time.

It seems, however, that the most illuminating observations on time have been recorded not by common men but by uncommon men, not by scientists, social or physical, but by artists and philosophers.

Lao-Tse the Chinese mystic simply noted that, "Time is a state of the mind." Omar Khayyam indicated the finality of the progress of time in his beautiful verse:

> The moving finger writes, and having writ,
> Moves on; nor all your piety nor wit,
> Shall lure it back to cancel half a line,
> Nor all your tears wash out a word of it.

In a related vein Henry Dobson answers a rhetorical question regarding time. "Time goes you say? Oh no! Alas, time stays, *we* go."

Omar Ibn Al Halif notes that regardless of whether we go or time goes, time does not come back:

> "Four things come not back:
> The spoken word
> The sped arrow;
> Time past;
> The neglected opportunity."

Einstein, speaking of visiting friends lingering (this is the artistic Einstein), stated; "They remind me of time—always going but never gone."

The pace of time is beautifully contrasted by Shakespeare and Oscar Wilde speaking of its slowness and Herrick and Tennyson speaking of its inexorable speed.

Macbeth laments:

"Tomorrow and tomorrow and tomorrow,
Creeps in this petty pace from day to day,
to the last syllable of recorded time."

And Oscar Wilde's sad, sad lines from the "Ballad of Reading Gaol":

"All that we know who lie in gaol,
Is that the walls are strong;
And every day is like a year,
A year whose days are long."

Contrast this tragic slowness of time with the light hearted challenge of the swiftness of time as presented by Herrick in his cavalier sonnet:

"Gather ye rosebuds while ye may,
Old time is still a-flying,
And this same flower that smiles today,
Tomorrow will be dying."

Tennyson's *Ulysses*, referring to the swift passage of time, bemoans the brevity of opportunity that the limits of just one life time impose:

"Life piled on life were all too little;
And of one for me—little remains,
And vile it were for some three suns,
To store and board myself."

Marcel Proust lucidly explicates the relativity of time:

"The time which we have at our disposal every day is elastic;
the passions that we feel expand it, those that we inspire
contract it; and habit fills up what remains."

In this day of such concepts as space-time, time-motion and the theory of relativity, the most appealing literary reference to time comes from Lewis Carrol. In *Alice in Wonderland*, that rich source of creative thought, the Mad Hatter speaks with Alice:

"If you knew Time as well as I do you wouldn't talk about wasting it.
It's him."
"I don't know what you mean," said Alice.
"Of course you don't" the Hatter said, tossing his head contemptuously,
"I dare say you never spoke to Time."
"Perhaps not," Alice cautiously replied; "but I know I have to beat
time when I learn music."
"Ah! That accounts for it," said the Hatter, "He won't stand beating.
Now if you only kept on good terms with him, he'd do almost anything
you liked with the clock. For instance, suppose it were nine o'clock in
the morning, just time to begin lessons; you'd only have to whisper a
hint to Time and round goes the clock in a twinkling! Half-past one,
time for dinner!"[1]

What, then, is this slippery concept time which has been so diversely described? A half facetious (and therefore more than half wise) definition states
that: "Time is the diminution of the future by the accumulation of the past."[2]

Historically, man has in fact judged time by periods or intervals. The
earliest such intervals were marked by natural events such as night and day;
Measurement
Spring, Summer, Fall, Winter; full moon, new moon; planting and harvest; etc.
It is somewhat ironical that just as man achieved precision and accuracy in the
measurement of intervals by the development of chronometers and by observations of the solar system, the concept of the relativity of time (subjectively
recognized by artists throughout history) was proposed by physical scientists. It
is therefore necessary to attempt to relate the views of the philosopher-artists on
the one hand and the physicists on the other hand before we can present a comprehensive social concept of time.

While physicists have long used time as a basis for measuring motion—
miles per hour for speed of motion or feet per second as a measure of accelera-
tion—they now view time as a concept without which motion and change cannot
exist. Time by definition now represents, rather than simply measures, change
or motion. Two or more differing and non-simultaneous images are required in
the perception of motion; non-simultaneous means time. For the physicists,
time is inextricably bound to change and motion. For the social scientists, this
change and motion is also seen in terms of the activity of people, of process, of
social change and interchange, and of the interaction of people.

Yet the social concept of time seems inextricably bound to our value system.
Thus George Woodcock, writing on the tyranny of the clock, suggests that the
clock was the most important instrument of the Industrial Revolution.[3] George
Soule, suggests that "The American Attitude" includes enslavement by and
reverence to the clock. This he relates directly to economic attitudes characteristic of the Protestant Ethic.[4] Thus we spend, waste, exchange, buy, hoard, sell,

Clock!

forget, save, use, kill, structure, beat, and pass time. Time itself: marches, flies, plods, creeps, passes by, and escapes. All these terms relate directly to action and process. While to the economist and worker time is money to be saved, spent or wasted just as material goods, time is also a dimension of activity, change, or process. In turn, time has several dimensions, including duration, intensity, extensity, quantity and quality.

DIMENSIONS OF TIME

Duration

This attribute of time may be viewed as a continuum extending from the infinite past to the infinite future. The present is an infinitesimal moving interval proceeding at a regular and unfailing pace from the past to the future. Time as the accumulation of the past by the diminution of the future fits this notion beautifully. Thus duration is measurable in terms of the regular passage of the present along the continuum of duration. Indeed this measurement has been so operationally accurate and economically useful that it has been literally reified in terms of an interval scale—the clock. This approach to time synchronizes smoothly with the notion of money, also an interval scale, to represent materially the value of man's time. Thus a man might say, "My time is worth $10.00 an hour."

There is, however, a subjective aspect of duration. The psychologists point out that time which is occupied with much pleasant activity tends to seem shorter than time which is devoid of meaningful activity. For example: one hour of playing baseball seems shorter than one hour of waiting for a bus. In retrospect, however, the reverse is true. The time which was occupied seems longer on recall than does that time which was relatively unoccupied.

Intensity

Since time is inextricably bound up with action, the subjective experience of any given action over a period will vary in intensity. What we must recognize is that regardless of the precise indices of time we use, we are in fact dealing with perceptions and feelings. de Grazia notes:

> "Thus by using a strictly quantitative assembly-line conception time—
> time as a moving-belt of equal units—one ignores the significance of
> much activity. A moment of awe in religion, or ecstasy in love, or orgasm
> in intercourse, a decisive blow to an enemy, relief in a sneeze, or death
> in a fall is treated as equal to a moment of riding on a bus or shovelling
> coal or eating beans."[5]

We can note the same intensity differential almost daily—bases full, two out, last of the ninth inning, the home team 2 runs behind, the count on the batter 3 and 2—is a significantly more intense moment than a ninth inning with 2 out nobody on and the home team leading 10-0. The subjectivity is clear in this illustration for in addition to the different intensity potential which is inherent in the setting and structure of the activity there is a distinguishable subjective intensity difference for the pitcher and outfielder, for the team managers and the umpires, for the players and the spectators, and among the spectators depending upon their emotional commitment to either team or the amount of their bet on the outcome of the game.

Extensity and Quantity

Under this heading consideration is given to the extent to which identifiable blocks of time are available. For example that block of time called a life time has doubled in western civilization during the past 1,000 years. This greater life expectation is increasing in extensity, i.e., it is becoming available to more people in more areas of the world.

Again—in western civilization—that block of time we identify as "work-time" is becoming more brief and this shortening of work time as a quantity of time is becoming more extensive. The obvious corollary is that non-work time increased in direct proportion to the decrease in work time. Again, speaking in terms of extensity, if we view non-work time as being mostly leisure time (as some do) we can state that, in Western Civilization at least, this is the age of mass leisure. No longer, as in Veblen's day, is leisure so restricted in extensity or so limited in quantity that we can speak of the leisure class. There is no longer a class identified by the fact that it alone has quantities of leisure.

Thus when we speak of time in terms of extensity, we are referring to the extent of the distribution of identifiable blocks of time. When we speak of time as quantity, we are speaking of the variations in measurement of particular blocks of time. Thus the 35 hour work week refers to the quantitative aspect of work time. The availability of the thirty hour work week to a given number of office workers refers to the extensity of this particular block of time.

Quality

The quality of time refers to those conditions that make it possible to classify a period as work, leisure, free time, idleness, etc. To a great extent the quality of time is culturally determined and inextricably dependent upon values. Most societies tend to dichotomize time and the tendency of western civilization is to do so in terms of work and non-work. To a large extent this particular dichotomy dates from the Industrial Revolution and is a reflection of the Protestant Ethic.

Other societies employ different dichotomies: e.g.,

> African Bushmen—Women's activities and Men's activities.
> Plains Indians—Peace and War.
> Baluchi of Pakistan—Obligatory and time of free will. Here the emphasis and status is on the latter.

In one respect the Baluchi point of view is easier for us to understand than is the view of the Plains Indians for, like us, they distinguish between an area of sober, mundane, practical activity and an area of play or free will.[6]

Work and Obligated Time

Work time in our society is that time required for maintenance or for material improvement of self and dependents. It is literally time spent in return for money or its equivalent. It is time *spent* to fulfill the obligation of monetary reward. One man spends his money for another man's time while reciprocally the other man spends his time for another man's money.

Obligated time may be divided into two types, although these are not always mutually exclusive:

1. Sleep and personal maintenance time. This would include time involved in personal toilet and for eating. Non-essential eating time can, however, on occasion be viewed as free time, leisure or recreation.

2. Non-work obligatory time. This involves time committed to one's primary role expectations outside the sphere of gainful employment. It is adequately illustrated by such characteristic suburban activities as upping and downing storm windows and screens, mowing the lawn, driving junior to his music lesson, the trip to the shopping centre and sundry obligatory "voluntary" activities. These may or may not be satisfying modes of behavior. No judgment is being passed on the value of these activities. For some they may challenge the mentality or spirit or simply be pleasant in themselves; for others they may be dull and "plonking."[7]

IDLENESS, RECREATION, FREE TIME, LEISURE

Idleness

In general use, idleness is a term of eprobrium although it can be an alternate for recreation, free time and leisure. It found wide currency following the Protestant Reformation when it was generally used in reference to non-workers.

As recreation came to be viewed as a contributor to greater productivity, the term idleness was reserved for those non-workers who were not refreshing or recreating themselves for more efficient work. Today the term has lost currency outside puritan oriented religious groups.

All four of the terms listed above represent the non-work side of our time dichotomy. We must recognize, however, that leisure is not the antonym for work but rather is the positive counterpart. The opposite of work is unemployment.

Recreation

This term in our society has been implicitly identified with the work category of time although it is popularly believed to represent the non-work category of time. Professional recreation workers identify recreation as activity indulged in voluntarily for the satisfaction derived from the activity itself and leading to revitalization, or recreation, of mind, body or spirit. In fact this is a limiting definition in terms of pre-determination as it is only by the result (revitalization) that recreation can be identified.

Nonetheless, our society assumes that certain types of activity are potentially recreative; music, sports, drama, cinema, social events, etc. Public, private and commercial organizations providing opportunities for these types of activities have proliferated in recent years. The question raised by the definition of recreation is: recreation or revitalization for what? Recreation promoted by business and industrial concerns, recreation as a medical prescription, and recreation as an adjunct to our educational system all emphasize the potential of such activities for revitalizing the individual so he can work more efficiently.

Will the role of leisure in relation to work undergo a basic change? Up to now our leisure as well as most other activities of our life has been work-oriented. Leisure is often thought of in terms of "recreation"—i.e., activities to be engaged in during non-work hours which will refresh or "recreate" the individual so that he may be a more effective worker upon his return to his job. Otherwise, it is regarded as idleness. With increasing leisure, will new types of pursuits emerge—goal-directed, useful, long-term, satisfying in nature—around which man may also focus his energies and ambitions? Will work once again in human history become a means to other ends—as visualized in Thomas More's *Utopia*—rather than an end in itself?[8]

Free Time

In general usage free time is considered as residual time after we take account of work-time, sleep-time and time for personal care. More precisely, free time may be considered as that time during which one is relatively free of primary role expectations. This approach ties the concept of free time into the theoretical framework of role theory. It derives from the notion that free time is time which is not restricted by occupational and family duties and obligations. Other obligations and duties then are considered secondary to an individual's family and occupational roles. Indeed occupational role may be considered as subsidiary to family role or as a specific aspect of that central role. Free time, then, is time during which one is relatively free of economic, social, or physical restriction or compulsion.

As with duration, free time and obligatory time can be conceived as the extremes of a continuum. Thus we may view time as relatively free or relatively obligatory. In terms of this conceptualization, absolutely free time is an ideal and probably unattainable.

Free time allows for relatively preferential behavior while obligatory time involves the expectation of a particular kind of behavior. During obligatory time an individual acts with reference to the norms and primary expectations of his occupational and family roles. While role expectation is not absent in free time there is not the same intensity of obligation to assume specific role behavior. If obligations to assume specific roles or to meet specific role expectations are present then the time during which such a role is performed is less free than when such obligations do not exist. During free time there is a greater opportunity for a person to select from a wide range of choices of behavior as he or she may pursue goals not necessarily related to economic or family expectations. It must be recognized that the individual is seldom, if ever, free of structural expectations. During free time he comes under the pressure of different norms which might be quite as restrictive as those operating during obligatory time.

Free time, then, presents the opportunity to exercise preferential behavior. The range and quality of choice may vary considerably in terms of the quantity and quality of time available. There is a difference in the quality of behavioral opportunity after ten hours of strenuous work and after eight hours of refreshing sleep. Also there is a great difference in the range of choice offered during a 15-minute free period at a factory ten miles from home and a free afternoon at a summer resort.

Leisure

Leisure, as opposed to recreation, does not describe activities and, as opposed to free time, is not time. The term "leisure time" as differing from "leisure" describes a particular type of time. On this basis *leisure* should perhaps be more logically compared with *freedom*, i.e., the two modifiers in the terms "free time" and "leisure time" warrant comparison.

Leisure has become a recent concern of the modern social science scholar whereas previously it was primarily the domain of the philosopher. We are not, however, dealing with a new concept but rather with a reconceptualization of a construct which has been a subject of philosophic discussion since the Golden Age of Greece. Most discussions of leisure take Aristotle's ideas as the point of departure.

Aristotle viewed leisure as, "a condition or state, the state of being free from the necessity to labor."[9] On occasion he used the term in such a manner as to suggest that it involved a time element, that is, the time during which one was in the particular condition or state referred to as leisure. The essential terms in this definition are "freedom" and "necessity." We must not be misled into believing that labor, in the sense of strenuous physical activity, is excluded from Aristotle's notion of leisure. What is excluded is the *necessity* or obligation to labor.

It must be noted, however, that freedom from the opportunity to labor does not constitute leisure if the necessity to labor is present. Thus the unemployed do not necessarily have leisure.

Pieper, commenting on Aristotle's view noted: "The provision of an external opportunity to leisure is not enough; it can only be fruitful if man himself is capable of leisure and can as we say occupy his leisure."[10] This suggests a value placed on the manner in which leisure is occupied: i.e., "fruitfully." Leisure thus has a positive connotation. If a man is free from the necessity to labor and does not employ himself "fruitfully" he is more likely referred to as idle than as at leisure.

A definition of leisure devoid of value is that offered by the *Oxford English Dictionary*: "The state of having time at one's disposal; time which one can spend as one pleases; free or unoccupied time."[11] This definition includes the notion of leisure as a state and of its freedom. It adds, however, the non-judgmental element of choice of use of time without specifying that the choice must be "fruitful" in order to qualify as leisure.

Thus we find a consensus that leisure is characterized by freedom, a sense of freedom that is in the mind of man as differing from environmental or socially determined freedom. This freedom can be considered an opportunity to act as one pleases within limits imposed by environment and social context. The idea that the action must be "fruitful" appears too judgmental and value oriented to be an essential aspect of the concept. In given circumstances, if we leave the judgment of leisure to criteria external to the concept, then we may speak of fruitful or non-fruitful leisure according to context.

When we divest the view of Aristotle and its restatement by Pieper of the value element, there remains the clear implication that activity is an aspect of leisure. The time during which one is in the state of leisure must be "occupied."

This occupation of time may include overt activity and also such "leisurely" pursuits as counting clouds on a sunny afternoon, or quiet meditation, or contemplation. Indeed Pieper considers the notion of non-activity an essential of leisure.

"Leisure is a form of silence, of that silence which is the prerequisite of the apprehension of reality: only the silent hear and those who do not remain silent do not hear. Silence, as it is used in this context, does not mean 'dumbness' or 'noiselessness;' it means more nearly that the soul's power to 'answer' to the reality of the world is left undisturbed. For leisure is a receptive attitude of mind, a contemplative attitude, and it is not only the occasion but also the capacity for steeping oneself in the whole of creation."[12]

Pieper adds that this ideal state of leisure contributes to happiness. The element of freedom as a precondition to leisure is explicated by Kaplan in terms of social role obligations. He suggests that during leisure a man can choose to assume obligations "voluntarily, and with pleasanter expectations than, for example, going to work on January 2 to which he is formally committed for a long period of time."[13] Our conceptualization of free time borrows the notion of freedom from social role obligation. We are, however, impressed with de Grazia's concern regarding the loss of free time by increasing family role expectations.[14] Our notion of leisure, however, goes further. Leisure is that time when one is free from the necessity of fulfilling primary role expectations. This means time not restricted by the demands of occupational and family duties and obligations. Clearly this concept does not limit leisure to free time.

It is possible to achieve leisure within the context of primary role obligation if the need or demand to act in a particular manner is not present. Thus a professional man may choose an activity while performing his professional role which is not necessary or demanded of him at that time. A worker on an assembly line lacks this choice. Similarly, a father may feel obliged to play ball with his son, which we would consider non-leisure, or he may choose to join his wife on the patio for a gin and tonic which would be leisure. The differentiating factors are the element of necessity and the element of freedom of choice.

Man is faced with an ever increasing block of time which is potentially free. Whether he keeps it free and is able to free himself to enjoy leisure is the challenge of our age. Meeting this challenge will not be facilitated by simplistic and often contradictory notions of time, of leisure, and of freedom. Conceptual clarity is essential in the use of designations. Games, play, idleness, contemplation, leisure, recreation, sports and cultural activities are clearly related terms. Yet just as clearly they are not synonymous or interchangeable when we want words to work with the precise denotations that are essential to knowledge building.

A more hopeful factor that might contribute to meeting the challenge is how man chooses to occupy his ever increasing potential inherent in free time. In a society of increasing unemployment, rapid replacement of workers by automation, earlier retirement, later entry to the work force, innumerable make-work jobs, and increasing income maintenance programs, it seems ridiculous to be concerned with full employment. Rather, maximum nonemployment might be a more reasonable goal for a post industrial society. Certainly, this would satisfy an essential precondition to a leisure society and free man's potential to occupy his time constructively and productively in terms of the quality of life. Towards this end, *time* is of the essence.

REFERENCES

1. Carroll, L. *Alice's Adventures in Wonderland.* New York: The Modern Library, 1920, p. 94.
2. Author unknown.
3. Cited in: Kaplan, M. *Leisure in America: A Social Inquiry.* New York: John Wiley and Sons, 1960, p. 265.
4. Soule, G. "The Economics of Leisure." *The Annals of the American Academy of Political and Social Science.* (September) 1957, pp. 16-24.
5. de Grazia, S. "How People Spend Their Time." In: Kleemeier, R. W. (Ed.). *Aging and Leisure.* New York: Oxford University Press, 1960, pp. 142-43.
6. Donahue, W. et al. (Eds.). *Free Time.* Ann Arbor, Michigan: University of Michigan Press, 1958, pp. 10-11.
7. A favorite Stephen Potter word meaning just what it sounds like.
8. Donahue, *Op. Cit.* p. 130.
9. de Grazia, S. *Of Time, Work, and Leisure.* New York: The Twentieth Century Fund, 1962, p. 11.
10. Pieper, J. *Leisure: The Basis of Culture.* New York: Pantheon Books, 1952, p. 71.
11. *Oxford English Dictionary.* Toronto: Leland Publishing Company, 1957.
12. Pieper, *Op. Cit.* p. 52.
13. Kaplan, *Op. Cit.* p. 23.
14. de Grazia, *Op. Cit. Chapter III.*

(no beep)

p. 32 is blank.

End of Chapter 2

Chapter 3

Is There Enough Time?

Thomas L. Goodale

> Hay mas tiempo que vida.
> *Spanish Proverb*

Being members of what Staffan Linder described as *The Harried Leisure Class*,[1] most of us would likely answer "no" to the title's question. Being more practically oriented than philosophically, we probably would answer the question with questions of our own: Time enough to do what? How long does it take? When does it start? When is it over? When does it have to be finished? In short, our response would be that of a people who are almost perpetually in motion going somewhere or doing something. We read that into the title's question. We do not read it as philosophical and have nothing comparable to the proverb Spanish people might offer in response: There is more time than life.

That notion, that there is more time than life, was nicely illustrated in a 1966 essay by Stuart Chase, an economist, authority on national and international affairs, and social philosopher. The question he put to himself and to each of us was, "Are You Alive?"[2] By life he meant absorption and vitality in contrast not to being dead but to merely existing. He then listed eleven states or situations in which he felt alive: when creating something, enjoying art, in the mountains or by the sea, at play, good conversation, sorrow, laughter, love, sound sleep, and when satisfying hunger or thirst. Mere existing included monotony, drudgery, anger, when senses were dulled or, and many philosophers have made similar comments, "when attending the average social function." He then calculated that during an ordinary week he was alive about 25 percent of the time; not a very high ratio he figured, but he guessed it was better than most Americans were able to manage. So the Spanish proverb is correct, there is more time than life. Perhaps we should be asking not about how much time there is but how much life.

WHAT IS TIME?

St. Augustine said that he knew what time was until someone asked. Then he had to admit that he did not really know. Probably most of us would have to make a similar confession. Alfred North Whitehead observed that the question, "What is time?" was one which humbles the human intellect. And if Aristotle's discussion of time in *Physics*, Book IV, was the only part of his work you had read, it would likely remain the only part you had read.

The word "time" has origins in the root *ti,* which means to stretch, suggesting length in reference to space or distance between events. Note how time and space are so commonly linked in our understanding, a matter elaborated upon in a coming section. The *ti* root is found also in tides, suggesting both rhythms and cycles, and in tidy, suggesting order and orderliness. Time also has origins in the Latin *temper* and in the romance languages: *tiempo* in Spanish; *temps* in French, and so on. We use the word temporal to refer to time, of course, and the root *temp* is found also in temperature, temperate and tempest, all of which in their original meanings suggest change and regulation.[3] The Greek *chronos,* the root of several English words, is another origin of time as we have come to understand it. In sum, time is a most complex concept, one with many origins and many meanings, of which sequence, duration, and temporal perspective (past, present, and future) are basic components upon which most students of time agree. Yet it is seems so simple until someone asks.

FREE TIME AND FREEDOM

Most people equate leisure with free time. Most students of leisure have abandoned that notion, mainly due to difficulties not so much with time, since we all know what it means (until asked), but with the modifier—free. By free time was meant time not required for work or other obligations: inadequacies of that meaning need not be belabored here. But other perspectives on the phrase free time (the above perspective is mainly sociological) help us think about time, and why we often think there is not enough.

One way of defining free is without cost or charge, gratis, a gift. Regarding time at least, we have little sense of that although that is a perspective taken by some philosophers, theologians, and others of similar ilk. They would point out that holy day is the origin of holiday. They would point out that in the beginning, in creating heaven and earth, God's day of rest was the seventh day; man's day of rest was the first day, since he was created on the sixth day. Josef Pieper[4] is particularly instructive about time being free in this perspective; a gift to be graciously received and committed to festive celebration.

The idea that time is not free and that there is never enough is drawn from an economic perspective. Just as we believe there is no such thing as a free lunch, we believe there is no such thing as free time. The Sabbath, the seventh day, is a day of rest earned by six days of work. We earn holidays and vacations and retirement. We earn time as we do money, and we save, spend, gain, lose, waste, and borrow it as if it were money, as Ben Franklin said. We treat it, then, as a commodity, trade it in the labor market, and so on. Scarcity is perhaps the central assumption of economics, and we think time is scarce. Hay mas tiempo indeed.

There is a third perspective, a political one. It is about power. In this case, it is about who decides what time is, how it is arranged, and particularly who imposes the meaning and the arrangement of time upon whom. *Time Wars,*[5] Jeremy Rifkin's interesting book with an intriguing title, is about the developing struggle over how time is conceptualized, arranged, and imposed; in short, our "lived" time and our experience of it. There are forces arrayed to speed it up; efficiency experts, for example, and the makers of high tech apparatus. Facing them are those living and advocating a more natural, biological time: the soft-energy, holistic health, and voluntary simplicity advocates, among others. Who prevails will influence how we perceive and experience time in coming years. Rifkin also suggested that history can be interpreted by who determined the temporal experience, the lived time, of whom. He argued, in fact, that the ability to shape the temporal experience of others is the central instrument of oppression.

That oppression is clear in the case of serfs and slaves, and of factory workers in the earlier stages of industrialism. As Bregha argues in the following chapter, all economic systems are oppressive, and part of that is because of their impact on our time and our experience of it. In hierarchical systems of superiors and subordinates, who decides whose time is to be used in what amounts and ways? What is the time experience of those with unchallenging work? Are they, Chase might ask, living or existing?

The matter of oppression via shaping temporal experience is central to the feminist movement and to the feminist critique not only of the distribution of free time but in fact the very meaning of it. To a husband a holiday may mean having a good time by having family and friends visit. To his spouse it may mean hours of work and worry. A family vacation can also have quite different meanings as well as quite different time demands. This, too, is part of the politics of time.

For most of us, when and how long we work, what we buy and how much we spend, and perhaps some of our obligations as well are influenced, if not entirely dictated, by others. If we feel harried and feel that there just is not enough time, we are unwittingly admitting that we are living by some other sense and arrangement of time than our own. We even resorted to talking about "quality time," usually in reference to the limited amount of time we spend with our own children and spouses. It was a transparent rationalization designed to protect us from admitting that we had lost control of our time, which is to say our lives.

FROM EONS TO NANOS

The main metaphors or symbols we use for time are the arrow and the circle;[6] the arrow representing linear time based mainly in physics, the circle representing cyclical time based mainly in biology. During virtually all of human life, time was conceived as cyclical, natural, and mostly biological. The seasons, tide, sun and moon, edible plants' growth, animal migrations, hunger, thirst, mating; these were the references for time. Calendars date back a mere two thousand years or so, clocks a few hundred, stop watches a bit over a century, photo and electric timing a few decades, nanos are of still more recent origin. Each of these developments has given us a way of reckoning time in increasingly precise and small amounts: from seasons to months, days, hours, seconds, tenths, and hundredths. A nano second is one billionth of a second: a one followed by nine zeros.

While this has been going on, we have also been learning more and more about vast expanses of time; the age of the universe, of the earth, of life, and of humankind. One would think such discoveries would have a limiting effect on the importance we attach to ourselves. Alas, it has not, and although Mark Twain's numbers are by now drastically underestimated, his perception of our sense of self importance seems about right:

> Man has been here 32,000 years. That it took 100 million years to prepare the world for him is proof that that is what it was done for. I suppose it is, I dunno. If the Eiffel Tower were now representing the world's age, the skin of paint on the pinnacle-knob at the summit would represent man's share of that age; and anybody would perceive that that skin was what that tower was built for. I reckon they would, I dunno.[7]

Our perceptions are based on nanos, however, not eons. That is probably because "real" time, as we understand it, is a product of physics. Time, in physics, is a product of dividing distance by velocity; $T = D/V$. Speed and space or distance are built into our understanding of time. Two hours = 120 miles divided by 60 miles per hour. The reference point is the speed of light, which is how the length of a meter was determined. The product of great velocities over great distances is light years. The product of great velocities over infinitesimally short spaces is nano seconds.

SHRUNKEN PERSPECTIVES—TIME AND LIFE

Our perceptions, then, are shaped by time and space, both of which we measure in smaller and smaller amounts. Time's arrow is shorter, time's passage faster. The real time, space and distance of physics have counterparts in our perception. For example, the more distant we are from an object, the slower it appears to be moving. Put another way, the wider our field of view, the longer an object takes to traverse it. The greater the distance from something, of course, the wider the field of view. Peripheral vision means they mosey along. Similarly, things close pass rapidly, things distant take their time. Time scarcity and the rush of events is mainly the result of shrunken perspectives of time and space. Here and now come to fill up that space and take on undue importance. Each of us, somehow, become the center of our own shrunken world. In each of those worlds, whirl is king.

The rush and scarcity of time are related to time's arrow, that is, linear, non-recurring time, for another reason. We know we are not immortal; we know we are going to die, and insurance actuarials give us a fair estimate of when. Life, we say, is short, our time is limited, we better make the most of it, and we can't take it with us. More than 150 years ago, Alexis de Toqueville described our restlessness, the "disquietude" he observed in us, as follows:

> A native of the United States clings to this world's goods as if he were certain never to die; and he is so hasty at grasping at all within his reach that one would suppose he was constantly afraid of not living long enough to enjoy them. He clutches at everything, he holds nothing fast, but soon loosens his grasp to pursue fresh gratifications.
>
> He who has set his heart exclusively upon the pursuit of worldly welfare is always in a hurry, for he has a limited time at his disposal to reach, to grasp, and to enjoy it. The recollection of the shortness of life is a constant spur to him. Besides the good things he possesses, he every instant fancies a thousand others that death will prevent him from trying if he does not try them soon.[8]

Toqueville also observed that a typical American tends to focus on a very puny object, himself. Today, more than 150 years after Toqueville wrote *Democracy in America*, scores of observers continue to note the same tendency. In recent years, our culture has become increasingly individualistic, witness the erosion of such institutions as family and community and their shared values which were, in a sense, the adhesives of collective life. What Toffler called the "psychologization" of the culture has sharpened our focus on individual experience, feelings, and the like. Existentialism has led us on a self-centered crusade to discover who we are by trying to experience everything, as if foregoing anything would foreclose on the prospect of self-actualization and realization of our full potential. Denial of anything came to be seen as a form of self-mutilation. The result has been further shrinking of perspective. Yankelovich neatly summarized this consequence of self-centering.

> By concentrating day and night on your feelings, potentials, needs,
> wants, and desires, and by learning to assert them more freely,
> you do not become a freer, more spontaneous, more creative self:
> you become a narrower more self-centered, more isolated one.
> You do not grow, you shrink.[9]

In addition to this shrinking of perspective, which makes even trivial matters loom large and all matters rush past our narrow view, our sense that time passes too quickly and is too scarce results from our belief that we must have and try everything. We think there is too little time because there is so much to do. Hurry this sale ends . . . Hurry, this offer expires . . . Hurry, there are only . . . shopping days before . . . As the bumper sticker says, "So many pedestrians, so little time." The new high tech slogan is, "Death to down time." And we are developing an entire language made up entirely of abbreviations and acronyms. Talk faster, we haven't got all day.

SAVING, DEEPENING AND DISCOUNTING TIME

One response to time scarcity, time famine some say, is to try almost anything that purports to save time. Nothing we have tried has saved as much as a moment because time cannot be saved. The only results have been to do more and to quicken the pace. That is why we observe others and ourselves waiting impatiently on computers and printers, instamatic cameras and bank tellers, microwave ovens and Minute Rice. If we are saving time, why are we increasingly impatient?

Another response to time scarcity or famine has been to practice time-deepening: doing more in less time, different things at the same time, and measuring time in smaller and more precise amounts. (At a workshop I attended recently, each speaker was allotted nine minutes, not ten, nine.) Current estimates are that 50 percent of Americans watch television during dinner and 25 percent of American commuters eat breakfast, such as it is, while driving to work.[10] They also shave, fix their hair, apply make up, and call home to make sure the children, of whom they see little, are up and getting ready for school and know where to go after school. At home, the children have "fax" machines for exchanging class and other notes with friends. Father, a time-management expert and a one-minute manager, is on a ten-day weight loss program and has a exercycle with a keyboard in place of handlebars. It is easy to make light of these examples of time-deepening. But one should not take lightly the consequences of time-famine and our attempts to cope with it. Some of those consequences are discussed in the next section. Suffice it to say here that it is making us sick and sometimes killing us.

Time famine also contributes to what economists call time-discounting or the preference for the present over the future. Its principal manifestation is indebtedness. Interest payments reflect the discount rate of time and how much more we are willing to pay to have something now rather than in the future. Much has been said about the federal deficit, the burden we are passing on to the next generation, the annual interest cost, and ways of reducing that deficit. As a way of understanding a deficit now measured in trillions of dollars, to retire the debt by making payments of $10,000 per minute would take 521 years.[11]

Our preference for the present over the future is also reflected in deferring costs, such as those required to maintain the infrastructure of our cities. Further decay, particularly in assuring safe water supply and sewage disposal systems, may be catastrophic. The cost of repairing or replacing them may also be catastrophic. Similarly, our treatment of the environment is a function of our present time preference and time discounting. Resource depletion is only part of the problem. Toxic waste, nuclear contamination, carcinogens, acid rain, greenhouse effects, ozone holes in the upper atmosphere and ozone concentrations in the air we breathe are just some of the potential catastrophes which time preference and time discounting led us to create and encourage us to ignore.

INSTANT GRATIFICATION AND THE POSTERITY PROBLEM

Instant gratification is another way of stating our preference for the present over the future. When once our ancestors, having more religious faith than we, deferred gratification to the hereafter; when once parents deferred gratification to improve opportunities for the next generation, now we have difficulty deferring gratification for even short periods. Our temporal perspective is focused almost entirely on the present. We discount the future, seldom giving it much thought. When we do think about it we are generally less optimistic, probably for good reasons, than were most previous generations, at least since the dark ages. One response to pessimism about the future is to enjoy the present, have and do all you can since you may not be able to in the future. The dilemma is that optimists make a similar response, assuming they can have it all now and in the future as well.

That is part of what Heilbronner called the posterity problem,[12] the problem of discounting the future and letting it take care of itself. Who cares about the future? Heilbronner asked. Why worry about it? What has the future ever done for me? Why shouldn't we maximize our own welfare and pleasure? The answer is:

"... that the welfare of the individual depends on the extent to which he can identify himself with others, and that the most satisfactory individual identity is that which identifies not only with a community in space but also with a community extending over time from the past into the future ... " There is a great deal of historical evidence to suggest that a society which loses its identity with posterity and which loses its positive image of the future loses also its capacity to deal with the present, and soon falls apart.[13]

Psychologists have pointed out the relationship between cognitive development, impulse control, delay of gratification, and time perspective. As children age, they become increasingly capable of delaying reward. They also understand temporal concepts better and develop more extended future time perspectives. These phenomena share a common cognitive substrate and pattern of development.[14] Moreover, there appear to be clear links between reward delay, temporal perspective, and the evolution of the brain. The ability to delay reward increases as one ascends the phylogenetic scale. Chimpanzees can delay rewards longer than cats, cats longer than rats, etc. Man has the greatest capacity to delay rewards. In addition, evolution of the central nervous system has entailed an increasing capacity to conceptualize and relate to more extensive spans of time. "It is possible," Melges observed, "that man's capacity for an extended sense of time and temporal relationships is his greatest evolutionary gift." Being able to take future consequences into account gives us "survival skills unprecedented in the animal kingdom."[15] The temporal and frontal lobes of the brain are among the more recently evolved portions, and they are also those most involved in our perception of time; sequence, duration and temporal perspective of extensive (past and future) time. Failure to exercise our capacity for deferral, our evolutionary gift and survival skill, may lead to our demise. That is one of the lessons evolutionary biology teaches.

IN SICKNESS AND IN HEALTH

The health of the future and of present society depend on our time concepts and temporal perspectives. It is also clear that the health of each of us is dependent upon how we conceptualize time, arrange and use time, and sense or fail to sense its extent. We have known about the health consequences of stress for some time, and about the consequences of disrupted biorhythms when clock time interferes with natural, biological time. Chronobiology continues to expose the health hazards and costs of time dictated and driven by clocks, from jet lag to shift work to deadlines and more. Most attention has been focused on physiological consequences such as the stress related diseases linked to Type A (time famine) behaviors.

There is also an interesting literature linking time perspectives to mental health and illness. Psychological time, or "inner" time, refers to "lived" or experienced time, which is often markedly different from "outer," physical time represented by the clock. All of us have had experiences during which time flies and others during which time drags. That is, inner time is moving slower than clock time, which seems to fly by. Usually this is when we are so absorbed as to not notice time passing. Time drags when inner time moves faster than outer time, as when we are bored. Other studies have explored temporal perspectives, sequence, presence or absence of awareness, and aspects of time other than duration. To summarize a large volume of complex material; inner time is one of the key elements of mental health and illness, and how we experience time is related to our extension of time, especially into the future.[16]

Perceptions of time which include the past and what we have acquired from it, along with the future and what we can foresee in it, are significant indicators of mental health and central to defining it. Those who have long term personal directions tend to be happy and in a good mood and also to have a secure sense of identity and esteem.

Conversely, those with shrunken time horizons tend to be tense, anxious, nervous, overly sensitive, and overly absorbed with themselves and the fleeting present. Psychopathology typically involves temporal disorientation, fragmentation, desynchronicity, disintegration of sequence, and other abnormal time experience. Schizophrenics typically confuse past, present, and future, have often wildly fluctuating estimates of the duration of clock time, and little extension to the future. Similar though less severe distortions and disruptions are found in mania and depression, anxiety disorders, and even personality and adjustment disorders.[17]

Time scarcity or famine and the sense that there is never enough time leaves us anxious if not neurotic. We over focus on the present, press to accomplish an endless series of short-term tasks, and sense a lack of control. We seem to have a whole culture suffering from anxiety disorders. For most of us, at least so far, this is a rather mild disorder, but one which has become so widespread it seems normal. It isn't. In addition, we have become obsessed with time and often compulsive about it, being brutally efficient, for example, or rigid in scheduling and sequencing our hours and days. We are obsessive about planning, often in detail, and compulsive about executing the plans, although there is little extension into the future. This, too, is so common as to seem normal. It isn't.

ILLNESS BEGETS ILLNESS

It is no wonder, then, that much of our free time is spent in one form or another of escape. Most of those forms are innocuous enough, although they are not always effective. Living vicariously rather than authentically, existing rather than living, is one of our principal forms of escape. Much of our daily contact with the media and some of our weekend and vacation activity is escapist. We speak these days of being "couch potatoes" or "vegging out" (i.e., becoming, for a while, a vegetable), in both cases becoming inanimate and thus escaping from the human environment, especially one made hectic by the pressure of scarce time.

But there is another form of escape, a detrimental one and one characterized by changing our awareness, sense, and perspective of time. We need no reminder that we live in a drug culture and substance abuse has taken on epidemic proportions. Americans consume about 60 percent of the world's production of illegal drugs and drugs are the danger of greatest concern to American parents. Drugs have many effects but altered consciousness of time is characteristic of all those drugs which concern us here. With them we escape present time and the presence of clock time. One of the earlier and better known descriptions of chemically altered time is Thomas De Quincey's, *Confessions of an English Opium Eater*, written in 1822.[18] In it he described staring at his shoes for an hour, which in reality was only a few minutes at most. There is an endless collection of similar, anecdotal evidence of the effects of drugs on time perception. Most users of marijuana, for example, report time slowing or coming to a halt, and diminished awareness of the presence of time. Clinical studies confirm the anecdotal record.[19]

"Uppers" typically accelerate inner time. Amphetamines, or "speed", is an example. "Downers" typically decelerate inner time. Opiates, hypnotics, psychedelics, stimulants, depressants, whatever—all change our awareness of time and sense of its passing. Alcohol is our most widely used and abused drug. As with the illegal drugs, alcohol changes inner time, slowing it down and thus making clock time pass more quickly. Often alcohol is used to block out the present, painful recollections of the past, or uncertain or fearful anticipations of the future.

Drugs, time and health are linked inextricably. The society's health as well as that of individuals is very much at stake. Time, as it is measured and as it is perceived, is at the center of this maelstrom. Our inability to conceive time as other than linear and scarce, our preference for the present over the future and our inability to defer gratification, our self-centeredness and shrunken perspective, our obsessive-compulsive personalities and anxiety laden neurosis in the face of time scarcity, our attempts at time saving, managing and deepening, our pursuit of the vicarious and the vegetative, and our escape into chemical euphoria and narcotic stupor—all this, quite literally, is killing us. There is another way.

OF THINGS INFINITE AND IMMORTAL

There are actually two ways. Perhaps there are many, although these two probably incorporate most of them. One is the flow phenomenon, first described at length in Csikszentmihalyi's *Beyond Boredom and Anxiety*.[20] Flow is used to describe the feeling of being carried along and away, gently, by the complete absorption of the individual in the activity in which he or she is engaged. It is the absorption, not the activity, that matters. Performing surgery, playing chess, climbing rocks or a thousand other activities can result in flow. One becomes part of what one is engaged in, the pre-occupied self disappears, and time disappears. We all know the experience of losing track of time. Children, in all their innocence, do it regularly. Innocence is just another way, although a profound way, of saying intrinsic motivation. There is no external goal, no agenda, hidden or not.

The experience of leisure or recreative life is a shaping of temporal experience, one which liberates rather than oppresses. It marks not an escape from linear time but a transcendence above and beyond it. We do not lose time, we lose only the awareness of it; it is free time in a new sense in that it is we who are free from the oppressive awareness of time. Priestly provided a colorful description of the flow of inner time:

> Notice how inner time behaves, as if it had centuries of chronological time at its disposal. As soon as we make full use of our faculties, commit ourselves heart and soul to anything, live richly and intensely instead of merely existing, our inner time spends our clock time as a drunken sailor his pay.[21]

He concludes, "We are not immortal beings, but we should often behave as if we were."

This appears paradoxical. We master time by forgetting it, by becoming oblivious to it. It seems also paradoxical that we gain time by losing it. Just as there is neurochemical evidence that laughter is the best medicine (see Norman Cousin's, *Anatomy of an Illness*), we know that the absorption and transcendence characterized by flow is good for our health. Its neurochemical counterpart is the flow of adrenaline, a recharged immune system, and the production of natural opiates and a natural "high."

A second way to master time is to give it away. This too seems paradoxical but there is some evidence to suggest that giving it away, giving time to others, may mean that you have more. We are finding, several centuries after his pronouncement, that Lao Tzu was correct in saying, "The invisible shield of caring is a weapon from the sky against being dead." This, it seems, is not only figuratively true, as in Chase's distinction between living and existing, but also literally true. People who give time caring for others seem to live longer.

American Health magazine, in March of 1988, reported on a ten-year study of 2,700 people in Tecumseh, Michigan. Among the results were that longevity was related to social contact and interaction: time spent alone correlated with an above average mortality rate. But the most significant predictor of longevity was doing volunteer work on a regular basis:

> ". . . doing regular volunteer work, more than any other activity, dramatically increased life expectancy. During the course of the study, men who did volunteer work on a regular basis were 2 1/2 times less likely to die than men who did no volunteer work."[22]

For women the results were less clear, but since women live about seven years longer than men, there is the hint that the traditional caring and nurturing activities may be partly responsible.

In evolutionary terms, that makes good sense. Nature cares about the species, not the individual. Thus, in the evolutionary process of natural selection, those who contribute to the welfare of others, to the whole or to the species, are likely to be selected for and enjoy greater health, vitality and longevity. Darwin, himself, said as much, the social Darwinians who think otherwise must have read *Descent of Man* through the brindled brown lens of their biases. Darwin spoke of such qualities as cooperation, sympathy, trust, group discipline, and others, and pointed out how our species benefits from them.[23] A brief sampler includes:

> In regards to certain mental powers . . . these faculties have been chiefly, or even exclusively, gained for the benefit of the community, and the individuals thereof have at the same time gained indirectly.

> Selfish and contentious people will not cohere, and without coherence nothing can be effected.

> Such social qualities (he was speaking of sympathy, fidelity, and courage), the paramount importance of which to the lower animals is disputed by no one, were no doubt acquired by the progenitors of man in a similar manner, namely, through natural selection aided by inherited habit.

There is much evidence that the stresses and strains of daily life, the principal source of which is perception of time, are ruining the health and welfare of individuals, communities and society as a whole. There is much evidence, too, that our attempts to cope with time, which we wrongly perceive to be scarce, are often of little help and often even more destructive than the original stresses and strains. But there is also much evidence, and on this biologists, psychologists, philosophers, theologians and poets agree, that some perceptions of time and patterns of activity over time can assure health and welfare all around.

In "The Marriage of Heaven and Hell" the poet William Blake wrote, "If the doors of perception were cleansed, everything would appear as it is, infinite. For man has closed himself up, till he sees all things through narrow chinks of his cavern." Our views are myopic and tunnelled. There is never enough time. Insignificant things take on extraordinary importance. Our anxieties and obsessions grow. We do not grow, we shrink. If the doors of perceptions were cleansed, time would appear as it is, infinite. If we are not immortal, we can still live as if we were. Since there is more time than life, we could easily give some away and we could become so absorbed in living that time simply fades away. There can be no harm in that. On the contrary, it appears that your life and mine depend on it.

REFERENCES

1. Linder, S. B. *The Harried Leisure Class*. New York: Columbia University Press, 1970.
2. Chase, S. *Are You Alive?* In: Berry, T. D. (Ed.). *Values in American Culture*. New York: The Odyssey Press, 1966, pp. 112-117.
3. Melges, F. T. *Time and the Inner Future*. New York: John Wiley and Sons, 1982, p. 7.
4. Pieper, J. *Leisure The Basis of Culture*. (Alexander Dru, Trans.) New York: Pantheon Books, 1952.
5. Rifkin, J. *Time Wars: The Primary Conflict in Human History*. New York: Henry Holt and Company, 1987.
6. Gould, S. J. *Time's Arrow - Time's Circle*. Cambridge, Massachusetts: Harvard University Press, 1987.
7. Quoted in Gould. *Ibid*. p. 2.
8. de Toqueville, A. *Democracy in America*. (R. Heffner, Trans.) New York: New American Library, Mentor, 1945, pp. 144-145.
9. Yankelovich, D. *New Rules: Searching for Self Fulfillment in a World Turned Upside Down*. New York: Bantam Books, 1982, p. 212.
10. Harper's Index. *Harper's Magazine*. 278:1666 (March) and 278:1670 (July) 1989, p. 17.
11. *Ibid*. 278:1668 (May).
12. Heilbronner, R. *An Inquiry into the Human Prospect*. New York: W. W. Norton, 1975.
13. Boulding, K. The Economics of the Coming Spaceship Earth. In: Daly, H. (Ed.). *Toward a Steady State Economy*. San Francisco: W. H. Freeman. 1973, p. 129.
14. Gorman, B. and Wessman, A. Images, Values and Concepts of Time in Psychological Research. In: *The Personal Experience of Time*. New York: Plenum Press, 1977, pp. 218-263.

15. Melges, *Op.Cit.* p. 12, 24.
16. *Ibid.* p. 14.
17. Gorman and Wessman. *Op.Cit.* p. 251.
18. De Quincey, T. *Confessions of an English Opium Eater.* London: Oxford University Press, 1934.
19. Newell, S. Chemical Modifiers of Time Perception. In: Yaker, H. et al. (Eds.). *The Future of Time.* Garden City, New York: Doubleday and Co., 1971. pp. 351-388.
20. Csikszentmihalyi, M. *Beyond Boredom and Anxiety.* San Francisco: Jossey-Bass, 1975.
21. Priestly, J. *Man and Time.* London: Aldus Publishing, 1964, p. 66.
22. Rockefeller-Growald, E. and Luks, A. The Immunity of Samaritans. *American Health.* (March), 1988, pp. 51-53.
23. Darwin, C. *The Descent of Man.* Akron, Ohio: The Werner Company, 1874, pp. 63, 132.

End of Chapter 3

Chapter 4

Leisure and Freedom Re-examined

Francis J. Bregha

In viewing some current definitions of leisure, one finds that many link leisure with freedom , even if only in the form of "free time." Two examples will suffice. de Grazia describes leisure as "the state of being free from the necessity to labor."[1] Neulinger affirms: "Leisure has one and only one essential criterion, and that is the condition of perceived freedom."[2]

Whether freedom is analyzed as an actual state of being or as a perception by an individual or a group, as suggested by Neulinger, it is evident that for many conceptual thinkers in our field, there is a profound and intimate relationship between leisure and freedom. How free do we need to be to enjoy leisure? Is professional intervention in leisure services enhanced or limited by the ethos of freedom? Does freedom, in fact, mean the ability of doing what one wants to do when one wants to? And if so, is leisure one of several possible outcomes of such an ability? Where do such questions lead us?

At this point, a word of caution: The purpose of this chapter is to raise questions more than to suggest answers. It is quite true that this old philosophical method of inquiry is rather unfashionable in our technological age in which answers have market value whereas questions tend to irritate. Moreover, we live at a time in which most believe that there must be an answer to everything, the growing evidence to the contrary notwithstanding. Therefore, this text should be read as an invitation to stop, to think, even to look into our own spiritual mirror and to reflect on the questions and answers that we find there.

It is a generally accepted belief that, as children, we first discover freedom, its delights and dangers, in playing. As formal education gradually replaces play, we all experience constraints, some of us rebelling, some adapting. Our freedom, as grasped and developed in childhood, is beginning a long process of adjustment that will last our entire life. But it is particularly in the world of modern work that the freedom of most of us will be subjected to its most severe restrictions. Whether because of standardization and uniformization of both products and production or whether because of the complex hierarchies of our bureaucracies, we can seldom, if ever, do what we would like. There is little place for a free, creative act, except perhaps one that brings in a new routine. Opportunity to do that is reserved for only a few. Hence, some people are actually unlearning the little freedom that may have survived their preparation for the working place. Freedom, like anything that is not exercised, atrophies. In Max Weber's words, "one does not work to live, one lives to work."[3] Marx spoke of alienation and Pieper brilliantly exposed the modern situation in *Leisure: The Basis of Culture*.[4] Finally, in old age many of us fall victim to institutional confinement, poverty or unkindly restrictive expectations of the younger generation. By that time, freedom may not have survived, even in memory or dreams.

If leisure and freedom are as closely related as current descriptions suggest, how can leisure survive whenever freedom is progressively curtailed, shrinking from birth to death? There is no freedom and therefore no leisure for those subjected to a routine, be it at work or elsewhere. Nor is there leisure for a prisoner, whether of conventions, social pressures or exhausted imagination. There is no leisure for anyone who has not maintained his freedom. Would, therefore, the maintenance of freedom throughout our lifetime not be the first and most important precondition of leisure; a sine qua non for its successful practice? Similarly, does such reasoning not suggest that, to be a professional in leisure services, means, among other things, the urgent need for helping people to rediscover their freedom, to define and maintain it? Surely a noble task, yet also one that is bound to lead to confusion if performed by those who are not free themselves.

ABILITY TO EXPERIENCE LEISURE

Going back to our initial question, whether leisure be the outcome of an ability to do what one wants to in a specific situation, one discerns the pivotal importance of the term "ability." It means several things: firstly, the possession of those qualities that enter into being able to do what one wants, essentially knowledge to compare options and then physical and spiritual capability to act on them; secondly, it suggests the availability of means required by such an option; thirdly, it connotes power and strength necessary for acting at all and living with the outcome of our own actions.

Let us look more closely at all three. Firstly, the possession of qualities that enter into being able to choose what one wants to do includes more than information on what is available or permissible. Something deeper is required: the knowledge of oneself as well as of one's milieu; the knowledge of what is good and what is wrong; the knowledge of various possibilities and of their consequences. Indeed, were such knowledge absent, then every choice would of necessity be a blind one, contradicting the very ability that is required. Thus leisure is linked to knowledge and to wisdom, both of which form part of the ability to choose with intelligence and responsibility. Furthermore, this analysis suggests the need of education for leisure. Throughout history we have increasingly accepted education for work: in fact, the working force in our century is vastly better prepared, more educated for work than ever before. Can humanity be left to its own devices in regard to leisure if we wish to occupy our leisure with intelligence and responsibility?

Secondly, there is the question of means. Throughout history, wealth was perceived as leading to leisure. The poor classes were excluded. Property and leisure went hand in hand, as noted in the expression "the leisure class." Leaving aside, then, the necessity for providing means to everyone who aspires to leisure, still a considerable undertaking even in our prosperous society, there remains the problem of our ability to use available means effectively and responsibly. The presence of means, however, is not sufficient. On top of it, man must have mastery over the means that his concept of leisure demands. Hence leisure cannot exist without training, apprenticeship, or whatever form of preparation the mastery over means may call for. Nor can it exist without a socially conscious management of means, especially for their conservation.

Thirdly, the ability to do what one wants is related to power and strength to act. Since few forms of leisure, except contemplation, can be practiced without at least passive consent of our neighbors or civic authorities, the ability we are seeking here addresses itself to the need for power arrangements that permit the seeker to proceed without fear or punishment. The incapacity to enjoy leisure may in many instances be due to the constant pressures exercised by modern states and their authoritarian institutional structures upon individuals, especially if those states are totalitarian or collectivist in character. Therefore, beyond knowledge, both practical and ethical, beyond accessibility to means and mastery over them, the ability that gives birth to leisure must also be based upon our secure power and strength to enjoy leisure in peace.

Assuming for a moment that such an ability can be developed and maintained through our lives, a phenomenon of extreme rarity in all history, what are the critical points at which our present world threatens to separate leisure from its roots in individual freedom? This is the most difficult part of our analysis as it forces us to reach beyond symbols with which we are increasingly bombarded in our communications-mad society, and to pierce through the thousand and one mirrors used by politicians, salesmen and propagandists of all hues to disorient us.

MANIPULATION AND LEISURE

The most obvious threat to leisure comes from manipulation of any kind, the problem being simply that few people know how much they are being manipulated. Many people do not know what they want. Quite practically, they want what they know—or what someone else shows or tells them. Although education may be presented sometime as an attempt to "draw out" the best that there is in us, in its actual form of schooling, training, or apprenticeship it clearly implies the transmitting of knowledge and skills from the outside to a more or less willing and ready learner.

Our economy may be painted in the bucolic colors of a free market in which free agents freely compete for the best supply-demand interaction—yet a moment of observation shows the ruthless manipulation of everyone by everyone else, the weakest, i.e., the poor, the unemployed, the consumers, holding the short end of the stick while the strongest, i.e., vertically integrated monopolies, are getting richer. One does not need to study Galbraith; personal experience is sufficient to show that, in our economy, there is little place for leisure rooted in freedom. In fact, all known economic systems use blatant manipulation to achieve their ends.

In politics, of course, manipulation parades as propaganda, lobbying pressure groups and, in extreme cases, as brainwashing or psychiatric treatment. At a more subtle level, none of us is exempt from some degree of political manipulation since we all deal in power relationships in our daily lives. There is no reason to think that leisure services are less receptive to bribery by politicians than other services, or that leisure professionals would confuse persons and principles or policy and expediency less frequently than anyone else. The freedom to act politically in Canada and the United States often reduces itself to biased reacting, to voting against rather than for something, to fighting first for self-interest and only second for common good. In short, manipulation in politics is easy because we offer it great opportunity and expect, even perversely enjoy, being manipulated by our leaders.

Manipulation, besides going unrecognized fully by many, presents the further threat of succeeding so well in some instances that the Orwellian 1984 is suddenly perceived as enduring social reality. "War is Peace," "Freedom is Slavery," and the brainwashed public is no longer able to discern even the sharpest value opposites. Manipulation, of course, thrives on gullibility and aims at the total elimination of all freedom, hence of all leisure, however cleverly labeled in the new doublespeak. The emergence of religious and ideological cults of exotic nature, effectively enslaving their adherents in a web of preposterous and sometimes dangerous beliefs; the amazing scope of phony commercial and financial operations; the readiness to accept as true the most clearly distorted new stories—an acquired taste to which a whole new industry is catering—are only a few current examples of the extreme situations created by successful manipulation in our midst.

We can now perceive the importance of what used to be called "inner strength," "independent judgment," even "character" before our times produced more ambiguous terms. These qualities constitute our defense against manipulation. Hence the ability to be independent, self-sufficient in judgment and its expression, is a fundamental condition of both freedom and leisure.

Beyond the massive manipulation by major forces to which we are subjected as learners of life, as consumers and as citizens, a variety of threats can make enjoyment of leisure problematic or impossible. A host of them reside actually in our very minds: feelings of guilt, especially when not working at something useful; fears reflecting religious or moral norms that appear contradicting what we wish to do; even the prosaic lack of imagination that instead of leisure in freedom generates boredom in idleness. These obstacles are as difficult to overcome as the more visible ones, created by explicit manipulation. Yet, no one is free who fears freedom; no one can be at leisure who feels guilty before an offered opportunity. The Greek advice of knowing oneself first of all remains valid today since the true independence needed for satisfying pursuit of leisure can never be achieved unless we get rid of what distorts us from within. Thus leisure frequently has to take the form of liberation, starting inside oneself.

Finally, environmental factors have to be considered. In a city where there are insecurity, noise, pollution of all sorts and hectic activity in all public places, leisure will be difficult, if not impossible, as no one can be at one with oneself in such conditions. Nor will a sensitive human being be able to enjoy leisure wherever nature is destroyed, exploited and beauty denied by functional utilitarianism. This describes so many of our modern surroundings that one can well raise the question: What chance for leisure here? There may be freedom though that freedom may only mean freedom to adapt or undertake the titanic tasks of environmental change. There may be "leisure activities" and "leisure facilities"—and yet little leisure can ever be experienced there. It is so because true leisure, like true freedom, can exist only in peace; in peace with oneself but also with one's surrounding.

LEISURE: AN IMPOSSIBLE GOAL?

The picture of leisure that is emerging from this discussion shows how difficult, fragile, almost impossible leisure is for modern man. Much less free than superficially believed, much more manipulated than publicly admitted, much less educated than generally thought, modern man appears to be lacking precisely those components of leisure that make it such an exacting state of being; self-knowledge and inner peace. Yet, were these two qualities added to those that we have identified as the basis of freedom, leisure would still not automatically follow. Boredom could still be with us, because leisure, to express freedom, requires choice; choice, in turn, requires awareness of preferences, hence a sense of direction, ultimately a goal. In other terms, leisure is as much freedom *to* something as it is freedom *from* something. Goalless leisure, then, is a contradiction which illustrates, even in our times, the difference between leisure and idleness.

These goals, of course, can be many. It is precisely the essence of leisure that they be almost without number since they define what is most personal, most unique in every one of us. At the same time, one suspects that these unique goals are not equal—in quality, morality or social relevance. Nor are they defined out of a vacuum. Besides individual predispositions, they reflect cultural influences and values constantly being absorbed and transformed. Leisure goals thus illustrate a state of society, probably better than any other single indicator. Obversely, the state of a society is perhaps the greatest determining factor is in shaping the leisure goals of its members. Using other terms: how well freedom fares in a given society will be the first measure of leisure opportunities in it.

One indirect result is that this diversity of leisure goals makes leisure as a social phenomenon so hard to grasp, to analyze and to classify. The study of commonalities leads to the development of theories—the study of unique particularities tends to resist scientific approach. Therefore, those social sciences that deal with leisure should not be astonished when their attempts at predicting or controlling, valid as these goals may be in regard to other phenomena, produce quite problematic results.

Much more important, though, is the inability of modern man to conceive worthwhile goals for himself. And yet, without a goal, he is condemned to an unleisurely life. As abhorrent as such a sentence might be to him, he falls victim to the all pervasive sickness of our times: the confusion of means and ends.

He starts with viewing education as a means to obtaining a job, then sees a job as means to securing a livelihood, considers work as means to getting rich, uses money as means to buy what he deems necessary to what would give him status and, finally, even that hardly acquired status becomes means to differentiating himself, a means to establishing his identity. Such a man lives in the world of means. There are no ends in his life that he does not use as means to still other ends and so, in growing confusion, his life results in what a poet once quite rightly described as "one damn thing after another."

Leisure, like freedom, is an end in itself. If perceived as means, it should be called recreation—a worthwhile but quite utilitarian concept. We do not occupy our leisure in order to become healthier or more productive. Leisure allows us to be free, to be what we want to be. Hence the importance of examining our own thoughts, desires and hopes and reflecting whether our lifestyle translates them or not into a coherent, meaningful life: an enterprise in which leisure counseling and education for leisure ought to play a role. The invitation to look into a spiritual mirror, issued at the beginning of this essay, is in fact a daily challenge. The questions that we shall find there, may not be answered immediately or by our effort alone. We need others as others need us. Beyond individual answers, we require societal ones and the understanding of their meaning. In this perspective, leisure professionals are both interpreters and builders of their communities.

It is for this reason that Aristotle's remark in his *Politics* remains so pertinent: "That is the principal point: with what kind of activity is man to occupy his leisure." He, over 2,000 years ago, as well as Pieper more recently, saw that activity related to divine worship. Leisure was part of celebrating God, exactly as Psalm LXV, II has it: "Have leisure and know that I am God."

This view is no longer shared by most contemporary analysts of leisure. Leisure's link to religion has been gradually weakened as religious festivities, rites and feasts occupy less and less of a place in our lives. Instead, modern technology has multiplied the means available for the pursuit of secular leisure while saying very little about their value or moral direction. It should be clear that we are possibly the first generation that faces a peculiar problem in regard to our leisure. As long as leisure found its origin in God and its expression in partaking in worship, its morality was beyond reproach. Now that a divorce has taken place and leisure is linked to freedom rather than to God, a vast question mark as to its ultimate purpose is before us. Who is to guide us through the maze of good and evil now that God is absent and freedom is perceived in many ways? This brings us back to the dichotomy of freedom *from* and freedom *to*. Historically, we have found it easier to define and to fight for freedom *from*. Although this process is far from finished in most of the world, in Canada and the United States the emphasis is slowly shifting towards the consideration of freedom *to*. Since the 1960s, significant sections of our population, particularly women, youth and some minority groups, have raised new questions that can be answered only in terms of freedom *to*—hence the considerable increase in conflicts over values, and also, therefore, such an explosion of new, morally untested leisure pursuits.

Is one type of leisure activity as good as any other? Are we to assume that, since leisure is the highest expression of our freedom and freedom, in turn, thrives best in our leisure time, there is not—there cannot be—an ethical conflict? Are leisure and freedom so good per se, in their essence, that neither can give birth to evil, under any circumstances? These questions flow naturally from linking leisure with freedom and necessarily lead into an examination of the moral dimensions of leisure. To say that modern leisure derives its meaning from personal self-fulfillment reached in various ways during free time is clearly no longer sufficient. All of us who in the past have been tempted into perceiving the ultimate goal of leisure in the Maslowian concept of self-actualization surely realize by now that such self-actualization cannot take place in a moral vacuum. The ethics of leisure, including the reconciliation of individual and collective goals within a coherent value system, thus form part and parcel of every serious inquiry into the nature of our freedom.

To sum up: leisure undoubtedly is the most precious and also most fragile expression of our freedom. Freedom remains leisure's pre-condition, its rewards being that freedom can flower best in pursuits that are leisurely. Whereas the maintenance of freedom becomes, then, our constant task and the defining of freedom *to* our greatest challenge, leisure itself still depends as much on the knowledge and wisdom entering into our options, on our ability to choose goals that will bring us happiness, on our inner strength and independence that affirms our unique character, and finally on an environment that is conductive to leisure because it offers peace, per chance beauty and quiet enjoyment.

REFERENCES

1. de Grazia, S. *Of Time, Work and Leisure.* New York: The Twentieth Century Fund, 1962, pp. 13-14.
2. Neulinger, J. *The Psychology of Leisure.* Springfield, Illinois: Charles C. Thomas, 1974, p. 15.
3. Cited in Josef Pieper. *Leisure: The Basis of Culture.* (Alexander Dru, Trans.). New York: Pantheon Books, Inc., 1952, p. 20.
4. *Ibid.*
5. Cited in *Ibid.*, p. 55.

End of Chapter 4

Chapter 5

Fantasy, Play, Creativity and Mental Health

Bill Michaelis

> ". . . with my anti-experimental bias I don't save myself from trouble,
> but it does have a lot of sideways opening effects."
>
> *Gregory Bateson[1]*

One of the ten rights of children as declared by the United Nations is the "right to full opportunity for play and recreation." The right to play should be also fully extended to adults. To discover what this means, it is important to reexamine the nature of play and to ask if our services are in line with our professional and theoretical knowledge. Our job as play professionals is not just to provide activities, teach skills, or fill people's time. It is also to educate them for leisure. Everything that we do, from the environments that we create for people to the type of leadership that we provide, should have this focus. The objective of leisure education is for people to have an understanding and actualization of the play experience in their lives. But what is play?

There are strong threads of interconnection between play and several other important concepts, notably fantasy, creativity, mental health and the "flow" phenomenon. Each of these has its own intricacies and muddled complexity. Each has relevance for human happiness. This chapter will explore those connections and suggest specific implications for the leisure services field.

PLAY AND MENTAL HEALTH: THE PRIMACY OF RIGHT BRAIN PROCESSES

A widely accepted definition of leisure is that it is primarily an existential state, a way of looking at the world. Gunter describes it this way: Leisure is ". . . a subjective state of the individual in his involvement with certain kinds of time, activity or lifestyle. This position is best known through the works of de Grazia but it also permeates the work of other well known writers."[2]

de Grazia himself would say that leisure has nothing to do with time or activity.[3] Play might also be viewed primarily as a 'mindset' (or a heartset). Some of its most significant components are fantasy, imagination and openendedness.[4] But there is more.

There has been much recent research on left and right brain functions. Psychologists tell us that we have primarily two modes of thinking. They are: (a) our right brain *primary* processes—our non-rational, dreamlike, emotional symbolizing modes; this is the powerful stuff of our tears, laughter, anger, hopes, fears, loves, loneliness and, yes, our play. And (b) our left brain *secondary* processes—our cognitive, reality-based, rational modes; this is our organizing, planning self.

Although play certainly contains aspects of rational planning, its magic and power lies in the attention to right brain, primary process elements. Eli Bower noted, ". . . that, for play and life in general, it is the primary process mode that is generally the more powerful, pervasive and satisfying of human symbolizing experiences, although secondary processes do serve an important organizing and planning function in our lives."[5] Bower also notes that a *balance* of both primary and secondary modes is necessary for mental health.

Erik Erickson confirms that play serves a very important mental health function. He reports that in a 30-year follow-up of people who had been studied as children, those subjects who felt they had had the most interesting and fulfilling lives were the ones who had managed to keep a sense of playfulness at the center of things.[6] Unfortunately our educational and leisure oriented institutions give too little attention to play and the right brain functions. Most people are taught to put away the "child" as they are subtly socialized into mass society.

PLAY AND CREATIVITY

Arieti describes the creative act in similar terms. He, too, uses the dualism of primary and secondary processes, but he postulates a third mode which he calls the *tertiary* process. He states that the task of this process is to fuse the irrational with the rational processes and thus produce an integrative balance and the magic synthesis of creativity. Both Bower and Arieti advocate that greater attention be paid to primary process development, the stuff that is the magic and power of play. Arieti states it this way: " . . . A society that urges the young to 'stop daydreaming and pay attention,' to 'stop playing and get to work,' is not one that encourages magic at all."[7]

Further evidence linking the right brain elements of play to creativity comes from the identification of blocks to creative lifestyles. Psychologists identify some of the main blocks to creativity as 1) the reluctance to play, 2) sensory dullness, 3) an impoverished fantasy life; 4) the reluctance to "let go", and 5) an impoverished emotional life.[8]

Corrine Hutt, in a series of longitudinal studies of 3-7 year olds, has shown that the opportunity for inventive and exploratory play affects a child's later creativity and social interaction. Feitelson and Ross also found that creativity is encouraged by the development of imaginativeness in play.[9] Bower summarizes our task when he states that "... a society concerned with producing a fair amount of creative and imaginative adults must protect the play modalities of childhood."[10]

PLAY, DREAMS AND FANTASY

Dreams and Daydreams as Play

Internalized fantasy or dreaming as a form of "play" has long been supported as valid by many play theorists. Sutton-Smith speaks of adult daydreaming as playing around in the head.

> "Play seems to parallel dreams in that it contains at least two types of processing: on the one hand the quite mundane assimilation of daily events and on the other the fairly elaborate and vivid construction of imaginary companions and the like."[11]

As children, most of us lived in a "never-never land" where we externally acted out our fantasies. It may have been the backyard, the imaginative worlds of dolls or cars, the forts built on bunk beds, the pickup games where the rules consistently changed, or the abandoned lot down the street. In many ways the whole world was accessible and limited only by imagination. We were not locked into a narrow conceptualization of everyday objects. A table would be a fort or, turned upside down, a ship or a motorcycle. But as we grew, powerful social forces buoyed by peer and adult pressure told us (overtly or covertly) to put aside that childlike freshness and creativity. Expressions of external fantasy were generally no longer legitimized or encouraged: play became more structured and reality became secondary process oriented. Bower suggests that much of the pain in growing up is the pull between the childlike fantasy and feelings of primary process and the demands of rational secondary process realities. It is clear, however, that as children grow to adulthood more of their fantasy and primary process activity is relegated to dreams and daydreams or internalized play. But these are still play and they do serve an important subconscious and conscious right brain function. But what if they are blocked?

Blocked Dreams (Internal Play) Lead to Dysfunctional Behavior

Recent dream research indicates that smooth functioning in the "awake rational reality state" is influenced by the integrative primary process function that is performed while we sleep. During sleep there are times when we wiggle our eyes and possibly dream a little. This wiggling has been called by sleep researchers rapid eye movement (REM). We know that if we consistently wake people up during REM, they will become irritable, dysfunctional, disoriented and even hostile in their waking state. Dreams seem to serve an important left and right brain integrative and sorting out process.[12]

This process that night dreams accomplish occurs in a subconscious state. But isn't the daydreaming that Sutton-Smith describes as one form of adult play also accomplishing this "sorting out" (bridging) process in a more conscious awake state? And isn't the spontaneous make-believe fantasy play that children externally act out also accomplishing this?

The Importance of Daydreams, Fantasy and Make Believe Play

Jerome Singer states that the nurturing of fantasy in our lives is vital for mental health:

> "Fantasies and daydreams, far from being irrelevant and insubstantial, may be the foundation of serenity and purpose in our lives . . .
> . . . those who have trouble using fantasy to enrich their experience or as a substitute for aggression run the risk of serious trouble at each stage of their lives. . . A well developed fantasy life seems to be partly responsible for independence, tranquility and realism."[13]

But the encouragement of fantasy still frightens a lot of people. Sutton-Smith, however, suggests strong linkages between fantasy and the development of creativity:

> "Teachers, even of middle-class background, still ask me whether a child with high levels of fantasy is not in danger of a nervous break-down. The answer is no; in most cases, he is only in danger of becoming an outstanding scientist, writer, scholar, or perhaps even an international chess player."[14]

But what if people have difficulty with daydreaming, fantasy and make believe play?

Blocked Fantasy and Make Believe Play Leads to Dysfunctional Behavior

Singer details studies with aggressive delinquents, drug abusers, and overweight people, among others, that seem to indicate a close relationship between their "problems" and their lack of elaborated fantasies. He suggests that the aggressive group may never have had the early contacts with adults that allowed them to try out in play and fantasy the complex and relatively self-controlled behavior of adults. The drug (including alcohol) abusers more than nonusers were found to be:

". . . subject to boredom and mind wanderings and their fantasies, though frequent, tend to be fleeting and undeveloped. They are not as interested in inner consciousness as in blotting things out or developing external sensations. Marijuana users were found to be the exception to this research and were generally found to be interested in expanding both their internal and external awareness."[15]

Singer also reports studies of school-age children and adults which indicate relationships between healthy fantasy development and behavior.

The development of imaginative play, which allows the exercise of right brain functions, becomes increasingly important in light of the often reported negative effects of heavy television viewing on children. Dr. Lawrence Friedman points out that regular television viewing has rendered children passive, thus denying them normal outlets for their fantasy and aggression. "All television, except in small doses, feeds children ready-made fantasy, at a time when *fantasy making* is crucial for their development . . ."[16]

It has been suggested that the power and magic of play lies in its attention to primary process right brain functions, and the balanced integration of these functions is necessary for health and creativity. Further evidence for this position comes from the phenomenological investigations of the psychologist Mihaly Csikszentmihalyi into "flow" experiences. Simply put, "flow" is enjoyment, and although enjoyment is made up of both rational (left brain) and non-rational (right brain) elements, it is argued that "flow" is also mostly influenced by the primary process, right brain mode. A look at the reported experiences and identified qualities of the phenomena suggests why.

TOWARD HIGHER CONSCIOUSNESS - THE FLOW EXPERIENCE

Csikszentmihalyi was interested in the feelings that emerged from activities found to be rewarding in and of themselves. He studied people in a variety of work-play settings—surgery, different sports, rock-climbing and artistic pursuits —and discovered that as individuals became totally immersed in a sport or creative act, they lost a sense of time and the external world and they experienced an ecstatic "flowing" feeling. His investigations indicated that this feeling approximated an "altered state of being" for those subjects:[17]

"In this state the person loses a self-conscious sense of himself and of time. He gains a heightened awareness of his physical involvement with the activity. The person in flow finds, among other things, his concentration vastly increased and his feedback from the activity enormously enhanced."[18]

Certain elements always emerged from the different descriptions. One of them was a merging of self with the environment or action with awareness:

> "One of the rock climbers put it this way: 'You are so involved in what you are doing you aren't thinking of yourself as separate from the immediate activity' . . ."[19]

Another element was the dreamlike sense of time:

> "In flow there is a sense of being lost in the action . . .'Time passes a hundred times faster. In this sense it resembles the dream state,' said a chess player. Sometimes the centering of attention produces a spatial alteration akin to the changed sense of time."[20]

In addition to a loss of self and time consciousness, a merging of action and awareness and a centering of attention on a relatively isolated and limited stimulus field, three other core qualities emerged. In the flow state, the subjects felt under control of self and environment, their activity was self-chosen and intrinsically motivated, and they received immediate and unambiguous feedback regarding their actions.

In addition to the peak arousal experiences of flow, there is also *micro flow* which is a small scale example of the same phenomenon. Dr. Csikszentmihalyi's studies identify six areas of microflow in descending order of reported frequency: a) social involvement (i.e., browsing, talking, etc.); b) kinesthetic (running, touching, moving, etc.); c) imagining type behavior; d) attending behavior (i.e., TV, radio, reading); e) oral pleasures, and f) creative work (i.e., writing, sewing, playing music, etc.).[21]

Play and Flow: Differences and Relationships

What is the relevance of the flow phenomena? In one sense, it appears to be closely related to the existential attitude by which play and leisure were defined earlier.

Although the two concepts are closely aligned, there are some differences. Sutton-Smith states that ". . . flow is a state of integration with reality, play is not."[22] Dr. Csikszentmihalyi clarifies this distinction and the relationship between the two concepts, especially emphasizing the *quality of playfulness* vs. trying to identify any one activity as *play*:

> "Flow describes a *process* of involvement in a given reality while playfulness refers to one's attitude towards the reality in which one is involved. One can experience flow in a routine activity whose goals and rules are consistent with the paramount reality; in such a case there wouldbe flow without playfulness. Or one could shift one's

perspective on what goals and rules applied in a situation, without
experiencing the intense involvement that characterizes flow. But,
by and large, the two processes tend to evoke each other. The
intensity of flow brings into question the value of everyday reality,
while playfulness usually provides the kind of opportunities for
action that make flow possible."[23]

It is clear that flow is one of the higher forms of pleasure, and it can occur in
a wide variety of work/play activities that are not limited to any set time frame.
Comprehending this holistic aspect of flow quite naturally leads to a greater
understanding of the weakness of the traditional work-play dichotomy, and the
application of the flow experience principles has tremendous potential for both
personal pleasure/play and professional practice. We can learn how to increase
flow in our own lives and in the lives of the people with whom we work and
serve.

APPLICATIONS

Csikszentmihalyi, the trio of Ellis, Witt and Aguilar, and this author, have all
suggested ways of applying what we know about flow.[24] The flow studies
suggest that in addition to changing environments (i.e., home, job, associates),
there are several principles that will increase the potential for flow, pleasure and
playfulness:

1. An activity ought to have a broad enough range of complexity and challenge
    so that one can fine-tune the balance between the perceived difficulty of the
    task and one's skill level (or the skill level of one's client). If the challenge
    is too difficult, it will cause anxiety. If it's too easy, the result will be bore-
    dom. If the challenge is fine-tuned, flow can occur. Among other things,
    this was certainly one of the advantages and playful attractions of the New
    Games Movement.

2. Attention needs to be focused, the stimulus field narrowed, and one's
    awareness merged with the activity in order to facilitate flow. Have you
    ever been totally absorbed in the concentration of the movement in a good
    ping pong rally, a musical piece, or a video game? When working with
    participants, one must first attract their attention. Ellis, et al., point out that
    being keenly aware of a client's preferences and using degrees of novelty
    and dissonance are extremely useful in gaining attention.[25,26] As this author
    pointed out in an article on game change and leadership, once attention is
    gained, limiting distractions along with fine-tuning the complexity of the
    task, provides greater access to flow, and very often playfulness.[27]

3. There is a need to focus on the process of being and doing the activity in the *present*. This implies minimizing: a) time consciousness; b) focusing on outcomes; and c) the promise of future extrinsic rewards. It also implies the elimination of a destructive anxiety-provoking competitive/comparative atmosphere. There is greater potential for flow, play and leisure when on is in the moment and neither racing nor chasing.[28,29]

4. There is a need to relax more and to become more aware of one's body and senses. The ability to achieve flow is enhanced by a relaxed body, an alert mind, and in general sensory awareness. Stress gets in the way. Dr. Jim Polidora, a professor at the University of California-Davis Medical School and a holistic play practitioner, uses guided imagery, dance therapy, the eastern martial arts, massage, yoga, and many other techniques to help reduce stress and actualize the play experience in their lives.[30] These methods have tremendous implications for the leisure service profession, but are still under-utilized.

5. Finally, for all of the above, there is a need for *immediate* and ongoing, positively reinforcing feedback about our relaxing and focusing on the process, and information or modifications that help us fine tune and be in the moment.[31]

Looked at from another angle, the steps just presented could be described as key elements of leisure education. By incorporating these steps into their lives, people can maximize the play state—the higher consciousness of flow. The ultimate result of understanding "the fun in fun" may be an increase in healthier, happier people and a redefinition of the work ethic.

BLOCKED FLOW

The flow experience is a form of higher consciousness accessible to all people. At least part of its power comes from its relationship to the right brain, primary process mode of symbolizing. The chess player, described earlier, referred to the time alteration experience in flow as a dreamlike state. If dreams and daydreams are forms of internal play that serve an important, integrative mental health function in human beings, then it may be logical to assume that make believe play and flow serve some of the same functions in a more activity oriented conscious state.

Further suggestive evidence for the connection of flow to such primary process activities as dreams, daydreams and make believe play comes from looking at what happens to people when their flow is blocked. Csikszentmihalyi discovered that when the people he studied attempted to inhibit their preferred forms of flow, for example daydreaming, talking, gaming, or watching, or when they were blocked in some other ways, they became very irritable, and experienced a wide range of mental health difficulties.[32] This mental health dysfunction is consistent with research cited earlier on blocked primary process (right brain) activities such as dreaming, fantasy and make believe play.

INTERRELATIONSHIPS

It has been suggested that the power and magic of play lies in its attention to the primary process mode of symbolizing, and that the active functioning of this mode, as evidenced in such things as dreams, daydreams, fantasy, make believe play and flow, is crucial for mental health. Also, the playful exercise of this mode is a key element in creativity. Mental health, then, might be more broadly defined as the actualization of a creative lifestyle—a lifestyle that is open to growth, sensitivity, and the universal quest for love and human happiness. Each of the concepts of fantasy, play, creativity, and mental health is complex, but they are indeed interrelated. It should be clear that one common denominator for creative lifestyles is play.

The understanding of the nature of play has important implications for enriching our lives and improving practices in the leisure services field. The job of all professionals in the field, as noted earlier, is to be leisure educators. If leisure service professionals are to help in the facilitation of creative lifestyles and human happiness, the environments and programs that they provide and the tools and leadership techniques that they use must be consistent with the theoretic understanding of play.

IMPLICATIONS: BRIDGING THE GAP BETWEEN THEORY AND PRACTICE

It is clear that more people today are engaging in more activities that have play and leisure potential.[33] Our complex, rapidly changing world makes the job of educating people about play that much more important. Too often the values of play that are professed by the leisure profession are not reflected in services. It is important for professionals to understand their clients' needs and to help meet them. But for leisure educators, there is a greater task: to provide not only for *what is* but also models for *what can be*. All programs, in reality, should be geared to educating people about healthy play values.

Leadership is increasingly important because it is clear that the people who take part in leisure service activities are also constantly being influenced by strong social forces that often confuse or distort healthy play values. For example, in an increasingly rapid-paced, depersonalized, technological, consumer oriented society such as ours, forces such as conspicuous consumption, escapism and self-destruction through media, drugs, and obligatory mass leisure, all have an influence on play values. Urbanism, the highly structured product orientation of capitalism, sexism, cultural stereotypes of such groups as the disabled, and early parental mixed messages such as withholding play as punishment or using it as a reward, also confuse the conceptions and values of play for many people.[34] And although it is changing, the work ethic is still alive and well. Leisure education cannot be viewed in a vacuum, and all of the above factors, as well as many others, make the job of value leadership that much more important. A more careful look at children's play and socialization further illustrates this point.

Play and Socialization

Recall that Bower suggested that a society concerned with producing a fair amount of imaginative adults must protect the play modalities of childhood. As children we had tremendous potential creativity within us and exercised it because in a very existential way we knew what play was all about. We had adventures, challenged ourselves, played made-up games with made-up rules, explored new areas of the world in our heads and through participating in activities. We knew what play was about because it included such elements as flexibility, change and spontaneity. Fantasies were allowed and feelings were exercised. Play had a healthy air of unreality about it; often loose and open-ended. Play was not without its "serious" moments, difficulties or hurt feelings, but things were worked out because we wanted to keep playing. For the most part we provided support for each other's play.[35] If lucky, we might have had support for playfulness from some significant adults in our lives. But something happened, to many of us, at least.

As we grew older, powerful social forces began to influence playtime and thus our conceptions of both play and the world. The message was to grow up and put aside that child self.[36] The abuses of two forces in particular have a very strong influence on children. The first is the existence of very structured, highly competitive, adult dominated youth sports leagues that emphasize a win-at-all-cost ethic. And the second is the power of the plug-in drug, television. Both of these forces, youth sports and television, can be playful, positive educational tools, but there is increasing evidence of their abuse. This abuse has had a strong influence on children's abilities to conceptualize and operationalize play alternatives.

More and more evidence continues to accumulate about the negative effects of heavy TV viewing on such things as creativity, the development of reading skills, the communicative emotional climate of the home, self-image, and healthy nutritional habits. Studies have also suggested links between heavy viewing and increased fears, violence and reality distortion.[37] And this is to say nothing of the exponential proliferation of media in general during the 1980s in the form of VCR's, video games, cable TV, etc. The effects of this proliferation on the development of healthy play patterns are not yet known, but the yellow caution flag is up.

The abuses of youth sports are also well documented. The "pro model" of big money, rigid structure and narrow definition of winning that includes only those with the highest score has filtered down to youth, with a strong push from the media. Although there are many well-meaning, caring adults in the youth sports, there are also those whose expectations of children are too high; they crush individuality and promote conformity by attempting to create little five and six year old warriors. They lose sight of the playful developmental process that is the true power of youth sports, and often their 'products' are increased violence, cheating, concern with bigger trophies and an increasing number of young athletic dropouts. Those who most need the positive reinforcement of healthy activity are often the first cut or spend most of their careers on the bench. Too often this aspect of childhood play has become over-institutional-ized and "adultocentric."[38]

Most professionals would state that they would like to have a hand in facilitating, more creative, independent individuals. However, too many leaders and programs foster dependence on structure and experts and create a group think mentality. All people have the potential for creative, playful independ-ence, but they are subtly socialized out of the magic, creativity, flexibility and individuality that is play. Children often buy into the media, abusive youth sports and other influencing social forces because they perceive very few alternatives. After all, adults *are* modeling their options. So children begin to perceive play as a narrow set of behaviors. Self-developed fantasy and pick-up games are things to be put aside. Play is to be structured to provide instant gratification or is something to pay for. Although there are many positive exceptions, leisure services still mainly reflect the confusing social forces influencing leisure rather than contributing to building a healthier future.

AND A CHILD SHALL LEAD

The main job of the leisure service profession is values leadership and that must include the nurturing of the positive child self and right brain elements for old and young alike. Education, for example, for all its innovations, is still mostly cognitive and career oriented, and based on faith and fear; drill and grill. Yet, the development of the affective primary process mode is crucial for creativity and mental health. And the operationalization of this leadership challenge and its programmatic manifestations will take many forms.

There is much to be done. In the broad sense, the profession must focus its attention on play as seen from the child's perspective. Traditional offerings, even of the most competitive type, still have an important place in the scheme of things. But the abuses must be eliminated and the value focus must once again be on the *process* of enjoying, on the playfulness that is central to our profession. Or, as Ellis et al., would say, we must see facilitating flow as an important and legitimate goal of our services.[39] Leaders must ask what's best for the development of mental health, human happiness and creativity. What messages are we giving people? Rather than running the serious risk of having "free" time dominated by left brain secondary processes and the stresses and anxieties that may accompany them, people need to be reminded not to take play too seriously. The non-rational 'unreality' of it is important. The magical right brain elements are the factors that free us from the boxes that we are in.

Meeting this challenge will require leadership; leadership that does not just provide what people have been taught to want, but expands into the areas where there is presently very little being done. There is still, for example, a paucity of cultural arts offerings in most public programs. It is clear that the full range of arts provide the much needed exercise of the right brain elements. They need as much (if not more) attention as sports programs currently command. Related activities such as intramural-type programs, movement education, theater, imagination and fantasy games, and the acclimatization movement in outdoor education all have potential to put people in touch with themselves and with the total environment. Important leisure education messages come from all these activities. That is: "It's okay to touch, to move, to feel, to dream, to giggle, to play, and to create adventure in one's daily life."

THE FUTURE: THE CREATION OF DIVERSE MODELS

People need options. It is interesting to note that some of the most innovative models for the encouragement of healthy play values come from outside the mainstream of the leisure services profession. These alternatives not only provide some future direction for the parks and recreation movement, but also help to remind those in leadership positions of the nature and importance of play. Not only are these programs important as models in and of themselves, they also contain many elements from which leisure service professional can learn. One does not necessarily have to always run, for example, a "New Games" program, but New Games leadership principles have broad based leisure education applications in schools, community centers, industry and many other areas of the public and private sector. What follows are a few short examples of alternatives. Additional information is available from the organizations themselves.

Adventure Playgrounds

What Adventure Playgrounds do is provide the space, materials and caring supervision for children to *create* and *own* their play experiences. In another article, this author has written extensively on the many growth and development values of Adventure Playgrounds.[40] The Adventure Playgrounds movement has been alive and well in Europe for over forty years, but has grown very slowly in the U.S. for a number of reasons, not the least of which is the power of the playground equipment industry in leisure service professional circles. However, with a little imagination the developmental, design, and child-centered leadership principles of Adventure Playgrounds can be applied in a variety of settings.

Project Adventure
Urban Outdoor Adventure Center

This rapidly growing movement has been described as both a "fun form of anxiety" and "adventure for big folks."[41,42] However, people of *all* ages and abilities have been playing Adventure Games, taking part in ropes courses, and sharing initiatives activities for some time now. Using activities that involve cooperation, initiative, challenge, risk and fantasy, the ultimate goal of the Adventure movement is to put people in touch with their physical selves, their abilities, and their feelings, as well as to connect with the people around them. There is probably no better short term way of getting in touch with the concept of 'flow' than through adventure activities. The U.O.A.C. has been particularly innovative in its use of adventure as a juvenile diversion tool and for team building in industry.

New Games

New Games continues.[43] The New Games Foundation has trained over 30,000 people in the last ten years in a style of play and leadership that encourages participation, community, and creativity. The Foundation offers a variety of services and has published *More New Games*[44] which details its philosophical underpinnings and the leadership techniques which have led to its success. And a key to that success has been that New Games and New Games leadership provide ready access to flow and playfulness.[45]

Cooperative Games
Playfair
Project PLAE

The Cooperative Games Movement pioneered by Terry Orlick, focuses on the *process* of enjoyable challenges.[46,47] In recent books, he shares a wide variety of resources, including international games, self-refereed intramural programs, cooperative games for all ages, and academic learning experiences. The focus is on playing and winning *together* to build positive self-concepts. One of the special features of Orlick's books is a section that details ways to modify traditional sports to rekindle a play and process focus. This is especially useful, given our sport-oriented culture, as an entree to games flexibility when working with community groups.

The Playfair group has been very successful in bringing cooperative play to college orientations throughout the U.S.[48] In the area of integrative arts, two recent works by Bob Gregson provide scores of nurturing creative arts ideas.[49] Gregson was one of the founders of 'Sidewalk' in Hartford, Connecticut, and has been very active in the children's museum movement.

Project PLAE (Play and Learning in Adaptive Environments) is an extremely creative community based program that is successfully using the interrelated arts and flexible environments as mainstreaming vehicles.[50]

The Family That Plays Together . . .

A recently formed San Francisco based creative play, community development and leisure education organization, *The Family That Plays Together,* has as its chief purpose the fostering of healthy family play as one part of a community-wide family support network.[51] Using a synthesis of the best of the above movements and fifteen years of finely tuned facilitation skills, T.F.T.P.T. . . . has a variety of vehicles to accomplish its objectives. These include The Family Funforall, Family Fun Festivals, family leisure education workshops for professionals and lay people, presentations and consulting. In both direct service and training, there is a strong emphasis on empowerment and intergenerational play.

CONCLUSIONS

The above are just a sampling of the many innovative play/leisure education models that exist. Yet, there is always room for more flowers to bloom. In fact, it might be suggested that an international computerized clearinghouse be established to connect the organizations and to provide information about them to interested parties. Until that time, leisure service professionals are fortunate to have a recently developed compendium of almost one hundred of the world's most progressive children's play programs. *Playing, Living, Learning: A Worldwide Perspective on Children's Opportunities to Play,* by Westland and Knight[52] contains a summary of the major issues related to children's play, as well as descriptions of healthy play programs related to nature, games, adventure, the arts, toys, culture, education, the family, mobile opportunities, and playstreets.

People need a variety of play options, and the gap between theory and practice needs to be bridged if the profession is serious about helping people actualize the play experience, and ultimately achieve greater "flow" in their lives. The challenge for the profession will be to create flow inducing environments. Initially, people may want just "more of the same" but once they appreciate the excitement, fun, and energy of these options, they will demand more. And leisure services will be transformed into a more viable vehicle for human happiness.

Csikszentmihalyi tells us that the evolutionary significance of play is not that it maintains an already existing reality, but that it provides alternatives to it. How, in fact, do we free ourselves in general for a more playful view of the world - to know that the rules are freely chosen and can be changed?[53] Sutton-Smith reminds us of the power of play.

When different groups celebrate together, when parents and children play together, they bring to their lives the kinds of vividness which we have earlier called play or flow. These have in them the seeds of a life which is more interesting and more connected in an age when many of the older forms of connections no longer seem so available or so meaningful:[54]

Teacher, let me swim in a puddle,
Let me race a cloud in the sky,
Let me build a house without walls

But, most of all . . .
Let me laugh at
Nothing things.[55]

REFERENCES

1. Bateson, G. "Both sides of the necessary paradox: Meditations on George Bateson and the death of the bread and the butterfly." *Harper*, 1973.
2. Gunter, B. G. "Properties of the Leisure Experience" In: Ibrahim, H. and Crandall, R. *Leisure: A Psychological Approach*. Los Alamitos, California: Hwong Publishing Co., 1979, pp. 3-43.
3. de Grazia, S. *Of Time, Work and Leisure*. New York: Anchor-Doubleday, 1962.
4. Berlyne, D. E. "Laughter, Humor and Play." In: Lindzey, G. and Aronson, E. (Eds.). *Handbook of Social Psychology*. Reading, Massachusetts: Addison Wesley, 1968.
5. Bower, E. "Plays the Thing." In: Bower, E. *Games in Education and Development*. Springfield: Charles C. Thomas, 1974, pp. 10-11.
6. Bruner, J. "Play is Serious Business." *Psychology Today*, 8(January) 1974, pp. 81-83.
7. May, C. "Study of Creativity and Sense of Magic." Review of: Arieti, S. *Creativity: The Magic Synthesis*. In: *Sunday Los Angeles Times Book Review Section*, January, 1977.
8. Kaufman, L. "Blocks to Creativity." Handout in E. Bower's Class, University of California, Berkeley School of Education, 1970.
9. Sutton-Smith, B. "The Useless Made Useful: Play as Variability Training." *School Review*, 83(February) 1975, pp. 197-214.
10. Bower, *Op. Cit.*, p. 11.
11. Sutton-Smith, *Op. Cit.*
12. Bower, E. et al. *Learning to Play/Playing to Learn*. Berkeley, California: University of California, Berkeley Creative Arts Printing, 1974. pp. 8-21.
13. Singer, J. "Fantasy, the Foundation of Serenity." *Psychology Today*, 10(July) 1976. p. 32.
14. Sutton-Smith, *Op. Cit.*, pp. 197-214.
15. Singer, *Op. Cit.*
16. Caplan, F. and Caplan, T. "Creativity Through Play." *The Power of Play*. Garden City, NY: Anchor Press, 1973, pp. 149-179.
17. Csikszentmihalyi, M. *Flow: Studies of Enjoyment*. Public Health Service Report: University of Chicago, 1974.
18. Furlong, W. "The Flow Experience: The Fun in Fun." *Psychology Today*, (June) 1976, pp. 36.
19. *Ibid*. p. 37.
20. *Ibid*. p. 37.
21. Csikszentmihalyi, M. *Beyond Boredom and Anxiety*. San Francisco: Jossey-Bass, 1976. See Also Csikszentmihalyi, *Op. Cit.*, 1973 and Furlong, *Op. Cit.*, 1976.

22. Sutton-Smith, B. "Play as Flow and Innovation: The New Meanings." Address at Press Conference, Frankfurt, Germany, March 12, 1979 (excerpted from *T.A.A.S.P. Newsletter*, 1979/80. p. 12.)

23. Csikszentmihalyi, M. "Some paradoxes in the definition of play" In: Cheska, A. *Play as Context*. West Point, New York: Leisure Press, 1981, pp. 24-25 (Proceedings of the 5th. annual meeting of T.A.A.S.P.).

24. Csikszentmihalyi, *Op. Cit.*

25. Ellis, G., Witt, P. and Aguilar, T. "Facilitating Flow Through Therapeutic Recreation Services." *Therapeutic Recreation Journal.*, Second Quarter, 1983, pp. 6-15.

26. Michaelis, B. "Flow/New Games." New Games Foundation Newsletter. San Francisco, California, Summer 1977.

27. —"It Power!—A Game Detergent." New Games Foundation Newsletter. San Francisco, California, Winter 1978.

28. Ellis, et al. *Op. Cit.*

29. deGrazia, S. *Op. Cit.*

30. Polidora, J. *Course Syllabus and Reading Guide for Behavioral Biology 451*. Davis Medical School, University of California, 1977.

31. Ellis, et al. *Op. Cit.*

32. Csikszentmihalyi, M. *Op. Cit.*, 1974 and Furlong. *Op. Cit.*, 1978.

33. Glasser, W. "Needed for America: The Kind of Recreation that Frees the Mind." *U. S. News and World Report*, (May 23) 1977. pp. 74-76.

34. Gunn, S. "Blocks to Play." National Recreation and Parks Association Congress, Las Vegas, Nevada, October, 1977.

35. Cf: Gaver, B. "Law and Order on the Playground." In: Bower, E. Games in Education and Development. Springfield: Charles C. Thomas, 1974. pp. 12-22.

36. Montague, A. "Don't be Adultish." *Psychology Today*, 11(August) 1977, p. 46.

37. Comstock, G. *Television and Human Behavior: The Key Studies*. The Rand Corporation, 1975.

38. Orlick, T. *Winning Through Cooperation*. Washington, D. C.: Acroplis Book Co., 1978.

39. Ellis, et al. *Op. Cit.*

40. Michaelis, B. "Adventure Playgrounds: A Healthy Affirmation of the Rights of the Child." *Leisure Today. J.O.P.E.R.* October, 1979. pp. 55-58.

41. *Cowstails and Cobras*: c/o Project Adventure, P. O. Box 157, Hamilton, Massachusetts 01936.

42. Urban Outdoor Adventure Center, 198 Seal Rock Drive, San Francisco, California 94121.

43. Cf: Fluegelmar, A. *The New Games Book*, Garden City, New York: Dolphin-Doubleday, 1976.

44. Fluegelman, A., (Ed.). *More New Games:* New York: Doubleday, 1981.

45. Sutton-Smith, B., "Play as Flow . . . " *Op. Cit.*
46. Orlick, T. *The Cooperative Sports and Games Book I & II.* Westmaster: Pantheon, 1979, 1982.
47. Michaelis, B. and Michaelis, D. *Learning through Non-competitive Activities and Play.* Belmont, California: Pittman Learning. 1977.
    Obispo, California 93406. 1980.
49. Project PLAE. 1824 A Fourth Street, Berkeley, California 94710.
50. Gregson, B. *The Incredible Indoor Games Book and The Outrageous Outdoor Games Book.* Belmont, California: Pitman Learning, 1982.
51. Michaelis, B. "The Family That Plays Together: Programming, Marketing and Delivering Family Play Ideas." *California Parks and Recreation.* Winter, 1984, pp. 38-42 (For further information about T.F.T.P.T., write: Michaelis, 338 Teiching Avenue, Pacifica, California 94044)
52. Westland, C. and Knight, J. *Playing, Living, Learning: A Worldwide Perspective on Children's Opportunities to Play.* State College, Pennsylvania: Venture Publishing, 1982.
53. Csikszentmihalyi, M. "Some Paradoxes . . . " *Op. Cit.*
54. Sutton-Smith, B. "Play and Flow . . . " *Op. Cit.*
55. Cullem, A. *The Geranium on the Window Sill Just Died, But Teacher Went Right On.* Holland: Harlin Quest, 1971.

End of Chapter 5

Chapter 6

On the Biological Basis of Pleasure: Some Implications for Leisure Policy

Stephen L. J. Smith

More often than not current speculations about the nature and value of leisure are either variations on a theme by Aristotle or a quantitative simulation of Veblen's observations of society. Many of our ideas about leisure are still strongly rooted in a school of thought 2300 years old or in the much more recent and mechanistic view that leisure is the leavings of time. We find ourselves in this condition because, it seems, we have forgotten a fundamental aspect of leisure: pleasure. Examine any recent article on any aspect of leisure and you will likely find a discussion of human rights, human dignity, social improvement, environmental quality, political action, holism, humanism or any of a shoal of other currently popular phrases and ideas. But you will find few, if any, references to pleasure. To ignore pleasure is a serious flaw. Pleasure is not trivial. It is absolutely essential to leisure, recreation and play, and we know very little about it. It is the answer to "why people play;" it is the reason for leisure and recreation. In this sense, "pleasure" has a much broader connotation than it does in Freud's concept of "pleasure principle" or in Aristotle's distinction between "pleasure" and "joy." Pleasure is used here to include happiness, joy, fun, sensuality, amusement, mirth and tranquility. These diverse emotions share one common quality—they make a person "feel good;" that is, they give pleasure.

Too often we try to better understand *why* humans play and recreate by ignoring pleasure and instead concentrate on the social structures that merely *shape* play, recreation and leisure. Much that has been learned by social scientists is useful for solving certain problems, but their work is neither fundamental nor universal. The subject which seems to offer more for the etiology of recreation, and thus pleasure, is neurophysiology.

Neurophysiology, the study of the nervous system, treats physical processes which are independent of the temporarily prevailing economy, political system or social mores. These external forces will result in different stimuli being perceived by the nervous system and in different material being learned, but the neurological processes of a person in the United States are the same as those of a person in the People's Republic of China. There is a common denominator in recreation which makes historical and cross-cultural studies academically meaningful and intriguing. That common denominator is pleasure—and pleasure is a neurophysiological phenomenon.

SOME BACKGROUND ON THE STUDY OF PLEASURE

A major step forward in the objective study of pleasure was made in 1954 as the result of an experimental error. James Olds,[4] a psychologist, was working on the mechanisms involved in the alerting response, the changes in an animal when it goes from a drowsy state to an alert state. Olds already knew that the process was due to some sort of electrical activity in a portion of the brain called the reticular activating system. He was working with a group of rats in which electrodes had been implanted in the reticular system to study in detail certain aspects of their alerting responses. The stimulation was not a particularly pleasant experience—with one apparent exception. One rat, when its electrodes were activated, showed no signs of alerting. It did exhibit a peculiar form of behavior, however, that caught Olds' attention. When removed from the corner of the cage where the electrodes were activated, the rat would try to return to that corner. Olds began to close the switch that excited the electrodes whenever the rat was in the corner and observed that the rat never wandered very far away. It stayed in the corner—apparently waiting for the next charge to its brain.

Examination of the rat by a curious Olds and his research team revealed that the electrodes had been incorrectly positioned. Instead of exciting the reticular activating system, they were stimulating an adjacent area called the limbic system. Very little was then known about the limbic system; some researchers, though, suspected that this primitive part of the brain was involved in several forms of behavior. This bit of serendipity implicated the limbic system as the biological basis of pleasure. In fact, a portion of the limbic system is now called the pleasure area of the brain. The process of pleasure-seeking the rat exhibited is called intra-cranial self-stimulation.

This form of direct pleasure stimulation of the limbic system quickly became an exciting new field for experimenters. For example, Olds devised an experiment to test the relative strength of the pleasure drive in rats. He gave the test animals one hour a day to obtain intra-cranial stimulation of the pleasure area or to eat. They consistently chose self-stimulation. The drive was so strong that the test animals completely forewent food. One animal starved to death; the researchers discontinued their experiments when other animals lost up to a third of their body weight.

The limbic system, with little change in structure and virtually no change in function, also exists in the human brain. So, as one would expect, work on other species eventually led to studies on human beings. Some notable experiments were with mental patients of Robert Heath at the Tulane School of Medicine.

Heath provided his patients with a set of implanted electrodes and a button. He noted that the patients used the buttons frequently. According to them, it felt good and made them feel happy. The improvement in their moods ranged from general pleasure, through intense excitement, to a profound euphoria that lasted anywhere from a few hours to several days. The variation depended on the strength and duration of the charge and the portion of the limbic system being activated.

Years of work and experimentation on these pleasure areas have determined that the pleasure drive is one of the strongest drives in animals (at least for vertebrates). Direct limbic stimulation offers the most powerful drive seen in animals, in the sense that "with the electrodes squarely in a pleasure area and a lever to activate them, the animal wishes to do nothing but press the lever and has no desire to engage in any other behavior whatever."[5] Direct stimulation of the pleasure areas is such a powerful drive that it overwhelms the desire for water, food, mating or protection of the young. What is being observed is "not merely pleasure in any parochial sense but what is clearly the ultimate pleasure, the font of all behavior."[6]

Intra-cranial self-stimulation clearly represents a totally new type of behavior although the idea of seeking pleasure is well-known in psychology and philosophy. However, no one could seriously suggest this kind of stimulation is "normal" behavior. Yet the pleasure areas of the brain, whether that of rat or man, are normally stimulated through our senses and internal nerve receptors in our daily round of activities. Indeed, the idea of seeking pleasure is a well-known idea of psychology and philosophy.[7]

SENSORY PLEASURE STIMULATION

Common experience tells us that not all sensory stimuli are pleasurable. Many mild stimuli and very sharp, intense stimuli are unpleasant; even painful. These forces activate another part of the limbic system which registers pain, but since we are dealing with recreation, and thus pleasant feelings, our focus is on the pleasure area. It was a similar interest in voluntary behavior (motivated by pleasure) which led Campbell, who had been studying intra-cranial stimulation (along with many other experimenters), to consider peripheral or sensory stimulation of the limbic system.

This new line of work did not rely on wires and electrodes or the conventional rewards of foods, water or sex for a deprived animal but on mere sensory stimulation of a healthy animal in a homeostatic environment. Campbell hoped to prove experimentally that animals would voluntarily engage in some behavior which would yield no reward other than the pleasure of doing that particular act. In humans we can call this play, leisure or recreation. Campbell's experiments included successful sensory stimulation (using a small external electrical

"tickle") of fish, newts, terrapins and a crocodile. The most significant successes, however, were with squirrel monkeys. His animals were kept in a
lighted environment with food, water, room to play and mate, noise and human
activity. Campbell provided his monkeys with a 500 watt lamp that would light
whenever the monkeys touched a capacitance rod. The advantages of the rod
included the fact that it had no moving parts to wear out, but most importantly, it
made no noise and, in general, was a rather dull plaything. During the initial test
sessions when the lamp was not attracted to the rod the monkeys touched the rod
about 30 times in 15 minutes. As Campbell describes their behavior, "unless it
(any new object) proves edible or can be made love to, the new object is soon
tired of and ignored."[8] After the lamp was attached, the monkeys required
several sessions to learn how to "operate" the switch and the lamp. Once this
education was accomplished they began touching the rod at the rate of 300 to
500 times in a 15 minute test.

The lamp used provided pure white light, which is not a stimulus readily
analogous to the monkeys' usual range of experiences. There is no reference or
symbolism to meat or mate or to free existence in the wild. All that was
operating was a meaningless flash of white light directly into the eyes. Unlike
intra-cranial stimulation which so absorbs an animal that it never stops voluntarily, peripheral or sensory stimulation will eventually become boring. When a
white light was made available continuously the monkeys stopped flashing it
within two hours. The same tapering-off or boredom was observed with any
color of light of equal brightness. However, when the colors of light were
changed every 15 minutes the monkeys kept flashing the light for over four
hours. Such behavior is not unknown in humans. Manufacturers in recreation
and other fields understand the value in bringing out the same old product in a
new container or new form. Boredom haunts all forms of recreation from
television to sex.

Psychologists, too, have discussed motivation based on intrinsic factors and
pleasure seeking. White's conceptualization is one of the most insightful,
although not physiologically based.[9] White noted that conceptualization of
intrinsic motivation is needed to account for both actual behavior and the
improvements in behavior animals and humans learn as they cope with their
environment. The new conceptualization White suggests is "competence" - the
ability of an animal to effectively cope with its environment. Learning, exploring, playing and thinking are among the activities that increase competence.
White described these competence-increasing activities as "motivated in their
own right;" that is, there is no motivation for them other than the feeling of
satisfaction derived from their performance. White is heading straight for the
recognition that pleasure is basic, that it is an element that cannot be simplified
or explained by a still simpler concept. However, he stops short and calls the
satisfaction of activity not pleasure or fun, but a "feeling of efficacy." This

phrase obscures the fundamental reality of fun and the fundamental importance of pleasure. White does acknowledge however that efficacy shows itself most clearly in the fun of play.

The point to be drawn from these ideas is that animals do engage in behavior solely for the pleasure derived. In fact, most activities in which an animal engages in the natural world, eating, copulating, or exploring, are done for pleasurable stimulation only. Fortunately, some of these activities keep the animal alive. The pleasure derived from eating concomitantly provides nourishment. But, and it is a critical distinction, an animal does not eat to get nourishment; it eats to get pleasure. If an animal's mouth is "numbed" so that there is no taste or feel of food sensed during the eating, an animal may starve to death. Research by Ziegler[10] indicates that over-eating may be due to a malfunctioning of the trigeminal nerve which registers oral tactile sensations such as kissing, smoking and eating. In his experiments the destruction of the trigeminal nerve not only stopped the sending of the pleasurable feelings of eating, but also stopped any interest in eating. The strength of the drive for pleasure through other forms of behavior, especially exploration, has been experimentally documented as early as the 1940s and 1950s by researchers such as Whiting and Mourer,[11] Montgomery and Markman,[12] and Berlyne.[13]

When a healthy animal reaches satiation (stops receiving pleasure) from eating or any other activity, such as looking at a flashing light, it does not stop behaving; it seeks out something new. If it did not constantly seek new stimuli that lead to pleasure it would die. For however pleasurable or beneficial any single act may be, it will not maintain homeostasis for the animal over any length of time (i.e., keep it alive). This is the fatal characteristic of intra-cranial self-stimulation: animals will push a lever until they drop. This also suggests, physiologically, the fundamental reason for most (perhaps even all) animal behavior—it is an unending search for renewed pleasure. Survival is not the motivation for the actions of an individual animal; the motivation is the seeking of pleasure.

The biological basis of pleasurable feeling (sensory and proprioceptive stimulation of the limbic system) is the same for all vertebrates and this necessarily includes man. Whatever one's feelings about an immaterial part of humans, a spirit, soul or whatever, man in his body and its processes is an animal. We feel pleasure in the same way that animals do.

THE HUMAN DIFFERENCE

There is one difference, however, in the ways that humans can attain pleasure. This is a way of seeking pleasure which makes some of us most of the time, and all of us part of the time, different from animals. We can obtain pleasure from thought, from the use of the tertiary portion of the human cortex - that part associated with creative thought and symbolic reasoning. Animals do not because they cannot. This includes the dolphins and whales whose large cortices are the subject of much popular speculation. There is no evidence the crustaceans use their large convoluted cerebrums for pleasure; they are too busy using their brain for the pursuit of the simpler pleasures of food, breathing and the companionship of their own kind.

The potential of conscious thought to control the older parts of the brain is a common experience. Almost all of us have experienced psychogenic insomnia—those nights when excited or angry thoughts have overwhelmed the call for sleep. The same barrage of electrical activity can be directed into the pleasure areas.

This organization and function of the brain provides the only unqualified, non-solipsistic and non-mystical difference between man and animal. The unique characteristic of Homo sapiens is that members have the potential for achieving pleasures from thought. To the degree that someone actualizes this potential and seeks pleasure from mental activity, he is acting human. To the degree he seeks sensory pleasure he is acting subhuman. These are unpleasant words, but we must face the truth, even if unpleasant, if we are to progress as human beings. The truth is: members of Homo sapiens often engage in decidedly sub-human acts.

With this simple distinction we can now perceive a pattern in recreation activities which is more basic than existing classification schemes such as the familiar indoor/outdoor dichotomy. Recreation activities, or anything else an individual does for fun or pleasure, can be placed on a continuum from purely sensory to purely intellectual and thus on a spectrum of sub-human to human activity.

This difference is not, in the first place, a philosophical one but an objective one (although there are many philosophical implications). In a rather over-simplified way the difference between acting human and acting sub-human is how you seek pleasure: stimulation by the cortex (human) versus stimulation by the peripheral receptors (sub-human).

While pleasure-seeking runs the gamut from sensual to intellectual, it can be approximated by three separate types of behavior. These three ways of pursuing pleasure have rather indistinct boundaries, but still provide a useful scheme for identifying different forms of pleasure-seeking behavior which is independent of prevailing social and political conditions. The three types of pleasure-seeking can be given the labels of (1) sensory, (2) expressive-cortical and (3) intellectual-cortical. The basis for differentiation is the relative importance of the cortex in generating the feelings of pleasure.

SENSORY RECREATION

Sensory activities include many popular and traditional activities: eating, some forms of children's play, much music (especially such primitive forms as rock), vandalism, hunting, sports, snowmobiling, flirting and rape. These apparently unrelated activities are grouped together because a person finding pleasure in any of them does so because the activity stimulates the peripheral receptors. Physical play, sports, hunting and snowmobiling involve the pleasurable use of muscles which is sensed by the proprioceptors (nerves sensing muscular movement).

Eating, drinking, loud rhythmic music and similar activities provide direct stimulation of the senses and, with allowances for variations in personal tastes, provide pleasure for all people. Other activities are enjoyable because of the visceral or autonomic pleasure they provide. David Klein, a professor at Michigan State and a commentator for National Public Radio in the United States, has suggested that the great popularity of snowmobiling in states like Michigan is due to the feeling of danger and personal confrontation with power it provides. These visceral pleasures (such as the tightening of the stomach) offset the blandness and tedium of jobs such as those on Michigan's automobile assembly lines. Klein suggested that snowmobiling could be greatly reduced (if this were deemed socially or environmentally desirable) by making snowmobiles safe, slow and quiet. Similarly, Campbell observed that the pleasure of mountain climbing comes primarily from the danger involved. Although the use of muscles, eyes, ears and nose must also provide pleasure it is the difficulty and challenge which draws climbers to their sport; thus "despite its apparent masculinity it reduces to the fairground mentality."[14]

Much so-called sexual pleasure also stems from the "fairground mentality." Caressing, kissing and intercourse provide many pleasurable stimuli, but not all apparently sexual activity is truly sexual. The first adolescent contacts between boys and girls generate great feelings of excitement and pleasure, but these are largely autonomic, arising from the pleasurable sensations in changes in the heart rate, respiration rate and movement of the stomach and intestines. Because these early pleasures (which also typically accompany any new contact between adults which has sexual overtones) are primarily autonomic, they inevitably decline as the two people become more familiar with each other. The mystery and intrigue is gone; sex becomes routine; the flame has gone out of their romance. Some change is necessary to rekindle the feelings: having sex in more exotic or naughty ways, in semi-public places or with new partners. Truly sexual feelings intensify with familiarity as the couple begins to draw together emotionally and become more skilled in their caresses. In brief, much so-called sexual attraction is basically pleasurable fear - like a roller coaster ride. In fact, a roller coaster is a not-unknown analogy in describing many love affairs.

EXPRESSIVE-CORTICAL RECREATION

The next group of recreation activities, expressive-cortical, are based on a mingling of man's sensory and intellectual characteristics. The expressive-cortical activities are those which use creative thought to produce something which also gives sensual pleasure (e.g., classical music) or which adds a major intellectual dimension to a sensory experience (e.g., winetasting). The arts and crafts: painting, sculpture, composing music, film-making, calligraphy and all the rest; sex based on emotional closeness; and certain occupations such as medicine and engineering provide this type of pleasure. Physical artifacts are used to give expression to an activity which is predominantly intellectual.

This category has especially confused borders. A composer of a piece of classical music will probably be closer to enjoying an intellectual-cortical pleasure than a sensual pleasure although his music can give sensual pleasure. The performer of that piece and the audience will tend to be successively more drawn to the sensual character of music. However, some mathematicians, for example, who have a taste for classical music have occasionally described perceiving profound mathematical structures in a musical movement. On the other hand, Einstein described some of his early ideas about relativity as mental dance images. His intellectual reveries took on, in his mind, sensual qualities. Beethoven, near the end of a life time composing powerful, sensual music, completed several works while deaf. His pleasure in the *Ninth Symphony* could hardly be called sensual since he lacked the sense to appreciate it. Similarly Adolf Gottlieb, a 20th century abstract expressionist, produced some of his best pieces after he became blind.

Some types of children's play are expressive-cortical. Any parent who has watched children play has seen them first enjoy physical activity with a plaything and then grow bored as they exhaust the initial possibilities for pleasure. Children will then attempt to renew the fun of the activity or plaything by increasing its complexity, by changing the rules of play, by using the toy for fantasy or, if all else fails, by taking the toy apart to see how it works. The phenomenon is one where a child can easily obtain pleasure from sensory stimulation, and when he grows bored, will seek new pleasure by changing the form of play. The change that overcomes boredom is the change that allows the child to use his intelligence and creativity. These observations are probably the objective origins for the play theories of Berlyn,[15] Maddi,[16] and Ellis.[17]

INTELLECTUAL-CORTICAL RECREATION

Intellectual-cortical, the final category of pleasurable behaviors, seems to belong to the realm of the thinkers. Actually, everyone obtains some pleasure from intellectual activities—those activities which provide pleasure without the use of sensory stimulation. Only a few people, however, derive most of their pleasure from such sources. They form an elite in any society which is regularly singled out for admiration or, as often happens, suspicion and ridicule. These are the philosophers, theologians, linguists, mathematicians, logicians, certain historians, theoretical physicists, mystics, and, at times, politicians. Any motor behavior associated with their seeking pleasure is only ancillary. Some physical action is necessary to obtain information, education or the resources to keep alive; their pleasure comes from their minds and not their actions.

The development and nurturing of a human mind capable of human pleasures is one of the greatest responsibilities a society faces. It would be a mistake, though, to believe that all intellectual pleasures are necessarily lofty and virtuous. There are a great many bad philosophers and theologians. Many intellectuals are as silly as non-intellectuals. The vast potential of the creative intellect can also be turned to fantasizing and daydreaming, which are surrogates for sensory pleasure. Still, other humans develop elaborate, twisted political philosophies which give intellectual pleasure but all too often find ultimate expression in sub-human, destructive terrorism and war. Fascism and the twisted science developed under Hitler are probably the major examples from this century.

Not all intellectual pleasure is constructive, creative, enduring and socially desirable. Only intellectual activities, however, have the potential for becoming so. Sensory pleasure virtually never does. Apparent exceptions are individuals such as the Wright brothers who experienced an exquisite aesthetic reaction as well as physical thrill in their early experiments with flight. But even in such cases the work is preceded by long periods of intellectual study and analysis which either gave or promised future pleasure and contributed the requisite scientific basis for a lasting contribution.

A FEW IMPLICATIONS

The identification and classification of phenomena is basic to any discipline, profession or body of practitioners. Researchers and academics are still searching for a paradigm which will help guide work and provoke questions for future study of recreation, leisure and play. Such a paradigm may be built out of the common denominator of these phenomena or pleasures. This chapter has described in brief terms some of the physiological importance of pleasure and in doing so pointed out an important dichotomy in the search for pleasure, vis., an objective is based on the origins of the stimuli received by the limbic system.

If a society holds the philosophy that the state exists to enable people to become as human as they can be, to emphasize and nurture good and enduring human values, then those social institutions that provide leisure services should take a careful look at their programs. Public recreation agencies, park departments, athletic leagues, youth groups, churches and schools (including universities) have the responsibility to evaluate their offerings in terms of their location on the sub-human to human spectrum. Few people would seriously suggest that we should not worry about preserving open-space natural beauty nor would they suggest that we can completely ignore physical health. The issue is one of relative emphasis, of budgets and of program resources. A flat statement that all recreation and park agencies are emphasizing the subhuman in us by virtue of their sensory-oriented programming is unwarranted. But we do have the responsibility to take a critical look at programs and honestly evaluate just what part of our human/animal personality we are developing and whether this is the appropriate role of a public or educational agency. Surely, the magnitude of sports programs in most schools deserves special attention. A comparison of the institutional support for intercollegiate and intramural sports with cultural recreation at the same institutions should be made and interpreted in light of the concepts argued in this paper. Societies and governments which provide so much support and place so much attention on events such as the Olympic games are highlighting and promoting sub-human behavior. Considering the recent events of terror, retribution, resource boycotts and other global acts of sensory pleasure-seeking (in the name of whatever ideology), the emphasis given the Olympics and world-champion prize fights is disturbing, to say the least.

The same pattern can be found at local levels. Recreation is often claimed to be a deterrent to juvenile delinquency. The causes of delinquency, as with most social problems, are diverse and diffuse. But it seems almost paradoxical to think that a recreation program which emphasizes some forms of sub-human behavior is going to have broad success in eliminating other forms of sub-human behavior. Fights and riots which too often accompany sporting events and rock festivals are evidence that sensory recreation may not be such a cure-all for socially undesirable forms of sensory recreation. On the other hand, rare indeed are plays, classical music concerts, lectures or other intellectual events which are followed by violent forms of sensory-oriented behavior.

All this is but one aspect of the new approach to recreation. There are many others, some philosophical, some scientific. A biological approach to recreation will place many familiar phenomena in new contexts and will challenge quite a few of our old comfortable beliefs about sports, athletics, arts, the humanities and science. It suggests that there is indeed something special and unique about being human—and that many people (perhaps most) do not act "humanly" for much of their lives. We have much, much more to learn about pleasure, the manifold ways people pursue it and the implications for fields of inquiry from management to evolution to theology. Through it all, the image of man as constantly striving to be happy, and being most human when he is pursuing "human" pleasures is an optimistic and hopeful image of humanity.

REFERENCES

1. A few of the many different approaches can be read in the works of the following authors: Veblen, T. *The Theory of the Leisure Class.* New York: The American Library, 1953; de Grazia, S. *Of Time, Work and Leisure.* Garden City, New Jersey: Doubleday and Company, 1964; Pieper, J. *Leisure: The Basis of Culture.* New York: Pantheon Books, 1952; Linder, S. *The Harried Leisure Class.* New York: Columbia University Press, 1970; Brightbill, C. *The Challenge of Leisure.* Englewood Cliffs, New Jersey: Prentice-Hall, 1960; Dumazedier, J. *Toward a Society of Leisure.* New York: The Free Press, 1967; Martin, A. R. "Leisure and Our Inner Resources." *Parks and Recreation.* March, 1975, pp. ia-ff.

2. Kuhn, T. *The Structure of Scientific Revolutions.* Chicago: University of Chicago Press, 1970.

3. A recent example is the debate over the acceptability of hang-gliding in the National Parks. Questions on appropriateness were raised in a *New York Times* editorial by Ronald Taylor, November 11th, 1975, "National Park Policy."

4. Olds, J. and Milner, P. "Positive Reinforcement Produced by Electrical Stimulation of Septal Area and Other Regions of Rat Brain." *Journal of Comparative Physiology and Psychology,* 47(1954), p. 419. See also Olds, J. "Differentiation of Reward Systems in the Brain by Self-Stimulation Techniques." In *Electrical Studies on the Unanesthetized Brain.* New York: Hoeber-Harper, 1960, pp. 17-49.

5. Campbell, H. *The Pleasure Areas.* New York: Delacorte Press, 1973, p. 25.

6. *Ibid.,* p. 24.

7. Among these would be Freud, S. *Beyond the Pleasure Principle.* (James Strachey, Trans.). New York: Liveright, 1961; Szasz, T. *Pain and Pleasure.* New York: Basic Books, 1975; Health, R. (Ed.). *The Role of Pleasure in Behavior.* New York: Hoeber-Harper, 1964.

8. Campbell, *Op. Cit.,* p. 49.

9. White, P. W. "Motivation Reconsidered: The Concept of Competence." *Psychological Review,* 66(1957), pp. 297-333.

10. Ziegler, H. P. "The Sensual Feel of Food." *Psychology Today,* August, 1975, pp. 62-67.

11. Whiting, J. W. M. and Mourer, O. H. "Habit Progression and Regression - A Laboratory Study of Some Factors Relevant to Human Socialization." *Journal of Comparative Psychology,* 36(1945), pp. 229-253.

12. Montgomery, D. C. and Markman, J. A. "The Relationship Between Fear and Exploratory Behavior." *Journal of Comparative Physiology and Psychology,* 48(1955), pp. 254-260.

13. Berlyne, D. E. "Novelty and Curiosity as Determinants of Exploratory Behavior," *British Journal of Psychology,* vol. 41, 1950, pp. 68-80.
14. Brown, Evelyn. "An Ethological Theory of Play." *Journal of AAHPER,* September, 1968.
15. Berlyne, D. E. *Conflict, Arousal and Curiosity.* New York: McGraw-Hill, 1960.
16. Maddi, S. R. "Exploratory Behavior and Variation-seeking in Man." In *Functions of Varied Experience.* Edited by D. W. Fiske and S. R. Maddi. Homewood, Illinois: Dorsey Press, 1961.
17. Ellis, M. J. *Why People Play.* Englewood Cliffs, New Jersey: Prentice-Hall, 1973.

End of Chapter 6

Chapter 7

If Leisure is to Matter

Thomas L. Goodale

Judging from the number of new periodicals with "leisure" in the title, or the pervasive use of the term in the literature and in conversation, or the jargon of leisure studies, leisure education, leisure research, leisure counseling, leisure services, etc., we are moving into the age of leisure at last. Unfortunately, that would be a hasty judgement because leisure is more common in our literature than in our lives and because the term leisure is usually used as little more than a substitute for words we have grown tired of.

Frequently, leisure is used where recreation would serve better; as in the phrase leisure services. Often leisure means no more than free time; as in the phrase leisure time. In addition, the term has been resurrected from antiquity to refer to a state or condition; that is, where one is at. When one is at leisure one is in a relaxed, contemplative condition. If we convey no more than one of these meanings when we say leisure, then we burden ourselves with being concerned about what is, *per se*, not very important. If this is all we mean, then leisure doesn't matter—not yet.

MISAPPROPRIATING ARISTOTLE'S THOUGHT

There is deeper meaning which does not come to the surface in most talk and writing about leisure. To find it requires a more careful examination of Aristotle's thought, and the thoughts of those like Pieper[1] and de Grazia[2] who have tried to guide us to and through Aristotle's philosophy. With few exceptions, our encounters with Aristotle's thought, as interpreted by many of those writing about leisure, are not very satisfying. Leisure seems simple, impossible, and unrelated to our lives. There is too little congruence between what we read and hear of it and what we experience everyday.

Seldom do we reflect on the complexity and subtlety of philosophical thought. Understanding Aristotle's writings is at best difficult. His style, as his subject, does not readily yield understanding. Too, there are few among us who read him in the original. Rather, what we read are translations, of which there are many, and notes and interpretations, also in great number. Indeed, Aristotle spawned an industry, as the shelves of any respectable library attest. Obviously, there are differences in the translations, notes, and interpretations. As a simple example, depending on the translation, Aristotle wrote either "one swallow makes not a summer" or "one swallow makes not a spring." The message, if not the season, is of great importance to us as is noted later. Surely, "leisure" is a much more complex notion than spring or summer. In fact, one of the better known translators, Benjamin Jowett, noted that Aristotle's "leisure" is "one of the most difficult notions to translate into English words and modes of thought."[3]

Aristotle was a product of a milieu so foreign to ours as to seriously tax our ability to comprehend. Consequently, it seems folly to wrench small bits of his writings from their context, transport them over twenty-three centuries, and set them down in an inhospitable place. This is especially hazardous as it is frequently noted that in Aristotle's thought, the existing order (i.e., what was) was an essential element in his thinking about what ought to be. The result is that there is much in Aristotle's writing that, quite simply, doesn't fit our time at all (for example, some notions about women, friendship and love, slavery and citizenship). He argues that friendship is a relationship between men exclusively, since it requires awareness and return of mutual affection. In relations between unequals, such as rulers and subjects or men and women, "the more useful of the two should receive more love than *he* gives."[4] And he writes, "Domestic authority is the best model for aristocracy, for the authority of the husband is founded on the superiority of his abilities and virtues."[5] One of Aristotle's contemporaries, a man named Aleman, in wishing to compliment some girls, could find no other way to refer to them except as "female boy-friends."[6] In Aristotle's Greece, women were simply not men's equals.

But all men were not equal either. Clearly leisure was not possible for all; or even many. As is widely known, Aristotle's concept of leisure, indeed many argue Greek civilization itself, was built on the backs of slaves. In most Greek cities of the time, slaves plus a few thousand non-voting metics and freemen, out-numbered citizens by ratios varying between 4:1 and 20:1.

In the context of the times, that posed no ethical dilemma. Citizens, in order to have time for government, war, literature, and philosophy, must have someone attend to their material concerns. To have leisure, one must be free from economic tasks. It is not necessary to be wealthy, but one must have means. Aristotle, if anything, was a preacher of moderation. To him slaves were animate tools, and he foresaw the machine age in recognizing inanimate slaves. He was, by all accounts, good to his slaves and to his women. But leisure was not for them; it was only for citizens. "Because mechanics and laborers cannot practice virtue while leading the life of mechanics and laborers they will not be included in the category of citizens."[7] Further, while slaves could enjoy "inferior pleasures . . . who will ascribe the happiness of a man to him who, by his character or condition, is disqualified from manly pursuits?"[8]

THE IMPORTANCE OF WORKING WELL

In the literature about recreation and leisure, one brief passage from Aristotle's voluminous writings is frequently cited. It is from *Politics, Book VII.*

> Nature herself . . . requires that we should be able to not only to work well, but to use leisure well; for as I must repeat once again, the first principle of all action is leisure. Both are required but leisure is better than occupation and is its end:[9]

Translators differ. Elsewhere one finds:

> Nature requires not only that we should be properly employed, but that we should be able to enjoy our leisure in an honorable way.[10]

There is agreement, however, that being able to work well, or to be properly employed is so evident as to be a foregone conclusion. Although that part of the passage is often neglected in the recreation and leisure literature, we are reminded of it in so many other ways.

It is said, for example, that Aristotle died of a stomach ailment aggravated by overwork.[11] Pieper, in referring to Aristotle's maxim, "we are unleisurely in order to have leisure," writes that the maxim is more weighty because Aristotle was, ". . . a cool-headed workaday realist."[12] Further, there is no mistaking the closing verses of Genesis, Chapter I and the opening verses of Chapter II. On the sixth day God reviewed his work and saw that it was good; on the seventh day, he rested from his work. Too, it seems clear that Jesus was proud of the fact that he could make a table because he was a carpenter.[13]

In *Politics, Book X,* Aristotle notes the roles of rest and recreation. They are good, but not the highest good.

> Happiness then, cannot consist in mere recreative pastime; for it is absurd to think that all our serious exertions and strenuous labors should terminate in so frivolous an end. We do not labor that we may be idle, but, as Anarchis justly said, we are idle that we may labor with more effect . . . The weakness of human nature requires frequent remissions of energy; but these rests and pauses are only the better to prepare us for enjoying the pleasures of activity. The amusements of life, therefore, are but preludes to its business, the place of which they cannot possibly supply; and its happiness, because its business,   . consisting of the exercise of those virtuous energies which constitute the worth and dignity of our nature.[14]

Rest and amusement are preludes to, and cannot replace business or happiness, the latter flowing from the former if by business we understand the exercise of virtuous energies.

VIRTUE, ETHICS AND LEISURE

Matters of virtue are found throughout Aristotle's *Politics*. This is so because
Aristotle wrote *Politics* in conjunction with *Ethics*. He considered them part of
one work. It is in *Ethics* that he identified happiness as the highest good, it
being an end in itself. And the wellspring of happiness is virtue. Happiness
doesn't come cheap; one has to be virtuous. That is the often repeated message
of *Nicomachena Ethics*; happiness derives from a lifetime of virtue:

> The proper good of man consists then in virtuous energies, that is in the
> exercise of virtue continued through life; for one swallow makes not a
> summer; neither does one day, or a short time constitute happiness . . .
> The multitude, indeed, pursue different pleasures, because they do not
> rightly apprehend in what true pleasure consists. But pleasure, strictly
> so called, is the delight of a virtuous man whose life needs not an
> appendag of false joys, containing the perennial spring of true pleasure
> in itself . . . In the estimation of a wise man, virtue is pleasant because
> it is honorable and good; his happiness is one regular whole; not broken
> and disjointed.[15]

Of course, Aristotle did note that leisure was better than work, or at least
better than work done by non-citizens, and he clearly linked leisure with the
contemplative life but, again, in far more complex ways than we generally
understand, because contemplation was inextricably bound to the divine in man;
to the somehow transcendent soul. Difficult a time as scholars have had with
the notion of leisure, it is as nothing compared to this. For Aristotle's notion of
contemplation was linked to his notion of God and God's own sense of pleasure.
To illustrate:

> Contemplation . . . is possible only by virtue of the divine element in
> man. We ought then not confine our thoughts to the ephemeral, but so
> far as possible we ought to seek immortality.[16]

> The life of good conduct—of morally good action—is the best human
> life, the completest expression of human nature . . . But there is in man
> an element which is either itself divine or the most godlike of elements
> in man: *vous*, or whatever that should be called whose nature it is to
> rule us and to take thought of things noble and divine. And in the
> activity of this element—in contemplation—man experiences the
> completest felicity.[17]

Work, leisure, contemplation and happiness are not the simple matters, at least
in Aristotle's argument, that we sometimes make them out to be. In most
contemporary discussions or writings about leisure, little is said about virtue and
less about the divine. The omissions destroy the meaning.

We Without Means

Leisure in the Aristotelian sense is troublesome enough for us on the most secular of grounds; i.e., having means. If to be at leisure one must have means, then what are we to do? Those without means, which is nearly all of us, are simply going to have to work. If, as de Grazia suggests, work and leisure live in two different worlds and free time lives in the world of work,[18] then what are we to do? We live in a world of work and we have no reason to think we should not. We are workers and have no reason to think we should not be, not because Calvin walks in the land but because the world's work (dare we say God's work?) remains to be done. Quite evidently, then, work will require us to exercise our virtuous energies more so than in the past.

If as Pieper writes, "Leisure . . . (is) utterly contrary to the ideal of 'worker' in each of its three aspects . . . as activity, as toil, as a social function,"[19] then what are we to do? We have no recourse but to reject Pieper's characterization of the "worker.":

> The 'worker' it has been seen in our brief analysis of that significant figure, is characterized by three significant traits: an extreme tension of the powers of action, a readiness to suffer in vacuo unrelated to anything, and complete absorption in the social organism, itself rationally planned to utilitarian ends.[20]

The description is not without merit, historically at least, including the recent past. It seems ill-fitted to the present and in any case there is no reason to cling to the characterization. Where it still fits perhaps it should not. Perhaps one of our major tasks is to assure that it does not. As long as we must work we must rid ourselves of hostility toward it. If leisure is to be a possibility for us, then it must infuse our work. Much more is involved here than the concepts of fusion or extension between work and non-work activities and roles. Our work should be what we choose to do; what we and others consider important. It should so absorb us, as W. H. Auden suggested, that in doing it we are, in essence, praying.[21] Would that Gibran's phrase, "Work is love made visible," was applicable. For if it is not, there seems little hope for leisure.

THE DIVIDING OF TIME . . .

A world of work such as ours suggests, a priori, that the most we can attain is free time. So leisure as free time becomes the focus. But free time is not a goal; per se it is not important and it cannot shoulder the burden too readily placed upon it. What is usually meant by free time is time free from work and other obligations. But even if by leisure we mean nothing more than free time, ours is still not an age of leisure and there seems little prospect of it. "One widely current illusion about the future needs to be dispelled. This is the illusion of great affluence and leisure . . . obtained via projections of increased productivity."[22] Productivity gains have not matched expectations for the past several years. Unemployment in mature economies has been increasing. The inanimate tools that Aristotle anticipated have not set us free; they have set us to work as servo-mechanisms. Sometimes they have set us aside. People now become redundant, a presumably sophisticated but actually grotesque way of saying unemployed. Economic and material growth was to have solved the problems of the unemployed and the poor. It has not, and it cannot, even if growth were to continue as in previous decades, and that seems most unlikely.

Free time unavoidably carries with it a connotation of subservient worth and value. That is a handicap and a burden. It is undermined by its own definition; it is unobligated time and it is free from work. But who is ever free from work and other obligations? Because one has some discretion about how his or her time may be used does not make it unobligated. In fact, the reverse is true. It is only when we have the opportunity to choose that our obligations become fully apparent. That, as noted later, is consistent with Aristotle's thought. Surely there is no end to the worthwhile work that must be done. Besides, do not each of us always have obligations to ourselves and to the cosmos and to most everything in between? Further, and particularly disconcerting about the notion of free time, is that it perpetuates the dichotomy between work and leisure as free time. The dichotomy deals leisure a heavy blow; probably a fatal blow. Jacques Ellul notes it well, among literally scores of other commentators:

> To assert that the individual expresses his personality and cultivates himself in the course of his leisure is to accept the suppression of half the human personality. History compels the judgement that it is in work that human beings develop and affirm their personality . . . When the human being is no longer responsible for his work and no longer figures in it, he feels spiritually outraged . . . The annihilation of work and its compensation with leisure resolves the conflicts by referring them to a subhuman plane . . . To gamble that leisure will enable man to live is to sanction the dissociation I have been describing and to cut him off completely from part of life.[23]

The work-leisure dichotomy does violence to our nature in so many ways, ". . . for one swallow makes not a summer; neither does one day, or a short time constitute happiness . . ." Evenings, weekends and holidays, however lengthened, are insufficient. A study in England revealed that a disproportionate number of suicides were committed on Sunday. Psychologists suggested that perhaps some of the victims of their own hand were not capable of facing another week of work.

AND OF LIVES

Much of the difficulty we face has been attributed to the factory system and the dehumanization of work, but people in comfortable highrise office towers show signs of a similar malaise. The factory system is, however, partly responsible for "the leisure problem" and for creating the work-leisure dichotomy, because it forced a separation; where one lived and where one worked became quite distinct, making the division of time a simple matter. Since then, the separation has been carried much further. Now we believe that working and living should be separate. One appeal of the suburbs, for many at least, is that they are not close to work. The space, and the time needed to traverse it, provides insulation between home and work, leisure and work, living and working. We are not supposed to take our work home; what goes on at the plant or office is supposed to be left at the plant or office. We can and do work at home, but that is a different matter. It is more imperative that one does not take home to work at the plant or office. So half our lives, for a period of 40 years or more, is supposed to be unrelated to the other half. It is errant nonsense of course. It is probably impossible as well. And to be constantly suppressing half of one's life inevitably carries a heavy psychological cost.

This is not just a matter of playing different roles. Even if it were, why must we be constantly playing roles? The main difficulty is that the roles have become not simply unrelated but worse, incompatible. Ruben Nelson makes the case powerfully, illustrating it with the story of a space engineer caught up in a project requiring long hours of hard work. On returning home, he was always surprised to find that his wife seemed just as tired as he was. He didn't think she had much to do but she claimed she had more to do than she had time for. So he arranged to take a day off and spend it with his wife—not on a dinner or family picnic, however. He did a time and motion study of her day. He determined conclusively that his wife's complaints of being overworked were unjustified, and henceforth paid no attention whatever to her complaints.[24]

PERSONS OR OBJECTS

Surely we all recognize how inappropriate was his response. But we also recognize that his response was not inappropriate to the world of work. So we have come to see ourselves and others in two lights—as persons in our private lives, and as things or objects in our public or working lives. We have come to live by two sets of rules—those for the role of worker, functionary, agent, official or whatever role we play in our public lives, and those for the role of parent, friend, spouse, lover or whatever roles make up our private lives. But the roles are incompatible. We cannot reconcile them.[25]

Publicly, as objects, we seek to maximize our profits, importance and status; in part by externalizing our costs and wastes. "Let the buyer beware." Don't require the vendor to be forthright. That is why we are advised not to do business with friends or relatives; the roles are incompatible. Privately, as persons, we share our profits and strengths, and internalize our burdens and those of others—that is what friendship is about. To Aristotle, the first characteristic of friendship was, "the promotion of another's good for his own sake."[26] Publicly, we are unrestrained except by law and regulation: sometimes not even that restrains us. For surely billions of dollars are spent each year to change, avoid or circumvent the law, always to the spender's advantage. Sometimes we are merely rule obeyers ("I'm only doing my job. Don't blame be, I don't set policy.") which is "an organized form of non-responsible behavior."[27] Publicly, as objects, we know only institutional restraint and avoid even that when we can. Privately, as persons, we restrain ourselves; we recognize and exercise personal responsibility. A place where personal responsibility no longer exists would be a good working definition of hell.

MEANING AND MATTERING

The notion of free time diverts our attention from problems which free time cannot resolve. The dichotomy of work and leisure as free time, the abandonment of people to incompatibly split lives, and the subsidiary value of free time is destructive as it recognizes—even emphasizes—selves as public "things" rather than private "persons." This creates not only confusion but also cynicism because we know that much of our work has lost its meaning; much of what we do does not seem to matter and so with our lives. That applies as often to those engaged in providing human services as it does to those providing goods or services for profit. Galper, [28] for example, notes that social workers are aware that many social services are of little benefit to people, thus they experience a sense of the limited value of their work. While individuals often feel the urgency and crisis, their institution often does not. As persons, they often feel that whatever they do will make little difference and they become dissatisfied with their own inadequate performance. Still, as things, they receive recognition and promotion in the system, perhaps for having resigned themselves to making the best of a situation which may be impossible. They learn not only that much of what they do may not matter, the institution conveys to them that it doesn't matter that it doesn't matter. Is it any wonder then that fatalism is on the rise, with not only more bingo and gambling in the usual sense but also with astrology and Tarot cards, religious and other cults (some of which have remarkably nasty streaks) and in privately and, increasingly, publicly sponsored lotteries, nearly all of which have been vastly more productive than their sponsors ever dreamed? There are even state organized lotteries for getting children into decent schools and those with too limited income into decent housing. What an incredible perversion. The losers are expected to blame their desperate situation on luck rather than on the failure of systems and institution. As Cohen notes:

> In the context of competitive culture the idea of luck may serve as a convenient stabilizer, convenient, that is, to the 'lucky ones' at the same time stultifying initiative and independent thinking. Daily emasculation of the reflective processes of millions, whose horoscopes are cast in the daily press, produces a potentially pliable mentality that sees the futility of social intervention if everything is ordained in the stars.[29]

Perhaps Cohen has cause and effect in reverse order, but it does seem that fatalism and a sense of futility go together.

Finally, the dichotomization of work and free time, the subservience and the abandonment suggested in the notion of free time; the fractioning of whole persons and whole lives as though no more than whole numbers, exacerbates what is generally regarded as the period of crisis in which we now find ourselves. Walter Lippmann addressed the issue directly, as noted in the editor's preface to his *A Preface to Morals:*

> Thus, Lippmann indicates, business, the family and the other preoccupations of men's daily lives are, in effect, 'religion's lost provinces.' This loss has inevitably made life seem less meaningful to many men. For with each province now autonomous, each having its own standards and its own modes of thought, there is no longer any strong central theme in men's lives; nothing seems to be organically related to anything else, and so nothing seems to be terribly important.[30]

Tillich, in *The Courage To Be,* comes to the same conclusion. He notes that the anxiety characteristic of our era is that of emptiness and meaninglessness, placing us ". . . under the threat of spiritual non-being."[31]

So the final problem with the notion of leisure as time free from work and other obligations is that it does not matter. It is without value or meaning. If we have a leisure problem it is not because we have too much free time, or too little work. What we have is too little meaning in our free time and in our work; in sum, in our lives.

In only one sense is free time a useful notion: the sense of discretion about its use. The opportunity and ability to choose is important. There is no other road to virtue because, to cite Aristotle once more, when he summarized his argument about the relation between virtue and voluntary and involuntary acts: "The habit of moral virtue implies the deliberate preference of one kind of conduct to another; and deliberate preference implies freedom of choice."[32]

IF LEISURE IS TO MATTER

Leisure is a useless notion if by it we mean merely free time or some contemplative state. Still, the Aristotelian view may inform and encourage us if we keep
his context. The context is virtue. The world of action is an essential corollary.
If happiness is the highest good and the product of contemplation, so it is also
the result of action; the exercise of virtuous energies. Well being and well doing
are parts of a whole; complementary and synergistic. That, not surprisingly, is
more compatible with our experiences than merely contemplating, even though
such experiences may be pitifully infrequent. For who has not felt the peace and
joy of having done something truly worthwhile, having done it well, and
knowing it?

Aristotle concerned himself with whole men leading whole lives. He saw
clearly that happiness was unattainable otherwise. Only if we perceive our lives,
including our work, congruently, can we come to grips with Aristotle or with an
endless collection of scholarly thought since his time.

What those in the recreation or leisure service fields should do about all this
is not entirely clear. It is characteristic of our time, perhaps because we are only
beginning to understand the crises before us, to have some ideas about what
needs to be done without yet knowing what to do. The recapture of selves as
persons rather than things; the exercise of virtue through a lifetime; the reintegration of all aspects of life into a varied but congruent whole; the recovery of
meaning; these are the tasks before us all.

If leisure is to matter, these tasks must be addressed more directly, and
probably more radically, than in the past. Until then, the judgement that leisure
has arrived is not only premature but also misleading, with consequences which
can only be dire.

REFERENCES

1. Pieper, J. *Leisure: The Basis of Culture*. (Alexander Dru, Trans.)
    New York: Pantheon Books, 1952.
2. de Grazia, S. *Of Time, Work and Leisure*. New York: The Twentieth
    Century Fund. 1960.
3. Steward, J. A. *Notes on the Nicomachean Ethics*. New York: Arno Press,
    1973, p. 446.
4. Kierman, T. P. (Ed.). *Aristotle Dictionary*. New York: Philosophical
    Library, 1962, pp. 137-138.
5. Gillies, J. *Aristotle's Ethics*. (John Gillies Trans.) London: Routledge,
    1886, p. 138.

6. Durant, W. *The Life of Greece*. (The Story of Civilization: Part II), New York: Simon and Schuster, 1939, p. 301.
7. Kierman, *Op. Cit.*, pp. 149-150.
8. Gillies, *Op. Cit.*, p. 361.
9. Kaplan, J. (Ed.). *The Pocket Aristotle*. (W. E. Ross, Trans.). New York: Pocket Books, 1958, p. 336.
10. Durant, *Op. Cit.*, p. 533.
11. Kierman, *Op. Cit.*, p. xii.
12. Pieper, *Op. Cit.*, p. 21.
13. Nash, J. B. *Philosophy of Recreation and Leisure*, Dubuque, Iowa: Wm. C. Brown Co., 1973, p. 222.
14. Gillies, *Op. Cit.*, p. 360.
15. *Ibid.* pp. 169-170.
16. Ferguson, J. *Aristotle*. New York: Twayne Publishers, 1972, p. 138.
17. Rees, D. A. (Ed.). *Aristotle: The Nicomachean Ethics*, (A Commentary by the late H. H. Joachim) Oxford: Oxford University Press, 1951, p. 287.
18. de Grazia, *Op. Cit.*, pp. 7-8.
19. Pieper, *Op. Cit.*, p. 40.
20. *Ibid,,* p. 39.
21. Auden, W. H. "Culture and Leisure." *Ekstics,* 144(Feb.) 1966, pp. 418-420.
22. Boulding, K. "The Future of Personal Responsibility." *American Behavioral Scientist,* 15:3(Jan./Feb.) 1972, p. 352.
23. Ellul, J. *The Technological Society*. (John Wilkinson, Trans.) New York: Random House, 1964, pp. 339-400.
24. Nelson, R. F. W. *The Illusions of Urban Man*, Ottawa: Information Canada, 1976, p. 34.
25. *Ibid.*
26. Ferguson, *Op. Cit.*, p. 137.
27. Nelson, *Op. Cit.*, p. 56.
28. Galper, J. H. *The Politics of Social Services*. Englewood Cliffs, New Jersey: Prentice-Hall, 1975, p. 58.
29. Cohen, J. *Chance, Skill and Luck: The Psychology of Guessing and Gambling*. Baltimore: Penguin Books, 1960, p. 66.
30. Lippmann, W. *A Preface to Morals*. New York: Time Inc., 1964, p. xiii.
31. Tillich, P. *The Courage To Be*. London: Nisbet and Comp., Fontana Library, 1952, p. 57.
32. Gillies, *Op. Cit.*, p. 194.

(no beep)

p. 96 is blank.
End of Chapter 7

Chapter 8

Recreation Rightly Understood

Daniel L. Dustin, Leo H. McAvoy, and John H. Schultz

In the novel *Catch-22*, Yossarian lay in a hospital with:

> "... a pain in his liver that fell just short of being jaundice. The doctors were puzzled by the fact that it wasn't quite jaundice. If it became jaundice they could treat it. If it didn't become jaundice and went away they could discharge him. But this just being short of jaundice all the time confused them."[1]

The park and recreation profession faces a condition not unlike that of Yossarian. In our case the perplexity stems from just falling short of knowing whether some forms of recreation are better than others. If we could prove it, we could deal with the implications. If we could disprove it, we could deal with that as well. But this just falling short of knowing all the time confuses us.

The problem is that we have yet to come up with a standard against which we can measure the goodness of one form of recreation over another. In the absence of such a standard, we have fallen victim to what philosophers call the hedonist error, the equation of the good with pleasure.[2] Since what pleases people varies from individual to individual, we assume that what is good for people varies similarly. It is up to each person, therefore, to pursue his or her own particular pleasures. And it is up to the park and recreation profession to facilitate that process. We proceed on the faith that the outcomes from this arrangement are bound to be good.

Exacerbating the situation is our inclination to equate freedom, as in "free time," with being able to do whatever one pleases. But to understand freedom only as an opportunity is to misunderstand its full meaning. Freedom also demands a sense of obligation to do the right thing.[3] To think otherwise, to embrace opportunity without obligation, is to mistake self-aggrandizement for self-fulfillment.

The purpose of this chapter is to illustrate the misguided nature of these patterns of thought and then to replace them with a different orientation to service. We do this by first correcting the hedonist error. Then we outline a standard of moral philosophy against which we might measure the goodness of one form of recreation over another. Third, we discuss the implications of such an ordering for the obligations attached to individual recreational conduct. Finally, we consider the implications for the park and recreation profession as well. By then the confusion should begin to go away.

CORRECTING THE HEDONIST ERROR

The hedonist error rests in the equation of the good with pleasure and the associated mistake of assuming that if what pleases people varies from person to person then what is good for people must vary also. From this perspective the quality of goodness is subjective and relative. But this is clearly not the case.

In the tenth book of *Nicomachean Ethics*, Aristotle argued that "the pleasure proper to a worthy activity is good and that proper to an unworthy activity is bad."[4] We need only think of the pleasures accompanying many self-destructive forms of human activity to appreciate this point. Drug-taking, excessive alcohol consumption, and smoking, to name but three, are all activities deemed unworthy by society, and their associated pleasures are considered bad as well.

A similar distinction can be drawn along a line from sensate pleasures to mental pleasures; or, put differently, along a line from the subhuman to the human.[5] Immediate sensory pleasures are subhuman in origin. They characterize the animal kingdom. Longer-term emotional, spiritual, and intellectual pleasures characterize human beings. They are not found at the subhuman level. If park and recreation professionals are to nurture that which is most human in us, there is, then, a second dimension along which we must differentiate between the good and the bad, or, as the ancient sages defined it, between true and false pleasures.[6]

The significance of these insights comes with the realization that there must be a standard of goodness external to pleasure in and of itself. Pleasures can thus be seen as more or less desirable based on some other criteria. But what are those criteria? On what bases can the goodness of our pleasures be ordered?

A STANDARD OF GOODNESS

According to the philosopher Mortimer Adler, the goodness of a particular pleasure can be ordered by the degree to which it accompanies right desire, the seeking of what we ought to seek.[7] If we can prove what it is we ought to seek then we will have a standard against which we can weigh the goodness or badness of particular recreational pleasures.

Adler goes on to state as the first principle of moral philosophy that we ought to seek that which is really good for us and nothing else.[8] He uses the word "really" to emphasize the distinction between those things that only appear good to us because we want them and those things that really are good for us because we need them to grow and develop fully as human beings. The task is to sort out the wants which differ from individual to individual from the needs which are universal to all people. In so doing, we should then be able to distinguish between real goods and apparent goods, or between those things we are obliged to seek and those we are not.

What things are really good for us? While this question has been debated throughout history, there does seem to be a general consensus among philosophers, social scientists, and lay people alike that we all have fundamental health-related needs followed by needs for love, belongingness, self-esteem, and ultimately needs related to personal growth and development. This hierarchy of human needs, popularized in the work of Abraham Maslow,[9] provides the skeleton of a standard against which the goodness of specific recreational pleasures can be measured. Things that are really good for us contribute to our physical and mental health, our sense of being loved and loving, our feelings of belonging and self-esteem and ultimately our personal growth and development. Things that work against the fulfillment of these needs are bad for us no matter how pleasurable they may be.

Contrary to popular opinion, however, human fulfillment is not predicated on an autonomous progression upward through Maslow's need hierarchy. This common misconception, decried by Daniel Yankelovich as the "me first" philosophy,[10] fails to recognize that there is more to the human condition than the singular self. To paraphrase the systems philosopher Ervin Laszlo, physiologically we are individual wholes, whereas sociologically we are integrated (or recalcitrant) parts. And since we are endowed with consciousness, psychologically we are both wholes and parts.[11] To the extent that we are attuned only to the individualistic part of our selves we are not following the path to human fulfillment in its larger sense. We cannot be fulfilled in life independent of the condition of those around us. Our self-fulfillment is wrapped up in the fulfillment of others.

What this means, ultimately, is that as long as even one person goes hungry in this world, as long as even one person goes without adequate housing, health care, or educational opportunity, as long as even one person goes unloved, each and every one of us goes unfulfilled. This is so because we are each part of the other. Their plight is our plight. Their struggle is our struggle. Their overcoming is our overcoming. Self-fulfillment, then, is akin to the stars. It appears beyond our reach. Yet we are obliged to try.

There remains the nagging question of, "Who says so?" After all is said and done, does it not still boil down to a matter of opinion? No it does not for the following reason. The prescriptive judgment that we ought to seek that which is really good for us and nothing else is a self-evident truth. "It is impossible to think the opposite. It is impossible to think that we ought to seek that which is really bad for us, or that we ought not seek that which is really good for us."[12] If we accept the premise that the fulfillment of our fundamental human needs is really good for us, then it follows that we are all morally obliged to seek only those things which contribute to the fulfillment of those needs—regardless of any personal inclination to do otherwise.

What we are driving at here is that recreation is not the laissez-faire issue we typically conceive it to be. It is not a case of whatever moves us. It is not anything goes. Recreation rightly understood is a matter virtuous conduct.[13]

ETHICAL EXTENSIONS OUTWARD

Were we to stop at this point, our thinking would not differ significantly from that of many other leisure philosophers. But what gives our argument its flavor is the way in which we conceive the "we" and the "us" in the first principle of moral philosophy, the exhortation that we ought to seek only that which is good for us and nothing else. We do not limit the "we-ness" or the "us-ness" to each individual or the human family as a whole. We extend the meaning of the terms to include all living things. Consequently, our sense of the goodness or badness of specific recreational pleasures is tied to their effect on the larger community of life. In our thinking, we are morally obliged to seek out those recreational pleasures which contribute to the physical and mental health, the sense of being lover and loving, the feelings of belonging and self-esteem, and the growth and development of life in its entirety. (Granted there is plenty of room for debate here as to whether or not other life forms have the capacity to experience "mental health," "feelings of love and belongingness," and "self-esteem." Would we still owe them the same degree of moral consideration if they did not? Perhaps not. But it can also be argued that regardless of their capacity to feel these things we ought to treat them as if they did if only as an expression of our enhanced humanity. This is the stuff of which the current environmental ethics debate is made.)[14,15]

Our position is an outgrowth of the thinking of Albert Schweitzer. In his book *The Teaching of Reverence for Life*, Schweitzer describes the human condition thusly: "I am life that wills to live, in the midst of life that wills to live. The mysterious fact of my will to live is that I feel a mandate to behave with sympathetic concern toward all wills to live which exist side by side with my own."[16] Accordingly, "ethics consist . . . in my experiencing the compulsion to show to all wills to live the same reverence as I do to my own."[17]

Widespread adoption of Schweitzer's philosophy could have a tempering effect on human conduct. It does not imply that we must "stop at everything"[18] in our interactions with the world around us. Obviously the land and its creatures play an instrumental role in our continued livelihood. But it does imply that we should place increasing emphasis on economizing. Sacrificing other life to sustain our life should be carried out with providential care reflecting our symbiotic relationship with all living things. The wanton destruction of life (referred to by Aldo Leopold as the "trophy mentality") should be diminished. Harvested resources should be stretched to their limits. These things should happen because of a universal understanding that one does not waste what is inherently valuable.[19] We must remember that although other life forms have economic value, they are above all else meta-economic.[20] They have not been created by humans. It is presumptuous to assume they have been created expressly for humans. They must, therefore, be viewed primarily as ends-in-themselves. Accordingly, they must be viewed with a good deal of respect and with a feeling for their intrinsic value.

Schweitzer's philosophy has important implications for our profession because it makes the nature of ethical recreational conduct explicit. "The essence of goodness," he says, "is: preserve life, promote life, help life achieve its highest destiny. The essence of evil is destroy life, harm life, hamper the development of life."[21] Those recreational pastimes which preserve life, promote life, and help life achieve its highest destiny are morally superior to those that don't.

From this perspective any recreational pursuits that are carried out with disregard for their effect on other people, or on other living things, are less good, even if they are highly pleasurable to the individual. This is so because what is ultimately good for the individual cannot be separated from what is ultimately good for the larger community of life.

TEACHING RIGHT DESIRE

Were we to apply this standard of goodness to the spectrum of recreation activities currently enjoyed by the American public, and were we to develop an ordering of them ranging from good to bad, what would it mean for individual recreational conduct? Would the individual be obliged to pursue only the good activities? In a moral sense the answer is clearly yes. The individual would be morally obliged to seek out those recreation activities that are really good for life in its entirety and nothing else. (This moral dictum allows an individual member of our species to act on the instrumental value of another as long as the action is based on a sense of respect for that species and does not jeopardize the existence of the species itself. The moral question would turn on the degree of wantonness accompanying any such act.)

Does it then follow that the park and recreation profession is also obliged to offer only those recreation opportunities that have been deemed morally good? The answer here is less clear. The essence of recreation has always been rooted in individual choice. To take that away, however good the rationale, would exact a heavy price. For our profession to dictate what is good and bad for people, no matter how strong the evidence, would be to deny the individual the freedom to choose. It would strike at the heart of what makes recreation special. Moreover, it would remove the question of virtue from recreation conduct. As Aristotle would remind us, only a freely chosen act can be virtuous. We cannot force people to behave virtuously.

This is not to say that the park and recreation profession has no leadership role to play. On the contrary, we believe the profession ought to embrace as its fundamental charge the enhancement of recreationists' moral development. We ought to be encouraging recreational conduct that is compatible with the dynamic structure of the whole. This does not mean that we make choices for people. It means that we do whatever we can to prod recreationists upward in their moral reasoning power, that we help equip recreationists with the cognitive and emotional tools to make responsible recreational choices, regardless of the choices themselves. It means we try our best to extinguish careless, thoughtless, irresponsible behaviors and replace them with careful, thoughtful, responsible alternatives.[22] It means we have a duty to educate people, to teach them right desire.

What, then, does all of this mean for recreational pastimes that are highly consumptive of limited non-renewable resources? What does this mean for driving for pleasure? What does this mean for recreational pursuits that tend to be destructive of other life forms? What does this mean for off-road vehicle use of the desert? For trophy hunting? And what does this mean for recreational activities that are pursued to the detriment of other people? What does this mean for boxing? For other combative sports?

The standard of goodness must be applied to each case. To what extent does this activity contribute to the physical and mental health, the sense of being loved and loving, the feelings of belonging and self-esteem, and the growth and development of life in its entirety? To what extent does it detract? To what extent does participation in this activity promote life, preserve life, and help life achieve its highest destiny? To what extent does it destroy life, harm life, hamper the development of life? To what extent, then, is this recreation activity morally good or bad?

Involvement in those activities deemed morally good should be encouraged, indeed celebrated by park and recreation professionals. Those deemed morally bad should be shown for what they are, and offered with an explanation of their moral deficiency. The individual should then be allowed to decide.

THE BURDEN OF REPONSIBILITY

To suggest that it is our professional responsibility to influence recreationists' decisionmaking processes has not come easily to us. Not only do we prize the individual's right to decide, but we also are reluctant to impose our values on others. We recognize that recreation may be one of the last bastions of choice in this increasingly regulated world. To interfere with those choices, even in the context of education, is not something we take lightly.

Nonetheless, there are compelling reasons to adopt a more pro-active professional posture. Foremost among them is the fact that no matter what we do as park and recreation professionals we will have an impact on the future. As the futurist Arthur Harkins reminds us, "inaction is a form of action, a sin of omission so to speak."[23] By simply serving up for people what they want, we are making history. Even though we are assuming a passive stance, we are still accomplices to whatever unfolds. What we are saying, in effect, is that we value the individual's right to decide more than we value what is harmed by the decision. That's okay as long as we recognize our position for what it is. But to leave the choice entirely up to the individual so that later on, if things turn sour, we can say, "It's not our fault," is not okay. We cannot shirk responsibility for the future. The question is what do we want to be responsible for?

Wallace Stegner puts the question to recreation land managers thusly:

> Do they exist to provide bargain-basement grass to favored stockmen whose grazing privileges have become all but hereditary, assumed and bought and sold along with the title to the home spread? Are they hired exterminators of wildlife? Is it their function to negotiate loss-leader coal leases with energy conglomerates, and to sell timber below cost to Louisiana Pacific? Or should they be serving the much larger public whose outdoor recreations of backpacking, camping, fishing, hunting, river running, mountain climbing, hang gliding, and, God help us, dirt biking are incompatible with clear-cut forests and overgrazed, poison-baited, and strip-mined grasslands? Or is there a still higher duty—to maintain the health and beauty of the lands they manage, protecting from everybody, including such destructive segments of the public as dirt bikers and pothunters, the watersheds and spawning streams, forests and grasslands, geological and scenic splendors, historical and archaeological remains, air and water and serene space, that once led me, in a reckless moment, to call the western public lands part of the geography of hope?[24]

Stegner speaks of a progression of responsibility, of movement toward a higher duty. Is this the way we see our professional calling? Are we, too, committed to moving people toward more desirable states of being through our professional practices? Or, as public servants, do we interpret our role simply as one of satisfying our constituencies' wants? Much like the politician who must decide whether he or she was elected to be a mirror of public opinion or to exercise his or her own special judgment and expertise in working for the public good, we park and recreation professionals must assess our own motives and responsibilities.[25]

We must also examine what a more active professional role means in the context of a democratic political philosophy. We must understand that:

> Aspiration and conventional behavior are in a continual battle. We are
> willing to impose coercion on ourselves to some degree . . . precisely
> because we recognize that left wholly to pursuit of our routine
> preferences we are not likely to do and be all that we want. A mixture
> of autonomy and self-imposed discipline is something we know
> very well.[26]

Without the discipline we would likely be involved in a free-for-all, each of us pursuing the object of our own desire. In a world of limited resources, such freedom would lead not to the good life, but to ruin.[27] Under the circumstances, a concern for the greatest good for the greatest number in the long run demands that we place limits on our individual freedoms for the sake of the group. In America, of course, this is a particularly bitter pill to swallow.

We are so accustomed to living in a society that stresses individualism that we need to be reminded that 'collectivism' in a broad sense has always been the more usual lot of mankind, as well as of most other species. Most people in most societies have been born into and died in stable communities in which the subordination of the individual to the welfare of the group was taken for granted, while the aggrandizement of the individual at the expense of his fellows was simply a crime.[28]

In a democracy, the critical concern is how we go about reaching decisions to impose limits on our individual freedoms. Due process matters greatly to us. But if we arrive at our decisions through a democratic process, what, if anything, is lost?

Some would say our individualism. But is that really the case? As Nathan Glazer reminds us:

> It is clear that some part of American individualism, whether we
> consider it 'rampant' or 'rugged,' is under severe restraint, and there is
> no hope that the restraints will become anything but more severe as
> time goes on. But it is necessary to point out that some kinds of
> individualism are under restraint only because another aspect of
> individualism is doing quite well. This is the political aspect of
> individualism, in which the single individual or individuals organized
> in private groupings battle for what they conceive to be their rights or a
> better condition.[29]

There are, Glazer continues, "Two faces of individualism: the more rugged economic and institutional individualism of the United States, hampered and hobbled by a new kind of individualism devoted to self-realization, to the protection for the environment, (etc.)."[30]

Thus, there is nothing inherently wrong with our profession drawing on its body of knowledge to nudge people toward a more desirable future. Indeed, to choose not to act in the light of our knowledge is reprehensible. In the final analysis, it is not a matter of whether or not we should become involved. It is a matter of what form our involvement should take.

We park and recreation professionals must decide whether our mission is to serve popular tastes for recreation or to elevate them.[31] The three of us are committed to elevation. The challenge is to cultivate a growing awareness that our human fulfillment is inextricably intertwined with the fulfillment of this larger organism that is the Earth itself. Such awareness is marked by ethical extensions outward from ourselves to other people, to the land and its creatures. To borrow once more from Aldo Leopold, our orientation to service should be to help recreationists:

"... examine each question in terms of what is ethically and esthetically right, as well as what is ... (personally) expedient. A thing is right when it intends to preserve the integrity, stability, and beauty of the ... community (of life). It is wrong when it tends otherwise."[32]

REFERENCES

1. Heller, J. *Catch-22*. New York, New York: Simon and Schuster, 1961, p. 7.
2. Adler, M. *Ten Philosophical Mistakes*. New York, New York: Macmillan Publishing Company, 1985.
3. Dustin, D., McAvoy, L., and Schultz, J. *Stewards of Access/Custodians of Choice: a Philosophical Foundation for the Park and Recreation Profession*. Minneapolis, Minnesota: Burgess Publishing Company, 1982.
4. Aristotle. *The Nicomachean Ethics*. New York, New York: Oxford University Press, 1980, p. 259.
5. Smith, S. "On the Biological Basis of Pleasure: Some Implications for Leisure Policy." In Goodale and Witt (Eds.) *Recreation and Leisure: Issues in an Era of Change*. State College, Pennsylvania: Venture Publishing, Inc., 1980, pp. 50-62.
6. Gillies, J. *Aristotle's Ethics*. (John Gillies, Trans.) London: Routledge, 1886.
7. Adler, p. 123.
8. Ibid, p. 125.
9. Maslow, A. *Motivation and Personality*. New York, New York: Harper & Row, 1954.
10. Yankelovich, D. *New Rules: Searching for Self-Fulfillment in a World Turned Upside Down*. New York, New York: Random House, 1981.

11. Laszlo, E. *The Systems View of the World*. New York, New York: George Braziller, 1972.
12. Adler, pp. 125-126.
13. Gillies, pp. 169-170.
14. See Nash, R. *The Rights of Nature: a History of Environmental Ethics*. Madison, Wisconsin: The University of Wisconsin Press, 1989.
15. See Hargrove, E. *Foundations of Environmental Ethics*. Englewood Cliffs, New Jersey: Prentice Hall, 1989.
16. Schweitzer, A. *The Teaching of Reverence for Life*. New York, New York: Holt, Reinhart and Winston, 1965, p. 26.
17. Schweitzer, A. *The Philosophy of Civilization*. New York, New York: The Macmillan Company, 1957, p. 309.
18. Goodpaster, K. "On Stopping at Everything: A Reply to W. M. Hunt." *Environmental Ethics*. 2(No. 3), Fall 1980, pp. 281-284.
19. Dustin, McAvoy, and Schultz, p. 61.
20. Schumacher, E. *Small is Beautiful: Economics as if People Mattered*. New York, New York: Harper & Row Publishers, 1973.
21. Schweitzer, *The Teaching of...*, p. 26.
22. Dustin, D., McAvoy, L., and Beck, L. "Promoting Recreationist Self-Sufficiency." *Journal of Park and Recreation Administration*. 4(No. 4), Winter 1986, pp. 43-52.
23. Dustin, D. "Leisure: A Futurist's Perspective." *California Parks and Recreation*. 35(No. 3), August/September 1979, pp. 10-11.
24. Stegner, W. *The American West as Living Space*. Ann Arbor, Michigan: The University of Michigan Press, 1987, pp. 42-43.
25. Dustin, D. and McAvoy, L. "Outdoor Recreation and the Environment: Problems and Prospects." *The Environmental Professional*. 9(No. 4), 1987, pp. 343-346.
26. Sax, J. *Mountains Without Handrails*. Ann Arbor, Michigan: The University of Michigan Press, 1980, p. 52.
27. Hardin, G. "The Tragedy of the Commons." *Science*. December 13, 1968, pp. 1243-1248.
28. Slater, P. *The Pursuit of Loneliness*. Boston, Massachusetts: Beacon Press, 1970, p. 5.
29. Glazer, N. "Individualism and Equality in the United States." In H. Gans, et al. (Eds.). *On the Making of Americans: Essays in Honor of David Riesman*. University of Pennsylvania, 1979, p. 131.
30. Ibid, p. 132.
31. Sax, p. 61.
32. Leopold, A. *A Sand County Almanac*. New York, New York: Oxford University Press, 1949, pp. 224-225.

End of Chapter 8 and
End of Section 1

SECTION II

Changing Services and Resources: Doing More With Less

INTRODUCTION

The end of World War II marked the beginning of three decades of unprecedented growth and affluence. Not unexpectedly—hindsight the aid that it is—the period was also characterized by turmoil; civil rights activists and campus radicals; moral crusades to end wars and conscription and then to save the environment. But through the same period public education, particularly postsecondary education, grew dramatically. So, too, did the provision of public recreation programs, facilities, and services.

During the 1970s and 1980s, the harbinger being the formation of the OPEC cartel, we saw gradual but accelerating shifts, including economic, large government deficits, high rates of both inflation (until recently) and unemployment, and growth rates lower than those of the 1950s and 1960s. Liberal governments of two decades ago have been replaced by conservative governments: from Kennedy to Reagan and Bush in the United States; Wilson to Thatcher and Major in England; Pearson and then Trudeau to Mulroney in Canada. In the communist world, the press for democracy has increased with the overthrow of governments throughout eastern Europe at the end of the 1980s.

These political, economic and social developments have already had significant impacts on public park, recreation and leisure services (and also universities) and appear destined to have even more in the years to come. We are faced with tighter limits and tougher choices. We are faced with the task of doing more, better and different than what has been done in the past and this must be done with fewer of the resources, especially financial, that we have relied upon for so long.

In the chapters comprising this section, "Changing Services and Resources," the need to change, and sometimes also the desire to change, is paramount. Some of the changes will be in response to governmental and economic forces; others will be proactive based on forces within the park and recreation movement itself.

The section begins with Irene Spry's discussion of "The Prospects for Leisure in a Conserver Society" (9) which builds on the issue of the appropriateness of certain activities over others developed by Dustin, McAvoy and Schultz (8) in the earlier section. The yard stick here is the need to make our consumption of leisure consistent with what is good for our ecosystem and our long term habitation of the planet. Spry also reinforces Godbey's (11) concern about our breakneck speed to consume time as well as material things and Goodale's (3) concern about the uses of free time and whether some activities are more appropriate to undertake than others. Spry's chapter is particularly interesting as she is a resource economist who has been extensively involved in multi-agency, multidisciplinary studies of the future. She is clearly hopeful that the recognition of limits will result in conserving resources and environmental quality by limiting consumptive pursuits that are destructive. In their place will (hopefully) emerge activities which are not only parsimonious but also characterized by intellect and imagination, beauty and good taste, social esteem and self-respect, all based on a life that has significance.

Building on the theme developed by Spry, Goodale (10) discusses some of the changes that must take place in ourselves and in the park and recreation system if we are to respond to the challenges of the 1990s and beyond. Godbey (11) paints some of the detail, noting a number of "sins" of omission or commission within the park and recreation movement. These have often been the result of governments' well intentioned interventions, growth in agencies leading to specialization and often splintering, and of the sense of complacency into which many were lulled by years of expansion and affluence. Godbey concludes his chapter with a major challenge, the result of people having accepted the meaning and significance of leisure in their lives, leaving many leisure service workers and agencies proselytizing each other.

Bannon (12) notes that change is a constant and that a better understanding of history would give us a better understanding of change in our own time. He shares Spry's concern that plenitude, not as past reality but as an enduring attitude, can only magnify the difficulty of change, and he appeals for an ecological perspective akin to the environmental ethic so widely discussed in the 1960s and early 1970s. In fact ethics weave throughout his exploration of the administrator's milieu, changed as it has due to accelerated technologies, gender equality in the work force and family, deteriorating environments and the like. Like Godbey (13), Bannon encourages imagination and innovation, and also a broad intellectual and humanistic approach to one's work in the field. He also makes a number of suggestions for administrators, including the use of modern management tools and the encouragement and use of research.

While the park and recreation services have increasingly turned to management tools developed in other parts of the public and private sector, their application in park and recreation settings may not always be appropriate. For example, as noted by Lamb and Crompton (14), measuring program success has too often relied on indicators of efficiency rather than effectiveness. On the other hand, Crompton (17), argues for the appropriateness of utilizing marketing principles derived from the private sector in the public park and recreation field.

Here Crompton, who almost single-handedly has introduced the marketing concept to the profession, deals with some causes of the resistance public service administrators often demonstrate toward the marketing concept, despite the fact that it involves much more than promotional activities. Recognizing its some-times unsavory history, Crompton argues that marketing is "neither snake-oil nor panacea," but one useful tool for administrators.

While Crompton notes that marketing is not, per se, a mechanism for raising revenues and does not necessarily lead to distorting priorities, Goodale (18) is even more emphatic about preserving the public service mandate under which public park and recreation agencies operate. He argues that the talk of "smaller" government is not only simplistic but also a seductive cover for political, economic and social values reminiscent of those holding sway a century ago. The increased emphasis on demand, costs, revenues, and efficiency may result in gradually bending the mandate in directions dictated by the current winds of change. Twardzik (24) and Duncan (25) carry that argument further.

An important example of Bannon's (12) call for the use of research to facili-tate the provision of recreation services is Kelly's (16) summary of years of research attempts to understand such a complex phenomenon as recreation. As he notes, our attempts to categorize activities and predict them according to socio-economic and demographic influences have not been especially fruitful. Kelly suggests what may be a more useful perspective, with core activities centering around home, family and informal social relations plus other, different activities serving to provide balance according to the individual's needs and interests at a particular but changing stage during the course of a lifetime. Kelly also notes that rather than the activity, i.e., what an individual does, we should consider style, i.e., how an individual goes about what he or she does.

Kelly particularly, but also all the authors represented in this section speak of a pluralistic society and culture. Godbey (11) focuses on the concept of pluralism with reference not only to behaviors but also to values. In this quotable chapter, Godbey contrasts single and plural culture societies to help point out their differences and the implications those differences have for plan-ning. In so doing, he is critical of the quest for a ton of experience for an ounce of investment. So he speaks of planning services to which people must make a commitment and for which something else must be sacrificed, a cold shower, perhaps for those for whom "me," "more," and "now" have become the criteria of daily life.

In a chapter with profound implications for the way recreation workers lead and provide activities, Bishop and Jeanrenaud (15) discuss the many potential roadblocks to creativity, expressing wonder that it survives at all. Their message reminds us of the centrality of the leader-participant relationship to the recrea-tion experience and reinforces Lamb and Crompton's (14) emphasis on effec-tiveness versus efficiency.

The chapters in this section are similar in that the necessity for and inevitability of change underlies each. Just as the future is uncertain, the outcome of change, whether chosen and pursued or coerced and resisted, is also uncertain. And that is a source, however great or little, of anxiety for us all. Obstacles and opportunities abound, as is evident throughout the chapters in this and other sections. It is also evident that within the recreation movement or (arguably) profession, much re-thinking is underway and much is needed.

End of Chapter 8

Chapter 9

The Prospects for Leisure in a Conserver Society

Irene M. Spry

Since Adam and Eve left the Garden of Eden human beings have dreamed of a life free from drudgery. In the last century in affluent western countries, the burden of incessant toil has largely been lifted from human shoulders. When the Toronto typographers, who in 1872 had won the right to organize a union, struck for a nine-hour day, the employers would not even meet them to discuss the matter.[1] Since then, the work week in Canada and the United States has contracted progressively. Average hours in manufacturing fell from 59 a week in 1890 to just over 40 hours a week in 1960.[2] Unions have fought long and hard for an eight-hour day,[2] and today a seven-hour day is not uncommon. A five-day work week is normal and experiments are being made with a four- and even a three-day work week. Besides longer week ends, most Canadians have ten or more paid holidays a year with two weeks or more paid vacation time. Pension plans have made possible retirement at an earlier age and the young stay longer at school and university before entering the work force. Besides, the unemployed have unwanted free time on their hands.

Side by side with this increase in time off from earning a living, there has been a reduction in the hours that must be spent on household chores. Washing machines and spin-dryers, mechanical ironers and electric and steam irons, vacuum cleaners and electric polishers, microwave ovens, juicers and blenders, Kleenex™ and throw-away diapers—a whole array of devices offer possibilities of cutting down the time and effort that must be spent keeping homes and their inmates clean and tidy and providing meals. Eating out at the local branch of a fast food chain, or buying ready-cooked fried chicken, pizza, or Chinese dishes make possible a further escape from housework.

Whether there has been a proportionate increase in time that is free to be spent as individuals choose is by no means clear. Many put in far more hours earning a living than the average work week, especially those who are self-employed, while women who combine work outside the home with household duties commonly have little if any spare time. Hours spent commuting and waiting in line-ups at the supermarket cash register and the like also erode leisure time.[3]

Whether the trend to shorter income-earning hours and reduction in the time that must be spent on household and personal maintenance will continue in the future is even more uncertain. If we are approaching limits to the growth of an energy-intensive way of life, and if the price of electricity and gasoline goes up still further, we may find that we must go back to using more human effort and more time in industrial, agricultural, and commercial activities as well as in household chores. It may be, however, that new discoveries of fossil fuels and new technologies, especially electronic devices, will, for a time at least, allow still further expansion in free time. This would intensify the already critical problems of the role of leisure in human happiness and of demands made by leisure time activities on material resources and on the environment.

SPARE TIME ACTIVITIES

Nearly all Canadians spend at least some of their time watching television, while some 15 percent of us spend a massive 30 hours or more a week in front of our TV sets. A large majority of us spend some time listening to radio each week, and nearly half of us listen to records, tapes, or cassettes, though no doubt, many of us do other things at the same time as we look and listen. Nearly two-thirds of us read newspapers and magazines, but only about one-sixth of us spend seven or more hours a week reading books as a leisure time occupation.

Only a small proportion of Canadians go to the theatre, opera, ballet or concerts, but more than a third of us go to the movies. Similarly only a few of us visit museums, art galleries and historic sites, but nearly a quarter of us spend at least some time attending sports events, some of us as regular spectators.

How many of us spend time wandering round the stores does not seem to be recorded, but this is undoubtedly one of the major diversions of the crowds that throng shopping malls and department stores, window shopping and "just looking." Eating out may be necessary at school or at work, it may be a quickie substitute for a meal at home, or it may be—and seems increasingly to be—a leisure activity, along with drinking.

Travel and tourism, ranging from Sunday driving and holiday camping trips to tours of Europe, and escape to sunny climes by refugees from a harsh winter, are becoming more and more important in our affluent and increasingly leisured lives. Some two-thirds of all Canadians indulge in recreational driving, while we spend billions of dollars in travel abroad.

A different type of leisure time occupation involves arts, crafts, music and hobby activities. A quarter of all Canadians spend some time, effort and imagination each week on such creative activities, though this estimate is uncertain as it is difficult to draw the line between such occupations as dress-making undertaken as a pleasing activity, for the fun of it, or as a necessary household chore. Twelve percent of us spend some time on hobbies, but only half as many of us give fifteen hours or more a week to those hobbies.

Substantially more than half of all Canadians spend at least a little while in sports and physical activities, a few in organized sports events and many of us in swimming (apparently the most common type of exercise right across Canada), jogging, hiking, and doing exercises, ice-skating, skiing, playing tennis and badminton or golf and other games.

Besides card games, chess, bingo and electronic games, there are other ways of spending free time, such as entertaining and socializing, lazing in the sun, indulging in more sleep than is physiologically essential to maintain health and strength, or just sitting around, like the old lady in Vermont who said, "Sometimes I sits and thinks and sometimes I just sits."

THE COST OF SPARE TIME ACTIVITIES

Of all these varied ways of putting in leisure time, some entail very heavy demands on material and environmental resources. Travel means jet planes, the fuel they use, and the cloud cover they create. Automobiles mean using up metals and gasoline and creating smog. Television means cameras and kleig lights, congested airwaves, production studios, elaborate transmitting and receiving equipment, including satellites and other apparatus of space technology. Movies mean cameras, sound recording equipment, filmstock, sets and costumes, cutting rooms, theatres and projection apparatus, to say nothing of the extravagances of the glamour industry. The record industry has similar requirements as does sport, both professional and amateur, organized as entertainment. International competitive sport has escalated jet set glamour and the kind of emulation that gives rise to Olympic extravaganzas. Even unassuming, personal participation in sport has become the raison d'être for promoting sales of elaborate equipment and clothing, while the record industry and night club dancing have become multi-billion dollar businesses.

Underlying the expansion of the mass media—TV, radio, records, computers, the press and periodicals—and their role in leisure time, is the proliferation of sales promotion and advertising. Shopping as a pastime simply adds to the perpetual pressure to buy more, have more, and consume more.[4] Increasing leisure time has become a market to be exploited through the ruthless promotion of the idea that more and ever more elaborate possessions and expenditure will add immensely to the satisfaction that can be won from leisure time. Power boats and snowmobiles, ten-speed bicycles and fancy skis, stereophonic record players and computers are becoming widespread items of household equipment, besides TV sets, radios, telephones and cars.[5] Emphasis is given increasingly to the apparatus used in leisure time activities. This is generally true of affluent societies.[6] Should leisure time continue to expand in the future as it has expanded in the recent past, and should emphasis persist on leisure as big business, leisure time activities will undoubtedly play a part in the continued expansion of our mass consumption economy. Increasing spare time may well become the focus of intensified consumption and sales in the entertainment industry, the travel and tourist industry, and the sports equipment industry. Even jogging and cross-country skiing are now the target for sales of special clothing, special footwear, and special equipment.

Paradoxically, increasing leisure time creates a need for so much increased expenditure that it induces people to undertake more income-earning activity, moolighting or mothers going out to work to procure the income to buy skates, skis, cameras and the like, or to pay the installments due on a color television or a car, or even on the labor saving equipment that is designed to increase leisure time. The choice does not seem to be a choice between more consumption and more leisure time, but between more consumption for leisure time activities and more consumption of other sorts.

Does this mean that more and more leisure time will inevitably reinforce other pressures in the direction of continued economic growth? Does the novel expansion of substantial leisure time to an increasingly wide range of classes make the possibility of a conserver society increasingly difficult to achieve? Is the transition from an economic system based on a high rate of material growth to a slow-growth economy, or even a stable economy,[7] all the more unlikely by reason of the growing demands of the expanding leisure market? The answer depends on the forces which shape our preferences and choices as to how we spend our leisure time.

LOW COST POSSIBILITIES

The TGIF ("Thank God It's Friday") view of the working week suggests that few of us get much satisfaction out of what we do to earn a living. In that case we must depend on what we do in our leisure time to give us a satisfying life. This raises the question whether modern conveyor-belt workers, either in a factory or in an office, when they finish a shift—even a short shift—of mind deadening work have enough energy and initiative, enough resilience, to launch into any mind or muscle stretching activity, even though they may have time to spare. Is there any impetus in their environment to stimulate them to creative effort? Do the mass media and the conversation of their associates suggest any possibilities other than seeking diversion and excitement from television, and spending more and consuming more? Ideas as to the good life absorbed from television programs and advertisements combined with conspicuous consumption to keep up with the Joneses mean continued, open-ended increases in consumption that bring very little satisfaction to the consumers. Thorstein Veblen's *Theory of the Leisure Class* is as relevant today as it was when he wrote it in 1899. Contemporary economists, notably Fred Hirsch and William Leiss, have developed the same theme.[8] One-up-manship means bigger and faster cars, more lavish household furnishings and equipment, up-to-the-minute power boats and snowmobiles, as well as travel to more remote and unusual places than those which neighbors and work-mates have visited. Emulation in consumption satisfies no one and there is no limit to the burden which it imposes on scarce environmental and material resources.

There are, however, a few straws in what may be a wind of change. The popularity of jogging, of trail skiing, and of cycling suggests that simple activities, without a great elaboration of apparatus, are coming into their own. Yoga and meditation, similarly, make very little demand on material support systems. Gardening, crafts, carpentry, and all sorts of do-it-yourself activities, ranging from home dress-making to household repairs, may actually conserve material and environmental resources, since they combine recycling of materials with satisfaction of the instinct of workmanship. Leisure time pursuits should be undertaken, not in the hope of winning Oscars or Olympic gold medals, but for their own sake, because they are fun or interesting, or because they contribute to a cause that is considered to be useful or worthwhile. Participation in the work of public interest groups intent on achieving desirable social objectives is an example of an activity that can give great satisfaction while making few demands on material or environmental resources.

Would a shift to such low consumption leisure time occupations mean serious losses in leisure time satisfaction? The answer seems to be that there is wide scope for increased leisure time activities of a type that would not increase consumption expenditures and might actually decrease demands on the resources of the biosphere, while contributing more to human happiness than do many of today's high consumption activities and entertainments. More and more satisfying leisure need not mean more expenditure; it might well mean less.

The most obvious use of leisure time is to give respite from stress, rest and relaxation, "re-creation" in the literal sense of restoration of depleted energies. More important, in a world of mass production conformity and monotony, leisure gives people a chance to exercise their own initiative, to follow their own inclination, to "do their own thing" in their own way. It is an opportunity for personal choice and self-expression, for the development of individuality, for exploring and cultivating the full richness of human diversity. In leisure time people can exercise cramped and atrophied bodies; exercise and develop powers of intellect and imagination and of independence of thought and character. In their time off from earning an income and doing necessary chores, they may cultivate the taste and sensibility which will allow them to enjoy the beauties of nature, and the glories of great art and architecture, the splendor of music, the bouquets of fine wines, or the nuances of cordon bleu cookery. They may themselves experience the joy of creative activities. It is on leisure time occupations that most of us have to depend for the stimulus and excitement that human nature needs for fulfillment, and to leisure time encounters that we must look for "laughter and the love of friends," for chances to meet satisfying sexual partners, and for the satisfaction of working with close colleagues to achieve a shared objective. In our leisure time we may do things that engage our abilities to their full capacity, we may contribute something of importance to the community of which we are part, so earning the social esteem and self-respect which can come only from lives that have some significance.

CONSUMPTION VERSUS SATISFACTION

Few of us are lucky enough to find in our working lives opportunities for all these varied satisfactions. Do we find them in our leisure time? Might we do so? How heavy would be the burden of such human fulfillment on the material and environmental resources of our space-ship planet?

Rest and Relaxation

For rest and relaxation we need some degree of comfort, tranquility, agreeable surroundings, and unexacting diversion. Many people, whose living conditions do not provide these requisites, escape into the image world of television, a world in which they may effortlessly join the jet set in gracious living. It is not a world that gives relaxed contentment; rather it generates restless discontent. It is a world in which the importance of having more and more consumer goods is relentlessly driven home, a world in which the emphasis is constantly on the apparatus of living, not on the quality of life itself.

Initiative and Individuality

Watching TV may open new worlds to the viewer, the world of ballet, of opera or of wildlife in the unspoiled wilderness of the far north, of the sweeping Pacific beaches, or of Newfoundland's cliffs and bays, but the message of the medium is more commonly that a finer car is essential, or a shinier floor polish or a zestier beer to ensure a good life. The emphasis is persistently on *having* things—the things that everyone else has—not on *doing* the things that interest you as a unique human being, nor on *being* that individual to the utmost limit of your powers. In the barrage of advertising, in the flood of thrillers and "sit coms" and "shows," is there any spark that would fire individual enthusiasm for striking out on some personal line of activity, for following some special interest?

Bodies and Beer

TV programs certainly foster admiration of physical prowess. The hockey or football star, the Olympic gold medalist is idolized, but what has the Stanley Cup play-off to do with the ordinary citizen's need for a stimulus to exercise neglected bodies? Hockey Night in Canada and Saturday afternoon sports programs are more likely to promote passive viewing, beer in hand, than physical activity. It is true that an occasional "Participaction" advertisement may exhort the viewer to keep fit by taking to some form of exercise, but the insistent model is that of a car-borne, candy and beer consuming way of life which is the antithesis of a way of life in which leisure is used to build bodily health and strength.

Despite the huge disparity between the number of Canadians who watch television and the number who engage at least occasionally in some exercise or sport, there does seem to be a new interest in getting fit and keeping fit. More and more Canadians "run for their lives" when they take to jogging but the figures for participation in swimming, skating, skiing, tennis, golf and other physical activities suggest that there is still plenty of room for higher standards of activity.

Intellect and Imagination

Some programs on television or radio provide food for thought and stimulate the mind and the imagination, evoking a creative response from viewers and listeners. For the most part, though, viewers and listeners are merely passive spectators or auditors whose minds and imagination are neither challenged nor stimulated by what they see and hear.

The much smaller number of people who go to live theatre, concerts, ballet and opera have more chance of a stimulating experience that requires an active contribution of thought and sensitive imagination. Visits to art galleries, museums, and historic sites also are likely to stimulate both mind and imagination. Continuing education plays its part in developing intellectual muscle and opening opportunities for creative experience, as may also be the case with some formal education. The activities of public interest groups and voluntary organizations, ranging from tenants' associations to Women's Institutes, stimulate thought and imagination, widen horizons, and offer opportunities for creative experience.

Taste and Beauty

Music on radio and television, ballet, and some dramatic performances present beautiful sounds and sights for those who have ears to hear and eyes to see. Some wilderness programs may allow city dwellers hemmed in by walls and concrete to experience in some small degree the delights of natural beauty. Sights and sounds which are lovely to some people, however, may give little pleasure or even be distasteful to others. Their enjoyment requires not only the time that must be spent in looking and listening, but, as well, time and experience are needed to cultivate the taste which will give the viewer or hearer the capacity to delight in them, just as an educated palate is necessary for enjoyment of subtle sauces and exquisite wines. Enjoyment of beauty involves a learning process that goes on through a lifetime of leisure experience. Only if a person seeking satisfaction can contribute sensitive perception can the full possibilities of the enjoyment of beauty be realized.

Creative Experience

The active enjoyment of beauty is a creative, not a passive, experience. The creation of beauty may give a still richer satisfaction, the satisfaction attained by a quarter of all Canadians, who take part in some kind of art, craft or musical activity. Playing a musical instrument, singing in a choir, drawing or painting what they see in the world around them, fashioning a carving or a sculpture, expressing their insights and ideas in poetry or prose, taking part in a play, or at a more practical level, making a lovely quilt or a handsome piece of furniture, growing a glorious garden, or baking a splendid cake, they need never be dull; there is always something exciting and rewarding waiting to be done. Such leisure time arts and crafts may give outlets for the instinct of workmanship if earning a living fails, as it often does, to satisfy this deep human need.

Stimulus and Excitement

Since jobs may be repetitive and deadening, it is leisure activities that must fill yet another fundamental human need: the need for stimulation and excitement. We no longer face the daily challenge of escaping from sabre-toothed tigers or running buffalo. It is true that driving a car or merely crossing busy streets gives some spice of adventure to our lives, but many of us seek an escape from boredom in purchasing every novelty that comes onto the market and acquiring a vast variety of consumer goods.[9] Such attempts to maintain an interest in life require continual escalation. The need for stimulus grows as it is satisfied. Similarly, neither television violence nor entertainment-sport can perpetually arouse interest and excitement without novel features and intensification of sensationalism. The only way in which we can hope to achieve a crescendo of interest, stimulation and excitement throughout a lifetime is pursuing some unfolding interest, achieving new skills, discovering new creative possibilities, exploring new ideas and widening horizons, developing a more and more lively creative imagination.

Arts, crafts, and musical activities can give such stimulation, such unflagging and developing interest; so can a variety of hobbies which lead the enthusiast on from one level of attainment to another, unendingly. In the last analysis it is not outside stimuli that can solve the problem of boredom; each individual must generate his or her own interest and excitement in life through activities that hold the possibility of progressive achievement, deeper perception, new invention and discovery. Competitive sports and the excitement of watching one's team win a contest give an ephemeral stimulus, but only playing a game oneself, one's own creative activities, one's own physical, intellectual and imaginative development will sustain interest and excitement that time and use will not dim, but constantly intensify. The solution lies not in a multiplication of consumer goods, or increasing indulgence, but in the development of human skills and non-material interests and activities.

Friendship and Team Work

Some people are so fortunate as to earn their living working with colleagues who are friends, with whom they can co-operate whole-heartedly. For many, if not most of us, this rewarding experience is more likely to be attained in activities undertaken in time off work, perhaps in sport, or in voluntary activities with a church organization, political party or other public interest group, or in a choir, an orchestra or band, or in a dramatic group. We have very little information as yet on how much time and energy is spent in spare time team work in such shared endeavors. That contact with other people is important for most of us, we do know, since more than three quarters of us spend part of our leisure time visiting friends and relatives. Apart from the cost of establishing and maintaining contact with voluntary colleagues and friends, telephone service, postage, travel, and the like, and perhaps the consumption of food and drink that ordinarily takes place on social occasions, such sociability and cooperation does not seem to require any extensive material support. The potluck type of formal entertainment may be necessary to ensure social esteem, but it probably contributes little otherwise to human happiness except insofar as it is the occasion for agreeable indulgences.

Social Esteem and Self-Respect

Social contacts may, however, mean conspicuous leisure, conspicuous consumption, and rivalry in lavish entertainment. All these have played a part in patterns of spending and patterns of leisure time activities. They have all been important as evidence of social status. They have all contributed to the association of leisure with lavish spending. Perhaps, as the idea of a conserver society spreads, other criteria of social worth and social respect may begin to make headway against competitive consumption. Just as concern is growing for the quality of life that cannot be measured in Gross National Product figures, so may concern be growing for human quality that is not demonstrated by lavish expenditures and an elaborate apparatus of spare time enjoyment. If ways can be found of gauging the character and caliber of what individuals and groups contribute to the community in creative stimulus, artistic achievement, constructive intelligence, and the assumption of social responsibility, there may be hope that, in the time in which people are free to do what they like, what they like to do will prove to be what will earn them the respect and esteem of the community. Such esteem is an essential element of a good life; even more important is the individual's own sense of contributing something of significance. If what one does to earn a living seems trivial, this vital sense of significance must be won in leisure time pursuits that are considered to be important in themselves or in the social results that may be expected from them.

A recent estimate puts average expenditure on recreation in Canada at some ten per cent of total personal expenditure. If one adds to that expenditure by governments at all levels on recreational services and facilities, to say nothing of the share of the cost of public goods (highways, waterways, education, communication and transport systems and the like) that is put to recreational use, the total becomes one of considerable significance. In addition, some family expenditures that are classified as expenditures on clothing and shelter, household operation, furnishings and equipment, and travel and transportation are probably related to recreational activities. What happens to leisure time and to leisure expenditures will, therefore, have an important part to play in future trends in consumer expenditure. Increasing emphasis on leisure time as an opportunity for the enhancement of human quality and the enrichment of creative experience, rather than as an opportunity for the elaboration of entertainment, escalation of self-indulgence, and multiplication of apparatus, would reconcile a trend to more leisure with a need for and the possibility of less spending.

CONSERVING THE SELF AND THE SURROUNDINGS

Pierre Falcon composed his ballads without any equipment other than his mind, his voice, and his enthusiasm for the feats of his compatriots, "ces braves Brois-Brulés." Shakespeare and his actors performed plays that have lasted through the centuries with little costuming and less scenery. They depended for success not on super-colossal spectacles but on splendor of language and perception of human problems. The winner of a recent contest (that elicited 10,000 entries) needed only a pen (or, perhaps, a typewriter) and some paper and a sensitive mind to produce her poem. One of the finest performances of *Hamlet* given in recent years was the work of amateurs in a chapel in off-hours with only one "prop," a bean bag, and one item of costume, a cloak made from a tablecloth. An Inuit theatre group from Greenland, using masks and costumes but neither scenery nor stage, created a deeply moving theatrical experience. A single flower can give enjoyment more exquisite than a mass of bloom. A family can have as much fun playing scramble-demon with old packs of cards as it might get out of a sophisticated electronic game. Spillikins or tiddly-winks can give more scope to precision of eye and delicacy of touch—and at least as much excitement—as playing a "one-armed bandit." Watching one live bird in the back yard can give more delight than watching an army of exotic creatures on the TV screen.

Leisure time activities stressing human perception and creative imagination and human thought and skill, put material accessories in their proper place as simply the instruments of human experience and human creativity. If this shift in emphasis is supplemented by a shift from stress on competition to cooperation, the pressure for ever more and more elaborate equipment would be still further reduced. Leisure occupations might then play a significant part in a movement towards a conserver society.

There will, of course, be enormous difficulties, difficulties in overcoming ingrained pecuniary canons of taste and tests of achievement; difficulties in breaking through barriers of lethargy to open up to everybody the excitements and rewards of do-it-yourself leisure activities; difficulties of dislocations in the business world and in the labor market, to say nothing of the unsolved problem of how to turn persistent unemployment into real leisure.

Perhaps the greatest difficulty of all, and one which is not just a problem of transition from a high consumption to a high activity leisure lifestyle, is the twin problem of space and of natural beauty. More and more space will certainly be needed for any massive expansion in creative activities. At the receiving end, all you need for TV viewing is somewhere to sit and a TV set. To act a play, to sing in a choir or play in an orchestra, to paint or sculpt, you need suitable space, and a good deal of it. For outdoor recreation you need playing fields, ski-slopes and beaches, lakes and rivers. For camping, wild river canoeing, mountain climbing, or bird watching you need unspoiled wilderness. When these delights become a wider part of the leisure life of growing urban populations with increasing free time, and, especially, bigger blocks of free time (three days at work, four days on the ski slopes), how can sufficient wilderness be made available to meet the demands that will be made on it? Here is a dilemma: Of all leisure time activities, experience of nature may be the most truly recreating, the most rewarding, and the most health-giving to mind and body. The need is evident but how can it be met? Throngs bent on wilderness experience destroy the wilderness. (The same problem already exists in the enjoyment of art and ancient buildings, as is illustrated in the congested condition of Florence and its galleries.) Perhaps, though, an end to high consumption life styles may release more wilderness for recreation by reducing the threat of destruction of wilderness beauty by hydro-electric development, lumbering or open pit mining.

Being and doing, not having; using only what is needed to realize human values, instead of consuming conspicuously; these are surely the keys to the future. They may prove the keys even to preserving unspoiled wilderness, our cultural heritage, finite resources, and, above all, personal and collective sanity.

REFERENCES

1. Innis, H. A. and Ratz, B. "Labour," Encyclopedia of Canada, Vol. III, Wallace, W. S. (Ed.), Toronto: University Associates of Canada, 1936.
2. Ostry, S. and Woods, H. D. *Labour Policy and Labour Economics in Canada.* Toronto: Macmillan of Canada, 1962, pp. 355-336.
3. Perspectives Canada II. Ottawa: Statistics Canada (Catalogue No. 11-508, 1977), p. 133.
4. Cordell, A. "Bye Bye to Buy Buy," *Conserver Society Notes*, 11:3 (Summer, 1977), pp. 5-18.
5. Household Facilities and Equipment. Ottawa: Statistics Canada (Catalogue No. 64-202).
6. Martin, W. H. and Mason, S. *Leisure Markets in Europe.* London: Financial Times Business Publishing Division, 1978.
7. See, for instance, Daley, H. (Ed.). *Toward a Steady State Economy.* San Francisco: W. H. Freeman and Company, 1973; and Stapenhurst, F. "Some Implications of a Conserver Society," *Labour Gazette* (November, 1977), pp. 511-513.
8. See, for instance, Hirsch, F. *The Social Limits to Growth.* Cambridge, Massachusetts: Harvard University Press, 1979; and Leiss, W. *The Limits to Satisfaction.* Toronto: University of Toronto Press, 1976.
9. Scitovsky, T. *The Joyless Economy.* Oxford: Oxford University Press, 1976.

End of Chapter 9]

Chapter 10

Of Godots and Goodbars: On Waiting and Looking for Change

Thomas L. Goodale

An often repeated short dialogue may be a useful beginning. It's a brief exchange between a native and a missionary.

> Native: "If I didn't know about God and sin, would I go to hell?"
> Missionary: "If you didn't know . . . well, no you wouldn't go to hell."
> Native: "Then why are you telling me these things?"

There is little doubt, anymore, that during the closing years of this century we will experience change; perhaps as rapid, pervasive, and dramatic as at any time in our history. And there is no doubt about which shoulders the burden of change rests upon, ... "the cutting edge of social change works at the level of the individual. Social change is change in an aggregate of individuals."[1] For a number of reasons, those working in the field of recreation, especially those employed by government at the municipal level, will be "front and center" through these years of change and will bear their share and more of the burden.

WE SHOULD CHANGE

First, even in a welfare state, the direct provision of recreation services is a peripheral rather than a central task of government. That does not, in any sense, diminish the importance of recreation or the legitimacy of government involvement. Rather, the nature of government involvement is at issue, as is the nature of recreation. The provision of recreation services through a large and complex organizational and institutional framework may, in fact, be antithetical to the nature of recreation; blocking rather than opening paths to the goals we espouse. This fundamental problem has been addressed by philosophers and utopians—Plato and Mill, Bellamy and Orwell for example—of every age. Bertrand Russell summarized it well more than 70 years ago:

> The problem which faces the modern world is the combination of individual initiative with the increase in the scope and size of organizations. Unless it is solved, individuals will grow less and less full

of life and vigor, more and more passively submissive to conditions imposed upon them. A society composed of such individuals cannot be progressive or add much to the world's stock of mental and spiritual possessions.[2]

WE MUST CHANGE

The second major reason why recreationists will be shouldering the burden of change is that most of the indicators of the decline (failure, demise, crisis, bankruptcy, etc.) of the present institutional order point to problems to which the recreation movement has always addressed itself. Perhaps the problems would have been worse if the recreation movement had not been concerned about them. And certainly recreation can't be faulted for the world's ills. Still, the problems remain, and remain the concern of recreationists in particular. Among indicators of failure, and consequently the need for dramatic change are, according to one of America's leading futurists, Willis Harman:

decreased sense of community;
increased sense of alienation and purposelessness;
increased frequency of personal disorders and mental illness;
increased rate of violent crime;
increased frequency and severity of social disruptions;
increased use of police to control behavior;
increased public acceptance of hedonistic behavior (particularly sexual), of symbols of degradation, and of lax public morality;
increased interest in non-institutionalized religious practices (e.g., cults, rituals, secret practices);
signs of specific and conscious anxiety about the future;
in some cases, economic inflation.[3]

[handwritten margin note: indicators of failure]

As has frequently been noted, recreationists have been trying diligently, through organizations and institutions, to forestall or resolve these problems and the recreation movement has been drawn along in the development of a vast, public, social service system during the past several decades. But the problems remain; some suggest that we have made conditions worse through our well intended efforts to make them better. More and better of the same, we now recognize, will not help. What is required is different; not re-doubling our efforts or even reform. What is required is change.

New genres of literature have emerged in the past several years; notably the literature of crisis and transformation. We have, it seems, a drug crisis, a population crisis, a housing crisis, an economic crisis, an energy crisis, an urban crisis, a government crisis, and an environmental crisis. At the root of all this is said to be a crisis in values. Much recent literature has been devoted to discussions of "old" and "new" values, transforming values, and shifting from these values to those. But another genre of literature has emerged which suggests a crisis related to but perhaps even deeper than the crisis of values. It is a crisis, variously, of spirit, hope, courage, or will evident in the writings of Fromm, Tillich, May, and many others. Unless that crisis is solved, none of the others can be. And without intending "gloom and doom," Alexander Solzhenitsyn, in his widely debated 1978 commencement address at Harvard University, noted that, historically, the loss of spirit marked the beginning of the end.

The difference between a crisis of values and a crisis of spirit, hope, will or courage is important in another respect. The former exists at the social, organizational, institutional level; the latter exists at the individual level. As Kristol writes:

"A crisis in values is something that happens *out there*. It is something you can cope with through rational manipulation of institutions, of beliefs, of ideas. A spiritual crisis is something that happens to *you* - deep down -and that you have to cope with. Therefore the phrase crisis in values can mislead by emphasizing what is essentially a technological approach to a problem that is not technological; this technological approach asks; how do we look at society; how do we manipulate it; how do we shape it in such a way that we don't have a crisis in values? I don't think that's the way. Real spiritual crises are resolved not by social science but by mysterious cultural processes which somehow reach inside every human being."[4]

Thus the indicators of widespread, systematic failures and the need for change relate particularly, but of course not exclusively, to the recreation field and the burden of change it must bear. And if the most fundamental crisis is not environment or population, or even values, but spirit and hope and courage and will, then the burden rests on the shoulders of individual recreationists and not on our agencies, organizations, or institutions.

Perhaps a brief, practical illustration will clarify the point and show the cutting edge in operation. A few years ago I had the opportunity to converse at length with about 35 recreationists employed in two Ontario municipalities. The informal interviews ranged into the future, dealing with goals, values, aspirations and the like for the society, their respective agencies and themselves. Materialistic and consumptive values and aspirations came under attack many times, and there seemed a longing for a conserver society and simpler and more authentic lifestyles. It was often mentioned, too, although with an air of chagrin, resignation or sometimes anger and frustration, that for the past three or four years, salary increases had been significantly below annual increases in the cost-of-living, consequently they were falling further and further behind. Can it be that materialism is an "out there" notion while falling behind in salary is something that reaches deep down?

WE WILL CHANGE

The third reason why the burden of change rests heavily on the field of recreation, on individual recreationists, and particularly on those working in municipal government agencies is that our social-political-economic situation is already bringing about change. Slow growth is the underlying characteristic of our situation now and for the foreseeable future. Slow growth in population, especially the decline in birth-rate to below replacement levels in North America and other "advanced" nations, is one element of this situation. The reshaping of age distribution from a pyramid to a diamond has consequences more far reaching than a shift from mainly child and youth oriented recreation services to serving adults and seniors more than previously. The impact on schools, teachers, local taxes, transfers of funds from other governments for education and other consequences is just one, albeit highly visible, example. Slow population growth also contributes to the present and foreseeable future situation of slow economic growth.

Inflation alone results in a smaller economy. Stagflation entered our vocabularies to cover an economic period characterized by high rates of inflation and unemployment, both at the same time. In a global village, every nation's economy is shaped by international economic forces; the cartel of the major oil producing nations and the increasing industrial capacity of developing nations, among them. Slow growth, and perhaps eventually no growth—material growth at least—is the major force already reshaping our present situation and certain to shape our future.

The consequences of these changes in the economy and in the age distribution of the population are already being felt by many. Some examples are widely recognized; affecting the world of work, families, and government, and they apply to recreationists as individuals as well as employees. Work: increased competition for jobs; less job mobility; slower advancement for younger employees; increased frustration with conservative managers and administrators at the top; those with several years in a position "locked in" or "priced out" of other positions; unemployment and underemployment. Families: more two-income families in order to acquire today's standard necessities and modest amenities; more children and teenagers on their own much of the time; pinched "discretionary" income forcing harder choices; more marital stress related to finances and to child rearing; alternative "family" groupings. Government: increasingly costly government sponsored social welfare programs for children and teens, the unemployed, and the growing number of retired and elderly persons; larger and costlier program to combat alcoholism and other social problems; higher taxes when there is already widespread public concern with the size and cost of government in relation to its perceived efficiency and effectiveness.

The dilemma confronting government—increasing demands for government sponsored programs and services on one hand, and increasing concern about the present size and cost of government on the other—is a difficult one. "Proposition 13," a phrase understood everywhere in North America and in overseas places as well, had, as one significant consequence, a serious demoralizing effect on the public service in California.[5] Low morale among government employees at all levels seems a universal problem.

The impact of increased demand and increased disenchantment about the size and cost of government is felt most, but not exclusively of course, at the local government level, despite the fact that most people believe the efficiency and effectiveness of local government is greater than that at federal, or state or provincial levels. Diseconomies of scale alone warrant that belief. That the impact is felt most by local government is related to accessibility and familiarity and also to the tax structure. The bulk of local taxes is raised through the property tax, an annual visible bite taken after other taxes (income, sales, etc.) have already been paid. In a sense, property taxes are paid out of "after tax" dollars. Despite the fact that only a small proportion of an individual's or family's total tax burden is for municipal purposes, the impact of taxpayers discontent is felt first, and most, at the local government level.

After two or three decades of successfully competing for local tax dollars and good treatment in the hands of local taxpayers and politicians, "leisure service" expenditures have declined as a proportion of municipal government spending during the past decade or so.[6] It appears, too, that personnel expenditures, while still taking the lion's share, are decreasing as a proportion of leisure service spending.

What seems clear from all this is that we have created a large and complex array of public agencies and have "institutionalized" recreation as part of the total government social service system. It also seems clear that the recreation institution, if not the whole social service structure, cannot be sustained and we are caught having created demands and expectations that probably can't be met. This point has been argued by many, but perhaps none more cogently than Geoffrey Vickers:

> If our world is to survive for another generation in any form which we today should regard as worth striving for, I have no doubt that for everyone, what we expect of ourselves and each other will have to go up and that for most of us in the western world what we expect of the system will have to go down.[7]

WE ESPOUSE CHANGE

The fourth reason recreation and recreationists must bear the burden of change is that for many years now, we have professed to want change. We even prided ourselves on being "change agents." And we have experienced in recent years a period of critical self-analysis, and either evolution or devolution to a philosophy suggesting quite different service modes than those characterized by direct provision of programs and facilities, telling our constituents about ourselves and encouraging them to participate with us.

Like Bertrand Russell, we want people to grow more full of life and vigor; we want to promote individual initiative. Is that not what we mean when we speak of learning, growth, development, positive health, self-actualization? Like Irving Kristol, we are concerned about what happens inside individuals, deep down. Is that not what we mean when we speak of individuation and holism, of qualitative dimensions and experiential qualities and therefore our subjective and intuitive selves? Like Geoffrey Vickers, we want people to rely more on themselves and each other rather than on the institutional complex of leisure services. Is that not what we mean when we speak of citizen participation and involvement and community development, and of self sufficiency and self-determination? These and so many other voices are not singing a dirge; they're singing our song. That it may sound like a dirge merely illustrates that change is difficult, and sometimes threatening and abrasive. It may mean, too, that recreation is not institutionalized but recreationists are.

The roles and functions we have defined for ourselves during the past several years, and thus a service mode different from programmer and provider, are widely accepted, at least among recreationists. So we have come to describe ourselves as educators, advocates, facilitators, enablers, catalysts, animators, encouragers, and developers. Still, this is more the idea than the practice.

WITHOUT GODOT OR GOODBAR

Godot, in the form of organizational or institutional change, is not likely to appear. What we get is reorganization. Petronius Arbiter, in 210 B.C., noted: "I was to learn late in life that we tend to meet any new situation by reorganizing; and what a wonderful method it can be for creating the illusion of progress while producing confusion, inefficiency, and demoralization." Creative organizations, we have found, tend to be characterized by small size and autonomy.[8] Neither of these conditions obtain in most municipal recreation agencies, and only size may be characteristic of others. Organizational development, however widely touted, may be beyond us. As Donald Michael has noted, this requires years of effort and a champion at the top who can control the organization's resources and boundaries; requirements not found in government. Further:

The personal and interpersonal skills needed to cope with the emotional and intellectual burdens of the changeover and the operating situation far exceed those that most people seem to possess, and certainly exceed those that organizations, particularly public agencies, reward.[9]

Chris Argyris carries the argument further in discussing "Some Limits on Rational Man Organization Theory." He notes a process by which individuals become passive, lose a sense of being an origin or cause, deny or suppress their own self-actualizing needs, and rationalize being passive and controlled by taking it as a measure of loyalty and maturity.[10] Warren Bennis, in exploring reasons why leaders can't lead, notes that all of us conspire in submersing ourselves in routine and formulates Bennis' Law (joining Parkinson and so many others) stating that routine work drives out important work. He, too, notes that change may be possible for small groups given enough truth and trust.[11] In most large organizations accounting to and informing everyone else about virtually everything one does has become a major task and a major source of succumbing to routine. Whatever arguments support this routine, it is still a symptom of generalized lack of trust.

Organizational change, like social change, results from change in an aggregate of individuals. Waiting for change is a non-exercise in futility; in the meantime an organizational climate conducive to change may deteriorate as incompatible demands from the outside are felt more and more. Too, the gap between the idea and the reality widens. Similarly, Mr. Goodbar, in the form of answers to questions or solutions to problems, may not be found no matter how harried our search. At issue is the nature of change, organizations, leadership and the like. Without that understanding, we might as well keep working on blue-ribbon task forces, which, Bennis argues, insures the status quo as "their reports get better and better while the problems get worse and worse."[12]

Organizations, anymore, are beleaguered by attempts to provide answers and solve problems. Technique after technique is adopted and soon discarded. Barely was the Management by Objectives technique understood before Management by Results replaced it. After struggling with Program Performance Budgeting Systems, we are now struggling with Zero-Bases Budgeting. We have sharpened and flattened pyramids changing steps in the hierarchy and span of control, and developed matrices and ad hocracies. Even if all these techniques contributed enough to off-set the drain from other efforts required in adopting them, the major effect seems still to be on organizational efficiency—an internal, system criteria—rather than on effectiveness—an external, service criteria. Organizational change does not appear to result from technical remedies for internal problems. The cutting edge of change is at the individual level.

SOME OBSTACLES

If the emerging philosophy of recreation service and the emerging social and economic forces point us in the same direction, then smooth and orderly change, and a smooth transition to a new service mode for the future should be expected. But the reality is that each of us resists change; each of us being products of our past; each of us better able to respond to yesterday's situation than tomorrow's. Understanding and managing change as a personal process is a requirement for all of us and there is a rich and growing literature to help meet it.[13] Along with obstacles to change which face everyone, recreationists have others, in addition to those noted or alluded to above, to overcome. A few are noted that seem sufficiently general as to apply to many.

1. Lack of union strength or professional status may result in some anxiety and insecurity. Difficulties in identifying specific and special competencies (a problem now being addressed in several quarters) adds to the problem.

2. Direct provision of programs and services is visible, tangible proof of a service being rendered. The roles attendant on the emerging philosophy—enabling, facilitating, and the like—are much less visible. There is some risk in foregoing visibility, since credit tends to be contingent upon it.

3. The development of successful programs, even if only measured quantitatively, is not always easy. There is an investment and some satisfaction of the need to be needed. The emotional task of letting go is difficult.

4. Recreationists do much simply because it's easier; that is, more efficient. Effectiveness may sometimes require a recreationist to do nothing, a task difficult enough in itself, and exacerbated by pressure from those who appreciate no objective except efficiency.

5. Success as providers, and the resulting dependency of the public on direct services, will be a source of stress and friction.

6. While recreationists are intent on enabling growth, learning, self-determination, development, involvement and the like, increasing stress on members of the public may mean that their primary objective in a recreational pursuit is simply escape.

7. Roles have been identified, however ill-defined, but less progress has been made in identifying goals and objectives and even less in establishing criteria by which to judge the success of the new service mode suggested by philosophy and identified roles.

The last obstacle listed is one which recreationists, as a group, can address so some fairly specific goals and objectives are suggested, not for adoption but for discussion and debate. While the goals and objectives relate to recreation service rather than individual change, they can only be achieved when the aggregate of individuals in their respective agencies, change. Some uncertainty, stress, risk, and failure will likely accompany change since the amount and pace of change is hardly uniform, and since organizations and institutions are not conducive to it. In the process we cannot expect much from our institutions. What we expect of ourselves and each other will have to go up.

SOME ASSUMPTIONS

By way of a summary and to re-set the context in which the suggestions are cast, six assumptions about our present and foreseeable future situation are noted.

1. It is assumed that the foreseeable future will be characterized by a slow growing and smaller economy: slow growing as population growth slows and at some point stabilizes; smaller as a result of inflation, resource short-ages and limits and the like.

2. It is assumed that the pressures of increasing demands for service and increasing concern about the size, cost and inefficiency of government will be felt first, and most, at the local government level.

3. It is assumed that what we expect of our institutions must go down and what we expect of ourselves and each other must go up.

4. It is assumed that the cutting edge of change is at the individual level. Institutions and organizations are not going to collapse, as some suggest, nor are they likely to change rapidly or markedly. Social change is the result of change in an aggregate of individuals.

5. It is assumed that there is already much individual stress in the society and that there will be much more. The reconstruction of viable, convivial institu-tions in family, neighborhood, and community groups and among colleagues will be essential if people are to have the necessary base of support form which to foster and manage change.

6. Finally, the fundamental assumption underlying all of this is that individuals and groups are fully capable, with support as needed, of generating most of their own recreational opportunities, including most of what is now provided by governments. The hesitancy and reluctance born of paternal dependence,

thus far agreeable to both the people and the government, is perhaps the overriding obstacle to change consistent with our professed beliefs and con temporary situation.

If the assumptions are not acceptable, then the suggestions certainly won't be because many will be difficult to accept in any situation. Each suggestion leads to many others, some of which may be even more difficult to accept. To suggest, for example, decreased budgets and personnel complements in the public sector is a direct challenge to our thinking about manpower, college and university enrollments and curricula, and a host of related matters.

SOME TASKS

Some objectives and criteria for the new service mode might be:

1. A smaller role for government: reduced program expenditures by government with no reduction in participation; reduction of total man hours of employment in the public sector; wholesale reduction in the number of rules, regulations, policies, and laws.

2. More assistance to others: redistribution of government resources to community groups via grants; sharing space, office supplies and equipment, technical administrative support, and the like; "no strings" support of voluntary, non-profit agencies; more incentives and more cooperation with the private sector.

3. Greater community identity and autonomy: decentralization of decision making authority throughout staff and back to community groups; indices of shifts of power away from government; re-emphasis on smaller, decentralized, and community controlled facilities.

4. More public (versus special interest group) service: increased emphasis on geographic community rather than communities of interest; increased shares of resources for the general public rather than special interests; increased integration of age and interest groups.

5. Less structure and rigidity: reduced "red tape" and faster response time; increased flexibility in scheduling; fewer leagues, teams, and classes; increased spontaneous activities and events.

6. More efficiency and (hopefully) effectiveness: improved coordination of current and comprehensive community information for all programs,

resources, social services and government affairs; increased coordination of all community programs, facilities and resources; increased use of all facilities in place; reduced debt service and current capital expense.

7. Less political alienation and social anomie: increased political sophistication and participation in the political process; decreased brutal, sensate, and escapist activity; reduced vandalism, alcoholism, and other indices of social malaise.

8. Increased individual assumption of responsibility: growth in volunteer services; increased neighborly sharing and self help; increased family activity; reintegration of the young and old in meaningful community service roles.

MOVING ON

Essential next steps include refining and consolidating appropriate objectives; redefining or "operationalizing" statements into measurable terms; identifying indicators by which progress or its lack can be observed; establishing baseline information. Another critical next step is to educate elected and appointed officials and the public about our situation, philosophy and assumptions about the next decade or so, and thus the efficacy of a different service mode and the objectives being pursued. Again, the service will become lower profile, if not invisible. Too, there is much evidence that the public is happy with the status quo based on direct provision of programs, facilities and services.[14] And if Lasch is correct in his depiction of a narcissistic culture,[15] these steps are very long ones and they're uphill all the way.

None of this will come about by "Waiting for Godot" or "Looking for Mr. Goodbar." Every individual recreationist is responsible for change. There are no easy or universal answers to our questions or solutions to our problems. The circumstances of every municipality are different. The circumstances, mandates, and resources of every agency are different. Problems and opportunities in one area do not exist in another; an appropriate strategy here would be inappropriate there. If the burden of change finally rests on the shoulders of each individual, then the ubiquitous question of how can only be determined by each individual according to his or her own lights, abilities and limits.

We began with a dialogue and end with one since the question of how we get from where we are to where we would like to go reminds one of the exchange between a tourist and a New York City cab driver.

Tourist: "How do I get to Carnegie Hall?"
Cab driver: "Practice, my friend, practice."

REFERENCES

1. Pizer, S. and Travers, J. *Psychology and Social Change*. New York: McGraw-Hill, 1975, p. 11.
2. Russell, B. "Individual Liberty and Public Control." In Desaulniers, L. (Ed.). *119 Years of the Atlantic*. The Atlantic Monthly Company, 1977, p. 272.
3. Harman, W. "The Coming Transformation." *The Futurist*, 11:2, (April, 1977), p. 197. That these are recreation's tasks see Weiner, M. E., "A Systems Approach to Leisure Services." In Lutzin, S. G. and Storey, E. H. (Eds.). *Managing Municipal Leisure Services*, Washington, D.C.: International City Management Association, 1973, p. 7.
4. Kristol, I. "Values in Contemporary Society." *Working Paper of the Rockefeller Foundation*, (March, 1974), p. 7.
5. From a conversation with Dr. David Gray, Vice President for Administration and Staff Development, California State University, Long Beach, January, 1979.
6. Crompton, J. L. and Van Doren, C. S. "Changes in the Financial Status of Leisure Services in Thirty Major U.S. Cities, 1964-1974." *Journal of Leisure Research*, 10:1(1978), pp. 37-46. This is also the case in Ontario cities according to data compiled by James Maxwell for presentation to a meeting of the Ontario Municipal Recreation Association, March, 1979.
7. Vickers, G. *Making Institutions Work*. New York: John Wiley and Sons, 1973, p. 15.
8. Steiner, G. (Ed.). *The Creative Organization*. Chicago: University of Chicago Press, 1965.
9. Michael, D. "On the Social Psychology of Organizational Resistances to Long Range Planning." *I.E.E.E. Journal*, SCM2:5(November, 1972), p. 583.
10. Argyris, C. "Some Limits on Rational Man Organization Theory." *Public Administrative Review*, 33:3 (May-June, 1973), pp. 253-267.
11. Bennis, Warren. *The Unconscious Conspiracy: Why Leaders Can't Lead*. New York: Amacom (A Division of the American Management Association), 1976, pp. 161-186. As to succumbing to routine, see especially Mintzberg, H. *The Nature of Managerial Work*. New York: Harper and Row, 1973.
12. Bennis, *Op. Cit.*, p. 33.
13. See Pizer and Travis, *Op. Cit.* and Adams, J., et al. *Transition: Understanding and Managing Personal Change*. London: Martin Robertson and Company, 1976.

14. Goodale, T. and Witt, P. A. "Goals for Municipal Recreation in Ontario." *Recreation Research Review.* 7:3(December, 1979), pp. 17-26.

15. Lasch, C. *The Culture of Narcissism: American Life in an Age of Diminishing Expectations.* New York: W. W. Norton and Company, 1978.

(no keep)

p. 136 is blank.

End of Chapter 10

Chapter 11

Planning for Leisure in a Pluralistic Society

Geoffrey Godbey

Leisure, in the sense of being free of the struggle for existence, is one of the oldest dreams of humans. To exist on one's own terms, to pass time in voluntary, pleasurable ways has been the ultimate transition hoped for by individuals in many cultures and the ultimate test of the few who partially achieved these conditions.

The situations which constrain leisure and those which shape it have varied historically among cultures. These different life situations, in large part, have been responsible for differing conceptualizations of leisure; different notions of what is meant to be free.

DETERMINANTS OF LEISURE

This chapter will examine some factors of our own society which are believed to be of great importance in shaping our potential for leisure, both at an individual and group level. Rather than defining leisure, a definition will be implied from examining its determinants. Particular attention will be given to implications for organized leisure services.

Work

Quantitatively, a higher percentage of the population now works for pay compared to the 1940s, because of both more female and more teenage employment. Additionally, a greater percentage of our population desires to work in some capacity. This trend, combined with rapid changes in the kinds of work available in our society and the educational requirements for such work, has brought about a break-up of the "linear life cycle" in which one received full-time formal education for one period of life, then pursued one career throughout his working life, and then retired.[1] Today, people starting second and third careers in midstream, taking an early retirement, or not retiring at all, returning to education in their middle-age, or switching from homemaking to part or full-time employment are redefining traditional patterns of work.

The content of our work has also shifted so that more people are involved in the production of services than the production of goods, and service occupations are devourers of time because service workers tend to be less efficient, live performance and personal contact are involved and capital cannot be substituted for labor. Thus, it is not surprising that the average workweek for the full-time employee has remained constant since World War II.

The increases in leisure which are occurring are due to increases in large blocks of time such as vacations and holidays. There is evidence that workers prefer that any future increases in leisure come in large blocks rather than slight decreases in the total workweek.

Many of the new jobs being created in our economy are repetitive, low-paying, and don't have many chances for advancement. Such jobs as fast food worker, janitor, retail sales, nurses and nurses aides, and other such positions have grown rapidly at the very time those entering the labor force have the highest levels of formal education they have ever had (and also perhaps the highest expectations concerning job satisfaction). This imbalance, combined with the fact that twice as many members of the Baby Boom Generation expect to move into middle management jobs as the number of such jobs which exist, means that much of the behavior which contributes to self expression and self identity will come from leisure behavior rather than work. Leisure, for increasing segments of the labor force, will be the arena in which personal statements are made about who one is and what is of personal importance.

Basic Values

When planners try to plan for leisure in our society, their focus must be on the total human experience. Vast changes have occurred in our techniques and meaning of work and there is increased unwillingness in much of the western world to accept the concept of fate.

In the last 300 years within the western world there has been increasingly less economic constraint on human behavior and yet an increasing inability of man to develop a meaningful reintegration with the rest of the living world. Our increased social and economic freedoms have been purchased at the cost of isolation and alienation from those systems which allow this world to survive and function. Our notion of God and theology have become increasingly vague yet people still long for the simple faith and answers of former times. Our machines have shown us the uninhabited heavens while parting the angelless clouds. At the same time, another part of our collective mind begins to see what we could do to become God by controlling nature. We can unlock knowledge by which we can live like a logical extension of the Earth. With such aspirations, it is perhaps natural that what we do or what we achieve is dominant over what we are. Our ascribed statuses: gender, race, age, religion, etc. are used less and less to convey who we are to other people. Instead, we become virtual composites of what we do, and it is doing something that keeps us from being nothing.

The rush to experience, particularly among those with high levels of education and income in advanced industrial societies, has led to "time deepening."[2] Time deepening occurs when the individual seeks to undertake more activity than can be accommodated with existing economic and educational resources. In other words, the more activities people undertake, the more they desire to undertake. Time deepening has three primary consequences for planners: (1) people do more and more activities in less and less time, e.g., eat lunch in ten minutes or get strenuous exercise in less than an hour with a game of racquetball; (2) people increasingly have the desire and ability to do more than one thing at the same time, e.g., to watch television while eating dinner or to listen to music while talking with a friend and reading the newspaper; and (3) people increasingly have the desire and ability to deal with more precise units of time, e.g., to schedule meetings at 10:36 a.m. rather than 10:30 or know within fifteen minutes how long a 300 mile drive will take. Time deepening is caused by and in turn facilitates experientialism, and it means that most of us approach both leisure and work activities with the same set of values and attitudes. These values and attitudes reflect our seriousness, rationality, hurried pace and lack of playfulness. They also reflect our doubt as to whether we belong in this world.

Democracy

Leisure has always been closely interwoven with political belief and shaped by political systems. The systems by which humans exercise power directly influences the quantity and quality of our leisure experience. The original notion of leisure, born in the Golden Age of Greece, was directly shaped by a political system in which only a minority of its residents enjoyed citizenship. Participation in the decision-making process was mandatory. The ideal of cultivation of self was more fully realized through the existence of an extensive slave system which freed the citizen from mundane work.

Unlike that of the ancient Greeks, our own democracy has been built around two key ideas: individual freedom and equality under the law. Over one hundred years ago de Tocqueville observed:

"When men living in a democratic state of society are enlightened, they readily discover that they are not confined and fixed by any limits which constrain them to take up with their present fortune. They all, therefore, conceive the idea of increasing it—if they are free, they will attempt it; but all do not succeed in the same manner."[3]

Thus, differences in well being were closely linked to one's personal efforts, to one's ability to compete, to one's level of aspiration, need or greed. Among those things early Americans pursued competitively was "happiness." Today happiness can be pursued by the acquisition of experiences as well as the acquisition of things. The struggle for the acquisition of material goods is more successfully undertaken by most people and the pursuit of happiness is today more a matter of individual self-expression than instrumental activities.

The combination of individual freedom of choice, voluntary action and technological capitalism have emphasized maximizing profit and production divorced from identified need. These have combined to change our notion of what is "voluntary" or "freely chosen." Since leisure is usually thought of as freely-chosen activity, this change of notion is important. "Voluntary" formerly meant a choice from among many alternatives which was freely and agreeably made by the individual, not externally constrained. Choice meant foregoing several attractive alternatives in order to gain the most satisfying one. In short, pleasure involved sacrifice.

People today are more nearly able to avoid sacrifice, seeking instead to experience all choices, do it all, see it all, and do it and see it now. In survey after survey, "lack of time" is cited more frequently than any other reason as a constraint which limits participation in outdoor recreation. Not money, or transportation, or crowding or health problems, but time. This could be taken as a statement of our system's success. Imagine a former generation saying that the main limitation on their leisure was neither capital nor technology but merely enough time to use them. This rush to experience, in one sense, indicates people have more democracy to do more and more chosen activities.

The lack of willingness to sacrifice one desirable activity in order to undertake another, however, suggests a new way of attempting to deal with our mortality: to deal with our greatest enemy, time, by doing more and more within a given period of time. Democracy has always dealt in finite terms, allowing us to choose either A or B. For a democratic government to work, people must be able to choose and accept, for example, either a cleaner environment or reduced taxes, either better health care for the aged or an alternative use of funds such as space exploration, either a president or prime minister with one set of beliefs (and faults) or another. Democracy involves sacrificing that which is potentially good for that which is potentially better. When we are no longer willing or capable of doing that or no longer allowed to, democracy will no longer function and we will enslave ourselves for one more utopian dream of life without limitation.

Cultural Pluralism

Our cultural pluralism also shapes our leisure behavior and values. The many ethnic, religious and political minorities who maintain their identity rather than completely assimilating further the process of pluralism. The United States has historically represented a model of cultural pluralism due not only to its historic ties with Britain, Europe, Spain and Africa, but also due to immigration policies which continued the immigration of new groups. Canada has also experienced a more pluralistic culture during the last few decades as immigrants from Europe, Asia, the Caribbean Islands and the United States transform the country from one which was dominated by the French and English to a multicultural nation.

The effects of cultural pluralism on the leisure behavior of a post-industrial society are illustrated in Table 1. The table attempts to identify the features of cultural pluralism in a mass culture which moves toward having even more things in common, primarily due to the pervasiveness of the mass media. Mass culture has been defined as:

> ". . . elements of culture that develop in a large, heterogeneous society as a result of common exposure to and experience of the mass media . . . The emergence of mass culture is a part of the process of the development of common unifying cultural values and attitudes in the new and vast population of modern national social units."[4]

Cultural pluralism emphasizes the role of leisure as anything the individual chooses to do for pleasure. The limits of such behavior are defined only by laws, with activity representing an expression of personal interest or "lifestyle" rather than one's culture. The social pressure resulting from fads and created leisure needs stimulated further innovation and a speeding up of the consumption of leisure experience. One solution to the accompanying uncertainty over what is worth doing is to do nothing, but a more prevalent reaction is to try to do or experience everything.

Self-Consciousness

Social psychologists claim that consciousness of self is what distinguishes us from other animals. Self-awareness is necessary and worthwhile for humans, but only within limits. Perhaps no society has been more self-conscious than our own. Our physical selves are seen instantly by cameras, we see ourselves dancing on our mirrored dancefloors or on the moon, and we receive advice concerning how to change ourselves for the better from a myriad of sources. We see and adjust ourselves daily in test scores, in beauty contests, in TV instant replays, in tape recordings, in factor analyses, in insurance company predictions and equations concerning our death, in newspapers, and, of course, in advertising. Advertising teaches us to be self-conscious. Am I succeeding? Am I having fun? Reaching for all the gusto? Am I in command?

Heightened self-consciousness shapes our leisure. It may limit our playfulness. Play is outside ordinary life, limited in time and space, and surrounded by an air of mystery. Self-consciousness allows us to dismiss mystery, to take the element of surprise out of ordinary life. We may actually take leisure counselors seriously, shy away from singing in public or reciting limericks to strangers, seek to rig our competition in advance or analyze why we like music. Thus, while leisure and play allow us to "get lost" in what we are doing, it becomes increasingly hard to get lost. Our heightened self-consciousness undoubtedly prevents us from doing some things in our leisure which would surprise or harm us. Additionally, it may make it more difficult to have fun. Fun, as Huizenga pointed out, is an irreducible category.[5] You cannot successfully analyze fun and break it down into component parts, although a number of social scientists are now trying. When you try too hard to analyze fun, it disappears.

Table 1

Leisure in Singular and Plural Cultural Societies

	Plural Culture Society	Single Culture Society
Concept	Leisure is anything the individual chooses to do which he finds pleasurable. Leisure is unlimited. An end in itself.	Leisure is a set of identifiable experiences which the individual is is taught to enjoy. Leisure is limited. A means to an end.
Variation in Behavior	Range of acceptable behavior wide.	Range of acceptable behavior narrow.
Standards to Judge Behavior	Laws set limits. No universally accepted mores by which to judge leisure behavior.	Mores and folkways set limits of behavior. Universal standards for leisure based upon perceived cultural necessity.
Role	Individual and subcultural identity linked to leisure behavior	National identity linked to leisure behavior.
Role problems	Difficult to judge leisure ethically. Dispute over leisure values. Lack of meaning.	Lack of experimentation or alternatives. Persecution of that which is foreign. Easy to use leisure as a means of social control.
Government's Role	Identification of recreation needs difficult. May provide only selected kinds of services or serve certain subcultures or groups disproportionately.	Identification of recreation needs easy. May provide services which serve as a common denominator.
Commercial Organization's Role	Commercial sector has more diverse opportunities. Can cater to individual or subculture's tastes. Easier to create needs.	Commercial sector has more limited opportunities. More difficult to create needs or cater to individual or subculture's tastes.
Mass Media's Role	Limited in its ability to reflect culture. Diversion and entertainment function.	Less limited in its ability to reflect culture. Transmission of culture function.

Post-Industrial Capitalism

Daniel Bell characterized post-industrial society not so much by the absence of certain traditional forms of material scarcities such as food and shelter, but by the development of new forms of scarcity.[6] Such new costs or scarcities include the cost of information, the cost of coordination, and the cost of time.

Information is mandatory in our society, and the rate at which we are bombarded with information increases daily. Every new social or political movement seeks to "educate the people." Thus, consumer activists want to provide more and more accurate information to the consumer to insure logical choice. This movement's success, however, is predicted upon individuals digesting large amounts of information, processing decisions, not unlike a computer. To buy the best tennis racquet requires extensive data not only concerning comparative price, but also on durability, flexibility of head, throat, and shaft; weight and weight distribution; head shape; size of "sweet spot"; racquet head torque; vibration; stringing pattern; grip composition; string type; string composition; and so forth. Such an approach assures that the individual pays for the racquet not only with money, but with his time, energy and added complexity to his life. Here the consumer movement becomes an apology for materialism, not usually questioning the need for products, just instructing the potential buyer on how best to choose among alternatives.

Similarly, our society is characterized by new costs of coordination. A more complex society means more interdependence and as our ability to interfere or do harm to each other increases, planning and regulating our society becomes more important and more complex. The necessity of interacting with increasing numbers of people and a greater number of social situations involves more travel. Such coordination is not just the prerogative of elites, but necessary for everyone to minimize the possibility of killing ourselves with our own cars, chemicals or radioactive wastes.

Both the need for information and coordination help create a third scarcity—time: the ultimate scarcity for those who wish to consume and experience at an historically unprecedented rate. Those who wish to achieve or conquer in such fashion have a problem which is, in many ways, a luxury to have: not enough time to do all the things they want to do. As Rifkin and others have argued, the computer has helped facilitate our illusion of a world without limitation and has sped up the pace of life even more—so much so that it is beginning to be a political issue.[7]

The desire to experience all things pleasurable, to be needed and involved in as many sets of human experience as possible, is, in many respects, the ultimate greed. Two things must be said about this greed for experience. First, it springs directly from the processes and mentality of economic capitalism, where competition for goods and the production process is divorced from need. It is natural that this progression has taken place. Much as the capitalist accumulates and invests money, we can see that the investment of time by individuals in diverse, pleasurable activity is a capitalist form of self-actualization: a competition with time as the scarce resource to find out who we are by literally recreating ourselves experientially.

Capitalism also sowed the seeds of experientialism by saturating us with unneeded material objects. As the ability of our economic system continually to create needs for new material products begins to find limits, these needs are transferred to leisure experiences. People are sold the experience of gambling, traveling through Europe, viewing other people's sexual activities, going down a wild river on a raft, learning tennis from a Zen Buddhist perspective, changing personal relationships through a multitude of therapies, making wine, and any other experience they will buy. What is produced is a wanderlust, not for other places but for other lives.

THE EMERGING LEISURE SERVICE PROFESSION

The industrial revolution was responsible for an increasing collectivization of work, concentration of power and the increasing organization of many aspects of our lives. The recreation and park movements in both the United States and Canada have historically represented an attempt to counter the negative effects of industrialization: the growth of urban areas without provision for children's play, the decreased contact of people with the natural environment, and the insidiousness of commercial recreation. Thus, it was a movement to reform, and reform takes organization. Yet a classic negative consequence was inevitable: in order to fight for their beliefs, those in the recreation and park movements were often forced to adopt the tactics and mentality of the system which produced the situations they were fighting to correct. To counter those who wished to plan, acquire and develop land for financial profit, parks people have had to maneuver in the same political arena with similar tactics to plan, acquire and develop land for the purpose of leisure. Rather than preserving leisure as it had been in pre-industrial society, it became more organized, more specialized, more scheduled in accordance with the demands of mass production, more influenced by consumerism and the increasing ability of the economy to produce "things" to play with, more fadlike, and so forth.

The movements for public recreation and parks, then, were not centered on freedom of leisure expression but with improved opportunity for participation in several forms of activity, such as outdoor recreation, sports and supervised play which were believed to be superior to the alternatives provided by the urban environment. The movement's founders were missionaries, seeking to convert people to forms of leisure expression they believed to be superior. Informed, rational choice, they believed, would lead people to the activities they advocated. The problems they fought against were real: children left with only the dangerous streets for playgrounds, men and women in the grim factories cut off from nature, the lack of recreation resources among the poor, and urbanites badly in need of exercise.

As these movements became institutionalized, recreation and parks became separate, then a combined function of local government. Both world wars, the depression, and the urban riots of the 1960s all served to heighten the growth of such agencies. Growth has brought a corresponding push for professionalization of employees, including specialized higher education curricula, attempts at certification of practitioners, professional societies and a specialized literature. Such professionalization has tended to minimize the advocacy role of most practitioners, and led to a posture where the recreation and park (leisure service) professional seeks to assume a role of only passively reacting to recreation need or demand, serving all people "equally" and reacting to rather than initiating societal change.

At the same time this professionalization is taking place, there is evidence that public leisure services, like many other functions of government, will have to adjust to the movement toward a sustainable culture. In such a culture, doing "more" will be less important than doing "better". Doing better will mean finding models of living which destroy less of the natural world but build human self-esteem and esteem for others.

PLANNING FUTURE LEISURE SERVICES

How can the emerging leisure service profession respond to the need for a sustainable culture? While the question is complicated, leisure planners will not have to invent things for people to do. They should provide a mechanism to encourage people to do things which are necessary for society but unfunded. In concert with the emerging decentralization of our society, public leisure service planners must abandon the large scale planning mentality which has ignored the quality of neighborhood life and substituted standardization, formality, efficiency and bigness. The leisure service professional is no longer viewed as a public servant, but as a bureaucrat lacking respect for variation in life style and particularly leisure life style. Public leisure services, in short, must reflect rather than create culture.

Each of the previously outlined situations call for some redefinition of leisure services. With regard to work trends, for example, as a higher percentage of our population becomes involved in part-time employment, as the linear life cycle of education, single career and retirement ends, and as leisure or non-work time becomes available in large blocks of time, the purposes or satisfactions from leisure activity may have less to do with refreshment or diversion from work and more to do with activity which is considered worthwhile or satisfying on its own merits. Relations between work and leisure may become far less systematic. The common work leisure cycle may become increasingly differentiated. For the leisure planner, services can no longer be confined to a few common periods of time such as weekday evenings, weekend holidays, and summer vacations.

While the relation of leisure services to work may in some ways be diminished, the impact of continuing inflation will be such that leisure service agencies will have to sponsor more activities which provide a useful end product as well as the pleasure of doing them. Gardening, cooking, crafts with useful end products such as furniture reupholstering will all increase in popularity as will voluntary activities which provide a useful end product for the community and a worthwhile experience for the participant.

The rush to experience in our society which has brought about time deepening, and the attendant diminished spirituality must be countered by the provision of leisure experiences which require commitment, sacrifice and a progression of skills. Timelessness, simplicity, joy and celebration are leisure values which must be promoted in such activities if leisure planners are to actually serve as advocates of leisure. Public leisure service, in short, should be concerned not only with "the pursuit of happiness" but also with "insuring domestic tranquility." Remember those phrases?

Our pluralistic culture makes if difficult for leisure service agencies to "create" culture. Rather, they must reflect the many cultures around them. This cannot be done without intensifying efforts to involve citizens in decision-making using a diversity of formats. This is not to say that the agency should be culturally neutral, having no values other than those interjected by various public lobbies and pressure groups. Rather, the agency cannot afford to be ignorant of public opinion and diversity of opinion among subcultures. Maintaining cultural pluralism requires that a delicate balance be maintained between ignoring differences in culture to the extent that those within specific sub-cultures are either alienated or surrender their identity, and recognizing such difference to the extent that members of society have little in common. Leisure service agencies must seek this balance.

Our heightened self-consciousness may indicate a greater need for opportunities for individuals to lose themselves in play and in service to others. While facilitating service to others may mean serving as a clearinghouse for voluntary action, promoting play will require much effort including redesigning many physical environments so as to encourage it.

In the future many unconventional types of property will be valued for their potential as a leisure resource. Cemeteries, for instance, are already undergoing a transformation from a burial place to one in which people may play. A spokesman for the archdiocese of Chicago said, "The trend is clear. Cemeteries will increasingly have more than one use. They have to. It's just good citizenship. In many areas the cemetery is about the last open green space left."[8]

Churches, schools, museums, shopping centers, and private organizations are increasingly providing recreation and leisure services, and leisure service planners must be aware of them in the planning process.

Streets also have a leisure potential which planners must seek to recognize, particularly in the urban areas. The Chief of Comprehensive Planning of Baltimore City Department of Planning recently pointed out that the conversion of streets into public play areas sometimes appears to be an ideal solution but in doing so the system of space management that exists is disrupted.[9] Since many urban residents, however, center their leisure activity around the sidewalk and street in front of their houses, he suggests the following:

> "Sidewalks should be widened, traffic lanes should be reduced and traffic speed cut down by using such devices as bumps in the road bed. Suitable space should be provided for sitting, playing games, congregating around activity nodes such as bookmobile stops, places for vendors of fruit, fish, vegetables, ice cream. These spaces should be suitably paved, well lighted, equipped with mailboxes, telephone booths, trash containers. They should have trees or some other shading devices."

Additionally, he suggests the demolition of old building in such areas, that windows be introduced into any standing blind walls, that playground equipment should *not* be introduced but that street furniture should be provided so that it can serve a recreation function. Steps should be wide enough for comfortable sitting and playing step ball, firehydrants should be made suitable for leap frog, paving surfaces should be useable by residents, adjoining residents should be encouraged to exercise surveillance over neighborhood playgrounds. Undertaking such steps would represent a revolution in thinking on the part of leisure service planners because it would be, in effect, creating a new leisure environment, rather than dropping a few pieces of playground equipment into a decaying environment and then expressing surprise when such equipment is not used or misused.

In all these undertakings, leisure services must help us to be humble; take ourselves less seriously. Help us attain a new tranquility which can come only with the sense of wholeness, the holiness, of this world. Those leisure services which are of greatest benefit to our world and for which we must plan will be those which help us see why it makes sense to celebrate this world and our very lives.

REFERENCES

1. See, for instance, Best, F., Bosserman, P. and Stern, B. *Changing Values Toward Material Wealth and Leisure in the United States*, Washington, D.C.: NEW, January, 1976.
2. See, for instance, Scheuch, Erwin, "The Time Budget Interview." In: Szalai, A. (Ed.). *The Use of Time—Daily Activities of Urban and Suburban Populations*. The Hague, Netherlands, 1972, p. 77.
3. de Tocqueville, A. *Democracy in America.* New York: Mentor Books, 1956, p. 161.
4. Theodorson, G. A. and Achilles, G. *Modern Dictionary of Sociology*, New York: Thomas Y. Crowell, 1969, p. 246.
5. Huizinga, J. *Homo Ludens: A Study of the Play Element in Culture.* Boston: The Beacon Press, 1950.
6. Bell, D. "The End of Scarcity." *Saturday Review of the Society.* (May) 1973, pp. 49-52.
7. Rifkin, J. Time Wars—The Primary Conflict in Human History. New York: Henry Holt and Company, 1987.
8. "Cemeteries Opening Gates for Recreation." *The New York Times,* (December 10), 1972, pp. 1, 76.
9. Brower, S. N. and Williamson, P. "Outdoor Recreation as a Function of the Urban Housing Environment," *Environment and Behavior,* (September) 1974, pp. 342-3.
10. *Ibid.,* p. 343.

End of Chapter 11

Chapter 12

The Impact of Change on Public Park and Recreation Administration

Joseph J. Bannon

"... living organisms don't just react to conditions – they actively and intelligently act to maintain and change them, as do the cells of the body, in order to keep the Earth at an optimum environment for life."

Mark Nathaniel Mead, et al.[1]

HISTORY AS CHANGE

One does not have to be a history buff to know that it is rarely dull. What is selected by historians and what survives the vicissitudes of time, are a multitude of dramatic events or experiences that are considered noteworthy. While there may be periods of relative calm between major events, change is a constant of all existence, from the minutest living organism to the burgeoning family of humankind. Stasis is often illusory, as nothing is fixed in time, but at some level is experiencing change or transformation. There is so much change and fluctuation, in fact, that from the microscopic level upward, the flux of life is a virtual patterned chaos.

Therefore, it is important not to forget the changes that are constantly occurring in our environments and lives. Change is endemic. There is little point served, therefore, in ignoring or denying transformations. There may be times when nothing seems to be happening and other times when too many things are taking place simultaneously to suit us. The whole point of leisure pursuits is to slow the tempo of activity, to step aside from the flux of life to catch one's bearings or recuperate from too hectic a tempo. But leisure is meant to be a change, a holiday from stress and work, not a permanent retreat. So for those of us in the leisure services professions, change is both a reality and a justification.

American life has always been frantic, though we preserve a mythological past of peace and quiet. Where this peace existed, and for how long, is one of the mysteries of recorded history. The golden Age of Silence never was, though there was room enough in earlier, less mechanized and congested centuries of this republic to allow the sounds of nature to dominate. That domination is swiftly disappearing so not only is change a constant but noise and distraction are also.

The flux of life and the inevitability of change are accompanied by the stresses of noise, 24-hour illumination, and nearly ceaseless action. Our cultural restlessness and our need for stimulation join with other forces of transformation to become almost unendurable and seemingly without purpose at times. Controlling these more noxious tendencies, while acknowledging the benefits of change, becomes a major challenge to address even before we can concentrate on specific changes that may affect us professionally. The change that we experience is different than that of the past-century because change itself is changing! Its hidden workings are becoming more manifest in many critical areas. Change is coalescing rapidly into crises and its impacts are multiplying. The interactions among a multiplicity of changes increase exponentially, hurtling us along, breathless, bewildered, uncertain, and challenged without reprieve. The roots of change have been torn up, and we face not a continuum of development and growth, but an aberration of transformations and challenges that have increasingly taken on global proportions.

The Context of Change

Historically, public administrators have been bureaucrats, which essentially means they are more likely to be reactive than causative.[2] Many bureaucrats lead a dual existence, or have split perceptions, being comprehensively aware of change while at the same time remaining pragmatically or politically passive. (They are also taxpayers, who may harbor ambivalence about funding social services!) When funds are available, public administrators are not so much innovative as expansive in their expenditures. Since leisure services are relatively recent in the public domain, the parks and recreation profession has not endured financial expansion and contraction very often. In the ups and downs of institutional survival we are relative novices, lacking the expertise for dealing with these cycles or fluctuations as have older bureaucracies who have endured them.

An ecological perspective was once an adequate framework for discussion since, while history may (or may not) repeat itself, the environment in which repetition or change occurs has drastically altered. Thus, reading of the many impacts of, say, the Industrial Revolution during the past two centuries, is to view a longer timeframe for event and implication, or cause and effect. Now even the ecological framework seems too limited, too systematic, as the very components of existence that comprise the ecological system are themselves experiencing dysfunctional change or destruction. No longer can we concentrate on examining subsystems or microsystems when the planet itself is ailing, and many of the ecosystems that comprise this earth are experiencing threatening changes.[3] We expand our framework, therefore, from an historical or ecological perspective to a global one where every concept or decision we consider invariably reveals multiple and universal implications and consequences. In addition to a United Nations of countries, we desperately need a United Nations of nature, to ensure that our continued uses and misuses of our habitat do not prove disastrous. The magnitude of these global problems is magnified by lack of awareness or myopia, so we are better served stretching our imaginations to encompass global systems that define and sustain our lives, both as professionals and private citizens. We should become world citizens in the finest sense of that term; conscious, concerned, ethical and wise, i.e., worldly.

Affluence and boundless resources have been an integral part of our experience. However, we have begun to sense that the older generation's fortunes were better and more secure than the younger's, rather than the traditional view that the lives of successive generations are always improving. The constraints we all face at all ages and levels, are no longer monetary, nor simply nonrenewable resources but climatic and natural dysfunctions that make affluence and abundance less meaningful, or even ironic. What good is financial ease, or ample operating funds, or discretionary income, if the air and soil are contaminated, the trees are destroyed at unparalleled rates, and worldwide economic systems are teetering on tightropes?[4]

MAJOR CHALLENGES

Awareness of many of the challenges we face can be traced to the end of World War II, though certainly the international and cultural tendencies were present for several centuries. But, by limiting our focus to recent decades, we can clarify the challenges that directly affect the administration of public recreation and park services. There is perhaps one great hope in all of these assessments, and that is that we realize—perhaps before it is too late—that each of us counts, that individual actions, whether personal or professional, accrue to create problems or solutions, resulting in crises or genuine stewardship of the finite resources we share and are responsible for.

Planetary Degradation

Our terms shift from environmental deterioration to those that are more alarming, and are meant to alert us to the seriousness of the situation. Our profession is at the heart of this crisis, though unfortunately not in a powerful position. That is, we hold or exercise little control ourselves over questionable manipulations of these resources. It is essential we go beyond being merely custodians of natural resources and seek to be guardians as well. As guardians, we would then be obliged to better understand the scientific and legal aspects of resource use (and abuse) as well as demonstrate an ecological perspective in all our professional activities. This control should not be forfeited to other professionals. Since much control over natural resources rests with various governmental units, we should seek to influence their policies and decisions, instead of observing and unquestioningly implementing them. Otherwise, we conspire in the accelerating destruction of the natural resources so essential to our profession. One must become either part of the solution or remain a part of the problem itself. The recreation and park profession is in the belly of the whale, reacting too often in piecemeal fashion to crises of a planetary nature because of a tradition of specialization, avoidance of politically and economically contentious issues, and reluctance to view mandates comprehensively.

A more global perspective is essential, and in some ways is easier to grasp because it is global. Rather than examining the multitude of effects a decision has on the immediate environment, we should school ourselves first to consider its broader impact. In many respects, this wider vision clearly reveals the best decision, rather than getting bogged down in endless detail. It is often a matter of right or wrong, harmful or useful, where value judgements—when applied to more planetary implications—are not as obscure.[5]

In most discussions of problem solving, one is cautioned to deal with the actual problem and not its symptoms. Of course, some symptoms are of such magnitude it is difficult to treat them as such, dealing with them in their own right as serious sub-problems. But the effort must be made—especially with ecological/environmental issues that have broader impacts—to widen the perspective within which a problem or its symptoms is perceived. This broad viewpoint is critical since planetary issues demand an equally planetary response. No more is each agency or unit an independent "Balkan State," but each is truly part of the global village.

What we also lack as a profession and as a society is an ethic of responsibility about individual actions, especially their impact on large systems or communities. The roots of this carelessness or ignorance are deep in our economic and social history which make it difficult for individuals to affect large systems in unselfish ways. We must realize that many actions are not private, especially when enacted in the public sphere. As public administrators, we can begin to outwardly portray less the behaviors of the rugged individualist and more the qualities of the conscious ecologist. Since our profession is responsible for many natural and cultural resources, we are in an excellent position to slow the impact of deterioration.

Financial Constraints

"One hundred ten billion, one hundred ten billion. B, billion."[6]

That was Senator John Glenn's attempt to drive home the huge cost of cleaning up the government's nuclear weapons manufacturing sites. "Clearly, the public does not accept the probalistic risk numbers. They just don't understand them."[7] That was Dr. Richard J. Slember's way of discussing strange, often incomprehensible numbers. Slember is vice president and general manager of the energy systems unit at Westinghouse, one of the nation's two major private nuclear reactor manufacturers.

Numbers are actually becoming more abstract and in some respects meaningless as they are difficult to comprehend. They are too large, so they are either ignored or used to serve merely symbolic or obfuscating purposes. Whether funds are available or not, whatever their magnitude, the financial deliberations of government continue luring us into believing that financial constraints are themselves illusory. On the one hand, we are flabbergasted at the amount of government debt, and on the other we are astonished at the level of ongoing governmental commitments—as if lawmakers had forgotten what they had been previously concerned about. Thus, it is easy for the parks and recreation profession—which unfortunately some regard as quite expendable—to lose sight of the fact there is a serious financial dislocation. Perhaps government finance is the charade of the emperor with no clothes. We should not be accomplices in that deception, or wag fingers about it, but continue our efforts to become more innovative and financially self-sustaining.

If there is global economic depression ahead as some predict,[8] our time is better spent now preparing for that possibility rather than raiding the treasury. Along with economic trends, a decade of political and social conservatism has produced government officials increasingly reluctant to finance social and human services at the rate they once did. Although minimal welfare increases are obtained after much struggle, it is not likely that substantial funding will be forthcoming from the public sector for leisure services. There is plenty of money, however, in the private sector for recreation and parks and related services. As our economy becomes more service oriented, as two paycheck families and well-paid young professionals seek leisure services, more people are prepared to pay for them, witness the proliferation of private leisure services that form an industry in the billions of dollars. The money is there, but is being spent directly by citizens seeking their own recreational activities, rather than paying taxes for public programs which have lost appeal and support.

Consequently, we must continue the trend of charging fees for our services and programs, offer programs comparable to those in the private sector, discontinue programs that attract only a limited clientele, and be more imaginative and innovative in anticipating the types of programs the public would respond to and be willing to pay for. In other words, be more competitive and entrepreneurial in the provision of leisure and recreation services.

Finally, the loss of public funding from property taxes or at least its drastic decrease this past decade,[9] is a long-needed reform, despite the immediate hardship imposed on and threat to leisure services. At such times, the habit of historical perspective is valuable, not only to weather the storm, but also to comprehend socioeconomic change, its inevitability, and where we might best concentrate our energies and the resources that remain. That requires soul searching and critical thinking about our mandates and missions.

Civil Rights and Gender Equality

Although economic constraints might be expected to retard the momentum of
other social changes, it is historically significant that the pressure for rights and
gender equality continues unabated, not dampened in the least by the loss of
funds. The greater the financial and ecological constraints, the more minority
groups and women seek an expanded role in social and economic decision
making. For the first time, these groups will not recede in the face of any
"larger" crisis, since many believe the roots of such crises lie with those who
are presently in power at all levels of society.[10] I recall the prediction of the
American Indian sage, who said his people would regain their land once the
white man had fouled his nest sufficiently to make it uninhabitable for himself.
Their historic patience is based on a faith in natural justice, in retributive justice
actually: that their due would become more evident through time. Their
expulsion from positions of power and influence, and that of women and other
minority groups as well, is reflected in the impoverished destiny of this naturally
rich continent. The viewpoints of these apparent outsiders are essential to our
well-being. Any public administrator would be committing professional suicide
to pretend otherwise.

During the 1960s, we were often criticized for failing to serve all groups
equally.[11] We were also questioned about the lack of minorities and women on
our staffs or in leadership positions in the profession. Without governmental
demands for affirmative actions, our employment record would be even worse.
Sexual, racial, and ethnic groups must be represented in our organizations in
comparable proportions to their numbers in society. Though many object to
quotas, there is no surer way of assuring an equal and just number of minorities
in the leisure services.

We must also give up the belief that minorities will automatically share and
assimilate our goals and values. As businesses diversify their product mix to
make themselves less vulnerable to market fluctuations, we must diversify our
staff and leadership to make ourselves more responsive to the actual conditions
in which we live and work. Perhaps the most important impact on our organization and values will be the influence of women. There are few women filling
leisure service positions presently,[12] though this is a career that attracts many
women to university study, and a profession that serves females in abundance.
Not only must we actively recruit women for leadership positions, we must
overcome any deep-seated male attitudes of superiority.

The Workforce

A major challenge for many public or private organizations lies in their relationship with and responsiveness to employees at all levels. In addition to client
satisfaction, leisure service administrators must now concern themselves with
employee satisfaction as well. Employees are complex; they bring their values,

aspirations, and problems to work. Organizations have increasingly begun to contend with these aspects of worker demands, from the executive suite to the mailroom. At all levels of the organizations, administrators are encountering new work values, as dissatisfaction with traditional hierarchal relationships increases, and as workers expect more monetary and nonmonetary benefits in the workplace.[13]

This change is basically a generational effect, although the influence of gender and ethnicity values are involved as well. While the growth rate of the overall labor force is slowing, those with these new work values are peaking in numbers. In addition to sheer numbers, the "baby boom" generation is also considered the best-educated workforce in history. While education certainly constitutes a great asset, it also poses a challenge to entrenched hierarchies.

Employee dissatisfaction is no longer confined to blue-collar workers. Groups of nontraditional workers continue to form or join white-collar unions.[14] If we are to attract and keep employees in public service, the response of leisure service administrators must be toward increased organizational democracy and harmony.

Salaries in the private sector are sometimes appreciably higher than those offered in the public sector. Many public leisure agencies face difficulties in staffing as a result. In some regions, the National Park Service offers salary differentials to attract workers, and even these are not sufficient to compete with private businesses and agencies, especially for clerical, secretarial, and computer staff. The combination of a traditional top-down style of management and noncompetitive salaries is not likely to keep our profession at the forefront of change in the working force.

The Tentacles of Technology

In response to challenges of worldwide economic and military competition, development and implementation of new technologies is expected to continue accelerating for the foreseeable future. Automation and technology are not always threats in themselves, but are harmful and potentially destructive when used to displace workers or threaten community survival for purposes of retaining or regaining a perhaps ephemeral economic superiority (e.g., substantial profits). Workers are often told that automated computers and robots will ease and simplify their life, granting greater leisure, while at the same time these mechanical inventions take away jobs and threaten the survival of communities. Ease and leisure, then, become meaningless and bitter compensations for such losses. Such losses are a daily reality in this country. The explanations offered are that inflation and reduced productivity have caused these grave problems, with companies helplessly at the mercy of an all-powerful economy; companies, incidentally, that are rarely hurt financially as they displace workers with technology.

The positions are clear, then, between those who seek to rely on advanced technologies in the quest of a competitive edge commercially—despite the cost to individuals and communities—and those who wish to minimize the impact of displacement technologies through compromise, modernization of existing plants, decentralization, shared decision making, reduced work-time, and shared power and profits in the operation of businesses and institutions. To know that eventually most offices and factories may be highly automated is not to accede to that probability, since alternative futures exist if enough citizens consider hegemony (either domestically or internationally) as too socially and humanly expensive to obtain, until we are ready.

Today's workers are likely to resist these changes because of their generally higher level of education, and the comparative leisure that permits them to think and confer, enabling them to perceive and comprehend the forces that contend in reshaping a post-industrial society. In essence, the struggle is to reconcile being economically successful (money-making) competitors, internationally, with having a more authentic, enriched, naturally paced existence, where machines are not dominant.

There are two aspects of technology that will likely continue as challenges for the remainder of this century: the relationship of technological change and innovation to human needs, and the impact of technology on natural systems. Experience with computers or telecommunications systems ranges from exceptional convenience to an invasion of privacy. If we object to the invasion of privacy, which the computer certainly facilitates, we must more directly object to the agency behind the equipment, rather than attack technology *per se*. Myopia in the use of any technology poses grave threats to our natural environment as well as our psychological and physical well-being. Since people control technology, the responsibility is ours to safely and humanely use such unprecedented technical resources. Technology may help us efficiently perform some tasks. It may also distract us from some tasks. Automated equipment is at the service and option of an agency. While newcomers often become enamored of these technologies, we should not be enslaved by such machines: they all have an "off" button.

Ethics and Accountability

Finally, public concern with ethics and behavior in business and the professions continues unabated, including the quality, necessity, and cost of goods and services. Private and public organizations operate far more in the public eye than ever before and are increasingly accountable for their products, decisions, service and behavior. It is becoming more difficult, especially for public organizations, to ignore the demand for accountability. Although as a profession we have a good reputation among lawmakers and citizens thus far, this image may suffer as pressures mount, or as we are tempted to cut corners and make deals to ensure our survival.

Since we are closely aligned with other social and human services, our ethical positions must be that the mix of social and human services presently available is essential in any advanced, civilized society. It is difficult to walk the line between political awareness and involvement, seriously depleted resource, and the maintenance of high operational standards. Whether we deserve public mistrust or not, we will be sure to earn it for any flaws, given the prevalence of governmental scandals, if our behavior is not above reproach.

THE ADMINISTRATOR'S RESPONSE

Leisure services administrators must be able to withstand enormous conflicts and pressures. This prospect poses more than a dilemma for managers; it represents the ongoing reality of managing within uncertainty. Apart from planetary or global cataclysms of which we run a serious risk, the next few decades will undoubtedly see the culmination of many issues raised in recent decades, as well as the emergence of other issues barely evident now. Those issues will affect park and recreation administrators just as they affect other organizations and institutions, public and private. The provision of leisure services, generally considered a positive cultural component in an advanced society, in no way frees our profession from the confusion of social, political, technological, and ethical pressures brought to bear on most organizations these days. It is naive to believe a public agency can avoid the political and monetary pressures private enterprise faces. In many ways, our continued accountability to taxpayers keeps us in the limelight.

Change is common, particularly in industrialized, competitive societies. The above challenges of ecology, finance, prejudices, labor and technology have been with us for decades. The administrative qualities needed to manage organizations in transition must include at least comprehension of these and other challenges. At the practical level, to successfully administer an organization, an administrator needs the following.

- Excellent organizational and interpersonal communications, reflecting a humanistic approach to administration. These skills include the ability to create workplaces that stimulate individual motivation and achievement. It is a waste of an administrator's time to ceaselessly motivate others. Through effective, empathetic communication skills, an administrator should counsel, coach, and inspire others to undertake their own self-development, and ensure a work environment that in no way opposes or contradicts more humanistic or personal values.

- A science based administration, using accountability systems such as PERT, Management-by-Objective, Zero-Based Budgeting, systems analysis, or other managerial models and programs. These management and accountability systems can be integrated with computers and other automated devices. In a time of increased accountability, the more so phisticated and accurate the planning and record-keeping systems, the greater the chances for improved performance and documentation of needs.

- A broad, eclectic intellect, not simply technical or administrative. Although technology and automated systems are important, administrators should avoid becoming over-involved with software or hardware. An administrator should obtain an overall knowledge of equipment and systems in an organization without gaining a specialist's comprehension of these technologies. The tendency to become an administrative technician should be avoided, as knowledge of machines often draws one away from concern with people, long-range goals, and prime administrative tasks.

- Understanding that what was once considered long-range planning must be treated in shorter segments. If forecasting is to be more meaningful, administrators must limit their time horizons while at the same time expanding their imaginative and speculative viewpoints.

- Proficiency in the use of evaluation techniques for staff and service performance, which are necessary for accountability and productivity assessments. An administrator does not have to use intuition or personal judgment in measuring an employee's ability or obtaining an operations evaluation of a service. Such personal assessments are both arbitrary and subject to poor judgment. They are also subject to challenge, legally and otherwise. Evaluation and accountability, especially in public organizations, go hand in hand. The more select and controlled the evaluation methods, the more likely administrators will avoid conflict with emergent work values, or a quality-conscious, resource-limiting public.

- Appreciation of research and readiness to contribute to and encourage original research in leisure behavior, reducing conflicts between theory and practice in parks, recreation, and leisure. While secondary data are not, in themselves, second-rate, there is a clear need for encouraging intellectual leadership and creativity in research.

The logical focus for such research is within the profession, not relying so heavily on other disciplines. As opportunities or discretionary income for leisure grow, our profession will be called upon to assess the phenomenon of people's diverse needs and responses. To bridge the gap between academics and practitioners, we need skillful and tactful interpreters of research. The snobbery of the intellectual, and the myopia of the hands-on practitioner, have no place in a progressive organization.

The most valuable skills during any transitional period are adaptive behavior and innovation. During periods of resource constraint, what is important as everything else shrinks is that our imaginations expand. While there are limited funds for traditional services and programs, it is surprising how much money is available to support new and innovative approaches. Unfortunately, many of these ideas and proposals are coming from private businesses and private contracts, or from administrators and employees who desert public agencies for the more lucrative atmosphere and salaries of private enterprise. Thus, the need for imagination and innovation in the face of change cannot be over-emphasized.

For this purpose, historical and intellectual perspectives are essential for effective, adaptive behavior. To understand what is happening at any point, one has to comprehend what has happened before, what has led up to or even caused circumstances to change or evolve. Comprehension is an intellectual habit, best acquired in youth, and invaluable in an administrator. Nothing happens in a vacuum, but is related and interrelated to a variety of factors and circumstances. It is not enough to accept what other present as causes, one must determine these for oneself, or at least go beyond simplistic analyses and rationales.

Although political realities are unavoidable, the larger constraint that parks and recreation faces as a profession is broader than politics, involving a planetary and ethical framework that takes up beyond self-interest and reactionary fear, that seeks to avoid anxiety, defensiveness or political conservatism. Change is inevitable, a form of temporal evolution essential to any vital existence. We should not regret what time has brought to bear, but rather confront the realities of the present day with the weight of history ever in mind, an inspiring burden in many ways if one has taken a proper measure of the centuries; taken the time, that is, to comprehend the forces of change in one's own time.

REFERENCES

1. Mead, M. "Whither the Trees." *Solstice*, 4(34)(Dec.-Jan. 1989), p. 65.
2. Bannon, J. *Leisure Resources: Its Comprehensive Planning.*
    Champaign, Illinois: Management Learning Laboratories, 1985.
3. McKibben, B. *The End of Nature.* New York: Random House, 1989.
4. Amin, S.; Arrighi, G.; Frank, A. G.; and Wallerstein, I. *Dynamics of Global Crisis.* New York: Monthly Review Press, 1982.
5. Bannon, *Op. Cit.*
6. In an interview regarding revised Department of Energy projections of the cost of cleaning up the nation's nuclear weapon production facilities.
7. Quoted in the *New York Times,* October 2, 1988.
8. Amin, *Op.Cit.*
9. Deppe, T. *Management Strategies in Financing Parks and Recreation.* New York: Wiley, 1983.
10. Bannon, *Op. Cit.*
11. Bannon, *Op. Cit.*
12. Bannon, J.; Busser, J.; and Lang, J. *An Analysis of Attitudes, Opinions, and Behaviors of Management Personnel in Leisure Service Organizations: Stress Management for Leisure Service Personnel.* Champaign, Illinois: University of Illinois, Department of Leisure Studies, 1986.
13. Bannon, J. and Unzicker, C. *An Analysis of Attitudes, Opinions, and Behaviors of Management Personnel in Leisure Service Organizations: Motivation — How It Functions in Leisure Service Personnel.* Champaign, Illinois: University of Illinois, Department of Leisure Studies, 1986.
14. United States Office of Personnel Management; Office of Employee, Labor, and Agency Relations, *A Survey of Union Representation Provisions in Federal Labor Agreements.* Washington: The Office of Personnel Management; Springfield, Virginia: For sale by National Technical Information Service, 1984.

End of Chapter 12

Chapter 13

Urban Leisure Services: Reshaping a Good Thing

Geoffrey Godbey

Urban park, recreation, and leisure services have a long and proud history in North America. These services have reflected a range of ideas concerning how urban life could be made better. Basically, the many social ecological interest groups which have made up the parks, recreation and leisure movements have attempted to bring about reform designed to improve the quality of everyday life for urban residents.[1]

For those interested in a career in urban leisure services, the good news is that urban areas continue to be in need of reform and our planet's inhabitants continue to move inexorably toward cities. Public leisure service agencies have been and continue to be the best value for money that urban government has to offer. For a sum as paltry as $15 per-year/per-resident, a huge range of leisure facilities and programs have been available to the public which, otherwise, would have been out of their reach. At their best, urban leisure services have expanded horizons, promoted a sense of community and contributed to our physical and emotional fitness.

Urban leisure services have a proud history. Their obvious successes, in the recent as well as distant past, are praiseworthy.[2] There are, however, a number of problems, relatively recent in origin, which need to be addressed and gradually alleviated. In addition, there is one central challenge.

PROBLEMS OF RECENT ORIGIN

Transition to a Close-Ended System

Administrators of public urban leisure services became accustomed to a model of open-ended growth in the 1960s, as did most of society, and became skilled in planning, acquiring, implementing and developing leisure services. They did not, however, get used to maintaining, conserving, incrementally changing, retrenching, protecting, substituting, or optimizing. Now they, like the rest of society, are having to learn. This is a particularly difficult task since federal legislation of the 1960s increased the agencies' hardware and infrastructure with no provision for maintaining it. Today, when maintenance is needed, local governments are often unable to supply the funds and are unwilling to seek more taxes to do so. Legislators will propose laws to establish new parks but not to maintain old ones. At the same time, "demand" for many kinds of leisure services is increasing from a public which is often not willing to either (a) pay more taxes, or (b) do it themselves. What is a poor leisure service administrator to do? The transition from quantitative growth to maintenance and qualitative growth is difficult and involves a change in basic mentality. The official American Prayer Book contains only one word—"more"—and leisure is the altar at which most praying is done.

Location of Park Land

During the last three decades there has been a tremendous acquisition and development of parks at the local, state, and national levels. A number of factors have brought this about, including mandatory dedication laws and state, provincial, and federal legislation providing partial funding for such acquisition. While this process has been, on the average, quite worthwhile, it has resulted in at least three problems: 1) Acquisition of cheap land away from population centers: 2) the dedication of flood plain and other undesirable land for local parks; and 3) disproportionate development of new parks in affluent areas due to matching fund requirements for cities in federal and state legislation.[3] Many parks in urban areas, therefore, are located on the least desirable land while state or provincial parks are not often accessible to the urban resident. Poor cities have benefitted least from federal and state park acquisition funds since they often could not provide matching dollars. In general, the mentality in regard to acquisition has been to think about how much land, rather than how useful or how beautiful the land was.

Inappropriate Use of Leisure Services to Address Social Problems

Because public leisure services are comparatively inexpensive, and because they can be altered quickly, they have often been used inappropriately by government to address other social problems. Perhaps the most dramatic example of this was during the urban riots of the late 1960s and early 1970s, when the Federal Government suddenly pumped money into the cities for summer recreation for inner-city residents.[4] The fundamental problems of such residents were housing, health care, education, transportation and, of course, employment. Recreation and park departments, however, were often the first to respond—a sometimes reluctant agent of social control.

The same argument can be made for the Comprehensive Education and Training Act and other public employment or so-called "job training" programs. Recreation and park agencies were persuaded to utilize so many of these temporary employees that, by 1975, CETA workers constituted 15 percent of all full-time leisure service employees at the municipal level. Never mind that there was precious little money for training. Let them cut brush. CETA employees sometimes replaced regular staff employees, often with disappointing results.

In less dramatic ways, public leisure services are used as tokens in political wheeling and dealing, particularly when some other requested commodity can not be supplied. While recreation and park administrators have often resisted such efforts, their resistance has frequently been futile.

Assignment of Urban Leisure Concerns to Federal Land-Managing Agencies

Federal involvement in urban recreation, park and leisure services, such as supplying technical information, administering federal funding programs, developing standards, and providing direct technical assistance has been entrusted largely to land managing agencies such as the United States Forest Service, National Park Service, Army Corps of Engineers, Bureau of Land Management, and others. Even the Bureau of Outdoor Recreation and its successor, the Heritage Conservation and Recreation Service, were staffed primarily by former personnel from federal land-managing agencies. Such staff were often largely ignorant of urban recreation and parks and displayed an anti-urban bias. Their background in recreation and parks was usually limited to situations in which recreation was the secondary use of large isolated land masses which had some other primary purpose. They were not often interested in the inner-city resident, the programmatic use of recreation areas, or establishment of high density recreation areas. Also, they generally did not want to work with other federal agencies (and vice-versa), let alone the private sector. No wonder the redevelopment of urban water fronts has gone on, largely successfully, without them. Their leadership has hindered urban leisure services.

Separation of Design, Program, and Maintenance Functions within Urban Agencies

One of the unfortunate consequences of attempts at professionalization of urban leisure agencies has been separation of design, programming, and maintenance of recreation areas. Architects and landscape architects have often worked in isolation as have recreation programmers and maintenance staff. Maintenance personnel are perhaps the most isolated, often relegated to a separate equipment storage area with a supervisor who occasionally make trips into the "main office." This method of operation has been a catastrophe. Maintenance, today, is often the number one urban leisure problem and it has to be approached in an integrated manner with the participation of all staff. Designers and programmers of urban park and recreation areas have to understand the maintenance implications of what they do before they do it. While survey after survey shows that the quality of maintenance and safety are the two biggest concerns of urban park users, the process of maintaining areas and facilities is not often systematically reexamined in terms of integration within the agency.

Emphasis on Activity Rather Than Process

Among the most serious kind of cultural lag exhibited by urban leisure service agency staff has been the tendency to think of what they are providing as "activities" or "facilities" rather than to conceive of their role as facilitators of a process which involves an activity or facility. The commercial sector has often understood this much better. "Going swimming" does not only constitute merely getting into a pool and swimming because one likes to swim. It happens for a myriad of reasons: a person is bored, or hot, or a competitive swimmer, or wants to be with girlfriends, or is forced to go by parents, or because there is a snack bar at the pool, or to watch the kids, or practice. The experience of swimming often includes driving an automobile, eating, drinking, sun-bathing, sleeping, reading, standing in water, card games, gossip, flirting, racing, floating, baby-sitting, snorkeling, listening to music, etc. Swimming is many activities done for many reasons and the design of the swimming area and the programming for that area must recognize this, but often such recognition is absent. While the British have begun, for instance, putting day-care facilities, pubs, sauna baths, and other amenities in their sports centers, our public sector has often avoided this approach. Leisure is a process, a complex process, and it must be intelligently thought through, rather than thinking, "Let's dump one more swimming pool in the ground at Location X." What does it mean that many "swimmers" spend more time out of the water than in? What does it mean that many swimmers who are in the water are more likely to be standing and talking than swimming? Leisure service professionals must know what these situations mean from a design, management, programming, and maintenance standpoint—to say nothing of marketing.

Inadequately Prepared Employees

The growth of employment in public leisure services has frequently taken place with little concern for or understanding of what these positions could or should entail. In many cases, no knowledgeable person or organization has "interpreted" such positions to employers. In other cases, employers simply did not care. This situation has resulted in a frequent pattern of employing staff with no appropriate post-secondary education, employing staff with low quality education in recreation or related areas, and employing staff based on partisan political motives. All of these patterns have resulted in problems.

There is a great tendency to think that urban leisure services are staffed by professionals. Such, to a great extent, is not the case. Appointments to urban leisure service departments are often made based upon partisan political motives. A survey of U.S. local recreation, park, and leisure service agencies by Don Henkel and me (1977) found that only 40 percent of full-time staff in local leisure service agencies had post high-school education specializing in recreation and parks or a related area.[5] Appointments to big-city agencies are even more disproportionately made as rewards by elected officials, regardless of the aptitude, educational qualifications or experience of the candidate. This is true in such cities as New York, Boston, and Chicago, and also in smaller communities. Parks and recreation is often the dumping-ground agency for the loyal party member who lasts in the job as long as his or her party is in office.

Civil Service sometimes helps the situation but can make it worse. In many cases, Civil Service exams are selectively administered, subjectively judged, and otherwise used to select the applicant that the political official in question wants.

In spite of problems of patronage, post-secondary education in parks and recreation has increasingly taken on the responsibility for professional preparation. Curricula grew rapidly through the 1960s and 1970s until an estimated 40,000 students were majoring in this academic area in the United States and Canada. Unfortunately, this growth often took place without a corresponding growth of qualified faculty. Universities sometimes viewed recreation and park curricula as an inexpensive program to initiate, which would compensate for declining enrollments in other areas, such as physical education. While the National Recreation and Park Association and Society of Park and Recreation Educators have made valiant efforts to bring about a meaningful accreditation program, to be accredited, a curriculum must have staff which often were graduates of the very second-rate curricula being evaluated. In any event, such accreditation is after the fact. The huge growth in curricula is over and natural market forces are now beginning to bring about declining enrollments.

Many recreation and park curricula have been intellectually sub-par, staffed by professors who have made a career of being "nice folks." It's important to be nice, but it's not enough. Curricular content is often a disgrace, utilizing a small body of knowledge to generate ten or twenty courses where three of four would do. Recreation and park curricula in urban areas have sometimes been diploma mills. Only a handful of curricula have had the desperately needed interdisciplinary involvement to adequately prepare students.

While increasingly needed, comparatively little continuing education is currently available for personnel of leisure services, and what does exist is often attended by those who need it least. A great flurry of research is underway, but much of it is suspect and almost none of it will be read by or interpreted to practitioners.

THE CENTRAL CHALLENGE

The previous problems, while vexing, are ones upon which we can incrementally improve. One other problem, however—really a challenge—confronts the
field. If it is not quickly dealt with, the previously mentioned problems of urban
leisure services won't matter much. This problem or challenge is central: to
rethink what we are about. To develop a better understanding of how leisure has
changed our society and react accordingly. The role of leisure in our society has
gone, in many instances, from a search for catharsis to pleasure to meaning. As
this has happened, leisure behavior has become of increasing importance to the
individual. This seems an obvious point. We spend a higher proportion of our
money for leisure than previously, rate it a higher component of life satisfaction,
increasingly use it as religious or spiritual expression, and find its contribution
to our self definition has grown greatly. Our field has grown so used to proselytizing about the importance of leisure that we seem not to have noticed that the
public believes it too, often more than we do. I remember once attending a conference where we all sat in the work-like atmosphere of the meeting room, our
name tags in place, listening to one more speaker drone on about the importance
of leisure and how we had to educate the public. Outside that room (it was a
beautiful day in the city), people were going to a nearby museum, picnicking at
a public plaza, sunbathing, playing tennis, running, talking and flirting in a
cocktail lounge, painting a picture of City Hall, sight-seeing, playing an accor-
dion, etc. We sat in our meeting room imploring each other to spread the good
news about leisure.

There are a number of indicators that urban leisure services will become
increasingly important to the public during the 1990s and that this increased
importance will bring about the need for changes in both the philosophy and
methods of operation of such agencies. One of the indicators of such importance was the findings of research done by the Presidents' Commission on
Americans Outdoors which found overwhelming evidence that the public was
willing to pay more for better park and recreation programs and facilities. "The
public responded that they would support additional taxes for some functions
and also pay higher user fees for others, evidencing a strong recognition of the
value of our programs."[6]

Not only is there survey evidence, but financial evidence as well. In California, for instance, where the tax-cutting revolution began under the name of
Proposition 13, voters recently approved the two biggest bonds for park,
recreation, open space and wildlife in the state's history. Between 1982 and
1986, a study prepared for the Academy of Park and Recreation Administration
found that 86 percent of 49 bond issues put to voters throughout the nation
passed.

Even at the federal level there is, at this writing, a move to reestablish the Land and Water Trust Fund as a self-sustaining trust. Since this has been the most important legislation allowing for the planning, acquisition and development of urban parks and outdoor recreation areas, the movement to reestablish this legislation is of fundamental importance to the well being of urban leisure services.

There is, in summary, reason to believe that urban leisure services are becoming more important in the eyes of the public and, while there is unlikely to be huge increases in spending for local government functions, parks and recreation will fare well in competing for resources with other functions of government if they can change with the times.

A number of situations account for this support. Children have become the new underclass in our culture and there is increased recognition of their plight. More than one child in five lives in poverty. Obesity among children is at an all-time high. Almost one-half will reside in a one-parent family before they are eighteen. They are often not competitive with their counterparts in other industrial nations in math and science attainment. Children are emerging as one of the most important political issues of the 1990s and urban recreation and park departments will be called upon to address children's needs in new ways.

The plight of children is just one manifestation of a more venerable society. We, as a nation, are getting older, the gap between rich and poor is increasing, more of us live alone, more of us are addicted, more of us live in urban areas. Government, particularly the Federal Government, has, in its recent policies, largely failed to recognize this fact. The majority of women, for instance, work outside the home for pay, yet public schools still operate as though a parent will be at home at four o'clock on a weekday and all the time during the months of June, July and August. Urban parks and recreation, in the 1990s, is going to be required to fulfill a function which has been talked about in our literature for many years—enabling. This will mean dealing with the public as it exists, not as government thinks it should. Enabling means that the mandate for such agencies will be broader. It means that the agency will need to be concerned with things like transportation; day care for both children and elderly (who live with their working children); highly technical legal matters concerning the ownership, use and rights to land for recreation; leisure counselling and education; closer interactions with the hotel and restaurant industry in conjunction with special events, tourism, and holiday celebrations; working relationships with numerous organizations who will increasingly use recreation areas and facilities as groups rather than an individuals (such groups will be as diverse as support groups for those with various illnesses, gay and lesbian organizations, members of Trout Unlimited, and members of labor union.)

While the enabling function may prevail, urban leisure services in the 1990s will increasingly be involved in the financial well being of cities and those who work for such agencies will need increasing sophistication concerning finance, marketing, and economic theory. Economic "enabling" will mean that many of those who work in urban recreation and park systems today will need retraining. Leisure experience will be an increasingly significant component of the economic well being of cities in the 1990s and recreation and park agencies will respond to this situation or be replaced.

If leisure is of increasing importance, a response is demanded by leisure service agencies and that response is to provide not more, but better. That response is to quit worrying about how many acres can be acquired and see if all of the litter can be removed from what exists; see if the elms can be saved; see if flowers can be kept in every public place.

That response is to stop sponsoring programs merely because people will participate—people participate more in watching television than any other leisure activity but most don't think it very important. That response is to stop hiring employees just because they have the right degree or will be dependable. In hiring employees, look for vision, ideas, curiosity, and a concern for the lives of other people.

If leisure is important, it will require cutting back some services which can't be done right (and taking the heat for it) and improving what remains. If leisure is important, it will mean that a constant dialogue with the public is necessary whether or not the public is interested in talking.

A new approach must be taken to judging the success of leisure services which allows for judgements about the qualitative aspects of the service by those who have experienced them or could experience them. One example of an approach to doing this is Importance-Performance Analysis, which starts by identifying what features or attributes of the given leisure service are important to an individual, having them rate these features in terms of comparative importance, and then rating them in terms of how well the leisure service "supplied" these features.[7] Such an approach allows the agency to understand what the participant thinks is important and how closely agency provision of the service corresponds to what is important.

It must be said once again that if leisure is important, urban leisure service organizations must play an enabling and facilitating role rather than one of direct service provision. This means, among other things, entering the consciousness of other organizations within the urban community and seeking to coordinate or cooperate with their efforts. The synergetic leisure service, in which many organizations contribute their resources, will have to become commonplace.

If leisure is important, then leisure services must reflect the unique characteristics of the city; no model can be transported. As Cranz points out in her remarkable book The *Politics of Park Design*, urban parks:

"... have been diffused from city to city and region to region through such media as annual reports, congresses, manuals, national professional associations, and universities. The process has led to design criteria with little living relation to particular cultures, climates, or people. Its antithesis, designing with local roots, could introduce regional character into the line of park design options."[8]

An urban park, in other words, doesn't really mean much until you put it into a specific environment. Designing a park is not a matter of technology, but one of cultural discovery. It distresses me to see essentially the same "fitness trail" in Sao Paulo, Brazil and State College, Pennsylvania; the same playground in Melbourne, Australia, and Philadelphia, Pennsylvania. If leisure is important, facilities cannot be "tacked on" to the environment.

In every post-industrial society, a decentralizing process is taking place, the nation state is an increasingly obsolete economic, political, and social institution, and a differentiation process is at work in terms of regions and sub-regions of the country. This process has profound implications for urban leisure services. Administrators must work from data concerning their own local area and this information must deal with qualitative aspects of local residents' lives as well as quantitative ones. Leisure services in urban areas are going to have to start from the specifics of people's lives and that means having administrators who understand what everyday life is like in each housing project in their community, understanding why old ladies go to the annual flower show, and what percentage of the "runners" of the city are interested in minimarathons.

Public leisure services in urban areas can seek to change the small problems they face incrementally. But the big issue, that leisure is now of central importance and that quality of experience is everything, demands an immediate response. In responding, urban leisure services must be recreated—and the process of recreation must be different in each urban area.

REFERENCES

1. See, for instance: Cranz, G. *The Politics of Park Design—A History of Urban Parks In America*. Cambridge, Massachusetts: MIT Press, 1982, p. 250. Dulles, F. R. *A History of Recreation*. New York: Appleton Century-Crofts, 1965. Duncan, M. "Back to Our Radical Roots." In *Recreation and Leisure: Issues In an Era of Change*, Chapter 25, this volume. McFarland, E. *The Development of Public Recreation In Canada*. Ottawa: Canadian Parks/Recreation Association, 1970.

2. For an accounting of the benefits of public recreation and parks, see *Winning Support for Parks and Recreation*, by the National Park Service, State College, Pennsylvania: Venture Publishing, 1983.

3.   One study which documented this situation in regard to the Land and Water Conservation Fund Act was Burdick, J. M. *Recreation in the Cities: Who Gains from Federal Aid?* Washington, DC: Center for Growth Alternatives, 1975.

4.   I remember working as an intern for a large city recreation and parks department which, during the period of the urban riots, had several million dollars almost forced upon it by a federal agency.

5.   Henkel, D. and Godbey, G. *Parks, Recreation and Leisure Services: Employment in the Public Sector*—Status and Trends. Arlington, Virginia: NRPA, 1977.

6.   Trudeau, R. C. PCAO—Where Are We Now? *Parks and Recreation.* October, 1989, pp. 50-55.

7.   Martilla, J. A. and James, J. C. "Importance-Performance Analysis for Developing Effective Marketing Strategies," *Journal of Marketing,* 4(1), Jan., 1977.

8.   Cranz, *Op. Cit.*

End of Chapter 13

Chapter 14

Effectiveness (Not Efficiency) is the Primary Measure of Program Success

John L. Crompton and Charles W. Lamb

> We really aren't talking about how many people pass across a park,
> but we are talking about such things as who had a better day
> because they saw the planting of azaleas on the way to work, or the
> wildflowers in bloom in a meadow, or the squirrel climbing that tree
> in an undisturbed area, or the handicapped child who learned to
> swim, and in later years saved somebody's life, or the senior citizen
> who learned a new handicraft. You cannot put a value figure on
> these experiences and attendance figures have nothing at all to do
> with it.[1]

The authors of this paper are concerned that, despite frequent utterances professing the need to be concerned about the quality of individuals' recreation experiences, we continue to use only quantitative measures to evaluate the success of recreation and park services. Theobold,[2] in a review of the literature, identified nineteen measures which have been proposed by a variety of authors for evaluating recreation and park services. Out of these nineteen measures only one addressed the perceived recreation satisfaction of citizens.

We do not mean to imply that the recreation and park field has not made progress in the area of evaluation. The early efforts at evaluation tended to focus more on inputs such as the number of acres of land, number of facilities, size of the budget, or range of programs provided. Now, at least, most agencies focus their evaluation efforts upon outputs. However, it is contended in this chapter that too much emphasis is currently placed on evaluating a program's output in terms of the *efficiency* with which it is delivered and insufficient attention is given to evaluating the effectiveness of a program's impact on patrons. *Efficiency* is usually measured in quantitative terms based upon the number of people who participate in, or use, a recreation and park program, or the cost efficiency of serving these people. Although measures of efficiency are necessary management tools, when used *alone* to evaluate the success of a program, they may be misleading. We contend that quantitative efficiency measures are of secondary importance and that primary attention should be given to measuring client satisfaction.

There are at least two good reasons why an agency's primary evaluation focus should be upon client satisfaction. First, many agencies have traditionally defined their purpose or objectives in such terms as: to enrich the quality of life; promote physical, mental, social and emotional development; and contribute to the self-fulfillment of all residents in the community. Hence, it would seem that appropriate measures of an agency's success should address how well it used its resources to achieve such psychological benefits rather than how many people used its programs or services.

As Weiss has pointed out, evaluation has a utilitarian purpose, it is not a pie in the sky phrase conjured up by some academic.[3] Its function is to provide evidence of the outcomes of programs so that managers can make wise decisions about those programs in the future. To the extent that a program is achieving its goals, evaluative evidence supports continuation, expansion and increased allocation of resources. But if evaluation discloses that a program is not achieving its goals then it should be modified, cut back or shut down.

The pressures for evaluation are increasing. Federal programs now demand evaluation of program outcomes and require a proportion of operating funds be budgeted to determine program effectiveness. At the local level the tax revolt has put increasing pressures on recreation and park agencies to prove their legitimacy in order to justify continued community support. The justification efforts of agencies have focused almost exclusively upon efficiency measures based upon the number of people served. These types of evaluation measures appear to represent the present state of the art in this field.

In the first part of this paper we review the use of attendance as a measure of evaluating a service's success. This is a frequently used criterion in the field. We discuss the rationale for using it and point out pragmatic and conceptual weaknesses in its use. We go on to distinguish between efficiency and effectiveness and argue that the reason the wrong primary criterion (quantity participating rather than quality of participation) is frequently used for evaluation is because we fail to correctly answer the question "What business are we in?" If this question is answered correctly, the objectives of the program will become clear and appropriate evaluative measures will be implemented. Finally, in the latter part of the paper we suggest measures for evaluating client satisfaction.

RATIONALE FOR THE USE OF ATTENDANCE AS A CRITERION OF SUCCESS

Traditionally, the most frequently used criterion for measuring the success of recreation and park programs has been attendance. In many cases, particularly in state or regional park systems, the use of this measure of success has led to financial resources being allocated on the basis of attendance. In other words, those parks or programs which have had the largest attendance in the past often receive the largest budget allocations in the future. Alternatively, those programs that have not demonstrated their success in terms of attendance (including new programs) have received relatively small budget allocations.

The popular use of attendance figures as the criterion for evaluating the success of recreation and park programs and services can be attributed to a number of factors. First, the method is intuitively appealing. Given a limited amount of funds to allocate among various programs or services, it seems reasonable to allocate the most money to those programs or services that are in greatest demand. Not only do these programs or services reach the largest number of people, but frequently they also have the lowest cost per participant.

A second reason for using attendance to evaluate success is that it is ostensibly politically appealing. It appears to adhere to the maxim of the greatest good for the greatest number of people. Hence, it is likely to be non-controversial. An important corollary to this strategy is the belief that more participants means more supporting votes for the program from both legislators and their constituents.

Another justification for using numbers through the door is the simplicity and apparent objectivity of the approach. Often instead of using absolute attendance figures for evaluating the relative merit of programs, a ratio of attendance to costs is derived. This gives the cost per patron served and may be used to determine which programs and services are most cost efficient. This approach seemingly eliminates any bias for or against particular individuals, groups or programs.

A fourth often stated reason for basing budget allocation on past attendance is the absence of alternative decision-making criteria. We use attendance because "it is not possible to measure the smile on a child's face." Attendance data are readily available, inexpensive to collect, and, hence, their use is expedient. Although some managers recognize that attendance is not an ideal criterion for evaluation, they continue to use this approach because they are unaware of any better way to measure success and allocate resources. Many also use attendance figures because they believe that this is the only basis for justifying their budget requests that will be acceptable to their superiors.

SHORTCOMINGS OF USING ATTENDANCE FOR EVALUATION

An obvious pragmatic limitation of using attendance to measure success concerns the difficulty of securing accurate data. If one knows that next year's budget allocation, or a supervisor's assessment of one's success, will be based upon this year's attendance, there is a strong incentive to produce large attendance figures any way possible. For example, if turnstiles are used to monitor the number of people entering a facility, it is a relatively simple task for employees to inflate attendance data by spinning the turnstile. This possibility also exists when traffic counters are used. Employees may inflate attendance figures by running their vehicles over the traffic counters as often as they like. In cases where electronic or mechanical devices are not used to monitor attendance, program managers or other employees often have considerable discretion in determining attendance. A playground supervisor may count casual walkers through the playground as facility users if he or she thinks this will aid promotion prospects or next year's budget request. Securing accurate attendance data is particularly difficult at programs or facilities for which no admission price is charged. If a price is charged, then receipts can be used to cross-check attendance records and the data are likely to be more accurate.

In addition to this pragmatic limitations, there are a number of conceptual weaknesses in using attendance to measure success. If resources are assigned to programs on the basis of participation, then *funding allocations may sometimes be the result of success rather than a cause of success*. Almost any program can be made to generate the attendance necessary to classify it as a success, given enough resources. For example, free admission or increased promotion would probably encourage more attendance. If admission is already free then providing the transportation and/or paying an incentive for people to participate would probably lead to increased attendance. Following this same line or reasoning, a program with low attendance may be considered relatively unsuccessful, but the reason for this may be that it has never had the level of financial support necessary to make it successful. If the program continues to have minimal financial support it is likely to remain unsuccessful.

The use of attendance to measure success ignores the fact that some programs or services are designed to appeal to smaller, yet equally important, client groups. For example, the potential market for a particular senior citizens' program may be smaller than the potential market for a youth oriented program. If a particular senior citizens' program attracted 100 participants which accounted for 80 percent of those capable of participating in the program and a youth oriented program attracted 300 participants which accounted for 10 percent of those capable of participating in the program, would the youth program be deemed three times as successful as the senior citizen program? Should it be funded at three times the level of the senior citizens' program? If programs are funded proportionate to attendance there is little incentive for recreation and park agencies to deliver services to smaller client groups. However, in some cases, this may be the most important justification for a recreation agency's existence. The welfare or public benefits accruing from serving smaller client groups may be much greater than the public benefits accruing from serving larger segments whose wants may more easily be met by other leisure services suppliers or other types of services.

And what about new programs? If resources are allocated based upon past participation levels, how is the funding level for a new program to be determined? It is possible that established programs no longer need the same level of financial support. These resources might be better used to launch new programs or to resuscitate programs that have previously received only modest support. Some new programs or services may require relatively more resources in order to become established, and some older programs may require relatively fewer resources. It takes time for new programs or services to become established and build up demand. They also usually require a substantial allocation of resources if they are to be successfully launched. Attendance may simply be an indicator of a program's stage in its life cycle. Higher attendance figures for one program over another may not indicate the superiority of the former. They may simply be a reflection of the length of time that the program has been offered.

Clearly, some programs require a larger per-participant expenditure than others. Programs requiring a small instructor-to-participant ratio or requiring special supplies, equipment, or facilities obviously are more costly per participant than programs requiring little supervision, supplies, equipment, or facilities. The attendance criterion, or the attendance/cost ratio criterion, often depict such programs as being inferior. Similarly, some programs have limited ecological and/or social carrying capacity. The use of an absolute attendance criterion as the measure of success ignores this. Because these programs have a lower carrying capacity it does not follow that they are inherently inferior. Indeed, to increase the numbers participating in such programs may destroy the experience sought by their participants. Furthermore, increased participation may lead to the decay, destruction, or imbalance of the recreation facility.

Some argue that quantity of participation is synonymous with a satisfactory experience since participants would not indulge in return visits or encourage their friends to participate if their experience had not been satisfactory. However, this ignores the possibility that there may be no substitutable alternatives. For example, if the public recreation and park agency own the only swimming pool in town, on a 95 degree day in the summer a large attendance is likely no matter how poorly it is operated. People will participate even though the experience may be considered less than optimally satisfying. Hence, numbers per se are not only incompatible with client satisfaction but are also likely to lead to erroneous conclusions if the numbers are interpreted as being synonymous with satisfaction. *Client satisfaction may result in large attendances, but large attendances are not necessarily indications that a service is providing high levels of client satisfaction*.

We noted earlier that advocates of the attendance criterion frequently equate increased attendance with increased support. This may be an erroneous assumption. Servicing a large number of people may be incompatible with having a well satisfied clientele. Frequently, large attendance or participation levels are obtained because the program is geared to appeal to the largest number of people within a community. Such a strategy suggests that relatively few participants will be well satisfied because compromises in the nature of the service have to be made in order to accommodate everybody. When the agency's budget comes up for review, it may be argued that the support of a relatively small number of highly committed people may be more desirable than a larger number of marginally satisfied people who will not miss the service sufficiently to fight for its retention in the budget. Politically, large numbers are not necessarily transferrable into increased support.

These shortcomings of using attendance as the criterion to measure the success or failure of particular programs suggests that it is an inadequate criterion used on its own. We do not advocate that attendance should be ignored. Attendance may be a useful measure of efficiency, but we argue that efficiency should be a secondary concern to effectiveness. There are times when it is useful to use attendance numbers for the purpose of gaining support from the public or from politicians who feel that their constituents understand and are sympathetic only to efficiency and do not recognize the weaknesses identified in the previous paragraphs.

If attendance figures are used for the purpose of gaining support, the recreation and park manager should be aware of their limitations. For example, major theme park operators use attendance figures for public relations purposes because large numbers generate good publicity. However, these operators are aware of the limited usefulness of these data for measuring their success. For their own internal measure of customer satisfaction, many theme park operators give a simple, one page questionnaire to a sample of 50 to 100 guests in the park at the end of each day, seeking to identify their level of satisfaction. These are used as a primary internal evaluation tool. They serve as a way to continually improve the services offered, so people will continue to attend and persuade their friends to visit the park. *Level of customer satisfaction is seen as the necessary prerequisite to sustained sales volume based upon repeat business.*

EFFECTIVENESS - NOT EFFICIENCY - SHOULD BE THE PRIME CRITERION

The first step to improved evaluation is to develop greater conceptual clarity about what recreation and park services are intended to accomplish. The use of attendance or attendance/cost ratio for evaluation reflects a concern for *efficiency*. Efficiency is concerned with the amount of effort, expense, or waste involved in delivering a service. Budgetary constraints have forced recreation and park managers to increasingly direct their attention to this criterion. This is important but should only be the second concern. Prime concern should be with *effectiveness*. Effectiveness is concerned with the impact or end result of the service on the clientele. As Kanter has pointed out, effectiveness is the more important criterion because doing the wrong things less expensively is not of much value.[4] Assessment of effectiveness focuses upon the extent to which goals are fulfilled. That is, effectiveness indicates how well the service succeeded in fulfilling the purpose for which it was established.

It is essential that a program's goals be established in a form that will permit evaluation. Unfortunately, some agencies use very generalized goal statements for a program which it is not possible to evaluate. Assuming that the intended benefits of a program are specified at the outset, the first question to ask in evaluating the success of a program is, "Does the program facilitate the benefits which it was intended to deliver to patrons?" Only when this question has been addressed is it appropriate to assess efficiency and ask, "Is the program being delivered in the least costly way?"

Efficiency deals with cost per participant and is a measurement designed to gauge if the program is doing things better or worse. Effectiveness, on the other hand, attempts to ascertain whether the program, through its stated objectives, is doing the right things in the optimal manner.[5] Efficiency is input-output oriented, effectiveness is patron oriented. The essence of this distinction was stated long ago by Gray and Greben in the following terms:

> We should have discovered long ago the nature of the business we are in, but we have not. Only now are we beginning to rethink what recreation is. In the emerging view it is not activities, or facilities, or programs that are central, it is what happens to people.

They go on to state:

> We must evaluate everything we do in human terms. The critical questions are not "How many were there? or "Who won?" The critical question is, "What happened to Jose, Mary, Sam and Joan in this experience?" . . . we must reorient our approach to services, to think not only in terms of activities and programs, but also in terms of human experience.[6]

If we reject the use of efficiency criteria as the sole means for evaluating performance and allocating resources, we need to propose methods of evaluating effectiveness.

ESTABLISHING THE RIGHT OBJECTIVES

Before an evaluation of the effectiveness of a program can be undertaken, there has to be a clear understanding of the impact that the program is intended to have on clients. That is, what are the objectives of the program? Appropriate objectives emerge in response to the question "What Business Are We In?" Often we lack clear vision as the to nature of our business. Our concern should not be limited to delivering programs or providing services. Rather our primary focus should be upon the end results which those programs facilitate. *People engage in leisure activities with the expectation of receiving benefits. Programs*

*have no value; only their benefits have value to patron groups. A program is
simply a means to an end.* Benefits, or ends sought include such things as social
interaction, prestige, excitement, security, relaxation or fantasy.

If an agency defines its business, and consequently its objectives, in terms of
specific programs, it is likely that it will measure its success in terms of the level
of efficiency in offering those programs, rather than in terms of their effectiveness in facilitating anticipated client benefits. Instead of specific programs, the
starting point should be identification of the benefits which client groups seek.
Agency objectives should be stated in terms of these benefits. Specific programs and services designed to meet these wants can then be selected. Program
performance can be assessed in terms of the extent to which it meets these
wants.

Because benefits are qualitative rather than quantitative, it does not mean
that program objectives cannot be written and subsequently evaluated. Failure
to establish objectives leaves an agency in the uncomfortable position of the
Cheshire Cat telling Alice that as long as she didn't care where she was headed,
any direction she took would be acceptable! If objectives are specified and
written in terms of benefits or what happens to people, then an effective evaluation measure must address these phenomena.

EVALUATING EFFECTIVENESS

Evaluating performance and allocating resources can be predicated on three
propositions. These are:

1.   The objective of recreation and park agencies is to satisfy client group
     wants;

2.   by translating client group wants into benefits sought, the agency defines its
     objectives in terms of benefits; and

3.   programs and services are the means to achieve ends, and not themselves
     ends.

If the agency accepts these propositions, it naturally follows that agency
objectives will be stated in terms of the *specific* benefits it intends to provide
selected client groups. Also, subordinates will establish objectives in terms of
benefits provided and not in terms of programs or attendance figures. After this
task has been completed, superiors and subordinates are in a position to assess
existing programs and services according to the extent to which they contribute
to the achievement of the specified objectives. They are also in a position to
determine what changes are needed in existing programs, what new programs
and services should be offered, and the various resources that are needed to
achieve desired outcomes.

What measures are available for assessing the extent to which an existing program successfully facilitates the benefits clients seek? There are four main approaches that can be used:[7] 1) unsolicited client response, 2) observation, 3) one-dimensional survey measures, and 4) two-dimensional survey saliency measures.

The *unsolicited client response* technique is the least rigorous of the four. This technique simply requires establishing a mechanism for clients to comment on their level of satisfaction if they so desire. Suggestion or comment boxes are commonly used. This approach has two important limitations. First, neither positive nor negative comments can be generalized to all publics, since the views of those who comment may be very different from the views of those who do not. Second, the absence of a large number of complaints cannot be interpreted as demonstrating a high degree of satisfaction because, as long as the service does not deteriorate below some minimal satisfaction level, many people may not make an effort to comment.

The *observation approach* represents an attempt to be a little more representative by directly observing and interacting with clients. A manager may visit a park, swimming pool, or recreation program and talk to participants or residents about their likes, dislikes, and suggestions for improvement of the program. This technique allows a manager to seek input from whomever he or she chooses, but again there is no guarantee that these people are representative of all members in each relevant public.

Both the third and fourth approaches to measuring satisfaction use a survey that potentially is more representative. Figure 1 shows a typical set of questions used in a *one-dimensional survey approach.* Directly asking people in this way

Figure 1
A One-Dimensional Approach to Measuring Satisfaction

How do you rate the following services provided by the Park and Recreation Department?

Service	Very Good	Good	No Opinion	Poor	Very Poor
Aquatics	___	___	___	___	___
Recreation Centers	___	___	___	___	___
Neighborhood Parks	___	___	___	___	___
Tennis Courts	___	___	___	___	___
Large Parks	___	___	___	___	___
Beaches	___	___	___	___	___
Arts	___	___	___	___	___
Athletics	___	___	___	___	___

what they think of the quality of particular services is, however, unlikely to be very helpful. As long as their level of satisfaction is within some adequate range, most will answer positively. A high percentage of favorable evaluations or satisfied responses does not necessarily reflect a high level of satisfaction; it merely reflects a lack of dissatisfaction. Indeed, it has been shown that a program's clients almost always report high satisfaction levels and predominantly favorable evaluations, even for programs that are not effective.[8] Only if the service becomes excessively bad are citizens likely to respond negatively to generalized questions.

The fourth approach, *two-dimensional saliency measurement*, also uses surveys, but it addresses the measurement of satisfaction differently. First, it attempts to break down and operationalize the concept "satisfaction" into a series of constituent parts. Each of the benefits that are perceived to accrue from a particular program and that when aggregated constitute "satisfaction" are identified. In Figure 2(a), respondents are asked to evaluate each of them on a scale (1 to 7, for example) ranging from extremely satisfactory to extremely unsatisfactory.

Figure 2

A Two-Dimensional Survey Approach to Measuring Satisfaction that Operationalizes
Service Satisfaction by Identifying Individual Benefit Components:
(a) Satisfaction dimension of individual benefits and
(b) Importance dimension of individual benefits.

	Extremely Unsatisfactory	Very Unsatisfactory	Slightly Unsatisfactory	Neither Unsatisfactory nor Satisfactory	Slightly Satisfactory	Very Satisfactory	Extremely Satisfactory
Opportunity to interact with others in this program is	1	2	3	(4)	5	6	7
Discussion generated among my friends by my participation in this program is	1	2	3	(4)	5	6	7

(a)

	Extremely Unimportant	Very Unimportant	Slightly Unimportant	Neither Unimportant nor Important	Slightly Important	Very Important	Extremely Important
Opportunity to interact with others in this program is	1	2	3	4	5	6	(7)
Discussion generated among my friends by my participation in this program is	1	(2)	3	4	5	6	7

(b)

This information alone is of limited value because it gives no indication of the relative importance that clients attach to each of the particular benefits that the program facilitates. For example, if the two scale items shown in Figure 2(a) are among those used to measure sociability and prestige benefits facilitated by a recreation program, both may receive a score of 4 on a 7-point scale (neither satisfactory nor unsatisfactory). However, sociability may be a very important benefit to participants in the program, while prestige may be of very little importance to them.

The necessary complement to the benefit evaluation is the second differentiating characteristic of two-dimensional saliency measurement, which is shown in Figure 2(b). The second series of questions seek to rate the salient benefit attributes sought by clients from a program. These measures are most useful for determining whether or not more effort should be given to improving dimensions of the service.

If clients rate the sociability and prestige benefits 7 and 2 respectively on this importance scale, then the previous satisfaction score of 4 for the prestige benefit may be considered adequate because a score of 2 shows clients consider it very unimportant. Thus it is of little concern that the program is not facilitating this benefit particularly well. In contrast, sociability is rated extremely important (a score of 7), so the agency should be greatly concerned if the program is not successfully facilitating this benefit. Unless the program is restructured in some way to increase its potential for encouraging interaction with others, client support is likely to diminish.

This approach can be presented very effectively in the form of a graphic action grid, shown in Figure 3. The importance and satisfaction scores for each

Figure 3
The Action Grid

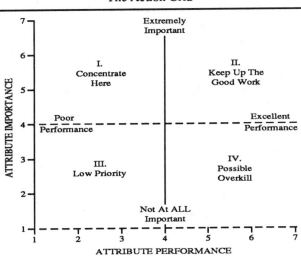

benefit attribute can be spatially located at a single point on the grid which specifies the marketing implications. In this way, a manager can quickly see those attributes of an offering that require remedial attention and those to which it may be possible to devote less effort.

CONCLUDING COMMENTS

We are not advocating that the key to success is maximizing client group satisfaction. This is an unrealistic expectation given limited resources. Furthermore, since all public agencies must satisfy many client groups, it is often necessary to reduce the satisfaction levels of some client groups in order to increase those of other groups. The goal should be to provide acceptable levels of satisfaction to clients within the constraints imposed by the agency's resource base. This goal can best be achieved by periodically monitoring the benefit expectations and satisfaction of clients.

By focusing our attention on the extent to which client wants are satisfied we can, as Gray and Greben suggest, begin thinking about recreation in terms of human experience instead of activities and programs. We can also begin thinking about successful performance in qualitative instead of quantitative terms.

REFERENCES

1.   Anonymous—Submitted to one of the authors in a term paper some years ago. The student's name was mislaid with the passage of time, but the vivid nature of the imagery remained.
2.   Theobold, W. F. *Evaluation of Recreation and Park Programs*. New York: John Wiley, 1979. pp. 84-89.
3.   Weiss, C. H. "Alternative Models of Program Evaluation." *Social Work*, (November, 1974), p. 675.
4.   Kanter, R. M. *The Change Masters*. New York: Simon and Schuster, 1983.
5.   Zabezensky, M. *Performance Accountability in Human Service Activities*. Indianapolis, Indiana: Board of Fundamental Education, 1974, p. 18.
6.   Gray, D. E. and Greben, S. "Future Perspectives," Paper presented at the National Recreation and Parks Association Congress, October, 1973.
7.   Adapted from Kotler, P. *Marketing for Non-Profit Organizations*. Englewood Cliffs, New Jersey: Prentice-Hall, 1982, pp. 66-76.
8.   Scheirer, M. A. "Program Participants Positive Perceptions: Psychological Conflicts of Interest in Program Evaluation" *Evaluation Quarterly*, 2 (February 1978), p. 55.

End of Chapter 14

Chapter 15

Creative Growth Through Play and its Implications for Recreation Practice

Doyle Bishop and Claudine Jeanrenaud

A cherished belief among many play specialists is that play enhances the development of creativity.[1] The fact is, the paths to play have many dead ends, detours, and debris that discourage instead of enhance the development of creativity. These bad road conditions are numerous and often not easily visible until it is too late. The traffic engineers, road crews, and patrolmen who manage the journey through play (i.e., parents, teachers, recreation leaders, therapists, and others) must work hard to remove these roadblocks. If they do not, play experiences will almost certainly help to make non-creative children and later adults.

We propose to demonstrate these roadblocks with a general model of the stages, or choice points, involved in play. This model is the authors' integration of diverse ideas about play as well as some that, up to now, have not been closely linked to play. The model is the result of the authors' many discussions between themselves and with students. The detailed ideas included in the model are not novel; we have borrowed heavily from previous research and theory. What is original is the particular ways in which we have tried to integrate the ideas to provide one view of play and its link to creativity.

It seems to us that our emphasis, in the model, on the importance of exploratory behavior and its balance against too much or too little directiveness and structure, as a path to creative growth, provides a focal point for examining some possible limitations of current recreation practice. In the last part of the chapter we explore those limits. But first it is important to look at the path to creative growth and the ways in which it can be blocked.

The main ideas from previous work that we have relied on are those of Hutt[2] and Linford and Jeanrenaud,[3] who laid the groundwork for viewing play as a series of critical stages; reinforcement theorists such as Hull[4] and Skinner,[5] whose principles of learning help to show how movement through the stages of play can be enhanced or retarded; arousal theorists, particularly Berlyne,[6] and Fiske and Maddi,[7] whose ideas about concepts like novelty, complexity, curiosity, and exploration help to define the distinctive crossroads on the path through play; personality and development theorists like Piaget,[8] Harvey, Hunt and Schroder,[9] and Eysenck,[10] whose ideas illustrate how different combinations of persons and environments, for both players and managers, can produce different outcomes at the different stages of play; and some investigations of play and creativity such as those by Torrance,[11] Lieberman,[12] Sutton-Smith,[13] and Bishop and Chace,[14] which have demonstrated that play is a powerful medium for inhibiting or enhancing creative potential. These authors and works are mentioned here so that the rest of the paper can proceed without continual reference to previous literature.

Refer to the diagram in Figure 1. For our purposes, a journey through play begins at:

THE ATTENTION STAGE

There is a story about an old farmer who used to periodically whack his mule on the snout with a stick of firewood. When asked why he did this, the farmer replied, "I can't l'arn him nuthin if'n I don't first git his attention!" Now, we do not recommend the whack-between-the-eyes method to get a kid started at play. But the farmer's wisdom, verified repeatedly by psychological research, is sound in principle: In order to begin learning anything, the person must first pay attention to some object or situation. No attention, no learning. No learning, no creativity.

NOVELTY

Novelty, or the extent to which an object differs, relatively or absolutely, from what has occurred before, helps to gain one's attention. So does the *intensity* of the object or situation—how much it stands out from the rest of its environment. Things that are familiar or plain will not grab our attention very often or for very long. How many of you have noticed the light bulb in your ceiling lately? If you have, our guess is that it had stopped producing light. When was the last time you marvelled at a gray cement wall that you passed?

Those with an economic motive, like top manufacturers, understand very well the old farmer's wisdom. Have you ever seen a child in a department store, grasping towards a brightly-colored toy and throwing a temper tantrum, because his mother is trying to pull him away? If so, you have witnessed first hand the significance of the attention stage of play.

Figure 1

Model of the Behavorial Stages and Blocks to Creativity Through Play

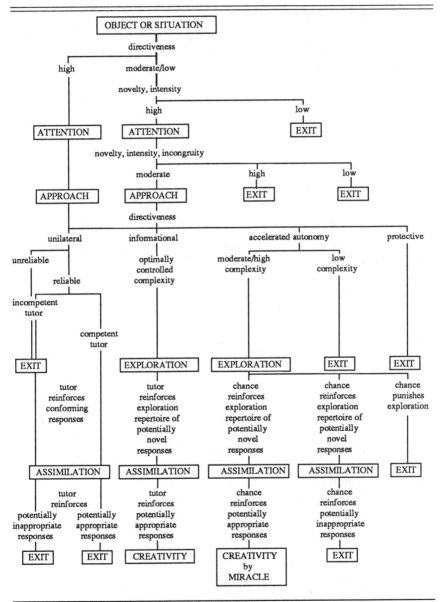

CURIOSITY

The *approach-avoidance conflict,* must be resolved into approach if play is to occur. Novelty and intensity also make a person approach or avoid a play object or situation. But their effects are a little different from those at the attention stage. Novelty and intensity are increasingly related to attentiveness: The more of them, the greater the attention. But they have an "inverted U" relation with avoidance-approach.

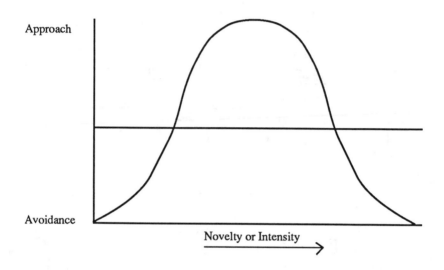

Approach

Avoidance

Novelty or Intensity

More novelty or intensity, up to a certain level, increasingly makes the person want to approach the play thing or situation. But beyond this critical level, adding more novelty or intensity produces greater avoidance. This effect seems to happen because too much novelty or intensity creates fear, not wonder.

Approach does not have to mean literally moving toward an object. It can also mean sustained interest, or not actively avoiding the object. This is an important distinction for spectator forms of play, where the play thing or situation is supposed to do something to the person, instead of him to it. This meaning of approach is illustrated by a circus performance that one of the authors attended. In part of the show, a gorilla escaped from his cage and his trainer to create havoc and fear among the other circus performers in the arena. This display riveted the interest of the children in the audience, who seemed delighted by these antics, until the gorilla leaped over the arena wall into the spectator section! The younger children, terrified, then began crying, clinging, and in some cases running for the exit. Soon the "gorilla" took off his hooded mask to reveal a man in a gorilla costume. The children immediately composed themselves and either returned to their seats or went over to the man-gorilla to get a closer look. Clearly, the children's approach tendency was close to or at the peak of the "inverted U," before the "gorilla" jumped out of the arena. The novelty and intensity were just too high and avoidance reactions followed. Finally, the object was transformed to one that was relatively familiar but still somewhat novel—enough to produce literal approach and even touching.

This example demonstrates that approach (or avoidance) can be psychological as well as physical. The example also shows that distance between player and object and the presence of barriers between them can affect the amount of approach or avoidance.

In summary, if you present a child with optimum amounts of novelty, intensity, distance, and barriers in a play situation, he will be inclined toward curiosity; he will resolve the approach/avoidance conflict in favor of approach.

EXPLORATORY PLAY

Exploration is the manipulation of the new object or situation in order to discover its properties. Berlyne distinguishes between two kinds of exploration: 1) *specific exploration*, aimed at finding a single answer to a problem or challenge and 2) *diversive exploration*, aimed at finding in the environment elements that can produce excitement or distraction. Exploration is the means (not necessarily conscious or deliberate) by which the individual acquires a wide range of information; it adds to the person's repertoire of possible ideas and responses. The availability of this repertoire at a later time makes it possible for the person to produce many ideas or actions in a given situation; this potential is a necessary, though not sufficient, condition for creativity to occur.

The *complexity* of the play thing or situation determines how much the person will explore it. A complex thing has many different parts and/or unusual arrangements or combinations of parts; so certain kinds of novelty affect exploration too. An object or situation that has many things to see, hear, touch, smell, taste, and manipulate, especially in unusual ways, is more complex than one with fewer of these features and is more likely to encourage exploration.

Imagine a cuckoo clock with a dial that permits choosing the cycle in minutes with which the cuckoo sounds. Now add complexity by providing three doors and three "cuckoos"—a bird, a lion, and an old car—with an unpredictable pattern of which one will come out of which door. Add more by allowing the three cuckoos to do different things when activated—the lion can croak like a frog or toot like a car's horn, the bird can roar like a lion or moo like a cow, and the car can bark as well as squirt water from a radiator leak. As more and more features like these are added and the child has some way of influencing, though not precisely determining, their occurrence, the frequency and duration of exploratory play should increase.

These rules about complexity and exploration hold, of course, only if the parts of the object did not produce so much intensity or novelty that an avoidance reaction occurred. Given that approach takes place, then complexity should be increasingly related to exploration.

ASSIMILATION

Assimilation or consolidation play is the repetition of behaviors or situations, which, during the exploratory stage, appeared challenging or were reinforced; such repetition permits the child to assimilate or master the behavior or situation. As a rule, unless other people impose the constraints that we discuss later, the child's assimilation play does *not* involve 100 percent repetition. Complete repetition of behavior, all the time, would seem to discourage the development of creative abilities. The natural tendency of the child, according to Freud and Piaget, would be to make subtle transformations in his play or the situation. These situations are the child's attempts to bring the object or situation within his range of comprehension or ability. These attempts are not diversive exploration but are forms of specific exploration that result in *mastery*; this word, although a good one to describe the outcome, does not necessarily mean that the child is diligently striving to master some specific skill, like a high school student strives to memorize the parts of the body for an anatomy course. Mastery or comprehension tend to follow (if not interfered with) not necessarily by the child's design or intent but often simply as a result of practice.

Assimilation play, along with formal training, helps the individual acquire proficiency in various responses; this proficiency is the other necessary condition for creativity.

CREATIVITY

Creativity is the production of *novel* responses that have an *appropriate* impact in a given context. If several truckloads of creativity were dumped in your front yard, this definition probably would not help you to identify it. But the definition does neatly summarize, if somewhat cryptically, the essence of extensive research and writing about creativity. Most people would probably agree that redundancy of ideas or products is not creative, but neither is novelty for novelty's sake; if the idea or product does not resolve some problem or affect established beliefs or practices, it is regarded as *not appropriate* and thus not creative, *for the given context*, although it might be appropriate in another place or time.

Our concern is to outline the general conditions that are likely to enhance or, more often, inhibit the person's ability to make novel *and* appropriate responses. According to the definition, if either of these abilities fails to develop, the person will be incapable of creative performance.

The first condition for creativity, the ability to make novel responses, comes primarily from the *exploratory play* experiences of the person; the attention and approach experiences are critical as well, but mainly because exploratory play cannot occur without them. In exploratory play the child learns the many different things that the environment can "do" and the many things that he can do to it. Over time, in many exploratory play situations, he accumulates a repertoire of potential responses that he can call upon, if and when he needs to. The more responses he accumulates, the greater the probability that at least one of them will be novel in some context, sometime. Also, the more there are the greater the possibility of combining several to yield a novel pattern of behavior, even though one response would not be novel in the given context. In short, exploratory play, by providing many potential responses, helps make the person *potentially creative*, in that he is able to emit those responses in some future context.

Exploratory play probably also increases the person's *motivation* to make novel responses, or at least reduces his fear of making them. Studies of humans and other animals suggest that fear of novelty is an acquired drive and that it is greatest in animals whose early environmental experiences are impoverished. We believe it was Piaget who said, "the more a child has seen and heard, the more he wants to see and hear." And we would add that this probably applies to the stimuli produced by the child's own responses.

The second condition for creativity, the ability to make appropriate or useful responses, comes primarily from the *assimilation-play* experiences of the person. It is during assimilation play that the person develops, through repetition and transformation, specific, known skills. He is not trying to find out all the things that the environment can do or that he can do to it, as in exploration; he is perfecting, within the limits of his existing abilities, his understanding of or skill at some particular situation or task. He is figuring out how to hammer a nail, throw a football, ride a bike, or why mother insists that he eat with a fork, not his hands, why he goes to the dentist, or later how a barometer, carburetor, or electric motor works.

In short, there is a kind of learning, distinct from exploration, that results in the acquisition of particular performance skills that are, or are intended to be, thorough and permanent. The more thorough and permanent the skills developed in a given domain of performance, the more likely it is that the person can make *appropriate* responses, and thus is *potentially creative*, in that domain. And the more frequently specific-skill learning is concentrated in one domain, the less potential creativity the person has in other domains: It is not likely that a professional novelist will help to invent a new breed of computers, and we would not expect an electronics engineer to win the Nobel prize for literature.

To briefly summarize, these are the major stages. By successfully progressing through these stages repeatedly, on many encounters with the environment during development, the person would become creative. Progression can be blocked, however, by environmental, social, and personality factors; the more often this happens, the less creativity will develop. We have seen how the degree of novelty, intensity, incongruity, and complexity affect these stages. Now we will look at some other factors that can block the development of creative ability.

BLOCKING PROGRESS TOWARD CREATIVITY

Control can be exercised by parents, older friends or relatives, teachers, etc. For lack of a better word on which most people can agree, they will be referred to as tutors. Tutors, then, can exercise control either directly on the child by means of directives and/or reinforcements (rewards and punishments), or indirectly through manipulation of the child's play environment, including its degree of novelty, complexity, intensity and incongruity.

Control can be exercised with over-directiveness, under-directiveness or moderate directiveness. Over-directiveness can take several forms. The tutor can draw the child's attention against his will, and show him how to handle an object or situation *before* the child has had time to be curious about it or to explore it. For instance, the tutor may say this to the child: "Here, come with me, I want to show you something: see this plane? I want you to play with it, and I'll show you how to hold it . . . " This condition is called unilateral since all the information passes from the tutor to the child, and none from the child to the tutor. If the plane flies and does not crash, the condition is considered as reliable.

Under this form of over-directiveness, reinforcement is contingent upon conformance to directions. So punishment might sound like this: "How many times must I tell you not to hold your ball with your left hand?" Because both curiosity and exploration were circumvented, the behaviors displayed during assimilation play are limited to the motions dictated by the tutor. Consequently, the child becomes fearful, dependent upon his tutor's instructions, imitative, conforming and non-creative.

If the tutor's directives are unreliable, i.e., produce undesirable outcomes or contradict previous directions, the child faces a multiple conflict: following directions does not necessarily lead to desirable outcomes; not following them certainly leads to punishment. besides having missed exploration, the child has no alternative solutions to the tutor's instructions. Consequently, he reacts with distrust and anger towards the tutor, and might try to oppose him. Often, therefore, behaviors opposed to directions and that escaped punishment are perceived as rewarded, even though they may be regarded as inappropriate by his society. So, the child might become rigidly anti-authoritarian and non-conforming—but not creative.

The tutor can also provide unnecessary assistance. For example, he might say this: "Here, this is too hard for you, I'll do it!" Under the *protective interpersonal* conditions, the tutor is over-responsive to the child's wants. While the tutor might interfere at any stage of the child's experience he tends to do so mostly when the child meets his first obstacle during exploratory play, thus preventing assimilation play. Therefore, while the development of novel responses might not have been affected as severely as under unilateral conditions, acquisition of proficient responses, whether appropriate or not, will have been inhibited.

One response, however, will have been fully explored and assimilated: manipulation of the tutor in order to elicit his assistance. The child might, therefore, become an expert at social manipulation, but without confidence in his own ability to achieve anything. So, he remains dependent on others to be creative in his place.

Under-directiveness occurs when the tutor exercises no control over the child. This is considered to be the *accelerated autonomy* condition. Spontaneous attention, curiosity, exploratory and assimilation play all occur, but in the absence of any guidance by the tutor. Reinforcement is dispensed by the environment. Behavior is rewarded whenever environmental consequences are pleasant, and punished whenever environmental consequences are adverse.

For instance, a child's attention has been caught by a toy which is lying on a table. He decides to explore the toy. Because he is too small to reach it, he grasps the table cloth and pulls on it until the toy falls on the floor. If the toy breaks, the child's behavior has been punished. If not, the child's behavior has been rewarded and table cloth pulling might become one of his favorite play activities.

As this example illustrates, the absence of adult guidance makes it difficult for the child to learn about his society's sense of appropriateness. So while he might have developed a wide repertoire of novel responses, few of them will be appropriate, thus limiting his creativity.

Moderate directiveness, as in the *interpersonal informational* condition, is most likely to lead to creativity. The tutor manipulates the environment so as to provide the child with an environment structured in such a way that the child will almost always proceed through a progression of experiences.[15] Although the child's approach and exploration are experienced as spontaneous, they actually follow a predetermined path leading to the discovery of appropriate responses.

For instance, if the tutor decides that the child will learn about cooperation, he sets up a game where success depends directly on the degree of cooperation between the players. He does not tell the child what to do. The child's desire to succeed motivates him to test alternative approaches, including the cooperative one. The consequences of the various approaches are compared. This information is stored and thus becomes available for combination with previously stored information, so that conceptual links can be drawn. In other words, the seeking of alternate solutions has been elicited, and concept formation made possible.

To that, the tutor may add social reinforcement by congratulating profusely the child for cooperating or initiating exploration. So, the behaviors likely to be learned during assimilation play are those rewarded during exploration as well as exploration itself. The child thus develops a wide range of appropriate and novel responses, the two necessary skills for creativity.

Table 1

Illustration of the Skills Developed under Each
Control Condition, and the Resulting Creativity

Control Conditions	Creative Skills		Resulting Creativity
	Novelty	Appropriateness	
Unilateral			
Reliable	—	+*	—*
Unreliable	—	—	
Protective	+	—	—
Accelerated			
Autonomy	+	—	—
Informational	+	+	+

* Note: + means existing skill; — means absent skill.

In summary (see Table 1), of the control conditions discussed above, only the last one offers the opportunity to develop both novel and appropriate responses. The unilateral condition, by bypassing exploratory play and emphasizing assimilation play, encourages the development of appropriate responses (at least when the tutor is competent), but discourages the development of novel responses. The protective condition allows some exploration, but no assimilation. Therefore, while some novel responses might develop, neither appropriate nor inappropriate learning occurs. Finally, in the accelerated autonomy condition, exploration and assimilation both take place, but the absence of guidance results in the learning of many inappropriate responses.

PERSONALITY OF PLAYER AND TUTOR

The environmental effects and tutoring practices that we have outlined are probably determined, in part, by the personality characteristics of both learner and tutor; some effects of personality are undoubtedly independent of what is actually present in the environment or what the tutor intends *at any given time*. On the other hand, the stages that we have discussed obviously help to shape the personalities of people in some ways. So movement through the stages and the participants' personalities are in a dynamic relationship; they influence one another. This dynamic interplay continues throughout development, which, though concentrated on one's early years, probably is a lifelong process.

The player or learner will be motivated or able to notice, approach, or explore things depending, in part, on his past experience in doing so. Some kids will approach and explore things that other kids will not even notice or will be frightened by. Piaget's phrase, "the more he will want to see and hear," is highly relevant to this point; so is the added notion: the more he will *be able* to see and hear. Fiske and Maddi's idea of high- and low-activation people (seekers or avoiders of stimulation) could be an example of a pertinent personality characteristic, which presumably develops out of experience.

Eysenck's introverted and extraverted types, which he believes are largely inherited, are other examples. The introvert has a nervous system characterized by high levels of cortical arousal and low levels of reactive inhibition (mental fatigue or boredom); the extravert is just the reverse. These differences suggest that introverts should be less impulsive, more conscious of details, more persistent at various tasks, and more capable of long-term memory than extraverts; these hypotheses have been supported by a variety of studies. Extraverts, because of their high boredom potential, presumably would attend to and approach novel stimuli more than introverts but would engage in less detailed exploration and less consolidation play. This reasoning would conclude that, given the same developmental circumstances, introverts have a better chance of becoming creative than extraverts.

Now consider the personality of the tutor. Even with the best of intentions for the outcome of his tutoring, what he can actually *do* will be partly dictated by his own personality. In fact, his intentions—what he thinks should be done —will be somewhat preconditioned by his personality. This, to us, is a vital point for the management of play experiences: A tutor, say a recreation leader, cannot simply decide to manage play for the betterment of the player and expect to do so entirely on the strength of his own motivation and game skills. His personality might be such that he cannot recognize or manage the delicate balance between exploratory and consolidatory play. If his aim is the enhancement of creativity, he will almost certainly fail (unless someone else plugs the holes that he leaves).

A highly extraverted tutor, for example, if Eysenck's meaning of extraversion is correct, would probably emphasize a great variety of novel but, for learning purposes, superficial experiences in play. This approach, if prolonged or used often enough, seems likely to produce a jack-of-all-trades-but-master-of-none kind of player. Such persons, though often interesting, are hardly models of creative production.

Because tutors were once players and learners, their personalities have been shaped by the developmental experiences that we have described. The methods of control used by tutors, outlined previously, were derived largely from the childhood training conditions described by Harvey, Hunt and Schroder.[16] Those authors claim that the different training conditions produce distinctive adult personalities, ranging from the highly concrete, authoritarian, rigid person to the highly abstract, open-minded, adaptive one. What this means, in our terms, is that tutors who were frequently exposed to directive, unilateral methods of control in their development are likely to become concretistic, authoritarian personalities who, as tutors, will employ directive, unilateral methods of control.

SUMMARY

We have not tried to give a precise and exhaustive rendering of relevant personality characteristics. We have merely attempted to point out the importance of personality, for both player and tutor, and to suggest a few directions for further thought and research. The reader might have concluded by now that in order to promote creativity in others a tutor must be creative himself. We do not disagree with that conclusion. Unfortunately, telling would-be tutors to "be creative" is about as helpful as telling an alcoholic that he really ought to stop drinking. Clearly, it is easier said than done.

We have presented a model of stages of play, which is really a view of developmental experience adapted to play, in order to reveal various roadblocks to creativity. Figure 1 (page 185) summarizes this model. We have not often referred to Figure 1 throughout our discussion. We hope that the figure, bolstered by the text, adequately summarizes our major points: a) the critical stages of play or, more generally, development, b) the dynamics between these stages and personality development, and c) the many roadblocks to creativity as well as the nature of the singular path that is likely to lead to it.

Recreation rhetoric sometimes extols the joys and wonders of play and its role in creative development. And researchers, including ourselves, have often looked to play as one source of creative behavior. We do not wish to squelch pretty thoughts or discourage positively-oriented research. But perhaps an alternative view should be heard and researched: If our model is somewhere along the right lines, the greater miracle is that anybody at all ever becomes creative.

IMPLICATIONS

This chapter has referred to childhood learning and experiences and their effects on later creativity. But "later" actually never comes. Recent research findings are beginning to re-emphasize what many individuals have always known but some of our institutions forgot: the need for creative development continues throughout the life cycle right up until death and, so far as we know, perhaps beyond it. Thus, fundamental ideas about the paths to creativity are relevant to adult behavior and development. And the recreation professionals who develop recreation institutions, programs, and the training of other recreation professionals are heavily implicated in that process, whether they want to be or not. Sometimes it seems that they do not want to be.

Recreation personnel are supposed to be "people-oriented." In their personal lives they most clearly are. Both casual observation and psychological test data show that recreation personnel are about as extraverted as you are likely to find. But in their professional behavior—what they do on the job, what they write books about, and what they try to teach others to do—many seem to show greater concern with things like organizational charts; staff assignments; budget preparation, defense and allocation; facility or resource design and maintenance; and the rules and regulations that shall govern people's recreation behavior. These activities smack of a love for *things* and their orderly arrangements rather than a genuine concern for people as such. It is fair to ask whether anyone, recreation professional or otherwise, can really be genuinely concerned with *people*. Perhaps most of us are only capable of being genuinely concerned with a person or two. As is often suggested, if you discover that your true friends can be counted on one hand, do not be dismayed — feel fortunate.

Nevertheless, one must wonder what this heavy emphasis on things and abstract process is doing to recreation's potential for fostering creative growth in child and adult participants. In the terminology of the model presented above, the recreation field sometimes seems like the unilateral, reliable (?), competent (?) tutor who reinforces conforming responses and expects participants to assimilate the response alternatives proffered. The sterility of many recreation programs and places and the apparent lack of concern for exploration (by professionals or by the public they serve) is notable. Perhaps most or all recreation professionals occasionally allow, consciously or unconsciously, exploratory behavior to appear. But, often, these instances seem too infrequent and too superficial.

Some counter arguments to this characterization of the recreation field need to be acknowledged. First, organizational charts, budgets, rules, etc. are necessary and serve valuable functions. It is hopelessly idealistic to imagine that parks, playgrounds, recreation centers, and some resources can manage themselves. We might be surprised, however, at the positive outcomes that would follow a loosening of the reins in some instances. Total loosening, or a *laissez-faire* philosophy, in addition to being disastrous in some ways, will not promote creative growth in participants, as we tried to show by the accelerated-autonomy form of directiveness. Partial loosening of the tight structure of planning and programming might, of course, lead to *less well-managed* outcomes. But as our model also shows, well managed tasks constitute only a necessary not a sufficient condition for creative development of players.

Second, there is the claim, related to that of poorly managed outcomes, that people will "muck things up" (the environment, facilities, other participants' recreation) if recreational experiences are de-controlled. This rationalization for emphasizing institutionalized processes in recreation reminds us of the one used by some hunters to justify the killing of other animals for "sport." The hunted animals, it is claimed, are deficient in natural predators or sustenance, so if men do not kill them, they will die anyway from overpopulation or competition for scarce resources. Some of these benevolent-minded sportsmen do not appear to question how their prey came to be in this unnatural predicament in the first place. Perhaps because of the actions of previous "benevolent-minded" men? To what extent does the perceived need to regulate recreation experiences stem from some consequences of having regulated them in the past? Is it possible that some "mucking up" behaviors are exploratory forms of protest against institutionalized processes that were conceived in order to prevent people from "mucking things up?" There is evidence that this is exactly what happens in some types of regulated work situations, such as assembly lines. It is ironic that the recreation profession promotes itself as the opposite of such situations, as the guardian of people's leisure—the freedom from constraints and from the necessity to be occupied. Exploratory behavior is an important quality of leisure, and, if our model is correct, is essential to one of the outcomes of leisure —creative growth. Yet, such behavior is often blocked by the very people who claim to be leisure specialists.

The irony of the discrepancy between recreation's words and deeds can be seen another way. It can be fairly said that recreation is not alone among the service professions in its bureaucratized ways. Medicine treats patients' diseases pretty well but often makes the recipients feel degraded and helpless in the process; many teachers teach well but seem unable to help students learn (and there is a difference); school administrators sometimes appear to forget both teaching and learning; counselors sometimes devote enormous energy to describing their clients' problems in terms of some personality model rather than helping to solve the problems; and some policemen are good at enforcing the law but forget to help and protect the public.

An important difference between recreation and these other fields is the distance between rhetoric and reality. Most doctors know that they are highly trained technician-scientists who can remove your ulcers, prescribe the right antibiotic for your infection, or possibly repair your malfunctioning heart. They do not claim to do more. Recreation is one of the few fields, along with certain branches of mysticism and Sunday-morning evangelism, that claims significant effects on crime reduction; family functioning and unity; social and community development; physical fitness; mental health and therapy; the development of attitudes, values, leadership, and character; psychological and spiritual growth; and "self-actualization."

One wonders how a field can know or do anything about family problems when it seems blissfully unaware that in this explosive, exploratory world there are two-parent families, one-parent families, no-parent families, nuclear families, extended families, childless families, living-together-but unmarried   .
families, married-but-living-apart families, homosexual families, communal families, and probably many more. As for self-actualization, Abraham Maslow's eternal sleep might be fretful indeed, if he knew that the existing practice of recreation is being touted as the pathway to that ultimate state of personality development.

People, especially in America, are today exploring a large variety of life-styles and leisure pursuits. Much of this is motivated by an urge for creative growth. Some do not participate much in the hubbub but, instead, observe it, investigate it, try to understand it. Whether as participants or observers, people in other fields appear to be more aware of leisure, its current stirrings, its myths, its possible futures, than many recreation professionals.

In *Psychology Today* a sociologist investigated the rapid growth of around-the-clock activity in American cities. He showed the banks, supermarkets, garages, restaurants, discotheques, theatres, tour agencies, laundries, and other privately owned facilities were adopting all-night hours to cater to this nocturnal life. No mention was made of public recreation facilities. Are they involved in this latest trend? Many recreation personnel can tell you who won last year's Orange Bowl game and the exact score or the latest attendance figures at the community swimming pool. But do they have a clue, or do they care, what people are seeking by wandering about in the middle of the night?

Economists and other social scientists are investigating possibilities for completely revising the calendar and work-leisure cycles—for instance, a nine-day week with alternating six-day/three-day, on-off cycles. The way in which we structure and allocate time goes to the heart of what leisure is all about. Yet, where are the recreators—the leisure specialists—in thinking innovatively about this most fundamental commodity?

It is perhaps in the area of research that the reluctance of many recreators to engage in or encourage exploratory behavior is most noticeable. Recreation practitioners often complain of the irrelevance of research, the researcher's apparent lack of concern for "meeting" the practitioner's needs. Despite decades of thought and careful research into the nature of creative thinking, these complainers still are unaware of a fundamental fact: Relevance is not something that is given; it is something that is conceived or created in an individual's mind. The internal creative flame often needs external sources of fuel to feed it. But the sources, in themselves, are neither relevant nor irrelevant. It is an exploratory attitude and behavior that make them so.

After these critiques, it is appropriate to acknowledge that there are some changes, which perhaps signify exploratory thinking, in the recreation field. There is a growing emphasis on the leisure problems of special populations that are not in the mainstream of American or Canadian life; there is increasing recognition of the importance of personality, the individuality of leisure, and the possible need for individual lifestyle counselling; in a few communities, recreation departments are "opening up" facilities to multiple and unusual uses, dictated by the felt needs, or whims, of the participants. These approaches had to grow out of some exploratory thinking, because they show a recognition of the idiosyncracies of human needs—those that cannot be handled by the standardized operating procedure given by organizational charts and activity schedules. In a field that claims to deal in a quality, leisure, that represents freedom from constraints and uniformity, these kinds of approaches should be the rule, not the exception.

REFERENCES

1. The part of this paper that describes the model of play and creative growth originally appeared in Jeanrenaud, C. and Bishop, D. "Road Blocks to Creativity Through Play." In Wilkinson, P. (Ed.). *Play in Human Settlements*, London: Croom and Helm, Ltd., 1979. We gratefully acknowledge the cooperation of Paul Wilkinson and Croom and Helm, Ltd. in allowing a different and expanded version of our original paper to appear here.

2. Hutt, C. "Exploration and Play in Children." In *Symposium of the Zoological Society of London*. 18(1966), pp. 61-81.

3. Linford, A. G. and Jeanrenaud, C. "A Behavioral Model for a Four-Stage Play Theory." In Kenyon, G.S. (Ed.) *Contemporary Psychology of Sports*. Chicago: Athletic Institute, Chicago, 1970, pp. 446-450.

4. Hull, C. L. *Essentials of Behavior*. New Haven : Yale University, 1951.

5. Skinner, B. F., *Science and Human Behavior*. New York: McMillan, 1953.

6. Berlyne, D. E. *Conflict, Arousal and Curiosity*. New York: McGraw-Hill, 1960.

7. Fiske, D. W. and Maddi, S. *Functions of Varied Experience*. Homewood: Dorsey Press, 1961.

8. Piaget, J. *Play, Dreams and Imitation in Childhood*. London: Routledge and Kegan Ltd., 1951.

9. Harvey, O. J., Hunt, D. E. and Schroder, H. M.. *Conceptual Systems and Personality Organization.* New York: Wiley, 1961.

10. Eysenck, H. J. *The Biological Basis of Personality.* Springfield, Illinois: Charles C. Thomas, 1967.

11. Torrance, E. P. "Education and Creativity." In Taylor, C. W. (Ed.). *Creativity: Progress and Potential.* New York: McGraw-Hill, 1964, pp. 49-128.

12. Lieberman, J. N. "Playfulness and Divergent Thinking: An Investigation of Their Relationship at the Kindergarden Level." *Journal of Genetic Psychology*, 107: (1965), pp. 219-224.

13. Sutton-Smith, B. "The Role of Play in Cognitive Development," *Young Children*, 22: (1967), pp. 361-370.

14. Bishop, D and Chace, C. "Parental Conceptual Systems, Home Play Environment and Potential Creativity in Children," *Journal of Experimental Child Psychology.* 12(2), (1973), pp. 212-232.

15. Harvey, et al., *Op. Cit.*

16. *Ibid.*

(no keep)

p. 200 is blank.
End of Chapter 15

Chapter 16

Sources of Leisure Styles

John R. Kelly

The observable diversity in leisure is almost beyond description. Let your imagination roam freely enough to picture some of the variety.

- There are countless environments for leisure: natural, and constructed, open and confining, quiet and clamorous, inviting and forbidding . . .

- There are the social contexts of leisure: solitary and intensely interactive, silent and communicative, unstructured and rule-intensive, cooperative and competitive, exploratory and role-rigid, strange and familiar, comfortable and threatening, mass and intimate . . .

- There are the mental states of leisure: relaxed and tense, detached and intensely involved, preoccupied and exhibitionistic, free and conforming, excited and bored, seeking novelty or defensive, sensual or rational . . .

And there are the activities themselves: from daydreaming to drag-racing, running to reading, contemplation to conversation, gardening to grappling, painting to parading, and devotion to drinking.

However, much more significant are the orientations of engagement. Exactly the same activity may have different meanings for participants of the same age depending on how they define themselves in the experience. For example, a teen may drink decorously in anticipation of adult status-group behavior or rebelliously in defiance of both law and parental preferences. A woman in mid-life may take an evening class as a pastime, an exploration of her potential to begin a career, or hoping to meet interesting others. Retirement men and women may have a familial style of nonwork life or be seeking new investments in personal development. The real issue of style is not what people do, but how they do it.

All this suggests that the variety in leisure styles may be even greater than is palpably observable. Not only are there thousands of activities that may be leisure, but there are the different meanings, intensities of engagement, and intentions for any activity.

This chapter will explore the seeming endless diversity of activities that may be leisure, and the different meanings, intensities of engagement and intentions for any activity. Three models depicting ways of viewing people's activity patterns will be explored as a way of bringing some order to the diversity noted above. This search for order in what people do will be followed by a discussion of why people undertake specific activities or a particular activity in a particular way and what may account for changing patterns over the lifespan. A role-identity model will be used to show that leisure may vary in meaning and environments, in intention and intensity. And the self we present or hope to become may vary from one context to another. Leisure, with its decisive element of relative freedom for action, is a social space for becoming, for developing and establishing personal and social identities. Whether an event or interstitial in a routine of obligations, leisure has meanings and consequences that are more than the fillings of leftover time. The issue to be addressed is how individuals develop the different styles that characterize leisure in modern society.

THREE MODELS OF LEISURE STYLES

The "how" of leisure engagement, the style of participation, may be approached in a number of ways. Three basic approaches have emerged in the literature. Each has some basis in research, but each also has the potential to be deceptive and misleading.

The Stereotypes Model

Stereotypes are a form of convenient classification, based on attaching a label according to some simple and generally observable factor. Leisure stereotypes presuppose that individuals are essentially monothematic in their leisure. A leisure style may be multidimensional, but a stereotype is reduced to a single dimension.

The stereotype of the blue-collar male is that he is so stifled by his work routinization that he seeks only escape in the relatively undemanding leisure of drinking with male companions, watching television (especially contact sports), and occasional masculine excursions into the back country armed to the teeth to slaughter some small animal. The stereotype of the history professor is that he drinks a dry white wine, reads thin books of poetry, listens to string quartets, and carries an umbrella when the sky is clear. Stereotypes of adolescent males focus on sports and sexual aggression; of older widows on loneliness and soap operas; of young mothers on discussing toilet training with other mothers; and of urban singles on specialized bars and one-night stands.

Of course, we seldom know anyone who fits the stereotype. Further, the support seemingly given by research in the 1960s has largely evaporated. Multi-variate analyses of national samples in North America now report that very little variation in frequency of participation in kinds of activities can be accounted for by discriminating variables of sex, age, income, occupation, education, and race.[1] Once the threshold of real poverty is crossed, remaining correlations are largely limited to the masculine dominance of team sports and drinking in bars, decreases in active sport participation with age, a female reluctance to go hunting, and a relationship between education level and certain elite arts interests. Other correlations are generally too small to be substantively significant or useful.

A major justification for presuming the existence of leisure stereotypes has been on-site observation. However, seeing 1000 teens on a beach does not tell us where the other 100,000 are at the same time. Knowing that 50,000 went to a rock concert of Friday does not tell us what they will do on Saturday. Most of leisure is not that observable, and the stereotypes tend to be based on the very biased evidence of impressions gained at public events.

Surveys have been analyzed by computer programs that sort activities or participants according to frequency of participation in selected activities. Results produced classifications such as "active-diversionary," "status-based," "sports," "water-based," "backwoods," and "fast living."[2,3] Typologies are to some extent an artifact of what is included or excluded in the list of activities. More importantly such classifications do not provide an answer to the question of "Why?" What are the sources of stylistic differences?

This does not mean that there are no single-minded individuals who pursue a "high-risk" sport, fine arts production, or some social group to the exclusion of almost all else. Nor does it mean that there are no significant differences in leisure styles, in how people do what they do. But for most of the population, stereotypes are blurred by the commonalties of leisure as well as by the relative diversity of interests and commitments.

The Balance Model

The second model is based on the evident variety of leisure common to most individuals and on the multiplicity of meanings that they find in their activities. The same activity generally has more than one meaning. Those meanings shift from one occurrence to another depending on a number of social and environmental factors as well as the predisposition of the actor. Further, anticipations and satisfactions often change for the same activity as we move through our life course.

Nor do most persons engage in only one kind of activity. Rather, we do a variety of things seeking many different outcomes. We seek to make new friends and deepen ongoing intimacies, to learn new skills and enhance old competencies, to relax and discover excitement, to gain interpersonal acceptance and self-development, to express our individuality and strengthen role relationships, to discipline our bodies and free our imaginations, to think quietly and subject our minds to maximum stress, to risk uncertainty and enjoy comfort and security. In our leisure histories, we have found that certain activities, locales, and social contexts are most likely to produce related combinations of outcomes for us. So we return to such opportunities when we seek the outcomes.

The balance we seek may change through the life course. Opportunity structures are different for children, students, establishment adults, and so on. We are likely to seek to explore sexuality in adolescence, develop intimacy in early adulthood, enhance the nuclear family in childrearing years, seek personal reintegration in midlife, provide a context for social integration in later years, and employ leisure to begin again when life is disrupted by trauma.

In the balance model, leisure style is not a monothematic stereotype. Style is the combination of activities and contexts through which we seek to work out the hierarchy of meanings for leisure at that time in the life course. Leisure style is a pattern, not a label; the shape of a process, not a caricature. Style is the set of investments with the personal and social meanings they have for us. A leisure style may not be a perfect balance. At a given time, it may tilt toward personal expressivity, family solidarity, physical development, or affective involvement. Such themes are related to culture, educational and work experience, opportunities, resources, gender roles, family circumstances, and other factors that change during the life course. Thus, according to the balance model, style is multi-dimensioned and changing, with contrast and complexity rather than a single color of unrelieved hue and intensity.

The Core Model

The balance model is a significant step beyond stereotypes. However, there are strong grounds for adding to it. The core model does not deny the diversity and richness of the balance model. Rather, it adds one simple element: the considerable commonality of adult leisure.[4]

In a national sample of adults surveyed in the United States, 91 percent read for pleasure, 58 percent walked for pleasure, 48 percent swam, 88 percent watched television, 62 percent listened to the radio, 83 percent spent evenings with relatives regularly, and 65-75 percent engaged in sexual interaction.[5] The point is simply that there are a number of relatively accessible, low-cost, and often home-based activities that most people do a lot. Some involve the media, especially reading and television. Many are social, informal interaction with intimates who most often are those living in the same household. Some are found in the midst of nonleisure settings, a bit of fooling around at work or school or task-inattention almost anywhere.

The best-supported model, then, is probably the "core plus balance" model. The core tends to cross social lines, partly because opportunities are available and resource-free. It continues in some form through most of the life course.

The balance part of the model is most likely to change through the life course. As opportunities, developmental orientations, and social roles change, we seek somewhat different satisfactions in our leisure. Further, that balance is not just the same for everyone. I may not be able to imagine my own life without both music and strenuous physical activity. However, the contexts of sport and arts investments have both changed considerably in the last ten years; and no doubt will change again.

THE LIFE COURSE

Having searched for an explanation of common themes in leisure involvements, further explorations are necessary to account for the changes through the life-course. How are the core and balance affected through the life course? The core may be more stable than the balance for most persons, but neither is untouched by either the passing years of our lives nor by alterations in our social institutions. Leisure must change as our identities and roles change. Leisure in which intimacy is developed and expressed undergoes transitions as we mature, leaving the parental home, marry, divorce, become parents, see our children gain their own independence, and either die or are widowed. The social identities accepted and reinforced in our cultures change in relation to age. Insofar as leisure is a major social space for the expression and exploration of who we are, then it must change with age.[6] Here a few examples will have to serve to suggest that complex process.

Social Role Change

The life course involves major changes in all our institutional roles. Only leisure totally segregated from the rest of life can fail to be influenced by our role transitions. In the preparation period of life, we are primarily students rather than producers, dependent members of a family of orientation, and engaged in a number of developmental tasks related to gaining autonomy and independence, establishing personal and sexual identities, and learning the modes of acceptable personal and social interaction. The environments of our lives move from home and neighborhood outward to incorporate school and community. The playyard is augmented by the playing field, the home by other homes, and the neighborhood by the shopping center and other meeting places.

The transition to early establishment involves shifts in aims as well as opportunities for leisure. On school-leaving, the locales of leisure shift from school facilities and commercial locales to the residence augmented by special events in exterior locations. Companions narrow to intimate dyads in many cases and then expand back to inter- and intra-familial groups. Leisure is more tied to the establishment of institutional roles for those in the early stages of employment and to inaugurating a family. There is a concerted effort to retain and develop some leisure that contributes to personal growth and expression, some leisure that individuals claim as really their own.

Middle years may include a number of traumas and transitions. The traumas include mental and physical health problems for the self or significant others, the death of intimates, disruption of primary relationships in marriage, work crises from disillusionment to unemployment, and geographical relocations. These impact the opportunities, social contexts, and often personal resources for leisure. In turn, a major leisure investment of the self can influence decisions and resource allocations for home, family, and work. The diminution in salience of any one role can lead to concentration on another. Failure in family or work may turn us to a leisure investment of fulfillment and meaning. Loss of a leisure resource, on the other hand, may cause us to reinvest in our families.

The later years of life, a time of culmination and integration for many, may also encompass a loss of leisure resources—financial, social and personal. Yet leisure and leisure contexts of social interaction may at the same time become more important to our schedules, priorities, and self-concepts. As provider and caretaker roles recede, leisure and intimacy take on even greater significance. The loss of work schedules that have given shape to the week, reductions in income, possible health impairments, and eventual loss of the primary leisure companion for the marital survivors all require reorientations of leisure contexts, resources, associations, and even aims.

Developmental Changes

However, shifts in roles are not the only changes important to understanding leisure styles through the life course. A major contribution of Rhona and Robert Rapoport in the past decade was to begin to combine attention to leisure with both human development and social roles.[7] In our life journeys, we change not only externally, in our roles and environments, but internally in our selfhood. We respond to the social and biological timetables that call for us to change in what we are able to do, how we act and enact our roles, and how we define ourselves.

Some examples have already been introduced. In early adolescence, the child has to learn to define him or herself as a sexual and sexually-identified being, to become a man or woman among significant same and other-sex others. Later retirement years usually entail defining the self as one who was a contributing worker and who now finds meaning and identity without that ongoing role.

Other illustrations abound: There is the home and family-invested woman who finds herself without a life companion. How does she refine herself when so much had been invested in being a supportive homemaker? What about the woman who chooses to make a work identity primary in her life? What about the man who is told that his skills are redundant in the labor market, the youth who can no longer explain himself as still getting ready for some unspecified future, the professional who "burns out" in his or her vocation, and so on?

We are not just units being processed by the computer of life, bytes of information to be sorted by the great machine. We are reflexive, thinking and self-conscious animals who try to make sense of who we are and what we may become. We are always in the process of becoming. That process involves not only social negotiation over who we are; it involves a process of self-definition and development that is never finally fixed. We are always at work on ourselves, on how we can conceive of ourselves, our competencies, our limitations, and our gifts.

The Career of Leisure

Leisure, then, has a career. Like work and family, there is a line of behaviors and actions undertaken primarily for their own sake that we call "leisure." In this career, there is both change and continuity. There are evident changes in opportunities and competencies through the years. There are less-evident shifts in intentions and identities, in the aims of our lines of action and how we define ourselves within them.

In this career of leisure that intersects with our other life careers, style is not static—learned once in the familial culture and retained rigidly ever after. Leisure careers develop in a series of historical events and social changes that impact our lives. Further, there are culture-specific attitudes, values, modes of communication, and learned behaviors that make up part of our life and leisure styles. How we present ourselves to others, communicate who we are among others—that is, our public leisure styles—are learned in our culture and historical epochs. As a consequence, our leisure styles are not quite like those of any other age group when they were or will become our age; just as our own styles change through our life journeys.

A PLURALISTIC APPROACH TO LEISURE

In brief, this means that leisure is neither separate from its historical, social, and cultural contexts; nor is it wholly determined by them. Leisure is both social and existential. Leisure styles are social in being learned in the context of institutions and relationships. However, styles are also existential with dimensions of decision to take caution in which we develop who are are and would like to be. We do chose something of the shape and content of our leisure styles, but we choose out of the times and places through which we make our way.

From a pluralistic perspective, there are multiple and interrelated sources of leisure style. Leisure is always of the culture, ethnic. It is developed in a social context and responsive to the social structures and role norms of the system. It takes place in varied environments and is influenced by their location, size, shape, and quality. On the other hand, the variety of leisure cannot be explained in any deterministic model. It is not simply the result of one or two variables—social class, status forces, market provisions, marketing, mass media, or childhood socialization. Identifying sources of leisure styles does not lead to the further step of labelling "determinants" of leisure.

The two dimensions of leisure, the social and the existential, are also the two polarities in the dynamic of leisure styles. If leisure is neither totally segmented and separated from other roles and relationships nor fully determined by them, then some sort of dynamic relationship is implied. This relationship may be conceptualized as a dialectic in which the social and the existential in tension, with both synergy and conflict, produce actual leisure choices and investments. The sources of leisure styles are in this dynamic interplay between the structures of society and the existential self-creation of the individual.[8]

Leisure as Social

From the social side of the dialectic, leisure is viewed as learned behavior We are socialized into leisure. We learn not only how to engage in activities and interact with others in leisure settings, but we learn culture-specific values and orientations for our leisure. The ethnicity of leisure is evident in its aim as well as contents.

In a differentiated social system, divided by cultural identification as well as by economic position, we make our life journeys with different sets of opportunities for leisure. Further, we do not all learn the same expectations for our roles. What it means to be a father or mother, son or daughter, student or worker, neighbor and citizen all vary according to our positions in the society. We learn the same roles in different ways. Insofar as leisure is connected with those roles, then we can be expected to vary in our leisure behavior. We may party, drink, compete and travel; but in different ways. We may argue, flirt, play games, inaugurate friendships, and demonstrate our gender identities; but with quite different vocabularies, symbol systems, and presentations. We do not all play our parts in our social dramas alike; and, to a large extent, the differences have been learned in our socialization histories.

Nor do we cease learning at some magic point in our development. Leisure style may be changed, both because of how others define and respond to us and because of how we have come to understand ourselves. Further, what is available to us changes and we learn to adapt to our opportunities.

The Existential Element

Such learning does not negate the existential element in leisure. There is always the "not yet" of life, a looking forward to what we might become. We seldom see ourselves as completed products with nothing more in life than to finish out what is settled and unchangeable. We are always in a process of "becoming," of dreaming, planning and deciding how we may enact our roles in ways that alter and enhance what we may be in the future. We develop lines of action with at least a direction, if not a clear-cut plan and final goal. In leisure we act with intention and purpose.

Leisure may, in some periods in the life course, provide the fullest space for such existential operation. If leisure is the most free of life's spaces, the least determined by necessity and structure, then we may use our leisure opportunities, activities, and relationships to explore the potential of tomorrow. In the interplay between what is and what we might become, we try out new portrayals and new parts. We may explore the possibilities of change. In the relative freedom of leisure, we take the first steps toward selfhood and contexts for living that are not quite like the present. Leisure, despite the centrality of the present experience, may also have a decisive openness to the future.

THE ROLE-IDENTITY MODEL

The crucial issue is just how we bring together these seemingly disparate elements in leisure—the social and the existential, socialization and becoming. What I propose is an approach that combines each side of the dialectic in a "role-identity model." If style refers to how we enact our roles, then we need both the role context and the decisive element of enactment in the model. Role identity combines the social context with our self-definition of who we are in taking a role and how we choose to enact it.[9] Style, then, becomes a melding of role content and enactment, a bringing together in the decision process of what we have learned and what we seek to become.

Rather than belabor definitions, we may advance the argument best with three analytical examples:

(1) The party: If a party can be considered a leisure event, then its taken-for-granted and agreed-on expectations for behavior can be assumed to be leisure roles. Depending on the complexity of the party, there may be roles of being host and hostess, intimate helper, familiar friend, official guest, companion of guest, guest of honor, stranger and so on. The interaction patterns, self-presentations, physical gestures, degree of cooperation, self-placement in a central or peripheral position, and other elements of action are role-related.

However, an individual may be in multiple role relationship with others at the party—spouse to one, boss or employee to another, colleague, partner, neighbor, schoolmate, lover, political opponent, parent, and others. The reciprocal expectations and mutual histories cause the ways party roles are enacted to change from one grouping to another. We may be in several roles at any given time as people move through our milieu.

As if that were not complex enough, each actor may define him or herself somewhat differently in each of the roles. Therefore, in a given conversation, there is the delicate negotiation of presenting an identity that is not inconsistent for those familiar with any of the roles and yet furthers the line of action desired at that time and place. We may present a self that is not too assertive for a work superior, affectionate enough for an intimate, aggressive enough to secure a place in the interaction, and reserved enough to allow for redirection. Every shift in composition of our conversation group slightly alters how we play our roles. The process of the interaction may even cause us to redirect our self-portrayal as our identity takes shape in the event. We may become funnier, quieter, more poised, or less passive. We may play scholar in one episode, good old chap in another, sensitive listener in a third, and aloof superior in a fourth. In the role mix, we retune our presentations to offer identities—role portrayals— that fit our aims in that particular situation. As a consequence, the party becomes the social context for an endless variety of role-identity offerings. In fact, the real content of the leisure event is the negotiation of such role-identities.

(2) Swimming: As another illustration of how role-identities give insight into leisure styles, take the common leisure activity of swimming in a public pool. The various styles of behavior—from lounging near the fence and main-taining consistent distance from the water to exhibitionist diving, a boisterous ball game, or solitary swimming of fifty laps—are more than preferences for dif-ferent degrees of physical exertion. Rather, they reflect how identities are pre-sented in that leisure context. Further, the behavior may change if only one new person arrives on the scene. The sequence of life-course roles and related identities is demonstrated by the quite different behaviors exhibited by frolick-ing children, self-conscious and posing teens, caretaking young mothers, card-playing students, and disciplined length-counting later-life men and women. The leisure environment, the pool, provides a social context for demonstrating and trying out a wide variety of portrayals that are the basis for the different styles.

(3) Day-dreaming: Even in the movement-free leisure of day-dreaming, we try out identities. We may enter a normaly inaccessible environment, acquire previously unattainable skills, and interact with formerly-distant others. The leisure of day-dreaming may leap all kinds of barriers. However, we are still ourselves in some recognizable form. Even more, we transcend some of our normal limitations to try out identities outside our normal reach, relate to others

actually continents away, and develop interaction sequences that may never come to pass. Yet, in all this we are still acting out who we would like to be—on the stage of the imagination. And often the portrayal is that of a wished-for leisure style and competence.

THE CENTRALITY OF LEISURE

How does all this come together? We began with the variety of leisure. Stereotyping approaches were rejected in favor of a combination of core and balance that together make up an individual's leisure style. The core of accessible and informal engagements seems to change somewhat less than the balance through the life course. However, both are affected by role shifts and developmental needs. Leisure was then analyzed as a pluralistic phenomenon, neither separate from our institutional roles and cultures nor wholly determined by them. Leisure is both social and existential, shaped by socialization and yet encompassing future-oriented decision. Leisure is experience, with intrinsic meanings rather than productivity aims; yet it is also a social space in which we may work out meanings of selfhood that are crucial to our identities and our primary reltaionships.

Leisure styles, then, are not the result of some simple set of determinants that can be run through a computer to produce a profile of predicted styles. Again, style is more a matter of how than what, or who we are than what we do. All approaches and models are faulty when they begin with the assumption that leisure is somehow residual, leftover in time and always secondary in meaning. At one time, leisure may indeed be simple rest, a change from duty and a recuperation from strain. At another time and place, leisure may be at the absolute center of our lives, exactly where we develop our most significant relationships, express our most profound emotions and desires, and portray our most crucial indentities.

Leisure, then, requires an existential element, that dimension of freedom that enables us to choose—at least within limits—the contexts of our role portrayals. This relative freedom makes possible the investment of self that leads to the fullest development of ourselves, the richest expression of who we want to become, and the deepest experience of fulfillment. This freedom to choose also enables us to relate most fully and expressively to those intimate others central to our lives, to develop trust and communication, to experience histories of enjoyment, and to weave color and texture into our ongoing relationships. Leisure is freedom—sometimes freedom to fill time aimlessly and retreat from ourselves and others; but also to invest ourselves most fully, to seek to become something more than we have yet become, and to add the reality of joy to our bonds of intimacy.[10]

REFERENCES

1. Kelly, J. R. Outdoor Recreation Participation: A Comparative Analysis. *Leisure Sciences.* 3, 1980, pp. 129-154.
2. Bishop, D. and Witt, P. 1970. Sources of Behavioral Variance During Leisure Time. *Journal of Personality and Social Psychology.* 16, 1970, pp. 352-360.
3. McKechnie, G. The Psychological Structure of Leisure: Past Behavior. *Journal of Leisure Research.* 6, 1974, pp. 27-44.
4. Kelly, J. R. Leisure Styles: A Hidden Core. *Leisure Sciences.* 5, 1983, pp. 321-338.
5. Kelly, J. R. *Leisure.* 2nd edition. Englewood Cliffs, New Jersey: Prentice-Hall, 1989.
6. Kelly, J. R. *Leisure Identities and Interactions.* London: George Allen and Unwin, 1983.
7. Rapoport, R. and R. *Leisure and the Family Life Cycle.* London: Routledge and Kegan Paul, 1975.
8. Kelly, J. R. Leisure Interaction and the Social Dialectic. *Social Forces.* 60, 1981, pp. 304-332.
9. McCall, G. and Simmons, J. *Identities and Interactions,* 2nd edition. New York: Free Press, 1978.
10. Kelly, J. R. *Freedom to Be: A New Sociology of Leisure.* New York: MacMillan, 1987.

End of Chapter 16

Chapter 17

Marketing: Neither Snake Oil Nor Panacea

John L. Crompton

An increasing number of managers in recreation and leisure settings are recognizing that marketing offers a useful framework for explaining and integrating many of the decisions involved in the delivery of services. However, few have had formal training in marketing with the result that there is a lack of insight and understanding of marketing principles and techniques. The simplicity of the marketing paradigm has a beguiling attraction. But beneath this attractive veneer there is a complex web of issues which require much greater consideration, knowledge, and understanding than they are generally accorded. Marketing is often presented as nirvana, a cure-all and solution to all management problems. However, much of what is currently applied under the name of marketing in this field is snake oil with minimal redeeming qualities.

This article discusses four common conceptual fallacies. They represent misapplications of marketing principles or techniques which are widely found in the field. These usually occur because the principles have been gleaned from a *superficial* awareness of what has been done successfully by others either elsewhere in the public sector or in the private sector. In some instances the principles are deemed to have failed because either the expectations associated with them were unrealistic, or because there was a failure to recognize the differences between the objectives and operating environments of public leisure agencies and the commercial sector. After discussion of the conceptual fallacies, the article concludes with two common failings of implementation. In these instances, there may be a good understanding of marketing principles, but lack of experience in implementing them has led to relatively disappointing results.

FALLACY #1:   MARKETING IS A EUPHEMISM FOR HUCKSTERISM

Although recreation and park professionals would be indignant at any suggestion that they were hucksters, many of them have unwittingly adopted the
approach of the huckster in their efforts to engage in marketing. Marketing is
two things. First, it is a philosophy, an attitude, or a perspective. Second, it is a
set of activities used to implement that philosophy. Many recreation and park
personnel, like the huckster, embrace neither the philosophy nor the full set of
marketing activities when they try to engage in marketing.

Acceptance of the philosophy is a prerequisite for successful implementation
of the set of marketing activities. The philosophy of marketing is simple and
intuitively appealing. It is a philosophy which states that the social and economic justification for an agency's existence is the satisfaction of customer
wants. It entails establishing a way for an agency to learn about customer wants,
and to use that information internally to create marketing programs that will
satisfy targeted clienteles.

This philosophy has evolved over time as the understanding of marketing
has passed through various stages in the recreation and parks field. These stages
may usefully be labeled the product era, the sales era, and the marketing era.
Although these three eras evolved sequentially, all three orientations still exist in
the field today.

Before the mid 1970s, public leisure agencies typically practiced what might
be called "minimal marketing." They assumed that demand for a service would
grow simply because they were offering it well. Thus, they did not consciously
perform marketing functions. Their thinking was, "Why should we have to sell
a worthwhile service?" Agency personnel were *product oriented*. That is, they
were primarily concerned with producing more of what they produced, rather
than with selling the services they produced, or trying to learn what clients
wanted them to produce.

Many recreation and park agencies are still product oriented. They regard
their primary task as providing the facilities, services, and programs which they
consider to the most appropriate, as efficiently as they are able, within the
resources that they have available. Their orientation is inward looking, dominated by programs, presumptions and processes. There is a presumption that it is
"our agency" rather than a recognition that it is the residents' agency. The
extent to which a service meets people's needs is not carefully considered. Such
agencies feel they have fulfilled their obligation by simply making the facilities,
services, and programs available.

A product-oriented agency decides what it can do best, or what it wants to
do, and then offers internally designed programs and services to the public.
Such agencies hope that the public accepts the programs and services and uses

them. Services are offered on a "take it or leave it" basis. If there is no response to an offering, these agencies are likely to conclude "The citizens missed a fine opportunity: we did our best."

The following are typical manifestations of a product-oriented agency:

- Day camp or summer programs which operate 9:00 a.m. - 4:00 p.m. This gives the program staff who come in at 8:00 a.m. an hour to organize their program materials and equipment before the children arrive. Similarly, they have an hour at the end to tidy up after the programs before they leave at 5:00 p.m. These hours are convenient for the staff but very inconvenient for client families in which both parents work 8:00 a.m.-5:00 p.m.

- A swimming pool at which loud, "heavy metal" pop music was played over the speakers. The pool was a small, shallow neighborhood pool used exclusively by parents and their young children. Teenagers went to larger more exciting pools elsewhere in the city. When asked, "Why is pop music being played?" the response was, "Because the teenage lifeguards like it." The musical preferences of the users were not considered.

In the late 1970s the situation changed for many agencies. When resources were no longer as plentiful, economic necessity forced them to go beyond the prevailing product orientation. There was a growing awareness of the need to adopt a more aggressive posture and persuade clients to use services in order for agencies to develop a constituency which would oppose budget cuts. The primary emphasis shifted from a product orientation to a *selling orientation*. However, emphasis was still on the service being sold rather than on the benefits that clients wanted to receive.

Agencies adopting a selling orientation decide what programs should be offered and make an effort to aggressively sell and promote them to potential users. Instead of merely offering programs and services on a take it or leave it basis, selling-oriented agencies attempt to convince prospective clients that they should participate in the program or use the service.

It is at this stage, when agencies ask "What do we want to offer that we must convince clients to support?" that similarities with the huckster emerge. There are three primary characteristics of a huckster. These are:

1. Hucksters will sell anything they can, irrespective of whether or not it satisfies a client's want or needs. They think of what the sale will do for them and their agency, rather than what it will do for their clients.

2. Hucksters focus on the immediate sale. They do not think about repeat
    business from their clients.

3. Hucksters will use intensive promotion in an effort to persuade a client to
    use a service, even if it is not to the client's advantage to do so.

In the 1980s some agencies recognized the limitations of this selling
orientation and moved one step higher up the evolutionary ladder to embrace
a *marketing orientation*. There was a recognition that what an agency thinks it
produces is not of primary importance to its success. What a client thinks he
or she is buying determines what an agency is, what it produces, and whether
or not it will prosper. Success is not determined by the producer, but by the
consumer.

Central to the concept of marketing is the attitude, "produce what you should
sell," rather than, "sell what you can produce." Thus, an agency is more likely
to succeed if it tries to understand people on their own terms, "looks through its
clients' eyes," identifies what the client wants, and then provides it. A well-
known marketing aphorism states: "To sell Jack Jones what Jack Jones buys,
you have to see Jack Jones through Jack Jones' eyes." This increased responsiveness to the client has led to the emergence of the marketing or consumer-
service orientation in a few recreation and park agencies.

Embracing the marketing concept requires agency personnel to determine
what client groups want, and then to provide services that meet those wants.
Consider the question, "How do you get street kids into recreation centers?"
This is a selling orientation which is doomed to failure. The marketing answer
to this question is, "You don't: you get street kids into street programs."
Whereas selling and hucksterism focus on the needs of the seller, marketing
focuses on the needs of the buyer.

> The aim of marketing is to make selling superfluous. The aim of
> marketing is to know and understand the consumer so well that the
> product or service fits him and sells itself. Ideally, marketing should
> result in a customer who is ready to buy. All that should be needed
> then is to make the product available, i.e., logistics rather than sales
> manship, and statistical distribution rather than promotion.[1]

Hucksters seek to achieve their sale through intensive promotion activities.
In contrast, marketers recognize that promotion is only one of six primary
marketing activities (Figure 1). It is the tip of the iceberg, the most visible
marketing activity and the one which arouses public attention. The marketer
recognized that each of the other five, which are below the surface and not as
visible, are just as important as promotion.

Figure 1

Six Primary Marketing Activities

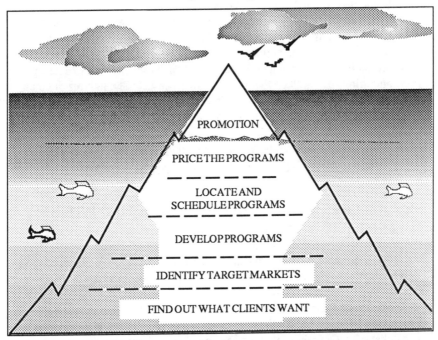

Three key questions provide insight into the extent to which an agency and its personnel are marketing oriented. The first question is: "Why do we do what we do today?" The answer should be, "Because our clients want these services and regard them as high priorities." Unfortunately, the real reason frequently is product oriented: because the agency has always offered this service, or because it is what the staff have been trained to do and they feel comfortable doing it.

The second question is "What are we doing differently than we were doing five years ago?" If the answer is "not much," then the agency is probably product or selling oriented because citizen needs and priorities are likely to have changed in the last five years.

The third question is: "How much market research does the agency do?" Frequently, the answer is, "none." Few commercial organizations with a multi-million dollar budget would dare to invest that magnitude of expenditure without engaging in research to monitor the investment to determine whether it was warranted. Without research to guide it, the agency is like a ship ploughing through the seas with great energy and effort, but without a compass to check whether it is heading for the rocks or a safe harbor. Sometimes the expressed rationale for not doing market research is, "It is a waste of money, we know what they want." A cursory review of the literature in this field will reveal a host of studies reporting what managers thought clients wanted and what clients actually said they wanted, and invariably the two lists are different.

A marketing orientation may appear to be expensive because it requires an investment of time, money, and personnel to find out what a clientele wants. However, a marketing orientation is, in the long run, likely to be less expensive than a product or selling orientation because it enables an agency to act responsively and minimize ineffective allocation of resources. The failures of an agency can usually be traced to its neglect of the basic wants and desires of its potential clients. As Aldous Huxley is alleged to have pointed out, it is not very difficult to persuade people to do what they are all longing to do. A marketing orientation is more troublesome, more bother, and more difficult, but it is also more rewarding, given its greater potential for success.

FALLACY #2: MARKETING IS CONCERNED WITH SELLING PROGRAMS

The most important marketing question a recreation and park manager has to ask is "What business are we in?" The answer to this question guides all marketing actions.

People spend their money, time, and energy resources with the expectation of receiving benefits, not for the delivery of services. Programs themselves are not marketable. Only their benefits have a value to client groups. This distinction has enormous implications for the way in which agencies define their business.

If an agency defines its business in terms of specific services, it is likely that it will miss opportunities to serve its clientele, for there is often a very wide range of programs through which peoples' wants may be met. Instead of specific programs, the starting point should be meeting client group wants. This may be achieved through a wide variety of services. For example, primary benefits people seek from using libraries are specific information, entertainment, and general-knowledge. These benefits can be facilitated through a wide variety of programs and services including books, movies, lectures, discussion groups, and trips. It is not the book that is important, rather it is the information, entertainment, or general-knowledge benefit derived from reading that the consumer seeks. By offering other services in addition to books, libraries are able to reach more residents and to better satisfy their existing clientele.

Those agencies and personnel who think of their job in programmatic rather than benefit terms are vulnerable to being afflicted by marketing myopia.[2] Too often public leisure personnel define their business in product terms such as athletics, aquatics, parks, or arts. These are programs and the marketing concept implies that our business should be defined in terms of the consumers' wants.

Charles Revson, who was responsible for building Revlon cosmetics into the thriving enterprise it is today, is reputed to have said, "In the factory we make cosmetics. In the store we sell hope." Women use cosmetics but they do not buy them; they buy hope. In a like manner the recreation and park agency develops and offers services and programs. Participants purchase benefits; the programs are simply a means to an end. These benefits may include such things as social interaction, prestige, relaxation or escape.

Taking a benefits approach helps us to understand that different people may participate in the same program but they will often be seeking different benefits. Similarly, people may be able to derive similar benefits from very different programs. Thus, instead of specific programs, the starting point should be meeting client group wants.

At a recent workshop, aquatic personnel were faced with a problem: attendance at the city pools had declined substantially in the past three years. The workshop participants identified their primary market as teenagers and, after discussion, determined that the primary benefit which teenagers sought at the pools was socialization. The workshop participants divided into groups for a brainstorming session in which they were asked to list all the program ideas they could think of which would facilitate socialization for teenagers in a swimming pool. After the 30-minute brainstorming session, 142 different program ideas emerged. The participants were surprised and elated at the result. Many of the ideas were new, exciting and feasible. Once they had moved away from defining their business in such product-oriented terms as "managing an aquatic facility" toward the marketing-oriented definition "facilitating socialization opportunities for teenagers," a new range of programs emerged which offered potential for reversing the attendance decline.

While the definition of an agency's business should be sufficiently broad to provide room for growth to respond to the changing environment, at the same time it should be narrow enough to give specific direction to the agency. If the definition is too broad, then it may not be useful for giving direction. For example, little useful guidance is likely to be gained by a manufacturer of lead pencils defining his or her company as being in the "communications business." There must be a common thread linking existing offerings and proposed new services. Expansion into service areas outside the leisure field for which the agency has no "feel" and no management expertise is unlikely to lead to client satisfaction or to enhance the agency's reputation.

In defining the business we are in, the key question is not, "What is the best way that benefits can be facilitated through the traditional leisure services we have offered given the resources available?" That would be a myopic approach. Rather the appropriate question to ask is, "What is the best way that sought benefits can be facilitated, given the resources available?"

All services are likely to decline over time, no matter how vigorous their present growth. In the present environment, a leisure agency's interpretation of the business it is in is not likely to be useful for longer than five to seven years.

Changes may occur either because client group wants and the benefits they seek change, or because competitors offer more effective programs for servicing those wants. If the agency does not change by reexamining its business definition and adjusting its program offerings accordingly, that agency is also likely to decline. In asking "What is our business?" agencies also need to add "And what will it be in five to seven years time, given the changes in the environment we can presently discern?"

Answering the question "What business are we in?" in terms of the benefits rather than programs or services has at least four important advantages:

- It ensures that an agency retains its focus on client groups and does not become preoccupied with programs, services, or the agency's internal needs.

- It encourages innovation and creativity of programs and services by suggesting that there are many ways to service similar client group wants.

- It stimulates an awareness of changes in client group wants as they occur, and hence services are more likely to remain relevant.

- It will probably lead to a broader definition of the role of the agency and thus contribute toward keeping its services abreast of society's wants.

FALLACY #3: MARKETING IS PRIMARILY AIMED AT GENERATING REVENUES

To many public recreation and park people, the term "marketing" is anathema because they perceive it to entail a shift away from the primary mission of encouraging human growth, toward a focus on generating revenues. Marketing frequently connotes an activity associated with the commercial sector's goal of maximizing revenue. Certainly, the crisis which stimulated an interest in marketing by many public leisure agencies was a reduction in operating revenues from tax sources which became prevalent in the late 1970s. It is no coincidence that at this time most of the agencies which are seriously committed to adopting marketing concepts and tools are located in those areas of the country which have been most subjected to financial constraints.

Many recreation and park managers have no formal training in marketing but they are aware that it is considered to be a key ingredient by commercial organizations in their efforts to generate a profit. Thus, marketing frequently is perceived as a promising approach for increasing revenues. However, the equation "marketing = more revenues" is overly simplistic and misses the point. Marketing offers a philosophy and a set of neutral tools which can be used to contribute to the attainment of desired objectives.

In the private sector, the desired objective is profit. However, in the public sector there are other equally important objectives. The "marketing = more revenues" equation is often inappropriate because public agencies are not commercial businesses. Their primary reason for being is not to generate revenue. They are social service agencies which are searching for new tools so they can be more efficient (or "business-like") in achieving their goals.

In the late 1960s and early 1970s considerable controversy was engendered in the marketing literature by the initial suggestion that marketing principles and techniques were appropriate for use by public agencies. Critics argued that marketing should be confined to market transactions characterized by the sale and purchase of goods and services by private sector firms.[3]

Over time it was realized that the set of marketing activities are neutral tools which can be used to assist an agency to achieve whatever objectives it established. It is this characteristic which makes their application as appropriate for use by public leisure agencies as in commercial enterprises. Marketing is a process concerned with maximizing the use of scarce resources to achieve whatever objectives a community seeks. The interrelationship of the set of marketing activities is shown in Figure 2 (page 222) and this model can be applied equally well in a public agency program which yields zero revenue, as it can in Disney World. For example, the market research or intelligence may reveal a need for wellness opportunities for senior citizens.

- The target market is senior citizens and this may be defined more narrowly using descriptors such as age (e.g., under 70 and over 70), income, ethnicity, singles and couples, etc.

- The program may involve physical recreation, mental health, financial planning, nutrition, counselling, or any other subject that contributes to wellness.

- Distribution involves decisions about where the programs should be offered and when they should be scheduled.

- Promotion involves communicating details of the program to senior citizens. How can seniors be effectively contacted? What media should be used? How should the content of the message be structured?

- Finally, price decisions have to be made. The decision may be to charge nothing. However, participants are still faced with a series of other costs they have to pay to use the program. These may include travel costs, the opportunity cost of their time, embarrassment costs associated with difficulties in interacting with others, and the physical effort or personal energy costs expended in getting to the program.

Figure 2
The Set of Marketing Activities

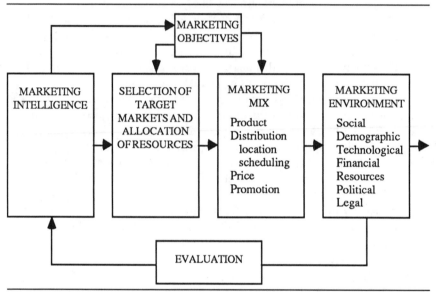

After these decisions have been made, the program is provided and its success is monitored. Feedback serves as market intelligence which may be used to adjust the product, distribution, promotion or price if the service is not as successful as had been anticipated.

The perception of marketing as focusing a department's attention on revenue production rather than human growth reflects a misunderstanding of its potential. Since discovering the marketing paradigm and its potential (around the late 1950s), the private sector has been the primary and most visible implementer of marketing, using the tools to maximize revenue. Much of the resistance to marketing by recreation and park practitioners would dissipate if there was an understanding of this. In 25 years time the connotations of marketing reflecting revenue production will probably no longer be paramount.

FALLACY #4: MARKETING IGNORES EQUITY

This issue is related to the misplaced tendency to focus on revenue generation when an agency initiates a marketing program. Most recreation and park professionals have failed to understand the important role of equity in implementing a marketing effort. All organizations strive to be efficient, effective and accountable, but in addition public agencies have to be equitable. There is often a conflict between efficiency and equity that is overlooked. The two concepts are defined in the following paragraphs.

Efficiency

Because efficiency is relatively well understood and has been discussed at length in the literature, it will only be briefly defined here.[4] Efficiency measures the amount of effort and expense involved in offering a service and is concerned with the question, "To what extent does the agency produce the output as inexpensively as it could?" It is measured in such terms as attendance days per dollars expended, subsidy per person in a program, acres maintained per dollars expended, or number of hours of operation per dollars expended.

Equity

The concept of equity has been explored in detail elsewhere,[5] but it has received relatively little attention in the recreation and parks literature. For this reason, a more extensive exposition is provided here.

In every resource-allocation decision there are winners and losers. Equity addresses this issue by asking the question, "Who gets what?" Because subjective, normative judgements are involved. There probably cannot be any "right" or "wrong" concept of equity. Indeed, three fundamentally different models of equity are commonly recognized. These are equal opportunity, compensatory equity and market equity.

Equal Opportunity is the most widely accepted model of equity. Its wide acceptance is probably a reflection of traditional values which recognize equal protection under the law. Equal opportunity entails allocating equal amounts of services to all citizens, regardless of need or the amount of taxes paid.

Compensatory Equity involves allocation of services so that disadvantaged groups, individuals or areas receive extra increments of resources. The operational objective of this equity model is to increase the compensatory role of public leisure services so opportunities for the underprivileged are improved. This requires that resources be allocated in proportion to the intensity of the need for them.

Market Equity entails allocating services to groups or neighborhoods in proportion to the tax or fee revenues that they produce. Market equity draws from the prevalent allocation model used in the private sector. Full commitment to this equity model would mean accepting the principle that residents are not entitled to equal access to outlets, and that residents' needs are not relevant unless they are backed up by dollar votes in the marketplace.

Demand Is An Inadequate Surrogate—it is not an equity model. However, it is included in this discussion since it is used extensively as a surrogate in lieu of a real equity model. The demand approach allocates resources on the basis of consumption and/or vociferous advocacy or complaints. It cannot serve to guide the allocation of services in a predetermined, agreed direction. Rather it is a complicating factor—a pragmatic, reactive approach to which agency personnel and elected officials frequently resort because it is administratively convenient. Its use is likely to result in an unpredictable and inconsistent set of winners and losers. Demand may lead to adoption of a pattern of services reflecting any of the three conceptual alternatives discussed previously, or it may fluctuate inconsistently among them.

The Dilemma

Traditionally, most recreation and park agencies have adopted either the compensatory or equal-opportunity equity models. However, as part of their efforts to be better marketers, and fallaciously believing that marketing implies increased revenues, many agencies are adopting higher prices. In so doing they are moving away from the two traditional models toward the market-equity model. The market-equity model enhances efficiency and responsiveness of resource allocation. Residents do not receive services they do not want, nor are they required to pay through the tax system for what other residents use.

This approach offers the most efficient use of resources but it ignores the social benefits associated with compensatory equity and equal opportunity. If market equity was completely adopted, then individuals and groups deprived by the operation of the private sector would be disadvantaged by the public sector as well. Adoption of this model would mean that, over time, recreation and park services would be substantially reallocated from poor neighborhoods to wealthier neighborhoods and directed exclusively at those client groups that can afford to pay.

The basic question is "What is our mission and whom should we be serving?" In the private sector, organizations usually give priority to developing target markets most likely to be responsive to particular offerings. However, park and recreation agencies seeking to service multiple potential markets face a dilemma. Potential client groups have differing abilities to pay and each market segment is likely to have a different price elasticity of demand. This means that when a price increase is imposed, it has a different impact on the quantity of demand from each group.

Which potential target markets should be given service priority? Is the agency to act like a private organization and ignore those segments likely to be less responsive to service offerings if prices are raised? If the role of the public agency is to facilitate delivery of a particular service to as many constituents as possible, and to complement the private sector, then public-sector agencies should be concentrating efforts on these less-responsive segments, leaving the more responsive segments to the private sector.

The development of marketing efforts aimed at relatively unresponsive target markets is a problem unique to marketers in public agencies. Indeed, the most critical question facing park and recreation agencies often is not how to develop marketing efforts to optimally service relatively responsive target markets, but rather what strategies are most useful for attracting those who are apathetic, disinterested, or reluctant to use service offerings.

Although many recreation and park services are initially justified on the basis of their compensatory contribution, their relative success often has been evaluated not in equity terms, but rather in terms of their efficiency and to a lesser extent their effectiveness. Two reasons have contributed to this inappropriate evaluation priority. First, because efficiency measures are more readily available than equity measures, it is expedient to measure recreation and park service delivery only in terms of efficiency. Second, budgetary constraints have forced agency managers to increasingly focus upon efficiency. The situation was summed up by one agency in these terms, "We do not render services to collect money. However, it is now necessary for us to collect money in order to render service." In times of financial scarcity it is relatively easy to secure increases in cost efficiency by changing from a compensatory to a market-equity perspective.

Park and recreation agencies have limited financial resources, which means that they are required to address the dilemma of who should be given priority in service delivery. The resolution of the dilemma is dependent upon how an agency interprets what constitutes a fair or equitable allocation of resources.

It is not sufficient to evaluate services only in terms of efficiency because this may result in an equity model deemed to be inconsistent with an agency's mission. Thus, although it is likely that an additional number of dollars may generate more recreation attendance at a program, and hence be more efficient if invested in one neighborhood, greater equality of opportunity or greater compensatory results to disadvantaged groups may be produced if it were spent in a different neighborhood.

Consider the case of a large traditional outdoor swimming area in a major metropolitan area operated by a public agency. Annual attendance was 120,000 visits. There was an admission charge of 50 cents and the facility was a break-even proposition over the course of a season. The agency then leased out the facility to an operator who transformed it into an aquatic theme park. The admission charge was increased to $8.50. In its first year 400,000 visits were recorded and the agency received $330,000 from the lease arrangements. This was cited by the agency as a good example of the results of its marketing efforts. But is it?

In terms of efficiency the agency has made a quantum step forward since the facility accommodated many more visits and net revenue increased by $330,000. But what about equity? Has there been some displacement? Are the users the same people who used it before the lease or have those people been squeezed out by the new high prices? If there has been displacement is the efficiency/ equity trade-off justified? There may be other inexpensive aquatic opportunities offered by the agency in close proximity to which displaced clients may gravitate. Further, the $330,000 revenue increase may enable new services to be developed for low-income groups for which previously there was no funding.

If efficiency/equity trade-offs such as this swimming pool situation are to be rationally addressed, three steps must be taken. First, an agency must determine what business it is in and adopt a statement of mission and objectives which will serve as the guiding criterion for all subsequent efficiency/equity trade-off decisions. Second, the impact of price on equity needs to be assessed by conducting surveys which monitor changes in user characteristics when price increases are implemented. Third, accurate cost-accounting data are required to measure the relative efficiency of delivering a service by identifying all costs associated with it.

Public-sector marketing is concerned not only with efficiency but also with equity, and it is this latter concern which is the primary characteristic distinguishing if from marketing in the private sector. Many public leisure agencies are rushing into marketing and seeking greater efficiency, but they are ignoring equity implications. This is not consistent with the mission of public agencies.

IMPLEMENTATION FAILINGS

In some instances there may be a good understanding of marketing principles, but lack of experience in implementation may lead to relatively disappointing results. Two such implementation failings concern the role of marketing specialists and the use of needs assessments.

There is often a belief that to have a successful marketing program an agency must have marketing specialists who are charged with the task of marketing the agency's offerings. Such specialists are likely to be helpful but it is important that they continue to engender awareness of the basic principles of marketing among all staff as well as to undertake specific assigned project responsibilities. If this general education function does not occur, then the hiring of a marketing specialist may be a step backwards rather than the anticipated quantum leap forward in the marketing effort.

The establishment of a marketing division may be an immediate signal to all other personnel that marketing is no longer their problem or responsibility. Thus, two percent of agency personnel have a marketing title and a marketing function, while 98 percent may comfortably return to being product oriented.

The attitude and actions of all personnel must be marketing oriented. A single employee may be the only contact a particular client has with an agency. Hence, in that client's mind, the employee is representative of the agency. A single person who is not client oriented can totally undermine the efforts of a marketing specialist. For example, if the person answering the telephone is abrupt or discourteous, that contact is taken by the client as being representative of the agency's orientation.

Those staff members who deal face-to-face with client groups are likely to be the first to learn about changes in client wants and to be most responsive to them. They provide key feedback. If they are not client oriented and sensitive to the implementation of the set of marketing activities, it is unlikely that the agency's marketing efforts will be successful no matter how many marketing specialists are hired.

It was noted earlier that too many agencies do not engage in any market research. Among those who do invest in it, some fail to interpret the findings correctly, because they do not understand the limitations and purpose of the research. Although there is general agreement that needs assessments should form the starting point of a marketing effort (Figure 2, p. 222), it is important to emphasize that they cannot replace professional judgement; they are an aid to it. Indeed, it is a dangerous fallacy to suppose that the answer to every marketing problem is more or better information.

Not all new service offerings, for example, ought to originate in response to a stated or obvious need, because needs are likely to be at least partially defined by clients' knowledge of the availability of services. There was no recognized need by consumers for powdered potatoes, xerography, computers, or windsurfing until they were available.

Preferences articulated by client groups must be mediated by sound professional judgement as to how sought benefits may be facilitated. The consumer is *not* king. If consumers were kings (or queens) they would know exactly what they wanted and demand it. However, we are all prisoners of our experiences. There is a well-known adage which suggests that "people don't know what they want - they only want what they know." Consumers have a limited set of experiences and are unlikely to assertively request anything beyond those experiences because they are not aware of benefits which may accrue from other potential offerings. For example, before the automobile was invented people knew they wanted transportation but could not articulate these sought benefits in terms of a motorized vehicle.

Consider the following example:

> If symphony orchestras always played what a majority of audiences
> requested, then Beethoven's Fifth Symphony and Tchaikovsky's
> *1812 Overture* could well be played every week! If the audience
> were to be given exclusive decision rights as to what is performed,
> then there is a danger that the classical music repertoire would be
> relatively narrow and sterile. However, human beings seek optimal
> arousal. They respond positively to new stimuli which avert
> boredom. Thus, there is likely to be a positive response to new
> artistic experiences of which audiences were previously unaware.[6]

Complete disregard of the potential for professional insight to improve
service delivery options means a very substantial resource in which the public
has invested would be ignored. The distinction is subtle between a product
orientation and discounting overt popular preference in favor of professional
judgment. The essential difference is that the latter approach focuses on the
long-term needs of the consumer, while the former approach exhibits no genuine
effort to be responsive to consumers' behavior or needs.

Interpreting the numerical responses to needs assessment surveys requires
considerable skill, experience and judgement. For example, if 70 percent of
residents prefer project A compared to 30 percent who prefer project B, does
that mean project A should be given highest priority? If A is a swimming pool
and there are several already in the city, whereas B is an ice-rink of which there
are presently none, then a decision to proceed with the rink rather than the pool
may be the right decision in order to provide a balance of leisure opportunities.
A public agency has to serve pluralities and not yield to the tyranny of the
majority, which is what happens if needs assessment numbers make the decision
rather than professional judgement.

The challenge is to study client groups, listen to them, observe them, and
then to *interpret* their input and behavior. It is inappropriate to implement what
consumers ask for on every occasion, because this usurps the opportunity to take
advantage of professional expertise.

Needs assessments are valuable tools for gathering information which
should lead to better decision making. They offer illumination and insights but
they do not make decisions. Some administrators see needs assessments as a
costly and time-consuming process that does not produce benefits sufficient to
justify their expense. This is an appropriate generalization often made by
managers who believe that experience and intuition are the only tools useful for
decision making. Both are necessary. While it is true that needs assessments
cannot eliminate uncertainty, it is equally true that they can substantially reduce
uncertainty. Failure to do market research of this type will lead to managers
remaining "permanently superficial" about the client groups they seek to serve.

FINAL THOUGHTS

The philosophy and set of tools which comprise marketing have proven to be an effective framework for the delivery of commercial sector services. Interest in their use in the public sector emerged only in the late 1970s. Marketing is in its formative years in the recreation and parks field. It suffers from frequent inaccurate conceptualization and inexperienced implementation. Marketing is in the early introduction stage of its life cycle. Trial and error and fine tuning are normal manifestations when launching any unfamiliar tool or product.

Marketing emerged in the commercial sector in the late 1950s and it is only in recent years that it has been widely understood. Given this experience, it seems reasonable to hypothesize that the widespread diffusion of a real understanding of marketing in the public recreation and parks field may take another decade. As the concept diffuses, we can look forward to a consistent rise in the quality of the performance of recreation and park agencies.

REFERENCES

1. Drucker, P. F. *Management: Tasks, Responsibilities, Practices*. New York: Harper and Row Inc., 1974, p. 64.
2. Levitt, T. N. "Marketing Myopia," *Harvard Business Review*, July-August 1960, pp. 45-56.
3. See for example Luck, D. J. "Broadening the Concept of Marketing Too Far" *Journal of Marketing*. 33(July 1969), pp. 53-55.
4. See for example Hatry, H. P., et al. *How Effective Are Your Community Services?* Washington D.C. The Urban Institute, 1977, p. 217, and Buchanan, J. M. *The Public Finances*, Homewood, Illinois: Irwin, 1970, pp. 452-453.
5. Crompton, J. L. and Wicks, B. E. "Implementing a Preferred Equity Model for the Delivery of Leisure Services in the United States Context" *Leisure Studies*. 7(No. 3), September, 1988.
6. Seales, D. P. "Marketing Principles and the Arts," in Mokwa, M. P., Dawson, W. M. and Prieve, E. A. (Eds.). *Marketing the Arts*. New York: Praeger Publishers, 1980, p. 69.

(no keep)

p. 230 is blank.
   End of Chapter 17

Chapter 18

Prevailing Winds and Bending Mandates

Thomas L. Goodale

Who has seen the wind?
Neither you nor I.
But when the trees bow down their heads
The wind is passing by.

Christina Rosseti

How frequently we allude to natural forces when referring to human affairs. We speak, for example, about political or social climate and we speak about the winds of change. We even offer each other prayers: "May the wind be always at your back." If, like a weather vane, one turns with the wind, it will always be at your back. It will also always dictate the direction in which you point.

The thesis here is a simple one. In adjusting to the prevailing winds, the park and recreation movement appears to be changing course. There is a need, then, to renew the dialogue of mandate and purpose; that is a dialogue of bearing, course, and heading. That is particularly needed with reference to public park, recreation and leisure services since they reflect our collective judgement and perhaps our collective purpose. A useful start would be to cut through the fog and haze of argument and rationale which has come to cloud our vision.

WHAT GOVERNMENT IS BEST?

"That government is best," said Thomas Paine, "that governs least." Modern reactionaires, parading slogans such as "getting government off our backs and out of our pockets," are rather fond of what Paine said, or at least that part of what he said that points downwind. The upwind part is more to the point. "Government, like dress, is a badge of lost innocence." Since that statement tells us more about ourselves than we care to know, we turn our backs on it. Innocence is pretty shaky ground for most of us to stand on. In the absence of evidence of recaptured innocence, the reactionary stance is hopelessly naive and wrong-headed. There is, in fact, much evidence suggesting we will have more government rather than less.

Pluralism or Nihilism

One principal reason is that the value concensus, which makes the social order self-regulating, is breaking down. We have prided ourselves on the emergence of pluralism by which we mean people derive their values from a variety of sources. The sources are human institutions such as the family, community, religion and education. But since these institutions have lost much of their influence, our value sources are not so much pluralistic as atomistic. There may already be too many value orientations, which is very much like having no value orientation at all. That is the inconvenient part. Similarly, we have come to pride ourselves for our tolerance which may be the convenient term for indifference. There is as much evidence of the one as of the other.

We seem to be experiencing what Geoffrey Vickers, in a seminal article, referred to as moral inversion and ethical nihilism, which he summarizes in these words:

> Moral criticism of human institutions is frequent: the acceptance of social constraints by the free individual is rare. This moral inversion is inconsistent with the survival of an increasingly interdependent society. Statements of human rights must be replaced by statements of human responsibility if we are to make the world viable.[1]

Over 50 years ago, Will Durant also noted the serious socio-political hazards when individuals are content merely with freedom in their gonads and in their cups.[2]

Legitimate Needs

The second reason why we may have more government rather than less is that there are needs to be met and they are costly ones. For example, the population aged 65 and over, now about 9 percent of the population, consumes about 35 percent of the cost of our health care system. Soon that population will be 12 percent, absorbing about 50 percent of the costs of health care. And the costs of the system are increasing dramatically. Similarly, the demographic forces of a baby boom followed by a sharply reduced birth rate means serious problems with our pension system around the year 2010 as the first of "the big generation" reaches 60 years of age. Currently, about six workers contribute to public and private pension plans for each person drawing from them. Soon, that ratio will be three to one.

Other major problems include the imperatives of international economic competition and the temptation to replace labor with technology, adding to the problem of income distribution. Too, a slowly growing economy will not produce enough "new money" to meet growing needs. Thus, existing financial resources will have to be redistributed, a task which seems beyond our present government.[3]

For cities, the gap between needs and resources is growing steadily. Long standing problems such as stable or shrinking tax bases and limitations on taxing powers remain, and despite all efforts to broaden the tax base, property taxes still provide the same proportion of municipal revenue as they did 80 years ago. Further, we are now painfully aware of the vast sums needed to repair and replace the aging infrastructure of most of our older cities: as much as 60 billion dollars during the next 10 years for New York City alone. Finally, the withdrawal of grants by senior levels of government raises serious problems. A number of students of the distribution of local government services have noted that without grants and transfers, services for the poor, including parks, recreation, cultural facilities and libraries, will be seriously curtailed.[4] Kenneth Boulding suggested that grants were either gifts motivated by love or tributes motivated by fear.[5] In that light, limiting or ending grants for such reasons as restraint or local autonomy sounds hollow. It has its convenient side—not paying tributes out of fear—and its inconvenient side.

Institutional Inertia

A third reason why we may have more rather than less government is that individuals and agencies involved in the provision and distribution of public services are not immune from the penchant for ideas and courses of action which are convenient. Nathan Glazer has noted that our intended services objectives may be distorted not only by the search for revenue but also by the search for "a comfortable, secure and well paid position with government."[6]

It is often noted that collective life, that is life in organizations, is conservative and bent on maintenance of the status quo. The present order, even if it doesn't work, is preferred to the potential disorder which often, perhaps necessarily, accompanies change:

> The normal state of an organization, therefore, as observers everywhere testify, is caution. It gets along by doing what it has always done. Before it does more, its bureaucrats, like other rational people, want to know whether they will benefit. Organizations exist to benefit their members. They have come to terms with their environment, terms that reflect existing relationships, not future ones. So they deal with the presenting problems, as social workers say, and do not go looking for trouble.[7]

Blame it on the Economy

This is one of our most convenient rationalizations. Just as individuals often use lack of time as the reason (read rationalization) why they do not participate in this or that activity, so agency personnel use lack of money as the reason for not providing this or that service. Even in the most vibrant economy, no government, agency, or individual can do everything. So the issue is not financial resource limits but rather priorities: the issue is not economics but political and social values. One must view with equanimity any claim of financial limits in a world in which 1.5 billion dollars *per day* is spent on the ability to make war—all for the purpose of not having one.

No doubt there is an economic limit to the total amount of goods and services that can be produced But within that limit, social and political values determine what is produced and who gets it. A budget, therefore, is an allocation based not on dollars but values: it converts resources into human purposes. By using the economy as a scapegoat, we avoid the central question of human purpose, including the purpose of government involvement in service provision.

Lacking a self-regulating social order which is the only real alternative to government regulation and control; confronted with growing needs to be met now and well into the future; unable to shake our penchant for the convenient, our inertia and our scapegoating, we have arrived at the point where the purpose, rationale, and mandate of public services may be bending. Perhaps that has already begun; certainly there is much potential for it.

GRADUALLY BENDING

That becomes evident when we examine the concepts and processes which shape the provision and distribution of local park, recreation and leisure services. These include concepts such as equity, merit goods and efficiency and activities such as reducing costs and increasing revenues. Though treated separately here, it is clear that these concepts and activities are inter-related. The starting point should be the concept of equity since a principal function of government is the allocation of resources. Private, market mechanisms do not always result in "fair" resource allocations. Public recreation services began for the purpose of making resources, thus opportunities, available in forms not otherwise provided and for people who would not otherwise have access. This is the fundamental rationale for public involvement in this field.

Equity

Equity can be conceived in several ways and there are different views about which type of equity measure to use. Still, some types are considered clearly inadequate by most. Five types can be identified and arrayed along a continuum according to the extent of resource reallocation resulting from each. From least to most redistribution they are: market equity; demand; equal input; equal opportunity; equal result.

Market equity is the receipt of goods and services exactly in proportion to the amount paid. It accomplishes no redistribution. Since those who can afford good services get them, the affluent benefit and the poor remain poor. Most students of government reject this criteria.[8] Yet in establishing fees and charges, the cost of comparable services provided by the private sector is one of the guides we use.

The second criteria, demand, is usually rejected, too. It is a pragmatic but often inappropriate criteria as it tends to be reactive and to favor those who are comparatively well-off: reactive since agencies react to demands placed upon them; favoring the comparatively well-off since they are the ones who know how to extract benefits from the agency.

Equal input, which is sometimes mistakenly taken to mean equal opportunity, is perhaps the most frequently used criteria for assessing the equity of service distribution. While it assures more of a redistributive effect than market or demand criteria, it is regarded as inadequate by some. According to Lineberry and Sharkansky, "Money spent is a commonplace, but not very good, index of service quality or productivity."[9] Wolman is even more emphatic, arguing that, "input equality is a ridiculous standard."[10]

Market equity and demand as criteria for service distribution are rejected in principle by nearly everyone although there is evidence, though perhaps not awareness, of their informal application in practice. These criteria are measurable although that is never easy. Equal input is also, with difficulty, measurable and is for many an acceptable limit to income transfers and redistribution efforts. Yet it is apparent that to equalize opportunity for many segments of the population a more than equal share of resources may be required. Opportunities for the poor, the handicapped and other sub-groups of the population may become equal only with a greater than equal share of resources.

Equal outcome or result is recognized as being unachievable and undesirable. On the other hand, there is a need to realize positive results from the public provision of services. As with any intervention, if it doesn't make any difference, why bother? There are some persuasive arguments for equity criteria which include measures of opportunity but also measures of results in desired directions.[11] The problems we confront in pursuing these equity objectives are two. The great difficulties we have in measuring opportunity and result is one about which several writers on the subject comment along with the consternation of not being able to detect results from increases in inputs. The second difficulty with opportunity and result measures of equity is that additional resources are required. Disparities in opportunity and result cannot be reduced by lowering the top but by bringing up the bottom; a leveling up rather than down. The criteria of opportunity and some indication of positive effect are the appropriate ones. But given the problems of measurement and cost, along with the real possibility that many service providers do not accept these criteria, equity is often judged from the standpoint of input, or worse, demand and market criteria.

Cost Reduction

Among the principle cost reduction strategies has been the adoption of means to save time and energy. Saving is realized with, for example, increasing use of computers to handle a variety of administrative and clerical functions; changing maintenance schedules; conserving gas, oil and electricity via design, monitoring, automated controls and the like.

A second principal cost reduction strategy is the increasing use of volunteers. There are, of course, other desirable objectives realized through the use of volunteers but philosophy and necessity are conveniently wedded here. To some extent we have come to incorporate self-service in the notion of volunteerism, in contrast to the traditional meaning of service to others.

A third principal strategy, an extension of volunteerism in some respects, is privatization of service delivery and contracting for service. Unquestionably, some local services can be delivered more economically this way. In the park and recreation field, some services have been effectively privatized. In Ottawa, Canada, for example, grants to neighborhood groups for the maintenance of natural ice skating rinks saves the city an estimated half-million dollars annually with no apparent decrement in service. But unlike other cost reduction strategies, privatization of recreation services is a contentious issue, however widespread the practice.[12]

Those opposed to privatization often base their opposition on such grounds as decreased service quality or at least decreased control over service quality. But another concern is that not only control but also public resources are turned over to those groups and agencies who already possess the resources, including organizational and administrative skills, with which to provide service. Too, privatized service is typically self-service, which is good. But services for those without resources must be assured somehow and that is a collective responsibility.

Efficiency

Cost reduction is one way of increasing efficiency as long as the quantity and quality of services available is not also reduced. One cannot be opposed to that. Still the efficiency criteria may result in distorting objectives. Often, efficiency is mistakenly accepted as a measure of effectiveness, perhaps in part due to the lack of effectiveness measures. Efficiency and effectiveness should not be confused. Efficiency tells us if we are doing things right: effectiveness tells us if we are doing the right things.

Attendance, for example, is often used as a measure of effectiveness. In fact it is a measure of efficiency in that user days or hours is part of the equation by which unit costs (such as cost per hour of participation) and efficiency criteria are calculated. Where unit costs are low, fees and charges can also be low and still realize significant cost recovery or revenue generation. The consequence of such decision making for the sake of efficiency results in agencies concentrating energy on doing what is easiest. Consequently, ease rather than need comes to shape service provision. Such an outcome, however, unintended, seems quite contrary to the objectives of public service.

While efficiency is a means of increasing production, it is not, or at least should not be, a criteria for determining what is to be produced. Further, production must be thought of as separate from, even if simultaneous with, distribution since the amount produced is independent of who receives it.

Where people are involved, one should not worship too long at the altar of efficiency. The work force was sometimes sacrificed at that altar, first by exploitation and more recently by displacement. Dictatorships are more efficient than democracies. And where leisure and recreation are concerned, efficient time use may simply mean we are all more harried. Something important may be lost in playing the Minute Waltz in thirty-seconds, or speed reading the novels of Mark Twain in a single evening—without laughing once.[13]

Merit Goods

The concept of merit goods provides the rationale for establishing fees and charges and, presumably, the amount charged. Briefly, there is no charge for public goods (available equally and indivisibly to everyone) and the charge for private goods (individuals benefit in proportion to amount paid) should cover the full cost. Unfortunately, despite the wide gamut of recreation and park services with which local government agencies are involved, there are very few services for which benefits are purely public or purely private. Most are "merit" goods which convey some public benefit and some private, but the task of determining how much is which is a very difficult one.[14]

It is generally recognized that in the provision of park and recreation services a minimum level of service quantity and quality should be available to all constituents. This, in a sense, is the level of service provision that would be considered public goods. Presumably, there would be no charge for such services. After such provision has been assured, merit goods can be provided and fees and charges established to recover the private goods portion as opposed to the portion which benefits the public and thus deserving public tax support. Obviously, the greater the private goods portion, the greater the revenue that can be generated and the greater the distortion of the public service objective. Until the basic level of service has been defined and opportunity to avail oneself of it assured to all constituents, merit and private goods, thus fees and charges, are premature.

Valuable as is the merit goods concept, there are other problems with it which are not always evident in the parks and recreation literature. One problem is that the merit goods argument is as valid for the private sector as for the public sector. There is some public benefit in people having recreational experiences regardless of the agency involved in its provision: fitness maintained at a private facility yields as much public benefit as that maintained at a public facility. In addition, the public benefit which merits support is, presumably, the same whether the individuals supported are rich or poor. The problem, of course, is that the public receives no benefit—the merit goods portion—from anyone who cannot pay the fees and charges for the private benefit portion. The situation is not unlike that of matching grants; the amount of the fee or charge being the portion which qualifies the grantee to receive support. So the rich get richer.

A third problem with the merit goods concept results from the difficulty of determining the public and private portion of a good. Consequently, the amount of fee or charge imposed depends on criteria other than merit, such as whether or not the fee is politically palatable, is appropriate vis-à-vis private sector pricing, is not so high as to result in lost revenue, and is not based on full cost because of the difficulty of determining full cost. So fees and charges are based neither upon merit nor cost. Consequently, we don't really know how equitably public resources are distributed though it is apparent that market and demand criteria are used in establishing fees and charges.

Increasing Revenues

Since tax support for park and recreation services is not expected to meet much more than inflation induced cost increases and sometimes not even that, increases in financial resources must come from contributions of various kinds or from revenue generated by services provided; that is, fees and charges. Contributions can come in the form of transfers or grants from a myriad of government and non-government sources, and increased efforts have been devoted to tapping those resources. More is being done to secure commercial and other sponsorships, local foundations to support park and recreational services are pursued more aggressively, and many other initiatives have been taken to secure additional financial support.

However, the principal source of increased revenue remains fees and charges. For several decades, this has been a contentious issue in the field of parks and recreation. In recent years, however, philosophy and necessity have shifted the issue from whether or not to charge to how much to charge. The other side of that coin is determining the level to which tax revenue should subsidize activities for which charges are made.

With any fees there will be some who do not have the ability to pay and who, therefore, will be excluded from the opportunity unless some special provision is made for them. In virtually every quarter, some kind of provision is made for at least some services, if not all. Passes, sponsorships, free periods, reduced fees and other provisions are made to provide access and, hopefully, if not always successfully, avoid stigmatization. Sometimes the poor pay in time (or inconvenience) while others pay in price.[15] Others note the utility of varying fees according to site quality or desirability as a means of distributing demand.[16] Thus both convenience and quality are trade-offs for ability to pay. They also argue that fees may work in favor of the poor for services to which the poor do not have access anyway. But they do not make clear what services the poor do have access to.

It has also been argued that discrimination does not result from user fees based on a study in which attendance at a park did not decrease as a result of establishing a modest parking fee.[17] The study did not address the question of discrimination, however, as the title and text presume. In the main, the fee successfully dislocated a use considered undesirable as the park was used as "a late night hangout for youthful beer parties (sic)." Again, there is no mention of what became of those youth. Clearly, there is no intention to discriminate and every intention to make provision for those lacking the ability to pay the fees and charges imposed. Discriminatory effects result nonetheless.

Virtually all fees and charges revenues come from two sources; participation in programs and use of facilities. Certainly programs and facilities are important agency products, but there are at least two others. One such product is information, including but not limited to agency provided opportunity, along with leisure education and perhaps counseling. A second product is community development, including all those activities described as enabling and facilitating, support services and the like. Much of the professional literature of the past several years has been devoted to the development of these two service products as opposed to direct provision of programs and facilities. By the very nature of information, education and community development services, fees and charges are seldom appropriate and unlikely to produce much revenue in any case. Consequently, perhaps inevitably, fees and charges push us back in the direction of direct provision of programs and facilities.

Among workers in the park, recreation and leisure service field and among the general public, there is a widespread agreement on two types of direct provision by the local government agency. One is the provision of parks and open space. The other is the provision of programs and services for those with special needs. A system of parks and open spaces is perhaps the best example we have of a public good provided by park and recreation agencies. Further, those with special needs quite often are those with least ability to pay. The likelihood of subsisting near or below the poverty level increases if one is elderly, non-white, in a female headed household, or has a mental, emotional, or physical impairment. But service provision may be distorted in the direction of direct services which convey private benefits for those who have the ability to pay.

Start V

WHO GETS WHAT?

In the determination of who gets what services, agencies engage in activities which either meet demand or, on a routine basis, attempt to discover needs. Agencies are judged to be reactive according to their demand, in contrast to need, orientation. Pro-active agencies are most persistently engaged in searching out needs. Resources for doing so are, of course, necessary. When resources are limited, search activities are too readily abandoned and demand rather than need comes to dominate service distribution and delivery decision making. The result has been referred to as "Adam Smith" agencies. Thomas Paine, writing without the encumbrance of Smith's invisible hand, would have called them by another name.

Revenue generation, efficiency, merit goods and related criteria may not only distort agency service objectives but in fact counter them. That is recognized in the literature but sometimes that recognition is unquestioned. According to one recently published textbook, programs which do not at least break even "will not be tolerated; in other words, the 'social welfare' approach to programming is rapidly being replaced by a capitalistic approach."[18] If so, there is no rationale for public sector involvement in park, recreation and leisure services. Similarly, it has been noted that with increasing wealth, the equity standards for services shifts away from market equity and toward the criterion of equal result.[19] The economy of the past several years has resulted in a shift toward market equity; a private enterprise rather than public service approach.

These trends are much in evidence. But trends are not laws, and social realities are not unalterable facts but products of political and social values. In light of these trends and what appears to be too ready accession to them, there is a need to renew the dialogue of purposes and objectives. As Poole writes:

> Rather than engaging in fruitless nickel and diming with local
> bureaucrats, we ought to raise a more fundamental question: why is
> local government providing a particular good in the first place?[20]

Answers to that question appear in a number of related phrases like distributive justice, equal opportunity, meeting needs, creating desirable outcomes, serving all constituents, providing public goods, and the welfare of people and community. They provide the rationale for local government services, park and recreation services significant among them.

Nearly a century ago, a void was created in a society dominated by Social Darwinists, Robber Barons, and the leisure class so deftly ridiculed by Veblen.[21] That void was filled by the reformers and radicals who founded the movement which has become public parks, recreation and leisure services. The playgrounds of Boston and Halifax and the community centers of Chicago and Winnipeg may not have recaptured our innocence but they reminded us of our neglect and our obligations to our children, our immigrants, and our poor. Amidst the clamor for smaller and less costly government, we shouldn't forget our origins or the rationale for public service provision. If we want less government, we must have more community. Clamoring won't help; commitment will.

The preservation of endangered species, fragile habitats and magnificent land and seascapes is a human responsibility. These are also public goods, even if the vast majority of people never experience them directly. The human spirit is recreated by the knowledge that we have shared in assuring that that is done. Similarly, as a measure of the quality and effectiveness of parks, recreation, and leisure services, perhaps we should make certain that the last person in our community, the one facing the greatest obstacles and handicaps with the fewest resources, has a good opportunity of having a good day. There is public good in the knowledge that we have shared in providing that opportunity. The welfare of the community is at stake, not simply the welfare of the individual.

> When the Stranger says:
> "What is the meaning of this city?
> Do you huddle close together
> because you love each other?"
> What will you answer?
> "We all dwell together
> To make money from each other?" or
> "This is a community?"[22]

REFERENCES

1. Vicker, G. "The Future of Morality." *Futures*, VII:5 (October, 1979), p. 371.

2. Durant, W. *The Pleasures of Philosophy*. Chapter XVII. New York: Simon and Schuster, 1953.

3. Thurow, L. *The Zero Sum Society*. New York: Basic Books, 1980.

4. cf., Levy, F., Meltsner, J. and Wildawsky, A. *Urban Outcomes*. Berkeley, California: University of California Press, 1974. Mladenka, K. and Hill, K. "The Distribution of Benefits in an Urban Environment: Parks and Libraries in Houston," *Urban Affairs Quarterly*. 13:1 (September) 1977, pp. 73-94. Farnham, P. "Measuring the Change in Urban Recreation Service Distribution: The Case of Oakland, California," *Journal of Leisure Research*. 13:4, 1981, pp. 353-364.

5. Boulding, K. *The Economy of Love and Fear*. Belmont, California: Wadsworth, 1973.

6. Glazer, N. "Toward a Self-Service Society." *The Public Interest*. 70 (Winter), 1983, pp. 66-90.

7. Levy, F. et al., *Op. Cit.,* p. 229.
8. Crompton, J. "Are Your Leisure Services Distributed Equitably?" *Journal of Physical Education, Recreation and Dance.* 53:4 (April), 1982, pp. 67-70.
9. Lineberry, R. and Sharkansky, I. *Urban Politics and Public Policy* (3rd Edition). New York: Harper and Row, 1978, p. 265.
10. Wolman, H. "Urban Public Benefits and Fiscal Retrenchment: The Distributional Impacts of Municipal Expenditure Reductions." In: Rich, R. *The Politics of Urban Public Services.* Lexington, Massachusetts: D. C. Health, 1982, p. 123.
11. Levy, F. et al., *Op. Cit.*
12. Contracting Out. *Recreation Canada* (Special Issue) 4:1(February), 1984.
13. William Baumol's suggestion of the thirty-second waltz is well known. The example of speed-reading Mark Twain was Carl Tucker's in "Racy Reading." *Saturday Review,* March 18, 1978, p. 72.
14. For a useful summary, see: Crompton, J. "How to Find the Price That's Right." *Parks and Recreation.* 16:3(March), 1981, pp. 32-40.
15. Becker, B. "The Pricing of Education - Recreation Facilities: An Administrative Dilemma," *Journal of Leisure Research,* 7:2, 1975, pp. 86-94.
16. Manning, R., Calliman, E., Echelberger, H., Koenemann, E. and McEwen, D. "Differential Fees: Raising Revenue, Distributing Demand." *Journal of Park and Recreation Administration,* 2:1(January) 1984. pp. 2-32.
17. Manning, R. and Barker, S. "Discrimination Through User Fees: Fact or Fiction? *Parks and Recreation,* 16:9(September) 1981. pp. 70-74.
18. Edginton, C., Compton, D., and Hanson, C. *Recreation and Leisure Programming: A Guide for the Professional.* Philadelphia, Pennsylvania: Saunders College Publishing, 1980, p. 18.
19. Crompton, J., 1982, *Op. Cit.*
20. Poole, R. "Objections to Privatization." *Policy Review.* 24(Spring) 1983, p. 105.
21. Veblen, T. *The Theory of The Leisure Class.* New York: Macmillian, 1899.
22. Eliot, T. S. "Choruses from 'The Rock'." *The Complete Poems and Plays: 1909-1950.* New York: Harcourt, Brace and World, 1971, p. 103.

End of Chapter 18 and End of Section 2

SECTION III

Rethinking Professional Status: A Word of Caution

INTRODUCTION

The first two sections of this book deal with (a) the need to clarify the conceptual basis of our field in order to improve our understanding of the phenomena (recreation, leisure, play, etc.) we are dealing with and (b) service provision changes that are necessary if we are to make the park and recreation movement more responsive to the needs of citizens in the 90s and beyond. The seven articles in this section deal with a variety of issues concerning growing professionalization within park and recreation movement.

The articles cover three sub-areas and a "final thought." In the first of these sub-areas, the authors raise issues and questions about the search for and benefits of professional status for workers in the park and recreation movement. Sessoms (19) begins the section by discussing the assumption that it matters whether the parks and recreation field becomes a profession. Witt (20) critically analyzes the motives for seeking professional status, by asking whether professional recognition is sought to achieve power for professionals or as a means of achieving better service for consumers. Lord, Hutchison, and VanDerbeck (21) examine the impact of professional practice on how consumers are served. Reynolds (22) challenges us to examine whether our professionalization efforts lead to too much social control over our "clients" by manipulating expectations and values. Witt (23) questions whether our efforts should focus on re-educating consumers about leisure or reforming a service system that does not fully meet people's needs. Together, these authors ask us to examine whether we inappropriately blame individuals for lack of motivation where in fact inadequate service provision may be equally at fault. They also ask us to determine whether we inadvertently disable individuals via too narrowly defined professional responsibilities, buckpassing, or misguided benevolence.

These first five articles present issues that are too often ignored by those who argue for the necessity of park and recreation workers achieving professional status. Sessoms (19) looks at five criteria by which professions are often distinguished from other occupational groups. He concludes that the park and recreation field is well on its way to meeting the criteria and that it is in the public interest that workers in the field achieve professional status.

One criterion, a mission or social concern, has been lost, Twardzik (24) argues. But Sessoms recognizes the difficulties in achieving status as a profession and he recognizes that one can behave and perform as a professional without the occupation being perceived by the public as a profession (and vice-versa, of course). Note that Sessom's discussion of ambiguity about the nature and scope of the field recalls the conceptual issues raised in Section I, and he touches on such questions as training or education, research or practice, questions also raised by Barnett (26) and Burdge (27) among others. Still, a reasoned case for continued growth toward professional status is made; a useful if not strictly necessary development.

Authors of the four chapters following Sessoms are not as convinced about the need for professional status. Together they question whether professionalism improves service or chances of survival. Witt (20), for example, raises questions that must be dealt with before the recreation and park movement rushes further into acquiring the trappings of professionalism such as accreditation, certification, registration, licensing, and a code of ethics. In essence, the authors that follow Sessoms are more concerned with the impact of professionals on people's lives than with the criteria for being a professional.

Woven through these first articles are a series of dilemmas which face any aspiring profession. One series deals with the thin line distinguishing between attempts at helping versus influencing or leading versus directing. Another series deals with means for preserving the delicate balance between independence and dependence of action or intrinsic and extrinsic motivation. In the rush to achieve status or authority, Lord, Hutchison and VanDerbeck (21) ask whether the recreation and park movement has failed to consider whether professionalization is consistent with meeting the needs of the people we intend to serve.

Indeed, as Reynolds (22) and Witt (23) note, it is not clear whether the people we serve are considered clients, recipients, or consumers. Although just labels, each designation has broad implications for determining the source of control, motivation, evaluation, and mandate for services.

Another theme that is touched on by a number of the authors is the growing uneasy feeling, perhaps even malaise, among many professionals that all is not right. Our public selves increasingly seek status, recognition, and security; our private selves wonder whether we are really fulfilling the kind of dream for the recreation and park movement that Duncan (25) sees many of our founding leaders as having. In a field dominated by civil service workers, and given the dilemmas and contradictions that daily haunt our decisions and practices, there is a tendency to ask too few questions. The conspiracy of silence thus threatens to become a pattern of "benign neglect." It is not clear whether the recreation movement as it has emerged in the later half of this century has the philosophic foundation or creative instinct to get beyond muddling through the difficult issues that lie ahead.

The final two chapters in this section explore the fundamental values upon which the park and recreation movement was founded and question whether current service attempts have moved too far away from the founding principles of the movement. Thus, Twardzik (24) decries the policies that put more emphasis on meeting high demand interests as opposed to service provision based on individual and community values. He goes back to the beginning of the movement and analyzes the values perspective based on an Aristotelian concept of happiness and other principles that formed the foundation for the efforts of the moral entrepreneurs who helped create the 19th century public park system. Twardzik sharply compares these ideas to the value free policies of our current park and recreation systems. He thus calls for a renaissance in the provision of public park and recreation services that would include more emphasis on developing community life and ultimately the public good. That is the practical side of conceptual issues raised by Bregha (4), Dustin, et al. (8), Goodale (7), Sylvester (33) and others.

Duncan (25) builds on Twardzik's concerns by persuasively reminding us of our roots and their implications for our present and future. The park and recreation movement had as its founders people who even today would be considered radicals and reformers. Gulick, Addams, Olmsted, Riis and Lee would feel comfortable with the discussion of purpose and concerns with professionalization contained throughout the book. Their focus was on people, needs (not wants), and ends (not means). Duncan's radicals would feel at home with Goodale (3), Spry (9), and Dustin, McEvoy and Schultz's (8) collective call for a society where "to be", "to produce," and "to participate" are valued more than "to have," "consume" and "to withdraw."

(no beep)

p. 246 is blank.

Chapter 19

The Professionalization of Parks and Recreation: A Necessity?

H. Douglas Sessoms

Our social structures reflect the status assigned various occupations. Where we live, with whom we associate, our views of the world, and our lifestyles are determined somewhat by our work, our occupation. Most revered among occupations are the ones we call professions.

Studies of occupational prestige are a favorite of sociologists. Look at any introductory sociology text and you will find a list of occupations according to their perceived status. In most instances, those occupations founded in the practice of medicine, law and theology will rank high. It is not surprising, therefore, that these three are most often mentioned as best fitting the classical definition of "profession."

But why this fascination with occupational prestige and professions, and what distinguishes a profession from other fields of human endeavor? Why do occupations strive to become professions? Does being a profession really make a difference? Researchers such as Goode[1], Wilensky[2], and Cheek[3] are among those who have analyzed these questions from a sociological perspective. In the field of parks and recreation, "recreation as a profession" has been the subject of doctoral dissertations and the basis of various articles in professional journals (Sorenson[4], Kauffman[5], and Shapiro[6]). Whereas the sociologists have been more interested in the characteristics of a profession and the means by which occupational groups seek to establish themselves as professions, recreation and park researchers have typically focused upon whether parks and recreation has become a profession. The question "does it matter whether recreation is a profession of not?" has rarely been addressed. The assumption is that it does matter, that parks and recreation's position in the order of occupations would be improved if it were granted profession status similar to that given to law and medicine.

DEFINING PROFESSION

How do professions differ from other occupations? If one is paid to perform a specific set of tasks, does that not make him/her a professional? With large numbers of individuals performing the same task or service, does that not qualify them to talk about their profession, their work, their uniqueness as an occupational group? Not so, according to the researchers. Whereas all professions are occupations, not all occupations are professions. Being paid to perform work may differentiate the professional from the amateur, but the work performed may not be that performed by a profession. As Neil Cheek succinctly stated:

> ". . . the symbol 'profession' has a variety of meanings attached to it.
> The arbiter of most definitional disputes, the dictionary, proves to
> be singularly unhelpful in this case. The main reason is that, in the
> vernacular, 'profession' is frequently a synonym for 'occupation'."[7]

A criterion approach is suggested and although there is no agreed upon set of criteria for determining a profession, most writers include the following in their analysis:

1. Professions align themselves with a social concern, the ameliorating of some social ill, and they frequently result from a major social movement.

2. Professions establish their body of knowledge, a set of concepts and procedures generally known to those within the profession.

3. Specified programs of education and training, generally involving internships, are need in order for one to learn the necessary concepts and practices of the profession.

4. To assure that programs of professional preparation are reliable, that individuals have the prerequisite skills and understandings to practice, programs of accreditation and certification are created.

5. Those within the profession create organizations to serve the profession. These organizations often establish codes of ethics, norms of practice which are enforced by the profession.

Some researchers go beyond these five major criteria and add other characteristics which they feel are necessary to differentiate professions from other occupational groups. Goode[8] made the point that professions are instrumental in creating their respective centers of learning (professional education), that they staff their licensing and admission boards and, for the most part, write the legislation which governs their practice. Also, he said professions were relatively free of external evaluation and control, citing that members of a profession are more strongly identified with their practices than are members of other occupational groups and therefore are unlikely to leave it for some other form of work. Abrahamson[9] supported Goode's position. He observed that professions tended to be free from organizational restraints, that their members work alone with individual clients, are oriented to their own set of norms and are free from responsibility to an immediate employing organization. Such a definition makes it difficult for any occupational group functioning in a bureaucratic setting to become a profession, a point Cheek also makes.

According to Cheek the social relationship which exists between the professional and client is critical in determining if the professional is a member of a profession. Central to Cheek's argument is the freedom of the client to initiate the relationship, the freedom of both the professional and the client to terminate the relationship, and the privileged communication which exists between the two. He also argued that the professional's expertise is based upon a body of knowledge which only those in the profession are capable of interpreting, that no transfer of techniques or skills is intended during the interaction, and that the professional's decisions cannot be counter-manded by some "outside" authority.[10]

The Cheek definition is certainly more restrictive than those of Goode, Wilensky, Sorenson and others, but is in keeping with the spirit that professions are unique in that their members have special knowledge, perform a specialized role and *have control over their occupation's structure, function, practice and destiny.*

PARKS AND RECREATION—A PROFESSION?

To answer, let us measure current practices and events in parks and recreation against these criteria, then, address the question: "Does it matter?"

Criterion One: Alignment With a Social Concerns

Most would argue that those involved in the delivery of leisure services, those who call themselves parks and recreation professionals, are involved with a major societal institution, are providing a necessary service (the provision of opportunities for meaningful leisure experiences) and, that their "profession" resulted from a social movement.

Parks and recreation is an amalgamated field of service. It did not result from one social movement, but is the product of several. One component—recreation services—resulted from the playground and scientific charity movements which occurred at the beginning for the 20th century. Leaders of those

movements were concerned about the quality of life for youth and the importance of play for all children. They believed in the inherent value of play, and
the responsibility of society to create and sustain organizations (privately and
publicly), especially comprehensive community centers which would promote
and/or provide play opportunities. They were against social injustices and
thought that proper play behavior would help the child grow into a healthy adult,
a good citizen.

A parallel but independent social movement was the conservation movement. Its leaders wanted to protect and maintain natural environments and were
not as concerned about the use of the environment as they were about its
preservation. They believed in the inherent value of wilderness, wildlands, and
open spaces. Preservation and careful resource management were their watch-
words; they were against exploitation and the loss of our natural heritage.

A third social movement which has claim on parks and recreation was the
formal educational movement. Its promoters viewed play as necessary release
from the tensions associated with study and long periods of physical inactivity.
Sports were viewed as a means for developing school spirit and school loyalties;
personal and community well-being were cited among its benefits.

Although these and other social reforms were occuring simultaneously and,
in some instances, interactively, different structures were created to foster their
goals. Joseph Lee (sand gardens), Jane Addams (settlement houses) and Luther
Gulick (school athletics) aligned themselves with the issues of human growth
and development, while John Muir and Horace McFarland were fighting to
protect our unique scenic and natural resources. There was no social movement
against boredom, no strong effort to make leisure behaviors the central behaviors of life, no concerns for leisure education and little attention to the leisure
activities of adults other than that they be socially acceptable, no concerns for
the acquisition of lands to be developed for adult amusement, and little tie
between travel and recreation concerns.

This diffused origin of the park and recreation movement has has a variety
of consequences affecting our programs and professional preparation, the organizational structure of our professional societies, and our perception of the
mission of the field. Are we leisure educators, therapists, entrepreneurs,
managers of leisure services, parks and recreation specialists, stewards of the
environment, social workers, what?

It may be that the most pressing issue confronting parks and recreation in its
attempt to become a profession is to define its parameters, to state its primary
mission. With what social concern are we aligned? Is leisure service a field of
work comprising many leisure service professions or is there a leisure service
profession and if so what is its mission? Who defines that mission: the public
or those serving the public? The lack of agreement in describing the profession's role says much about where we are in becoming a profession.

Criterion Two: Body of Knowledge

Although the mission of the "profession" may be unclear, there is evidence that we are developing a body of knowledge to give direction to our efforts. Unfortunately, some of that research and scholarship is disconnected, not related to theory or practice. Earlier on, much of it was done by social and biological scientists, trained in a variety of disciplines, not in parks and recreation. Their concerns often dealt with participant motivation, the carrying capacity of a resource, and the need for developing models to measure demand. More recently, however, some writers have attempted to get at the problems of delivery, developing a basis for pricing structures, designing more effective maintenance procedures utilizing computer based programs, and perfecting techniques for assessing attitudes toward leisure experiences. The results of these studies speak to this criterion.

Prior to 1968, scholars interested in recreation and leisure either had to publish their work in the journals of sociology, psychology, forestry and the like or in one of the trade publications, e.g., *Parks and Recreation*. Most books written on the subject of parks, recreation and leisure services were done as texts. The exceptions, such as Dumazedier's *Toward A Society of Leisure* or de Grazia's *Of Time, Work and Leisure*, were written by persons tangential to the profession and who had no identity within the profession. However, their contributions did stimulate and support a growing interest among a select group of academics, most often employed as members of a park and recreation faculty, to research the leisure phenomena. As one might expect, a division of interest developed between those who conceptualized parks and recreation as a profession and those who viewed leisure as a subject of study, an academic discipline, in its own right.

The body of knowledge developed by a profession is quite different from that developed by a discipline. The former results from the application of concepts and techniques applied to solving a social problem or maintaining a societal function or system, not from a theory to explain or control behavior or from a treatise about man's nature as often is the case with a discipline. Disciplines create knowledge; professions apply it. Present day activities would suggest that those interested in furthering the methods and techniques of leisure services are in the minority. Most of our researchers are interested in issues related to their discipline; the body of knowledge of practice remains woefully undeveloped. It largely consists of adapting techniques developed in other areas of management to the delivery of leisure services, not in a set of unique practices and methods known primarily by those who provide that service.

Criterion Three: Professional Preparation

Training efforts to upgrade the skills of recreation and park personnel began to appear shortly after the first playgrounds opened. As volunteers tired of watching children play or of working with immigrants in a settlement house, they employed others to perform these tasks for them. The volunteers remained in positions of authority, comprising the committees which set policy and/or generated public support and funds for their efforts. As the number of employed playground supervisors increased, so did the number of workshops and short courses designed to orient these workers to their roles and responsibilities. Some of the workshops were conducted by the emerging service and professional organizations; others were sponsored by urban universities. By 1921, several universities had developed either a certificate program or an undergraduate concentration (generally in physical education or sociology) to prepare personnel to work with youth as "recreation leaders."

The conservation movement traveled a different direction. Its leaders recognized, early on, that if the forests were to be properly managed and lands protected, two kinds of personnel were needed: protectors (rangers) and biological scientists (naturalists and foresters). Beyond these, there was also a need for resource planners and designers (landscape architects). Those agencies created to protect the resources could be managed effectively by its public administrators and the political system. Nearly all the training efforts involving the preparation of park and forest recreation personnel were done at our land grant colleagues.

For years the logic behind these two separate programs of professional preparation was not questioned since parks and recreation were viewed as separate and distinct concerns requiring different types of personnel and operations. Recreation service was grounded in the social sciences; parks and natural resources in the biological sciences. This view changed, however, following World War II. By 1960, the rapid expansion of park and recreation systems and the public's growing interest in outdoor activity had caused both park professionals and recreation professionals to rethink the purpose, structure and content of their programs of professional preparation. The system needed administrators, people with an understanding of the relationship of activity to resources. Nationally, municipalities were combining their park departments with their recreation departments to form a single administrative unit, a department of parks and recreation. Major park and recreation profession organizations were to merge—why not park and recreation curricula?

Several questions arose as a result of these and other changes. What should be the focus of an undergraduate education to prepare park and recreation professionals? What was the ideal location, administratively, of these education units: Education, Forestry, Sociology? What about the other settings in which recreation services were administered, e.g., industry, medical settings, military installations—did they not require specialized information and, therefore, personnel with specialized training? Could all the educational needs of so many different types of practitioners—administrators and specialists—be met in one degree program and at the baccalaureate level?

Those who study professions are in agreement that (1) the length of training and (2) the degree of selectivity used in determining who is to be trained are factors in determining if an occupation is moving toward profession status. The established professions require extensive training and are highly selective. They control not only the training efforts of the profession but also the numbers of those who will enter the profession. Furthermore, nearly all of these programs of professional preparation involve extensive internships and rarely occur at the baccalaureate level. They are post graduate programs, generally culminating in the awarding of a professional degree rather than a traditional academic degree.

When the curricula merged, programs of professional preparation of recreation and park personnel did not follow the traditional profession pattern. The demand for personnel was so great that selectivity was not a major issue. Most programs were at the baccalaureate level so the length of training was relatively short. To meet the demand for faculty, universities employed either recent doctoral graduates who had a minimum of experience as practitioners or those trained in one of the disciplines related to parks and recreation, individuals more interested in leisure studies than in recreation and park management. Like so many of the elements of professional development, the educational component was growing without focus, responding more to the marketplace than to a concept of mission and role. Yet there was clear identity of the creation of distinct programs of professional preparation.

Criterion Four: Accreditation/Certification

Partially in response to the proliferation of park and recreation curricula (the number of universities declaring a recreation and park major increased from 144 to 206 between 1971 and 1978[11]), and partially in response to a growing sense of wanting to be a profession, efforts to accredit curricula and to certify personnel were undertaken. Of the two, accreditation is furthest along as a functioning reality.

In October, 1986, the Council of Postsecondary Accreditation (COPA), an organization created by university presidents to control the accreditation process, gave approval to the accreditation program of the National Recreation and Park Association in conjunction with the American Association for Leisure and Recreation. Prior to that, the NRPA/AALR Council on Accreditation had functioned for nine years as an informal accrediting agency of the profession.

Although some educators may view accreditation as an unnecessary action, one which might inhibit creativity and restrict institutional freedom, most agree that it has had a significant effect upon professional preparation. In general, it has given direction to curriculum planning and has deterred some institutions from continuing to offer the park and recreation major when their programs obviously could not meet the standards set by the Council. By 1989, nearly 100 universities and colleges had had their undergraduate curriculum in Recreation and Parks accredited by the Council. Some may view this as a service to the profession and to the public at large; others might view accreditation only as an effort to protect the profession. Both acknowledge its growing influence.

The issue of protection is central to the accreditation and certification processes. When the Council on Accreditation presented its case to COPA, it had to demonstrate that recreation and parks was a profession and that the public would be served by the accreditation process. That case seems to have been made—at least in the eyes of COPA. Advocates of certification argue that certification is necessary to assure the public that it will be served by professionally qualified practitioners. Others see it as one means of upgrading the profession and adding to the practitioner's worth (salary).

The certification process is more diffuse and its results more uncertain. Various professional organizations have implemented their own certification plans. Some have tied certification to continuing education efforts; others based certification only upon the training and experience of the candidates or to some examination procedure. Some states have enacted certification laws and licensing plans. This is especially true for therapeutic recreation personnel. Most states, however, have not; certification remains primarily a voluntary program operated by professional organizations.

Certification is a powerful tool in the hands of a profession. It governs practice and, along with accreditation, tends to standardize procedures. It can be a negative force when it restricts creativity, or dictates practice and since certification tends to be decentralized, a matter for state legislatures and special interests groups, the problems are numerous. Each certifying body is defining in its own way the nature of our practice. The more diffuse that practice, the more specialized the certification requirements, the greater is the tendency toward fragmentation. The need for cooperative efforts between the various certifying and accreditation bodies is essential if a central view of the profession is to emerge.

Criterion Five: Professional Organizations and Ethics

Although identified as the fifth criterion, the creation of professional organizations may be the first step toward becoming a profession. Certainly, the forming of professional bodies to represent the "profession," to advocate its services and to improve the standards of those who practice and identify themselves with the profession should be expected. It seems only natural that those who have a like interest and who do similar work would join together for mutual benefit.

Professional organizations always identify in their name the professional body or social concern they represent. The identity factor is paramount. So is the belief that "in unity is strength." Interestingly, the formulation of bodies to represent the profession may also signal the end of the social movement which brought the "profession" into being. Once the professionals take over, the involvement of the laity, the social advocates, tends to diminish.

Initially, there were only two national organizations representing park and recreation interests. They were the Playground Association of America (the forerunner of National Recreation Association) and the American Institute of Park Executives. The later group was comprised of executives of various governmental park systems; groups such as the Sierra Club and the National Wildlife Association represented the general public's interests in conservation.

The Playground Association of America, formed by philanthropists and advocates of the playground movement, attracted both professionals and lay members. Its mission was to represent those interested in assuring that every child has a right to play and its structure was such that contributions to the Association (hereafter referred to a the National Recreation Association) were, for tax purposes, charitable gifts. It established regional offices to assist local communities in developing their playground and recreation programs and to aid in fund raising. In their work, Hartsoe and Knapp[12] describe in detail the formulation of this national organization, its organizational structure and contribution through 59 years of service. The National Recreation Association ceased to exist in 1965 when it merged with four other national recreation organizations to form the National Recreation and Park Association. Although the National Recreation Association underwent several name changes, its basic structure remained the same throughout its history. Its control was in the hands of a board of trustees which employed a professional staff to operate the organization. Its membership was non-voting; it viewed itself as a service, rather than a professional organization.

In addition to the NRA and AIPE, several other recreation/park organizations were formed during the first half of this century, most in response to the need of "professionals" working within a given interest area to promote that speciality's identify and growth. Among the more notable were the Conference on State Parks; the National Employee Recreation Association; the Recreation Division of the American Association for Health, Physical Education, Recreation and Dance; the National Association of Recreation Therapists and the American Recreation Society. The latter organization was the largest of the group and merits special mentioning.

The American Recreation Society was formed in 1938 as an organization for recreation workers. Its appeal was to the professional. It was broadly based with state chapters, a board of governors, and officers elected by the general membership. To accommodate the many interests of its members, it formed special interest divisions, such as hospital recreation, county recreation, recreation education, military recreation, and the like. It viewed itself as an organization by and of the "profession." Only those laity involved as recreation board and commission members could join the American Recreation Society but their membership was without a vote.

Recognizing the inherent problems in having so many diverse professional groups speaking for the "profession", the leadership of these and other professional organization created, in 1953, the Federation of National Professional Organizations for Recreation. The Federation sponsored various projects, involving one or more of the professional groups, but was never able to generate much support or influence. Allegiance continued to be to the individual professional body representing the special interest of the practitioner; unity in the profession seemed to be beyond the movement's grasp. However, that changed in 1965 when five of these major organizations, including the NRA, AIPE and ARS, merged to form the National Recreation and Park Association.

It was hoped that combining these many professional interest groups would give the "profession" one voice, one identity—Parks and Recreation. In deference to the National Recreation Association and its strong history as a service organization and to its many members who had no professional affiliation with parks and recreation but who supported the recreation movement, the National Recreation and Park Association developed an organizational structure to accommodate both professionals and the interested public. It also established branches to satisfy the interests of those professional members who wanted to retain some sense of the uniqueness of their speciality: military recreation, therapeutic recreation, state parks, recreation education, etc. It also allowed state organizations to become affiliates rather than chapters and employed a professional staff to respond to the needs of the profession and to continue the service activities formerly done by the National Recreation Association.

THE ORGANIZATIONAL DILEMMA

It was the hope of the founding fathers of the National Recreation and Park Association that it could do something no other national organization had ever done—represent both professionals and the laity. Also, it had hoped its members would identify with the larger movement of parks and recreation, while responding to their special interests through its branch approach. But, in so structuring its organization, it was going against the history of professions and violating one of the major characteristics of a profession; it was creating a professional organization not controlled by the profession and was perpetuating the fragmentation of the profession's identity. Its by-laws state that the Chairman of its Board of Trustees must be a lay person, the majority of the members of the Board of Trustees are to be non-professionals and that only the Board of

Trustees can vote on policy issues or elect its officers. Trustees are either chosen by the Board of Trustees or come to the Board as a representative of one of the branches or regional districts, units representing the various state affiliates. Branches are given autonomy to develop their own programs and conduct their business but they have no power to employ personnel or control their budgets. Those powers are retained in the hands of the Board of Trustees. Although active in serving the profession through publications, national and regional meetings and by interacting with other national organizations, the National Park and Recreation Association has been unable to unify the movement or attract a large membership, lay or professional. Its size has remained about the same—16 to 22 thousand members—since its creation.

Those who criticize the Association's approach most often argue that the Association is not a professional organization, and that its branch structure encourages special interest identification rather than with the profession at large. However, in defense of the Association's approach, it should be acknowledged that lay boards and commissions still manage many local recreation and park systems and than it is natural for workers to identify with those colleagues who work in a similar setting. If practitioners see their specialization as a profession in its own right rather than a speciality within a larger profession, it is probably due to the field's failure to define its central mission, its parameters of service and who is to deliver that service, not the fault of an organization's structure. Without a well-defined focus and identity, fragmentation of the "profession" is inevitable. The emergence of additional professional organizations recently to represent those employed by commercial and resort recreation agencies or those recreation therapists who work in clinical settings should have been expected.

The National Recreation and Park Association and other professional organizations and societies have contributed significantly to the concept of professionalism. Had it not been for the interest of the National Recreation and Park Association and the American Association for Leisure and Recreation (formerly the Recreation Division of AAHPE&R), it is doubtful that parks and recreation would have had its accreditation program approved by the Council on Postsecondary Accreditation. Likewise, had it not been for the lobbying effort on behalf of recreation by these associations, the inclusion of a recreation requirement in federal legislation requiring recreation services for the physically disabled might not have occurred. These accomplishments demonstrate both the impact professional organizations have on making sure the public is better served while at the same time enhancing the status of those who provide the service.

Has our approach to the creation of our professional organizations been effective? Should we push for only one body to represent the profession? Or should each special interest have its own voice, its own advocacy? Perhaps a federated approach is best, yet this has not been the pattern with the more established professions of medicine and law. The American Medical Association and the American Bar Association are not federations, yet they provide a structure which allows for specialists to identify with their specialty while not dissociating themselves from the larger profession. Parks and recreation has not done that. Why? Is it because our professional bodies have not represented the needs and interests of their constituents? Is the field too encompassing for one or two organizations to represent adequately? Is it due to the heterogeneousness of the professional background of those who practice in the "profession"?

Some might argue that our professional organizations have tried to be too many things too many interests, that they have attempted to be both advocates of the movement and ministers to the membership. Our national meetings rarely deal with critical issues or have the profession take a political position. Rather, they take on the air of a trade show with entertainment and general educational sessions. They attempt to update skills and provide new information, but with content that is more general than specific.

Is this the fault of the profession itself or is it a reflection of the stage at which parks and recreation is in its evolution? Perhaps it is a function of its multiple roots, its heritage and the public's satisfaction with its performance. Perhaps it is the changing nature of our delivery system with emerging specialities such as ski resort management. Perhaps it is the self-defining character of the recreation experience which makes it difficult to view parks and recreation as a profession. Yet there are those who believe it is and have worked diligently to professionalize their activities and services. Most of those who have done so identify themselves as park and recreation professionals and are employed by public park and recreation agencies. This is also the group which has the strongest tie to the past, to those social movements which gave rise to their concerns and functioning. They tend to recognize that they are only one of the many groups involved in the delivery of leisure services, that other agencies, too, employ similarly trained personnel but that only parks and recreation makes an issue of maintaining profession identify and has taken the steps necessary to reach profession status. This has occurred through professional societies and associations, adding to a body of knowledge, and programs of accreditation certification and professional preparation.

Most of these efforts toward creating a profession have been done by those within the movement. The public at large has not asked parks and recreation to take these actions but, according to Haug and Sussman,[13] that is generally the case with emerging professions. Public recognition often occurs as a result of the profession's activities to become a profession; it is not the causative factor. The public has never mandated park and recreation professionals to be guardians of its leisure nor has the public viewed leisure as a major social concern. It has accepted the importance of parks and recreation as an area of governmental activity to operate certain types of facilities and resources where the public can pursue its hobbies, be at leisure, recreate. And, as long as these resources are reasonably provided and operated, the public will not concern itself with who is the provider. While recognizing the existence of park and recreation specialists, it also tends to identify their role responsibilities in a more restrictive manner than do those who envision parks and recreation, even leisure services, as a profession.

A COURSE OF ACTION

What then must occur if parks and recreation is to become recognized as a profession, assuming that is a desirable goal? First and foremost, the profession must clearly define itself and its mission, and in terms different from those used to describe itself as a field of employment. Leisure services, albeit a nice term, describes an area of work but so does the term parks and recreation. If leisure services is the field of employment, is parks and recreation the profession? If parks and recreation is the field, then is leisure services the profession? Standard nomenclature is needed.

Secondly, it must be recognized that professional identity does not result from the place of employment but comes from the roles and responsibilities one performs. Parks and recreation and leisure services employ a variety of specialists, many of whom also function in other areas of human service and who do not identify themselves as members of the park and recreation profession—nor should they; an accountant is an accountant no matter who employs her. Likewise an architect is a member of a profession because of his training and role functions, not his job title or the name of the employing agency. In the field of health care, there are a variety of health care professions but only one role set assumed by those identified as physicians. Their role set is well defined and both the public and the practitioner (the physician) have similar expectations of the service to be performed.

The role of the professional within parks and recreation has yet to be clearly defined. What is the unique role set for the leisure service professional that distinguishes her as a member of the profession separate from all others who practice their craft in an organization or agency providing leisure services? What is it the recreation professionals can do which differentiates them from other workers? It certainly is not leading activities or managing operations. Like members in any profession, they must have the knowledge and ability to problem-solve, to identify the goals of their work consistent with a philosophy or mission of the profession, and create a plan of action to achieve those goals. Such action implies an understanding of the required resources, the method appropriate for utilization of those resources for goal achievement and the ability to monitor the process. It also implies the utilization of other professions, trades and even volunteers in the accomplishment of those objectives. The role set suggests management responsibilities, but management is not a unique role function. Others also manage. What it does require is an understanding by both the profession and the public of the role the profession is to assume and the major social concerns to be addressed.

The clearer the mandate, the less ambiguity there will be between the public's perception of the profession's role and that of the profession itself. The more closely the profession can identify and articulate the social concern it is addressing, the easier the task. Failure to define fully the field or to identify the social mandate does not negate the importance of the function of leisure services. Those who manage or operate recreation and park systems, serve as recreation therapists or work as recreation specialists in a resort setting perform valuable functions whether they are viewed as members of a profession or not. However, their functioning may be improved and their job title or vocation enhanced by the actions of those who wish to make parks and recreation a profession.

Recognizing the distinctive difference which exists between a discipline and a profession is critical. Parks and recreation is moving toward becoming a profession, not a discipline. Leisure studies may become the latter although it may remain primarily as an area of multidisciplinary and interdisciplinary work. The two—parks and recreation and leisure studies—may be interrelated, but their objectives are different. Leisure studies is not concerned about methods and techniques of service delivery; parks and recreation is. The implications of this separateness has curriculum consequences.

Perhaps more professional preparation should occur at the graduate level. The movement might best be served if undergraduate education was preprofessional education. Such an action should not prevent baccalaureate degree holders from finding employment in the field of parks and recreation, but would suggest that graduate study was the appropriate means for becoming a professional. It would also address the issues—length of study and selectivity of those admitted to the profession—raised by Goode.

Acceptance by employers and those who represent the public of the value of certification would also enhance the status of the field. By demonstrating to them that those who have a particular set of experiences and training can best serve the public, perhaps some of the ambiguity between the perceptions of practitioners and the public can be resolved. Requiring certification as a prerequisite for certain jobs suggests that those jobs are positions which can only be filled by members of the profession. That, too, would help but in the final analysis it will be the action taken by its professional organizations to enhance the status of parks and recreation that will make the difference.

Our move toward profession status is more than an exercise, it is a needed and worthwhile enterprise. The more the public and the "profession" come to expect park and recreation practitioners to have graduated from an accredited curriculum, to adhere to a professional code of behavior, to become involved in matters of public policy affecting parks and recreation, the better the service rendered. We will have also elevated the public's expectations of performance and by doing so, we may also elevate the expectation of the practitioner to perform as a professional.

As nice as it might be to have one organization speaking for the movement, that may be impossible. In fact, it may be advantageous to have many voices speaking on our behalf, each voice representing its special interest, as long as there is an understanding among each of those interests that they are not *the profession*, but are a part of a field of service striving toward professionalism. The bottom line is that, to a great degree, professions must and do control their destiny. Therefore, professionals must be in control of their professional organizations, their accrediting and certifying bodies, and develop and articulate the rationale for their existence as a profession. They must clearly identify their mandate, define their area of expertise and differentiate their role from all others who might practice within the same sphere of work. Until that is done, all steps toward profession status will be futile even though potentially beneficial to the delivery of services.

REFERENCES

1. Goode, W. J. "Encroachment, Charlatanism and the Emerging Professions: Psychology, Sociology, and Medicine." *American Sociological Review.* 25(December) 1960, p. 903.
2. Wilensky, H. "The Professionalization of Everyone?" *American Journal of Sociology.* 120:2, 1964, p. 145.
3. Cheek, N. H. "The Professions: Specialization and Bureaucratization" in Abrahamson, Mack. *The Professional in the Organization.* Chicago: Rand McNally and Company, 1967.
4. Sorenson, R. "Professional Maturity." *American Recreation Society Quarterly.* (May), 1953 in Sessoms, H. D. *Introduction to Leisure Services.* Englewood Cliffs, New Jersey: Prentice-Hall, 1984, p. 288.
5. Kauffman, E. *A Critical Evaluation of Components Basic to Certain Selected Professions With a View to Establishing Recreation as a Profession.* Unpublished doctoral dissertation, New York University, 1963.
6. Shapiro, I. G. *A History of the Professionalization of Recreation Administration from 1930 to 1970.* Unpublished doctoral dissertation, University of North Carolina, 1970.
7. Cheek, *Op. Cit.,* p. 9.
8. Goode, *Op. Cit.,* p. 903.
9. Abrahamson, *Op. Cit.,* p. 7.
10. Cheek, *Op. Cit.,* p. 13-14.
11. Stein, T. A. "Recreation Education in the US and Canada." *Leisure Sciences.* 6:3, 1984, p. 340.
12. Knapp, R. F. and Hartsoe, C. E. *Play for America.* Arlington, Virginia: National Recreation and Park Association, 1979.
13. Haug, M. R. and Sussman, M. B. "Professionalism and the Public." *Sociological Inquiry.* 39, Winter, 1969, p. 57.

(no keep)

p. 262 is blank.
End of Chapter 19

Chapter 20

Gaining Professional Status: Who Benefits?

Peter A. Witt

Is there any documented correlation between possession of a recreation degree and innovative leadership within the profession and community served? Are there any concrete data which demonstrate that recreators who have degrees in social work, teaching, psychology, or even English are less effective than those with degrees in recreation?[1]

Since the merger that formed the National Recreation and Park Association (NRPA) in 1965, achieving full professional status for workers in the park and recreation field has been a steadfast goal. However, concern within the field for instituting accreditation and certification goes back to the 1930s and 1950s respectively. In the 1980s, NRPA and the American Alliance of Leisure and Recreation (AALR) implemented procedures in these areas. Along with defining a body of knowledge, establishing a code of ethics, and achieving other trappings of a profession, these efforts have been hailed by workers in the field as giving them the status and recognition they feel they deserve in addition to potentially protecting the public via improved quality of service delivery.

While acquisition of the accoutrements of professionalization has been a central goal of the park and recreation field, professional status, power and the ability to provide service to consumers is being increasingly questioned in a variety of other fields. Although park and recreation workers are basking in their new found status, it seems appropriate to examine why there is increasing agreement with George Bernard Shaw's observation that "professions are a conspiracy against the laity." While continued efforts to professionalize the field are inevitable, understanding the increasing concern over the power and status of professions may help the park and recreation field achieve the advantages of professionalization while avoiding some of the pitfalls.

COMPETING EXPLANATIONS

While there has always been a bit of suspicion of the power and prestige held by professionals, societies (especially western) have fostered the growth of professions despite Shaw's warning. In most instances the public has been willing to grant special power and privilege to specific occupational groups in exchange for dedicated service. Larsen notes that:

> Society grants these rewards because professions have special competence in esoteric bodies of knowledge linked to central needs and values of social systems, and because professions are devoted to the service of the public, above and beyond incentives.[2]

This view is similar to what Cullen labels the "exchange-structural" explanation for why occupations develop professional elements. Exchange-structuralists argue that accomplishing intellectually complex tasks in occupations centered on working with people "necessitates occupations having features such as long training, ethical codes, licensure, high income and high prestige."[3] Thus, granting professional status is a bargain struck between society and a given occupation by which individuals agree to acquire the knowledge and education necessary to perform a complex task in exchange for power and privileges. Society gives professions the right to monitor their members' performance and prescribe educational curricula and standards. Professions, in return, give dedicated, quality service.[4]

An opposing view of professions to that of the exchange-structuralists is the "power orientation' perspective. This orientation questions the underlying motivation of occupational groups in their quest to be recognized as professions. Power and prestige rather than quality of service are viewed as the major motivation for development of a profession. While the exchange-structuralist view implies a free market system of rational exchange of status for quality service, the power orientation views professions as monopolies based on self-interest:

> Consistent with their critical position, the power theorists are quick to argue that many of the occupations considered as non professions are qualitatively no different than the accepted professions—yet, because they lack the necessary resources and power, these non-professions are not successful in convincing society of their needs for autonomy.[5]

While the exchange perspective views professionalism as a means, the power perspective sees professionalism as an end.[6]

The difference between these two views of why professional status is sought or granted can help us understand why professionalization is viewed as a direct benefit to society by some and as conspiracy by others. The exchange view sees the trade off value of what professionals receive in return for service while the power theorists are suspicious that status and prestige have been usurped under false pretenses primarily for reasons of self-interest.

Cullen offers further contrasts between how the exchange and power perspectives approach certain criteria used to define a profession. Three are discussed here in order to more fully understand the differing approaches: the code of ethics, long formal training, and licensure or credentialing.[7]

Criteria Defining Professions: Two Views

In the exchange view, a code of ethics is the "institutionalized manifestation of the service ideal and colleague control."[8] The need for a code of ethics arises due to the competency gap between clients and professionals. Only fellow colleagues are thus thought to be able to monitor the performance of their professional peers. A code of ethics also promotes the interests of the client by specifying criteria for judging service delivery and quality.

Power theorists argue, on the other hand, that a code of ethics is simply a public relations tool. Friedson has noted that:

> A code of ethics may be seen as one of many methods an occupation
> may use to induce general belief in the ethicality of its members,
> without *necessarily* bearing directly on individual ethicality.[9]

In the case of long formal training, exchange theorists believe that the complexity of professional work necessitates this commitment. On the other hand, power theorists contend that the presumed necessity of long formal training is just another smoke screen or attempt to sell the earned nature of power and prestige to the public. Power theorists point to studies showing the lack of a direct relationship between length of formal education and actual job performance.

Similar contrasts can be made between the exchange and power perspective on licensure and credentialing. Exchange theorists view the license or credential as a method of the profession and a mandate by the society for establishing standards that limit entry to professional practice to only those individuals with the capability of serving the public interest. Federal and State regulatory agencies assess whether or not such a mandate should be extended to a given occupational group. In essence, these regulatory bodies do not establish standards. In most cases they give the profession the right to judge, for example, whether an individual possesses sufficient knowledge or expertise to be credentialed or licensed. What constitutes sufficiency or expertise is also usually left to the profession to decide:

Noting both the competence gap associated with highly professional-ized   occupations as well as the 'institutionalized altruism' (Merton, 1975) built into the ethical code and other norms of professional behavior, exchange- structuralists see autonomous self-control as necessary for the professions because they believe it is a viable mecha-nism by which society can be protected from dangerous exchange relationships with 'quacks.'[10]

On the other hand, power theorists see potential for abuse in a system that can be utilized to monopolize the job market by using licensure and credential-ing as means to decrease the supply of practitioners and increase occupational rewards. Because education is often used as the standard for defining whether an individual is qualified to be credentialed, licensing laws can specify strict accreditation and educational standards that limit enrollment or the number of graduates. While these laws may seem on the surface to be aimed at protecting the public by promoting quality education and in turn improved practice, power theorists are again suspicious that the implied monopoly may encourage abuses and laxness based on self-interest:

> As a result of acquiring this highly specialized knowledge, professions demand autonomy and independence for their actions. They demand immunity from the consequences which result from intervention (except by peer evaluation). In a sense, professions which are accorded [this status] are removed from the competitive marketplace . . .   Once an occupation is able to subordinate the consumers' freedom of choice, it has monopolized services.[11]

The resulting monopoly may create a situation, for example, where salaries are artificially inflated because demand for workers outstrips the sanctioned supply and where quality of service is controlled by occupational standards as opposed to consumer criteria. Often this means that the profession, rather than the consumer, controls the basis, rationale, and mechanics of service delivery. Professional control of entry, knowledge to be acquired, and standards of practice may give it undue autonomy and powers of self-regulation.

Power or Exchange

Cullen has conducted an exploratory, yet complex, study designed to ascertain whether either the exchange or power perspective is supported by available data concerning the relative impact of both power-related and exchange-structuralists determinants of professionalism. While no formal theory was tested, Cullen's findings led him to several propositional conclusions. In essence, Cullen concluded that in most professions functional reciprocity (exchange) and power act concurrently. He noted that (a) "occupational task-complexity and intellectual sophistication are the major determinants of professionalism's characteristics" (ex. educational requirements) and (b) "to the degree that professionalism's characteristics are not determined by task complexity/intellectual sophistication, they are determined by the occupational group's power."[12]

Cullen's propositions do not indicate that task-complexity and intellectual sophistication are necessary for an occupation to achieve status. Indeed, occupational groups involved in work requiring lower levels of task-complexity and intellectual sophistication may be able to achieve designation as a profession via increased use of power (ex. influence or use of the financial resources of the national association). Power alone, however, in the absence of perceived task complexity and intellectual sophistication of the role requirements, may be insufficient for achieving professional status. Regulatory bodies and public suspicion probably will prevent creating a profession based purely on the use of influence or organizational resources.

From the foregoing discussion, it should be clear that there is probably no such thing as a pure profession or only one route by which an occupation becomes recognized as a profession. Listing a set of characteristics that typify a profession and checking off how many of these elements a given occupation possesses fails to take into account which characteristics are the most critical under the law (i.e., laws that grant rights to license or accredit) or in the eyes of the public. In point of fact, many occupations possess some elements that have been used to designate a profession. The label "profession" may be in fact misleading and subject to abuse.

It is also necessary to keep in mind that occupational groups seek professional status for differing reasons (i.e. exchange or power). Thus, a discussion of the role, value and legitimacy of a given occupation's claim to professional status should be based on an assessment of the motives of the occupational group, benefits of the perceived status to society *and* the occupational group, and also the costs or negative consequences of granting such status.

LEGITIMATE PURSUIT?

Do current efforts to achieve the professional designation for the park and recreation field arise out of the belief that the occupational tasks involved are *complex* and the knowledge base for practice characterized by *intellectual sophistication?* Or, do efforts at achieving professional status depend primarily on the use of influence and organizational resources (such as NRPA's staff and the hard work of members)? Or, as noted by Cullen, are there elements of exchange *and* power at work in the field's quest to be designated as a profession?

There is little hard evidence to support the contention that exchange or power alone or some combination of the two motivations are driving current efforts at professionalization. My own view is that some combination of exchange and power motivated efforts to achieve recognition of the AALR-NRPA accreditation process by the Council on Professional Accreditation, the national body responsible for legitimizing an occupation's desire to accredit educational programs. Elements of exchange and power also seem to be the motivation for establishing certification procedures, a recognized code of ethics, parameters for defining a body of knowledge and other elements that are considered essential to defining an occupation as a profession.

While my own inclination is to agree with Shaw's conspiracy view of professions, it is also easy to understand why the park and recreation field would seek professional status from an exchange perspective as well as self protective reasons independent of exchange.

Increasingly, achieving designation as a profession is seen as one way of defining job specificity, legitimizing control over working conditions, and meeting the needs of society for quality performance. While this may sound like a restatement of the power view, it is more a recognition of the degree of status and prestige accorded to recognized professions and the desire of a wider group of occupations to achieve the resulting rewards. Successful democratization of access to status and rewards in the last 20 years will probably only lead to redefinition of criteria for determining acceptance and designation of a given occupation as a profession. But, for the time being, it appears that many occupational groups involved in work without evidence of task-complexity or intellectual sophistication are seeking professional designation.

On the sole basis of "keeping up with the Jones," the park and recreation field probably has good reason to seek professional status. If we believe remuneration is too limited and differentiation of occupations on the basis of professional recognition is an important determination of remuneration, self protection in an age of specialization seems mandatory. Of course we should not delude ourselves as to our motivation by believing our own pronouncements on the irreparable societal consequences of failing to grant the park and recreation field the status of a profession. While we may need to develop an elaborate "story" to sell our claim, we should be cognizant of the impact of the game on the quality of service we ultimately render to the public. In other words, whether professional status is achieved as the result of exchange or power, or as requisite to occupational survival, we need to ask the more fundamental question: Are the needs of consumers ultimately served? The following section will briefly discuss several consequences of professional status that may be potentially detrimental to the consumer and in some cases even the professional These consequences include: (a) inappropriate socialization of potential workers and (b) failure to meet consumer needs.

THE SOCIALIZATION PROCESS

One of the potentially negative consequences of the accreditation/certification/ licensure process is the establishment of a process of socialization that individuals must go through to gain the right to practice. Thus, individuals are selectively admitted to degree granting programs, educated with regard to a particular body of knowledge, taught accepted skills and techniques, and reinforced for absorbing a prescribed set of occupational values and attitudes. The more rigid the accreditation (what can be taught) and certification/licensure (what should be learned) processes, the more rigid the socialization process.

It has been observed in the literature dealing with a variety of professions that each profession tends to develop a paradigm based upon:

> ". . . a taken-for-granted conception of what the issue is, and how it
> is solvable. Each profession tends to see the world in terms of
> its own characteristic conception of problems and solutions . . ."[13]

Thus, professions tend to become like social movements:

> They recruit only certain types of persons, they develop highly
> elaborate ideologies and supra-individual values, they have
> their own mechanisms of socialization and they often attempt to
> proselytize and bring new members into the fold.[14]

Implicit in these statements is the danger that the paradigm may cloud professionals' perceptions of consumers' problems and needs and thereby diminish the prospect of successful service delivery.

Two major sources have been identified to account for the development of a professional paradigm: 1) the personality and other characteristics of individuals who self-select or are chosen to enter a particular profession; and 2) the training and socialization process that individuals go through prior to and during their professional careers. Both of these sources have the potential of developing filters or biases concerning the problems a particular profession chooses to address and the solutions adopted for dealing with the perceived problems.

Bishop, et al. found significant differences in selected personality traits and achievement measures between students in recreation and those in other university departments.[15] Of particular interest was that recreation students were shown to be exceptionally high in extroversion when compared to students in other departments or to general population norms. Based on these results and on similar test results involving recreation students at four other universities, and taking into account Eysenck's[16] theory of extroversion-introversion and its behavioral implications, Bishop observed that:

Many recreation students (and in our judgement many recreation professionals) tend to be socially oriented and dependent, somewhat conventional, need fairly large amounts of temporal variation or change, tend to prefer action over thinking . . . All of the characteristics cannot be explained by extroversion. They do suggest a consistent recreology character or type, however, of which extroverted tendencies appear to be an important part.[17]

Added to Bishop's results are observations that recreation students tend to have a significant history of recreational involvements through which they developed the requisite skills to participate and the motivation for continued involvement. Many of these interests are in physical activities although recreation students currently seem to have more diversified interests than previously, when recreation was largely associated with physical education and a "jock" mentality. In addition, most students entering the recreation field have had significant contact with some form of recreation service agency through part-time work.

The socialization and training process that potential professionals are subjected to via educational experiences prior to entering the field and on an ongoing basis via inservice training and contact with fellow workers, exposure to a common group of educational and professional materials and so on, also has a significant impact on the development of a paradigm.[18] These experiences are usually endorsed by educators and practitioners alike as necessary to successful professional development and socialization.[19] There is a tendency to adopt a fairly consistent in-group philosophy of the need for recreation services, the benefits of participation and the best means of organizing recreational opportunities. Many of these perceptions will be "correct," i.e., they will prove useful in meeting needs as defined by consumers. However, in some cases professionals seem to develop a paradigm either for the rationale or the methods of offering services that differs dramatically from citizens' perceptions of what needs to be done. As Hughes notes, "Professions profess. They profess to know better than their clients what ails them or their affairs."[20]

Most people feel the need to identify with some group. Combining this need with the tendency of the in-group to preserve itself via subtle pressure to conform to ideas and working practices may lead workers in most professional areas through an acculturation process wherein the social values, behavioral norms, and symbols of the occupational group are internalized.[13] In this way, the philosophy and practices of a given profession are institutionalized and protected from erosion from outside influences. Most professions tend more toward the status quo led by an old guard that depends heavily on tradition and years of experience rather than an ongoing process of questioning assumptions and practices as a basis for future services. Of course, every profession also has its "black sheep" and its radicals, those who resist the acculturation process. They, in fact, play a valuable role by questioning underlying assumptions and providing a basis for innovation and change.

There are some other potential costs in the accreditation/certification/professionalization process. Standardization of practice and knowledge, for example, can be good but it can also squelch innovation, experimentation, etc. One wonders whether, if people in Columbus's day had a professional body to adhere to, we still might think the world was flat and rests on the backs of a group of turtles.

I am also concerned that we will make the entire focus of university education to get a job, i.e., to prepare students to enter a profession. This refocusing of *higher* education on *hire* education and job training violates the basic tenets of being an educated person. While a liberal arts education may also be abused, there are advantages to understanding the world in which we live in more general terms than professional education will allow.

RISING CONSUMERISM

As a result of the socialization process, recreation professionals may develop and protect assumptions about consumer needs that do not match consumers' perceptions of their own needs. Thus, professionals may over- or under-estimate the extent to which particular barriers such as lack of time, money, or equipment, are problematic for consumers. For example, recreation professionals may see lack of motivation, inability to maintain commitments, or even lack of physical fitness, as problems of greater magnitude than they actually are. Such "conclusions" may be self-serving in that they can be used to justify the development of services to overcome professionally perceived barriers. Service professions need people who need services.

Another example of where professionals and consumers may differ is over how to define what is a "wholesome" leisure activity:

> Obviously, it can be viewed differently by the provider of park and recreation services and the consumer. Therefore, the critical question becomes this: who is to determine what is wholesome, the consumer or the professional? Should the profession impose its value upon the consumer or should the consumer exercise control over the profession . . . ?[21]

It should be noted that professional "biases" may actually be based on facts or knowledge not available to or ignored by consumers such as the relationship between fitness and health and the demonstrated low level of fitness in the populace. On the other hand, it could be argued that citizens are as fit as they want to be, are aware of the implications of fitness for health, and do not share the profession's concern with developing a fit society. Who is "right" raises numerous questions for professionals, such as whether to be proactive or reactive or adopt a leadership as compared to a followership posture. Who has the right to make decisions is another issue; professionals have the responsibility to do so. The biases upon which professionals make those decisions is at issue.

One result of the growth of professionalism and the tendency toward developing professional paradigms has been a corresponding emergence of consumerism. Consumerism involves an attempt to insure that the type, quantity, and quality of goods and services provided are in keeping with needs and standards as defined by the ultimate user as opposed to the supplier. As professionals have moved toward increasing autonomy and control, consumers have fought back by demanding greater involvement in all aspects of the planning and provision of needed goods and services. Thus, for example, the delivery of park and recreation services is being increasingly affected by the emerging awareness, sophistication, and competency of consumers. As consumer involvement in decision making processes affecting the delivery of services increases, a clearer understanding of the relationship between the rights, needs and obligations of consumers and providers must be established.

One result of emerging consumerism is an increasing responsibility to clearly identify the source and validity of professional assumptions and practices. Constant attention needs to be given to sorting out whose interests are served by service provision efforts. Professionals need to avoid self-serving ideologies that preserve the status quo in the face of evidence that those ideologies are inappropriate. On the other hand, professionals should avoid seeking change simply because it avoids routine or appears progressive.

Thus, ways need to be found to overcome professionals' perceptions based on personal needs or orientations of the provider and to adopt outlooks that give more credence to consumer generated perceptions of needs, problems, and solutions. Ways need to be found to return control over service conceptualization and delivery to those whom the services are designed to benefit. This will help avoid dependency that professionalism often entails. It will also help overcome the mentality that professionals' views take precedence because of the supposed advantage accruing to those who have studied in a given area or devoted their working lives to solving a particular problem or issue. We must overcome the mentality that the capacity for solving problems is narrowly distributed within the society, existing only in the realm of the professions. Recognizing that being certified and graduating from an accredited school guarantees access to a job, but not necessarily the ability to do the job, may help alleviate some of this problem. Where is the evidence that degrees, certificates, and titles assure expertise and competence?

Raising consumer expectations and worker obligations (and perhaps expectations) is another of the undesirable and potentially dangerous side effects of accreditation, certification, and licensure. These practices create an aura of knowledge and infallibility which may in turn, lead to dependence and unfounded expectations of success. The medical and legal fields are replete with stories of clients who grow to expect too much from professionals rather than being taught how to do for themselves.

TOWARD INCREASED COLLABORATION

In the final analysis what is needed is a renewed spirit of collaboration between professionals and consumers. While professionals may have specific interests in gaining a personal measure of status, authority, and autonomy, it should not be accomplished at the expense of consumer needs or rights. Expertise has its place but professionals need to recognize that they serve at the behest of consumers and not in opposition. The granting of special powers and privileges through processes such as accreditation, certification, and licensing should only be done to the extent that tangible benefits to consumers can be shown. In the case of the park and recreation field, we need to ascertain more clearly the unique knowledge or skills that recreation professionals possess that would justify certification or licensing or the unique roles played by park and recreation curricula that would justify accreditation.

Ultimately, recreation workers may be simply playing a game within a structure established by perceived necessity and reality. However, to confuse economics, job protection, and liability limitation concerns with actions which purport to protect the interests of consumers is misleading and potentially dangerous. Creating a union, while less glamorous, may be more appropriate.

REFERENCES

1. Yale, D. R. "Certification and Registration: A Mistake." *Parks and Recreation.* 1975, 10, pp. 24-25.
2. Larsen, M. S. *The Rise of Professionalism: A Sociological Analysis.* Berkeley: University of California Press, 1977, p. x.
3. Cullen, J. B. *The Structure of Professionalism: A Quantitative Examination.* New York: Petiocelli Books, Inc., 1978, p. 2.
4. *Ibid,* pp. 48-57.
5. *Ibid,* p. 67.
6. *Ibid,* pp. 58-64.
7. *Ibid,* pp. 64-70.

8. *Ibid*, p. 65.
9. Friedson, E. *Profession of Medicine*. New York: Dodd, Mead and Company, 1970, p. 187. Quoted in Cullen, *Op. Cit.*, p. 66.
10. Cullen, *Op. Cit.*, p. 68.
11. Edginton, C. R. "Consumerization and Professionalization," *Parks and Recreation*. 11(9), 1976, p. 42.
12. Cullen, *Op. Cit.*, p. 204.
13. Friedson, E. *The Professions and Their Prospects*. Beverly Hills, California: Sage Publications, 1973, p. 31.
14. Denzin, N. K. "Pharmacy: Incomplete Socialization." *Social Forces*. 46 (3), 1968, p. 376.
15. Bishop, D. W. *In Investigation of Some Temperament and Ability Differences Among Advanced Undergraduates of Selected Departments at the University of Ottawa*. Mimeo paper, 1979.
16. Eysenck, H. *The Bilogical Basis of Personality*, Springfield, Illinois: Charles C. Thomas, 1967.
17. Bishop, D. W., *Op. Cit.*, p. 29-30.
18. Pavalko, P. M. *Sociology of Occupation and Professions*. Itasca, Illinois: Peacock, 1971.
19. McChesney, J. C. *Professional Development and Involvement of Recreation and Park Students*. Unpublished Doctoral Dissertation, Indiana University, 1974.
20. Hughes, F. C. "Professions." *Daedalus*. 92, 1963, p. 67.
21. Edginton, C. R., *Op. Cit.*, p. 84.

End of Chapter 20

Chapter 21

Narrowing the Options: The Power of Professionals in Daily Life and Leisure

John Lord, Peggy Hutchison and Fred VanDerbeck

Choice, risk, and involvement are vital elements in growth and development and human experience In our society, however, adults have become less playful and more security-oriented. Many of our institutions are dominant and unresponsive, making it difficult for people to feel a sense of purpose and control in their daily lives. To regain a willingness to risk and change, we need to increase the options in our lives, beginning at the personal level and moving to community and social system levels. So it is necessary to examine the inter-relationships between our creative, playful selves and the systems of professional dominance which narrow our options. It is timely to analyze this process in the field of leisure services because of the current thrust toward certification. standardization and professionalization. An exploration of the power of professionals in daily life and leisure will help us to clarify the relevant issues and to come to an understanding of our role in creating more options for ourselves and our communities.

NEGATING PLAY THROUGH PROFESSIONALISM

Professionals often destroy or exclude play and playfulness by disregarding and institutionalizing the central elements of play. Spontaneity and exploration are obliterated by a preoccupation with teaching and structure. Internal motivation is weakened by imposing rewards and external controls. We become dependent upon professionals, rather than relying on ourselves and our community of friends.

We have become serious about ourselves and our work, unable to be playful, and unable to recognize opportunities for play. Most of us probably smile when we observe children laughing, sharing, creating, and exploring at play. But do we smile only because we fondly remember how important play was to us? In other words, is children's play an external event to us, rather than something which we feel comfortable joining?[1]

Perhaps some of us wonder why we have lost our ability to play and self-generate. One possibility is that professions which dominate our lives lower people's trust in themselves to generate energy, ideas, and alternatives. Our lives are permeated by services which create dependency on the part of both the client and the professional. Dependency for the client means that the capacity for self-development is narrowed to the choices offered by the experts in a particular field. Dependency for the professional means that his or her actions become nearly synonymous with the profession's need to help and to create needs.

Play is also negated or destroyed by control and fragmentation, two characteristics of professionalism. Both these elements have had an impact on children by the time they are six years old. Children at school soon learn that play is relatively unimportant and that the only valuable knowledge is formal knowledge which is acquired primarily from professionals. It is in this sense that professionals and institutions control the lives of children and adults. As several researchers and social critics have emphasized, children's sport and recreation programs reflect the dominant social values, as indicated by competition, leader-directed activity and exclusion.[2,3]

Beliefs which permit professionalism to dominate and control our lives lead people to separate their work and play. This kind of fragmentation makes it difficult for people to have meanings and understanding in an increasingly complex world. Many people with whom we have spoken see their lives as routine and unconnected. The way we separate our lives into units for leisure, work, family, and sleep are disabling, particularly as recreation and leisure become residual events in our lives. Play is no longer a space for exploration and learning but becomes a space, like work, for the accomplishment of narrowly defined tasks. The negation of play by professionalism, then, is a serious paradox for recreation, since play and professionalism have become fundamentally antithetical practices.

THE GROWTH OF PROFESSIONALISM

Two important historical periods have been identified with the rise of professionalism in western culture. The first took place in the middle of last century with the development of cities and a corresponding rise in commerce. From these influences, a middle class emerged which resulted in increased inequalities of wealth distribution.[4] The idea of individual career patterns and upward mobility, in contrast to community sharing as a way of meeting human needs, became important. This historical perspective remains relevant today since most professionals continue to support inequality and social hierarchies. Consider how human service workers at the direct programming level are devalued, both in terms of social status and financial remuneration.

The second period associated with the rise of professionalism was the middle part of this century when professions became more dominant in people's lives by acquiring authority and control.[5] This period was in contrast to earlier times when professionals had a more benevolent role. For example, a medical practitioner made home visits, diagnosed sickness, and recommended a variety of prepared and home remedies. In contrast, the medical profession today controls health-related matters and provides impersonal service.[6] It has been suggested that medical practices themselves stimulate further problems by focusing on illness rather than health and prevention.[7] Doctoring today is thus an industry, not a service. A second example concerns recreationists who, in the past, cooperated with citizen's groups in order to provide a variety of formal and informal leisure opportunities for the community. Again, this is in sharp contrast to many current recreation professionals who feel they need to institutionalize our leisure and organize our time. Have you ever tried to go skating in a municipal rink more than once or twice a week? Schedules, leagues, and narrow age groupings for organized sport dominate most hours of the day and night.

THE MAKING OF A PROFESSIONAL

In our society the professional occupies a privileged position. She/he did not get there because of innate individual characteristics, but rather because of our particular societal organization. However, the power of the person who is a professional is also dependent upon the willingness of that person to conform to the standards created by his/her profession.[8] Professionals view themselves as owners of their area of expertise and as custodians who have the right and responsibility to control access to the occupation. The definition of a profession, then, is largely determined by:

> . . . the professional's authority to define a person, as client, to determine that person's need, and to hand that person a prescription which defines this new social role.[9]

Thus, this relationship of mutual dependency creates a social distance between the client and professional and reinforces the idea that one needs a service which is best provided by an expert. In essence, this is a *political* relationship, since it legitimizes the professional in the role of policy and decision-maker for the client. Rather than fostering a sense of shared responsibility for the problem, the professional behaves in ways which are designed to maintain awe of and respect for the profession.

Our daily lives are a source of constant confrontation with such professional enhancement. Haven't we all had the experience of waiting in line at an agency office and hearing a person introduce himself or herself as a Doctor, Attorney, or

Professor? Is this done as a means of identification or is it a professional claim to be placed ahead of the people waiting in line? Perhaps it would be useful for all of us to try an experiment to test the reality of this system. Introduce yourself, either in person or on the telephone, using your usual name one time, and a professional designation another time. See if the tone of voice, the demeanor of the person to whom you are talking or the quality of service changes. For even more impact, try slurring your words or add a foreign accent and see if the response is any different.

This way of acting develops during a period of training in which the professional acquires a certain self-concept which gives legitimacy to these actions in her or his mind. This training consists of absorbing a particular way of thinking about oneself and one's society which emphasizes success over support and nurturing. We are taught to get to know people according to their accomplishments rather than for their human characteristics. Upon meeting someone, we are most often concerned about their status (assembly line worker, housewife, vice-president), rather than the possibility of a shared relationship or learning experience. Contacts such as these tend to reify and depersonalize human relations. This superficial way of interrelating becomes dominant in everyday interactions. It would require a very different way of thinking about ourselves and our society for us to become more humanly and less technically concerned about our fellow persons.

Those of us in professions know very well the narrow, procedural training we received. We can remember the emphasis on technical solutions to social problems and moral dilemmas. Jeffry Galper reflects upon the process of professional training:

> Students, for example, are encouraged to think analytically, but not to connect the material before them to the major emotional dynamics in their lives. Similarly, the survival needs of many workers dictate that they not feel, in any profound way, the emotional poverty of the work situations. . . To encourage people to deny and compartmentalize their emotions, therefore, serves to maintain a public myth about the acceptability of the social order, since it encourages the belief that the pain people experience is idiosyncratic. (In addition) this serves to isolate the professional from the fullest awareness of the amount of pain that exists in the society an the relative powerlessness of the professional to deal with it.[10]

Certification is an attempt to ensure that professionals will acquire their profession's view of what is best for people. Unfortunately, both the client and professional too easily conform to expectations each has of the other and therefore both maintain the status quo. This established hierarchical form is generally restrictive and constraining to human development and human relationships.

UNDERLYING IDEOLOGIES

It is helpful to reflect on the dominant ideologies and values in our society which create and support this professionalized training. One underlying ideology emerges from the examination of worker alienation as technological changes are introduced into the workplace. The worker moving from being a crafts person to a baby-sitter on an assembly line illustrates this ideology.[11] Technology tends to dominate the workplace, thus allowing a system of cost effectiveness to emerge, which devalues human being. Purpose and meaning give way to narrow productivity measures and work and leisure are subordinated to specialized, industrial functions. When this occurs, it is difficult for individuals and groups to feel a sense of control over their own lives. Rather than confronting this dilemma, professionals and others rationalize its necessity. Using this ideology of rationalization, professionals often focus upon facts, objective data, and procedures as a way of explaining social problems, rather than trying to understand the political-economic and human issues underlying a problem.[12] Unconsciously then, rationalization has become a way of explaining and resolving daily life issues.[13]

To what extent do recreationists accept the rationalization of leisure by assuming that play is what you do away from work? Does professional education for recreationists reflect the strong conservative bias which seems to dominate professions in general? Examining the leading books in a field is one interesting way to decipher these questions. Our reading of the recreation literature suggests a consistent theme, which focuses upon the present and future growth of leisure and recreation as a result of technology. Some textbooks on leisure services argue that diversion and escape from a highly complex industrial society are central to the growth of mass leisure.[14] Many recommendations for organized recreation emerge from this assumption. Based upon this material, one clearly gets the impression that social, political, and economic systems are accepted unquestioningly. This simplistic focus on leisure as diversion is contradicted by the increasing evidence about the impact of technology and unemployment on both body and soul.[15]

Recreationists educated in such a narrow focus will continue to promote recreation as a means of coping with or avoiding oppressive and alienating work. Our leisure, however, is hardly more fulfilling than our work. Workers currently employed in unsatisfying jobs know that the "frustration and tension of the job are not easily left at the plant gate."[16] It is in this sense that recreationists often use leisure as a way of placating people. For example, disabled people are offered recreation programs but not jobs, often with the rationalization, unlike normal expectations, that they are fortunate not to be working, and that free time should be used more constructively. As a second example, recreation focuses upon activity, skills, procedures, participation, and programs. It seldom, if ever, emphasizes self and community development, women's groups, workers' study groups, political, theatre, or participant-directed activities.

A second ideology is known as positivism. The positivist tends to accept the status quo and dominant ideology that emphasizes bureaucratic rationality, modern technology, centralized authority, and scientific control.[17] Thus both the positivist and rationalist way of knowing and organizing the world presuppose the existence of objective knowledge and decision-making processes which devalue subjectivity in order to maintain control. This approach legitimizes technique at the expense of human interrelationships.[18] The contrast illustrated by the chart below, adapted from Harold Hodges Jr., clarifies the socialization process which occurs as young people become professionalized.[19]

THE CHILD	THE PROFESSIONAL
spontaneous, unrestrained	self-restrained, inhibited
risk-taking, adventuresome, change seeking	cautious, fearful of unfamiliar, security-oriented, stability seeking
intuitive, affective	logical, cognitive
open-minded	close-minded
innovative, exploratory	conventional, custom-bound
at ease with chaos, complexity, disorder mystery	fearful of the unstructured, undefined

In our view, these dominant values represent social processes which create daily life situations which avoid the real problems, support hierarchical relationships, and view people as commodities. The irony for recreation and leisure is that while recreation professionals often are characterized by items in the right hand column they are at the same time supposed to nurture the values in the left hand column through play and leisure. (See illustration above).

PROFESSIONAL DOMINANCE OF HUMAN SERVICES

In recent years there has been a rapid expansion in social, medical, and human services. Jeffry Galper, in a penetrating critique of social services in the United States, views current social services as a logical extension of capitalism.[20] Galper presents a great deal of data to support the viewpoint that social services allow the dominant ideology and commodity relationships discussed earlier to be maintained. Obviously, this approach will dismay many liberals who see welfare, homes for the elderly, and minimum wage laws as progressive and humane practices. In reality, however, many of these are band-aid arrangements which delay the implementation of fundamental changes in social services and political-economic structures. The myriad of existing human services which are constantly increasing to respond to yet another need is society's way of approving professionalism. In this sense, the human service industry serves as professionalism's stamp of approval.

Professionalism in human services is maintained by a belief in a political and value system which is supportive of competition as natural process, people as commodities, and hierarchies as the logical means of organization in people's lives. Thus, recreation departments teach primarily competitive values, slot people into programs, and force individuals and consumer groups to compete for artificially scarce resources. The cruel paradox of this value system is that individuals are often blamed for problems which are, instead, created by this unjust system. For example, in one community, a fitness program for senior citizens was run on Sundays from five to six-thirty. When few attended, the recreation department blamed the seniors for being poorly motivated.

Four practices help to maintain and institutionalize professionalism in human services.[21]

Narrow Focus

Professions develop a narrow frame of reference by focusing upon one aspect of a client or a problem. Such specialization narrows the range of solutions which are considered possible. In fact, real problems are often avoided and any solutions apply more to the symptom than to the cause of the problem. For medicine this means that a headache is viewed as the problem, and thus, treatment is aimed at eliminating the headache. In developing a broader frame of reference, professionals would spend less time trying to ameliorate existing problems and more time on prevention and self help. For example, in recreation, many problems and solutions tend to revolve around the issue of activity. We struggle to determine how to get and keep people active, but seldom do we undertake an analysis of meaning and purpose in people's lives.

Professional Detachment

Professions emphasize that their members should not become emotionally involved with their clients. It is ironic that many so-called "helping professions" train people and deliver services based upon these values. By "helping", we have come to mean doing something for someone without involvement. To *not* be neutral is to be involved and might mean cultivating a sense of wholeness.

This includes playfulness, empathy, and support for enabling others to view their own oppression collectively and the facilitation of alternative courses of action. This issue creates a dilemma for the recreationist. To be professionalized means the recreationist loses a certain degree of involvement and playfulness. Once these vital personal ingredients are lost, recreation becomes another commodity, another marketplace item to be packaged and sold. Thus, recreationists need to be deeply reflective about the growing professionalism in their field. Godbey is one of the few recreation professionals to express concern at the growing professionalization of recreation. He wonders whether:

> ... the recreation and parks movement, in seeking professional status, has moved toward an inappropriate model to bring about its initial ideals, such as restoring a sense of community through recreation, provision to the poor, and increased recreational self-sufficiency for citizens ... (professionalism) may increasingly alienate the practitioner from the social reform ethic and "grass roots" approach to community involvement.[22]

We must ask ourselves whether increased professionalization in the field of recreation will lead to further degradation of play values which are inherent in the minds and spirits of children, but which have lost their impact and meaning for most adults.

Professional Service Ethic

Professionals develop an ethic of service based upon their standards and expectations. Lack of cooperative efforts between the professional and client ensures that this process continues. For example, games are not adjusted for *mutual* participation when disabled individuals, health-impaired persons, or children wish to take part. The standard of performance continues to be the professional sports player. Some recreationists segregate participants of unequal capabilities and do not even consider changing the rules to permit the inclusion of all persons. This is another illustration of the permeation of the competitive ethic in our society. For many participants socialized in this society, the game would lose its meaning if the rules were changed. Thus, service to others is most often seen as the service *needed by the client*, in order to adjust him/herself to the requirements of the existing structure of power in any society.

Impartial Service Delivery

Human service providers generally claim impartiality in terms of the allocation of their services. Race, creed, and sex, for example, are said to be irrelevant factors in the distribution of resources. In practice, however, people start at very different levels when seeking services, and thus require different degrees of support. As Galper puts it:

> To guarantee equality of opportunity without assuring equality in the places from which people start to compete is to assure that equal opportunity will mean unequal outcomes.[23]

In order to show how this is part of our social-economic lives, we need to examine the unequal basis from which people begin. First, we recommend the study of income distribution and poverty in North America.[24] Second, despite improvements in recent years, there is evidence that women and minority groups with equal training compared to white males earn considerably less on entry into the labor market.[25] Third, consider the claim many community recreationists make that their services are equally available to all citizens. In reality, few recreation facilities are physically accessible to all persons, costs are often prohibitive, and opportunities for particular age groups are lacking.

Professionalism reflects a strong conservative bias in human services. Professional control serves to dampen personal and collective action and to encourage dependence on professional remedies. The human service and leisure industries support this dependence by serving as a link in the institutionalization of professionalism. The diagram on the following page illustrates the relationships among several components which serve either to institutionalize or change professionalism.

WHY THE TRUST YET THE QUESTIONING?

In a society where professionalism has become dominant, people continue to have tremendous trust in the process of professionalism:

> It is one of the maddening facts of our time that people believe themselves incapable of dealing with the most ordinary human conflicts without the aid of a 'specialist.[26]

Professionalism engenders trust because it penetrates and controls most aspects of our lives. Three of the ways in which professionalism affects people and gains trust follow.

First, the institutionalization of professionalism (see Figure 1, pg. 284) has resulted in a trust of institutions rather than community, and a trust in professionalism instead of self and others. We have been taught to believe that something that we need. For example, knowledge is of value only when given by an expert; therefore, learning must occur at school. Thus, it has become difficult for people to self-generate or put trust in oneself for learning the essential nuances of our day. Similarly, we believe we can't play without a recreationist, get better without a doctor, or gain rights without a lawyer.

Figure 1
Institutionalizing Professionalism

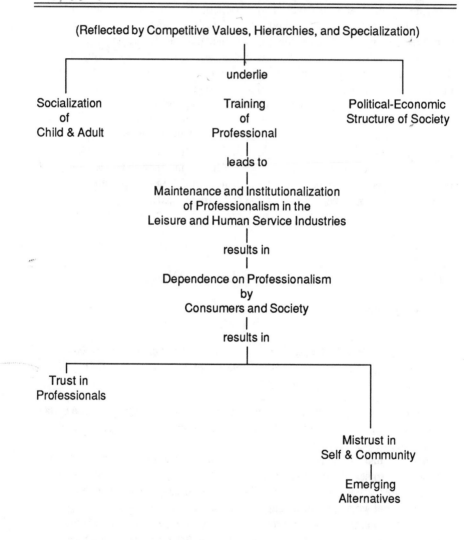

Dominant Ideologies
of
Rationalization and Positivism

(Reflected by Competitive Values, Hierarchies, and Specialization)

underlie

Socialization   Training   Political-Economic
of   of   Structure of Society
Child & Adult   Professional

leads to

Maintenance and Institutionalization
of Professionalism in the
Leisure and Human Service Industries

results in

Dependence on Professionalism
by
Consumers and Society

results in

Trust in
Professionals

Mistrust in
Self & Community

Emerging
Alternatives

Second, the trust in professionalism should not be so surprising, when one considers how professional power is subtly and effectively enshrined in our common speech. In an excellent book by one of the few persons to examine the relationship between power and helping language, Murray Edelman wrote:

> Consider a common usage that staff, clients, and the general public all accept as descriptive of a purely professional process: the term 'therapy.' In the journals, textbooks, and talk of the helping professions, the term is repeatedly used as a suffix or qualifier. Mental patients do not hold dances; they have dance therapy. If they play volleyball, that is recreation therapy. If they engage in a group discussion, that is group therapy.[27]

In other words, the professional's relationship to the client is based upon controlling the other's context by defining the possibilities for the client in professionally advantageous ways. By calling a relationship or an activity therapy, an immediate power hierarchy is established which makes it difficult for the devalued client to develop any self-help skills except those sanctioned by the professional. The client comes to rely on a professional for cues which will indicate the appropriateness of behavior and thoughts. Linguistic support for this situation is emphasized in professional jargon: solitary confinement is called a quiet room; an attempted escape is referred to as attempted elopement; and compulsory personal revelations at group meetings are defined as "benefiting from peer confrontation."[28] There is implicit power in these new terms and clients readily respond to the professional's orders.

Third, public policy is shaped, to a large extent, by our dependence upon, and trust in, professionals. An example occurred during National Health Week in Canada, when the former Minister of Health and Welfare was discussing health problems. He emphasized that:

> " . . . of all the problems we face, motivation of Canadians has to be singled out as the crucial one which will ultimately decide whether our strategy will be a success or failure . . . public education therefore cannot be overemphasized. Although education alone has only limited success in the past, there are exciting new approaches to be explored by scientists, psychologist, professional educators, social workers, and all professional workers."[29]

Professional intervention is thus seen as necessary for overcoming people's needs which have been described as deficient. By seeing the problem within the citizen, a fertile climate for professional dominance is maintained. Individualizing the problem leads to blaming the victim, when the root causes of health and leisure problems are much deeper. Examples of causes include: the dominance of professions and corporations in dictating our needs; political-economic priorities which devalue certain citizens; loss of citizen control of schools, the work place, and the community.

It is understandable why professionals are able to acquire so must trust and control in our society. It is people's feeling of personal powerlessness combined with an expectation that they should be able to get ahead and solve problems by themselves (individualism) that leave people susceptible to relying on professionals. When acting alone, we become the only integrators of our experience and our perceptions of ourselves become as fragmented as the world in which we live. We get caught in a vicious cycle of believing ourselves to be fragmented, and thus share with others in fragmented ways. It is at this point that we become even more susceptible to the influence of professionalism.

Despite this professional encapsulation of our lives, or possibly because of it, cracks are appearing in the dominant trust of professionalism. In our view, two major thrusts account for this questioning. First, citizens and their families who have been systematically devalued by the society have often had the courage to speak out about the oppressive nature of professionalism. For example, a young couple gives birth to a baby who is mentally retarded. They oppose the overwhelming advice of physicians and social workers to have their baby institutionalized. Such people are tired of professionalism and all its trappings, its bureaucracy, and its inequality. The result is a growing advocacy effort by parents, disabled persons, and their friends directed toward changing the human service industry.

A second attack on professions has come from social critics who see professionalism as avoiding the root causes of problems. In fact, some critics point out that professionalism contributes to our problems, rather than resolving them. For example, John McKnight asks:

> "Why are we putting so much resource into medicine while our health is not improving?
>
> Why are we putting so much resource into education and our children seen to be learning less?
>
> Why are we putting so much resource into criminal justice systems and society seems less just and less secure?
>
> Why are we putting so much resource into mental health systems and we seem to have more mental illness"?[30]

While many citizens are beginning to echo these concerns in their daily life experiences and dialogue, it is interesting to note the response of professionals to the growing criticism of professionalism. Some appear shocked and claim that any wrong-doing or problems in the profession are rare and must be the result of incompetent individuals. If one pushes the critique further, the professional may ask: "Are you in this field?" This defense, which assumes that one must be certified in a field in order to understand and criticize, squelches any attempt to critique professionalism on the basis of human values and system problems. These defenses serve as excuses which function to limit the creation of new options.

BROADENING THE OPTIONS

Developing alternatives to professionalism means broadening the options which people believe they can create to transform our society and daily lives. We suggest three broad approaches which we believe can have an impact on daily life and leisure. We also trust that readers can generate more specific alternatives and applications which are appropriate to their contexts.

New Vision

Creating serious alternatives to professionalism involves developing a vision of a different kind of society. As Margaret Mead once said:

> "Periods of social disorganization invite correction in two directions, one an order imposed by force . . . the other a radical transformation of society that relies on the creation in individuals of a spirit of deep dedication to new social goals".[31]

A new vision would involve new social goals which enable *all* individuals to develop to their fullest capacities. Social reconstruction would entail a deep concern for the quality of life of every citizen. Society would no longer be based on the principle that the individual is respected only insofar as she/he is profitable.[32] We need to acknowledge that we have a very crucial identify as persons separate from our role in economic and institutional life. Valuing people as developing human beings would mean new goals and new priorities for human and leisure services. For example, elderly people, disabled people, minority group individuals, and native people would no longer be systematically devalued. We would link the oppression of these groups to our own lives. Professional practices would cease to assume that people's needs are best resolved by psychological and specialist answers. Recreationists would ensure strong consumer input and control in planning services. And the quality of the leisure experience would take precedence over the quantity of services. Cooperation and collective understandings become central to these values. Too often, our sense of self is tied directly to our individual, professional goals. If we truly valued the potential of sharing with others, we would transform our work and leisure. Decision-making would become decentralized. Egalitarian relationships would replace professional domination and hierarchies. And leisure services would become a community and neighborhood project rather than a professional responsibility.

Changing Relationships

The professional-client relationship must change significantly. It must be viewed as an inter-relationship rather than a controlling relationship. In practice, professionals must not only share knowledge in a natural way, but struggle into the unknown with their clients through shared experiences and shared reflections. Barry Kaufman writes in a deeply human manner about his struggle with professionals in seeking effective approaches with his autistic son.[33] All professionals either had rigid prescriptions or responses which clearly indicated that nothing could be done. Finally, one professional was willing to explore the unknown and to converse with Kaufman about a range of options. It is in this sense that broadening the options means that professionals must be open to altering their theories in response to ongoing experiences in which alternative realities have been demonstrated. This also involves shared control over contexts rather than professional domination in relationships. Lack of consumer input into decision-making and planning in recreation makes it unlikely that recreation professionals will either alter their perceptions or relinquish control through cooperative efforts with citizens.

Advocacy

Recreationists must advocate to ensure that professionalism does not dominate the field of recreation. The recreationist as an advocate can work to deprofessionalize recreation and to deindustrialize the leisure industry.

A deprofessionalized view of recreation restores community and play as central to the recreation movement. Advocates will cooperate with others to identify barriers to community and play. They will infuse their jobs and their lives with a sense of community and a sense of playfulness. In practice, this will mean having a support group of deprofessionalized friends and colleagues who share the commitment to create a more just and humane society. It also entails being comfortable with negotiation and confrontation about the practical issues in everyday life. Creating links with community groups to ensure that consumers gain control of community resources is one example.

Recreationists as advocates can also begin to deindustrialize the leisure industry. First, this requires a fundamental critique of who controls our leisure needs. Corporate permeation of our lives through television and advertising creates expectations in which pursuit of material things is the major goal.[34] Second, most people in the leisure field unquestioningly accept the notion that a technological society frees people for more leisure. As we have emphasized, however, failure to confront this notion contributes to the technological permeation of our lives. Instead, we need to take learnings gained away from the job and vice versa and fuse them into a work-place. Common phrases such as "stop talking about the office, we are here to have fun" need to be confronted. And participating in a shared, cooperative venture in a leisure setting raises consciousness about the possibility of such sharing in other environments.

Is it possible that bottom-up change, with cooperative efforts of recreation advocates and others, could change the leisure delivery system? The alternative is more professionalism and more recreation leaders imprisoned within their allegiances and loyalties to the organization and the profession. Fortunately, alternatives are emerging in people's lives which involve cooperation, shared knowledge, and a different set of social goals. Change is fundamental to this search and struggle. It challenges us to reemphasize collectivity, self-worth, advocacy, and responsibility in social affairs. As Richard Bach states in *Illusions*, change is perfection; the sea and the sky are changing every second, but they are always a perfect sea and sky![35] Can we find security in changing ourselves and our society?

REFERENCES

1. For a delightful, yet extremely important, analysis of children's potential to grow and develop through play and natural learning, see Pearce, Joseph Chilton, *Magical Child: Rediscovering Nature's Plan for our Children.* New York: E. P. Dutton, 1977, esp. pp. 138-145.
2. Orlick, T. *Winning Through Cooperation: Competitive Insanity: Cooperative Alternatives.* Washington, D C: Hawkins and Associates, 1978.
3. Sage, G. H. "American Values and Sport: Formation of a Bureaucratic Personality," *Leisure Today.* October, 1978, pp. 10-11.
4. Bledstein, B. J. *The Culture of Professionalism.* New York: W. W. Norton and Company, Inc., 1976, pp. 21-22.
5. Illich, I. "Disabling Professions." In: Illich, Ivan, et al. *Disabling Processions.* London: Marian Boyars, 1977, pp. 15-21.
6. Heidenheimer, A., Heclo, H., and Adams, C. T. *Comparative Public Policy.* New York: St. Martin, 1975, p. 14.
7. Illich, I. *Medical Nemesis: The Expropriation of Health,* New York: Bantum, 1977.

8. Smollet, E. "Schools an the Illusion of Choice: The Middle Class and the 'Open' Classroom," In: Martell, G. (Ed.). *The Politics of the Canadian Public School.* Toronto: James Lewis and Samuel, Publishers, 1974, pp. 92-102.

9. Illich. "Disabling . . ." *Op. Cit.* p. 50.

10. Galper, J. *The Politics of Social Services.* Englewood Cliffs, New Jersey: Prentice-Hall, 1975, p. 95. Jeffry Galper's book continues to be the primary reference for those interested in a radical critique of social service delivery systems. Our four practices in systematizing professionalism follow his suggestions with adaptations. See also Allan Moscovitch and Glenn Drover (Editors). *Inequality: Essays in the Political Economy of Social Welfare.* Toronto: University of Toronto Press, 1981.

11. Shaiken, H. "Craftsman into Baby Sitter." In: Illich, I., et al. *Disabling Professions.* London: Marian Boyars, 1977, p. 120.

12. Fay, B. *Social Theory and Political Practice.* London: George Allen and Unwin, 1975, p. 44.

13. For a valuable analysis of the rationalization of the conduct of life, see: Goldman, R. and Wilson, J. "The Rationalization of Leisure." *Politics and Society.* 7:2(1977), pp. 127-156.

14. See, for example: Sessom, H. D., Meyers, H. D. and Brightbill, C. K. *Leisure Services: The Organized Recreation and Park System.* Englewood Cliffs, New Jersey: Prentice-Hall, 1975. And Shivers, J. S. *Principles and Practices of Recreational Service.* New York: MacMillan Company, 1967.

15. Sharon, K. *Unemployment: Its Impact on Body and Soul.* Toronto: Canadian Mental Health Association, 1983.

16. Shaiken, *Op. Cit.* p. 122.

17. Quinney, R. *Critique of the Legal Order.* Boston: Little, Brown and Company, 1974, p. 24.

18. See especially two essays: "Technical Progress and the Social Life-World," and "Technology and Science as 'Ideology'." In Habermas, J. *Toward A Rational Society.* Boston: Beacon Press, 1970.

19. Hoedges, H. M., Jr. "The Humanistic Intellegentsia." In Gella, A. (Ed.). *The Intellengentsia and the Intellectuals.* Beverly Hills, California: Sage Publications, 1976, pp. 157-158.

20. Galper, *Op. Cit.*

21. *Ibid.,* pp. 91-98.

22. Godbey, G. "The Professionalization of Recreation and Parks in the Public Sector: Implications for Social Development." *Society and Leisure.* 1:2(November, 1978), pp. 280-81.

23. Galper, *Op. Cit.* p. 98.
24. See for example, Johnson, L. A. *Poverty in Wealth.* Toronto: New Hogtown Press, 1977.
25. Baker, S. and Levenson, B. "Earnings Prospects of Black and White Working-Class Women." *Sociology of Work and Occupations.* 3:2 (May, 1976), p. 123.
26. Henley, N. and Brown, P. "The Myth of Skill and the Class Nature of Professionalism." In: Radical Therapist Rough Times Collective (Ed.). *The Radical Therapist.* Middlesex, England: Penguin Books, 1974, p. 61.
27. Edelman, M. *Political Language:* Words That Succeed and Policies That Fail. New York: Academic Press, 1977, pp. 59-60.
28. *Ibid.,* p. 61.
29. Lalonde, M. Quoted in: *Halifax Mail Star,* (March 18, 1978), p. 2.
30. McKnight, J. "Professionalized Service and Disabling Help." In: Illich, I., et al. *Disabling Professions.* London: Marion Boyars, 1977, p. 75.
31. Mead, M. and Heyman, K. *World Enough.* Boston: Little, Brown and Company, 1975, p. 56.
32. de Beauvoir, S. "Old Age: End Product of a Faculty System." *Saturday Review,* (April 8, 1972), p. 42.
33. Kaufman, B. N. *Son-Rise.* New York: Warrier Books, 1976.
34. Hamelink, C. *The Corporate Village.* Rome: IDOC International, 1977, p. 138.
35. Bach, R. *Illusions.* New York: Delacorte Press, 1977.

(no beep)

p. 292 is blank.
End of Chapter 21

Chapter 22

Leisure Services and Social Control

Ronald P. Reynolds

> "... to submit to however wise a master planner is to surrender an illusion that may be the bedrock on which life flourishes ... "[1]

While those concerned with the study of "leisure" and/ or the provision of leisure services have yet to reach a consensus regarding its exact substantive definition, there is general agreement that the element of choice or freedom from constraint is one essential aspect of the phenomenon.[2] Conversely, *control* or imposed external influences affecting the leisure participant may preclude the achievement of the desired leisure state. With the notion of personal freedom as an atmosphere engendered by the absence of external control, the ideal society for promoting leisure is one which allows and encourages the individual to exert maximum autonomy over his or her own lifestyle. Sites describes such a set of social conditions:

> A good society then is a society which is structured by allowing optimum control possibilities to each person of his own life experiences within the framework of an identity which he has been free to work out, maintain, or change on his own terms, so long as he does not infringe upon the possibility of others doing the same thing.[3]

There are increasing indications which suggest that North Americans may not count themselves members of the "good society" nor perceive that they have adequate control over their own life experiences, including leisure. Cult organizations, Equal Rights Amendment movements and taxpayer revolts represent divergent attempts to regain or insure personal control of one's own religious ideology, human rights and monetary resources. Concern for leisure autonomy also prevails in our society as individuals turn to leisure counselors seeking dispensation to enjoy their free time and business executives forsake established careers to hand-fashion boats and sail the world.

In the midst of increasing discontent with personal and leisure lifestyles in a fast changing and unpredictable society, members of the leisure service profession must address several critical questions relative to the notion of social control. To what extent has the field of leisure services contributed to the personal autonomy of the individual? What has been and what will be the response of the leisure service profession to threats upon individual control and freedom. Has our field in general functioned to maintain the status quo at the expense of the freedom of the individual? Are we subtly, yet effectively, shaping and promoting subservient behaviors for our "clientele?" In responding to those with special needs are our notions of therapy, as Angel[4] suggests, "obsolete, elitist, male-centered and obsessional, clinging to concepts often outmoded and rarely questioned?" Has recreation therapy today become a commodity? A means of social control?

THE INFLUENCE OF OUR "ROOTS"

As a profession, the Recreation and Parks field traces many of its historical ties to the discipline of social work as practiced in the early 1890s. Despite its eventual emergence from social work, the leisure service profession has retained and continues to model many practices exhibited by social workers who promote and perpetuate the social service system today. Recent critics of this system have charged that the social service delivery structure "fosters particular behavior patterns in clients both as a condition of usage and as a consequence of service,"[5] thus denying personal control and autonomy to individuals served by this system. Three such practices: economic responding, functionally specific professionalism, and "socio-psychologism" found in the social services also appear to permeate the field of leisure services. A brief examination of each concept reveals the potentially deleterious effect which adherence to these practices may have upon the type and quality of service provided by contemporary recreation and parks personnel. Also suggested are some future directions which leisure service providers might explore to insure the leisure autonomy of our "clients" in the 1990s and beyond.

ECONOMIC RESPONDING AND LEISURE SERVICES

A basic criticism of today's social service practices relates to the system's perception of the good society as one exhibiting an overriding commitment to economics and materialism, which in turn causes the state to "view human needs as being primarily economic and serve the needs of private capital in many ways."[6] Competitive behavior is viewed as an inevitable part of the human condition and welfare programming is designed to prepare people to excel through practicing individualism and self aggrandizement. Work in turn in viewed as being a means to high levels of leisure consumption.

In several respects, the field of leisure services plays a major role in reinforcing a materialistic and competitive orientation to leisure thereby perpetuating a form of economic control on the recipients of its services. This practice is effected both through the *types* of activity offerings provided and the *method* in which participation in recreational experiences is structured. The largest proportion of content of our professional magazines is devoted to private and commercial enterprises proclaiming the necessity to install $100,000 fiberglass skateboard parks, purchase vanilla ice-cream bars "wrapped in attractive sports motif foil" for concessions or appropriate funds for peacocks as "exotic accents" for parks. This is symptomatic of our growing tendency to respond to the leisure needs of the public in an overly materialistic fashion.

Similarly, we frequently find ourselves in the uncomfortable position of denouncing the work ethic in our writings and teachings while continuing practices such as offering community recreational pursuits which stress activities requiring high initial monetary outlays, the purchase of expensive consumer goods, the consumption of fossil fuels and the construction of extravagant facilities. Practices such as these are particularly disconcerting in times of high inflation when rising prices and decreased discretionary income mean increased work hours to purchase leisure goods and services The dilemma is apparent—individuals are encouraged to utilize their leisure in a more personally satisfying manner but to work longer and consume more in the process.

When scarce time is found for leisure participation, an inordinate emphasis is placed upon individualistic, competitive pursuits. Recreation program texts suggest a plethora of competitive events varying from sports and drama tournaments, sandcastle sculpturing contests and spelling bees to baking contests, shingleboat races, flower arranging contests and sidewalk chalk art competitions. Elitist sport for disabled and non-disabled athletes consumes a disproportionate amount of our human and physical resources while comparatively little energy is expended for development of activity programs for the non-competitor at the grass roots level. Our largest single effort to promote activity for mentally retarded persons, the Special Olympics, is modeled after the highest echelon of competition, the Olympic Games.

Lest there be misunderstanding relating to competitive endeavors between and among the sexes and disabled persons, current texts provide the following advice concerning sport:

"... there is organized support for recognizing limitations, which says that a big bosom and throwing things are incompatible. Menstrual cramps don't contribute to record-making physical outlays. But then these are foreseeable handicaps, perhaps more psychological than physiologically restricting. A fat boy doesn't throw too well either, nor does a mentally or physically depressed male rise to great efforts in recreational activity."[7]

Sports medicine clinics continue to cater to a younger and younger clientele. As a recent article points out: "For the anxious mother of a little league player or a mosquito, a sports injury is a nightmare which she must hope is never played out."

Programmatic interventions designed to rehabilitate disabled persons have also fallen prey to the paradox extant in the economically oriented philosophy of the mental health field which defines emotional well being as "the active pursuit of a career, the engagement in competition within the rules of the game, the focus on recreation (asceticism) and on purposeful activity in general (utilitarianism).[8] The current controversy over the inclusion of recreation services in sheltered workshop settings for mentally retarded people speaks to our confusion regarding the relationship between work and leisure in "therapeutic recreation" service.

FUNCTIONALLY SPECIFIC PROFESSIONALISM AND LEISURE SERVICES

According to critics of the current social service system, professionalism, characterized by functional specificity, is a second critical issue threatening the autonomy and self control of its clients. Briefly, functional specificity may be defined as:

> ". . . the condition whereby professions are characterized by their development of technologies. As a result, . . . clients and professionals are prevented and "protected" from forming relationships which transcend this orientation. As a consequence of this ideology, the professional tends to concentrate on one facet of a client's life to the exclusion of other areas. In short the person is viewed only in terms of their problem."[9]

Undesirable by-products of this orientation appear to be emotional indifference toward clients and faulty perceptions and practices relating to the delivery of service. The field of leisure services has in no way remained immune to the development of functionally specific professionalism or the undesirable consequences of this practice in removing control of personal leisure lifestyles from our "clients." As we move toward another decade of service, the following questions must be addressed: Have our technologies prevented us from forming meaningful relationships with colleagues in our own field, with others in related disciplines and with the individuals served by our profession? Does the leisure service field as a whole concentrate on certain facets of a "client's" life to the exclusion of other needs and interests? To what extent has our own "functional specificity" resulted in a loss of autonomy and control by the individual consumer? A brief examination of two current practices in our field—specialization of training and compartmentalization of services illustrate the extremes to which unchecked overspecialization may lead in the next decade.

Functional Specificity in Professional Preparation

Specialization appears rampant in professional training in the field of leisure services. A cursory glance at our professional preparation institutions reveals that individual curriculums provide program options in "Public Recreation," "Commercial Recreation," "Resource Planning," "Church Recreation," "General Programming," "Private Recreation," "Turf Management," "Vocational Corrections," "Recreation for the Socially Deviant," "Agriculture Teaching," "Ranger-Enforcement," "Naturalist-Historian," "Social Service Agencies," "Recreation for Minorities," "Youth-Family Leadership," "Maintenance," "Industrial Recreation," "Volunteer Management," "Community Schools." Junior colleges specialize in the training of "technicians." Four year curriculums spawn graduates who aspire as "leaders," "supervisors" or "administrators." Competency based graduate education attempts to develop "Educators," "Researchers," "Master Administrators" or "Clinicians." The "Researcher - Practitioner" dichotomy controversy periodically rears its head in our professional writings and conferences illustrating the real or imagined rift between "providers of service" and "generators of new knowledge." "Special groups" personnel segregate themselves from "community recreators" in professional societies and universities. "Therapeutic Recreation Personnel" frequently see themselves as concerned exclusively with one particular "clientele" (visually impaired mentally retarded persons), setting (institutional, hospital or community), or media (art therapist, crafts specialist, physical activities instructor). The effects of this overspecialization on the autonomy and control of the individuals served by the leisure service profession can be profound. As therapeutic recreation specialists and community recreators isolate themselves, those trained in "T.R." will lack a working knowledge of leisure service provision in the public sector and consequently will be unable to influence this system and act as advocates for their "clients." Similarly, those trained in "community recreation" will not be imbued with an awareness and understanding of the needs and abilities of disabled persons. The current rift between institutions and community based services will remain, thus depriving disabled persons of the right to participate in generic services. While functional specificity reigns supreme, landscape architects and resource planners will continue to design aesthetically pleasing environments and facilities which are architectural nightmares to disabled persons. All leisure service providers lacking extra-disciplinary study in economics, political science, sociology and human development will continue to perpetuate economic control in leisure services as previously described.

Compartmentalization of Services

A second manifestation of functional specificity exhibited by those charged with the provision of leisure services concerns the fragmentation of leisure experiences offered to recipients of our program efforts. By limiting our attention to certain aspects of a "client's" life, we inadvertently assign and perpetuate stereotyped roles and sets of expectations on the basis of our preconceived notions of the characteristics of groups of individuals. Labeling, a commonly used technique to insure functional specificity in therapeutic recreation, controls people's lives and potential through:

> "...categorical judgments about individuals' interests, skills, level of functioning and previous experience. This practice has the effect which I am sure we do not intend, of proving to others that persons with a particular illness are "within their category," "alike in all respects" and "distinctly different" from the non-ill, non-disabled, non-special in all respects."[10]

Once this labeling process is complete, the removal of control from the disabled person is inevitable. The recreator provides packaged programs" or activities based on the diagnostic label of the "client" which exist in a vacuum devoid of other skills, abilities or interests of the individual. Functional specificity prevails—mentally retarded people receive one regimen of activities, the aged another, and so on. Compartmentalization of activities also extends to the time frame in which leisure pursuits are scheduled. This condition is dramatically illustrated in the account of an ex-mental patient:

> It's a pretty dull existence in which everything you need is handed out in neat little packages—even the therapy—not when you need it most, but again at specific times."[11]

While the labels utilized by the "community recreator" are not as mystifying as those adroitly adopted by the "therapeutic recreator," they too have the effect of perpetuating social control through stereotyped responding to the leisure lifestyles needs of the general public. A cursory examination of commonly used municipal recreation labels identifying program offerings include: Boys, Girls, Men's, Women's, Adult, Child, Novice, Advanced, Intermediate, Teen, Handicapped, Special. Women's programs are still offered primarily during the day ignoring the fact that over 40 percent of married women are now gainfully employed. Children's activities are scheduled at times so as not to interfere with adult activities or disturb family cohesion. Program levels such as beginner, intermediate and advanced stratify ability levels and promote competition.

Specialized instructors are relied upon to provide technical expertise rather than general assistance in planning a leisure lifestyle. Leisure counseling and education necessitating personal contact and familiarization with all aspects of the "client's" life remain low priorities of parks and recreation agencies. "Handicapped" programs insure that groups of individuals sharing only one common feature will congregate at a certain place at a certain time. Functional specificity again promotes social conformity and control in leisure services.

"Socio-Psychologism," Leisure Services and Social Control

A third factor threatening the personal control of "clients" served by the leisure service profession is the profession's adherence to the concept of "socio-psychologism." Briefly stated, socio-psychologism is the practice or philosophy of emphasizing or focusing on the problems which an individual has in his or her personal interactions with the social order, rather than exhibiting a concern for the underlying basic nature of the social order. In terms of the social services:

> If a diagnosis does not incorporate a concern for the way in which the whole society may be pathological and produce pathology in individuals as a normal condition of functioning, then the condition of pathology that is shared by all will be, paradoxically, the standard of behavior and existence toward which treatment is directed.[12]

The implications of the application of this orientation in the field of leisure services are obvious. If all existing values of society are embraced as a given, service efforts will center around the adaptation of the "client" to existing conditions thereby exerting a form of social control. Our professional interventions tend to be "time limited" and "technological" and treat symptoms of discontent within the "client" rather than dealing with the fundamental environmental sources of the person's discomfort. The following points will illustrate the prevalence and effects of socio-psychologism in the field of leisure services.

Like the social services, leisure service providers seem most willing to interact with individuals who do not exhibit major differences in behavior and lifestyle. By selectively excluding persons who manifest significant deviations from commonly accepted norms, leisure service providers are spared the cognitive dissonance which would be engendered if the environment instead of the individual was viewed as being pathological. For example: an individual of lower socioeconomic status is parolled to a community from a correctional facility. He or she is motivated to become involved in community recreation and leisure opportunities. After locating the recreation department, the individual finds the program offerings foreign to his/her previous experiences.

Secondly, no one is available in the department to offer assistance in developing the skills necessary for participation or to suggest the alternative forms of leisure pursuits. The "parolee" returns to his or her former lifestyle, the environment influencing this deviance remains unchanged, and the socio-psychological orientation triumphs.

When the recreation field is involved in providing service to devalued or disadvantaged people, it also frequently adopts a socio-psychological "time-limited," "technological" intervention. To illustrate—leisure programs and services to delinquent youths are frequently aimed at altering the "clients'" beliefs, values, attitudes and actions without attempting to change the pathological environment which may be responsible for the behaviors of the person. By ignoring economic, familial, and social conditions, such interventions are doomed to failure. Partington graphically illustrates the results of adopting a strict socio-psychological approach to aiding disadvantaged individuals. Commenting on the failure of a wilderness project to engender measurable changes in delinquent youths, he laments:

> Perhaps the most crushing inference to be drawn from this project is that in retrospect it is seen to rest on a suspect assumption; namely, that troubled youth can be helped by making them think more like "normals"—to expect that they can influence outcomes in their own lives. Unfortunately, changing expectations without changing realities may arouse frustration and resentment. The WILD program, like most current therapeutic interventions, was not designed to change the actual reward structures in the schools and communities to which these participants returned. Moreover, no efforts were made to change their future probability of success through social—economic—political engineering to create broader potential occupation opportunities. Maybe the 86 percent of WILD participants who chose not to complete the four trip program understood this conceptual error.[13]

Our approaches to leisure counseling and education are also frequently colored by a socio-psychological and technological orientation. If an individual becomes motivated to seek assistance in his or her leisure planning, what is frequently offered is a value laden "choice" of activities to fill the individual's time. Usually these pursuits are predominantly middle-class in nature and are "prescribed" without concern for altering the environment which has caused the basic dissatisfaction with the person's current leisure lifestyle. For example, a counselor might urge a person in a disadvantaged area to select an activity or series of activities limited by the existing resources in the community rather than working with the individual to secure new and better leisure resources in the individual's neighborhood. Additionally, many recreation departments fall victim to the socio-psychologism approach in their attempt to assume sole responsibility for the provision of leisure opportunities in communities. This role is undertaken in lieu of providing services not currently offered by other existing generic agencies and organizations *and* instead of lobbying for leisure environmental changes which would ultimately result in improved services to all community members. As a result of this orientation, energy is expended providing "patchwork" diversional programs which could be better used in analyzing what services are needed and (if so) what agencies could best provide these services.

Meanwhile the practices of the public sector of leisure services exhibit a subtle socio-psychological approach. The area of leisure services to and for "special populations" blatantly embraces this orientation. Even a casual review of past and current literature reveals numerous examples of technological approaches aimed at the changing the person to fit the environment rather than dealing with the pathology of the external conditions impinging on the individual. The social control function which is attributed to recreational activities in many institutions (and community based program) is ample testimony to the orientation. Obvious examples are the diversional and inappropriate activities offered in correctional settings and residences for mentally retarded people. The purpose of these activities is the distraction of the individual from their living conditions (in which they may have cause for rebellion) and the release of surplus energy which they may misdirect toward themselves or their keepers. In both instances, social control prevails.

In psychiatric settings, a more clandestine form of social control through recreation exists. Individuals have the following idea communicated to them in many subtle (and not so subtle) ways:

> Healthy people take part in recreation. You are currently unhealthy and therefore don't take part in recreation. Your participation in recreation will be taken as a sign of getting well. Therefore, if you want to get out of here, you had better participate!

Consequently, a great deal of stress is placed on participation in highly structured and controlled activities which are often inappropriate to time, age, and skill level of people. (Has anyone else observed "mentally ill" adults throwing bean bags in a day room at 9:00 AM?)

A more direct form of social control through socio-psychologism and technological intervention is evidenced by the persistent "prescription" of activities for disabled persons in institutional settings. This interventionist strategy by definition "precludes the voluntary aspect of recreational activity."[14] Ironically, this belief and practice may be the last remaining vestige of choice, control and autonomy of the individual. Behavioral technology poses a similar threat to the personal freedom of the individual. Recent experimental investigations[15] in which participation in "client" preferred activities was made contingent upon participation in therapist "prescribed" activities raises some serious questions concerning our rationalization for mandatory activities and the degree to which individual choice (control) over participation must be respected in all leisure service settings.

RETURNING THE LOCUS OF CONTROL

With the previously outlined threats to client autonomy exposed, it is imperative that the field of leisure services develop new orientations and strategies resulting in more personally responsive, consumer-controlled leisure lifestyles. To meet this end, the following directions and practices are suggested:

1. *Future Recreators Must Encourage the Development of Leisure Lifestyles Which are Consistent With the Means and Therefore Under the Control of the "Client."* If the vicious circle of spiraling work and extended credit to meet high levels of leisure consumption is to be overcome, individuals must learn to locate, utilize and enjoy leisure opportunities which are geographically and economically accessible. Over the past decade, inflation and increases in the cost of living, including higher gasoline prices, have plagued customers. Developments such as these will necessitate an increased use of leisure resources within the home, community and neighborhood in which the individual resides. Trips of 500 miles in fuel and aerodynamically inefficient vehicles to distant facilities will become untenable. Vest-pocket parks, home-centered family leisure participation and low-budget "new games" will prevail. Leisure interest finders may be redesigned to emphasize noncommercial leisure activities which do not reinforce or create materialistic "wants' for their users. The artificial work/leisure dichotomy may disappear from out therapeutic interventions as occupational and recreational "therapists" de-emphasize professional boundaries in favor of providing opportunities meeting the total lifestyles need of the individual. "Vocational" and "avocational" counseling interventions will merge into client-centered educational experiences fostering an integrated rather than fragmented lifestyle in which work and leisure needs are complementary, realistically achieved, and under the control of the "client."

2. *Recreators Must De-emphasize Limited Technological Interventions in Favor of Developing a Fundamental Understanding of the Phenomenon of Leisure.* By departing from traditional, functionally specific educational training and professional placement, several changes in service delivery would take place, resulting in increases in "client" autonomy. First, by

emphasizing the exploration of the underlying human needs and motivations relevant to the leisure experience, future service providers would be less likely to stress traditional facility planning and the provision of stereotyped activities. As concepts such as "activity substitution" are substantiated, consumers will be provided with *choices* of several leisure pursuits within cognates of low-cost, readily available activities which satisfy a basic leisure need. This practice will be in sharp contrast with current practices of offering a finite number of highly structured "programs."

Secondly, "client" leisure autonomy will be enhanced as professional recreators are encouraged to view individuals' leisure and lives in total rather than a series of compartmentalized activities. Those individuals involving public and quasi-public agencies will take an interest in the consumer's leisure beyond the four walls of the agency. Activities within institutions will cease to be served up in "packages." Rather, opportunities for free play and social interaction of the "client's" own choosing will predominate. The role of the recreator must hence be shifted from that of a therapist or programmer to that of a facilitator.

3. *Recreators Must Recognize Participants as the Only Reliable Monitors of the Effectiveness of Their Services.* Contemporary leisure research[16] has tended to reaffirm early notions of leisure as being a state of mind or a personal perception of the individual engaged in a "leisure experience." Despite the growing recognition of leisure as being subjective (participant defined) rather than objective (second party defined), recreators continue to offer narrow, structured, time limited programs which ignore the subjective feelings of the "client." In seeking a solution to this situation, Ellis[17] admonishes recreators to "consult more with individuals regarding their leisure perceptions and recreations and abandon the orientation that any activity provide for people is recreational." In the public sector, this may mean polling individuals as to their needs and wants and altering community centers from program facilities to places for consumer-centered leisure counseling and resource referral. In institutional settings, this orientation may involve the abandonment of the weekly activity schedule, the initiation of free choice of activity on the part of the "client" and the right to refuse recreational treatment. The "client" must in fact play the most significant part in the restoration of his or her own health if personal autonomy is to be insured.

4. *Recreators Must Engage in Reciprocal Relationships With "Clients" Which Stress the Development of Independent Leisure Skills.* A final step in insuring the personal leisure control of the individual involves a re-definition of our relationships with our "clients" in both public and "therapeutic"

recreation settings. No longer must the recreator be seen as the mentor or ultimate source of expertise in handing down or prescribing activities for the consumer. Rather, the "client" must be viewed as having the primary responsibility for the quality of his or her own leisure. This does not suggest that the recreator has a diminished role to play in achieving this end. It does however, suggest a fundamental change in our interventions with our "clients." Fifty-minute-hour, counselor oriented leisure counseling sessions stressing computerized activity matching must give way to more personal reflection on the part of the "client." Counselors and other personnel in municipal recreation and institutional facilities must "de-mystify" their techniques to the point where the "client" may understand and adopt these practices to his or her own betterment. In short, recreation personnel in general cannot afford to become privileged and unaccountable at the expense of the freedom and control of the individuals they serve.

When people create their own meaning they take possession of the world; when they do it recreatively with style and dignity, they stage the dream of human life as only it can be staged.[18] Perhaps our greatest challenge of the next decades will be the creation of a climate of personal freedom in which this "dream" can be realized.

REFERENCES

1. Lefcourt, H. M. "The Function of the Illusions of Control and Freedom." *American Psychologist*. (May, 1971), p. 425.
2. Neulinger, J. *The Psychology of Leisure*. Springfield, Illinois: Charles C. Thomas, 1974.
3. Sites, P. *Control: The Basis of Social Order*. New York: Dunnellen Co., 1973, p. 214.
4. Angel, J. *The Radical Therapist*. New York: Ballantine Books, 1971, p. XV.
5. Galper, J. F. *The Politics of Social Services*. New Jersey: Prentice Hall, 1975, p. 47.
6. Galper, *Ibid.*, p. 22.
7. Tillman, A. *The Program Book for Recreation Professionals*. California: National Press Books, 1973 p. 63.
8. Galper, *Op. Cit.*, p. 54.
9. Galper, *Op. Cit.*, p. 92.
10. Meyer, L. "A View of Therapeutic Recreation: Its Foundations, Objectives and Challenges," Paper presented at New England Therapeutic Recreation Society Meeting, Durham, New Hampshire, October, 1976, p. 15.

11. Angel, *Op. Cit.*, p. 50.
12. Galper, *Op. Cit.*, p. 123.
13. Partington, J. "Project Wild: A Wilderness Learning Experience for High Delinquency Risk Youth," *Leisurability.* 4:2, (1977), p. 40.
14. Shivers, J. "Why Not Recreational Therapy?" *Leisurability.* 4(4), (1977), p. 4.
15. Quilitch, H. R. and de Longchamps, G. "Increasing Recreation Participation of Institutional Neuro-Psychiatric Residents." *Therapeutic Recreation Journal.* 8:2, (1974), pp. 56-60.
16. Shaw, S. "The Problem of Leisure: A Comparison of Subjective and Objective Methods of Calculating Leisure for Males and Females." Unpublished Master's Thesis. Dalhousie University, Halifax, Nova Scotia, Canada, 1978.
17. Ellis, M. J. "Some Leisure Studies—Review and Preview." Paper presented at the Allen V. Sapora Symposium on Leisure and Recreation. University of Illinois, Champaign, Illinois, May, 1977, p. 10.
18. Becker, E. *The Structure of Evil.* New York: George Braziller Co., 1968, p. 213.

* The term "client," when utilized, appears in quotes to symbolize the incongruous relationship those in the recreation and parks field have established with both disabled and non-disabled service recipients. As the basic methods and content of this interaction change over the next decades, it is hoped that leisure service professionals will develop alternative perceptions of individuals as "consumers" or "citizens."

(no keep)

p. 306 is blank.
End of Chapter 22.

Chapter 23

Buckpassing, Blaming or Benevolence: A Leisure Education/Leisure Counseling Perspective

Peter A. Witt

Several professional stances can be taken toward an individual in need of service. On can act with benevolence, attempting to "do good" relative to meeting the expressed needs. On the other hand a posture of "it's not my concern or within my professional domain" can be adopted. Or we can blame the one in need for causing his/her own misfortune and subsequently hold them responsible for extricating themselves from the causes and consequences of their own actions. As recreation and leisure services begin to move toward "enabling" and "facilitating" services, adopting a philosophic stance toward the cause, responsibility and remediation of problems of leisure functioning will become an increasingly important concern. Whether to act with benevolence, pass-the-buck or blame the victim will become an increasingly difficult moral and practical issue.

Nowhere is the problem of focus more acute in the realm of recreation and leisure services than in the burgeoning attempts to conceptualize and initiate leisure counseling and leisure education services (LC/LE).[1] In general, theory and practice have tended to develop along the twin paths of the "helping relationship" and educational models. Remediation or learning has been largely assumed to be client, student or participant focused. School systems, recreation programs and counseling relationships have been seen as the locus for some kind of intervention. All of these developments have emerged within a general framework that has emphasized individuals learning to cope with problems or barriers that block leisure fulfillment.

While there is every reason to believe that the LC/LE movement will further crystallize its methods and broaden it base of support, there are several issues which it must come to grips with if it is to make a lasting impact on peoples' leisure functioning. Of particular concern is the fact that, to date, most of the attention has been focused on helping individuals change or modify some combination of their values, attitudes, skills or knowledge concerning leisure. Little attention has been directed toward dealing with systematic problems that support the work ethic, productivity, and societal definitions of usefulness as basic criteria for success, well-being and meaning.

The belief within LC/LE seems to be that individuals need to be educated or counseled to fit into society and its institutional structures. Little attention has been given, however, to changing the basic social, economic and political conditions within the society that affect an individual's ability to undertake personally meaningful leisure experiences. It is not clear whether "changing" individuals will have any significant impact on the values and attitudes expressed by the institutional structures of the society as a whole. It seems more likely that efforts to educate or counsel individuals will be significantly overridden by the basically conservative and slow nature of social change that will continue to support the status quo and a work-ethic-dominated definition of success and personal well-being.

While we should not abandon attempts to help individuals develop the tools necessary for a personally meaningful leisure lifestyle, significant attention should be directed toward reforming the social institutions that support the dominance of the work ethic (at least to the extent that it undermines leisure lifestyle). This stance does not necessarily imply supplanting work by leisure or downgrading attempts to create a society that meets the material needs of its populace. Rather, this position is aimed at helping to create a society that provides a climate conducive to leisure. While it is not being proposed that work be made obsolete, the work environment and its accompanying ethic of production, quantity and conformity does need to be humanized to make the possibilities of leisure more achievable and meaningful at the individual level. Significant attempts must also be made to make recreation environments more "hospitable" to human needs for play and leisure.

BLAMING THE VICTIM

Up to now, leisure education and leisure counseling have proceeded based on a "blame the victim" model. Thus, we blame individuals as the source of their own problems and "justify inequality by finding defects in the victims' inequality."[2] Ryan explains that the stigma, defect or fatal difference (whether it be an inability to read, the failure to obtain or maintain employment, or the failure to achieve a personally satisfying leisure lifestyle):

> ". . . is still located within the victim, inside his skin. With such an elegant formulation, the humanitarian can have it both ways. He can, all at the same time, concentrate his charitable interest on the defects of the victim, condemn the vague social and environmental stresses that produced the defect (some time ago) and ignore the continuing effect of the victimizing forces (right now). It is a brilliant ideology for justifying a perverse form of social action designed to change, not society, as one might expect, but rather society's victims."[3]

Thus, Johnny can't read because Johnny is not smart enough to read and is poorly motivated as opposed to looking at factors such as poor teaching methods an inadequate reinforcement. In the case of leisure "problems," we tend to overemphasize the "defects" in an individual's values, attitudes, skills and knowledge regarding leisure without giving proper attention to the service provisions and reinforcements provided by the society which influence leisure choices and outcomes. Further, we fail to give proper weight to factors such as unequal distribution of income, social stratification, inequality of power, plus mechanization and urbanization as the source of significant portions of the "leisure problem" for many individuals.

Overcoming the "blame the victim" mentality of LC/LE requires that we pay more attention to why, for example, poor leisure habits arise in the first place; why individuals are unprepared for increased free time; why playfulness is considered only the prerogative of children, and only then if it's the work of the child in his quest to grow up to be a productive adult; and why competition versus cooperation, and physical versus artistic and intellectual activity, are the socially accepted and reinforced bases of leisure involvement through our tendency to overprogram and plan for people to the point where "many are almost incapable of creating their own satisfying activities or of finding lasting meaning in what they do."[4]

Orlick provides numerous examples of children, as they get older, dropping out of competitive, hierarchically based sports programs because these programs are not conducted at an appropriate skill and competitive level for their needs.[5] Of course, we can undo Orlick's evidence by "blaming" the drop-outs as being unmotivated and insufficiently competitive. We may even rationalize that they have learned an important lesson in life by failing and being rejected. It is in this context that some have argued for the need for LC/LE to help dropouts deal with rejection and failure when a better system of opportunity and matching skill or interest levels may be what is really required.

Preparing people to cope better with an unfit, dehumanizing and non-growth encouraging environment is only part of the answer. Rendering the environment more hospitable is the necessary correlate.[6] Lane goes even further by suggesting that we place too much emphasis on individuals as if they had personal power and choice and on human behavior as if it was primarily determined by enduring and consistent characteristics of the individual. "We perpetuate the cult of individualism by refusing to consider the existence of interrelated power structures as necessary if not sufficient variables in determining behavior."[7]

START

BLAMING THE ENVIRONMENT

In recent years several other authors have suggested placing more emphasis on a change (blame) the system versus change (blame) the individual approach to leisure services. Most have voiced their opposition to the medical model approach to the problems of special populations. For example, Rusalum suggested what he called the ecological model as an alternative to the therapeutic model in therapeutic recreation. This model:

> ". . . is built upon the belief that the overwhelming majority of disabled and disadvantaged persons do not need therapy. Despite their limitations and a denying society, they are relatively well-integrated emotionally healthy persons struggling to survive in a given unrewarding, inhospitable environment . . . For example, America's urban areas are polluted, crowded, unattractive, inconsiderate of people's need for intimacy and warmth, poverty-stricken, inconvenient, dangerous, and most important from the vantage point of the exceptional individual, intolerant and inflex ible in relation to extremes of human differences."[8]

The ecological approach would significantly "shift professional emphasis from the therapy of people to the therapy of environments."[9]

Thibault outlines three general approaches that can be taken to leisure education.[10] Under the *traditional education model* leisure activities are offered by service providers that are judged appropriate and good according to the dominant values of the society. Individuals are then informed via advertising of the availability of these opportunities and sensitized to the value of participating in them.

The *psycho-education model* assumes that individuals lack self knowledge regarding leisure values and attitudes. A variety of individual and group counseling methods are used to help individuals develop personally appropriate values and attitudes.

Finally, the *psycho-socio-education model* sees actual leisure involvement as a result of the interaction between economic, social and political influences of society and the individual's own will to actualize his needs, values and attitudes. The aim of leisure education is to demystify the actions of these social forces thus enabling the individual to perceive and act differently relative to his/her leisure. This demystification is accomplished by working to reduce the pressure of the social forces and impinging systems within the society as well as influencing the individual's perceptions by offering social alternatives that make real choice possible. Thibault seems to favor this model as it has the most potential for influencing the perception of options available and resultant outcomes for leisure lifestyles.

Edginton and Compton also have taken a middle ground position in the system versus individual change controversy by arguing for more attention to consumerism and advocacy as essential service approaches for those working with special populations. Consumerism will help individuals develop "personal competency in making qualitative and quantitative judgments about goods and services received and consumed."[11] Advocacy involves efforts to improve the quality of goods and services rendered to deal with the environment and bringing about significant environmental change to meet the needs of individuals.

Whether to blame the victim or the environment is a controversial issue in a number of other helping professions as well. Of particular relevance is the controversy going on in both the psychology and the health fields. For example, Lewis and Lewis argue that a preventive or developmental approach to community mental health problems is more efficient than a remedial one.[12] The intent of prevention is "to anticipate future problems and move to prevent them by providing individuals or groups with needed skills or by creating changes in the environmental so as to prevent the development of problems."[13] These authors do not argue against the validity of direct efforts to help people deal with the problems they confront in their lives. Rather they see the need for equal attention to changing the social surroundings that affect people's lives. To accomplish this Lewis outlines four programmatic approaches to intervention:

Extensive-experiential: programs that provide direct experiences available to the population as a whole.

Intensive-experiential: programs that provide special experiences to individuals or groups that need them.

Extensive-environmental: programs that attempt to make the entire community more responsive to the needs of all its members.

Intensive-environmental: programs that intervene actively in the environments of specific individuals or groups, so that their special needs can be met.[14]

Rappaport et al. suggest that we tend to place too much emphasis on problems, whether a victim or environment blaming model is adopted. As community psychologists, they argue that services should emphasize building on "community strengths and aiding in the development of those, while leaving amelioration of deficits to physicians, clergyman, social workers and clinicians."[15] This point of view may have a valuable parallel when trying to delineate the responsibility of recreation professionals to remove leisure deficits of individuals.

Building on strengths via community development and enabling functions may be much closer to both the traditional roots and the training of most recreation professionals. Creating new avenues to desired goals and helping to transfer skills from areas of already existing competence via identification and utilization of community resources may be better avenues than attempts to repair weaknesses. This calls for emphasis on a "what are you good at" versus a "what can I help you with" model.[16]

IMPLICATIONS AND FUTURE DIRECTIONS

The preceding ideas have a number of implications for the ways that the recreation and leisure services profession should conceptualize and deliver services aimed at dealing with people's leisure problems or deficits. Emphasis should change from trying to initiate person-centered, remediation and counseling approaches to strategies emphasizing consumerism, advocacy, environmental change and education, particularly in community settings. Because it is new and sounds "professional," jumping on the leisure counseling bandwagon may appear to be a more attractive alternative than services aimed at redistributing opportunity, removing barriers to participation, and providing a humane environment in which people can make personally meaningful leisure choices. However, given the roots and basic expertise of the leisure services profession, our real mission lies in helping to reshape the opportunities available for leisure involvements, whether these be municipally, school or privately sponsored, as well as providing the supportive and skill training services that would facilitate participation.

In addition, the leisure services profession also has a vital role to play in educating itself, other professionals and citizens regarding a new outlook on the benefits and potential of leisure experiences. This education process should probably begin at home with the staff of existing recreation, park and leisure services. Workers in these areas need to assess their own attitudes toward play, recreation, leisure and work. Workers should analyze how their own biases and philosophies become a filter through which the problems and needs of others are viewed. As Friedson points out:

> Embedded in the claims of each of the professions is paradigm, a taken-for-granted conception of what the issue is, and how it is solvable. Each tends to see the world in terms of its own characteristic conception of problems and solutions.[17]

The paradigm within recreation and park services has been based on seeing the essential problems as 1) re-creation, i.e., involvement in activity that would prepare an individual to go back to work refreshed; 2) idleness, i.e., people need something to do to fill the time freed from work due to automation; 3) catharsis and compensation, i.e., helping people act out frustrations derived from dehumanizing work and living environments. We have avoided blaming ourselves for our service conceptualization and provision failures by passing judgment on participants. This paradigm has led to a system of park and recreation services which has generally served the interests of a society committed to the work ethic. In many cases the profession has been the handmaiden of a bread-and-circuses, social-control approach to serving the public good. Arguing that what is currently being provided is what people want ignores the process by which people learn to want. It ignores the fact that the delivery system is a value giving, reinforcing and reflecting entity that shapes and reinforces particular patterns of activity within the population.

Up to now, the recreation profession has had a basically conservative focus. It has been largely a civil service profession, allied closely with the purposes of preserving status quo governmental priorities and assumptions. These assumptions have led to a mainstream system of park and recreation opportunities that reinforce existing values and keep people busy or entertained. The profession must do some serious soul-searching and self-evaluation if a revised set of assumptions, and eventually services, is to become a reality. The "bankruptcy" warnings of Grey and Grebin[18] and the need to adopt a more holistic and humanistic perspective, as suggested by Murphy,[19] must be seriously examined.

Perhaps Charles K. Brightbill best summarized the basis for a new paradigm when he stated:

> If we are to educate for leisure, it will be necessary to change many of our basic values. It will be necessary for us to revise our ideas of what constitutes success in life. We shall have to think less of bank accounts, fur coats and estates to leave to our children and cherish more the wonders of nature, the arts, the zest of leisurely physiological release, as well as service to our fellow man. We shall have to want more time not to produce and consume more material goods, but rather, to live more of life.[20]

In addition to adjusting our own paradigm, the profession must also place substantially more emphasis on becoming a catalytic change agent in the society at large. The profession must become more active in the political and social development process to help foster a better understanding of leisure needs and barriers to leisure fulfillment. The profession must also help to foster a social, political and economic environment conducive to leisure fulfillment. This will require the profession to become an active force in promoting an awareness of leisure's potential among political leaders, school officials, the clergy, business leaders and social service workers; an awareness that goes beyond a work ethic definition of recreation.

The profession must also help to overcome the emphasis on competition (to the detriment of cooperation), busyness (to the detriment of involvement and meaning) and consumption (to the detriment of experience and quality). On a wider scale, this involves seeing the role of leisure in fostering personal autonomy and growth; building a foundation for personal expression and self-defined meaning, and building on the potential of leisure to add to an individual's life — rather than repair problems created by interaction with the work or urban environment. Increased emphasis must be placed upon prevention and building on strengths rather than remediation and overcoming weaknesses.

REFERENCES

1. Epperson, A., Witt, P. A. and Hitzhusen, G. *Leisure Counseling: An Aspect of Leisure Education.* Springfield, Illnois: Charles C. Thomas, 1977. Compton, D. M. and Goldstein, J. E. (Eds.). *Perspectives of Leisure Counseling.* Arlington, Virginia: National Recreation and Park Association, 1977.

2. Ryan, W. *Blaming the Victim.* New York: Vintage Books, 1976, XIII.

3. Ryan, W., *Op. Cit.* pp. 7-8.

4. Czurles, A. "Art Creativity vs. Spectatoritis." *Journal of Creative Behavior.* 10, 1976, p. 107.

5. Orlick, T. *Winning Through Cooperation: Competitive Insanity: Cooperative Alternatives.* Washington, DC: Hawkins and Associates, 1977.

6. Witt, P. A. "The Art's in a State." In: Compton, D. M. and Goldstein, J. (Eds.). *Perspectives of Leisure Counseling.* Arlington, Virginia: National Recreation and Park Association, 1977, pp. 1-8.

7. Lane, M. K. "A Reconsideration of Context: Perspectives on Prediction-Mote in the Eye." *American Psychologist.* 32(12), 1977, p. 1056.

8. Rusalem, H. "An Alternative to the Therapeutic Model in Therapeutic Recreation." *Therapeutic Recreation Journal.* 7, 1979, p. 12.

9. Rusalem. *Ibid.* p. 15.

10. Thibault, A. *La Situation Professionnelle des Travailleurs en Loisirs du Quebec comme Determinant de la Possibilite Differentielle de l'Education au Loisir.* These de Doctorat, Universite, Laval, 1979.

11. Edginton, C. R. and Compton, D. M. "Consumerism and Advocacy: A Conceptual Framework for Therapeutic Recreation." *Therapeutic Recreation Journal.* 9(1) 1975, p. 27.

12. Lewis, J. A. and Lewis, M. D. *Community Counseling: A Human Services Approach.* New York: John Wiley Sons, Inc. 1977, p. 16.

13. Morrill, W. H., Oetting, E. R. and Hurst, J. C. "Dimensions of Counselor Functioning." *The Personnel and Guidance Journal.* 52(Feb.), 1974, p. 357.

14. Lewis and Lewis, *Op. Cit.*

15. Rappaport, J. *et al.* "Alternatives to Blaming the Victim or the Environment." *American Psychologist.* 30(4), 1975, p. 526.

16. Rappaport, *et al. Ibid.* i a the Some place

17. Friedson, E. "Professions and the Occupational Principle." In: Friedson, E. (Ed.). *The Professions and Their Prospects.* Beverly Hills, California: Sage Publications, 1973, p. 31.

18. Gray, D. E. and Grebin, S. "Future Perspectives." *Parks and Recreation,* 9(July), 1974, pp. 26-56.

19. Murphy, J. F. *Recreation and Leisure Service: A Humanistic Approach.* Dubuque, Iowa: W. C. Brown, Co., 1975.

20. Brightbill, C. K. *Man and Leisure.* Englewood Cliffs, New Jersey: Prentice Hall, Inc., 1961, p. 193.

(no keep)

p. 316 is blank.
  End of Chapter 23.

Chapter 24

The Overdue Renaissance of Public Park and Recreation Services

By Louis F. Twardzik

Park and recreation professionals and policy makers have lost the early idealism of their movement which was to contribute to each individual's pursuit of happiness by providing "worthwhile" recreation opportunities. Today almost all North American communities support a public park and recreation agency. Almost all of them operate within a policy framework that has effectively removed individual and community values from their interpretation of the public good through recreation service, and replaced them with policies that attempt to meet only those interests that are in high demand.

Public parks and recreation policy and services should be dedicated to assuring that all people, not only the majority, shall have opportunities to pursue happiness. If happiness is the highest good and if assuring opportunity to pursue happiness is the primary purpose of park and recreation agencies, then the provision and allocation of opportunities to pursue it should not be taken lightly. Can the right to pursue happiness, self-evident and inalienable, be denied without damage to core political and social values? No, it cannot. When public agencies' core values are damaged, what anchors their being breaks loose, leaving them adrift.

Local park and recreation agencies seem to have lost those original values and ideals from their public service mission. As a result, the public is losing interest and a renaissance of public interest is needed. The success of the renaissance will depend largely on how the universities change their approach, including the courses of study, and the resulting education and training of park and recreation professionals, the quality of public policy makers and the response of state, national and international organizations that represent the interests of park and recreation professionals and educators.

THE PURSUIT OF HAPPINESS AND PUBLIC RECREATION POLICY

Charles Murray called attention to a number of interpretations of happiness from which we may choose. He noted that prior to the 18th century the traditional view of happiness was based on the thinking of Aristotle and Aquinas. Locke provided an alternative view, but the most serious breech with the classic concepts of happiness occurred in the 19th century when Jeramy Bentham and John Stuart Mill, leading "utilitarians," maintained that happiness was a matter of pleasure over pain thereby refuting the Aristotelian position of higher (intellectual and civic virtue) pleasures over low (sensate) pleasures. In his famous passage Bentham wrote: "Nature has placed mankind under the governments of two sovereign masters, pain and pleasure. They govern us in all we do, in all we say, and in all we think."[1]

Nevertheless, classic notions, until recently, produced "an undercurrent of an agreement about how man achieved happiness. It was not until the 20th century that social science dispensed with the intellectual content of both traditions and began to define happiness by the responses to questionnaire items."[2]

Aristotle, Aquinas and others developed an ethical basis for happiness which the Framers recognized and used in the Constitution. Nevertheless, the central importance, as of life and liberty, of the pursuit of happiness as a right for all people has not really caught on, either as an ethical or as a public policy imperative. Perhaps the problem is because of apparent confusion and misgivings about "the right to happiness," rather than "the right to the pursuit of happiness." As Murray notes "only the pursuit of happiness can be a right. The achievement of happiness is not within the gift of any government."[3]

Aristotle's disquisition of happiness is found in the *Nicomachean Ethics* in which he developed the concept of happiness as the ultimate good-in-itself:

Honor, pleasure, intelligence, and all virtues we choose partly for themselves. For we would choose each of them even if no further benefit would accrue from them—but we also choose them partly for the sake of happiness, because we assume that it is through them that we will be happy. On the other hand, no one chooses happiness for the sake of honor, pleasure, and the like, nor as a means to anything at all.[4]

Goodale carries the discussion of happiness further:

Leisure is a useless notion if by it we mean merely free time or some contemplative state. Still, the Aristotelian view may inform and encourage us if we keep his context. The context is virtue. The world of action is an essential corollary. If happiness is the highest good and the product of contemplation, so it is also the result of action, the exercise of virtuous energies. Well being and well doing are parts of a whole; complementary and synergistic. That, not surprisingly, is more compatible with our experiences than merely contemplating, even though such experiences may be pitifully infrequent.[5]

During the 20th century we seem bent on replacing those theories of happiness based upon rational thought with the notion that happiness is based exclusively upon individual perceptions of pleasure and pain void of any commitment to higher individual or social good.

Moral Entrepreneurs

Gaylen Cranz vividly described the role of moral entrepreneurs of the 19th century public park system.[6] They were the early park commissioners, community leaders, and men of high social standing who developed public park policies that reflected their personal moral sensibilities. As a result, for example, there were separate times and days for bathing for males and females and water fountains were liberally sprinkled throughout the parks to discourage the drinking of beer.

Consider public park and recreation services during the past century with and without the guidance of those moral entrepreneurs. On the positive side they were able to add a sense of morality to the early public policies and practices. This meant that they added a value to the public system, they gave this new service a collective, social purpose and direction. Without such direction, the public would have been free to pursue whatever pleasures they wished. In other words, the early parks could have been havens for all people to pursue their notions of happiness without any of the value constraints, as is often the case today, of religion, home and community.

Because of those early park and recreation policies, public parks were islands of clean, open space where adults and children were expected to act with a decorum often absent in other public places, including the streets and neighborhoods of the early industrial cities. This kind of public behavior was possible because policies were translated into park rules which dictated how park users would behave. Children could run and play in specified areas, but not on the grass or paths, and adults could not spit in the park.

The early park and recreation commissioners were recognized community leaders. They assumed a certain level of civilized behavior for themselves and translated it into public policy for park users. Their values defined appropriate and inappropriate pursuits of happiness in public places called parks. This is the Aristotelian interpretation of happiness: it is a value sensitive policy. The public is free to pursue happiness but only within the constraints of higher values, not exclusively the individual's values, but those that represent the community's interests. The commissioners, of course, represented community interests and values. They were appointed or elected for that purpose.

If park and recreation commissioners represent the idealism of the early "moral entrepreneurs" who have experience in leisure and a concern for the social good, we can expect an orderly and comprehensive system of parks and recreation service. This value sensitive system provides the public with options for activities that go beyond the popular and attempt to assure more opportunities to pursue happiness for more people. If, on the other hand, the political system requires an egalitarian commission which represents the entire social and political spectrum of the community, top to bottom, one that is more often experienced in the latest play and recreation trends, then the public is more apt to get public policy that results in maintaining the most popular programs and services, but not necessarily those that expand the opportunities for happiness for all the various interests in the community.

Happiness is Value Laden

The early park commissioners considered the public happiness as something beyond personal pleasures. Happiness was, instead, achieved through the higher standards of social behavior with great emphasis on families and communities, the basic units of society, and their interpretation of what constituted good. That sense of family and community, rather than individual pleasure, was expressed by Murray's note that "happiness is what Mother Teresa does, happiness is not a new car."[7]

Misguided epicureans and utilitarians advanced a view of happiness opposite that of the Aristotelians. It was based on the notion that pleasing oneself was necessary to achieve happiness. This individual expression of self-importance becomes a major socio-cultural problem when excessive and exclusive self-love, narcissism, becomes a social norm.

Public policies that shape park and recreation resource distribution and use are usually sharply divided between value sensitive happiness and self-pleasing happiness modes. And, interestingly enough, it is largely an urban and rural resources split in emphasis that determines which approach to happiness is taken in the public policy of parks and recreation.

"Value Free" Policies of Urban Park and Recreation Systems

Urban park and recreation policies and programs today are largely based on what the public wants. Typically, these wants are determined by marketing activities, the essence of which remain "give them what they want and what they are willing to pay for."[8] Other than adding individuals' desires, such policies and programs are non-sensitive to values, or "value free."

Policy is increasingly determined through marketing research and techniques. Invariably, the public is surveyed to determine what they would like in the way of recreation and how much they would be willing to pay for it. Planning of public areas and programs then proceeds on the basis of what respondents said would make them happy, which is based on their perception of happiness, and what they think the community can afford and will provide. Policy makers and professional managers and staff proceed with plans and programs that reflect the individual wants of the greatest number of people.

This is a non-value sensitive or value free process. This process requires little intellectual contribution from either policy makers or professional park and recreation managers. The process is instead characterized by techniques of surveying the public to determine what they want and then developing policies, plans and programs to help them get it. Many professional managers of local park and recreation agencies have been trained to merely serve as conduits between what constitutes the public's perception of need (wants) through a scientifically sound survey, advising policy makers to this effect and then implementing their decisions without reference to professional views, values or judgments.

Value Sensitive Policies of Natural Resource Park and Recreation Systems

The concept of happiness that is associated with natural resource based park and recreation areas and systems is not as apt to be based exclusively on user wants. There are some instances where value sensitive happiness policies are *in extremis*, as for wilderness areas, for example, where the actual presence of the user is merely tolerated and held to a minimum in order not to compromise the natural order. In wilderness areas the user does not have a choice in recreation other than those nonconsumable experiences that emanate from nature. To accomplish this as a matter of public policy nature is first, not the sum of individuals' desires.

The nonvalue sensitive policies of some urban park and recreation systems are anthropocentric, largely based on user demand, and are managed accordingly. This is not the case with the value sensitive policies and programs found in natural areas. Users cannot impose hedonistic views upon the policy of natural parks because the value of nature preservation and appreciation is permitted to override them. Policy makers and professional managers of natural areas use this ecocentric policy model because they believe that the integrity of ecology and environment represent a greater good than do individual preferences of users.[9]

The most important distinction between these approaches to opportunity for happiness in public park and recreation policy is that the ecocentric approach has a moral and ethical dimension lacking in the anthropocentric model. The value sensitive approach to happiness is most evident in the intergenerational rationale inherent in the ecocentric policies wherein the preservation of nature "for the enjoyment of future generations," is paramount. Concern for the happiness of others is an ethical position for both individuals and society. It represents the value sensitive happiness that we can associate with the philosophy of Aristotle and the example of a Mother Teresa.

It is apparent that public policy for parks ad recreation is characterized as functioning at these extremes; self-serving and nonvalue, usually seen in urban park and recreation systems, and ethical and value sensitive, usually seen in the natural park and recreation systems. County and regional park and recreation systems are consistently able to develop policy that incorporates both urban and natural systems.

PROBLEMS WITH LOCAL PARK AND RECREATION SYSTEMS

It seems that for economic considerations, and now a rapidly growing public perception that local public parks are amongst the least safe places in the community, that public parks and recreation services are losing their once solid reputation as contributors to the public good we call opportunity to pursue happiness. This erosion of credibility is occurring not only in North America but in many parts of the world, especially the United Kingdom and New Zealand, where the private sector's ability to compete with the public sector in performing traditionally public sector functions is recognized.

The upper classes have always been well acquainted with opportunities to pursue happiness, and could afford to pursue them. The role of the early public park and recreation agencies was to provide a greater number and variety of programs for the middle and lower classes in order to expand their opportunities to pursue happiness. The private sector philosophy of public park and recreation services may lead them to provide only those services and activities in profitable demand. That is the nature of private investment. The result, invariably, will be a program of popular activities for everybody, twenty-four hours a day, indoors and outdoors, supported by local commercial enterprises as well as an increase in spectacular special events and programs and any other kinds of activities that can attract high public participation.

Many local park and recreation agencies already have changed from their original mission of providing value sensitive opportunities to pursue happiness to the non-value system. As a result, opportunities for people of all ages and socio-economic levels to grow and develop emotionally, aesthetically and intellectually, and find a resource of happiness through public park and recreation services, have already diminished considerably in many communities.

Our current situation is a socio-cultural inversion in policy formulation. The original public system for parks and recreation, nurtured by public policy makers of the upper classes for the lower classes, has gradually been replaced by a libertarian system wherein local public policy is often determined by a classless group for the upper, middle and lower classes. But with a limited sense of "wise use" of leisure time, egalitarian public policy makers thereby limit the offerings of the public system to high demand programs. As a result, the public system is now providing a variety of high demand activities and programs, many of which the private sector is capable of producing. Since facilities and programs cater to mass participation in mass culture, they are increasingly ignored by the upper and middle class users who pursue private sector or other activity alternatives. With the market of users reduced to the lower classes, the need by the public park and recreation agency to produce greater attendance and revenue becomes more difficult. As a result we can anticipate that "spectaculars," with large crowds and commercial sponsors, will become a more important part of the public park and recreation programs.

It is difficult to justify public policy and services that can be as well provided by private, for-profit organizations. In essence, the public policy makers and professional staff in some communities have purposely emphasized a non-value program of services, one that has as primary values attracting crowds and producing revenue. Not knowing any better, the public accepted it. Now the public is reacting: If this is what public parks and recreation is all about, why not purchase it from the private sector at lower cost?

The non-value, high demand, self-interest focus of public park and recreation agencies is not what public service is all about. If the original value sensitive policies of the moral entrepreneurs were followed the public system would not be an attractive candidate for "take-over" by the private sector. Instead somewhere during the past one hundred years professional managers and policy makers should have had sufficient vision and courage to gradually develop a more meaningful mission for their agencies, one not limited to isolated islands of parks and service. The parks and playgrounds, community centers and sports areas were an important beginning point. But instead of growing conceptually with a changing society and culture, professional vision and guidance in public parks and recreation stayed at the level of a "one-product company" in a fast changing market.

Therapeutic recreation professionals and services for special populations may be excepted from this critique. Therapeutic recreation is a model of how professional and educational leadership can identify a public need and then, in concert, act on it. An outstanding example of how their program interprets public agency responsibility for all is that they have legitimized the entire culture of American sports and athletics, which traditionally recognized only championship caliber play, by assuring that now, finally, the pursuit of happiness through sports is available to all in the community including those with disabilities. This is happening in the arts as well. That is in keeping with their efforts to promote integration and the principles of normalization throughout the community.

SOME PROMISING DIRECTIONS

The public policy of parks and recreation during the past century did not
sufficiently respond to needs of a changing society it was expected to serve.
The agencies did not grow with and into the community. As the communities
grew and their needs changed, the contribution of parks and recreation agencies
remained limited to their isolated islands of parks and recreation services.

Developing Communities—in Parks

The future of local park and recreation agencies as a viable public service is in
their ability to see and meet the needs for service beyond its islands of facilities
and open space and contribute its unique services and talents as a public agency
to the total community. If local park and recreation agencies are to survive as
viable public service systems, it will be necessary to change the mission of the
agencies from providers of high demand opportunities in separated spaces to a
mission that recognizes happiness should be pursued throughout the community
as a condition of living. The framers of the Constitution made that paramount
right abundantly clear. The public good, including the pursuit of happiness, was
not limited to facilities and activity islands. Policy makers, educators and the
profession of parks and recreation have yet to fully rise to the challenge of that
mission.

Doing so will necessitate greater involvement in aesthetics, education, commercial and cultural development of the community; provision of amenities such
as shade trees where people live; comprehensive educational program that will
assist the lower income groups in learning a variety of skills; working with the
private sector in demonstrating how easy and economical it is to upgrade many
neighborhoods with paint and plant materials; transforming refuse filled alley-
ways into attractive pedestrian ways; leading environmental stewardship;
providing "community gardens" cooperation with local courts in developing
programs to rehabilitate young offenders by learning work skills (e.g., stone
masonry and landscape maintenance in parks); providing more and varied
opportunities in the fine arts; and so on.

The Child's Right to Play

Play for children, since establishment of the Boston Sand Gardens in 1885, was
the emotional vehicle used by the recreation movement and political leaders to
advance community or public recreation. During the past half century, recreation became a movement for all people, of all ages. Still, play programs for
children on a year-round basis remained an important service in communities
throughout the country during the first half of this century. But this level of
programming for children is seldom seen today.

This is especially unfortunate because society and its norms have changed and parents often no longer assume the responsibility of supervising the life and play of children because of other interests and responsibilities. Public school systems are still largely committed to the play and education of children starting at age five. This issue of what to do with pre-school aged children while parents are unavailable is a serious contemporary national issue and is the basis of proposed federal legislation. After school and summer care have also become issues and problems.

The importance of each child's formative years is well documented. As The International Association for the Children's Right to Play stated, play, along with nutrition, health, shelter and education, is vital for the development of the potential of all children.[10] Programs that address children's development and thus public good are, by tradition and professional commitment, park and recreation agency responsibilities; responsibilities probably best met cooperatively with local public school systems and with private companies. The questionable ethics of shifting primary child care responsibility for parenting from parents to public agencies is overridden by the developmental risks to children when no responsible person is available to supervise their pre-school play years. There are also heavy social costs.

Commissioners and Their Policies

Perhaps enough of the public values of parks and recreation remain to begin the process of change. If so, the policy process has to be first, not so much how policy is formed, for which we train everyone to be administrators, but what policy is formed and by whom. There are potential commissioners inclined toward providing all members of the community with opportunities which truly represents the public good, and not merely its immediate and trendy pleasurable appetites. But they have to be found and recruited.

Until the 1950s, local park and recreation commissions, the policy making group, were usually composed of community leaders who were recognized for their strong sense of civic duty. They were also people with the necessary social skills and economic influence to effectively represent the community's park and recreation interests before political and legislative bodies. Park and recreation advisory committees, on the other hand, were made up of representatives of local interest and constituent groups. After World War II an egalitarian movement was started to assure that major interest groups, already represented in advisory boards, were also represented on the policy making commission. Community and social leaders were elbowed aside or gradually drifted away to serve on boards in other community oriented organizations.

Whatever the reasons, the last several decades there has been a noticeable drift of community leaders away from membership on local park and recreation policy making boards and commissions. They are increasingly found in the service of other local organizations such as zoological societies, symphony orchestras and art councils which, as a result, enjoy increasing public acceptance and support.

As the lead professional person in the agency, the director has an ethical and professional obligation to advise the policy makers, with or without an invitation to do so. It is his obligation to contribute professional, value sensitive judgement to the public policy process when he perceives that the commission's visions would benefit from it. Without the exercise of that ethical and professional obligation there is no reason not to appoint someone's relative as chief executive officer of the public's park and recreation systems and services.

Accreditation of Local Park and Recreation Agencies

The reasons behind public resistance to increasing expenditures for park and recreation services is obviously based on a perception that they are not receiving sufficient value. One way that this growing public attitude can be addressed is to establish a credible method of evaluating the agency's performance and services. Yet, "Not quite one-half of local departments nationwide reported using a systematic program evaluation system. Many respondents currently not involved reported interest in adopting an evaluation system."[11] The long recognized model of outside peer evaluation, which is characteristic of how the academic community evaluates itself, has high public credibility and should therefore be given consideration by professional park and recreation organizations. The National Recreation and Park Association, which is involved in accrediting university park and recreation curricula, is well positioned to take what would seem to be a most logical extension of its responsibilities by cooperating with the American Academy of Park and Recreation Administrators in developing a system to accredit local park and recreation agencies. This could be a national program in which everyone would benefit; the public with improved services, the local departments with guidance on how services can be improved and on improved public perception of the value of these services.[12] Through the initiative of the American Academy of Park and Recreation Administrators, which has established a special study committee on accreditation, there is a growing national interest in the subject.

THE COLLEGES AND UNIVERSITIES

The beginning of the long road to again achieve acceptance and support of policy and programs for the pursuit of happiness through recreation is now in the hands of those colleges and universities that offer undergraduate and graduate degrees of study in parks and recreation and/or leisure studies. In the

1970s there were almost 500 colleges and universities in the U.S. offering degrees in some form of parks and recreation and/or leisure studies. Many programs were in institutions ill-equipped to offer anything that resembled an experience in higher education or a program of professional studies in recreation and leisure. As a result, a nationwide accreditation program of colleges and universities was initiated in 1975 by the National Recreation and Park Association and the American Association for Leisure and Recreation, largely because of the need to keep marginal curricula from proliferating.

The long-range value of the program is now in question. Whether it can adjust its criteria to meet the fast moving changes in curricula development and standards and maintain the interest of its constituents in higher education in meeting them, is the question. Will the program of accrediting park, recreation and leisure studies curricula be part of the renaissance or an impediment to it?

University Strategies and Constraints

Change is a condition of American higher education. The organizational changes that are occurring in the nation's colleges and universities are driven almost exclusively by external interests, chiefly finances. The inevitable result of financial limitations in all public and private investments is to reassess institutional priorities. The classic formula in ordering program priorities in colleges and universities is for the disciplinary based academic programs to remain at the top. Of these, the basic disciplines: biology, mathematics, psychology, physics, chemistry, philosophy and the arts are first. They are followed by the recognized applied disciplines; medicine, geology, forestry, sociology, botany, agri-culture and so forth. It is safe to assume that, being both a new addition to college and university programs of study and a second generation program in the applied fields, recreation, leisure, parks and tourism seldom enjoy high priority.

There are several ways college and university curricula can survive the present and anticipated cutbacks in many universities. First and most obvious is for the park, recreation and leisure studies departments to become an integral part of a department that represents a recognized basic or applied field of study: psychology, geography, economics, business, sociology, forestry, fisheries, and wildlife, etc. The important point is that these departments are protected by status as recognized disciplines that engage in disciplinary research. There is a recognized fall-back position for the universities and colleges in times of financial stress; first, cut the departments without recognized disciplinary linkage.

As noted in a study on improving undergraduate education at Michigan State University:

> The university must offer carefully conceived patterns of study in all of the basic disciplines and those particular professional and applied fields which it chooses to develop. The distinction between these two—the basic disciplines and their fields of applications—is worth drawing for no other reason than to suggest again that while the university can choose to offer, or not to offer, a program in an applied field, it has no choice with the basic disciplines in the arts and sciences.[13]

This means, in effect, that only those university curricula that are associated with a basic discipline have tenure as a program of study, even in the best of times. So it behooves faculty in park, recreation, leisure and tourism studies departments to plan their future in a program area that if not part of a basic discipline, is at least part of a highly regarded applied field.

The conundrum faced by university departments of parks, recreation, leisure and tourism studies I noted previously:

> If departments of park and recreation administration continue to build faculties of an interdisciplinary nature rather than ones with training in parks and recreation, they might find themselves with faculties more inclined toward research and the traditional academic reward system. However, students trained under these faculties are ill-prepared as recreation and park practitioners. The profession may discover that universities are no longer preparing students for practitioner roles; university curricula may discover that their students are no longer as employable or interested in employment as recreation practitioners. The same phenomenon occurred in sociology some years ago as sociology ceased to be interested in the preparation of social workers. Consequently, social work evolved its own curricula and program of professional preparation.[14]

Burdge addresses this complex problem and recommends that leisure studies should seek an institutional home that will permit leisure researchers to work in an environment which recognizes that "Leisure is broader (than parks and recreation) and research derived from its study has wider implications than simply the evaluation of park and recreation programs."[15] This further demonstrates the need for university curricula in parks and recreation to become affiliated with other compatible academic fields and administrative units. However, if university and college park and recreation departments are to achieve academic status as a recognized applied discipline, it is critical that the faculty include researchers who are committed to addressing the research needs of the providers of park and recreation services as well as those of their discipline.

Without proper institutional linkage and support within the colleges and universities, the future for curricula that are committed to the study of parks, recreation, leisure and tourism and the education of professionals in park and recreation systems of public service is not bright. It is apparent that college and university curricula and their academic departments of parks, recreation, leisure and tourism, without a viable constituency and without a recognized disciplinary linkage, will not be part of the renaissance.

More important than the institutional arrangement is the quality of the teaching and research programs. Local park and recreation systems of service suffer from a tradition that limits the notion of public service to traditional facilities and program areas. The new curricula should incorporate the principals and dynamics of community service and development. This change in curricular focus will assure that park and recreation agencies will eventually break away from their dependence on islands of green and recreation centers and deliver recreation opportunities throughout the community.

If university curricula do not address the concept of the community as a park there is no reason to expect that this social and professional goal will become part of the mandate of park and recreation practitioners. Unless the entire profession of parks and recreation is once more directed by important values, the renaissance of local public park and recreation agencies will not occur and many will not survive as identifiable units.

Until community leaders can be attracted back to the policy making functions of the local park and recreation commission wherein they can add vision to its mission as a public service, while also representing and legitimizing its new policies before mayors and city councils, the possibilities for a renaissance are bleak.

The renaissance of public park and recreation agencies will depend largely on how well they are able to meet the public's interest in returning to value sensitive policies and increasing the range of opportunities to pursue happiness. Chief among these will be changing the mission of the agencies to embrace the concept of creating a park community. There is too little community, it seems, and brambles are driving out the flowers.

The field of parks, recreation, leisure and tourism needs to be burned-over and sterilized to permit some new and some original seeds, free to be nurtured in newly conditioned soil, to bloom once again into a movement and service enriching us all.

REFERENCES

1. Murray, C. *In Pursuit of Happiness and Good Government.* New York: Simon and Schuster, p. 39.
2. *Ibid.* p. 39.
3. *Ibid.* p. 34.
4. *Ibid.* p. 28.
5. Goodale, T. L. "If Leisure is to Matter" In: Goodale, Thomas L. and Witt, P. A. (Eds.). *Recreation and Leisure: Issues in an Era of Change* (Rev. Ed.). State College, Pennsylvania: Venture Publishing, 1985, p. 54.
6. Cranz, G. *The Politics of Park Design: A History of Urban Parks in America.* Cambridge, Massachusetts: MIT Press, 1982, p. 157.
7. Murray, *Op. Cit.* p. 26.
8. cf., Crompton, J. F. and Lamb, C. W. Jr. *Marketing Government Social Services.* New York: John Wiley and Sons, 1986.
9. Doell, C. E. and Twardzik, L. F. *Elements of Park and Recreation Administration* (Fourth Edition). Minneapolis, Minnesota: Burgess Publishing, 1979, p. 77.
10. Westland, C. and Knight, J. *Playing, Living, Learning: A Worldwide Perspective on Children's Opportunities to Play.* State College, Pennsylvania: Venture Publishing, 1982, p. 7.
11. McDonald, B. L. and Cordell, H. K. *Local Opportunities for Americans: Final Report of the Municipal and County Park and Recreation Study.* Alexandria, Virginia: National Recreation and Park Association, 1988, p. 93.
12. Twardzik, L. F. "Accreditation: A Method for Evaluating Public Park and Recreation Systems.: *Parks and Recreation.* 22(3), 1987, p. 60.
13. Michigan State University Committee on Undergraduate Education. *Improving Undergraduate Education.* East Lansing, Michigan: The Committee, 1967, p. 3.
14. Twardzik, L. F. "A Case for the Study of Ethics in Professional Recreation Education and Practice." *Leisure Sciences.* 6(3), 1984, p. 375.
15. Burdge, R. "Leisure Research and Parks and Recreation Education: Compatible or Not?" In: Goodale, T. L. and Witt, P. A. (Eds.). *Recreation and Leisure: Issues in an Era of Change* (Rev. Ed.). State College, Pennsylvania: Venture Publishing, 1985, p. 349.

Chapter 25

Back to Our Radical Roots

Mary Duncan

The most dangerous woman in America, a civil-rights newspaper columnist, a man who started a playground at his own expense, a publicist who exposed filthy tenement conditions and advocates of socialism and leftist politics are frequently cited as being the founders or cornerstones of the park and recreation movement. Unfortunately, these facts are seldom stated in our recreation textbooks. One has to read biographies, autobiographies and other publications before these facts become evident.

Why haven't our textbooks dealt with the personalities, commitments, failures, and political views of our professional predecessors? Is it because the authors were not aware of it? Has there been an unspoken conspiracy to make our new profession more "respectable" by glossing over our founders' sometimes unsavory and controversial pasts?

In order to fill these voids in our literature, herewith is a brief foray into the lives of Frederick Law Olmsted, Jacob Riis, Jane Addams, Luther Gulick and Joseph Lee. In many ways they were the radical counterparts of Eldridge Cleaver, Jane Fonda, Caesar Chavez, Gloria Steinem and Ralph Nader. They continually fought city hall, organized labor strikes, marched in the streets, gave public speeches, and wrote award-winning articles deploring the living conditions of the poor. The issues and problems they faced were well defined: slavery, the aftermath of the Civil War, thousands of new immigrants, slums, child labor, disease, the suffrage movement, World War I, and a rapidly industrializing nation. America was striving to develop its abundant natural resources and was also enjoying a booming economy. The work ethic and the free-enterprise system flourished, thus creating a paradox of strong economic growth at the expense of human suffering and exploitation.

Our founders faced these issues. They were not meek and mild, easily intimidated or swayed by local politicians. They worked in, around, and with the political system. The political battles they fought gave them the skills needed in order to establish the park, playground and recreation services we enjoy today. With these thoughts in mind, let's look at their radical pasts. Perhaps it will provide some insights into the present, and hopefully provide a model for the future.

FREDERICK LAW OLMSTED (1882-1903)

Frederick Law Olmsted, a political columnist, writer, traveler, farmer, and landscape architect, was also an abolitionist who later become one of the designers of Central Park. His biographer, Elizabeth Stevenson, states that his early years laid the groundwork for his dedication to public service.

His childhood was unusual and set the course for his interest in landscape architecture. Even though his family were prominent merchants and lived in Hartford, Connecticut, Fred was allowed to roam free in the nearby woods. At the age of seven, he was sent to live with a series of ministers where his formal education vacillated between very good and very bad. He was not always happy, but learned to cope by escaping to the woods for solitude and adventure.[1] Later he visited England where he was impressed with her parks and wrote that in "democratic America there was nothing to be thought of as comparable with this People's Garden."[2]

Even though he was not a good student, writing his thoughts seemed a natural habit for him. This ability led the liberal editor of the *New York Daily-Times* to employ Olmsted to travel South and write his impressions about slavery. While Olmsted's columns were simple and unemotional, they vividly portrayed the brutalities, both physical and psychological, of a slave society. Writing in a letter to a friend he said, "I would take in a fugitive slave and shoot a man that was likely to get him." One of his columns was attributed to influencing Abraham Lincoln to emancipate the slaves.[3]

Prior to the Civil War, Olmsted, who had "tried being clerk, tried being sailor, and failed at farming," was determined to be the Superintendent of Central Park. He succeeded and immediately ran into opposition from Chief Engineer Egbert Viele. When Calvin Vaux's and Olmsted's plans for Central Park were later adopted, Viele charged them with stealing his plans. Viele had designed a drainage system for the park, and based on that was initially awarded a court settlement of $8,000.[4] But the jealousies between the men did not deter the progress of Central Park.

For a while, Olmsted resisted entering the Civil War. He considered Lincoln to be "lacking in firmness and dependent upon others for direction." Later he changed his mind and became Secretary of the Sanitary Commission, which dealt with the health needs of Northern soldiers.

Following the war, Olmsted designed numerous other private and public parks. Almost as if he were psychic, he recommended that San Francisco's Golden Gate Park be designed to act as "a barrier of protection to large districts . . . during great conflagrations." Although he didn't design Golden Gate Park, his suggestions were followed and during the fire that followed the 1906 earthquake, the park served as a firebreak and later was used to house thousands of homeless people.[5]

Both Vaux and Olmsted served as consultants to the New York City Park Department, but were fired in 1870 when the Tweed Ring took over New York City. In spite of the political setbacks, they were later reinstated and continued to guide the development of Central Park.

During these years, his wife Mary cared for their children and also advised him on professional matters. Partially because of this he was not upset by the Suffrage Movement. "If an occasional woman was found to be doing a man's work . . . he was not alarmed." He welcomed Elizabeth Bullard, of Bridgeport, Connecticut, into the "brotherhood" of landscape architects and recommended her for several jobs.[6]

Conservation and preservation were also Olmsted's concerns. He continued to fight for maintaining the natural scenery of such places as the Niagara Falls area and Yosemite.

The tumultuous years of Civil War, corrupt politicians, suffrage, and increasing urban problems did not deter the thousands of immigrants who flooded our shores. Among them was twenty-one-year-old Jacob Riis, a Danish citizen.

JACOB RIIS (1849-1941)

Jacob Riis was a troublemaker. Using his position as a police reporter, he expanded his beat to include dramatic stories about the horrors of slum conditions in New York City.

Stressing the theme of two Americas, he wrote that "slums were an evil cancer born of public neglect and nurtured by private greed."[7] His book, *How the Other Half Lives*, recommended tighter health laws, the prohibition of child labor and improvement of public schools.

Lectures, photo displays and articles facilitated his meeting influential people. Together they conducted tours of the tenements and pressured politicians to clean up the filth. Philosophically he wanted to solve the problems by going further than simple charity but stopped short of socialism. His biographer stated:

> "Riis's programs of social, economic, political and humanitarian reform aimed to beautify the environment and to reestablish the position of the home, the school, and the neighborhood in the lives of the poor . . . Riis wanted school buildings to be open in the evenings, on weekends, and during the summers for recreational, cultural and civic use."[8]

Highly critical of organized religion, he admonished the churches to wipe the soot from their windows and take up the gospel of service. Settlement housed to him were the best example of practical Christianity.

Parks and playgrounds were high on his priority list of urban needs. He believed cities should provide parks for "the rest and recreation of the poor," rather than "for the pomp and parade of the wealthy."[9] Like other members of our movement, he wrote that creative play was necessary for teaching proper citizenship. As local politicians grew tired of his crusades, Riis resorted to other methods. One of his favorites was to send women to the mayor's office because "they could worm a playground or small park out of him."[10]

Jake's concern for parks and play areas was undoubtedly a result of his rural youth environment. Like Olmsted, he preferred rivers, hills or trees to the structured classroom. The son of a schoolmaster, he enjoyed high social status but on an austere family income. He once commented that his father "was the one link between the upper and lower strata in our town . . . enjoying the most hearty respect of both."[11] In order to support fourteen children, the elderly Riis wrote columns for a local newspaper. It was as his father's young assistant that Jacob decided he wanted to be a news reporter.

Distressed by the rejection of his sweetheart, Elisabeth, and the lack of work, he travelled by steamer to New York in 1870. From that time until 1877, he lived on the brink of poverty, hunger, loneliness and humiliation. Cheated by several employers, Riis finally turned to the Danish consul who gave him shelter, clothes and a job.

His social life revolved around the Lutheran Church where the young people played "particularly energetic kissing games" because the pastor despised dancing.[12] But he still longed for Elisabeth, who was now engaged to another man in Denmark. Finally, after years of effort and taking classes at a business school, he secured a job as a reporter. From here he embarked on his career as a social reformer and, when established, was able to marry Elisabeth.

Throughout his life he struggled to bring the "two Americas" that he knew so well—one rich and the other poor—into harmony with one another. Believing in the integrity of neighborhoods, he emphasized community rehabilitation by the families, schools and churches rather than distant experts.

On these points, he and his friend Jane Addams concurred.

JANE ADDAMS (1860-1935)

Jane Addams is frequently lauded for having started a playground next to Hull House in Chicago. Photos of her depict a kindly woman chatting with children. Addams was also a "women's libber" who helped organize labor unions for women garment workers, investigated child-labor practice, established a day nursery for the children of working mothers and struggled to help women gain the right to vote. In spite of her personal wealth, she chose to work among the poor. Her clientele consisted of immigrant settlers, sweatshop toilers, unwed mothers, the hungry, sick and aged. Programs at Hull House encompassed a myriad of social, educational and recreational services.

As an ardent supporter of Theodore Roosevelt, she seconded his nomination for President under the now defunct leftist Progressive Party. Her endorsement of him waned when he became a "hawk" regarding World War I while she was an avowed pacifist. Along with several other women she organized the Women's Peace Party and organized a large peace demonstration in Washington. Later in 1931 she was awarded the Nobel Peace Prize for her efforts.[13]

Psychoanalysts could offer some insights into what motivated Jane Addams. She was the daughter of a wealthy man whom she adored, but his attention to her was diverted by her stepmother. Marriage probably did not seem appealing because her mother died in childbirth; her father's remarriage disrupted her emotional ties to him and her sister's marriage was marred by much bitterness and recrimination. Her personal relationships revolved around Mary Rozet Smith, who was a donor to Hull House and Jane's closest friend, confidante and companion. For many years they lived together and when apart exchanged what only can be described as love letters. Her biographer Daniel Levine wrote, "there can be no doubt that each of the women filled some of the emotional requirments a spouse might have filled had either married. Whether emotional intimacy ever led to physical intimacy no one can say. Probably the strong sexual inhibitions of the age and of both women prevented it."[14]

What really matters, though, is that she channeled her energies into projects like Hull House and into creating a more humanistic society. Other wealthy women might have succumbed to their tensions, and retreated to a pampered, self-indulgent lifestyle. Jane Addams dealt with her world and in the process touched many lives including Joseph Lee, the father of the American playground movement.

JOSEPH LEE (1862-1937)

Joseph Lee and Jane Addams both served as officers in the Playground Association of America and he, like her, came from a wealthy, prominent family. While Lee would not be considered as radical as Riis or Addams, he continually fought to make recreation a viable part of American life. Appalled by the jailing of children for playing in the streets, he established, at his own expense, an experimental playground in Boston.

His Harvard education, law degree, European travel and happy childhood provided a solid foundation for pursuing his interests in youth, delinquency and family life. His book, *Constructive and Preventive Philanthropy*, stressed the importance of recreation in molding youth development. Another of his books, *Play and Education*, focused on the relationships between play, recreation and the social problems facing our cities.[15] Lee, philosophically, felt that recreation was an integral part of everyone's life, both adults and children. His definition of recreation included many aspects of leisure time activities such as visiting museums, use of school fields and parks as well as children romping on play-grounds. Recreation, to him, was one important factor in life which also had to be integrated with the educational, political, social, religious and economic realities of neighborhoods and cities. To use today's terminology, Lee advocated utilizing an holistic approach to recreation services. This approach was shared by Luther Gulick, a pragmatic man who identified needs in our society and then created organizations or programs to meet those needs.

LUTHER GULICK (1865-1918)

The dignified and mustached Luther Gulick was shoved into the swimming pool, along with several other officers of the newly created Playground Association of America. Graham Taylor, who wrote "Everybody Played," cited this as the high point of that organization's first Chicago convention in 1907.[16] This playful and spontaneous prank was indicative of Gulick, who was described by his son as a "great initiator, a vigorous man who was fun, jovial, very inventive, and an energetic outdoorsman. He derived his greatest satisfaction from working with youth-serving agencies and once established, moved on to other projects." Halsey goes on to recall that his father "had a great interest in the suffrage movement. He fought battles with the New York City School Board in order to incorporate girls into the physical education classes, and organized an elaborate girls folk-dance festival at a time when dancing was considered immoral."[17]

Frustrated by the lack of recreational opportunities for his three daughters, Gulick and his wife started a camping program which later became the Camp Fire Girls. He was also instrumental in promoting the YMCA and designed the triangle which symbolizes that organization.

As the first president of the Playground Association of America, the forerunner of the National Recreation Association, and the National Recreation and Park Association, Gulick struggled along with Jane Addams, Jacob Riis, Joseph Lee, Henry S. Curtis and Howard Braucher to establish recreation services as a proper function of government. President Theodore Roosevelt, honorary president of the Playground Association of America, heartily supported their efforts.

Gulick's parents were medical missionaries in the South Seas. One can only guess at the influence this had on Gulick's sense of strong moral purpose and commitment to the recreation movement. In spite of his strict, biblically based religious childhood, he was an evolutionist, a man with world vision. Many of his thoughts and ideas are expressed in his book, *Philosophy of Play*, and in his formal address at the Chicago Convention. Unlike many other people, Luther felt that play was an absolute necessity for the maintenance of democracy in an industrial society. He and Addams both espoused a new social ethic which stressed society's responsibility to recognize and solve social problems.[18] This differed significantly from the prevailing philosophy that problems were separate, and segmented and could be examined on an individual basis.

Gulick argued that this social ethic could only be learned by experience and in an atmosphere of considerable freedom. Playgrounds and sandpiles were where children learned about self-control, mutual rights and the awareness and importance of group effort.

As a professor at Massachusetts' Springfield College he taught this philosophy and continued until his sudden death to promote progressive camping, physical education and recreation programs.

SUMMARY

In many ways, Olmsted, Riis, Addams, Gulick and Lee represented the left wing of Theodore Roosevelt's Progressive Party. They advocated government support and regulation of parks and playgrounds while Riis and Addams in particular wanted government to also control nickelodeons, penny arcades and pool halls.

Many of the problems they faced have been solved only to create a fascinating paradox. Immigrants and foreign laborers are now actively discouraged from entering our country. Our efforts to industrialize were so successful that now, in the 90s, we face dramatic energy shortages. Children who were once exploited in the factories are now economically dependent on their parents until their late teens or early twenties.

The slavery issue has been resolved, but racial injustices still exist. Others feel that white people or Anglos are discriminated against and have filed reverse discrimination suits involving college admissions and employment opportunities. Antibiotics and modern sewage systems have irradicated most communicable diseases only we now find that cancer and stress-related diseases like heart attacks have taken their place. Government at all levels has recognized its role in providing park and recreation services for the people but a growing taxpayers' revolt now threatens some of those same services. Women have been able to vote for many years but are still struggling to pass the controversial Equal Rights Amendment which guarantees equal rights to everyone regardless of sex. Infant-mortality rates remain high among minority groups and the poor while the conservative right wing attacks abortion laws which allow women to control their own bodies. Even the traditional family concept has been broadened to include the alternative lifestyles of singles, couples without children, divorced people and gay or homosexual relationships.

It's difficult to second guess how our founders would have dealt with these issues. But based on their past records one can imagine Riis marching with the Mexican migrant farm workers; Addams leading the fight to ratify the Equal

Rights Amendment and opposing the Vietnam War; Olmstead an active member of the Sierra Club and writing columns opposing nuclear reactors and the commercialization of our state and federal parks; Lee financing adventure playgrounds with his own money and Gulick initiating recreation programs on rooftops and under freeways and continually lobbying with government officials for better recreation services.

Some people may question if these leaders were really radical. When looking at definitions of "radical" one finds the following explanations: "A person favoring drastic political, economic or social reforms; advocates extreme change of the social structure."

It would be difficult to deny that there have been "drastic political, economic and social reforms" since the early 1900s. Our founders were an integral part of those reforms. Now as we look to the future, what role will park and recreation professionals play in addressing today's issues?

REFERENCES

1. Stevenson, E. *Park Maker: A Life of Frederick Law Olmsted.* New York: The MacMillan Company, 1977, p. 113.
2. *Ibid.*, p. 55.
3. *Ibid.*, p. 72, pp. 112-131.
4. *Ibid.*, p. 335.
5. *Ibid.*, p. 268.
6. *Ibid.*, p. 383.
7. Lane, J. B. *Jacob A. Riis and the American City.* New York: Kennikat Press, 1974, p. 50.
8. *Ibid.*, p. 91.
9. *Ibid.*, p. 113.
10. *Ibid.*
11. Riis, J. A. *Making of an American.* New York: The MacMillan Company, 1904, p. 22.
12. *Ibid.*, pp. 14-16.
13. Levine, D. *Jane Addams and the Liberal Tradition.* Madison, Wisconsin: State Historical Society of Wisconsin, 1971, p. 203.
14. *Ibid.*, p. 71.
15. Lee, J. *Play and Education.* New York: The MacMillan Company, 1916.
16. Taylor, G. R. "How They Played at Chicago." *Charities*, XVIII (August 3, 1907), pp. 471-480.
17. Gulick, H. Personal interview with the author, May 1979.
18. Gulick, L. H. "Play and Democracy." *Charities*, XVIII (August 3, 1907).

End of Chapter 25 and End of Section 3

SECTION IV

Questioning Research Paradigms: Tight Methods, Loose Concepts

INTRODUCTION

The chapters in Section IV deal with attempts to develop research for the recreation field and the emerging directions that are necessary to improve research development efforts to meet future needs. The eight chapters cover a variety of topics, but running through them is the implicit theme that increased, improved and more relevant research needs to be undertaken concerning park and recreation issues. What type of research to increase, the standards by which improvement should be judged, and how to judge research relevance form the basis of the discussion. The explicit thrust of the chapters is directed toward how to improve park and recreation research and future directions that the research should take.

Barnett (26) opens the section with a point/counter-point discussion of three issues underlying park and recreation research: (1) Is leisure research a discipline and can leisure research be considered science?; (2) Does leisure research lack relevance to practice due to the pursuit of research agendas that are overly esoteric and relevant only in a university environment?; and (3) Have researchers over-emphasized field and questionnaire-based research at the expense of the controlled laboratory experiment? These three issues—theory, relevance, and method—strike at the heart of whether leisure research is accepted within either the academic environment of the university or the "real world" of the practitioner. While Barnett's chapter does not mend the splits implicit in each of the issues she raises, her conclusion is compelling: Whatever one's views about what research is or should be undertaken, "leisure research is a very good thing."

While Barnett focuses on fundamental problems in the undertaking of leisure research, Burdge (27) discusses the struggle to create a viable body of knowledge that would add credibility to the park and recreation movement's claim for professional status, and the quest by researchers from a variety of disciplines to find an institutional home for leisure research. Goodale (28), extends Barnett's and Burdge's insights another step by outlining some of the fundamental problems or biases that are inherent in the conceptualization and methodology of leisure research.

Burdge (27), like Sessoms (19) in an earlier chapter, asks whether leisure research can exist within professionally oriented park and recreation departments. He notes the name changes many of these departments went through in the 70s and early 80s to include the ideas of "leisure" and "studies" along with or as a replacement for recreation and parks. Burdge is concerned that discipline oriented leisure researchers (sociologists, economists etc.) may have difficulty living within the expectation and support systems of these renamed units. More importantly, Burdge is concerned with whether leisure research will be supported by the profession. Thus, he sees a growing separation of leisure research from parks and recreation education programs whose central concern is professional training. Many of the reasons that the leisure research might not be supported by the profession were previously outlined in Barnett's (26) chapter.

Goodale (28) explores some the underlying issues impinging on the quantity and quality of leisure research. He notes, for example, the problems of aligning discovery with a publish or perish university environment that rewards production. Thus, journal editors receive more manuscript status inquiries as tenure time approaches and investigators often gear research efforts to areas where funding is available as opposed to undertaking a line of inquiry consistent with their own interests. Goodale also points to our rewarding atomistic approaches as opposed to theory building and overview efforts. This concern is a further elaboration of the fundamental nature of theory as the basis for meaningful research begun by Barnett (26). Finally, Goodale looks at what we do and do not research. For example, demand and wants seem more prevalently investigated than need. Does this exemplify a society of affluence or is it a result of our inability to operationalize difficult concepts?

Together Barnett (26), Burdge (27) and Goodale (28) raise the level of discourse about the purpose and support systems for leisure research. Combined with articles in the previous section, they expand the debate about whose interests are served by professional status, research undertaking, and professional preparation programs.

While a body of knowledge, research efforts, and some kind of organizational structure are considered essential to the development and legitimacy of a profession, Barnett, Burdge and Goodale point to the dilemmas and contradictions in creating processes, symbols and substance. The diversity of matters is clear and the complexity of alternatives overwhelming. Consensus as to purpose and methods, in the final analysis, may be unachievable.

The chapters by Ellis and Witt (29), Kelly (30), and Glancy (31) address in more detail some of the issues raised by authors of the first three chapters in the section. Ellis and Witt (29) summarize attempts to operationalize the concept of leisure. According to the authors, operationalization is necessary to move the study of leisure from the realm of philosophy to a legitimate social science. To this end, the authors summarize attempts to operationalize leisure, whether it is defined from an objective (time), subjective (experience), or dispositional (personality) perspective. While not advocating any one approach to defining leisure over another, the authors strongly advocate the need to move beyond current word definitions of leisure to instruments and methods that will allow quantification in measurable terms. Only then are studies of service impact, benefits of leisure involvement, and leisure needs possible.

Kelly (30) takes issue with the strong emphasis on quantitative methods proposed by Ellis and Witt (29), arguing for the increased utilization of qualitative methodologies in the pursuit of leisure research. Kelly argues that qualitative methodologies may be more appropriate in some cases for capturing and preserving the meaning of leisure and in fact may have better potential for leading to the development of fundamental theory, the lack of which was emphasized in the chapters by Barnett (26) and Burdge (27). Thus, Kelly discusses the role of collaborative interviews, participant observations, and projective techniques as useful additions to, and in some cases substitutes for, the arsenal of survey techniques so commonly utilized by leisure researchers.

Glancy's (31) chapter concerns the androcentric approach taken by most leisure researchers. A growing group of women, and some men, have recognized the dominance of theory and research methods that are biased toward conceptualizing, studying, interpreting, and planning for leisure from a male perspective. Thus, Glancy argues for a "gender-conscious view of leisure," a perspective that will recognize, honor and appreciate differences between women and men. While the leisure literature in this area is in its infancy, Glancy builds upon the mounting evidence that leisure may be experienced differently by women and men. She uses Jung's explanation of archetypes to show some of the origins of a male-dominated world and the implications of this dominance for the way women experience leisure. Glancy's analysis leads to the conclusion that women need to be more central in defining and interpreting their own leisure, research methodologies need to be employed that will allow gender differences to emerge, and the outcomes of this approach to research need to be more fully reflected in the development of leisure theory and practice.

The final two chapters in this section by Mannell (32) and Sylvester (33) concern the increasing prominence of definitional structures and research methods that emphasize the subjective view or state-of-mind view of leisure. Mannell (32) wonders about the desirability of the social and psychological engineering applications which may result from our quest to achieve the perfect leisure state-of-mind. He raises questions concerning the emergence of "experience" as the focus and objective of recreation and leisure services. Psychic rather than material gratification has increasingly become the motivation of what advertisers tell us is the "now" generation and social critics tell us is the "me" generation. Mannell thus warns us against the "psychologization of leisure services" where "experience engineers" manipulate "psychic loadings" and the like. How far is it from here to the "feelies" and "solidarity services" of Huxley's *Brave New World?*

In the concluding chapter to the section and book, Sylvester (33) also discusses some of the pitfalls of the emerging emphasis on the subjective view of leisure. He decries the misrepresentation of Aristotle's concepts of happiness and freedom by those seeking to justify a state-of-mind leisure perspective. Echoing some of Twardzik's (24) concerns about basing the provision of leisure services on a high demand rather than an ethics perspective tied to the survival of community life, Sylvester describes how classical leisure was an intersubjective or public experience rather than a subjective or private one. Thus, the goal of leisure is not feeling good about oneself; rather "self-esteem and self-respect [grow] out of virtuous action." In addition, Sylvester challenges the notion that happiness can be simply judged on the individual basis of perception rather than being judged by what people actually to with their lives. These ideas challenge much of the current trend toward a social-psychological interpretation of leisure and thus the approaches to leisure research that are currently being undertaken. They also bring us full circle to the definitional problems and issues raised in the first section of the book. Thus we are reminded once again that definitions and philosophy form the foundation for practice, our efforts to develop a profession, and the development of theory and research.

Chapter 26

Leisure Research is a Very Good Thing

Lynn A. Barnett

A major sign that something is amiss with current research is that prominent leisure scientists frequently express discontent with its outcomes. Concerns are raised about the theoretical bases and aspirations of the research, the methodological techniques and approaches employed, and the practical utility or relevance of the results. These three overriding issues (theory, relevance, method) are the basis for several specific questions that have been posed and remain unresolved. For example: Should research in leisure and recreation be directly relevant to practice? Are findings obtained in other fields, such as sociology or community psychology, relevant to leisure and recreation? Do studies conducted in laboratory settings have any bearing on leisure practice? Should correlational findings based on nonexperimental designs be taken seriously? Are subjective conclusions reached during the course of recreational practice scientifically sound? What is the role of theory in guiding leisure research?

Questions about theory, relevance and methodology arise from a number of interrelated sources. However, Kuhn's[1] approach to science suggests that these issues remain unanswered because leisure educators and researchers disagree about the goals of science, leisure, and research. We lack a *disciplinary matrix*, or *paradigm*[2], a shared set of fundamental beliefs, exemplars, and symbolic generalizations. Therefore, disagreements about what makes for good leisure research and how leisure research related to improving professional practice are inevitable.

Kuhn's concept of paradigm suggests that one path to the resolution of the current methodological and epistemological debate is to carefully and openly examine our undergirding, paradigms, and assumptions. This chapter is an attempt to draw from Kuhn by highlighting some of the major issues underlying current debates in our field. In so doing, it is the goal of this paper to provide the material from which we can understand, ponder, argue, and perhaps even resolve some of these issues. As a step toward this goal, each of the three major issues of theory, relevance, and methodology is presented in a point-counterpoint format.

ON THEORY: SCIENCE AND LEISURE RESEARCH

The debate over whether the study of leisure is a discipline or whether it is merely a topical area of inquiry is not new, but it still continues.[3] A variety of discussants have come to essentially the same conclusion: we are making progress, but we are not (yet) there. One recurrent theme in this reasoning is that we borrow too heavily from other disciplines, and as such, we have yet to establish our own body of knowledge.[4] And, without a unique body of leisure knowledge, we are not at a level of comparable discourse to those of our neighboring disciplines.

A second thread that runs through much of the leisure identity argument is that our empirical thinking about leisure is more concerned with practice than with theory.[5] This is commonly labelled the distinction between "basic" and "applied" research, with the former being regarded as the *sine qua non* and the latter considered to be short-sighted and overly specific. Many authors draw a distinction between these two types of research, and suggest further that they cannot be interlaced. They argue that the concern for directly applicable leisure research has short-circuited the scientific process and inhibited rather than encouraged the use of creative thought. In the two sections that follow, the contrasting views that leisure research is science (point) versus that leisure research is not science (counterpoint) are presented.

Point: Leisure Research is Science

Philosophers of science often note that basic science is not the same thing as applied science. For example, Bunge[6] emphasized their divergent goals by noting that systematic knowledge is the essential goal of basic researchers, whereas the applied scientist seeks information that will increase knowledge while also proving itself to be relevant to some particular problem. Bunge also proposed that research questions originate from different sources in basic and applied research. The basic researcher, according to Bunge, is interested in investigating some puzzle or problem that is suggested by theory. He or she says, "Let's compare 'what is' with 'what should be' to see if the theory is adequate." In applied science, the research may spring from practical concerns rather than from theoretically relevant hypotheses. In essence, the applied researcher says, "Let's understand the nature of this problem so we can do something to resolve it."

However, in the final analysis, basic and applied leisure research are more similar than different, for both are science rather than technology. Both accept the long-term goal of increasing knowledge and understanding. Both involve relating observations back to theoretical constructs that provide the framework for interpreting data and generating predictions. Both insist that the test of theory lies in objective, empirical methods rather than logical claims or subjective feelings. Both involve striving for consensus among members of the discipline concerning acceptable, unacceptable, and to-be-evaluated explanations of empirical observations.

Thus, recreation and leisure research, characterized by basic or applied concerns, is science rather than "technology," "social engineering," or "community research." Problems relevant to recreation and leisure are the initial source of research questions, but these applied concerns are ultimately placed into a theoretical context, and the long-term goal of research includes testing the adequacy of assumptions and hypotheses that make up the underlying theory. Theory therefore is not solely used to develop some product, such as an instrument that can be sold for profit (technology), a procedure that will satisfy the needs of some community agency (social engineering), or a cost-effective structured training workshop (community research). Rather, theory is examined by gathering information relevant to predictions derived from theory. Furthermore, the adequacy of the theory and the value of any products or useful information obtained from application to practice is usually determined by methods recognized as acceptable by other leisure researchers in the field.

Not only is there scientific unity of basic and applied leisure research, but leisure research is also united with other branches of social science. Although the unique characteristics of recreation settings pose special problems for researchers, the unification perspective argues that leisure researchers and investigators in other areas of the social sciences share the superordinate goal of increasing our understanding of human behavior. As such, we need not be so critically preoccupied with generating our own unique body of knowledge since we are an integral part of this larger effort.

In contrast to a unificationist viewpoint, other investigators have advocated a dualistic approach to leisure research. Proponents of dualism suggest that leisure is so unique that its processes and dynamics cannot be explained using principles of human behavior derived from any other branch of the social sciences. In arguing against dualism, dissenters emphasize the shared goal of social scientists: to develop and test generalizable principles of human behavior. If these "laws" of behavior make reference to specific leisure settings, then the inevitable changes in these leisure settings that take place over time and across situations undermine the generalizability of the laws themselves. Because leisure researchers should strive to explain individuals' actions in terms of general statements that hold across many situations and times, findings obtained in other branches of the social sciences that bear on these general statements are necessarily relevant in evaluating their adequacy.

Evidence concerning the adequacy of a general principle of human behavior should be drawn from all available sources, including both basic research and applied research within and outside recreation and leisure. As Merton[7] long ago noted, applied researchers cannot afford to adopt a myopic, single-discipline focus: practical problems often involve variables that do not fall within the scope of any particular subfield. Leisure research must draw on the findings of other fields to be successful, and not condemn itself for sharing a knowledge base.

Homans emphasized the importance of empirical evidence when judging the sciences. To Homans, "When the test of truth of a relationship lies finally in the data themselves, the data are not wholly manufactured—when nature, however stretched out on the rack, still has a chance to say 'no!'—then the subject is a science."[8] This viewpoint, although a simplification of science, nonetheless underscores the importance of data in scientific research. In addition, it also suggests that leisure scientists must remain eclectic by drawing on findings generated in fields other than their own. That is, leisure researchers should use any and all scientific means possible to gather information concerning the leisure construct under investigation. Whether experimental, correlational, field-based, laboratory, role-play, or analog, no opportunity to further our understanding of leisure should be bypassed. As Hilgard noted, in order to "satisfy the criteria of 'good science,' the researcher must cover the whole spectrum of basic and applied science by doing sound (and conclusive) work all along the line."[9]

Arguing that leisure research is science is essentially a unificationist view. Researchers working in the many and varied subfields of recreation and leisure are united in their professional identity (they are all scientists), their goals (they seek to extend our understanding of human behavior), and their empirical outlook (they all strive to collect data relevant to the research questions at hand). Thus, we must work toward the integration and synthesis of leisure theory and research dealing with recreation and leisure-related topics.

Counterpoint: Leisure Research is Not Science

The state of research in recreation and leisure is generally poor by any yardstick. The quality of research design, including methodologies, instrumentation, and data analysis is poor; the relationship to the larger theory and data is not specified; the impact and relevance of the research to leisure and recreation practice is not made explicit; and research productivity by leisure researchers is lacking.[10]

The scientific study of leisure cannot proceed without an integration of theory with research. The apparent sterility and lack of relevance of research to practice as well as the current controversy over the generalizability of research results are inevitable consequences of inadequate attention to the role of theory in scientific leisure endeavors. Graduate training in recreation and leisure focuses on the technology of collecting and analyzing data, with a special emphasis on applying findings to recreational situations and problems. The vital and creative steps of generating transituational propositions from observed relationships are bypassed. The result is the reduction of the scientific study of leisure and recreation to technological inquiry. Technicians are being trained rather than scientists, and the products of their situationally limited work are of little value to practitioners.

A solution to these limitations of training and research lies in more fully developing the theoretical side of social science and integrating theory and research. Although the logic and methods of science can be described in many ways, descriptions of the scientific inference process emphasize the dual importance of theory construction and theory testing. Leisure researchers must also be cautious so that they do not become so preoccupied with theory testing that they overlook the critical role played by theory construction. Granted, leisure investigators are highly proficient in finding hypotheses to test, operationalizing concepts in the specific settings examined in the study, determining the statistical significance of the results, and even relating the evidence back to the initial hypotheses. But leisure researchers often fail to develop strong, applicable theoretical systems to support their work. Consequently, very few theories of leisure and recreation possess the characteristics of good theories; simplicity, interpretability, usefulness, generality, testability, disconfirmability, and logical internal consistency.

As to integrating theory and research, how often do leisure researchers conduct research programs that facilitate "strong inference"[11] by devising alternative hypotheses, pitting rival hypotheses against one another in carefully designed studies, and refining the theory through the development of subhypotheses? Likewise, how many researchers follow the scientific steps recommended by Popper's "sophisticated methodological falsifictionism"[12] approach to science by focusing on unexpected, disconfirming findings rather than on confirming evidence?

Although we are often more gratified by supporting rather than disconfirming evidence, failures to corroborate hypotheses invite us to abandon our preconceived notions and creatively reconstruct our perspective to better account for observed relationships. Popper and other philosophers of science suggest that the greatest advances in leisure science will occur when leisure researchers focus on unexpected irregularities in their data, seemingly trivial observations, and even subjective impressions that are inconsistent with the best theories they can construct.

Science is based on the accumulation of evidence and fact, but such an accumulation is not the only goal of science. Facts are used to spin theoretical systems or support existing frameworks, but they should not be considered the endpoint. Unfortunately, many leisure researchers consider themselves to be finders of facts, striving to answer such questions as: "What impact does X type of publicity have on user participation rates?" "Is therapeutic effectiveness related to client gender?" "Does leadership style A work better than leadership style B?" "Is a high score on a certain subscale of the Leisure Diagnostic Battery an indicter of leisure pathology?" "Are recreation directors' religious values related to their administrative style?" Although all of these questions raise important issues, such studies cannot advance our understanding of leisure unless the obtained findings are relevant to transituational statements dealing with leisure behavior. Specific facts—or, as in this case, empirical findings— are not themselves generalizable, but the hypotheses they either support or disconfirm are.

For example, the investigator who finds that targeted flyers increase participation rates 16 percent compared with general program brochures or store signs, may be tempted to tell practitioners to produce a good number of specialized flyers. Unfortunately, the specifics of the setting—the type of program, the content of the flyer, the mode of distribution, the type of agency, the formatting and appearance of the publicity—all limit the generalizability of the "fact" that special flyers increase participation levels. If, however, the leisure researcher had been studying a higher order theory—such as marketing strategies in public service agencies—then the study has implications beyond the obtained data. In this case the leisure researcher would be scientifically justified in suggesting that marketing campaigns be developed for certain types of agencies and programs.

We must develop higher order hypotheses to guide and summarize leisure research. However, the leisure researcher should keep in mind Hempel's requirement of testability: "the statements constituting a scientific explanation must be capable of empirical test."[13] Seeking broad, generalizable explanations of leisure behavior is a laudable goal, but these explanations must not be so general that they are untestable or so empirically bound that they are merely accidental generalizations.[14] The investigator must therefore strike a balance between generality and specificity in his or her theoretical thinking.

ON RELEVANCE: THE LEISURE SCIENTIST-PRACTITIONER DEBATE

There are those who would vehemently argue that applied research is not truly scientific research at all if it is merely fact-finding, that is, seeking to answer a specific question about a specific recreational setting, time, place, or client. And, because of their mutability and situational specificity, facts are of little long-lasting value in leisure science. Further, these individuals would harshly conclude that the concern for directly applicable research has short-circuited the scientific process in leisure research and inhibited rather than encouraged creative thinking about leisure. This obsession with relevance has led to a "knee-jerk mentality" in leisure research consumers who automatically dismiss meaningful leisure research solely on grounds of artificiality or lack of applicability.

Others would just as strongly (if not convincingly) respond that the scientific study of leisure cannot proceed without an interweaving of both basic and applied research. These individuals would becry the perceived irrelevance of leisure research to practice and argue about the lack of generalizability of research findings. If today's students are not taught how or expected to produce research bearing on issues of relevance to practice, how can we expect recreation and leisure services to be increasingly data-based? Without relevance to practice, the researcher or student-researcher works to institutionalize research, further insulating the academic from the applied environment. These opposing views about the need for relevance in leisure research and the viability of the leisure scientist-practitioner model are very much a part of our current debate, and they are further expounded below.

Point: Leisure Research Needs to Relate to Practice

As early as 1900 John Dewey recommended unificationism in the study of learning: that is, linking theory and educational practice with each pursuit stimulating the other. The unificationist view suggests that leisure research should be applied as well as basic. There is something desirable about the involvement of leisure professionals in posing research problems and in their ultimate critique and evaluation. (As an example of how this view is embraced in our field, the *Journal of Park and Recreation Administration* requires all submissions to contain an "Implications" section, and the review process involves at least one practitioner.) Whether or not leisure professionals are equipped to conduct the research and design may be another matter, but the general perspective and concerns of leisure professionals must be reflected in the design of research, lest all the research conducted and its results be so far removed from the immediate practical purposes of the research.

In addition, it can be argued that the epistemology of practitioners is more closely affiliated with humanistic values. Thus, the practicing professional "knows" in terms that are related to valued human outcomes. The practitioner uses this or that approach, theory, or technique because he or she "knows" it works. The quality of recreation research is defined in terms of what seems to lead to or produce desired outcomes. Although practitioners would like assurances that their methods are supported by research of high "quality", they often will forego nomothetic conclusions in a given instance because they recognize that each intervention is experimental in nature with the client, group, family, or community serving as its own "control." They also *believe*, based usually on accumulated but often unsystematized data, that a given leisure service or intervention will lead to a given (desired) outcome.

Research and professional education should be melded early in the educational process. For example, educators could use professionally interesting examples to teach statistics,[15] teach students to ask professionally relevant questions, and then teach them the experimental means to test those questions.

Course work on basic professional theory teaches students to think critically about the content of the theory, so why not teach students to test the theories experimentally? Interest in research would also be enhanced by placing a value on professionally based studies, which gain recognition in the department by being the subject of colloquia. In sum, research should not be only an academic exercise. Students' research projects should be valued and encouraged for public consumption. Thus, students would learn the practical skills associated with producing research.

Counterpoint: Leisure Research Doesn't Need to Relate to Practice

Although it has been argued earlier that basic and applied leisure research share scientific unity, the counterposition states that problem solving activities are best described as technology rather than science. Even though the distinction is not always clear, attempts to solve a specific problem in a specific situation without concern for increasing our general understanding of leisure and human behavior are more akin to technological research or social engineering than to science. Technological researchers may borrow the theories of science to guide their problem solving, but their efforts are not designed to test generalizable propositions derived from these theories. Technological research may generate information that is useful in leisure settings—such as providing an indication of what variables are important in a given recreational setting, stimulating leisure research, or refining methodological tools and innovations—but the research is so problem- and situation- specific that generalizations to other settings are limited.

Leisure science and leisure technology are further distinguished because leisure scientists must strive for a consensus of rational opinion over the widest possible field. Technology does not attempt to gain consensus, for it is focused on solving a specific problem; it provides the "means to do a definite job"— provide a junior aerobics program, generate corporate support for a decathalon event, produce a better agency brochure. In consequence, the technological leisure investigator owes primary responsibility to his or her employer rather than peers.

Although the actual practice of leisure and recreation may involve a "scientific attitude", it is not science *per se*.[16] For example, although a good theory of recreational benefits may state that increases in factors A, B, and C will benefit clients with D, E, and F characteristics, technological research may be needed to determine the optimal levels of A, B, and C, approaches to varying these factors, and ways to assess D, E, and F. Few theories in leisure are so precise that they yield mathematical statements describing the magnitude of important variables, and so recreation practitioners must turn to situation-specific and client-specific research to obtain the precision they require.

It is precisely this predominant concern with the specific that fuels the thesis that leisure research does not need to come directly from, or relate directly to, every day practice. Instead of being overly preoccupied with practical application, we should rather be working to generate systems and models that will interrelate service, interpersonal, and therapeutic variables. Instead of being concerned about how similar a specific leisure time/space event of a study is to a specific leisure time/space event in service or therapy, we should creatively reconstruct how the relations among events differ in various leisure environments or settings and induce transituational statements about these differences. Rather than limiting our focus only to therapeutic settings, we should generate theories of such wide scope that they apply to a host of interpersonal situations.

Leisure will not be better understood by overvaluing generalizability of findings, but by the energetic application of the scientific model to generate a theory of biological, social, interpersonal, and psychological relationships that specifies how the dynamics of leisure and nonleisure situations differ. In addition, increased effectiveness of leisure delivery systems will not come from direct application of research results to practice, but from the application of theory to practice. Events generated for research purposes are applications of theories to a specific time and place, just as recreational therapy is an application of a theory to a particular client with a particular problem in a specific treatment location. Theories that explain leisure outcomes must, in many ways, be capable of explaining outcomes in many other types of settings.

ON METHOD: THE "ARTIFICIALITY" OF LEISURE RESEARCH

The current controversy over the need for research to drive practice, versus the need for practice to drive research is complicated further by debate over the methodology to be meaningfully employed in such research. While in many ways the issues of focus and method cannot be divorced, nevertheless, the debates about setting and experimental rigor may be independently raised and presented. With the appropriate acknowledgement that the research question (however "relevant") must precede the choice of methodological design, the critical issue of appropriate settings and types of leisure research are discussed.

Point: The Laboratory Experiment is the Acme for Leisure Research

The "relevance" issue raised in the preceding section is an important issue for leisure research, however, research findings cannot be relevant to anything if the empirical efforts generating them are not valid. Without data that we can trust and believe, leisure theory and knowledge cannot progress. The validity of our methods plays a large role in determining the course and direction of our future research efforts.

A true laboratory experiment offers the ultimate in control; it has been referred to by Kerlinger as "one of man's greatest achievements".[17] In the ideal experiment, the investigator has control over the environment in which the research is conducted, and is able to hold constant or otherwise control the composition of the experimental and control groups, generally by assigning subjects to these groups by matching or randomization. A third type of control in a true experiment is control over the independent variable; the investigator ideally has actual physical control over the independent variable and administers this variable to the experimental group but not to the control group. Finally, the experimenter has the ability to measure the values of the dependent variable both before administering the treatment and after administering it.

Often because of practical limitations, the experimenter is unable to exercise all four forms of control. However, in field-based research, the researcher can control virtually nothing, as the study is conducted in the natural environment rather than in the laboratory. In the natural setting, there are a potential wealth of extraneous factors which could be impinging at any one time during the study, and which are usually outside of the control and often the knowledge of the investigator.

The basic goal of science is theory.[18] The goal of any theory is to go beyond description to explain and predict; theories attempt to answer the why and how questions. Experimental research offers the opportunity to demonstrate causal relationships, and thus to develop and test theory. The higher degree of potential control which is characteristic of experimental research allows the researcher to generate cause-and-effect conclusions from his/her data. There is virtually no possibility for such causal conclusions in field-based research.

Many laboratory studies certainly involve highly artificial situations, however, they may still be relevant to recreation problems if they examine theoretical generalizations that are transferable to these applied problems.[19] For example, suppose a recreation therapist is asked to choose between two therapeutic approaches. The first, approach X, has never been applied to a clinical population, but in over two dozen laboratory studies the approach has perfectly predicted behavior change. Approach Y, in contrast, has never been tested in the laboratory, but in one study conducted with clients at a Veterans Administration Hospital, several of the factors emphasized in the approach were positively correlated with improvement. What approach should be used? To many therapeutic recreators, approach Y may seem to be the more appropriate choice because it was supported by field research. However, what if the clients are verbally skilled female teenagers, and the subjects in the study of approach Y were Vietnam War combat veterans with only limited verbal abilities? In contrast, what if the laboratory studies examined the effects of dietary factors on behavior and found that the behavior the recreation therapist wished to increase could be reliably obtained by modifying the client's diet?

The generalizability of a theory from one situation to another depends more on the theory than on the results that support it. Although approach Y was corroborated in a field setting, if its theoretical structure cannot explain what effect gender, age, verbal skill, type of agency, etc. have on the therapy outcome, then it does not generalize to the new situation. If, however, approach X is based on a physiological explanation of behavior that applies to a wide range of individuals, then its generalizability is far greater. In summary, generalizability is determined more by the structure of the theory—its scope, specificity, and universality—than by the location of its supporting research.

Counterpoint: The Laboratory Experiment is Not the Acme for Leisure Research

Although many authors try very hard to keep the door open to all kinds of research methods, eventually it becomes clear that most view the controlled experiment as the ultimate refinement in leisure research.[20] Other methods may be all right for exploratory stages, but when push comes to shove, when we want to demonstrate cause-and-effect, it's the controlled experiment that will do the job. Perhaps that position is valid in the physical sciences, but it makes some huge assumptions when applied to the behavioral sciences. (There are exceptions in the physical sciences, too. Consider the work of Darwin, Einstein, Shapley, and Leakey. Are they not scientists and researchers? In psychology, among the giants are Freud and Piaget. Were they scientists?)

Labelling the experimental design "precise" or "rigorous" does not make it so. Random assignment of individuals, for example, might mean something if one were dealing with hundreds of people. But in small sample studies, it is a huge assumption to believe that just because they have been assigned to the group at random the few individuals in the experimental group are comparable in all important qualities to those in the control group. Statistical tests of significance are no substitute for the simple logic that says: You need a large number of cases before you can assume that the process of random assignment will provide two groups that are reasonably equal in all important variations (including those we don't know are important).

Further, it is beyond reality to assume that any experiment can actually control all pertinent factors save the independent variable. We don't begin to understand what the pertinent factors are in people, in clients, in situations, and in the interaction of all these variables with each other and with other possible causal factors. So the frequent assumption that the experiment can, and does, identify cause-and-effect is rarely realized in the practice of leisure research.

Another flaw in the reasoning that would have us generalize from controlled laboratory experiments to real life is that in real life people do not get assigned to each other, to problems, and to time and place at random. If we really want to shed light on leisure, we must either study real life or simulate in the laboratory *all* the conditions in leisure in real life that might possibly be important in determining cause-and-effect. From this point of view, the ultimate test would be a naturalistic field study that is done with whatever rigor is possible.

Even if we knew what the pertinent factors are, "rigor" assumes that we can indeed measure each pertinent variable with some degree of precision. Compared to measurement in physics and chemistry, our measurement is so crude as to be hardly worth calling measurement. Of course, we must be as systematic and precise as reality permits, but at the same time we must recognize that we may delude ourselves into believing that thousands of numbers carried out to several decimal points and spewed forth quickly by a computer are evidence that the data underlying the numbers are indeed being measured precisely. Atoms and chemical events don't have self-consciousness, perceptions of each other, values, attitudes, or feelings. People do have all these complex qualities, and more, a fact that undoes most dreams of real rigor and control in research designs of all kinds.

CONCLUDING COMMENTS

On Theory . . .

As leisure researchers, it is our goal to harness the powers of science in a manner that will help us refine human services. This might sound like a rather straightforward undertaking, requiring only a knowledge of scientific methods and the opportunity to apply them to problems of setting X or individual Y. As it turns out, however, few undertakings are quite as ambitious as the scientific study of human interactions. This may be due in part to our poor understanding of the nature of science. At this point in time, for example, no acceptable criterion has been established for the demarcation of science from nonscience. We must therefore proceed with humility about our understanding of what it is that constitutes "good scientific research" and show considerable tolerance for statements that convey relativity and tentativeness.

On Relevance . . .

Leisure research should be as basic as it is applied. Basic research provides the initial evidence concerning theoretical propositions and hence represents the first hurdle that any explanation of human action must possess. The second hurdle, however, is the successful application of the theory to practice. As in medicine, basic research should be inextricably linked with applied research to guard against the limitations of each pursuit. If too applied, research can become theoretically simplistic, situationally restricted, and technologically oriented. In contrast, basic researchers sometimes develop elaborate theoretical conceptualizations that have little relationship to reality or lose sight of the social value of their findings. Leisure scientists can reach their goal of helping others only if applied researchers make use of theories *and* basic researchers develop theories that can be applied to important problems.

On Method . . .

The perfect experiment has yet to be designed and is, in some sense, inconceivable.[21] Even if it were conceivable, however, it is a safe bet that it would be impossible to execute. Among other things, the human element in science makes research an inevitably fallible endeavor. Let us therefore dismiss the notion of an ideal experiment and instead devote our attention to the continuum of fallible effort along which all experiments must fall.

A phenomenon may be examined from different perspectives. A leisure activity can be approached in terms of the physics of movement, economics, the psychological state of the participants, in medical terms, and so on. Such accounts may all be true; they are complementary or orthogonal, not conflicting. Thus, let us not condemn one type of methodology or hail one particular context over another. Today's science may well be tomorrow's alchemy. It is imperative that we learn from our previous research efforts to continue our attempts to refine our empirical study of recreation and leisure.

Finally . . .

Several decades ago at a renowned midwestern university, Professor Morris took her teaching assistant aside and said:

> Today, Jules, I am going to teach you a lesson you will never forget. When you teach undergraduate students, it doesn't matter way you say, it's how you say it. No matter how trite a statement is, no matter how banal, no matter how meaningless, you can easily get undergraduate students to write it down in their notebooks.

Jules followed Professor Morris to their class on "Research Methods in Parks, Recreation, and Leisure." Professor Morris began the lecture to 38 undergraduate students in her usual manner, but midway through the hour she stopped. In the silence that followed she looked each class member in the eye for a brief instant, then jabbing the air with her finger as she slowly enunciated each word, she said, *"Leisure research is a very good thing."* Scribble, scribble, scribble went thirty-eight pens in thirty-eight notebooks as every undergraduate student wrote down those seven precious words.

I think of that incident now because there is an implicit supposition in this chapter that research about leisure is a very good thing: we don't do enough of it, and sometimes we don't do it very well, but we surely should be doing it more often and better and we should be training even our youngest students to do it. As the three issues raised in this chapter attest, even those who are actively doing the leisure research don't agree about "What is quality leisure research?", "What is meaningful leisure research?", or "How can the quality of our research be improved?" These issues are raised to stimulate thought, provoke discussion, and perhaps cause us to question some of our underpinnings and ultimately aggressively address these questions.

Despite these issues, criticisms, and misgivings, I believe the future of our profession rests upon our unanimously assenting to this one proposition: *Leisure research is a very good thing.* Write it down.

REFERENCES

1. Kuhn, T. S. *The Structure of Scientific Revolutions.* Chicago, Illinois: University of Chicago Press, 1962.
2. Kuhn, T. S. *The Structure of Scientific Revolutions (2nd ed.)* Chicago, Illinois: University of Chicago Press, 1970.
3. For example, see: Burton, T. L. "The maturation of leisure research." In Goodale, T. L. & Witt, P. A. (Eds.). *Recreation and Leisure: Issues in an Era of Change.* State College, Pennsylvania: Venture Publishing, 1980, pp. 373-385. Thorsteinson, W. "Beyond professionalism." *Ibid.*, pp. 269-279. Witt, P. A. "Capturing the service market: Licensure, certification, accreditation." *Ibid.*, pp. 280-286.
4. For example, see: D'Amours, M. "Leisure sciences and studies: Indicators of interdisciplinarity?" *Leisure Sciences.* 16(3), 1984, pp. 359-373. Thorsteinson, *Op. Cit.* Van Doren, C. S., Holland, S. M., and Crompton, J. L. "Publishing in the primary leisure journals: Insight into the structure and boundaries of our research." *Leisure Sciences.* 16(2), 1984, pp. 239-256.
5. For example, see: Burdge, R. J. "Leisure research and park and recreation education: Compatible or not?" In Goodale, T. L. and Witt, P. A. (Eds.). *Recreation and Leisure: Issues in an Era of Change (2nd ed.).* State College, Pennsylvania: Venture Publishing, 1985, pp. 343-351. Burdge, R. J. and Beckers, T. "Breaking the one-way mirror: The increased isolation of North American leisure research." *World Leisure and Recreation Association.* 1984, pp. 11-16. Iso-Ahola, S. "Concerns and thoughts about leisure research." *Journal of Leisure Research.* 18(3), 1986, pp. iv-x. Smith, S. L. J. and Haley, A. F. "Ratio ex machina: Notes on

leisure research." *Journal of Leisure Research.* 11(2), 1979, pp. 139-143.
Tinsley, H. E. A. "Limitations, explorations, aspirations: A confession of
fallibility and a promise to strive for perfection." *Journal of Leisure
Research.* 16(2), 1984, pp. 93-98.

6. Bunge, M. "Towards a philosophy of technology." In Michalos, A. C.
(Ed.). *Philosophical Problems of Science and Technology.* Boston: Allyn
and Bacon, 1974, pp. 28-46.

7. Merton, R. D. *Social Theory and Social Structure.* Glencoe, Illinois: Free
Press, 1949.

8. Homans, G. C. *The Nature of Social Science.* New York: Harcourt, Brace
and World, 1967, p. 4.

9. Hilgard, E. R. "Toward a responsible social science. *Journal of Applied
Social Psychology.* 1, 1971, pp. 1-6.

10. For example, see: Burdge and Beckers, *Op. Cit.*: D'Amours, *Op. Cit.;*
Riddick, C., DeSchriver, M. and Weissinger, E. "A methodological
review of research in *Journal of Leisure Research* from 1978 to 1982."
Journal of Leisure Research. 16(4), 1984, pp. 311-321. Tinsley, H. E. A.
"Application of multi-variate analysis procedures in leisure research."
Journal of Leisure Research. 15(4), 1983, pp. 285-289. Tinsley, 1984,
Op. Cit.: Iso-Ahola, *Op. Cit.*: Howe, C. Z. "Possibilities for using a
qualitative research approach in the sociological study of leisure."
Journal of Leisure Research. 17(3), 1985, pp. 212-224. Kelly, J. R.
"Leisure and quality: Beyond the quantitative barrier in research." In
Goodale, T. R. and Witt, P. A. (Eds.). *Recreation and Leisure: Issues in
an Era of Change.* State College, Pennsylvania: Venture, 1980,
pp. 300-314. Howe, C. Z. "Using qualitative structured interviews in
leisure research: Illustrations from one case study." *Journal of Leisure
Research.* 20(4), 1988, pp. 305-323.

11. Platt, J. R. "Strong inference." *Science.* 146, 1964, pp. 347-353.

12. Popper, K. R. *The Logic of Scientific Discovery.* New York: Harper, 1959.

13. Hempel, C. G. *Philosophy of Natural Science.* Englewood Cliffs, New
Jersey: Prentice-Hall, 1966.

14. Goodman, N. *Fact, Fiction, and Forecast (3rd ed.).* New York: Bobbs
Merrill, 1973.

15. Barnett, L. A. "The why, what, and how of research methods." *SPRE
Annual on Education.* 1, 1986, pp. 107-132.

16. D'Amours, *Op. Cit.*

17. Kerlinger, F. N. *Foundations of Behavioral Research (2nd ed.).* New
York: Holt, Rinehart and Winston, 1973, p. 104.

18. *Ibid.*

19. For example, see: Mannell, R. C. "A conceptual and experimental basis for research in the psychology of leisure." *Society and Leisure*. 2, 1979, pp. 179-196. Mannell, R. C. and Bradley, W. "Does greater freedom always lead to greater leisure? Testing a person x environment model of freedom and leisure." *Journal of Leisure Research*. 18(4), 1986, pp. 215-230. Mannell, R. C., Zuzanek, J. and Larson, R. "Leisure states and 'flow' experiences: Testing perceived freedom and intrinsic motivation hypotheses." *Journal of Leisure Research*. 20(4), 1988, pp. 289-304.
20. Iso-Ahola, *Op. Cit.*
21. Weimer, W. B. *Notes on Methodology*. Hillsdale, New Jersey: Lawrence Erlbaum, 1977.

End of Chapter 26

Chapter 27

Leisure Research and Park and Recreation Education: Compatible or Not?

Rabel J. Burdge

Assessment of the structural and organizational problems that confront the future of leisure and recreation research is critical to both those in academic settings and in recreation service agencies alike.[1] While discussion still persists within the academic community about whether or not leisure represents a body of knowledge, there is increasing agreement that leisure represents an important area of study both for its theoretical and practical implications. Among practitioners there is at least respect for the role that research can play in providing insights that can potentially lead to more effective and efficient service delivery. Yet acceptance of the value and role of recreation and leisure research is not universal and rarely unequivocal by either practitioners or academicians.

Problems in accepting leisure as an appropriate area of study may be traced to difficulties in defining the term and what the use of leisure means for the maintenance of a "healthy society." A well adjusted person uses free time properly for individual enhancement. Inappropriate use of free time can lead to breakdowns in the normative structure of society. If leisure time is not used properly by large segments of the population, it is seen as a social problem. Leisure research has become more important as we have sought to understand expressively and intrinsically motivated human behavior as opposed to maintenance or productive activity. Attempts to deal with the "leisure problem" are represented by the development and distribution of recreation programs and facilities.

Recreation and leisure research has had trouble finding a home in either traditional disciplines such as economics or sociology, or in academic departments focusing on professional park and recreation education. Nevertheless, recreation and leisure research has received increased attention over the last twenty-five years. But what of its future? Where will leisure research be "housed?" How well will it be supported and promulgated by academicians within degree programs focused on educating recreation professionals? Is there a place for recreation and leisure research within such traditional disciplines as sociology or economics?

Most of the early social science research on leisure and recreation came from persons trained and housed in traditional disciplines (mainly sociology) with little output from persons located in "park and recreation" type departments. However, few departments of sociology, economics, psychology or geography had the resources to devote portions of their programs to the study of leisure. As a result, Ph.D.'s from traditional disciplines with an interest in the study of leisure sought positions in park and recreation departments.

The renaming of traditional park and recreation departments to leisure studies, recreology or even leisure sciences, was an attempt to lay claim to the study of leisure while continuing to train professionals for park and recreation management careers. Furthermore, the emphasis on leisure as a topic of scholarly study is a reflection of the increasing need of these departments to achieve respectability within the larger academic community. The key question is: Has renaming departments enhanced and expanded leisure research? To shed light on this question, I have reviewed the history of leisure research and the difficulties inherent in pursuing leisure education and leisure research within the same department.

THE BACKGROUNDS AND LOCATIONS OF RESEARCHERS

In the 60s, Kaplan, Burch, Dumazedier, Meyersohn, Foote, Berger, Parker, Clawson, and Brightbill, among others, were the dominant scholars in the emerging field of leisure research. A different generation is now writing the articles and doing the research. However, we are not so much interested in who is doing the work as the disciplines the researchers represent and the contribution of the different disciplines to the supply of refereed leisure research articles. Knowing the background of leisure researchers helps us understand the major theories and methods that have shaped the body of knowledge. In addition, it is useful to examine the disciplinary background and institutional location of editorial board members of major journals that publish leisure research. Editorial groups, which include editors, associate editors and book review editors, are important because they are both the promoters and the gatekeepers of research. Editorial groups decide what gets into print and what is kept out and promote their product by encouraging submissions.

Two journals are recognized as preeminent in the leisure research field: the *Journal of Leisure Research (JLR)* and *Leisure Sciences (LS)*. The editorial boards of both *JLR* and *LS* reflect the multidisciplinary and applied nature of the field. In the early 70s persons from the traditional social science disciplines were dominant. In the late 70s and early 80s persons with degrees from parks and recreation and forestry represented the emerging majority on the editorial boards.

The discipline of the authors whose articles were printed in these two journals has been, and through the early 80s remains, based within the traditional social sciences. Sociologists continue to hold the lead in authorships with persons from forestry a close second. Persons with degrees from park and recreation type departments increased their share of contributions in recent years, but continue to lag behind both forestry and sociology.

Articles published by economists dropped significantly in the last part of the 70s and that pattern continues today. Several of the applied disciplines not normally associated with leisure research, including urban and regional planning, landscape architecture, engineering and business administration/marketing, published a number of articles in the early years of *JLR*, but those contributions have since stopped.

Leisure research is done by persons in a variety of disciplines located in diverse institutional settings. The institutional location of scholars determines the constraints on their research, how they are rewarded and the type of research problem they select. Equally important, their institutional setting influences the way they review and select manuscripts for publication, thus also the focus of the publication.

In the first seven volumes of *JLR* (through 1975), persons from recreation and park departments had the most representation on the editorial boards, with forest experiment stations having significant representation. At about the time that *JLR* was established (1969), the U. S. Forest Service was expanding its recreation research program. This was also a period when attendance was increasing at federal recreation facilities and much research was focused on management problems. Sociology and agricultural/resource economics had the most representation on the editorial boards among the traditional social sciences.

During the late 70s and early 80s, departments of parks and recreation and forestry totally dominated the editorial group of *JLR*. Persons housed in traditional sociology and economics departments had measurably less involvement in the later part of the 1970s; leadership and control of the editorial group had shifted to persons in the applied departments. The institutional location of the *LS* editorial group is proportionally similar to the first seven volumes of *JLR* (through 1975), with the important exception that well over one-third of its members were located in departments of parks and recreation and leisure studies.

The institutional location of authors for both journals underscores the basic trend of where leisure research is done. There are more contributions from authors affiliated with applied departments and less from traditional social science departments. For example, forestry and parks and recreation made up about fifty percent of the authorships in *LS* through the first five volumes. Sociology and geography had slightly more contributions than *JLR* during the late 70s and early 80s, but that may have been because these represent the disciplines of the two founders and co-editors.

There are also important similarities between institutional location of the editorial group and authors of the two journals. The traditional social science departments of sociology and geography as well as the applied discipline of forestry are underrepresented in the editorial groups compared to the amount of materials they publish. On the other hand, parks and recreation departments and forest experiment stations have more editorial representation than authorships.

If these trends continue, we can expect that more of the editorial group, at least of *JLR*, will be concentrated in departments of forestry and parks and recreation. Being an independently owned journal, the editorial board of *LS* will probably maintain a good diversity in institutional location. The authors of articles published in both journals will more likely come from the applied departments as rewards for multidisciplinary research decrease in traditional social science departments.

In total, the authors and the location of leisure research has shifted from traditional social science departments such as sociology and economics to applied departments like forestry and parks and recreation. But can leisure research be properly nourished in departments that must provide professional training for park and recreation practitioners?

THE LOCATION OF TEACHING AND RESEARCH PROGRAMS

The mission of park and recreation departments has been, and continues to be, one of training practitioners for positions in leisure services agencies. When research was added as a requisite for academic credibility, many faculty resented the additional requirement to publish, particularly if they had not obtained the research skills during their graduate student days. Professors in applied departments were accustomed to addressing problems defined by the practitioner or professional in the field. They were not as supportive of scholarly research directed toward the accumulation of knowledge about leisure. Furthermore, the interconnections between research and teaching was not always perceived or understood by persons in departments that emphasized professional training. The quality and quantity of research produced by departments of recreation and parks may be characterized by an emphasis on application, a disdain for intellectualism and the lack of a research tradition.

In North America, and most particularly the United States, parks and recreation had its roots as a teaching program within Colleges of Education, generally housed within Departments of Health, Physical Education and Recreation. In many universities those departments are now colleges, with each area designated as a separate department. Recreation was taught as a series of skills, which were then combined into recreation and park programs. The content of the classroom materials was based on what seemed to work best for the practitioner.

Chronicling of individual experiences in developing good recreation programs was labelled as research. Research was defined in an "experience" sense rather than by scientific procedures of accumulating verified knowledge. Parks and recreation teaching materials tended to have narrow applicability and seldom could be generalized from one situation to the next. Being applied in orientation, the information base for recreation programs was not the stuff upon which a science is built.

However, teaching from experience is perfectly appropriate for professional training. No conflict would have been present if the graduate programs in parks and recreation that inevitably arose in the quest for academic respectability had not been increasingly staffed by faculty from traditional social science departments. When this happened, graduate programs that emphasized social science research bore little resemblance to undergraduate programs that trained managers to operate park and recreation programs. Park managers need skills ranging from turf management to accounting. The early graduate programs in parks and recreation had a tradition based in the College of Education, which taught methods and techniques. The shift to the study of leisure and recreation behavior represented an attempt to establish leisure as an area of scholarly concern. The process has produced faculties split between undergraduate professional education and graduate research programs.

The previous discussion raises a policy question: should park and recreation departments recruit and retain faculty who have a background in the study of leisure but not practical experience in the field? Perhaps so, but the realities of the university tenure system may not allow the retention of faculty immersed in park and recreation teaching and public service activity but not involved in scholarly research. A recent article by Sessoms helps to further clarify the dilemma:

"... if departments of park and recreation administration continue to build faculties of an interdisciplinary nature, ... rather than ones with training in parks and recreation, they might find themselves with faculties more inclined toward research and the traditional academic reward system. However, the field of parks and recreation may find that students trained under these faculties are ill-prepared as recreation and park practitioners. The profession may discover that universities are no longer preparing students for practitioner roles; university curricula may discover that their students are no longer as employable or interested in employment as recreation practitioners. The same phenomenon occurred in sociology some years ago as sociology ceased to be interested in the preparation of social workers. Consequently, social work evolved its own curricula and program of professional preparation."[4]

LEISURE RESEARCH AND PARK AND RECREATION PROGRAMS

If the amalgamation of parks and recreation and leisure studies is to be successful, then research generated under the umbrella of leisure studies should eventually translate into a body of useful and useable knowledge for the many practitioners in the field. Although accumulated knowledge about leisure has increased, the link to recreation programs has been spotty. Practitioners have
complained that research such as that published in *JLR* and *LS* is incomprehensible and therefore useless for their programs or facilities. They seem much
happier with the "research by experience" reported in *Parks and Recreation*
magazine. There have been several abortive attempts to halt the publication of
JLR by practitioner oriented groups within the National Recreation and Park
Association (NRPA). However, all have failed, because publication of the
journal provides legitimacy for the educational and research functions of NRPA.

Being housed in an applied curriculum, where the interests are practical, has
limited the chances of leisure researchers to address important theoretical and
methodological issues. Research is often funded by organizations interested in
the improvement of leisure delivery systems or the removal of obstacles to
program implementation. Under such a system, each researcher must identify a
management problem and then look for a theoretical framework within which to
study it. In essence, the research problem determines the selection of theory and
methods. For example, if the management problem is campsite vandalism, then
that behavior is singled out for study. The emphasis is on how to get rid of
vandalism, rather than how leisure settings differ from other settings in the
frequency and type of vandalism. The emphasis on management precludes the
findings from the study being placed within the leisure literature. Under the
pressure to be practical and relevant we may not be pursuing the theoretical and
methodological advances that an emerging field so badly needs.

FUTURE DIRECTIONS

Can leisure research be conducted within the same department that conducts
park and recreation education? In the late sixties the union seemed promising.
"Leisure studies," a nebulous and uncertain problem area, found an organizational home within an already established university department. The university
administration was excited because research and measurable publication standards would come to a department that previously had little taste for scholarly
writing. The more thoughtful leaders among park and recreation educators saw
a chance for practitioner oriented students to receive a more "liberal" education
made possible by a broader leisure studies curriculum.

The discovery of an administrative home within the university community may ultimately prove to have hampered leisure research. Leisure is broader and research derived from its study has wider implications than simply the evaluation of park and recreation programs. In the process of coming under the parks and recreation umbrella, the number of persons interested in leisure research who felt they could fit within these units declined. As a result, many of the leisure researchers that were not inclined toward the park and recreation movement either sought different organizations or continued their research in the relative isolation of their disciplinary departments. At the same time, the departments of parks and recreation that attempted to label their graduates as leisure studies majors were having difficulty marketing students to practitioners who operated the leisure services systems.

Given the above problems, what steps need to be taken to insure the further development of leisure research? The following are a few suggestions on how the problem might be dealt with and perhaps provide the opportunity for both leisure studies and parks and recreation education to flourish in the decades ahead.

1. One solution, at least in the short term, would be for Institutes of Leisure Studies to be established. People trained in traditional disciplines could return to their home discipline and hold joint appointments in that department and the research institute. Thus, they could teach within their own field, while working with a multi-disciplinary research team in their interest area. Graduate students could receive training within these institutes but would earn their degrees within an established discipline. The institutes would retain ties to park and recreation departments but would not be identified solely with them. Parks and recreation departments could then concentrate on providing quality professional preparation for undergraduates and terminal master's degree students and be evaluated on that basis, rather than research productivity, assuming tenure and promotion criteria permit it.

2. The American Leisure Studies Association should be established as a meeting ground for scholars and scientists representing the breadth of disciplinary interests in leisure. Here they could meet, exchange ideas, and present papers on leisure and recreation theory, methodology and the substantive accumulation of findings. As the name implies, the Association would have as its central focus the theory and methods of leisure studies. One would attend the meeting to exchange research findings on that topic. The American Leisure Studies Association, like its counterparts in other parts of the world, would be supportive of organizations devoted to training leisure service delivery professionals as well as the applied aspects of leisure research.

3. A separate Department of Leisure Studies would, of course, be an optimal solution. However, in North America, only at Trois Riviere, in Quebec, has the study of leisure flourished on an independent basis. A few leisure studies type departments and institutes are active in Europe, where a distinction is made between theoretical and independent research in scientific institutes and applied research done by non-academic, commercial organizations.

In an earlier portion of this chapter, it was shown that editorial control of leisure research has shifted to persons housed in park and recreation and forestry departments. It may be that in a period of reduced funding levels and hiring freezes that the study of leisure as a scholarly pursuit can only be kept alive by support from an applied department. If those are the short-term political realities, then the issues raised in the later portion of this chapter must be understood and discussed by faculty members in departments where both "leisure studies" and "park and recreation education" is practiced.

Regardless of the location of leisure studies, the university research community, as well as state and federal governments, must recognize that the study of leisure is necessary for understanding social change in post-industrial societies. The importance of understanding leisure for individual and societal development has already been established for other countries and will become important in North America as all those trends in leisure we have talked about over the last three decades begin to come true.

REFERENCES

1. This chapter was adapted from: Burdge, R. J. "Making Leisure and Recreation A Scholarly Topic: Views of a Journal Editor," 1972-1982. *Leisure Sciences.* 6(1), 1983, pp. 99-126.
2. Discipline refers to the major department from which the Ph.D. or Ed.D. was obtained, even though the place of employment may be different upon graduation. Data supporting the conclusions in this section are detailed in Burdge, R. J. *Op. Cit.* pp. 110-117.
3. Portions of this section are taken from: Burdge, R. J. "The Coming Separation of Leisure Studies from Parks and Recreation Education." Keynote paper for the annual meeting of the Leisure Research Symposium, Orlando, Florida, October 21, 1984.
4. Sessoms, H. D. "Research Issues in Park and Recreation Education: An Overview." *Leisure Sciences.* 6(3), 1984, p. 333.

End of Chapter 27

Chapter 28

Spirits Sacred and Secular: Context as Bias in Leisure Research

Thomas L. Goodale

A professor at the California Institute of Technology has suggested a method for determining the credibility of works of a theoretical nature. So along with Murphy's Law, Parkinson's Law and Peter's Principle, David Politzer suggests what might best be called "The Volkswagon Criterion." It states:

> Never believe a theoretical paper unless you can fit all the authors into a Volkswagon. If there are more than that, it means no one person has thought the whole thing through.[1]

In science and in art, creative individuals often "think the whole thing through." The more precise the questions to be answered and problems to be solved, the more likely individuals can and do provide answers and solutions. But more questions and problems are complex. And so we have deliberative bodies, panel discussions, think tanks, and interdisciplinary teams for this and that. That is also why the search for relationships, understanding theories, facts and laws is conducted publicly. Thus research literature accumulates, publicly and communally, into a body of knowledge.

This exploration of the biases of (or in) the body of leisure research is an individual one, but also a public one. It is for sharing, perhaps also for shredding. Whatever the result, the more important matter is that the issue be joined. What are the biases in leisure research, where do they come from, and what difference does it make?

The perspective here is that of one neither immersed in nor divorced from leisure research. From that perspective, it appears that—all considered—the body of leisure research is in adequate health. To be sure, there remains some pseudo-sophistication, an example being a phrase like "peripheral parameters of the age cohort." (I have tried to figure that out: I think it means age range.) To be sure there is an air of stridency around some of it, including appeals to each other for constantly improving the quality of leisure research. To be sure there remain communications among researchers in which the art of civility appears to have been sacrificed to the faculty of criticism. All that is understandably the exuberance of a still young science.

In addition to that, leisure research encompasses a variety of viewpoints; perhaps biases is the appropriate term. Some, for example, are concerned that too few leisure researchers are well versed in multivariate statistical techniques;[2] others wonder whether or not the quantification imperative may not be too limiting for a young science.[3] Views as diverse as this are a sign of good health. Further, it is axiomatic that the skepticism integral to the practice of science be applied to one's own work as well as to the work of others. Thus when highly respected researchers note that perhaps it is fortunate that the research output is far behind attempts to formalize scientific planning and design of leisure experience,[4] one can be assured of a healthy skepticism and a healthy body of research.

Perhaps there is a health-maintaining system "built in" to leisure research. Since freedom, or at least perceived freedom, is a fundamental attribute of leisure, the pursuit of explanatory power by would-be autonomous persons is bound to incorporate a certain amount of ambivalence; most of us would like to be exempt from the laws we are trying to discover. Consequently, while appreciative of the analysis and insights of many informed commentators, it may be that leisure research is not seriously plagued with biases, or conversely, is plagued by such a variety of them that the body of leisure research remains in reasonably good health.

Three related observations, biases if you will, about leisure research are briefly discussed in the following pages. First, the bodies of leisure researchers are occupied by spirits other than the spirits of curiosity and inquiry. Second, the biases that may be evident in leisure research are not so much the biases of leisure research as the biases of the culture in which leisure research takes place. Third, the biases are evident not only in what is present in, but also what is missing from, the body of leisure research.

SPIRITS IN CONTEXT

Curiosity and the spirit of inquiry are the sacred spirits moving within us. Were there only sacred spirits, the body of leisure research would likely be different: probably smaller, conceivably better. The voluminous work on intrinsic and extrinsic motivation points to the likelihood of such an outcome.

However, extrinsic motivations, secular spirits if you will, are evident in a variety of ways. When Greg Buhyoff stepped down as editor of the *Journal of Leisure Research*, he observed cycles of recurring phenomena in the life of an editor. One such phenomenon was the increased number of telephone calls inquiring about the status of manuscripts during those weeks prior to updating vitaes and resumes for submission to deans and committees charged with assessing department, faculty and university personnel.[5]

A second manifestation of secular spirits at work results from the pursuit of funding. In most universities the number and amount of grants received by individuals and departments is an important evaluation criteria. Thus there are, among researchers, whether in leisure or any other domain, those who do research on anything that can be funded. That is not necessarily a bad thing, but it is a force which shapes the kind of work undertaken, thus also the kind that is not. Individuals' research interests may be deferred or lost in the process.

This is an old argument, of course, though the state of the economy and the financing of universities raise the question anew. Many universities are redoubling efforts to attract private financing, much of which takes the form of contract research. University overhead charges are often a substantial percentage of the contract amount. Too, the flow of funds available for academic or noncontract research has become a trickle, a highly politicized trickle.

In the quest for private-sector financial support, the dominance of faculties of medicine, science and engineering, law, and more recently commerce or business may become even greater than at present, probably to the detriment of the arts, humanities and social sciences. Even in psychology, private funding likely favors experimental psychology and such hyphenated fields as psychopharmocology; clinical psychology a poor second and social psychology a poorer third, and social psychology is one of the main disciplinary bases of leisure research. The concern, then, is the potential distortion not simply of leisure research as of the tradition and provision of liberal education. But even with funding, among those extensively involved in contract research on parks, recreation and leisure-related topics are those who perceive their own work as hack research, devoid of much of the intellectual challenge, creativity and fun. Without those attributes, academic undertakings of every kind become merely work, usually harried work.

Another manifestation of secular spirits at work is that leisure research is anything but leisurely and becomes, necessarily, geared more to production than discovery. As funding sources change their priorities, or as old sources are replaced by other sources with other priorities, research tends to become the result of sporadic forays into this subject or that. Conversely, when topics are pursued in a sustained, long-term fashion, articles appear which report not so much completed research as work in progress. Deans and personnel committees are singularly unimpressed with vitaes which report work in progress. So whether sporadic foray or work in progress, the result is a literature more fragmented than one might hope. Of course the breadth of the field and the limited number of outlets for some of the work contributes to producing the same effect.

Because secular spirits demand productivity, they also demand efficiency, especially of a researcher's time. Money for leisure research usually enables the researcher to buy the time and services of others. Thus within a research enterprise, specialization and division-of-labor increase efficiency. But they also tend to shape the methods and techniques employed. Not every kind of research lends itself to division of labor such as is possible, for example, with surveys. Perhaps that is one reason for the preponderance of surveys in leisure research, and the lack of other methods.

The other secular interest served by methods permitting such specialization is that the Volkswagon may be crowded, if not overflowing, with co-authors, thus dramatically increasing the passenger miles per gallon.

CULTURAL BIASES WRIT LARGE

This is not so much a criticism of leisure research as a gnashing at the secular bits by which it is held in tight rein: not so much a comment on the biases of leisure research as the cultural context which shapes it. Among the characteristics of that context has been the shift from monism to pluralism, perhaps extending even to atomism. So it is not surprising, then, that social philosophies like utilitarianism and pragmatism find expression at the individual level. It is also not surprising to find within the body of leisure research much diversity, leading to fragmentation and growing splits between this and that. The volume of information alone requires increasing specialization which reinforces the trend.

The growing split between leisure research and parks and recreation has been noted in the previous chapter. Not long ago Steven Smith and Arthur Haley commented on the apparent divorce of theory and empiricism, noting the atheoretical nature of much empirical work and the lack of empirical support for work of a theoretical nature.[6] One might also argue that research is increasingly divorced from scholarship or that scientific creativity and imagination is increasingly divorced from scientific methodology and techniques. The cultural dualism dividing the artistic and literary group from the scientific, noted by C. P. Snow some 25 years ago, seems also to have evolved to pluralism and perhaps atomism.[7] It is often jokingly observed that even within a discipline, sociology is the common example, those from one section of the country have trouble understanding those from other parts.

Yet there is much that is compelling in the parallels in the creative process in science and art and much compelling in depicting sociology, again by way of example, as an art form.[8] The best science and the best art does not sacrifice imagination, creativity or the desire to communicate to jargon or to the methods or techniques at hand. Among many possible examples are two from the work of former colleagues in Canada. A young psychologist, now at McGill University, observed how pleased those engaged in various self-improvement courses seemed to be with their progress, though empirical evidence was lacking. He discovered a strong tendency for people to depreciate their level of competence at the start of their self-improvement activities. His thesis, "Getting What You Want by Revising What You Had" was imaginative, technically sound, literate and fun.[9]

Another psychologist, this one at Carleton University, has been engaged the past few years in "personal projects" research.[10] Its focus is not upon subjects, instruments and experimental situations important to researchers but on the projects large and small that individuals are engaged in in the context of everyday life. One of the preliminary findings will be mentioned later on. The principal point is that the many splits and divisions that seem increasingly characteristic of the body of leisure research are understandable but not inevitable. Works that are imaginative, comprehensive and literate can be just as scientific as work in which some of these attributes are compromised by limiting designs to those projects for which methodological tools are available.

Other researchers have noted the fragmentation and have advanced suggestions and made efforts to help bring more coherence and comprehensiveness to the leisure research literature. In undertaking a book-review editorship, Tinsley, among others, encouraged comprehensive reviews of a body of literature rather than reviews of single books in which reference to other recent, related materials is usually absent.[11] Similarly, Iso-Ahola, in assuming a journal editorship, expressed receptivity to review articles and to occasional theme issues.[12] These are encouraging efforts. But here again, secular influences may restrain such efforts. Review articles however well done, do not have the status, in many quarters, of research articles. Reviews contribute much more than reward struc-tures reward. The preparation of such reviews is difficult academic work which, once references have been gathered, does not lend itself to efficient divisions of labor. Book reviews, even comprehensive ones full of good insight and analysis, count little—if at all.

BIAS BY OMISSION

The volume of research articles published by those trained in psychology seems quite consistent with the dominant notion that leisure is an individual matter and the dominant socio-cultural trend toward individualism and individuation. Second largest in volume of articles published is from the area encompassing natural resources, resource economics, and forestry. This, too, is understandably part of traditional recreation resource interests and reflects the opportunity for research not only in academia but also resource-oriented agencies of government, particularly those at national, provincial or state levels.

The balance of the leisure research reported is scattered over a dozen or more fields of study.[13] Thus psychology and natural-resource orientations are predominant. Surely there are biases within these orientations though the greater bias appears to be not within what is present but between what is present and what is not.

Among the social sciences, the disciplines of economics and political science are notably under-represented in the leisure research literature. Yet leisure, which is generally operationalized as time free from work and other obligations, is a dependent variable. At the collective level it is profoundly dependent upon economic and political forces. No doubt there are a number of reasons for the comparative dearth of materials from these disciplines in the body of leisure research. But among those reasons may be the almost exclusive focus upon leisure as an individual as opposed to a collective phenomenon. Perhaps, too, except for econometrics, economics and politics are inextricably tied not only to each other but to value-laden social, political and economic philosophies. This is uncomfortable terrain for value-free inquiry. Again, there appears to be a parallel between tendencies in the culture and leisure research. The transition from monistic to pluralistic and perhaps atomistic value systems comes at some point to mean that there may be so many value systems as to have, essentially, none. There seems also a tendency in the culture to perceive human institutions as incapable of any right and individuals as incapable of any wrong.[14] Nonetheless, political scientists and economists have few difficulties wading into value-laden waters to explore human institutions including work, leisure, income distribution, welfare, democracy, community and so much more. Most of them are quite explicit about the values involved, often including their own value positions. Presumably we all value leisure, work, democracy, community and all the rest. Despite that, leisure at the collective level, deeply interpenetrated with social, political and economic forces, has not been incorporated into the body of leisure research.

This seems the case, at least, for the body of research reported in the *Journal of Leisure Research* and *Leisure Sciences*, arguably the two most prestigious North American leisure research journals. Work reflecting more of a collective focus and more of a political and economic orientation is more likely found in European and British publications such as *Leisure Studies* or even the publication emanating from (mainly French) Quebec, *Loisir et Societe*. This, in turn, appears to reflect if not biases then surely traditions of the different cultures.

The growing split between leisure research and parks and recreation may be in part a function of this void in the body of research. Parks and recreation, including both public- and private-sector involvement, is inextricably bound to political and economic forces. Secular as well as sacred spirits move among practitioners, too. And those secular forces make the gap between leisure research and park and recreation practice even wider.

The split may be unfortunate for all concerned for there seems to be much fertile ground upon which leisure research and parks and recreation could grow. At the present time, park and recreation practitioners are in great need of effectiveness measures. In recent years, evaluation research has become topical in many agencies and programs. In Canada, there is growing interest in "comprehensive auditing," particularly of public-sector activities. The comp-audit includes effectiveness, in addition to the traditional auditing of economy, efficiency, and accountability. Value for money is being demanded at all levels of government. Leisure research could contribute more. Practitioners' difficulties with evaluation, effectiveness or benefit measurement is partly the result of ill-formulated problems: that is, non-researchable problems. Yet implicit in most decision making are hypotheses of an if-then nature which can be reformulated in researchable ways. Problems of measurement, of course, are difficult. Further, limited resources and constant public and political surveillance may preclude much experimentation. They may also make it difficult to fail, and what kind of research is it that cannot support a null hypothesis?

Related to this is the fact that the concept of need has almost totally disappeared from both the research and professional literature. This is especially true at the collective level—how much of what service does this community need? —but also at the individual level—has someone's affiliation need, for example, been met? Rather we speak of wants, desires, preferences and demands. Perhaps the concept of need is simply to ambiguous. Perhaps people do not need much. But perhaps we have abandoned the concept of need because it begs a question that is evaluative. Wants and desires contain their own closures: that is, we want what we want because we want it. Need is without closure. The concept demands explication. We don't need something because we need it, we need something in order for something else. Whatever that something else is, it is value laden and collective in a way that parallels the process of counter reinforcement. We attempt or do not attempt to meet needs according to judgments about the purposes to be served by so doing. If we cannot be explicit about our purposes, we cannot engage in evaluation or effectiveness research.

The lack of work on recreation benefits and on service effectiveness is only one of many voids in the literature which leisure researchers might appropriately address. Matters related to the distribution of work and thus the distribution of both income and non-work time are clearly of interest, as are matters related to the political processes of distributing leisure resources. Technological impacts and assessments of them are important to our understanding, such as the studies undertaken by the Office of Technology Assessment of the United States Congress. The Conference Board in Canada, a highly respected, private, economic research organization, has engaged in a major study of the implications of a three-day work week. Surely the lists of subjects which leisure research might encompass could be a very lengthy one.

One of my biases, related to leisure research and to university education, favors renewed emphasis on liberal studies and reduced emphasis on specialized training. In particular, subjects like history and anthropology should be stressed, and much more historical and anthropological research on leisure would be greatly appreciated. For it seems clear that a broader perspective of ourselves and our times would contribute much to leisure. Perhaps not, though on this matter the arguments of historians and anthropologists are persuasive. Myopia surely contributes to anxiety, and anxiety is a fatal enemy of leisure.[15]

Finally, the personal projects research, noted earlier, is very much a study of leisure, comprehensive and fully integrated into daily life. The starting point is whatever projects people are engaged in. Projects could range from getting some letters written to building a boat and sailing around the world or even to transforming western intellectual thought. Participants in the study also answer dozens of questions related to their projects and to other aspects of their lives, including verbal and other measures of health. Some interesting relationships are emerging from preliminary results. One of the correlates of poor health is that no one else seems interested in the projects engaging the respondents.[16] Are we beginning to identify the limits of individualism and atomism? Are we beginning to identify the break point between tolerance and indifference? Are these, indeed some of the health hazards of our current cultural biases? If that is so, then we should weigh very carefully the values and attitudes shaping our culture and thus our work.

REFERENCES

1. Politzer, D. Cited in: *The University of Ottawa Gazette*, 19:12(July) 1984, p. 13.
2. Tinsley, H. E. A. "Application of Multi-Variate Analysis Procedures in Leisure Research." *Journal of Leisure Research*. 15:4, 1983, pp. 285-289.
3. Cf. Kelly, John R. "Leisure and Quality: Beyond the Quantitative Barrier in Research," In: Goodale, T. L. and Witt, P. A. *Recreation and Leisure: Issues in an Era of Change*. State College, Pennsylvania: Venture Publishing, 1980, pp. 300-314.
4. Mannell, R. "The 'Psychologization' of Leisure Services," In: Goodale, T. L. and Witt, P. A., *Op. Cit.* p. 107.
5. Buhyoff, G. Editor's Notes. *Journal of Leisure Research*. 15:3, 1983, p. iv.
6. Smith, S. L. J. and Haley, A. J. "Ratio ex Machina: Notes on Leisure Research." *Journal of Leisure Research*. 11:2, 1979, pp. 139-143.
7. Snow, C. P. *The Two Cultures and the Scientific Revolution*. New York: Cambridge University Press, 1959.
8. Nisbet, R. *Sociology as an Art form*. New York: Oxford University Press, 1976.
9. Conway, M. "Getting What You Want by Revising What You Had." (Unpublished Master's thesis) University of Waterloo, Department of Psychology, 1983.
10. Little, B. R. "Personal Projects: A Rationale and Method for Investigation." *Environment and Behavior*. 15:3(May) 1983, pp. 273-309.

11. Tinsley, H. E. A. "Some Parting Thoughts." *Journal of Leisure Research*. 10:1, 1978, p. 5.
12. Iso-Ahola, S. "Editorial Philosophy and Policy." *Journal of Leisure Research*. 15:3, 1983, p. v.
13. Cf., Burdge, R. "Making Leisure and Recreation Research a Scholarly Topic: Views of a Journal Editor 1972-1982." *Leisure Science*. 6:1, 1983, pp. 99-126.
14. Cf., Vickers, G. "The Future of Morality." *Futures*, VII:5(October) 1979, pp. 371-382.
15. This is discussed at greater length in Chapter 3.
16. Little, B. In a graduate research seminar, Department of Psychology, University of Ottawa (April) 1982.

(no keep)

p. 376 is blank.
        End of Chapter 28

Chapter 29

Conceptualization and Measurement of Leisure: Making the Abstract Concrete

Gary D. Ellis and Peter A. Witt

What is leisure? The question is simple enough, but the answer is complex. In the preceding chapters, a variety of perspectives and definitions have been offered. But are we any closer to knowing what constitutes leisure? Why is deriving a definition of leisure critical in the first place? Is definitional precision a necessity when we all "know" what the term means anyway? If we have a ballpark notion of what constitutes leisure, isn't that enough?

Achieving definitional understanding and agreement would be nothing more than an intellectual exercise to be pursued by university professors if definitional clarity didn't ultimately relate directly to how public and private recreation services are justified, planned, and evaluated. Just as medical services are dependent on whether health is defined as the "absence of illness" or in terms of quality of life, leisure services will be fundamentally different in purpose and provision depending on how leisure is defined. To better understand the impact of definitions on service delivery, it is necessary to delineate several different approaches that have been taken in defining leisure.

Traditionally, definitions of leisure have been categorized into three groups: time, activity, and state of mind. More recent developments suggest the appropriateness of regrouping these into three major paradigms of leisure: objective, subjective, and dispositional. Neulinger[1] has distinguished between the objective and subjective paradigms. He labels the "time" and "activity" approaches "objective," because criteria external to the experience of the individual can be used to determine what is and what is not leisure. In contrast, the state of mind approach is labeled "subjective" because, under that model, what is and what is not leisure depends upon the perceptions and interpretations of the individual. Further, a "dispositional" approach may be identified which focuses more on characteristics of people's personalities rather than on discrete events and activities. A summary of basic characteristics of these approaches is included in Table 1.

Whether analyzed from the objective, subjective, or dispositional perspectives, it is evident that leisure remains an elusive and abstract concept. Nevertheless, many attempts have been made to define what leisure is, with each

Table1
Major Paradigms of Leisure

PARADIGM	DESCRIPTION	EXAMPLES	MEASUREMENT OF LEISURE
I. OBJECTIVE	CRITERIA EXTERNAL TO THE INDIVIDUAL DETERMINES WHAT IS AND IS NOT LEISURE.	PLAYING A GAME TRAVELING LISTENING TO MUSIC	TIME DIARIES
II. SUBJECTIVE	WHAT IS OR IS NOT LEISURE DEPENDS ON THE OPINION AND PERSPECTIVE OF THE INDIVIDUAL.		
POST HOC SATISFACTION APPROACH	THE QUALITY OF A LEISURE EXPERIENCE IS DETERMINED BY THE SATIASACTION ONE REPORTS FOLLOWING PARTICIPATION.	SATIFACTION WITH OPPORTUNITY FOR RISK TAKING. SATISFACTION WITH RELAXATION EXPERIENCE. SATISFACTION WITH EXPERIENCING NATURE.	RECREATION EXPERIENCE PREFERENCE (REP) SCALES
MEANING AND DEFINITIONAL APPROACH	LEISURE IS ACTIVITY THAT PARTICIPANTS CONSIDER TO BE LEISURE.	ANY ACTIVITY CAN BE CLASSIFIED IN TERMS OF THE EXTENT TO WHICH IT MAY BE DESCRIBED AS LEISURE.	PARTICIPANTS ARE ASKED TO RATE THE EXTENT TO WHICH AN EXPERIENCE WAS LEISURE OR THE SEMANTIC MEANING OF LEISURE IS MEASURED.
IMMEDIATE CONSCIOUS EXPERIENCE APPROACH.	LEISURE IS AN EXPERIENTIAL STATE THAT OCCURS DURING A WELL DEFINED SEGMENT OF TIME.	FLOW AROUSAL PLEASURE FEELING OF "WORK" FEELING OF "JOB"	ESM MEASURE OF FLOW PROFILE OF MOOD STATES. PSYCHOPHYSIO-LOGICAL MEASURES (EDA. EMG. EEG. SKIN SURFACE TEMPERATURE)
III. DISPOSITIONAL	LEISURE IS A RELATIVELY STABLE CHARACTERISTIC OF THE PERSONALITY THAT LEADS ONE TO BEHAVE IN CERTAIN WAYS AND PERCEIVE AND INTERPRET STIMULI IN CERTAIN WAYS.	PERCIEVED FREEDOM IN LEISURE. INTRINSIC MOTIVA-TION ORIENTATION. SELF AS ENTERTAINMENT. LEISURE AS BOREDOM.	LEISURE DIAGNOSTIC BATTERY INTRINSIC MOTIVATION PERSONALITY DISPOSITION SCALE. SELF AS ENTERTAINMENT SCALE. LEISURE AS BOREDOM SCALE.

end of Table 1

position adding unique implications to understanding the role of leisure in people's lives as well as adding different perspectives on leisure service planning, delivery, and evaluation. This chapter is intended to help "make the abstract more concrete" by describing objective, subjective, and dispositional paradigms of leisure and summarizing major efforts to actually quantify leisure within each paradigm.

THE OBJECTIVE PARIDIGM

The objective paradigm includes perspectives on leisure as time and leisure as activity. Under the *time* view, leisure is conceptualized as time left over after the necessities of life have been taken care of. Work, household chores, and other obligations are usually included under the heading of necessities. In this sense, the time approach is a "freedom from" definition. One is free from necessity or obligation. The definition, of course, is fraught with problems. What is obligation or necessity to one person may not be to another. Thus, rather than being objective, the definition is actually subjective since it is based on an individual's perception of what constitutes necessity. Of course, individual perceptions could be ignored and a societal definition of what constitutes obligation and necessity derived. Thus, there would exist a shared, and in that sense objective, understanding of leisure as time left over after work and other obligations have been completed.

Leisure defined as *activity* has also been a popular approach to cutting through the definitional morass. Use of a period of time would be considered leisure if the activity undertaken appeared in an agreed upon list of leisure activities. On the surface, this seems straight forward and objective. If asked, we would probably all include baseball, quilting, and painting on the list. But what if one plays baseball for pay, quilts to create warm clothing for the family, and paints the house so that the exterior surfaces do not deteriorate? Would card playing be included on the list by everyone or does that depend? Would sex be included if it involved adultery, or would that, too depend?

According to some views of the activity approach, to be considered leisure the activity must be moral, wholesome, and contribute to the betterment and welfare of the individual. The morass thickens. Clearly, each of these criteria involves a series of judgments about what is moral or wholesome, etc. It is easy to see why there is so little agreement on what constitutes leisure. In the final analysis, the activity approach seems to be largely based on a subjective perception of moral, wholesome, betterment and a host of equally difficult to define criteria. This approach may be comforting but it is hardly objective.

THE SUBJECTIVE PARADIGM

State of mind, or "subjective" approaches to defining leisure are based on the assumption that leisure resides in the mind of the participant. According to this view, we can never be sure that we are directly observing someone at leisure until we gain an understanding of that person's perspectives, moods, perceptions, thoughts, and feelings at the time that he or she is being observed. There are various state of mind orientations ranging from mood states to psychophysiological "arousal" responses. In typically insightful fashion, Roger Mannell[2] has proposed a classification scheme for the organization of major subjective approaches.

According to Mannell, three major orientations within the subjective paradigm may be considered: the post hoc satisfaction approach, the immediate conscious experience approach, and the definitional/meaning approach. Each of these involves a different set of assumptions about subjective experiences.

The Post Hoc Satisfaction Approach

Under the post hoc satisfaction approach, leisure experiences are equated with participants' levels of satisfaction or dissatisfaction following participation in a recreation activity. Implicit in this model is the assumption that individuals are motivated to participate in activities in order to obtain specific benefits. An individual might choose to spend an afternoon hang gliding, for example, in order to experience risk, feel challenged, or relieve stress associated with his or her daily life. The hang glider's satisfaction with the afternoon's hang gliding experience may be determined after the recreation engagement has ended by determining the extent to which the activity provided the individual with an opportunity to obtain the benefits that he or she was seeking. In this example, those benefits would be risk, challenge, and relieving stress.

The post hoc satisfaction model has been the dominant approach among scholars interested in outdoor recreation resource management.[3] Improved resource management decisions are thought to result from managers' awareness of the benefits being sought by recreationists who visit the areas they manage. If a sizeable number of visitors seek a learning experience by visiting a site, for example, managers might strive to increase interpretation activities and other methods of enhancing the educational opportunities for visitors. Major challenges faced by advocates of the model are the weak correlations between measures of congruency of expectations and outcomes and global measures of satisfaction, the myriad of potential benefits sought, and individual differences in benefits sought.[4]

The Immediate Conscious Experience Approach

The immediate conscious experience approach addresses specific experiential states of individuals during identifiable segments of time. The focus is on such factors as thoughts, feelings, moods, images, and vividness of perceptions. Certain combinations of these factors are considered to be characteristic of leisure experiences. Tinsley and Tinsley[5], for example, presented a comprehensive theory of the leisure experience, suggesting that leisure experiences are characterized by total absorption in the activity, lack of focus on self, feelings of freedom, and enriched perception of objects and events, increased sensitivity to sensations, increased sensitivity to emotions, and decreased awareness of the passage of time. Similarly, Gunter[6] identified the following as characteristics of "pure leisure" experiences:

1. A sense of separation
2. Intense pleasure and enjoyment
3. Freedom of choice
4. Spontaneity
5. Timelessness
6. Fantasy
7. Adventure and exploration
8. Self realization

The common element of these two examples and other "immediate conscious experience" approaches is that they focus on the "actual content"[7] of experiences occurring during leisure behavior.

The impact of the immediate conscious experience approach on recreation and leisure studies has been enormous. Both the "flow" model, which has captured the attention of numerous scholars in recreation and leisure and the "optimal arousal" model, which is of major historical and contemporary significance, clearly fall within the parameters of the immediate conscious experience approach.[8,9]

The Definitional/Meaning Approach

A third perspective on subjective leisure involves the assessment of the extent to which individuals believe that their experiences may be described as leisure. This "definitional" approach does not impose preconceived notions of the facets of experience on people, but instead enables them to define leisure in a way that is most consistent with their personal interpretations of that term. The definitional approach, therefore, is not directly concerned with such factors as the identification of benefits received, "flow" experiences, arousal levels, or mood states. Rather, it is directed at the *meanings* individuals ascribe to experiences; leisure is whatever leisure means to the individual.

Several studies have been conducted that are representative of the definitional approach. Definitional leisure has been found to be different for males and females, for different social situations, and for individuals involved in activities with different degrees of motivation, perceived freedom, and relationship to work.[10,11] Further, the semantic meaning of different activity types has been found to differ across cultures and activity types.[12]

Dispositional Approach

A disposition is a prevailing tendency of an individual toward particular outlooks, moods, or ways of behaving. A few efforts have been undertaken to define leisure as a disposition. These approaches do not focus on specific activities, time, or subjective experiences, but rather on relatively stable beliefs people hold about themselves and ways of responding to different situations. Leisure thereby becomes a part of one's personality, with leisure related dispositions exerting influences on ones' leisure behavior and subjective experiences.

An example of the dispositional approach is Weissinger and Iso-Ahola's concept of orientation to intrinsic leisure motivation.[13] While we generally think of intrinsic motivation as being characteristic of a situation, (e.g., we participate in an activity for intrinsic rewards), Weissinger extended that notion, proposing that some people have a general tendency (disposition) to engage in activities that are intrinsically motivating. In other words, some people ". . . may be more predisposed (than others) to experience a wider range of activities as intrinsically motivating."[14]

Other examples of the dispositional approach to defining leisure are Roger Mannell's "Self as Entertainment" concept.[15], Iso-Ahola and Weissinger's "Leisure as Boredom" concept,[16] and the "perceived freedom in leisure" variable that has been studied extensively by Witt and Ellis.[17] The self as entertainment concept describes the extent to which individuals are able to keep themselves challenged and satisfied in the absence of external stimulation. The leisure as boredom concept is concerned with people's perception of leisure. Boredom, from a dispositional standpoint, is thought to contribute to "deterioration (of) psychological and physical health."[18] Finally, perceived freedom describes individual differences in perception of ability to successfully participate in personally fulfilling leisure activities and thereby placate personal leisure related needs.

SO WHAT?

Besides providing interesting dialogue in leisure studies courses and at park and recreation conferences, what does it matter that differing approaches have been taken to defining leisure? As noted previously, do the definitions impact on how services are actually conceptualized and carried out? The answer is, inevitably, "yes." In brief, if the objective view of leisure is accepted, then we are largely in the free-time activity business. Public or private agencies would be responsible for planning activities that are defined as leisure during non-work, non-obligated periods of time. On the other hand, if leisure is subjectively defined, we need to know more about what is perceived as leisure by each potential participant. The objective approach lends itself nicely to counting how many people show up at a given activity, for leisure is seen in terms of participation in given activities during free time. The subjective approach necessitates our asking what motivates people to participate in an activity and what does each person experience during participation. Success is determined by the individual participant.

While definitions of what constitutes leisure have important implications for the actual delivery of leisure services, only recently have steps been taken to bring a degree of precision to our definitions so that service delivery implications could be fully realized. Whether approaches to defining leisure have been from an objective, subjective, dispositional, or combined perspective, earlier approaches have been based on what Hollander has referred to as social philosophy.[19] Approaching the understanding of leisure from a social philosophy perspective means that we have relied primarily on ideas independent of testable data. We have concerned ourselves with what "should be," resulting in endless debates, excessive rhetoric, and conjecture. The approach has proven to be frustrating in an environment that demands a greater degree of objectivity (i.e., "hard" data or evidence) than found in philosophic discussion. Many of the perspectives described earlier (objective, subjective, dispositional) have, until recently, been approached from primarily a conceptual and pseudophilosophical perspective. Thus, we have argued that leisure is time free from obligation or participation in an "approved" activity. We have only recently embraced what Hollander refers to as social empiricism or social analysis in our attempts to understand leisure.

Social empiricism goes beyond speculation and conjecture. While *social philosophy* deals in what should be, social empiricism focuses on understanding what is. Thus, as noted by Iso-Ahola,[20] in the 1960s the study of leisure began to include time budget studies, attitude and interest surveys, and other means to identify *what* people did in free time or what kind of leisure services were desired.

The *social analysis* approach to understanding leisure has been far less prevalent. Social analysis focuses on *why* people do what they do. It results in theory testing and the verification of hypothesized relationships between variables. It is dependent on "operationalizing" variables such that measurement is facilitated and comparison with other studies is made possible. A social analysis approach allows us to more definitively answer questions such as the following:

- does a relationship exist between perceived freedom and leisure?
- does leisure contribute to health and well being?
- is a particular service meeting its stated objectives?

We are faced with a growing need to provide evidence that our services achieve what they are designed to achieve. To this end, it is not enough to simply assume that either leisure is a necessity in the lives of people or that provided services facilitate people achieving benefits from leisure. Accountability concerns alone necessitate our moving beyond a social philosophy approach to service provision that is based on social analysis. Although progress has been made in that regard, our literature is still woefully weak in taking this approach.

MAKING LEISURE CONCRETE

The social analysis perspective (or, more generally, positivist science) requires measurement. That is, we must not only have agreed upon definitional perspectives in order to understand leisure, but we must also translate those understandings into concrete, quantifiable statements. Quantification allows us to make statements about how much leisure is present in a given set of circumstances. These "how much" questions have important implications to leisure service delivery. How much leisure was produced by my softball tournament? How much did I improve the leisure functioning of my client through leisure counseling? How much did I enhance the quality of visitors' leisure experience by changing the format of my environmental interpretation program? It is through such quantification that we can begin to study and gain knowledge about the conditions which create leisure and the costs, benefits, and outcomes of leisure.

The uninitiated typically cast a doubtful glance on comments about quantification of leisure. How can we assign meaningful numbers to something that is elusive and often subjectively defined? Can pleasure, excitement, and semantic meaning be captured in a petri dish and scrutinized through a microscope? It is, of course, not possible to study experience by looking through a microscope. Rather, one must think of leisure, and other psychological variables, as being like the wind; we cannot see it, but we can learn of its existence by watching its effects on objects in our environment. When the windmill turns the wind is present. This presence has a certain quantity (speed), duration, and interval, each of which we can quantify by observing the effects of the wind on the windmill. We must learn to think of subjective and dispositional leisure in a similar manner. We never really *see* leisure, but by observing its effects on responses to our questionnaires and other measures, we become confident of its presence. In the following section, efforts to measure leisure within each of the three paradigms are illustrated.

MEASUREMENT WITHIN THE OBJECTIVE PARADIGM

The challenge of measurement within the objective paradigm is to derive a quantitative summary of units of expenditure of minutes of mechanical time or some estimate of people's frequency and duration of participation in recreation activities. Two major approaches have been used to obtain such estimates: time diary methods and use of the experience sampling method (ESM). Time diaries are simply records people keep of how they spend their time. In a recent study utilizing time diary methods, Shaw[21] asked 120 couples living in Halifax, Nova Scotia to keep a 48 hour record of time use, spanning a period of one week day and one week end. Extrapolating these data for a one week period, Shaw was able to estimate the average "free time," "leisure time," and "recreation time" for residents over the one week period. Among her many interesting findings were that unemployed housewives had the most "free time" of any other group, but also had the least amount of time that they considered to be "leisure time."

The experience sampling method (ESM) was originally developed to gain data on subjective experiences (immediate conscious experience model), but is also quite useful in generating "objective" measures of leisure. In ESM studies, subjects carry electronic paging devices, typically for a period of one to two weeks. At randomly selected times over the study period, signals are sent to the pagers. When subjects receive a signal, they complete a short questionnaire, which may include "objective" measures of where they are, in what activity they are involved, and with whom they are involved in that activity. Typically, measures of "subjective" variables are also taken at that time.

Voelkl and Birkel used the ESM to gain insight into the time use of nursing home residents.[22] Important differences and similarities in time use were observed for each of five residents. "Sara," for example, spent 44 percent of her time watching television or listening to the radio. In contrast, "Andrew" and "Emily" spent very little of their time watching television or listening to the radio (about 3 percent). Instead, most of their time (65 percent for Andrew and 42 percent for Emily) was spent "thinking and sitting." Other differences were observed in terms of location and companionship. Therapeutic recreation treatment implications for each client were identified from the ESM data. This study provides an important example fo the practical implications of quantification of objectively defined leisure.

MEASUREMENT WITHIN THE SUBJECTIVE PARADIGM

Measurement of Post Hoc Satisfaction

Several noteworthy efforts have been undertaken within the various facets of the subjective paradigm. Within the post hoc satisfaction approach, the most significant effort has been the development of the Recreation Experience Preference (REP) Scales by Driver and his colleagues.[23] The REP scales represent an attempt to measure the major categories fo outcomes that people desire and expect to receive through recreation participation. A total of 16 scales were developed to measure such outcomes as sense of achievement, independence/autonomy, risk taking, social contact, security, and family togetherness. People completing the REP scales are typically asked to indicate their reasons for participating in an activity. Examples of items from some of the scales are "To test the extent to which I can do it," "I thought it would help me feel like a better person," "So I could become better at it," and "To feel my independence."

Use of the REP scales has been widespread in recreation resource management research. Driver and his associates used the concept of focusing on psychological outcomes to develop an "experience based setting management" model for the management of such resources.[24,25] Measurement related issues faced by scholars interested in the future development of these scales include managing and systematizing the myriad of existing and potential outcomes of recreation activities, developing an understanding of the various factors that can affect REP scale scores and developing a more complete understanding or the conceptual link between these measures and the more general concept of recreation satisfaction.[26,27]

Measurement of Immediate Conscious Experience

Most attempts to measure subjective leisure from the post hoc satisfaction approach have followed the model of Driver and his associates. In contrast, a variety of approaches to the measurement of leisure from the immediate conscious experience perspective have been undertaken. These approaches range in scope from self-report questionnaires on daily experiences and mood states[28,29,30] to electronic, psychophysiological measures of activation.[31] Two approaches will be reviewed here: the "optimal arousal" model and the "flow" model. interest in these two models has been widespread among scholars in recreation and leisure studies.

Measurement of arousal. One of the most widely known conceptualizations of subjective leisure in terms of immediate conscious experience that included a measurement component is Machael Ellis' explanation of play as arousal regulating behavior.[32] In *Why People Play*, Ellis reviewed such early theories of play as the recapitulation theory, the relaxation theory, the surplus energy theory, learning theory, and the compensation theory. Ellis' thorough review of these "classical" and "recent" theories clearly showed their inadequacy as explanations for the very complex phenomenon of play. This led Ellis to propose a "modern" theory of play, based on the work of such "arousal" theorists as Berlyne, Hebb, Duffy, Lindsley, and Malmo.

Application of the arousal seeking theory to play behavior led Ellis to the position that play is caused by a constant, physiological need for individuals to maintain an optimal level of interest or alertness. This optimal level of arousal may be maintained by adjusting the novelty and complexity of input from the environment. Thus, a child needing to heighten his/her level of arousal to the optimal might think of new uses for an old toy (increase novelty and complexity) and a frightened youngster during his/her first visit to the dentist might reduce a too high level of arousal by playing with a familiar toy (reduce novelty) which an insightful parent encouraged him/her to bring. Play, therefore, become a mechanism by which individuals regulate their levels of arousal.

The application of the arousal seeking theory to the study of play was a significant departure from earlier efforts because arousal is a measurable, physiological phenomenon. Unfortunately, early play researchers found the measurement of arousal to be quit complex. Three studies in which play researchers sought to"...observe the arousal mechanism in action"[33,34,35] led to the conclusion that "new and more robust measures" were needed before meaningful studies could be conducted on play as arousal regulating behavior.[36]

The absence of related follow-up studies suggests that play researchers have not actively pursued "new and more robust" measures of arousal. Researchers in psychophysiology have noted consistently weak intercorrelations between different measures of arousal and now distinguish between different forms of arousal.[37] Rather than assuming the existence of a strong arousal "common factor" affecting various systems equally and simultaneously as the studies of play assumed, arousal is now conceptualized as being comprised of a number of unique factors, each associated with a different subsystem within the overall nervous system.[38] Measurement of the impact of each of these unique factors may be more meaningful than an attempt to measure a single common factor. Measures of arousal within the autonomic nervous system, for example, include heart rate, pupil dilation, blood pressure, and skin conductance. Central nervous system arousal can be measured with an electroencephalograph (EEG), and an electromyograph (EMG) can be used to measure arousal within the somatic nervous system. Arousal, obviously, is a very complex phenomenon. Any explanation of play based on arousal theory must take into account its various dimensions. Although the methods of measurement of the different dimensions of arousal are relatively well established, considerable updating is needed of the conceptualization of play as arousal regulating behavior.

Measurement of flow experiences. Another "immediate conscious experience" model of a leisure realted phenomenon that includes both conceptualization and measurement components in Csikszentmihalyi's "flow" model.[39] In
developing this model, Csikszentmihalyi conducted several studies with
individuals who participated regularly in activities demanding intense involvement and optimal challenge. Individuals studied included surgeons, chess
players, rock climbers, and dancers.

Through discussions with these individuals, Csikszentmihalyi was able to
develop a description of what we call the "flow" state. A typical description of
flow was provided by a rock climber:

> Your concentration is very complete. You mind isn't wandering, you
> are not thinking of something else; you are totally involved in what you
> are doing. Your body feels good. Your energy is flowing very smoothly,
> you feel relaxed, comfortable, and energetic.[40]

Six characteristics of flow which Csikszentmihalyi derived from such descriptions were as follows:

1. A merging of action and awareness;
2. A centering of attention;
3. Loss of self consciousness;
4. Perception of great power and control;
5. Noncontradicting demands for action and clear, unambiguous feedback
   concerning the person's actions;
6. The absence of a need for external rewards.[41]

This "flow state" is assumed to result from a balance between the challenges
of the activity and the skills of the participant. When the demand for the activity
outweigh the individual's skills, anxiety is present. When the individual's level
of skill outweighs the demands of the activity, boredom occurs. When the
demands of the activity match the skills of the participant, an individual may
experience a state of "flow."

Like the arousal theory explanation of play, Csikszentmihalyi's flow model
includes a measurement component. Using the flow model, Csikszentmihalyi
and his colleagues have conducted experiential studies in a variety of settings
and have found the model to be useful in the prediction of adults' subjective
perception of well-being.[41] Eight components of the flow model are typically
assessed: self-consciousness, skills, challenges, mood, motivation, sense of
control, how much is at stake, and difficulty in concentrating.

With the exception of mood, each is measured with single items with each
rated on a 10 point scale. The self-consciousness item, for example, is "How
self conscious were you (during the activity)?" "Not at all" is rated zero, while

"very" is scored as a ten. The "mood" component has two parts: affect and activation. Affect is measured with four bipolar adjectives, on a sever point scale: happy-sad, irritable-cheerful, angry-friendly, and lonely-sociable. The activation component is similar, but includes five adjective pairs: alert-drowsy, strong-weak, active-passive, involved-detached, and excited-bored.

This approach to measurement of flow has worked quite well in studies of experiential states. Major challenges that lie ahead include accounting for findings that show less positive experiences at low challenge, low skill tasks and developing an understanding of the role of the self in determining experiences.[42] As leisure research continues the quest for antecedents and outcomes of leisure experiences, the flow model serves to reinforce the position that what happens to people during an activity is also of great interest and concern.

MEASUREMENT WITHIN THE DEFINITION/MEANING APPROACH

The definitional/meaning approach involves an attempt to elicit individual meanings of leisure rather than imposing a-priori assumptions about particular mood states, dimensions fo satisfaction, or other assumptions. In order to avoid imposing these assumptions, it is necessary to measure leisure using methods devoid of extraneous information. One popular approach, therefore, requires asking people to respond to a single question: To what extent do you consider this experience to be leisure?[43,44,45] Responses are made along a ten point scale, ranging from "not leisure at all" to "absolute leisure."

Although this approach has produced results that are consistent with hypotheses, it falls short in providing insight into what leisure actually means to people. Results of studies that utilize this single item measure provide information about the conditions under which definitions *change*, but they do not provide insight into meaning people ascribe to leisure. Within the definitional model, an approach seems to be needed that both provides insight into meaning and enables comparisons to be made across different personal and environmental contingencies.

One solution may be the utilization of the extensive research that Osgood and his colleagues conducted on semantic meaning in the 1950s and 1960s.[46] The general interest of this research group was in identifying the major dimensions people utilize to understand things. Subjects in Osgood's studies were presented with an ambiguous stimulus in the form of a written word (e.g., federal spending, socialism, United Nations) and were asked to indicate the meaning of those stimuli in terms of such bipolar adjectives as good-bad, fast-slow, strong-weak, and happy-sad. Through statistical analysis, Osgood identified three major dimensions along which people make judgments about items: evaluations (e.g., good-bad, beautiful-ugly), potency (e.g., strong-weak, large-small), and activity (e.g., active-passive, fast-slow). Other dimensions such as receptivity, novelty, and aggressiveness appeared in other studies, but were not as stable as evaluation, potency, and activity.

The research of Osgood and his colleagues provides us with an alternative method of measuring the meaning of leisure. Subjects might be presented with a leisure related stimulus and asked to respond along continua of bipolar adjectives representing domains of meaning. Such an approach has been advocated by Tinsley and Tinsley and others[47,48] and one study has actually used that approach[49]. In that study, Ramos compared the meaning of leisure across two cultures and four different activity types, represented in pictures. Results showed significant differences on the meaning in terms of potency and activity across the two cultures and across the activity types. This study provides a basis for future work within the definitional model based on Osgood's work with semantic meaning.

MEASUREMENT WITHIN THE DISPOSITIONAL APPROACH

The previous models focus on leisure as a transitory state, which may vary with such factors as novelty, complexity, demands of the activity, skills of the participants, perceived freedom, and motivation. As discussed previously, the dispositional paradigm provides a major contrast tot he view, focusing on personality characteristics. An example of the dispositional approach that has been the subject of a considerable degree of research is the Leisure Diagnostic Battery.[50]

The Leisure Diagnostic Battery (LDB) conceptualization assumes the existence of a relatively stable perception of self which is maintained over time and which predisposes an individual to have positive experiences. The "perceived freedom" concept, which is the focus of the LDB conceptualization, therefore, is "dispositional;" it describes tendencies of people toward particular outlooks, moods, and ways of behaving.

The LDB defines perceived freedom as a unitary concept, consisting of perceived leisure competence, perceived leisure control, ability to satisfy leisure needs through participation in recreation, ability to achieve depth of involvement in activities, and playfulness. Individuals who are high in perceived freedom are assumed to have a high degree of self sufficiency in leisure. Most of their leisure activities are intrinsically motivated. They have a high propensity to experience the "flow-like" states, they feel comfortable with their levels of skill and involvement in recreation activities, and they exhibit a high degree of satisfaction with their leisure. Individuals who are low in perceived freedom, on the other hand, are assumed to perceive a sense of helplessness in leisure. Their leisure involvements are generally extrinsically motivated, they lack confidence in their ability to successfully participate in recreation activities, and they are unhappy with their leisure.

Attribution theory has been used to explain the process by which this relatively stable sense of perceived freedom is established and maintained. Of particular interest are patterns of attributions for success and failure. Following a win in an athletic contest, for example, an athlete might attribute success to his/her skill, effort, an over-matched opponent (task difficulty), and/or to luck.

The LDB conceptualization asserts that certain patterns of attributions determine an individual's perceived freedom. Individuals who are high in perceived freedom attribute success to such internal factors as skill and effort. "The painting is beautiful because I am a good artist," an artist high in perceived freedom might conclude following completion of a work of art. Failures of individuals who are high in perceived freedom are attributed to such external and unstable causes as bad luck and/or not enough effort. "I lost because of bad luck," an athlete who is high in perceived freedom might conclude. This attributional pattern is assumed to protect the individual's sense of perceived freedom in leisure.

Individuals who are low in perceived freedom, on the other hand, are assumed to adopt an attributional pattern which reinforces their low perceived freedom. Successes are attributed to luck or to an easy task and failures are attributed to a lack of ability. This pattern is assumed to reinforce the individual's perception fo lack of freedom in leisure.

Readers familiar with attribution theory will recognize the above conceptualization a the familiar "self serving" attribution hypothesis. That hypothesis has been the subject of numerous studies and conflicting results have been obtained. Some studies have provided evidence of the phenomenon and other studies have provided no support. One of the important issues facing the further development of the LDB conceptualization, therefore, is the validation of an attributional explanation of perceived freedom.

Although conflicting results bring to question the validity of the attributional explanation of perceived freedom, considerable evidence exists concerning the validity of the LDB as a tool for the measurement of perceived freedom. Two forms of this tool exist. One form is a ninety-five items summative rating scale which was originally designed for use in the assessment of the leisure functioning of adolescents with disabilities. The second form of the LDB is a twenty-five item short form which was derived from the original version. Adult versions of both forms have also been created.

Several studies have suggested that the LDB provides a valid measure of perceived freedom in leisure for different populations.[51] Populations with which the LDB has been used include 9-14 year-old junior high school students, teenage deaf individuals, substance abusers, elderly individuals, participants in a summer playground program, and college students. Studies involving these groups have produced significant correlations with such theoretically related variables as self concept, self-esteem, life satisfaction, and lack of perceived barriers to leisure involvement. In addition, the hypothesis of a unitary concept has been supported through factor analysis. Thus, the most pressing need in LDB research seems to be to examine the validity of the attributional explanation of how perceived freedom is established and maintained, not the measurement of the perceived freedom concept itself.

DISCUSSION

The conceptualizations and operationalizations described in this paper suggest that progress has been made in moving our understanding of leisure from a social philosophy and social empiricism to social analysis. The described approaches differ from what Ellis[52] has termed the "classical" or "recent" theories because they are more universally applicable, lend themselves more easily to operationalization, and to date have led to instruments that produce more valid data.

The various approaches have also produced instrumentation that has potential for helping to determine the effectiveness of public and private agency leisure services. Instrumentation that is capable of measuring the leisure state of mind of participants prior to, during or after participation could help supply more effective measures of program success than attendance counts. Although these approaches and methods are still of the "first generation" variety, they do show much potential. They enable us to move far beyond attitude and interest inventories or philosophic pronouncements about the avowed benefits of the leisure experience.

Our task in the future is to continue to sharpen our conceptualization of leisure followed by even more sophisticated attempts to operationalize developed theory. Until the concept of leisure is brought into sharper focus and sufficiently operationalized so as to provide valid measurement tools, our ability to understand the central phenomenon we are dealing with, and our ability to ascertain if leisure is the benefit that we presume it to be, will be severely impaired.

REFERENCES

1. Neulinger, J. *The Psychology of Leisure*. (2nd Edition). Springfield, Illinois: Charles C. Thomas, 1981.
2. Mannell, R. C. "Problem, Progress, and Usefulness of Theory and Research on Leisure." In *Abstracts from the 1986 Symposium on Leisure Research*. Alexandria, Virginia: National Recreation and Park Association, 1986.
3. Williams, D. "Great Expectations and the Limits to Satisfaction: A Review of Recreation and Consumer Satisfaction Research." In *Proceedings of Benchmark 88 USDA Forest Service Conference*. Tampa, Florida, in press.
4. Williams, in press.
5. Tinsley, H. and Tinsley, D. "A Theory of the Attributes, Benefits, and Causes of Leisure Experience." *Leisure Sciences*. 8, 1986, pp. 1-45.
6. Gunter, B. "The Leisure Experience: Selected Properties." *Journal of Leisure Research*. 19, 1987, pp. 115-130.
7. Mannell, 1986.
8. Csikszentmihalyi, M. and Csikszentmihalyi, I. (Eds.). *Optimal Experience: Psychological Studies of Flow in Consciousness*. New York: Cambridge University Press, 1988.
9. Ellis, M. J. *Why People Play*. Englewood Cliffs, New Jersey: Prentice-Hall, 1973.
10. Iso-Ahola, S. E. *The Social Psychology of Leisure and Recreation*. Dubuque, Iowa: Wm. C. Brown, 1980.
11. Unger, L. and Kernan, J. "On the Meaning of Leisure: An Investigation of Some Determinants of the Subjective Experience." *Journal of Consumer Research*. 9, 1983, pp. 381-392.
12. Ramos, C. *Cross Cultural Variation in the Subjective Meaning of Leisure*. Unpublished thesis, University of Utah, Salt Lake City, 1987.
13. Weissinger, E. and Iso-Ahola, S. "Intrinsic Leisure Motivation, Personality, and Physical Health." *Society and Leisure*. 7, 1984, pp. 217-228.
14. Weissinger and Iso-Ahola, 1984.
15. Mannell, R. "Personality in Leisure Theory: The Self as Entertainment Construct." *Society and Leisure*. 7, 1984, pp. 229-240.
16. Iso-Ahola, S. "Leisure as Boredom: An Analysis of Causes and Effects." In *Abstracts from the 1984 Symposium on Leisure Research*. Alexandria, Virginia: National Recreation and Park Association, 7, 1986.
17. Ellis, G. and Witt, P. "The Leisure Diagnostic Battery: Past, Present, and Future." *Therapeutic Recreation Journal*. 22, 1986, pp. 31-47.
18. Weissinger, E. and Iso-Ahola, S. "Intrinsic Leisure Motivation, Personality, and Physical Health," *Society and Leisure*. 7, 1984, pp. 217-228.

19. Hollander, E. *Principles and Methods of Social Psychology.* (2nd Ed.) New York: Oxford University Press, 1971.

20. Iso-Ahola, 1980.

21. Shaw, S. "Leisure, Recreation or Free Time? Measuring Time Usage." *Journal of Leisure Research.* 18, 1986, pp. 177-189.

22. Voelkl, J. and Birkel, R. "Application of Experience Sampling Method to Assess Clients' Daily Experiences." *Therapeutic Recreation Journal.* 21, 1988, pp. 23-33.

23. Driver, B. *Item Pool for Scales Designed to Quantify the Psychological Outcomes Desired and Expected from Recreation Opportunities.* Fort Collins: USDA Forest Service, Rocky Mountain Forest and Range Experiment Station, 1977.

24. Manfredo, M., Driver, B., and Brown, P. "A Test of Concepts Inherent in Experience Based Setting Management for Outdoor Recreation Areas." *Journal of Leisure Research.* 15, 1983, pp. 263-283.

25. Driver, B. and Rosenthal, D. *Measuring and Improving the Effectiveness of Public Outdoor Recreation Programs.* Washington: George Washington University, 1982.

26. Williams, D., Ellis, G., Nickerson, N. and Schaffer, S. "Contributions of Time, Format, and Subject to Variation in Recreation Experience Preference Measurement." *Journal of Leisure Research.* 20, 1988, pp. 57-68.

27. Manfredo, M. "The Comparability of Onsite and Offsite Measures of Recreation Needs." *Journal of Leisure Research.* 16, 1984, pp. 245-249.

28. I.P.A.T. *Manual for the Eight State Questionnaire.* Institute for Personality and Ability Testing. Champaign, Illinois, 1976.

29. Russell, J. and Pratt, G., "A Description of the Affective Quality Attributed to Environments." *Journal of Personality and Social Psychology.* 38, 1980, pp. 311-322.

30. Csikszentmihalyi, M. and Csikszentmihalyi, I. "Introduction to Part IV." In Csikszentmihalyi, M. and Csikszentmihalyi, I. (Eds.). *Optimal Experience: Psychological Studies of Flow in Consciousness.* New York: Cambridge University Press, 1988.

31. McGuigan, F. J. *Psychophysiological Recording of Covert Behavior: A Guide for the Laboratory.* New York: Halsted Press Division of John C. Wiley and Sons, 1979.

32. Ellis, 1973.

33. Ellis, M. J., Barnett, L. A., and Korb, R. J. "Psychophysiological Correlated of Play." *Annual Report of the Motor Performance and Play Research Laboratory.* Champaign, Illinois: Children's Research Center, 1973.

34. Barnett, L. A. *An Information Processing Model of Children's Play.* Unpublished thesis, University of Illinois, 1974.

35. Barnett, L. A., Ellis, M. J., and Korb, R. J. "Arousal Modulation as Function of Visual Complexity." *Annual Report of the Motor Performance and Play Research Laboratory.* Champaign, Illinois: Children's Research Center, 1974.
36. Ellis, M. J. and Scholtz, B. J. L. *Activity and Play of Children.* Englewood Cliffs, New Jersey: Prentice-Hall, 1978.
37. Barry, R. J. "A Factor-Analytic Examination of the Unitary OR Concept." *Biological Psychology.* 8, 1979, pp. 161-178.
38. Buck, R. *Human Motivation and Emotion.* (2nd Edition). New York: John Wiley and Sons, 1988.
39. Csikszentmihalyi, M. *Beyond Boredom and Anxiety.* San Francisco, California: Josey-Bass, 1975.
40. Csikszentmihalyi, 1975.
41. Csikszentmihalyi, M. and Csikszentmihalyi (Eds.), 1988.
42. Csikszentmihalyi, M. "The Flow Experience and its Significance for Human Psychology." In Csikszentmihalyi, M. and Csikszentmihalyi, I. *Optimal Experience.* New York: Cambridge University Press, 1988, pp. 15-35.
43. Unger and Kernan, 1983.
44. Iso-Ahola, S. "Some Social Psychological Determinants of Perceptions of Leisure: Preliminary Evidence," *Leisure Sciences.* 2, 1979, pp. 305-314.
45. Unger, L. "The Effect of Situational Variables on Subjective Leisure Experience," *Leisure Sciences.* 6, 1984, pp. 291-312.
46. Osgood, C., Suci, G., and Tannenbaum, P. *The Measurement of Meaning.* Urbana, Illinois: University of Illinois Press, 1957.
47. Tinsley and Tinsley, 1986.
48. Bishop, D. "Stability of the Factor Structure of Leisure Behavior: Analysis of Four Communities." *Journal of Leisure Research.* 2, 1970, pp. 160-170.
49. Ramos, 1987.
50. Ellis, G. and Witt, P. "The Leisure Diagnostic Battery: Past, Present and Future," *Therapeutic Recreation Journal.* 20, 1986, pp. 31-47.
51. Ellis and Witt, 1986.
52. Ellis, 1973.

(no keep)

p. 396 is blank.
    End of Chapter 29.

Chapter 30

Leisure and Quality: Beyond the Quantitative Barrier in Research

John R. Kelly

Research does not exist in a separate world of its own. While there is a developmental process in cumulative "normal science" that may be disrupted or redirected by internal crises,[1] there are also factors outside the research act that influence its nature. In leisure research, a practical issue has had an impact on research. That issue is the formulation of decision criteria for providers of leisure resources, both public and commercial. Especially when financial and logistical support for research has been supplied by government agencies with specific missions of recreation resource provision, research has been designed to meet their needs for resource allocation.

Partly in response to this practical aim as well as to narrow norms restricting "science" to mathematical modes of analysis, research in leisure has tended to be concentrated on quantitative studies of participation and the development of methods and formulas of prediction. The goal has generally been the eventual development of an econometric prediction model that can be computer-programmed and universally applied.

At the same time, a central intention of bureaucratic functionaries in any modern social or economic system is to achieve personal career stability. One rule of bureaucratic survival is to minimize risk by employing standard and accepted methods of administration, problem-solving and decision-making. The dangers of being responsible for judgments can frequently be reduced by having what appear to be "hard" quantitative data to apply to a statistical set of decision criteria. Regardless of the implicit assumptions underlying the quantitative model, it gives the appearance of objectivity.

At the same time, there are also accepted premises and even theoretical models that shape research aims and designs. In leisure research, the "functional" or "systemic" model has been dominant.[2] This model has led to social research employing survey techniques that attempt to explain behavior with indicators of institutional roles and positions. Most often economic positions have been assumed to be determinative for such "secondary" behavior as leisure, community, political, and even family roles. In sociology, those studying leisure have not often been daring enough to employ non-standard theory or methods. Rather they have either explicitly accepted the dominant paradigm or have implicitly followed its conventions in what appeared to be a-theoretical designs.

Research, then, has two aims: the practical purpose of providing a useful basis for resource allocation and the scientific purpose of building coherent and explanatory theory about the phenomenon. Leisure research, shaped by public funding and by theoretical timidity, has for the most part adopted familiar methods to examine traditional questions. Most often, leisure sociologists have used the correlational analysis of survey data to investigate the determinative power of social position on leisure behavior.

This chapter is complementary to an analysis of theoretical approaches to leisure that call for more variety in research methods and strategies.[3] The analysis will concentrate on the methods themselves. Following a brief review of past quantitative approaches, mainly in North America, I will outline transitional methodologies that lead to a set of qualitative research models that may yield new and significant theory formulations. Finally, I will outline possibilities for a more inclusive research strategy in leisure studies. Surprisingly, the new strategy may have a greater potential to answer crucial practical questions than the old model.

The Issue of Appropriate Methodologies

The basic issue is really a simple one. Methodologies are servants, not rulers. Research methods are chosen only after the phenomenon to be investigated is given preliminary analysis and the aims of the research clearly delineated. Then, methods appropriate to the specific task are selected, modified, and integrated. The unused and even misplaced mountains of survey data on recreation in the United States are evidence enough that starting with a method, however safe and acceptable, rather than with the problem generally yields results of little value. When a theoretical model is implicitly and uncritically accepted or the method is adopted a-theoretically, the result tends to be a failure to explain anything important.

In the case of research on leisure, the accepted methods have been quantitative. They have stressed the statistical analysis of aggregated numbers. Whatever the implicit notions of "science" underlying this approach, the consequence has been a failure to develop satisfactory theory about leisure—even in the terms of the model.

Is it possible that the phenomenon itself—leisure—requires other modes of research? Are the accepted methods valid within their scope, but unable to cope with fundamental questions about leisure such as *how* decisions are made, what satisfactions are gained, and the effects of providing new or different resources? Current developments in leisure research and theory-building suggest that both the nature of leisure and critical practical problems are requiring different research strategies.

RETROSPECT: QUANTITATIVE RESEARCH IN LEISURE

While government-funded research, especially in outdoor recreation in the United States, has frequently been labelled "mindless empiricism," it might be more appropriate to understand national and community surveys as the application of common methods based on unquestioned premises. When economists are presented with a research problem, they tend to think in terms of adapting an econometric equation. Social psychologists select a scale. Sociologists are most likely to develop a survey instrument that will be analyzed with social positions and status as the independent variables correlated to social behavior.

Participation Surveys

The underlying theory for most leisure sociologists has been one of an institutional social system operating functionally with status-differentiated roles. The familiar method, now escalated in sophistication by packaged computer programs, has been correlational analysis of survey data. While such surveys have been commissioned in several countries, repetition has characterized efforts in the United States and Canada. Not only national outdoor recreation surveys beginning with the ORRRC effort in 1962, but a series of inconsistent follow-ups have worked over the model.[4]

Some alterations have been made as factors of regional resources, distance and attractiveness of sites, and variation in tastes have been suggested as significant.[5,6] Despite the lack of consistency in format, some indications of trends can be extrapolated from data that have not been mislaid or lost by the sponsoring agencies as well as from sources such as national marketing surveys.[7] Further, there have been countless state and community surveys combining participation questions with common demographic information.

To what extent has such research proven useful? Several indications of problems are evident: (1) Very few scientific or theory-building papers have been based on such data. (2) The use of such data in planning has been rendered suspect because of the determination of current participation rates by available opportunities. (3) Their is little evidence that respondents will reliably behave in accordance with expressed interests and attitudes about future recreation. (4) The predictive capability of such models has proven to be quite low, accounting for 30 percent of the variance at most and more recently less than ten percent.[6]

Time-Diary Studies

A second quantitative methodology has been employed in comparable ways in several nations and thus provided rare cross-cultural comparisons. The time-budget or time-diary method is perhaps the most purely quantitative in its approach. Subjects are instructed to report their activity, location, companions, and other such information through a day or week in brief time segments. The activity is then classified and generally reported as daily and weekly means by population aggregates.

Differences among countries[8] and in one population at different times,[9] while not fully explained by the data, can be compared with some reliability and provide an initial basis for analysis over time and space. One appeal of the method, along with such comparability, is that it is so purely quantitative. It seems to have no ideological or political connotations and carries an aura of "objectivity."

However, the reports themselves illustrate the limitations of the approach. By themselves, time-diary studies explain almost nothing. Tables of average hours spent by aggregates on arbitrarily-classified activities give a general "time map" of the employment of clock time. However, to the map we must add our interpretation in order to account for the data. Some explanations are not difficult. Differences in proportions of automobile or television ownership account for major nonwork variation among national cultures. In the United States changes in family structure provide a partial explanation for decreases in average family-task engagement between 1965 and 1975.[9] However, those interpretations are from outside the data.

Further, from time-diaries we do not know such basic information as whether a person is walking for transportation, leisure, health, companionship, or some combination of reasons. Rather, it is assumed that the form of the activity tells us whether it is work or leisure, required or discretionary, valued or dreaded. Like a road map, time-diary research gives us a one-dimensional sketch of activity, but requires considerable supplement for us to even begin to understand what it all means. Such limitations are recognized and have led to designs in which time-diary data is augmented by interviews or other methods that offer dimensions of meaning to the map.[10]

TRANSITIONAL METHODOLOGIES

A number of problems and anomalies in results of the survey and time-diary methods along with entrance into leisure research of scientists with somewhat different theoretical orientations has led to adaptations of the standard methodologies. Not only the failure to account for major proportions of variance in participation rates, but raising questions about the socialization process, differential satisfactions, and the relationship of leisure to other non-work roles and special spaces has prompted a number of adapted strategies.

Space and Access

At the same time that sociologists were concentrating on social position, resource economists were attempting to develop predictive equations for the recreation use of new or expanded public and commercial resources. While a number of complications both in application and theory have kept the effort from reaching finality, at least two major determinative factors were consistently identified. They are distance from user population to the site and the attractiveness of the resource itself. Along with price, some measure of predispositions of potential users, competing resources, distance, and resource attractiveness have been included in all such models.[11,12]

As a consequence, sociologists also began to include some measure of access and attractiveness in a few research designs.[4] In one comparison of communities, variation in resources and differential access was a major explanatory factor in differences between communities.[13] In Canada, regional differences in outdoor recreation were found that were directly related to geographical and environmental factors.[5,14]

While sociologists have not entered the study of distance, access, and environmental factors in leisure with enthusiasm, their employment in program-oriented research requiring results of some predictive substance has helped break the rigid focus on social structure and stratification. The method employed has still been that of the social survey, but with new elements of environment introduced.

Immediate Communities and Socialization

Even when it was agreed that social status did identify some differences in leisure patterns, the process producing those differences was left to speculation. While socialization into leisure through institutions of the social system was assumed to take place in ways differentiated by social status, little had been done to examine just how persons inaugurated and continued particular kinds of leisure activity.

When such research was undertaken, the methods tended to be only adaptations of survey approaches. While personal interviews that could obtain some greater richness of data[15] as well as self-report survey instruments with items on the history of participation[16] were employed, the approaches tended to be rather superficial. Rather than following the history of a person's participation in a set of activities from childhood on, discrete items on childhood participation, context of introduction, and first participation were identified. Some advance, however, has been made in relation to sport participation by obtaining more sequential data from youth and adult participants.[17]

Satisfactions and Decisions

Two approaches to the issue of leisure meanings or satisfactions were also being developed, for the most part after 1979. One was built on the work of Robert Havighurst[18] and employed sociological design. The second was more closely related to "need" theories in psychology[19] and began the use of scales adapted to leisure research. Both approaches recognized the necessity of dealing with the attitudes and definitions of leisure participants rather than only with behavior and social position.

The sociological strategies sought to place leisure in a context of institutional roles and investigate how they were interrelated. In the Havighurst study, a variety of methods were used to go beyond what middle-life adults were doing in non-work time to questions of association, styles, satisfactions, modes of participation, and the relation of psychological to social factors.[18] While results were too diffuse to have an impact on conventional research commensurate with their significance, the importance of elements other than social position and the richness of multiple methods and instruments was demonstrated.

This approach was adopted in the United States in efforts to delineate the relationship between leisure and other social role constraints and opportunities,[13,15] the social contexts of leisure decisions for youth,[20] and contexts of socialization.[21] For the most part, respondents were directly asked questions about leisure companionship, perceived constraints in decisions, relationship to work and dominant satisfactions. In one research sequence from open-ended interview formats, a self-report instrument was developed that examined meanings, contexts, and satisfactions.[15]

At about the same time, social psychologists were beginning to apply their tools to the study of leisure satisfactions and attitudes, both in general and in relation to specific activities. Scales were developed in relation to outdoor recreation and environments,[22] self-concepts and clusters of perceived satisfactions among students,[23] and the identification of types of leisure satisfactions.[24] The value of scales that can be validated for reliability and validity and administered to a variety of populations has been combined with new statistical techniques of factor analysis, cluster analysis, and multi-dimensional scaling. Such techniques are increasingly being employed with nonstudent populations. The focus on the attributes of summed experiences is now leading to valuable connections between the nature of activity and meanings to participants.[25]

These transitional methodologies are an important expansion of the limited data of the traditional social survey. Issues raised in an earlier era[26] about social contexts, personal meanings, and environments have been reopened. Leisure socialization was approached more as a process and leisure as a multi-faceted phenomenon. Nevertheless, the analysis has been still for the most part quantitative with data gathered in structured self-report formats and a cross-sectional

time frame. Nevertheless, new issues have been raised, new variables introduced, and more varied analytical techniques employed. The possibilities of
using quantitative methods to investigate questions of meaning and perception
are being drawn into the study of leisure.

NEW METHODS IN LEISURE RESEARCH

There are two sources of innovative research methods in contemporary leisure
research, one external and the other internal. The external source is the persis-
tence of other theoretical paradigms in sociology that have consequences for
research.[23] While conflict or neo-Marxist theory leads to several critical research
issues for leisure, the paradigm with special affinity for the existential and social
phenomenon of leisure is the "interpretive" or Weberian. This perspective
stresses questions of meaning to social actors, the constructed and problematic
nature of social structures and collectivities, and the processual character of
interaction. It, therefore, appears to be peculiarly suited for the investigation of
a phenomenon that is defined in terms of freedom, intrinsic and social meanings,
and some possibility of distinction from the world of necessity and major
consequences.[3]

The internal source is derived from the kinds of issues increasingly being
raised in leisure research and theory-building.[27,28] When leisure is understood
as a complex and multi-dimensional set of behaviors and meanings that may
change through the life course,[29] simpler strategies and designs are patently
inadequate. If the same activity may have different meanings for the same
person in different social contexts of life-course periods and different activities
much the same meanings, then both the contexts and the meanings must be
included in the research design. Restricting data to who does what and where
seems to yield little that is explanatory from either a statistical or substantive
perspective.

As a result, at least three standard "interpretive" methods have been added
to the leisure research repertoire. While none of the three is intended either to
supplant quantitative analysis or to provide the final word on leisure, each makes
special contributions to leisure sciences.

Collaborative Interviews

Collaborative interviews are those in which the subjects do more than respond
to questions and scales. Rather, they are engaged in the process of seeking
understanding and encouraged to join in the interpretive and theory-building
process. While there have been several inaugural uses of this approach in the
study of leisure, the most path-breaking is that of Rhona and Robert

Rapppoport.[29] Taking the life-cycle framework and adding to it the developmental perspective of Erik Erikson and others, they have sought to understand the relationship of leisure to the changing roles and identities of persons in various periods of their life courses.

The method includes open-ended questions, checking with others close to the collaborator, full explanation of the aims of the study, recording partial histories of past roles and relationships, and probing for explanations from the respondent.[30] Other research has included methods such as meeting for the interview in past or current leisure environments, joint interviews with significant others, and "what if" projective techniques of using imagination and fantasy to seek meanings. While collaborative interviewing is directed toward research goals, the aim is to be inclusive rather than predetermine what is relevant. Further the subject is consulted when profiles are written and interpretations offered by the researchers. The persons being interviewed join in the interpretive process.[31] This method is especially valuable for placing current leisure patterns in a context of personal histories.[31,32]

Although collaborative interviewing has its dangers and limitations, it has the strength of dealing with the perceived worlds of persons rather than a world structured externally by research aims and assumptions. Various means of cross-checking both data and interpretations are possible that minimize the impression-management process that is part of any interview.[33]

Participant Observation

Perhaps a more radical departure from traditional methods is one that has been employed in social research for decades but has remained on the fringes of mainline sociology. Participant observation has been a central part of community studies since the 1930s. There has been an acceptance of the orientation and insight provided by systematic, first-hand observations in examining community behavior at specific sites such as playgrounds and bars. Often the method is accepted as an exploratory tool that leads to different strategies. Sometimes it is combined with other methods in a "grounded" theory-building strategy.[34] In locations with clear boundaries, observation can even yield quantitative data. However, participant-observation data is more likely to be reported as interpreted by the observer.

In recent years, there have been initial uses of this method in research on outdoor recreation, especially at campgrounds[35,36] and on playgrounds.[37] In these cases, the observation is dominant and participation in a selection of community events and enterprises may be used to assess leisure styles and obtain informally the interpretations of participants while they are engaged in the activity. A study of a sports group demonstrates how a sequence of research studies the game as a process.[38] Analysis of the kinds of leisure behavior and events that are most amenable to such an approach suggests that observation may lead to an emphasis on public styles and datable events while participation and interviews lead to a focus on similarities in orientations and behaviors.

When social interaction is viewed as a process of symbolic meaning and exchange, a negotiation of self-presentation and identity establishment and a problematic construction of social structures, then only research that can encompass and follow that process can deal with its nature. Participant observation or observant participation can yield data on how the process develops, how the situation is defined and redefined, and on the dialectical nature of the interaction. Recognizing that no two situations are identical, multiple observations—especially when systematically recorded, compared, and verified—can produce explanatory generalizations grounded in the social world under investigation.

Kinds of leisure with face-to-face interaction, essaying of identities, dealing with problematic outcomes, and temporary suspension of external role status and norms[39] may be best studied with a method that follows the complexities of the social process. Especially when the freedom and suspension of external realities turn the event into play,[40] participant observation possesses an openness that does not predetermine behavior classifications and salient variables. Bar behavior, card games, cocktail parties, beach and swimming pool interaction, the outdoor play of children, and camping are only a few of the leisure situations that have been examined through observation with results that have already enriched our understanding of social leisure. As long as considerable leisure consists of socializing[39] and just "fooling around," then one-time methods that freeze the process will be inadequate to explain the behavior and its meanings.

Projective Techniques

Just being introduced into leisure research are some of the projective techniques that have been more familiar to psychologists in the past. They have been given attention by those who seek a systematic and reliable way to investigate what leisure activities, events, associations, and locales mean to persons in relation to their self-definitions, anticipations for the future, and personality characteristics.

One method relies on fantasy. Drawings, unresolved situations, or other stimuli are introduced to initiate an imaginative construction of behavior, attitudes, and interactions by the subject.[41] Such techniques have several advantages over more structured approaches. They do not close off possible responses through predetermination of categories or limit the scope of information to past behavior. Projective techniques seem to open the possibility of probing into the future. If leisure is defined in terms of freedom and even directed toward self-actualization and fulfillment, then research that deals with the past limitations of opportunities, prior socialization, and social expectations fails to introduce the free and existential element in leisure.

Most often such projective techniques will be employed in conjunction with various instruments that assess personality characteristics, value structures, and motivational orientations. Past concentration on social and economic factors in leisure has led to neglect of a central possibility for leisure understanding—that there are elements internal to social actors that are a part of their decision-making. Investigating social position and socialization history does not exhaust the personal elements in our thinking, feeling, initiating, responding, and deciding. Leisure research, to recognize the freedom element in leisure, must include methods that tap the existential as well as the social.

THE PROBLEM OF SYSTEMATIC ANALYSIS

Of course, there are problems with qualitative research. Beyond the quantitative barrier is a world with many uncertainties as well as possibilities. Perhaps the major problem is in the systematic comparative analysis of data. It is, in the jargon, the problem of reliability.

One response is to bypass the issue. If social interaction is understood as a process, then no two events, situations, or exchanges would be expected to be just alike. Outside the laboratory, neither conditions nor individuals can be controlled, replicated, or guaranteed consistent. Rather, social research seeks to extract the consistencies from human behavior with the aim of developing explanations for regular behavior and common conditions. What is surprising from one perspective is that behavior is as consistent as it is, that for the most part we can enter new situations with some assurance that we know how interaction will develop and what will be expected of us. Therefore, consistencies in the process may be identified and even predicted in terms of statistical probabilities.

But how do we compare data from a number of life histories, a series of collaborative interviews, community studies with participant observation, or imaginative constructions based on projective stimuli? A number of strategies of comparison, theory-building, theoretical sampling, evaluation, and case-study presentations have been developed and tested for many different kinds of social interaction.[30,33,42] One means of presentation often found useful in summarizing data and analyzing the interrelationships of the various elements in the social process is the writing of "profiles." When the varieties of types of situations, groups, communities, social actors, or role definitions are distinguished, a profile of each significant type can be presented in a way that introduces critical factors in their processual development.[31] Thus, the "over time" nature of social interaction is not lost in the attempt to measure the quantitative effects of variables as though they were simultaneous.

In some cases, such qualitative analysis in profiles and typologies may become the basis for a sophisticated quantitative design. However, in other cases, a quantitative study can provide a beginning that leads to processual research in some depth. A survey may give something of the "lay of the land" as in aerial photography which then needs to be followed up on the ground. Social explanation in this Weberian rather than structural mode consists of more than concomitant variation of statistical aggregates.

THE VALUE OF QUALITATIVE RESEARCH

The foremost value of the qualitative study of leisure is that leisure is studied with methods that correspond to its nature. If leisure is defined as a qualitative experience rather than designated time or activities[3,43,44] then data that omits meaning, satisfaction, social definitions, and other elements of the quality of the experience may deal only with indices and contexts rather than with leisure itself. If leisure is an experienced process rather than a category of behavior, then research should examine the nature of the experience over time. Collaborative interviews, life histories that focus on particular relationships or transitions, observations, participation analysis, and projective techniques along with some of the adapted methodologies examine leisure as defined rather than some arbitrarily designated behavior.

However, there are other values as well:

1. Qualitative research "brings people back in" to the study of leisure. Knowing that so much of the meaning of leisure is in the definition of the actors, they are dealt with as thinking, feeling, deciding, experiencing, and changing beings. They are not simply digits in a computer printout.

2. The presentation of qualitative data and analysis is understandable by those who are not technically proficient in quantitative analysis. A profile, case history, set of quotations from interviews, or grounded typology may gain the attention and comprehension of providers, planners, advisors, political decision-makers, and others who need to understand the implications of their decisions.

3. A model that can encompass changes and continuities over time provides a scope of explanation far richer and more inclusive than one that must place a single number on every element in the analysis. The process of life, including leisure, is more like a story than a diagram.

4. Qualitative designs allow for the introduction of new elements into the explanation that were not anticipated by the scientist. Not only the diversity but the complexity of human experience suggests that significant factors in leisure may be found *in* the research rather than identified prior to the investigation.

5. So much leisure is a face-to-face interaction process with the interchange of symbols and gestures, negotiation of meanings, and slow or abrupt alterations of reference that explanation requires observing, assessing, and analyzing the total event. After all, one of the appeals of much social leisure is that it is problematic and unpredictable in outcomes; it has elements of play, games, and the suspension of rules and roles.[39]

7. Perhaps most important, such research can begin to identify the satisfactions sought and found in various leisure events and settings in relation to social identification. The relationship between movement through the life cycle and changes in leisure interests suggests that providers can, in time, respond to the needs of their service populations by designing programs based on the meanings and priorities of the potential users. Planning may be based on need and potential interest rather than on participation rates shaped by current opportunities and provisions.[45]

LEISURE RESEARCH IN THE FUTURE

Leisure is not so fully researched that it is appropriate to focus too narrowly on a few issues or concentrate on only one or two methodologies. Each method outlined here—traditional quantitative, adapted transitional, and qualitative—has particular values. Each does some things well and is most useful in relation to certain issues. Further, leisure is such a multi-dimensional phenomenon that each approach has the potential of furthering our understanding of some dimension.

One problem is that methodological models have been prematurely limited. Correlational analysis of survey data and time-diary studies have so dominated the field that "research" has often been identified with quantitative designs. The preference for studying leisure in natural settings or from household-based data rather than experimental laboratory studies has narrowed design to survey and structured self-reports. The unanswered questions, unresolved issues, and unsatisfactory performance of most research even by its own predictive criteria has led to attempts to adapt or expand such methods.

The argument here is that theory-building in the sense of substantive explanation requires the inclusion and acceptance of a number of qualitative methods. Further, the nature of leisure as experience calls for such research. Research strategies are not just a matter of familiarity, convenience, personal bias, or even professional acceptance. Developing a research strategy means beginning with the nature of the phenomenon and the particular aims of the research. There is no single method that can begin to encompass, much less exhaust, a complex phenomenon such as leisure.

Quantitative research has certain values related to replication, statistical analysis, comparative data bases, standardization, size and representativeness of samples, compactness of presentation, and inclusion of a wide range of variables. It is often useful for both exploration and confirmation.

Qualitative research has values related to depth, the definitions and perceptions of social factors, unobtrusiveness of some designs, inclusion of subjects in the research and discovery process, openness, analysis of process and history, personal and event histories, examination of decision elements and processes, and richness of presentation. Further, it has a special affinity to modern definitions of leisure that stress the quality and meaning of the experience to the participant.

At least for the next decade or so, some emphasis on such qualitative approaches would seem appropriate. If there has been a strong tilt toward the traditional quantitative methods for the past decades, then some compensatory strategies would seem in order. Such emphasis should not eliminate the use of surveys, time-diaries, and other cross-sectional methods when they are clearly appropriate. However, it is time that those doing leisure research admit to their repertoire those methods especially suited to study freedom, satisfaction, processual action and interaction, and personal development—the central elements in leisure.

REFERENCES

1. Kuhn, T. *The Structure of Scientific Revolution*, 2nd edition, Chicago, Illinois: University of Chicago Press, 1970.
2. Kelly, J. Sociological Perspectives and Leisure Research. *Current Sociology*, 22, 1974, pp. 128-158.
3. Kelly, J. R. *Freedom to Be: A New Sociology of Leisure*. New York: MacMillan, 1987.
4. Cichetti, C. "A Review of the Empirical Analyses that have been based upon the National Recreation Surveys." *Journal of Leisure Research*, 4, 1972, pp. 90-107.

5. Zuzanek, J. "Social Differences in Leisure Behavior: Measurement and Interpretation." *Leisure Sciences*. 1, 1978, pp. 271-293.
6. Kelly, J. "Outdoor Recreation Participation: A Comparative Analysis." *Leisure Sciences*, 4:1, 1980.
7. Kelly, J. R. *Recreation Trends toward the Year 2000*. Champaign, Illinois: Sagamore Press, 1987.
8. Szalai, A. *The Use of Time: Daily Activities of Urban and Suburban Populations in Twelve Countries*. The Hague: Mouton, 1972.
9. Robinson, J. *Changes in Americans' Use of Time: 1965-1975*. Cleveland, Ohio: Communications Research Center, Cleveland State University, 1972.
10. Shaw, S. "The Meaning of Leisure in Everyday Life." *Leisure Sciences*. 7, 1985, pp. 1-24.
11. Knetsch, J. *Outdoor Recreation and Water Resources Planning*. Water Resources Monograph, No. 3. Washington, DC: American Geophysical Union, 1974.
12. Krutilla, J. and Fisher, A. *The Economics of Natural Environments*. Baltimore: The Johns Hopkins University Press, 1975.
13. Kelly, J. "Leisure Styles and Choices in Three Environments." *Pacific Sociological Review*. 21, 1978, pp. 187-207.
14. Beaman, J., Kim, Y. and Smith, S. The Effects of Recreation Supply on Participation. *Leisure Sciences*. 2, 1979, pp. 71-87.
15. Kelly, J. Situational and Social Factors in Leisure Decisions. *Pacific Sociological Review*. 21, 1978, pp. 313-330.
16. Yoesting, D. and D. Burkhead. "Significance of Childhood Recreation Experience on Adult Leisure Behavior." *Journal of Leisure Research*. 5, 1973, pp. 25-36.
17. Spreitzer, E. and Snyder, E. "Socialization into Sport: An Exploratory Path Analysis." *Research Quarterly*. 47, 1976, pp. 238-245.
18. Havighurst, R. The Leisure Activities of the Middle Aged. *American Journal of Sociology*. 63, 1957, pp. 152-162.
19. Maslow, A. *Motivation and Personality*. New York: Harper and Row, 1964.
20. Noe, F. and Elifson, K. "The Pleasures of Youth: Parental and Peer Compliance Toward Discretional Time." Paper at the American Sociological Association, Chicago, Illinois, 1975.
21. Kelly, J. Leisure Socialization: Replication and Extension. *Journal of Leisure Research*. 9, 1977, pp. 121-132.
22. Driver, B. "Quantification of Outdoor Recreationist's Preferences." In: van der Smissen, B., Compiler, Penn State HPER Series, No. 11 (N.D.).
23. Tinsley, H., et al. "Leisure Activities and Need Satisfaction." *Journal of Leisure Research*. 9, 1977, pp. 119-120.
24. McKechnie, G. "The Psychological Structure of Leisure: Past Behavior." *Journal of Leisure Research*. 9, 1977, pp. 110-120.

25. Tinsley, H. and D. Tinsley. A Theory of the Attributes, Benefits and Causes of Leisure Experience. *Leisure Sciences*, 8, 1986, pp. 1-45.
26. Lundberg, G., et al. *Leisure: A Suburban Study*. New York: Columbia University Press, 1934.
27. Harper, W. The Experience of Leisure. *Leisure Sciences*. 4, 1981, pp. 113-126.
28. Gunter, B. The Leisure Experience: Selected Properties. *Journal of Leisure Research*. 19, 1987, pp. 115-130.
29. Rapoport, R. and R. N. *Leisure and the Family Life Cycle*. London: Routledge, 1975.
30. Denzin, N. *The Research Act: a Theoretical Introduction to Sociological Methods*. 2nd edition. New York: McGraw-Hill, 1978.
31. Kelly, J. *Peoria Winter: Styles and Resources in Later Life*. Lexington, Massachusetts: Lexington Books, D. C. Heath, 1987.
32. Shank, J. An Exploration of Leisure in the Lives of Dual Career Women. *Journal of Leisure Research*. 18, 1986, pp. 300-319.
33. Webb, E., et al. *Unobtrusive Measures: Nonreactive Research in the Social Sciences*. Chicago, Illinois: Rand McNally, 1966.
34. Glaser, B. and Strauss, A. *The Discovery of Grounded Theory*. Chicago: Aldine, 1967.
35. Burch, W. "The Play World of Camping: Research into the Social Meaning of Outdoor Recreation." *American Journal of Sociology*. 70, 1965, pp. 604-612.
36. Campbell, F. "Participant Observation in Outdoor Recreation." *Journal of Leisure Research*. 2, 1970, pp. 226-236.
37. Lever, J. Sex Differences in the Complexity of Children's Play and Games. *American Sociological Review*, 43, 1975, pp. 471-483.
38. Glancy, M. Participant Observation in the Recreation Setting. *Journal of Leisure Research*. 18, 1986, pp. 59-80.
39. Simmel, G. "Sociability" Chapter 3 in K. Wolff, Ed. *The Sociology of George Simmel*. New York: Free Press, 1955.
40. Bateson, G. "A Theory of Play and Fantasy." *Psychiatric Research Reports*. 2, American Psychiatric Association, 1955, pp. 39-51.
41. Nunnally, J. *Introduction to Psychological Measurement*. New York: McGraw Hill, 1970.
42. Schatzman, L. and Strauss, A. *Field Research: Strategies for a Natural Sociology*. Englewood Cliffs, New Jersey: Prentice Hall, 1973.
43. Murphy, J. *Concepts of Leisure: Philosophical Implications*. Englewood Cliffs, New Jersey: Prentice Hall, 1974.
44. Neulinger, J. *The Psychology of Leisure*. Springfield, Illinois: Thomas, 1974.
45. Kelly, J. *Leisure Identities and Interactions*. Boston: Allen and Urwin, 1983.

(no beep)

p. 412 is blank.
End of Chapter 30.

Chapter 31

The Androcentrism Complex

Maureen Glancy

Gender is an issue little explored in the field of recreation and parks. Yet women and girls continue to be underrepresented in most user categories of public and commercial programs and facilities. Furthermore, there is no satisfactory explanation why female recreation and parks students generally outnumber male students at the baccalaureate and masters levels, but at the doctoral level, men lopsidedly outnumber the women.[1] Moreover, in the parks and recreation recreation profession and in institutions of higher education, women hold lower ranked and technical positions while men hold the broader management and higher administrative jobs.[2] If we are what we claim, why don't we do more for, and with, women and girls since females outnumber their male counterparts.

While these disparities persist, this is also a time of transition for leisure service professionals—a time when the profession is challenged by calls for equity in its mission, philosophy, policies, leadership, and everyday roles in public life. Thus it is appropriate to explore some of the disturbing gender discontinuities in the field of leisure. These concerns relate to the broader issue of androcentricity in leisure: *the condition of male domination in positions of power, in structures that control access to power,* and *in the way leisure is interpreted.*

To successfully explore the gender issue requires an expanded knowledge of our collective mentality and potential motives for the current state of our affairs. Professional practice, education, and research in the field of recreation and parks is a collective experience in studying, interpreting, and responding to matters related to play, recreation, and leisure. This suggests that we have a shared psychological existence; we are a collective entity. In various ways, our history, philosophy, traditions, and current concerns are responsible for our shared perspectives. While many of our actions are a consequence of the way we consciously view the world and see our collective self in action, they are also a function of unconscious knowledge, attitudes, and feelings.

The purpose of this essay is to go beyond what is conscious in our everyday behaviors and consider the extent to which androcentrism is unconsciously a factor in decision-making related to recreation and leisure service delivery and participation.

A GENDER-CONSCIOUS VIEW OF LEISURE

In the course of daily life, women and men share a great deal, but they do so with differences we are just discovering.[3] When it comes to leisure, women have very little of it by men's standards of free time or recreational activity.[4] This, however, does not mean women lack leisure or men's leisure is wanting. A recent spate of research into the qualities of leisure suggests that men's leisure is segmented from work and family life by virtue of generations of experience, leaving the household to work and to carry out civic roles in the community.[5] In fact, this has been suggested as the basis for men's positive attitudes about rational leisure structures such as a particular time set aside, rules to follow, a place to play, or a challenging personal goal.[6]

In contrast to men's preference to compartmentalize facets of their lives, women are used to experiencing a sense of holism in their lives. Being at home for generations, they have traditionally taken pride in how smoothly they manage the sphere of the household and express themselves creatively through related responsibilities.[7] Most constrained are mothers of young children and employed mothers since voluntary effort is principally done by women and children's roles have expanded into the community. Few women experience separation of work, family, leisure, and homelife.[8]

Women experience feelings of leisure interwoven within some of their work tasks;[9] leisure is emergent and unplanned. Similar to men, however, women want to feel some sense of choice, the pleasure of effort, and intrinsic motivation.[10]

Also high on women's list of leisure priorities are opportunities for relational[11] and nurturant experiences.[12] Since they appreciate relating emotionally or spiritually to friends, family, and things in general, many women are apt to want to do something that is less structured than men would choose. They want to fit it into unscheduled demands of family and household and to allow opportunity for relationships with their children or friends to emerge or develop without constraint. This may explain why many women enjoy cooking, crafts, visiting, and entertaining, all of which can be invaded by interruptions and may relate to bonds with others. Men, however, are usually more interested in doing, being active, agentic.[13] Probably that is why so many men seem to have an interest in mastering sports, hunting and fishing, and using equipment like boats and off-road vehicles.

To be leisure for women, then, certain qualities, rather than conditions, must be present.[14] An activity is the container in which leisure can occur for women while it *is* leisure for men.[15] In terms of the profession, it may be the emphasis on activities and planned program and facility structures that attract men more often than women. Dissimilar attitudes suggest something different underlies women's and men's choices and experiences.

THE COMPLEX ISSUE OF ANDROCENTRISM

What keeps women from enjoying leisure in the same way men do? Perhaps it is the feeling that men control public places and create an unpleasant or uncomfortable atmosphere for women.[16] Public places like bars, restaurants, and theatres have been identified by Dixey as problematic to women along with most leisure settings such as city parks and gymnasia-weight room-locker room facilities.[17] Of interest to women, she reported, is a place they feel is their own, one that is safe, asks nothing of them, where they can go unaccompanied and share in meaningful interactions with other women. Where do women congregate on their own?—in semi-public places like bingo halls, support group meetings, and shopping malls.

There are numerous points of view about gender differences in leisure and recreation. Principle explanations center around four concepts: (1) whether women are free enough of traditional female roles and expectations to adopt leisure lifestyles and ethics that are comparable to men's; (2) whether stereotyping women's capabilities suggests they cannot enjoy leisure in the same way as men; (3) whether real or perceived powerlessness prevents women from gaining control over constraining conditions; (4) and whether women and men function in social-psychological settings which allow them to form different meanings from their leisure experiences.

At present, there is a debate about the role of leisure in women's lives. Some scholars seem to believe that women are constrained and deprived of rightful opportunity for development because of their inability to experience leisure according to masculine definitions. To this group, the fault lies in the patriarchal nature of our social systems which deliver and/or interface with leisure.

Other scholars seem less concerned with women's recreation and free time being equal to men's and propose existence of another view of leisure which has not yet been broadly explored, a women's sphere. That, too, is subject to the patriarchal system of social structure and knowledge, and the implication is that it has rendered women invisible or illegitimate. Since most research has studied men or has failed to differentiate between women and men, existing descriptions of leisure expose rationalized knowledge of men's leisure; results often do not reveal the expressive side of leisure which may be women's primary orientation. Thus, the way we study leisure and provide leisure opportunities is a result of androcentrism.

Of course, androcentrism is not just a modern problem. Because division of labor traditionally separated people by gender, with men leaving home to labor and participate in community affairs, women have spent innumerable generations at home, shut out from the public sphere of activity. Women learned to lead privatized lives and, consequently, public life has been in the hands of men as caretakers. It is possible that this history is more than a record called into consciousness by school studies, research, and romantic novels. History can yield a subtle imprint that unconsciously affects everyday life.

THE UNCONSCIOUS ROOTS OF ANDROCENTRISM

Our potential to do or be is not solely the product of conscious logical intent or experience. Underlying many of our actions is what Jung called the *collective unconscious:* a "reservoir of latent images,"[18] or ways of being, common to all people, archaic to modern, regardless of race or nationality. Why have we thought of the earth as "mother" and the sky as "father" from the beginning of time? Everything is not learned firsthand; each individual carries within her or him these instinctual patterns. While we cannot know what is in the unconscious part of the mind directly, we can understand some of its contents by analyzing the predispositions exposed in our decision-actions.

According to Jung, our collective unconscious is partially characterized by archetypes, meaning archaic pattern-types. Jung's research revealed that these patterns have universal meanings retained generation-by-generation. Every ethnic culture and era has created myths that contain the archetypal metaphors. We experience an archetype connection when we are touched, and we resonate, or feel linked, with a stimulus event or person.[19] The connecting image is sensed, though not necessarily directly interpreted. By way of symbols and metaphors created in poetry and myth, archetypal meanings are conveyed as forms underlying words.[20] No words are needed as winter is transformed into spring or taps is played.

Other examples exist as well. Numerous metaphors are used for the hero. Our modern myth of Spiderman is comparable to earlier models such as Robin Hood or perhaps Hercules. In the face of great odds, the archetype portrayed is a hero who saves the downtrodden. The hero is filled with an exuberance of life and is seen as courageously disregarding conventions to achieve the higher moral purpose of the greater good for others.

Facing conflicting social expectations, goddess Vesta (or Hestia), Golda Meir, and Katharine Hepburn represent the undefiled woman who maintains her purity of purpose. They symbolize the virgin woman who, in being true to her own self, is empowered to warmly embrace and uplift humanity. The virgin actualizes herself in the world without violating her principles. Women resonate with this archetype which implies women's contradictory tensions of simultaneously being attractive, gracious, and nurturant in feminine ways but not yielding in principle.

Offering an heroic figure for women, the virgin, like the hero, is adored for holding true to the greater good in herself. However, even though her strength of character provides a vision of the capable and kind woman, the virgin is a model who many women feel powerless to equal due to social convention.

In both accounts, the images suggest ways of coping with life: the message is social. Moreover, the messages conform to stereotypical typologies which mediate behavior unconsciously. No direct link can be identified between what is consciously observed and how we interpret it.[21] Thus concepts underlying myths, parables, legends, and symbols can shape how we understand reality and behave today.

Because western society is founded on the ancient Greek philosophical tradition espoused first by Socrates and systematically institutionalized by Plato, the roots of androcentricity have been useful in helping each generation live within its androcentric reality; therefore, little psychological stress was noted. Today, however, social and economic changes have given women increased access to the public sphere of life, and psychological adjustment is not necessarily easy for women or men.

Jung's concept of the collective unconscious offers archetypal keys for understanding the stressful imbalance caused by changes that threaten previous androcentric regulation of our lives. The collective unconscious is a resource of images which produce the attitudes and feelings surrounding issues experienced unconsciously in day-to-day life. The collective unconscious is the source of intuitive knowledge, most of which never reaches our conscious thoughts, but continues to affect our moods, preferences, day dreams, and decisions nonetheless.

Jung described four areas of the collective unconscious by characterizing the different function of archetypes associated with each one. These include the *anima, persona, shadow,* and *Self.* These archetypes provide a useful framework for analyzing androcentrism issues and perhaps some direction for future changes that would impact the way leisure services and opportunities are conceptualized and offered for both men and women.

The "Anima" Archetype

According to Jung, we carry with us a learned sense of ourselves that has been rendered socially unacceptable. However, this is also the part that guides the kind of relationships we form with members of the opposite sex. It is composed of the opposite gender stereotype, an archetype which fits the opposite-gender person closest to us during infancy and childhood. In men, the archetypal feminine is called the *anima,* and in women the archetypal masculine is the *animus.* Whether positive or negative, the *anima* or *animus* shapes an unconscious "ideal" type in our choices of opposite-sex partners.

The "opposite gender orientation" is observable in adolescent leisure use patterns. Through research that examines girls' and boys' leisure choices, it becomes apparent that youth are concerned with fulfilling sexual stereotypes by rejecting certain activities as options.[22] Without social influence, it would be easy for women and men to express both aspects of their gender; however, due to social sanctions, people learn to hide the unacceptable character traits. To achieve a sense of wholeness, a person must be thoroughly conscious of her or his own opposite-gender nature. For most people, however, their opposite-gender qualities are met only in others, not recognized in themselves.

In regard to leisure, we have repressed the feminine principle because decision-making has been in the hands of men. We can expect that men would prefer to show what they have been led to believe is their "good side", what they have learned works for them. To accommodate social expectations, men try to distance themselves from anything that could be construed as feminine, or from their own *anima*. (Note also that women are just as often gripped by their *animus*.) In a man's life, the *anima* can be a positive force (nurturant, cooperative, kind, sensing) or a negative force (moody, controlling, manipulative). Unfortunately, what we have learned from Jung is that repressed motives and capacities are not simply out of sight, thus out of mind. They affect us in undetermined ways so long as we keep them in primitive or undeveloped states hidden from our consciousness.

The form of men's positive anima in the profession. *Anima* forces are reflected through our profession's actions and decisions in ways we cannot explain. While some men may be comfortable in expressing their *positive anima*, other men will be very doubtful about such ideas or actions. For instance, interest in humanistic and new-age styles of thinking appear to follow feminine principles, yet there is a small, but growing cadre of men assuming leadership toward these ideals in our field. Participative management is another example that could reflect a predisposition toward *positive anima* capacities that can function in rational work institutions. Our gradual acceptance of qualitative research methods and study of the subjective experience, a feminine way of understanding, is not the result of women's actions alone; men, too, have adopted subjective research methods. The whole service ethic which emerged as the philosophical core of the playground and recreation movement at the turn of the century was probably associated with men's positive feminine component because it represented men's nurturant or helping motive.

Form of the negative anima. Dispositions to control, to consume creativity rather than nurture, or to manipulate services of offices causing dependent relationships are suggestive of *negative anima*. It is apparent that institutional leadership and college professorship are principally male privileges and decisions are dominated by male managers and office-holders. In some instances, being in positions of control may have followed an assertive or even deviant course, while at other times, office-holders may have emerged as the result of a non-conflicting path of events. It is unlikely that many persons in powerful positions consciously exert their power in ways to stifle women's development, but it is the unconscious influence on decisions and acts that we are concerned with here. To maintain appearances of control, *negative anima* tendencies may have surreptitiously invited incorporation of androcentric structures and meanings under the claim of rational ways of undertaking responsibilities in our field.

We need to know more about how the *anima* manifests itself; otherwise, this structure will remain a hidden agenda that can undermine rather than enhance our outward orientation. Consciously called upon, the *anima* is a genuine complement to the competitive, masterful, analytical, ruthless potential of the masculine principle; it is compassion, nurturance, emotion-capable, sensing, flexible, and cooperative.

The "Persona"

Jung called the *persona* a mask for outward looking. Responding to social expectations of how people should behave, Jung explained that we construct an appropriate archetypal mask or masks to conform. This is a sham inasmuch as we must be conscious that we use the mask. The objective is to gain public acceptance, cooperation, favors, advantages, and the like. In the profession we speak of professional image, codes of conduct, accreditation, and certification as well as the "life be in it" symbol, and publicized honors and events. These images portray our ideal self. All of this is a way of presenting our face to the public in ways that will be beneficial.

Becoming dependent on the mask can result in *persona* inflation; the person becomes the mask.[23] Acting as if "life be in it" or the accreditation process really are what the leisure profession is all about are illustrations of mask inflation. Do our masks convey or repress a feminine side to leisure? How are we viewed by the public?

Examples of the persona in parks and recreation. Historic symbols associated with our field include physical structures like parks, stages, play fields, and gymnasia. We also call upon historic human forms. The Discus Thrower, Winged Mercury, or the Olympian athlete are meant to suggest achievement for us. Daniel Boone or Paul Bunyan are cited for adventuring in the hills or a great Indian chief like Seattle is noted for identifying humility in stewardship of wildlands. To signal our own elite, we cite former leaders and service providers who established praiseworthy standards of honor.

Many myths and symbols in parks and recreation come from the pronouncements of the early leaders in our field. For example, in 1911, Joseph Lee addressed the Playground Association, saying that play builds character because it calls up the fighting instinct in boys. Boys should not be without difficult and dangerous exploits to bring out the hero that is "stamped in our inheritance."[33] Calling on classical mythology, Lee offered images as "elements of the divine within every man." Using the highly fictionalized interpretations still popular at the turn of the century, Lee idealized the virgin knight, Sir Lancelot, Diana the Virgin Hunter, Apollo the healer and patron of the arts, the Muses of music and poetry, and the warrior Mars. Lee also spoke of the tragedy of civilization's influence — "the defeat of [the] inner life," suggesting that civilizing technology turned youth from an expressive life to an instrumental life.[24]

Do we ask ourselves what meaning there is in the fact that most of our significant role models are masculine? Are there any other trait-clusters to be inferred? How much of our ego is invested in our masks: our facilities, activities, trophies, or the rhetoric of slogans?

The "Shadow"

The *shadow* is responsible for how we relate to members of the same sex in contrast to the *anima* or *animus* which helps us relate to the opposite sex. If we consider the corporate entity of our profession to be primarily masculine, then the *shadow* is a male archetype, containing all the repressed, primitive elements of the very best and the very worst that the ideal man can be. The *shadow* is our unactualized, unconscious possibilities and destructive darkside potential.

We have all heard tales of the *shadow* at work when socializing with old friends at a conference. Conversations reiterate programs that will never be forgotten and personalities who reached their heights under masterful direction. There are also things we would just as soon never talk about again: disasters and fiascoes that divided the members or meant great losses, leaving us dispirited and needing to rebuild after an uncontrolled unleashing of power. The *shadow* cannot keep its competence hidden behind a mask of what is expected; it has a legitimate contribution to make in the field. Kept hidden, the hero can become a villain.

The shadow in the profession. Greek philosophy affects us far more than simply providing the basis for understanding leisure as contemplation. In his *Republic,* Plato wrote of the perfect state which was governed by citizens who were rational, logical, and self-controlled. Women, whom he saw as weak, emotional and unreliable, could never become guardians because the repressive Athenian system denied them citizenship.

In adopting Platonic ideals, men sought to bring themselves under strict control and to exert control over all that was their dominion. They repressed all emotion and distanced themselves from women who might lead them to lose emotional control. To dwell fully in the mind in a state of contemplation was the ultimate experience for which men of class prepared themselves. Women were considered incapable of rational, logical, mental control, however, and were abandoned to their sensate ways, legally confined to their households with

only their children and servants for companionship. Except for social obser-
vances such as funerals and weddings, women were not allowed to participate in
public life, and association with their husbands was limited to procreation.
Plato's systematic plan idealistically and socially divided women from men and
formed the basis for two different views of life.[25]

According to Schott, the Kantian paradigm for science of philosophy and
scientific methods of investigation has its origin in Greek philosophy. This
paradigm forms the basis for science today. It is rooted in the Aristotelian logic
of natural law: form rules over matter, reason rules over passion, and active rules
over passive. Only what can be objectively observed and logically derived
describes reality. Schott observed that philosophy is "an articulation of relations
in the social world."[26]

The Greek experience, as conceived by men, defined leisure as self-willed
control to achieve a mental state devoid of emotion and physical experience, the
willing of pleasure confined to a time period, and the realization of pleasure
from engaging in a particular form of activity other than work. These views of
leisure were not, and still do not appear to be, leisure for women. In twentieth-
century life, these views may not be an authentic, or complete, representation of
leisure for men either.

Men in leadership positions are apt to repress their feminine side that normally would aid interaction with women. They are also accustomed to relating
to each other competitively, aggressively, and without mercy following the
Greek model contained in their *shadow* sides. On the other hand, many women
do not feel comfortable with adopting masculine characteristics believed to be
necessary to achieve and be successful in positions of power.[27] Thus, maintaining an androcentric model of relations within our profession, in our philosophy,
and by our enabling actions is a natural and necessary, though unconscious,
effort to control men's feminine archetypal forces. The model also is effective
in limiting women's access to positions of authority which might threaten men's
sense of control.

The "Self"

The collective unconscious offers many possible archetypes, but what we truly
are is a composite archetype of what is possible in our own special way. As the
organizing concept of who we are, the *Self* archetype is our guiding factor. To
the the field of recreation and parks, it alone is the "truth" of the potential of our
profession. The *ego* of our profession may determine our actions, but it does not
mean that we are using the potential the *Self* has to offer. The more conscious
we are about the absolute nature of our collective *Self*, the more chance we have
of attaining the sense of harmony and rightness desired.

As a field, we unthinkingly confront archetypes in our use of historic symbols,[28] but historical insight into our collective meaning and significance has erred due to biased interpretations made popular in the 19th century.[29] However, our philosophical development has remained limited. Judging by the few authors involved in original thinking, none consider the significance of lore and tradition on the profession or field. The focus is usually on rational analysis of concepts enduring from classical philosophy such as freedom and work or the existential basis for leisure. Our self-knowledge will be constrained as long as we fail to recognize the significant meaning of the archetypes in our corporate psyche.

MAKING THE INVISIBLE VISIBLE

Based on ideas already discussed, it becomes clear that we may have a problem being conscious about our masculine self. There also needs to be more consideration of the feminine side, men's collectively repressed *anima* as well as women in their own right. Since women also are part of the corporate psyche, resolving the dilemma of androcentricity does not simply mean we need to liberalize our gender-consciousness. To achieve the psychological harmony which a good professional image and relations truly can be, we need to act together in a soul-searching process to identify the unique *Self* that we are collectively: a *Self* that is neither male nor female in being. Perhaps change is already underway.

Search for Female Archetypes

Gradual change in woman's sphere of influence has taken place within recent years. Today, women and girls feel less social constraint; self-constraint may be the greater issue. However, leisure still lacks a heritage of positive archetypes for women and girls emanating from the feminine principle. Without political power to wield, women cannot directly express their full selves satisfyingly in the public sphere. Just examining illustrations in our profession-related periodicals suggests the Aphrodite image of youth and beauty is significant for females. What images does history provide that invite girls and women who would break from tradition?

The effect of a negative archetype. The female counterpart of the stalwart, self-controlled, and youthful Olympian is the Amazon—a mythical race of women endowed with great physical power and courage, so much so few men dared to face them lest they be consumed. The term Amazon is familiar to women athletes so we should not be surprised to learn that, in the elementary

years, even with equal opportunity, girls' interest in sport does not equal boys'
Early in high school, girls' sport participation wanes sharply. The idea that
women must have "special strength of character" to enter into the man's world
to play[30] revives the Amazon image. Despite the Amazon inference, many
women enjoy sports and play extremely well, but why they play suggests a
different set of motives and traits than we find in men. Joy, with no sense of
obligation, characterizes women's sports participation while their male peers
more often play to fulfill social expectations of masculinity.[31]

The Archetype of Wholeness

Whether an emergent trend or simply an unobserved phenomenon, women have
recently been credited with adopting the archetype of wholeness: the androgenous personality which blends strong feminine qualities with strong masculine
qualities. Women athletes are more likely to express androgenous personalities
than masculine, feminine, or undifferentiated personalities,[32] and women with
masculine and androgenous personalities are less apt to feel constrained by
barriers to recreation participation.[33]

The resilience of tradition. While many women still function in sex-stere-
otyped clerical, program specialist, or supervisory positions, it is interesting to
note that during the war years, women held most of the management positions at
all levels. Many women feel they face a double standard which implies repress-
ing feminine characteristics in favor of masculine characteristics necessary for
professional role success,[34] yet women who occupy top positions by virtue of
their own legitimate power use the same array of leadership skills that men do in
the work environment.[35] Once at the top, gender does not seem to be noticed;
administrators of either sex are likely to be attributed as androgenous.[36]

Women who learn to maintain a balance between masculine and feminine
traits, in other words behave androgenously, can be successful in the traditional
bureaucratic environment.[37] Androgenous women also seem to be more capable
of maintaining a multiple-role lifestyle than women with feminine orientations.[38]
Yet, women seem to accept the differential status they have in the leisure service
delivery system. Due to the absence of alternative, effective, socially acceptable
archetype models, many women react by denying or by acquiescing to socially
limiting options for personal expression and development. They cannot imagine
themselves acceptable as other than they are.

The Developed Feminine Archetype

Despite their lack of power in the profession, woman are making changes that will affect their leisure involvements. Feeling repressed, unrepresented, invisible, and unsatisfied, women have been driven to express their *shadow* sides to make leisure more satisfying to themselves. Although they cannot be a dominant force, neither can their *shadow* be dominated. As examples, we might consider women's social and service organizations. On the surface these may appear to be mirror images of men's institutions, but careful study of the YWCA or Girl Scouts and other similar kinds of groups will show a different mission guiding women's operations compared to men's.

Women have begun to effect changes in recreation institutions, demanding child care to help enable adult programs, more evening activities as a result of increased daytime employment, and facilities adapted to their needs. Equal right to membership in many traditionally male activities or groups has also been gained. The developed feminine archetype in our women members may be responsible for the quality of leadership and program innovation in our institutions since the great majority of direct leadership is at the hands of women. Women's influence may likewise be reflected in replacing the traditional spartan gymnasium, natatorium, and office with complexes of meeting rooms, lounges, and specialized art and dance facilities distinctively decorated and furnished to invite socializing and relaxation.

Legitimize Women's View

The evidence that women and men do view leisure differently is beginning to be reflected in the work of scholars like Bella, Bialeschki, Deem, Henderson, Kelly, Neulinger, Shaw, and Talbot. Their efforts are leading to a broad definition of leisure that genuinely means leisure to both women and men. We are also beginning to undertake critical resource analysis: where are the women and what is the quality of the experience where they are found? Already, we know that men enjoy public places; whereas, women are drawn to semi-public settings offering safety, congeniality, and limited imposition of schedules, regulation, or activity expectation. The impact of signs and symbols on the mind has also been discussed and efforts need to be made to respond to the "space-of-her-own" concept.[39]

Restructure organizations integrating feminine and masculine.
Since we have reason to believe that it is partly the way organizations are structured which causes women to refrain from participation or making moves upward in our hierarchies, we need to learn what qualities of organization resonate with women's style of interaction and work. We also need to examine ways to incorporate these qualities in structures, devising new organizational

systems where necessary. For example, by eliminating hierarchical structure and promoting independent, intrinsically motivated action, the matrix organization could be useful to our field. Job descriptions, leave policies, workstyles, programming systems, control systems, publicity techniques, and marketing strategies also need to be examined and adjusted.

Continue building the subjective knowledge-base. Strange as it seemed to our field a decade ago, qualitative research into everyday life is contributing significantly to knowledge about leisure. Qualitative approaches have helped expose women's lives and leisure and resulted in finding that many differences do exist when women's and men's experience is examined separately and in detail without *a priori* assumptions.[40]

Through the incorporation of qualitative approaches, we can become aware of the complexity with which people make decisions and take action. Providing richly detailed description is making it possible for us to envision reality in other than dichotomous terms.[41] We are becoming adept at abstracting the data of discourse, but still struggling with how to locate the central concepts without falling victim to quantification's misleading simplicity.[42] In this process, woman has emerged. She is subjectively observable in her own ways, and man is subjectively different in his ways.[43] The woman researcher has emerged, too. Qualitative research may eventually become a prime interest to women scholars in our field.

SUMMARY

The profession of recreation and parks is a psychological entity, made real by virtue of the collective experience of professional colleagues who comprise its service, education, and research interests. As a psychological entity, we are responsible for both our consciously and unconsciously motivated behavior. The purpose of the discussion was to construct a means of understanding how the issue of androcentricity could exist psychologically and, further, to provide a basis for intervening in the process which keeps androcentric systems functioning. Achieving a state of internal balance would be the key concept. A variety of alternatives have been offered centering on the idea that the profession does not know its *"Self."* Most of the suggestions require searching for answers while beginning to construct new models of thinking, organizing, and doing. Of greatest potential value is the overall process of self-analysis which is needed and the involvement of all professional women and men in honest dialogue.

REFERENCES

1. Gitelson, R. "1986 PSRE Study: Park and Recreation Program in Higher Education." *Parks and Recreation.* 22: 11, 1987, pp. 38-42.
2. Several sources support this along with Gitelson's report. For example: Peterson, H. *The Status of Women in Public Recreation and Park Agencies.* An unpublished masters thesis, The Pennsylvania State University, August 1981. White, J. "Women in Leisure Service Management." In Wimbush, E. and Talbot, M. (Eds.). *Relative Freedoms: Women and Leisure.* Milton Keynes. England: Open University Press, 1988, pp. 147-160. In addition, preferential funding for men's professional development is common according to DiGrino, B. Nicholas and Brian Seeger. "Organizational Commitment to Professional Development of Male and Female Recreation and Park Practitioners." Paper presented at the Fifth Canadian Congress on Leisure Research, Halifax, Nova Scotia, May 1987.
3. White, J. W. and Gruber, K. J. "Gender Differences in Leisure-Need Activity Patterns." *Sex Roles.* 12, 11/12, 1985, pp. 1173-1186.
4. Wearing, B. and Wearing, S. " 'All in a Day's Leisure': Gender and the Concept of Leisure," *Leisure Studies.* 7, 1988, pp. 111-123.
5. Gihring, T. A. "Leisure-Time Activities in an Urban Nigerian Setting: Attitudes and Experience," *Journal of Leisure Research.* 15: 2, 1983, pp. 108-124.
6. Deem. R. "The Politics of Women's Leisure." Paper presented at the Leisure Studies Association International Conference, Brighton, England, 1984.
7. Bialeschki, M. D. and Henderson, K. "Leisure in the Common World of Women," *Leisure Studies.* 5, 1986, pp. 299-308.
8. Chambers, D. A. "The Constraints of Work and Domestic Schedules on Women's Leisure," *Leisure Studies.* 5, 1986, pp. 309-325.
9. Several authors make this point. See for example: Bialeschki, M. D. "Women and the Dichotomies of Work and Leisure." Paper presented at the NRPA-SPRE Leisure Research Symposium, Dallas, Texas, October, 1984. Shaw, S. M. "Gender and Leisure: Inequality in the Distribution of Leisure Time," *Journal of Leisure Research.* 17:4, 1985, pp. 266-282.
10. Bialeschki and Henderson, *Op. Cit.*
11. Bella, L. "Women and Leisure: Beyond Androcentrism." In Burton, T. L. and Jackson, E. (Eds.). *Understanding Leisure and Recreation: Mapping the Past, Charting the Future.* State College, Pennsylvania: Venture Publishing, 1990.

12. Shank, J. W. "An Exploration of Leisure in the Lives of Dual Career Women," *Journal of Leisure Research.* 18:4, 1986, pp. 300-319.

13. Kleiber, D. A. and Kane, M. J. "Sex Differences and the Use of Leisure as Adaptive Potentiation," *Loisir et Societe /Society and Leisure.* 7:1, 1984, pp. 165-173.

14. Henderson, K. A. and Rannells, J. S. "Farm Women and the Meaning of Work and Leisure: An Oral History Perspective," *Leisure Sciences.* 10:1, 1988, pp. 41-50.

15. Shaw, S. M. "Leisure, Recreation or Free Time? An Empirical Comparison." Paper presented at the NRPA-SPRE Leisure Research Symposium, Dallas, Texas, October 1984.

16. Green, E. and Woodward, D. "Gender Relations and Women's Leisure Patterns." Paper Presented at the Leisure Studies Association 1984 Conference, Brighton, England, 1984.

17. Dixey, R. "It's a Great Feeling When You Win: Women and Bingo," *Leisure Studies.* 6, 1987, pp. 199-214.

18. Hall, C. S. and Nordby, V. J. *A Primer of Jungian Psychology.* New York: NAL Penguin, Inc., 1973.

19. Hillman, J. *Archetypal Psychology: A Brief Account.* Dallas, Texas: Spring Publications, Inc., 1981.

20. Jaffé, A. "Symbolism in the Visual Arts." In Jung, C. G. (Ed.). *Man and His Symbols.* New York: Anchor Press, Doubleday, 1964, pp. 230-271.

21. Jung, C. G. "Approaching the Unconscious." In Jung, C. G. (Ed.). *Man and His Symbols.* New York: Anchor Books, Doubleday, 1964, pp. 18-102.

22. Glancy, M. "The Relationship of Adolescent Leisure to Adult Success and Satisfaction: A Twenty-Four-Year Panel Study." An unpublished doctoral dissertation, The Pennsylvania State University, November 1982.

23. Jung, C. G. *Aspects of the Feminine.* Translated by R. F. C. Hull. Princeton, New Jersey: Princeton University Press, 1982.

24. Lee, J. "Play as an Antidote to Civilization." Reprint 89 from *The Playground*, July 1911.

25. Shehadeh, L. R. "Plato's Paradoxical View of Women," *Feminist Issues.* 8:2, 1988, pp. 67-74. Schott, R. M. *Cognition and Eros: A Critique of the Kantian Paradigm.* Boston: Beacon Press, 1988.

26. Ibid, viii.

27. Talbot, M. " 'Their Own Worst Enemy'? Women and Leisure Provision." In Wimbush, E. and Talbot, M. (Eds.). *Relative Freedoms: Women and Leisure.* Milton Keynes, England: Open University Press, 1988, pp. 161-176.

28. von Franz, M. L. "Science and the Unconscious." In Jung, C. G. (Ed.). *Man and His Symbols.* New York: Anchor Books, Doubleday, 1964, pp. 304-310.

29. Bernal, M. *Black Athena: The Afroasiatic Roots of Classical Civilization.* Vol. I, New Brunswick, New Jersey: Rutgers University Press, 1987.

30. Kleiber, D. A. and Hemmer, J. D. "Sex Differences in the Relationship of Locus of Control and Recreational Sport Participation." *Sex Roles.* 7:8, 1981, pp. 801-810.

31. Kleiber and Kane, *Op. Cit.* in the work cited

32. Kleiber and Hemmer, *Op. Cit.*

33. Henderson, K. A., Stalnaker, D. and Taylor, G. "The Relationship Between Barriers to Recreation and Gender—Role Personality Traits for Women," *Journal of Leisure Research.* 20:1, 1988, pp. 69-80.

34. Horner, M. "A Bright Woman is Caught in a Double Blind," *Psychology Today.* 3(November) 1969, pp. 36-38+.

35. Kanter, R. M. *Men and Women of the Corporation.* New York: Basic Books, 1977.

36. Kennison, J. "Sex-Role Stereotypes and Evaluations of Administrative Performance by Municipal Recreation and Park Administrators," *Journal of Recreation and Park Administration.* 3:2, 1985, pp. 45-60.

37. See: White, "Leisure Service" and Bialeschki, M. D. and Henderson, K. A. "The Personal and Professional Spheres: Complement and Conflict for Women Leisure Services Professionals," *Journal of Park and Recreation Administration.* 2:4, 1984, pp. 45-54.

38. Bialeschki and Henderson, "Personal and Professional." Hirschman, E. C. "Leisure Motives and Sex Roles," *Journal of Leisure Research.* 16:3, 1984, pp. 209-223.

39. Henderson, K. A., Bialeschki, M. D., Shaw, S. M. and Freysinger, V. J. *A Leisure of One's Own: A Feminist Perspective on Women's Leisure.* State College, Pennsylvania: Venture Publishing, 1989.

40. Wimbush, E. "Mothers with Young Children—Understanding Their Leisure Needs." Newsletter Supplement of the Leisure Studies Association, Fall 1988, pp. 13-26.

41. Glancy, M. "Participant Observation in the Recreation Setting," *Journal of Leisure Research.* 18:2, 1986, pp. 59-80.

42. Howe, C. Z. "Possibilities for Using a Qualitative Research Approach," *Journal of Leisure Research.* 17:3, 1985, pp. 212-224.

43. Shaw, *Op. Cit.*

End of Chapter 31

Chapter 32

The "Psychologization" of Leisure Services[1]

Roger C. Mannell

Today we are often exhorted to think of leisure as a state of mind or as a subjective experience. Unfortunately, clear and unambiguous descriptions of this state or experience are all but non-existent. Most of us would be unable to say with conviction whether or not we had encountered one of these mysterious experiences. While "experts" have dodged describing the characteristics of the leisure experience, some view it as being achievable by only a select few,[2] yet others consider it approachable by anyone at almost anytime.[3] Most agree that it is *pleasurable*, yet criteria have not been forthcoming to allow us to distinguish between leisure and non-leisure states.[4] Are religious, mystical, aesthetic, amusement, intense competitive sport, and experiences during altered states of consciousness leisure experiences? With these questions unanswered it is not surprising then, that leisure services have not developed planning strategies specifically to encourage and promote experiencing during leisure or developed evaluation techniques to assess the success of such efforts. Similarly, leisure research, until quite recently, has all but ignored examining the factors which affect the experiential component of leisure.[5]

Now we find ourselves on the threshold of an *experience revolution*—a revolution for which our leisure delivery systems may be unprepared. Numerous Canadian studies by futurists predict that we will devote increasing amounts of time and energy to creative activity, personal growth and self-actualization endeavors.[6] Over the last few years there has developed a tremendous interest in esoteric eastern philosophies and psychologies, western psychotherapies and personal development programs on the one hand, and high risk outdoor pursuits and the hunt for fantasy and amusement experiences on the other. These trends, if they continue, may mean an increase in the search for and collection of exotic, novel and exciting blends of experiences. This experience revolution has many potentially positive aspects, yet like the failure of increases in discretionary time and affluence to lead inevitably to a leisure society, the emerging experience revolution may bring us no closer to achieving leisure lifestyles or self-development.

We must, then, explore the notion of an experience revolution and some of its implications for the delivery of leisure services. And we must look critically at the notion of an ideal human condition of personality and the "experience vendors" who are emerging to meet the demand for experiences that will lead to this state of development. Should leisure services become experiential and compete with the private entrepreneur for their share of the "experience" market? Is there another role that leisure services can play? Will the current interest and efforts in a psychology of leisure result in information that will serve as a basis for some form of "leisure experience engineering" to support leisure services in providing experience oriented (psychologized) services?

DO WE NEED A MAN-OF-LEISURE PROTOTYPE?

In more optimistic times, times pre-dating the energy crisis and the appearance of ecological and environmental concerns, the eventuality of a leisure society seemed assured. Though the details of the nature of such a society have always been obscure, the need to do little or no work, accompanied by abundant amounts of discretionary time and resources to pursue a wide variety of interests seem to characterize this vision. The psychological, economic, political and social changes necessary to support leisure lifestyles for our citizens have not been considered comprehensively other than through the occasional writer's literary construction of a utopian community or society. Similarly the phrase "leisure lifestyle," so frequently used these days, has not been defined, or the types of activities or behaviors comprising this mode of living agreed upon.

During the last decade there has emerged a growing concern that the movement toward a workless society has not resulted in a shift to a leisure society. Increases in discretionary time and affluence have not guaranteed the adoption of leisure lifestyles whatever they are! Some social critics have argued that one of the major barriers to the achievement of a leisure ethic, besides a lingering work ethic, has been its subversion by the consumer ethic.[7] The consumer ethic, a refinement of Veblen's notion of conspicuous consumption, suggests that we have not become leisurely but rather have used increases in discretionary time and resources to purchase and expend more. This consumption oriented lifestyle supposedly allows us to "shore up" our personal identities and establish our social status on the basis of what we spend rather than on the basis of our work. The achievement of a "true" leisure lifestyle would seem to imply that social status needs are to be abandoned and self-esteem result from the personal development allowed one in a leisure society.

More recently there has even been a loss of optimism that we can sustain a continued movement away from a work society, with the appearance of energy crises, population pressures and economic competition with newly developing nations. Yet, in spite of these problems and the spectre of economic collapse the consensus of futurists is that developments still hold the possibility of a society with a substantial amount of leisure. Fewer young people, smaller families, shorter working hours, increases in discretionary time are familiar predictions that continue to be made. However, the authors of these reports hasten to caution us that prosperity is not assured, and that our consumption patterns must be made a little more modest since we may be obligated to redefine our concept of prosperity.

Of particular interest is the apparent consensus in the predictions of changes in our values:

> "New values will gradually take over as the dominant, decision-making values of our society. There will be a decline in values associated with materialism, private ownership, capitalism and unqualified economic growth. Increasing emphasis will be placed on concepts such as the quality of life, self-actualization, creativity, individualism and humanitarianism."[8]

The one recurring theme of most futurist predictions is that there will be an increasing demand or need for opportunities to be more creative and self-actualized, that is, for opportunities for personal development. Apparently then, it is still possible that if man fails to "cremate himself equal" in a nuclear holocaust or crowd himself off the earth, he may be condemned to the horrible fate of a workless society—the victim of automation. What type of person shall inherit this leisure world? Will the survivors possess a huge arsenal of recreation skills and the surviving society be one populated with Renaissance men— the ultimate recreators? Is there a suitable prototype for all members of a leisure society? Is a life based on intellectual and rational pursuits, as well as the pursuit of the cultural arts and recreation able to sustain the total population or only a small elite segment of the population?

We have a need for a "man-of-leisure" prototype, and for a clearer notion of the types of activities and experiences that will sustain this individual and contribute to a meaningful lifestyle. Is this to be a leisure lifestyle? Leisure service professionals are being urged to devote more organizational time to leisure counseling and education which are espoused as suitable mechanisms for shaping the prototype man of the future. What are the features, options and capabilities of this new model of man? What exotic blend of experiences will be needed to "power" leisure man in his search for happiness and self-development?

Today we encounter a variety of competing views regarding the appropriate model for living. These views have been at various times stated in terms such as oneness with the universe, Christian virtue, manhood, proper taste, or self-actualization.

Ideas about the *ideal person* and how he should relate to his world come from many sources. In Western society Christianity contributed to the ideal of *Spiritual Man* whose present life is a preparation for an afterlife where people are to be free and equal. With the European Renaissance the ideal of *Intellectual*

Man evolved with the belief that our salvation was to be found in this world and achieved through the application of human intelligence to our problems. The extension of this belief into the political sphere fostered the ideal of a *Political Man* who was to be actively involved in modifying the political institutions of his society to further the quality of life. With the industrial revolution the image of *Economic Man* evolved with the belief that man would achieve the good life through his contributions to economic growth and development.[9] Of course, during this evolution of various notions of the ideal man the development of the scientific method and science contributed to the belief that man could solve all his problems with an objective, rational, and scientific approach. Most recently it has been suggested that a new ideal of *Psychological Man* has emerged with the belief that we are moving into an era in which we are achieving a clearer understanding of human needs and will more completely meet them.[10] Psychological Man is contemporary man with a developed self-awareness who has shifted his attention from the external world to his own nature. Much has been written over the last thirty years concerning the barriers preventing contemporary man from achieving a "free," "self-actualized," and "happy" existence. Numerous models of the ideal orientation to life and means to self-development have been suggested, supposedly based on modern psychological principles.

Other models for the ideal person also exist; the hero/intellectual, the artist, the mystic, the saint and the prophet. These models all suggest different emphases on what are desirable or ideal human traits. While most models of man recognize the need for some kind of psychological growth, there is no universal view of the ideal human condition.[11]

Unfortunately, we are faced with a bewildering array of models of the ideal person which does not help us decide what prototype we should be encouraging in leisure counseling and education. We are not even sure that a society in which most persons did not have to work would be a society where man could survive and adapt in such a way that his life would be perceived by himself as happy and fulfilled. Is a man-of-leisure prototype suitable for all persons, only for an elite, or for no one? Implicit in many of our activities and thinking is the assumption that man—the masses—can be counseled or educated into adopting a leisure lifestyle which will sustain him, provide meaning and purpose in his life, prevent him from becoming a social nuisance, and he and his fellows collectively from becoming a social problem.

The essence of a *leisure problem* would seem to be a question: can man, when biological survival is no longer problematic, adjust his goals and find activity in which to engage that allows him to perceive himself as happy. When work and consuming no longer preoccupy us, we may finally have to personally confront the purpose of our lives. What new goals shall we seek? Can man convince himself that the exploration of his own psyche, the search for self-actualization or personal development is sufficient to provide direction, meaning and importance for his life? How are leisure services evolving to provide for these needs of Psychological Man?

THE EXPERIENCE INDUSTRIES AND THE PSYCHOLOGIZATION OF LEISURE SERVICES

Critics have been pointing out the need to focus a concern not on how much we consume or participate but on the quality of our experiences. As a result leisure is currently viewed by those in the "know" as a state of mind or a subjective experience. Pessimism has been expressed about the possibility of the masses being able to achieve this state. More optimistic futurists predict that the future will see an increasing concern for personal development. Toffler, writing before the appearance of the energy crisis, predicted an experience revolution. He was optimistic that the current preoccupation with acquiring goods and material possessions as an avenue to happiness would pass as merely a stage in the adaptation of man to an affluent society where his needs were readily met:

> As rising affluence and transience ruthlessly undercut the old urge to possess, consumers begin to collect experience as consciously and passionately as they once collected things.[12]

Toffler predicted that the manufacturing sector would direct more resources into the conscious design of "psychological distinctions and gratifications" with the development of experiential industries which would also keep the economy growing as the production of goods went beyond our material needs. "We are moving from a 'gut' economy to a 'psyche' economy because there is only so much gut to be satisfied."[13] The term "psychologization" coined by Toffler, labels this predicted shift from providing goods and services simply to meet functional needs to also generating experiences:

> We shall go far beyond any "functional" necessity, turning the service, whether it is shopping, dining, or having one's hair cut, into a pre-fabricated experience.[14]

Writing before the advent of the energy crisis and our current economic difficulties, Toffler's predictions are still relevant. We will need to focus more and more on psychological or psychic gratifications (experience) because excess materialism beyond a "comfortable" level will be wasteful and costly in a world of scarce resources and large populations.

Will the shift from the acquisition of material goods mean that suddenly we are going to achieve a happy and satisfying life as a society? Toffler, himself, wondered what would happen when industry began to produce experiences for their own sake that " . . . blur the distinction between the vicarious and the non-vicarious, the simulated and the real?"[15] As well, we may give up our need to possess more and more material goods only to replace them by a similar fascination with collecting experiences. One would expect that the simple clamoring after experience does not mean that the road to self-development will be better guaranteed.

THE SEARCH FOR EXPERIENCE

What is the nature of a lifestyle that is centered around the pursuit of experience? Are we now not continually experiencing our surroundings every waking minute? To say there will be an experience revolution seems to suggest that greater concern will be given to "engineering" our experiences and the situations which give rise to them. The purpose of this "experience engineering" would be to create experiences that are somehow of greater quality than in the past, that are perhaps more memorable, that give greater satisfaction, and that perhaps lead to a fuller life or more complete personal development. What types of experiences are likely to attract man if he is given the opportunity to pursue experience for its own sake?

Education and the Search for Knowledge

The formal education institutions of the West have not fostered the "development of the mind" through intense and exotic experiences. Personal development has been based on the slow and gradual acquisition of factual information and the development of intellectual, rational and scientific modes of thought. The education system has been very work oriented. Unfortunately, universities have backed themselves into a corner by stressing their ability to place graduates in jobs instead of the less fashionable and tangible ideals of a liberal education. They are now scrambling to develop and market continuing education programs as self-development opportunities to meet the problems of shrinking enrollments as the number of young people in our population decreases, and, also, they avoid the university since its brand of experience no longer guarantees jobs.

Experience Seeking: Growth or Addiction

A current psychological view of man is that he is constantly motivated to maintain an optimal level of arousal. That is, man attempts to maintain enough change or novelty in his life to avoid boredom or anxiety from too little or too much change respectively. When the challenge of survival is no longer available to provide this arousal as would be the case in a leisure society, man will play or leisure to maintain the optimal level of arousal.[16] When this physiological model is translated into subjective or experiential terms the conditions providing for an optimal level of arousal often lead the human organism to experience "flow" or a peak-like experience which is pleasurable and highly involving.[17] In a workless society many people are likely to search out situations which will provide this type of experience. What role do these types of experiences play in the development of psychological well-being and personal development? For example, the pursuit of high risk activities appears to generate intense and highly involving experiences. Contemporary psychological theory has generally viewed this type of behavior as negative or abnormal, particularly the behavior of those who devote a whole life to its pursuit. Is this merely a hold-over from the Protestant work ethic?

If one engages in activities in which one's skills develop so as to make that activity less challenging or novel, then higher risks or novel forms of the activity must be found. In the case of high risk sports this cycle has been seen as addictive:

> Stimulus addiction implies the derived need to expose oneself repeat-
> edly to situations where the balance among fear, danger and anxiety
> remain within the boundaries of personal control. The cyclical need to
> extend oneself to the absolute physical, emotional and even intellectual
> limits is the quest to escape from bland tensionless states associated
> with everyday living.[18]

We might expect increasing numbers of people when freed from the constraints of work and thoughts of survival, no matter how indirect, turning to a more immediate and direct flirtation with survival. Experiences derived from balancing on the edge of survival/non-survival may produce an intoxication that cannot be provided by any other type of activity. The removal of the need to work for one's living or survival, no matter how indirect the connection in our society, may lead us to erect artificial barriers which we then challenge in the face of fear. This activity must take a form that is accepted by society such as play and sport. The endless search for novelty and experience is already underway:

> There is a whole set of leisure environments that are becoming a part
> of American life. These "ultra mod" settings include: electronic game
> parlors; computer games in people's homes; amusement parks which
> offer the latest in simulation and fantasy; and lazer light and music
> entertainment centers.[19]

The Mind Field or the Consciousness Technologies

While our educational institutions have stressed the rational, intellectual and logical approaches to understanding, there has been a trend to seek experiences which provide for self-development and knowledge through more intuitive and experiential modes. Many persons in our society in the search for this self-development are sampling western psycho-therapies and encounter groups as well as various degenerate forms of the esoteric Eastern psychologies currently being marketed. We have embraced transcendental meditation, astrology, biofeedback, gurus and trantrum yogas. The need to explore the intuitive side of

our natures has caused many " . . . to flock, unthinkingly, to rudimentary spiritual sideshows, which are quick, cheap, and often flashy"[20] . . . and an earnest
individual " . . . encounters innumerable freaky, peaky psychologies and associations, advertisements in the Sunday newspapers for courses in instant self-
improvement . . . and tiresome loonies of almost every persuasion."[21] While the
types of experiences provided by these "growth" fads are undoubtedly self-
indulgent and sensational, recent physiological and psychological research on
brain function and human cognitive capabilities suggest that man has two modes
of thinking or knowing (perhaps even three), and a variety of techniques that
have evolved in many esoteric eastern psychologies may allow us to explore one
of these ways of knowing.[22] As a nonverbal, nonlinear, nonintellectual approach
to knowing ourselves and the world, this mode sharply contrasts with the usual
Western approach which utilizes rational, intellectual and verbal modes of
thought. Is the search for mystical, religious and peak experiences synonymous
with the search for leisure experience? What role will leisure services provide to
potential consumers?

LEISURE EXPERIENCE ENGINEERING

Toffler has argued that the psychologization of services will mean that " . . . no
important service will be offered to the consumer before it has been analyzed by
teams of behavioral engineers to improve its psychic loading."[23] Psychological
research on leisure is only now beginning to study mental experience during
leisure. The field of psychology abandoned the study of consciousness early in
its own history and has only recently begun to consider these processes as
legitimate areas of inquiry. The small amount of leisure research done has
focused on the motives or needs for leisure and recreation preferences, while
leisure experiences have been overlooked. This view of leisure as a state of
mind or experience has made it difficult to study from the perspective of the
social sciences with their emphasis on the collection of objective data. A
handful of studies though, have emerged over the last several years attempting
to measure leisure experiences themselves. Several studies have measured
recreators' moods over the course of a recreation engagement using measures
of the changes in positive and negative moods as unidimensional indicators of
leisure experience. In my own research I have attempted to develop several
parallel measures of leisure experience. By monitoring changes in subjects'
moods, time perception and awareness of their surroundings, I and my colleagues have been able to monitor the impact of environmental factors, such as
the degree of freedom to participate and the level of competition in the setting,
on experiences during leisure. As well, the effect of personal characteristics on
one's leisure response to these environmental factors can be examined:

"... the identification and monitoring of these experiences (leisure)
will hopefully lend itself to a systematic effort to discover those
features of situations, activities, and persons which inhibit or enhance
the experience of leisure. The impact on leisure experiences of such
factors as freedom of choice, intrinsic and extrinsic motivations, work
and leisure attitudes, personality, and man-made and natural environments could be tested experimentally."[24]

Unfortunately or perhaps fortunately, the research output is far behind any
attempt to formalize scientific planning and design principles which could
provide the tools for leisure service professionals to become "leisure experience
engineers."

THE ROLE OF LEISURE SERVICES IN THE EXPERIENCE REVOLUTION

Is there a role for public leisure service agencies in a society in which experiences and consciousness technologies are marketed and sold? Should public
leisure services jump into the race and compete for a "piece of the experience
market?" Perhaps the private sector should be allowed to evolve unimpeded to
meet these experience needs. Public leisure service agencies are unlikely to
have the investment monies needed to pioneer the development of the facilities
and programs that will be demanded to provide exotic experience opportunities.
Perhaps public leisure service agencies should become monitoring and consumer
protection bodies to ensure that the experiences entering the market are "safe,"
"sanitary" and "enriched." We will then need to have knowledge concerning
what experiences contribute to growth states and consciousness raising and to
discern leisure from non-leisure states. We will have to establish criteria for
what are "good" experiences and develop standards. A complementary role
to the consumer protection and product monitoring role would be to take
responsibility for leisure counseling and public education to ensure that people
become wise "experience consumers."
     Our professional preparation programs in the universities and colleges would
have to adapt to these changes. What skills should our students depart with, and
where will our students find jobs? Should we be training "leisure experience
engineers" able to apply leisure experience principles that have been developed
by researchers in the social sciences concerned with human experience and
leisure. If we are to take this route there is a need to train some of our students
to be behavioral and experiential researchers. Also the majority of the jobs for
our students, certainly the most exciting jobs, will be in the private sector,
therefore we should better train them to operate and function in the commercial

sector both as innovative inventors of experiences and as knowledgeable private entrepreneurs. To ensure the quality of commercial leisure services and the availability of jobs for our graduates, we should press the government to pass legislation requiring the licensing of leisure experience engineers. It would be expected that the designer of a leisure experience would be suitably trained as would be the designer of a bridge. Commercial leisure service firms would, as a matter of course, hire our "engineering" students. There also would be positions in government. Leisure experience inspectors would be needed to police and monitor existing services and new varieties of experience introduced to the market. The experience revolution will mean a whole new role for leisure service professionals and leisure services as they are psychologized.

REFERENCES

1. Toffler, A. *Future Shock*, New York: Random House, 1979, p. 188. Toffler coined the term "psychologization."
2. de Grazia, S. *Of Time, Work, and Leisure*. New York: Twentieth Century Fund, 1962.
3. Gordon, C., Gaity, C., and Scott, J. "Leisure and Lives: Personal Expressivity across the Life Span." In: Binstok, R., and Shanas, E. (Eds.). *The Handbook of Aging and the Social Sciences*. New York: Van Nostrand
    Reinhold, 1976.
4. Mannell, R. "A Conceptual and Experimental Basis for Research in the Psychology of Leisure." *Society and Leisure/Loisir et Societe*. 1979, 2, pp. 179-196.
5. Mannell, R. "Social Psychological Techniques and Strategies for Studying Leisure Experiences." In Iso-Ahola, S., (Ed.). *Social Psychological Perspectives of Leisure and Recreation*. New York: Charles C. Thomas, 1980.
6. Balmer, K. *The Elora Prescription: A Future for Recreation*. Toronto: Ontario Ministry of Culture and Recreation, 1979.
7. Kando, T. *Leisure and Popular Culture in Transition*. St. Louis, Missouri: Mosby Co., 1975.
8. Balmer, *Op. Cit.*, pp. 9-11.
9. Drucker, P. The End of Economic Man: *A Study of the New Totalitarianism*. New York: John Day, 1939.
10. Tolman, E. *Behavior and Psychological Man: Essays in Motivation and Learning*. Berkeley, California: University of California Press, 1951.
11. Coan, R. *Hero, Artist, Sage, or Saint?* New York: Columbia University Press, 1977.

12. Toffler, *Op. Cit.*, p. 193.
13. *Ibid.*, p. 201.
14. *Ibid.*, p. 192.
15. *Ibid.*, p. 201.
16. Ellis, M. *Why People Play.* Englewood Cliffs, New Jersey: Prentice-Hall, Inc., 1973.
17. Csikszentmihalyi, M. *Beyond Boredom and Anxiety.* Washington, DC: Jossey-Bass, 1975.
18. Ogilvie, B. "The Stimulus-Addicts, A Psychosocial Paradox." In: Schwank, W. (Ed.). *The Winning Edge*, Washington, DC: American Association for Health, Physical Education and Recreation, 1974, pp. 49-50.
19. Fridgen, J. "Leisure Behavior: An Environmental Perspective." *Leisure Information Newsletter*, 5:4(Spring, 1979), pp. 6-9.
20. Ornstein, R. *The Mind Field.* New York: Pocket Books, 1976, p. 11.
21. *Ibid.*, p. 20.
22. Ornstein, R. *The Psychology of Consciousness.* Markham, Ontario: Penguin Books Ltd., 1972.
23. Toffler, *Op. Cit.*, p. 209.
24. Mannell, "Social Psychological . . . ," *Op. Cit.*

(no beep)

p. 440 is blank.
End of Chapter 32.

Chapter 33

Recovering a Good Idea for the Sake of Goodness: An Interpretive Critique of Subjective Leisure[1]

Charles Sylvester

Among the several branches of the psychology of leisure, the subjective view is gaining acceptance as "the most valid conceptualization of the leisure phenomenon."[2] Judging from its visibility in the professional literature and the ubiquitous use of the term "perceived," subjective leisure is certainly one of the most popular ideologies among researchers. Before it is crowned the supreme paradigm, however, I wish to raise several submerged issues that have moral, social, and epistemological implications. First, though, some background is required.

Neulinger's widely recognized definition typifies the basic premises of subjective leisure.[3] He defines leisure as a "state of mind," a subjective experience consisting of two essential conditions—perceived freedom and intrinsic motivation. The former is quintessential, for "leisure has one and only one essential criterion, and that is the condition of perceived freedom."[4] Thus, an "activity is leisure if it is perceived as leisure by the individual participant,"[5] meaning that "no activity is inherently not a leisure activity."[6] Regardless of the actual content, context, or consequences, *anything* counts as leisure as long as the individual avows a subjective experience of freedom. Applying to illusions as well as real events, the potential for leisure is virtually boundless. If you experience leisure, then leisure it is, for there is no disputing the truth of subjective states of mind.

The conceptual roots of subjective leisure have been traced to Aristotle in fourth century, B. C., Greece.[7] Regarding any "state of mind" view as a direct descendent of classical leisure, Neulinger claims that "probably the most critical aspect of this classical view is the fact that leisure is considered to be a state of mind."[8] His own subjective model "attempts to phrase these conditions in modern terminology, and may thus be considered a direct offspring of [classical leisure]."[9]

A comprehensive critique of subjective leisure, though overdue, cannot be accomplished in this brief chapter. My limited aim is just to clear some of the conceptual thicket surrounding the subjective theory of leisure by exploring several ironies. First, subjective leisure *is not* descended from classical leisure.

Second, classical leisure and subjective leisure are ethically opposed. Third, classical leisure relies on a method of inquiry that has been either rejected or largely abandoned in favor of empirical-analytic methods. Each of these ironies exposes morally and intellectually compelling implications for research and practice.

THE SUBJECTIVE ERROR: ARISTOTLE TURNED "OUTSIDE IN"

Transporting classical leisure over the span of 23 centuries from one civilization to another poses formidable problems. Language is particularly perplexing. Aristotle's moral vocabulary is not readily rephrased in the terminology of modern psychology. Erroneously considered a precursor of subjective leisure by some writers, Sebastian de Grazia observed that the language of classical leisure is philosophical, not psychological.[10] Although psychology evolved from philosophy, treating the language of classical leisure and modern psychology as interchangeable produces anachronisms that can lead to serious interpretive mistakes. Unfortunately, this has not discouraged some modern writers from using Aristotle to their advantage. Honoring him as their starting point, they proceed to "develop and justify [their] own particular ideas in ways that have little to do with [Aristotle]."[11] As Goodale observes, the results have been disappointing.[12]

I have chosen three examples from Aristotle's works to expose the disparity between subjective and classical views of leisure. They include the topics of happiness and freedom, moral conduct, and the context of leisure.

Happiness and Freedom

In the *Nicomachean Ethics* Aristotle discusses the good life and asks how it should be lived. He answers from the beginning that the best life is *eudaimonia*, which most translations interpret as happiness, some as well-being. But what kind of life deserves to be called *eudaimon*? In line with modern versions of happiness, proponents of the subjective view suggest that happiness is essentially psychological, a "state of mind" characterized by *feelings* of contentment and satisfaction. Although often affected by social factors, happiness is not dependent on them. In short, happiness is in the head.

Psychological happiness, however, is not what Aristotle meant by *eudaimonia*. Commentators reject the remotest relation between classical *eudaimonia* and the modern conception of happiness viewed as a subjective state.[13] Zeller is especially forthright, declaring that "Aristotle finds the criterion by which the conditions of happiness are determined *not in subjective feeling but in the objective character* [italics added] of the activities of life.[14] Above all, happiness is not a state of mind. Happiness is an action, moreover a good action. In Book I of the *Nicomachean Ethics* Aristotle explains that:

> ". . . it makes, perhaps, no small difference whether we place the chief good in possession or in use, in state of mind or in activity. For the state of mind may exist without producing any good result . . . but the activity cannot; for one who has the activity will of necessity be acting, and acting well."[15]

A complete explication of happiness would exhaust limited space and lead us too far afield. Clearly, though, happiness is not a subjective state of mind. Aristotelian happiness is "activity of soul in accordance with complete excellence."[16] Greatly simplified, happiness is having the conditions needed to choose and engage in worthy pursuits according to a standard of excellence.

Thus, happiness consists substantially of goodness or excellence and "is thought to depend on leisure."[17] The condition of leisure is the freedom needed for happiness and "leisure activities are the constituents of happiness."[18] Therefore, treating leisure as a state of mind results in a logical contradiction. Because happiness is an action, its constitutive parts must also be actions.

Aristotle is further explicit that leisure is fundamentally a social condition, defining it as "freedom from the necessity of labour."[19] Hannah Arendt calls this freedom:

> ". . . the *essential condition* [italics added] of what the Greeks called felicity, *eudaimonia*, which was an *objective status* [italics added] depending first of all upon wealth and health. To be poor or to be in ill health meant to be subject to physical necessity, and to be a slave meant to be subject, in addition, to man-made violence. This . . . 'unhappiness' of slavery if quite independent of the actual subjective well-being of the slave."[20]

Aristotelian leisure, therefore, was not acquired through subjective dispositions, such as feelings or attitudes. Rather than being descended from *eudaimonism*, subjective views are historically linked to the Stoic *theory of assent*. It suggests that people can subjectively control their circumstances, using wishful thinking to clear life's traumas and troubles from the path of happiness. In other words, no matter how wretched the circumstance, you can always willfully choose your attitude and thus be subjectively happy and free in the face of ruin and constraint.

Yet Aristotle largely rejected Stoicism. The lack of objective freedom, particularly when brought on by war or poverty, produced *unleisure*, "the narrowing of the field of action" necessary for the activities of happiness.[21] The assumption that leisure can be produced by a change of mind contravenes classical leisure and is one of the more egregious propositions of subjective leisure. No matter how convincing an illusion psychologists are capable of engineering, the poor, the disenfranchised, and the politically oppressed do not have leisure.

Moral Conduct

Sociopolitical freedom is just the beginning of leisure. Aristotle observes in the *Politics* that the cultivated ability to use leisure rightly is the basis of a person's entire life. Choice and conduct imbue leisure with moral substance. Leisure is therefore intended for worthy purposes performed well. Discussing classical leisure, Owens explains that:

> ". . . choice characterizes all moral action . . . If choice is [also] made the distinguishing characteristic of leisurely action, then the topic of leisure and the topic of morality will coincide in Aristotle. *Leisure conduct and moral conduct will become the same* [italics added]."[22]

The freedom of leisure is not for doing anything one pleases. That is license, which leads to licentiousness, not happiness. Molded by habit and directed by reason, moral conduct—leisurely action—involves consistently making the right choices among life's myriad alternatives and doing them well.

Conversely, any choice, including the illusion of choice, qualifies as subjective leisure as long as it produces a feeling of freedom. Since leisure is derived from private feelings, logically valid and empirically verifiable moral judgments are not relevant, exposing the subjective view as implausible and potentially repugnant. Rooted in subjective feelings, "no activity is inherently not a leisure activity."[23] As such, making "snuff" films, the depraved and horrific practice of kidnapping children for pornographic purposes and then torturously murdering them, subjectively counts as leisure alongside family strolls in the park. Yet the classical view considers moral conduct and leisure conduct synonymous. As a result, only worthy activities are inherently leisure. Unless morality can be verified by brainwaves, subjective and classical leisure reside in different ethical worlds.

The Context of Leisure

The final disparity involves context. While subjective leisure may be influenced by social conditions and practices, it originates from individual perceptions, making it inherently individualistic. The world of subjective leisure is *private*, needing nothing but one's feelings and perceptions.

Classical leisure was nurtured by a much different source. It acquired meaning and significance in the context of *intersubjective* (public) rather than *subjective* (private) experience. Aristotle observed that human beings are social animals who come together for survival. People stay together, however, for *eudaimonia*, the good life. An individualistic conception of leisure was inconceivable to the Greeks. The conditions required for personal leisure and happiness were located in the political domain of the Greek city-state *(polis)*.[24] It was only as the city-state fell into decline that despairing philosophers withdraw to individualistic and subjective philosophies like Epicureanism.

The public domain provided two vital conditions for classical leisure. First, individuality was only possible in the presence of others.[25] Tacit and explicit understanding of the meaning and significance of individual life, including the worthy use of leisure, were derived from public life. Without commonly understood beliefs and values to provide moral moorings, leisure dissipated into a vaporous subjective morass. The modern quest to "know thyself" often implies a journey into the private psyche in search of the "real" self. For the Greeks, identity and worth were mainly gained through a vigorous public life.

Second, excellence required, in addition to a "field of action," an arena to appear, a place where one's outstanding efforts could stand out. This, too, occurred in the *polis*. Arendt writes that:

> ". . . excellence, *arete* for the Greeks and *virtus* for the Romans, has always been assigned to the public realm where one could excel, could distinguish oneself from other . . . excellence by definition, [requires] the presence of others . . . "[26]

Personal esteem and respect were not produced by inducing people to feel good about themselves. Self-esteem and self-respect grew out of virtuous action. Accordingly, Greek life was characterized by *agon*, the spirit of challenge and struggle, giving rise to excellent action.[27] Thomas Green, who has not received the audience in leisure studies he deserves, recovers this spirit in his modern critique of work, labor, and leisure.[28] Using *effort* as a conceptual category, Green distinguishes between meaningful effort (work) and futile effort (labor). The modern problem of leisure involves discovering opportunities for meaningful effort, resulting in experiences of potency and joy. Finding meaningful activity—a work to do in one's leisure—demands "the discovery of an area of wrestling, of a sphere of activity in which the self is tested and disclosed."[29] Green labels these modern versions of the *polis* "spheres of action" or "publics." Adapted to modern pluralism, he calls for a "diversity of spheres of action . . . in which different kinds of persons may test themselves and disclose themselves."[30]

Therefore, while classical leisure was profoundly personal, it was also inextricably public. Reducing classical leisure to a subjective experience sequesters it is private feelings, leading to mystification. The excellence of classical leisure objectively resulted from reciprocal enrichment between personal and public life.

In sum, the preceding examples reveal that subjective leisure is neither descended from nor distantly related to classical leisure. Reconstructing classical leisure into a subjective model turns Aristotle's views "outside in," misappropriately shifting them from ethics to psychology. Moreover, psychologism distorts the meaning and significance of classical leisure, obscuring critical moral implications.

THE MORAL MESSAGE: THINK POSITIVE

Among several issues, one of the major ethical problems of subjective leisure is evident in Seppo Iso-Ahola's discussion of leisure, happiness, and the perceived quality of life. Nestled in his critique of consumerism, materialism, and status-seeking, Iso-Ahola espouses a core ethical tenet of subjective leisure. He declares that "the quality of life is in the mind. No matter how much or little a person owns or does, he can be happy and satisfied with the life if he so decides."[31]

Here we witness the Stoic theory of assent in operation. The radical implication is that people can transform their lives from troubled to contented and from empty to enriching by the power of positive thinking. Happiness is mainly psychological adjustment, an exercise of mind over matter, as suggested in the following passage from an article entitled "A 10-Day Plan for Happiness.":

> Actually, as the experts would tell you, that lost feeling—those Sunday afternoon blues—can't be blamed on your hard or boring life. It's all in your head. *What you need is scientific guidance to help you regain true perspective* [italics added] and start living life fully again. This ten-day plan does that. Its simple psychology should work for you.[32]

Whether life is really fulfilling along such lines as respect, challenge, accomplishment, and excellence is moot as long as people can either convince themselves or be persuaded to feel happy and contented. Therefore, the task for social psychological engineers—descended from Stoicism, not Aristotelianism—is *"how to induce or convince people to be satisfied with what they are and what they have now."*[33]

Anticipating criticism, Iso-Ahola cautions that his ideas should not be construed as support for the status-quo.[34] Yet if social justice can be achieved by inducing perceptions of contentment and well-being, why bother with material changes in work, housing, education and leisure? Convincing people to feel contented avoids the far messier and more difficult problem of providing substantive opportunities for authentic accomplishments so people have something in their lives worth feeling good about. In subjective terms, social justice starts with equality of experience and distributive perceptions instead of fair distribution of resources and equal opportunity.

Subjective leisure draws much of its support from research which correlates perceptions of control, competence, novelty, intrinsic motivation, and self-determination with such benefits as health, enjoyment, and psychological happiness.[35] These findings are impressive. Yet the ethical argument they support is specious.

Charles Murray, a social critic and political theorist, agrees that challenge, autonomy, competence, intrinsic motivation, and self-determination are the wellsprings of enjoyment and the pillars of happiness.[36] Yet he disagrees that subjective perceptions are adequate foundations for lasting and substantive happiness. Murray contends it is not enough for people to feel *as if* they are free, autonomous, challenged, competent, and self-determining if in fact they are not. He asserts that happiness depends on what people actually do with their lives. Substituting dreams, illusions, or subjective perceptions for actual deeds is mistaken, inauthentic, and an implausible basis for personal happiness and social policy. The challenge is not to persuade people to lead pretentious lives by having psychological tailors outfit them in the emperor's new clothes. Instead, it is to organize society so "people are authentically in control of their own lives and possess authentic competencies in which they can take pleasure."[37] Murray concludes that "these fundamental wellsprings of human satisfaction must rest on reality. The test that any proposed program must meet is that is *really does* contribute to them."[38]

In his discussion of work, labor, and leisure, Thomas Green also rejects radical subjectivism.[39] Acknowledging that the meaningfulness of effort relies on the individual's interpretation of the action, he warns:

> If the difference between work [meaningful effort] and labor [futile effort] is purely a matter of individual appraisal and corresponds to no real distinction in kinds of human activities, then it would seem that the universal meaningfulness of work could be achieved by the successful propagation of a mass delusion. The very idea is offensive to one's respect for truth.[40]

Grounded in emotions, subjective leisure offers no rational foundation for evaluating the meaning and significance of moral actions. If leisure is whatever the individual experiences, and if experiencing leisure is inherently good,[41] we are cast adrift in murky and turbulent waters with nothing to guide us besides the shibboleth, "If it feels good do it."

The quality of life requires something more substantive and authentic than ephemeral feelings and mental states. Iso-Ahola, for instance, correctly acknowledges the importance of shared human relationships and "feelings of mutual respect."[42] On what basis, though, should we grant respect and gain self-esteem—perceptions or performance? Surely both are involved, and therein lies the resolution to the subjective-objective dichotomy. But subjectivism alone is morally vacuous. Self-respect and respect for others is based on understandings among people of the kinds of acts worthy of moral regard. If I damage the environment or participate in racist activities, I am undeserving of respect regardless of what I may perceive. Individual interpretations of leisure gain meaning and significance in the context of shared understandings. Charles Taylor thus argues that:

> Not just any new definition can be forced on us, nor can we force it on ourselves; and some which we do gladly take up can be judged inauthentic, or in bad faith, or just wrong-headed.[43]

Subjective leisure lacks such a framework for judging ways in which leisure can be authentic, right-headed, and in good faith. Peter Witt's and Gary Ellis' comments about the morality of leisure are therefore instructive. Discussing what they call the "leisure-as-activity approach," they explain that:

> To be considered leisure the activity must be moral, wholesome, and contribute to the betterment and welfare of the individual. The morass thickens. Clearly each of these criteria involves a series of judgements about what is moral or wholesome, etc. It is easy to see why there is so little agreement on what constitutes leisure. In the final analysis, the activity approach also seems to be largely based on a subjective perception of moral, wholesome betterment and a host of other equally difficult to define criteria. This approach may be comforting but it is hardly objective.[44]

They are wrong that the "activity approach" is necessarily based on subjective perception. Values can be rationally validated and empirically verified. Yet they are also correct. Ethics does require reasoned judgment, and criteria are often tough to define and validate. Nevertheless, valid, verifiable criteria do substantiate the claim that Gandhi was a better person than Hitler and that the poetry of Robert Frost is preferable to child pornography. Of course most value judgments are far more difficult than these to assess. Still, rational value inquiry is both possible and necessary. Aristotle, who took a "leisure-as-activity approach," accepted this as his objective in the *Nicomachean Ethics*. He wished to help us face the difficult and paramount challenge of becoming good people.

He knew ethics was not easy. As such, he took great pains to explain the kind of knowledge needed for the sake of goodness. Yet proponents of subjective leisure, in their expedient use of Aristotle, have obscured and therefore missed one of his most important points.

THE RISE OF RATIONALITY AND THE DECLINE OF REASON

> The existence of experimental methods make us think we have the means of solving the problems which trouble us, though problems and methods pass one another by. Ludwig Wittgenstein[45]

Leisure drew little attention from science prior to the advent of "leisure science" in the second half of the twentieth century. In the past several decades, however, efforts to "operationalize" and *make* leisure susceptible to scientific analysis have grown. Pioneering the psychology of leisure, John Neulinger wrote that his subjective model "attempts to translate [classical leisure] into contemporary scientific language."[46] Other proponents of subjective leisure have also espoused empirical-analytic methods as the most positive and progressive way to gain knowledge of leisure.[47] Referring to the canon "that the *nature* of the phenomenon . . . directs the methodology," Christine Howe asserts that "a major contributor to the increasing sophistication in leisure research is the way in which leisure is being defined as a psychological state."[48] Thus, truth and method ostensibly join in the psychology of leisure, exposing a final irony related to classical leisure.

Leading proponents of subjective leisure at once embrace the heritage of classical leisure while advocating methods of theoretical science. One of the first to observe that method is a function of the subject, Aristotle did not believe, however, that theoretical science was the principal method of inquiry for the subject of leisure. Therefore, if we accept the narrow rationality which limits legitimate knowledge and research to "social empiricism and social analysis,"[49] we abandon the kind of inquiry Aristotle deemed most appropriate for understanding leisure.

Aristotle does not give a scientific explanation of goodness in the *Nicomachean Ethics*, writing that "the present inquiry does not aim at theoretical knowledge . . . (for we are inquiring not in order to know what excellence is, but in order to become good . . .)."[50] Nor does he attempt a scientific account of leisure. Usually precise and thorough on subjects of theoretical science, Aristotle discusses leisure just enough to explicate how it is acquired and how it should be used in relation to happiness. Indeed, "the writing of the *Ethics* . . . is not a work of science proper but of *practical wisdom* (italics added)."[51] It is *ethical* inquiry into the practical problem of how to achieve happiness. What, though, does "practical wisdom" mean? And what is its connection to theoretical science and leisure? At the risk of oversimplification, I wish to sketch their relationship.

In its traditional sense, theoretical science is knowledge of absolute and immutable truths, such as the laws of motion and gravity. The purpose of theoretical science is to explain the causal nexus of nature in order that it may be understood. It assumes, therefore, the existence of an orderly, enduring, and universal structure underlying natural phenomena that can be described and explained using empirical and statistical methods. Theoretical science has amassed a remarkable record of elucidating how nature works. The success of natural science at predicting and controlling the physical world has also fostered and sustained the dogma that theoretical science can similarly discover the laws governing social life.

Yet Aristotle considered social and physical life fundamentally different. Physical life is governed by forces that are permanent, universal, and determinate. For example, all else being equal, gravity in ancient Athens operated the same as gravity today in Los Angeles and Istanbul. Social life, on the other hand, is mutable, relative, and indeterminate. Rather than absolutely true, it is contingent, existing, as Aristotle observes, "only by convention, and not by nature."[52] Aristotle means that human beings creatively contribute to the "nature" of social life through the beliefs, customs, norms, and cultural practices they adopt. Beliefs and practices differ among and within societies. They also change over time, resulting in new and different cultural forms. Reasons can be identified using scientific methods to explain social life, providing general knowledge conditioned by time and by place of the myriad factors shaping it. Explanations cannot, however, be stated as foundational laws, eternally and universally true.

Each progressive moment of social life, then, is complex, diverse, variable, and never exactly the same. Social life cannot be subsumed neatly under global scientific principles. It is open, changing, and, to a degree, self-caused. Reflection and judgment are required to mediate between general social scientific principles and the contingencies of particular social situations. Aristotle referred to this kind of knowledge and method of inquiry as *phronesis* ("practical wisdom").

Phronesis is similar to judicial reasoning. Judges base their decisions on laws. Law, however, cannot determine the one right decision for every case since all cases are not alike. Judges, therefore, must interpret the law relative to the unique features of each case, reaching their judgments by deliberation rather than scientific equation.

Just as judges decide cases, people choose how to life. Beyond basics— food, water, shelter—the answer to the question "How should I conduct my life?" is open to diverse possibilities. Moreover, this question cannot be answered with scientific certitude. Science, for example, can inform us of diseases which affect our lives. It cannot tell us, however, whether we should tend to the sick or protect ourselves from them. Ethical understanding is needed to guide judgment and choice in concrete situations where no definitive rule of action exists.

Moral choice is also a central element of classical leisure. Suppose science finds that social relations, public service, physical fitness, intellectual pursuits, and aesthetic expression and appreciation are all activities that contribute to the "quality of life" (a modern synonym for happiness). Should I do just one or all of them? What if I am not artistically inclined or simply do not like physical activity? What about my obligations to family and community? Lacking a law, equation, or absolute standard, how can I decide what I should do? Practical wisdom is a mix of knowledge and insight that enables one to evaluate the use of leisure *relative* to one's abilities, interests, circumstances, and development. Guided by general principles (scientific reasoning), particular actions require deliberation and judgment (moral reasoning) in order to do the right thing, at the right time, and in the right way. Scientific reasoning and moral reasoning, unlike the separate departments they are today, were complementary ways of understanding in Aristotle's eyes.

Of course Aristotle reflected on leisure without the advantage of modern scientific methods. As a result, he was limited to conjecture or "social philosophy."[53] Conversely, modern researchers, equipped with sophisticated scientific methods, are apparently in positions to discover what leisure really is.

Yet I do not think so. Leisure is not an independent object "out there" in the world of nature (the fallacy of reification). It is invented in the interplay of thought, language, and cultural practices, including the practice of science. Consequently, leisure has been differently "valid" throughout history. An ancient Athenian and a contemporary New Yorker could speak intelligibly with each other about a stone well-shaped for skipping on water. Conversation about leisure, however, would leave them perplexed with each other's incommensurate views. Modern "conceptualizations" of leisure are no more independently valid than the conceptions of Renaissance Italy or classical Greece. *All* theories of leisure tacitly embody cultural beliefs and values. Reflecting the historically embedded desires, interests, intentions, and ideologies of their creators, theories of leisure are originally *prescriptive* rather than descriptive or explicative. We call leisure what we think it *should* be, not what it *is*; for it is theoretically no more than a *choice* of theories. The question, then, is not which theory is more "true." There is simply no neutral way to decide. Rather than the "pure and naked truth," the issue is how we can arrive at *better* ways of thinking about leisure whose truth is believable and functional to the demands of modern life.[54] As social and intellectual conditions change, so will our theorizing, leaving the "nature" of leisure an open question subject to infinite inquiry.

For the present, I have argued that subjective leisure is neither plausible nor functional. Furthermore, I have challenged the strain of rationality evident in leisure science that considers empiricism the answer for the "problems which trouble us," most of which are moral rather than technical. Theoretical science indeed has an essential role, providing knowledge that permits "more discerning judgments"[55] of how to live our lives as well as we can. Nevertheless, as something free, personal, purposeful, and "which conditions the deepest fiber of moral conduct,"[56] leisure also requires reflection, judgment, and choice.

Finally, interpretation permits conversations between past and present horizons. Understanding what Aristotle was trying to say to us would assist leisure studies to come of age by recovering an important part of its classical heritage. He tells us that practical wisdom is indispensable "if leisure is to matter."[57] Curricula may never include courses on *phronesis* to complement and direct theoretical knowledge. But for the sake of leisure and goodness it would not be a bad idea.

REFERENCES

1. I wish to thank John Hemingway, Ken Mobily, August Bartlett, and C. Mousse for their assistance.
2. Howe, C. "Possibilities for Using a Qualitative Research Approach in the Sociological Study of Leisure." *Journal of Leisure Research.* 17 (1985), p. 212.
3. Neulinger, J. *To Leisure: An Introduction.* Boston: Allyn and Bacon, 1981.
4. Neulinger, J. *The Psychology of Leisure.* Springfield, Illinois: Charles C. Thomas, 1974, p. 15.
5. Witt, P. and Ellis, G. "Conceptualizing Leisure: Making the Abstract Concrete," *In Recreation and Leisure: Issues in an Era of Change,* In: Goodale, T. L. and Witt, P. A. (Eds.). State College, Pennsylvania: Venture Publishing, 1985, p. 106.
6. Neulinger, *The Psychology of Leisure,* p. 35.
7. See Iso-Ahola, S. *The Social Psychology of Leisure and Recreation.* Dubuque, Iowa: Wm. C. Brown, 1980, pp. 28-29. Neulinger, *To Leisure.* p. 33.
8. Neulinger, *To Leisure.* p. 18
9. Ibid.
10. de Grazia, S. Letter to author, 25 May 1989.
11. Owens, J. "Aristotle on Leisure," *Canadian Journal of Philosophy.* 11 (1981), p. 714.
12. Goodale, T. L. "If Leisure is to Matter," in *Recreation and Leisure: Issues in an Era of Change,* In: Goodale, T. L. and Witt, P. A., pp. 44-45,. *Op. Cit.*

13. For example see Cooper, J. *Reason and Human Good in Aristotle.*
    Cambridge, Massachusetts: Harvard University Press, 1975, p. 89.
14. Zeller, E. *Outlines of the History of Greek Philosophy.* (L. R. Palmer,
    Trans.), New York: Meridian Books, 1957, p. 207.
15. Aristotle. *Nicomachean Ethics* trans. (W. D. Ross, Rev. J. L. Ackrill and J.
    O. Urmson, Trans.), London: Oxford University Press, 1980/originally
    published 1925, pp. 1098b33-1099a3.
16. Aristotle. *Nicomachean Ethics* trans. (W. D. Ross, Rev. J. O. Urmson,
    Trans.), in *The Complete Works of Aristotle*, Vol. 2, Barnes, J. (Ed.).
    Princeton, New Jersey: Princeton University Press, 1984, p. 1102a5.
17. Aristotle. *Nicomachean Ethics.* p. 1177b4.
18. Adler, M. "Labor, Leisure, and Liberal Education," *Journal of General
    Education.* 6(1951): p. 45.
19. Aristotle. *Politics* (E. Barker, Trans.) London: Oxford University Press,
    1946, p. 1269a.
20. Arendt, H. *The Human Condition.* Chicago, Illinois: University of
    Chicago Press, 1958, p. 31.
21. Stocks, J. L. "Leisure," in *Reason and Intuition and other Essays.*
    Emmet, D. M. (Ed.). London: Oxford University Press, 1939, p. 155.
22. Owens, "Aristotle on Leisure," p. 718.
23. Neulinger, *The Psychology of Leisure.* p. 35.
24. Arendt, *The Human Condition.*
25. Ibid.
26. Ibid., pp. 48-49.
27. Ibid.
28. Green, T. F. *Work, Leisure, and the American Schools.* New York:
    Random House, 1968.
29. Ibid., p. 141.
30. Ibid.
31. Iso-Ahola, *The Social Psychology of Leisure and Recreation.* p. 380.
32. Quoted in Jones, H. M. *The Pursuit of Happiness.* Cambridge, Massachu-
    setts: Harvard University Press, 1953, p. 161.
33. Iso-Ahola, *The Social Psychology of Leisure and Recreation.* p. 393.
34. Ibid.
35. See Iso-Ahola, S. *The Social Psychology of Leisure and Recreation* for an
    extensive discussion of research related to the social psychology of leisure.
36. Murray, C. *In Pursuit of Happiness and Good Government.* New York:
    Simon and Schuster, 1988.
37. Ibid., 157.
38. Ibid., 296.
39. Green, *Work, Leisure, and the American Schools.*
40. Ibid., 28.

41. See Neulinger, *The Psychology of Leisure.* pp. 155, 165.
42. Iso-Ahola, *The Social Psychology of Leisure and Recreation.* p. 394.
43. Taylor, C. "Interpretation and the Sciences of Man," in *Interpretive Social Science*, Rabinow, P. and Sullivan, W. (Eds.). Berkeley, California: University of California Press, 1979, p. 37.
44. Witt and Ellis, "Conceptualizing Leisure: Making the Abstract Concrete," 106.
45. Wittgenstein, L. *Philosophical Investigations.* (G. E. M. Anscombe, Trans.) New York: MacMillan, 1953, p. 232e.
46. Neulinger, *To Leisure.* p. 33.
47. See Iso-Ahola. *The Social Psychology of Leisure and Recreation.* Witt and Ellis, "Conceptualizing Leisure: Making the Abstract Concrete."
48. Howe, "Possibilities for Using a Qualitative Research Approach in the Sociological Study of Leisure," p. 216.
49. Iso-Ahola, *The Social Psychology of Leisure and Recreation.* p. 48.
50. Aristotle, *Nicomachean Ethics.* p. 1103b26.
51. Ross, W. D. *Aristotle: A Complete Exposition of His Works and Thought* Cleveland, Ohio: The World Publishing Co., 1955, pp. 211-212.
52. Aristotle. *Nicomachean Ethics.* p. 1094b16.
53. "Social philosophy" has been used pejoratively by some proponents of subjective leisure to imply shallow conjecture and emotivism. Their choice of words is unfortunate since social philosophy is a serious and important intellectual endeavor. Ironically, once again, proponents of subjective leisure practice social philosophy all the while they belittle it.
54. Green, *Work, Leisure, and the American Schools.* p. 7.
55. Gergen, K. J. "Social Psychology as History," *Journal of Personality and Social Psychology.* 26(1973), p. 317.
56. Owens, "Aristotle on Leisure," p. 723.
57. Goodale, "If Leisure is to Matter," p. 54.

End of Chapter 33. "About the Contributors" follows.

CONTRIBUTORS

Serena E. Arnold is Professor Emeritus at U.C.L.A. where she served as Chair of the Department of Kinesiology and formerly Chair of Recreation Education. She received her doctorate from Indiana University while serving as Recreation Consultant for the State of California. She has served as area supervisor, Federal Works Agency (WPA), county recreation planner, and superintendent of parks and recreation in a California municipality. Recipient of numerous awards, she has held offices in several state and national professional organizations. Her principal academic interest is play behavior.

Joseph J. Bannon, Professor and former Head of the Department of Leisure Studies, University of Illinois, is founder of the Management Learning Laboratory and of Sagamore Publishing. Author of three texts and numerous articles, he has given dozens of workshops on problem solving, human resource management, decision making, and other management related topics. He has been a trustee of the National Recreation and Park Association and Chairman of its National Council, president of the Society of Park and Recreation Educators, and recipient of several awards from national professional organizations. His Ph.D. is from the University of Illinois.

Lynn A. Barnett is Associate Professor, Leisure Behavior Research Laboratory, Department of Leisure Studies, University of Illinois. She is the author of numerous articles and chapters on children's play, reflecting interests in theoretical explanations for play and relationships between play and children's cognitive and emotional development. She has consulted on the design of playgrounds and play materials for maximizing children's expression and development. She recently edited *Research About Leisure,* and has written and spoken extensively on research methodology and issues related to conducting research in recreation and leisure.

Doyle Bishop is currently Senior Research Analyst at National Demographics and Lifestyles, Denver, Colorado. He holds a Ph.D. Degree in Psychology from the University of Illinois and was a professor there and at the University of Ottawa. He has an extensive background of research and writing in psychology and leisure research and has been an editor and reviewer for several research journals. His research interests focus upon personality as it influences leisure pursuits, creativity, physical and mental health, and lifestyles as they relate to consumer behavior.

Francis J. Bregha, now retired, was Professor in the Department of Recreology at the University of Ottawa. Previously he was Professor and Chairman of the Community Development and Social Change Program, School of Social Work, University of Toronto. He has been writing about leisure since 1970. Interested in demographics, employment, social planning and community development, recently he has been examining the philosophical and ethical basis of our ideas about leisure. Member of several federal and provincial commissions and task forces in Canada, he was the first Canadian representative of the Inter-American Development Bank in Central America.

Rabel J. Burdge, Professor of Rural Sociology at the University of Illinois at Urbana-Champaign, is affiliated with the Institute for Environmental Studies, the Department of Agricultural Economics, Leisure Studies, and Urban and Regional Planning. A graduate of Ohio State University, his Ph.D. is from The Pennsylvania State University. Former editor of the *Journal of Leisure Research* and founding co-editor of *Leisure Sciences,* he is co-editor of *Society and Natural Resources.* He has authored numerous articles and co-authored a text on rural sociology. He has taught at Universities in the Netherlands and Australia as well as at the Universities of Kentucky and Washington and the Air Force Academy.

John Crompton is Professor of Recreation, Park and Tourism Sciences at Texas A&M University. He is the author or co-author of three books and numerous articles which have appeared in the recreation, tourism and marketing literature. He has given invited presentations in eleven countries. His interests center around marketing and financing recreation, park and tourism services.

Mary R. Duncan received her Ph.D. from the United States International University and is Professor and former Chair, Department of Recreation at San Diego State University. She has published several articles regarding recreation and violence in Northern Ireland and co-authored *Supervision of Leisure Services.* She also wrote *The Underground Guide to Job Interviewing.* She has traveled extensively and lectured in Europe, India and the Arab Gulf as well as the Smithsonian Institution in Washington, DC, where she lectured on "Play, Terrorism, Revolution and Radical Politics."

Daniel L. Dustin is Professor of Outdoor Recreation Planning and Policy at San Diego State University. He has a B.A. in Geography and an M.S. in Resource Planning and Conservation from the University of Michigan, and a Ph.D. in Education with an emphasis in Recreation and Park Administration from the University of Minnesota. He is the principal author of *Stewards of Access/ Custodians of Choice: A Philosophical Foundation for the Park and Recreation Profession,* and the author of numerous essays on outdoor recreation planning and policy, interpretive techniques, and environmental ethics.

Gary D. Ellis is Associate Professor and Director of Graduate Studies in the Department of Recreation and Leisure at the University of Utah. He also serves as Director of the Western Laboratory for Leisure Research at that institution. His research interests are in conceptualization and measurement of leisure, research methodology, and the social psychology of leisure.

John Farina, now retired, was Professor of Social Work at Sir Wilfred Laurier University, having taught previously at the University of Toronto and the Chinese University of Hong Kong. He earned the Doctor of Social Work degree at Washington University, Saint Louis. Prior to teaching he was Assistant Superintendent of Recreation in Tacoma and Superintendent of Recreation in Edmonton, Alberta, and was Executive Secretary for Group Work of the Canadian Welfare Council. He has authored numerous articles and reports on social work and social welfare, as well as leisure and recreation.

Maureen Glancy is Visiting Assistant Professor, Department of Leisure Studies, University of Illinois, with previous experience at Western Illinois University, The Pennsylvania State University, Virginia Tech, University of Maine, and Northeastern University. She has served as State Director of HPER and Camping for the YWCAs of Greater Rhode Island, Co-Founder and Assistant Director of Spruce Mountain Environmental Center. She was Director of Strategic Planning for the Commonwealth Educational System at The Pennsylvania State University where she received her Ph.D. in Recreation and Parks with a minor in Social Organization. Her interests include qualitative research methods and using social theory to understand the meaning and significance of leisure.

Geoffrey Godbey is Professor of Leisure Studies at The Pennsylvania State University. He is the author or co-author of six books and numerous articles concerning leisure behavior and services. His interests include aging and leisure, leisure ethics, urban parks and recreation services, research methodology, international aspects of leisure services, futures research and histories of leisure behavior. He has given invited presentations in fourteen countries and is Editor of Venture Publishing.

Thomas L. Goodale is Professor and Coordinator of Parks, Recreation and Leisure Studies at George Mason University, Fairfax, Virginia. He received the Ph.D. degree from the University of Illinois at Urbana-Champaign and has taught at the State University of New York-Cortland, The University of Wisconsin-Green Bay and the University of Ottawa, Canada. Author of numerous articles and chapters on leisure and related topics, he recently co-authored *The Evolution of Leisure*. He is Past-President of the Academy of Leisure Sciences and currently Editor of *Leisure Sciences*.

Peggy Hutchison, Ed.D., consultant and educator, has been doing research and writing on integration, deinstitutionalization, consumer participation and empowerment, and friendship through the G. Allan Roeher Institute (GARI) in Toronto and the Centre for Research and Education in Human Services in Kitchener, Ontario. She is currently active with Conestoga College developing a new program in Community Integration. Her latest books *Friendship* (published by GARI), and *Community, Integration, and Leisure* with J. McGill (published by Leisurability Publications) are a culmination of her last five years of work on leisure and disability.

Claudine Jeanrenaud, formerly an Associate Professor, Department of Recreology, University of Ottawa, earned her Bachelor's of Art Education degree at the University of Lausane, Switzerland; her M.S. and Ph.D. at the University of Illinois, Department of Leisure Studies. Her main interests lie in the area of conceptual and creative development as reflected in graphic expression of adults and children, as well as the environmental and personality determinants of such development. She is currently a student of analytical psychology, and has a private practice providing individual psychotherapy and group art therapy.

John R. Kelly is Professor of Leisure Studies and Director of the Office of Gerontology and Aging Studies at the University of Illinois. His Ph.D. is in sociology from the University of Oregon and he has received master's degrees from Yale, Oregon, and the University of Southern California. His recent books include: *Leisure; Freedom to Be: A New Sociology of Leisure; Recreation Business; Leisure Identities and Interactions*. Leisure roles, contexts, and meanings through the life course are his principal academic interests.

Charles W. Lamb is the M.J. Neeley Professor of Marketing at Texas Christian University. His interests include the application of marketing philosophy, techniques and knowledge to the solution of problems faced by nonprofit organizations and government agencies. He has published over 50 articles and research papers on marketing for nonprofit organizations and co-authored two books in this area of specialization.

John Lord is currently with the Centre for Research and Education in Human Services in Kitchener, Ontario. He has been a school teacher, a recreation worker, and has worked in program development, planning, and evaluation. He was, for seven years, a faculty member at Dalhousie University. Author of several articles, and two books in the area of integration, advocacy, recreation, community development, and human service planning, he is an Associate of the National Institute on Mental Retardation.

Roger C. Mannell is Professor and Chair of the Department of Recreation and Leisure Studies at the University of Waterloo. He is a research psychologist having received a doctorate in Psychology at the University of Windsor. Previously he directed the government and university sponsored Center of Leisure Studies at Acadia University in Nova Scotia. His teaching an research interests include the psychology of leisure and program evaluation.

Leo H. McAvoy is Associate Professor and Head of the Division of Recreation, Park, and Leisure Studies at the University of Minnesota. He holds a B.A. in Psychology from Loras College, an M.S. in Recreation Administration from San Francisco State University, and a Ph.D. in Education with an emphasis in Recreation and Park Administration from the University of Minnesota. He conducts research and writes about recreation resource management, outdoor program leadership, and wilderness policy.

Bill Michaelis, Ph.D. is a Professor of Recreation and Leisure Studies at San Francisco State University. He chairs the Parks, Beaches and Recreation Commission for the city of Pacifica, California, and is Director of both "Children Together" and "The Family that Plays Together," two play event and training organizations. Bill has written, taught and consulted extensively in the area of play and its applications to learning and development. He has provided over 300 presentations and workshops to various recreation, education and human service organizations throughout North America and Europe. He is the author of *Learning Through Non Competitive Activities and Play* and was a contributing author and editor of *More New Games.*

Ronald P. Reynolds is Professor of Recreation, Parks, and Tourism at Virginia Commonwealth University where he coordinates the therapeutic recreation option. He received the Ph.D. degree from the University of Illinois and has been editor of the *Therapeutic Recreation Journal,* and co-editor of the *Journal of Leisurability.* In addition to contributing numerous articles and book chapters, he has co-authored two texts: *Problems, Issues and Concepts in Therapeutic Recreation* and *Therapeutic Recreation: A Helping Profession.*

John H. Schultz is Associate Professor in the University of Minnesota's Division of Recreation, Park, and Leisure Studies. He earned a B.S. in Physical Education from Valparaiso University, an M.S. in Recreation Administration from the University of Illinois, and a Ph.D. In Education with an emphasis in Recreation and Park Administration from the University of Minnesota. In addition to serving as Division Head for the past fifteen years, he has authored several articles on legal issues, funding, and the philosophical underpinnings of the leisure services profession.

H. Douglas Sessoms is Professor and Chair, Curriculum in Leisure Studies and Recreation Administration, University of North Carolina at Chapel Hill. He has authored over one hundred articles and several texts. A graduate of the University of North Carolina (AB), University of Illinois (MS), and New York University (Ph.D.), he is a charter member of the Academy of Leisure Sciences. He has chaired the Council on Accreditation and the National Certification Examination Committee of the National Recreation and Park Association. His primary interests are group dynamics and leadership, curriculum development, and the professionalization of park and recreation services.

Stephen L. J. Smith, Professor and former Chairman of the Department of Recreation, University of Waterloo, completed his bachelor's and master's degrees in Geography. His Ph.D. in Recreation and Resources Development is from Texas A&M University. His research activities include the geography and economics of leisure, park planning, tourism, and the philosophy of leisure research. He is the author of *Recreation Geography and Tourism Analysis,* and former editor of *Recreation Research Review.*

Irene M. Spry is Professor Emeritus of Economics at the University of Ottawa. Educated at the London School of Economics, Girton College of Cambridge University and Byrn Mawr, she previously taught at the University of Toronto and University of Saskatchewan. She represented the Federated Women's Institutes of Canada with the Associated Country Women of the World, an international non-governmental organization engaged in community development and continuing education activities, serving as administrative chairman and Deputy President. Co-editor of *Natural Resource Development in Canada*, she was a Senior Research Associate of a multi-university, multi-disciplinary study of the prospects for a conserver society. Several Canadian scholars compiled an anthology of original essays to honor her many scholarly and humanitaran contributions .

Charles Sylvester is Associate Professor in the Department of Physical Education, Health, and Recreation at Western Washington University. He received the B.S. and M.A. degrees at the University of Maryland and the Ph.D. at the University of Oregon. He directed and continues to volunteer for recreation programs serving persons with disabilities. He is a student of the history and philosophy of play and leisure.

Louis F. Twardzik is professor, Department of Park and Recreation Resources, Michigan State University and was Chair for 13 years. Earlier he served 10 years as State Recreation Consultant, Tennessee Division of State Parks. He has a B.S., University of Notre Dame, M.S. and Director degrees from Indiana University. He also serves as a specialist in park and recreation policy and administration for the Cooperative Extension Service, served as advisor to four successive governors of Michigan, has held offices in several professional organizations, and travels extensively. He co-authored *Elements of Park and Recreation Administration* with Charles Doell, and has authored scores of papers bulletins and plans.

Fred VanDerbeck has been involved in policy and advocacy related to child development services for disabled and non-disabled children. He worked with the East Mountain Centre, an integrated preschool in Westfield, Massachusetts, and has an extensive background in political science.

Peter A. Witt is Associate Dean of the Graduate School, University of North Texas and Professor and former Chairman of its Division of Recreation and Leisure Studies. He previously taught at the University of Ottawa after completing his Ph.D. degree at the University of Illinois. He was the founding editor of Leisurability, former editor of *Therapeutic Recreation Journal* and *Leisure Commentary and Practice*, and currently edits the *Journal of Leisure Research*. Author or editor of numerous articles and books, his main interests are psychosocial determinants of leisure, leisure education, and recreation for special populations. Awards include the AALR Outstanding Achievement Award and NRPA's Roosevelt Award for outstanding research.

End of Contributors and
End of Book: Recreation and Leisure:
Issues in an Era of Change, edited by
Thomas L. Goodale and Peter A. Witt,
3rd edition.

BOOKS BY VENTURE PUBLISHING

Acquiring Parks and Recreation Facilities through Mandatory Dedication:
A Comprehensive Guide
by Ronald A. Kaiser and James D. Mertes

Adventure Education
edited by John C. Miles and Simon Priest

Amenity Resource Valuation: Integrating Economics with Other Disciplines
edited by George L. Peterson, B.L. Driver and Robin Gregory

Behavior Modification in Therapeutic Recreation: An Introductory Learning
Manual
by John Dattilo and William D. Murphy

Beyond the Bake Sale—A Fund Raising Handbook for Public Agencies
by Bill Moskin

The Community Tourism Industry Imperative—The Necessity, The
Opportunities, Its Potential
by Uel Blank

Doing More With Less in the Delivery of Recreation and Park Services:
A Book of Case Studies
by John Crompton

Evaluation of Therapeutic Recreation Through Quality Assurance
edited by Bob Riley

The Evolution of Leisure: Historical and Philosophical Perspectives
by Thomas Goodale and Geoffrey Godbey

The Future of Leisure Services: Thriving on Change
by Geoffrey Godbey

Gifts to Share—A Gifts Catalogue How-To Manual for Public Agencies
by Lori Harder and Bill Moskin

International Directory of Academic Institutions in Leisure, Recreation
and Related Fields
edited by Max D'Amours

Leadership and Administration of Outdoor Pursuits
by Phyllis Ford and James Blanchard

The Leisure Diagnostic Battery: Users Manual and Sample Forms
by Peter Witt and Gary Ellis

Leisure Diagnostic Battery Computer Software
by Gary Ellis and Peter Witt

Leisure Education: A Manual of Activities and Resources
by Norma J. Stumbo and Steven R. Thompson

Leisure Education: Program Materials for Persons with Developmental
Disabilities
by Kenneth F. Joswiak

Leisure in Your Life: An Exploration, Third Edition
by Geoffrey Godbey

A Leisure of One's Own: A Feminist Perspective on Women's Leisure
*by Karla Henderson, M. Deborah Bialeschki, Susan M. Shaw
and Valeria J. Freysinger*

Outdoor Recreation Management: Theory and Application, Revised
and Enlarged
by Alan Jubenville, Ben Twight and Robert H. Becker

Planning Parks for People
by John Hultsman, Richard L. Cottrell and Wendy Zales Hultsman

Playing, Living, Learning: A Worldwide Perspective on Children's
Opportunities to Play
by Cor Westland and Jane Knight

Private and Commercial Recreation
edited by Arlin Epperson

The Process of Recreation Programming Theory and Technique, Third Edition
by Patricia Farrell and Herberta M. Lundegren

Recreation and Leisure: An Introductory Handbook
edited by Alan Graefe and Stan Parker

Recreation Economic Decisions: Comparing Benefits and Costs
by Richard G. Walsh

Risk Management in Therapeutic Recreation: A Component of Quality
Assurance
by Judy Voelkl

Schole: A Journal of Leisure Studies and Recreation Education

A Social History of Leisure Since 1600
by Gary Cross

Sports and Recreation for the Disabled—A Resource Manual
  by Michael J. Paciorek and Jeffery A. Jones

A Study Guide for National Certification in Therapeutic Recreation
  by Gerald O' Morrow and Ron Reynolds

Therapeutic Recreation Protocols for Treatment of Substance Addictions
  by Rozanne W. Faulkner

Understanding Leisure and Recreation: Mapping the Past, Charting the Future
  edited by Edgar L. Jackson and Thomas L. Burton

Wilderness in America: Personal Perspectives
  edited by Daniel L. Dustin

Venture Publishing, Inc
1999 Cato Avenue
State College, PA 16801
814-234-4561